TRAVEL AROUND
CHINA

TRAVEL AROUND China

Foreword

I am always troubled by a dilemma when vacation finally comes: Should I stay at home to relax my mind or take a trip to immerse myself in nature? You might say it depends on one's disposition whether to choose physical or mental relaxation. *Travel Around China* may give you a completely fresh inspiration—going on a trip does not have to be an exasperating and ennervating experience.

In contrast to conventional travel guides, this book presents an in-depth picture of scenic spots and, in addition, offers special features with photos showcasing the magnificent views in China. Using this guide and starting in western China, the most beautiful area in the country, you can travel every corner of China, enjoying the wonderful natural scenery and historical and cultural landmarks in different regions. This guide also provides for your reference information about travel routes, special food, shopping, and the best travel season.

Travel Around China opens a window on China and serves as a comprehensive guide for your next travel destination.

TRAVEL AROUND

CHINA

CONTENTS

6-191

SOUTHWEST CHINA

192-323

NORTHWEST CHINA

324-411

NORTH CHINA

412-447

NORTHEAST CHINA

Tibet Autonomous Region

Geography at a Glance

Tibet Autonomous Region lies in the southwest of China on the Qinghai-Tibet Plateau. It is bounded to the north by Xinjiang Uygur Autonomous Region and Qinghai Province, to the east by Sichuan Province, to the southeast by Yunnan Province, and to the south and west by Burma, India, Bhutan, Sikkim, and Nepal. The region covers an area of around 475,800 square miles, which accounts for 12.8 percent of the total area of China.

With an average altitude of over 13,120 feet, Tibet Autonomous Region has very complex topography and falls into three geographic parts: the west, the south, and the east. The west part, known as the North-Tibet Plateau, lies between the Kunlun Mountains, Kangdese Mountains, Tonglha Mountains and Nyainqentanglha Mountains. This part takes up two-thirds of the total area of Tibet. The southern part of Tibet consists of valleys and lies between the Kangdese Mountains and the Himalayas. The eastern part is made up mostly of canyons, and the entire area is marked by a gradual decline in altitude interrupted by small mountain systems called the Henduan Ranges.

Nearly all Tibetans follow Tibetan Buddhism, known as Lamaism, with the exception of approximately 2,000 followers of Islam and about 600 Roman Catholics. In its infancy, Tibetan Buddhism was greatly influenced by Indian Buddhism, but after years of evolution, Tibetan Buddhism developed its own distinctive qualities and practices. A well-known example is the belief that there is a living Buddha, who is the reincarnation of the first, a belief not held by Chinese Buddhists.

(From CFP)

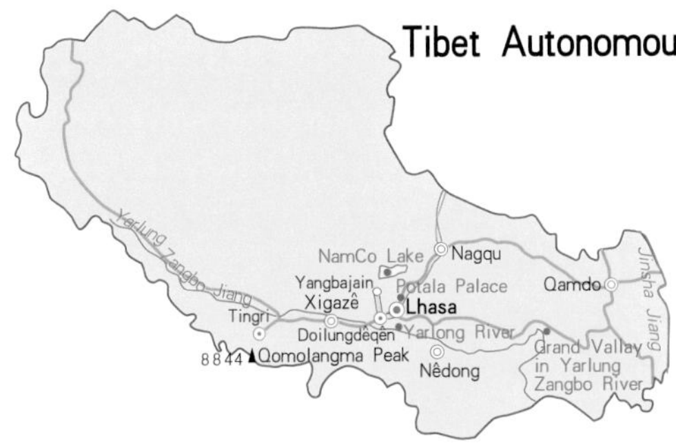

Tibetan clothes (From ImagineChina)

The climate varies greatly in different parts of Tibet. In southeastern Tibet, it is mild and temperate, with an average temperature of 46°F. In western Tibet, the average temperature is below 32°F. In Lhasa and the central part of Tibet, the climate is temperate and nice for traveling. Visitors would be neither too cold in winter nor too warm in summer, especially from March to October, the best seasons for traveling. Most rainfall comes in the rainy season that lasts from May to September. The precipitation gradually decreases from 196 inches in the lower part of the southeast to just 2 inches in the northwest.

Featured Cuisine

Tsampa (roasted barley flour), momo (steamed or fried dumplings), stir-fried meats, thukpa (noodle soup with meat or vegetables), carrot cake, banana porridge, lamb with radish, caramel tea, soja (butter tea), barley ale.

Note: Tibetan cuisine is somewhat bland in taste. No spices other than onions and garlic are used.

Featured Commodities

Herbal Medicines

Saffron crocus, aweto, glossy ganoderma, gastrodia tuber, musk.

Local Handicrafts

Tibetan swords, Tibetan carpets, Thangkas, aprons, masks, wooden bowls, Chamdo boots, Lhasa pottery, prayer wheels.

Transportation Tips

By Bus

Major roads in Tibet include the Chuanzang Road (from Chengdu to Lhasa), Qingzang Road (from Xining to Lhasa),

Notes 

❶ Office hours in Tibet are from 9:00 a.m. to 12:00 noon and from 3:00 p.m. to 6:00 p.m. It is best to deal with important business in the morning.

❷ Since many students in Tibet end their summer vacations and leave for school by plane in late August, it is advisable to book plane tickets in advance at this time of the year.

Xinzang Road from Yecheng to Pulan, Dianzang Road from Xiaguan to Mangkang, and Zhongni Road from Lhasa to Kathmandu. Only the Qingzang Road is open for traffic all year round. Most foreign travelers prefer to enter Tibet via the Zhongni Road.

Mani stone (From ImagineChina)

■ **By Plane**

There are two civilian airports in Tibet. Gongga Airport in Lhasa has the highest altitude of any airport in the world, and has direct flights to Chengdu, Beijing, Chongqing, Chamdo, and Kathmandu. Bonda Airport in Chamdo, on the other hand, offers

POPULAR FESTIVALS

Tibetan New Year

Tibetan New Year is the most important festival in Tibet. Tibetan families reunite and hope that the coming year will be a fortunate one.

Butter Oil Lantern Festival

It's held on the 15th of the first lunar month. (It's impossible to use Western months on such occasions, since a lunar year consists of only 355 days, which means a lunar date does not correspond to a fixed date in the Western calendar.) Huge yak-butter sculptures are placed around Lhasa's Barkhor circuit.

Bathing Festival

It is believed that when the sacred planet Venus appears in the sky, river water becomes purest for curing diseases. During Venus's one-week appearance, usually at the end of the seventh and beginning of the eighth lunar months, Tibetans go to rivers to wash away the dirt and/or sins of the previous year.

Shoton Festival

This is one of the major Tibetan festivals, also known as the Tibetan Opera Festival. The founder of the Gelugpa (Yellow Sect of Buddhism), Tsongkhapa, set the rule that Buddhists must seek only indoor entertainment in summer, in order to avoid killing other creatures carelessly. This rule must be carried out till the seventh lunar month. Then Buddhists go outdoors, eat yogurt made and served by local people, and in general have fun.

Harvest Festival

This festival is celebrated when the crops ripen, usually around August. The festival is observed only in farming villages. People walk around their fields to thank the gods and deities for a good year's harvest. Singing, dancing, and horse racing are enjoyed by all.

Nakchu Horse Race Festival

Nakchu Horse Race Festival is a very important folk festival in Tibet. In early August, Tibetans gather and build tent cities for this annual horse race. They dress themselves and their horses in finery, and thousands of herdsmen participate in the thrilling horse race. There are also archery and horsemanship contests. Other folk activities and craft fairs take place as well.

flights only to Lhasa and Chengdu. Air travel is the best and quickest way to reach Tibet.

Recommended Routes

Featured Routes

Six-day pilgrimage tour of Lhasa and Namtso

Day 1 Arrive in Lhasa (Gongga Airport) →Yarlung Tsangpo River. Lodging: Lhasa Hotel.

Day 2 Potala Palace→Jokhang Temple→ Barkhor Street. Lodging: Lhasa Hotel.

Day 3 Drepung Monastery→Sera Monastery. Lodging: Lhasa Hotel.

Day 4 Namtso. Lodging: Dangxiong Hotel.

Day 5 Namtso→Lhasa→Barkhor Street. Lodging: Lhasa Hotel.

Day 6 End of tour.

Five-day tour of historic sites and Tibetan landscape

Day 1 Arrive in Lhasa. Lodging: Lhasa Hotel.

Day 2 Potala Palace→Jokhang Temple→ Barkhor Street. Lodging: Lhasa Hotel.

Day 3 Lhasa→Qushui Bridge→Mount Gambala→Yamdrok Yumtso Lake→Kanuo Glaciers→Gyangtse→Palkhor →Monastery →Gyangtse Dzong Fortress→Shigatse. Lodging: Shigatse Hotel.

Day 4 Tashilhunpo Monastery→Yarlung Tsangpo River→Lhasa. Lodging: Lhasa Hotel.

Day 5 End of tour.

Five-day tour of lakes and forests

Day 1 Arrive in Lhasa. Lodging: Lhasa Hotel.

Day 2 Potala Palace. Lodging: Lhasa Hotel.

Day 3 Lhasa→Cuogao Lake. Lodging: Basongco.

Day 4 Nyingchi→Niyang River. Lodging: Nyingchi Hotel.

Day 5 End of tour.

Eight-day tour of Mount Qomolangma

Day 1 Arrive in Lhasa. Lodging: Lhasa Hotel.

Day 2 Potala Palace→Norbulingka. Lodging: Lhasa Hotel.

Day 3 Lhasa→Yamdrok Yumtso Lake→ Kanuo Glaciers→Dzong Fortress→ Gyangtse→Shigatse. Lodging: Shigatse Hotel.

Day 4 Shigatse→Xieger. Lodging: Shigatse Hotel.

Day 5 Tingri→Base Camp of Mount Qomolangma→Tingri. Lodging: Tingri Guest House.

Day 6 Tingri→Shigatse→Tashilhunpo Monastery. Lodging: Shigatse Hotel.

Day 7 Shigatse→Lhasa→Jokhang Temple→Barkhor Street. Lodging: Lhasa Hotel.

Day 8 End of tour.

Traditional Routes

Four-day tour of Tibet

Day 1 Arrive in Lhasa.

Day 2 Lhasa→Potala Palace→Jokhang Temple→Barkhor Street.

Day 3 North Tibetan grasslands→ Yangpachen.

Day 4 End of tour.

Addresses and Phone Numbers

Lhasa Hotel	1 Minzu Road, Lhasa	0891-6832221
Balangxue Hostel	8 East Beijing Road, Lhasa	0891-6338040
Jiri Hotel	12 East Beijing Road, Lhasa	0891-6323462
Ya Hostel	100 East Beijing Road, Lhasa	0891-6323496
Nyingchi Hotel	25 Shuangyong Road, Bayi, Nyingchi	0894-5821300
Nyingchi Guest House	21 Yongjun Road, Bayi, Nyingchi	0894-5821078
Shigatse Hotel	12 Middle Shanghai Road, Shigatse	0892-8800336
Gangtse Hotel	2 East Shanghai Road, Gangtse, Shigatse District	0892-8172222
Zhangmu Hotel	Zhangmukouan, Shigatse District	0892-8742222

Qinghai-Tibet Railway (From ImagineChina company)

Nine-day tour of eastern Tibet

Day 1 Lhasa→Duilongdeqing→Yangpachen→Dangxiong Pasture→Tanggula.

Day 2 Nakchu→Source of the Nujiang River.

Day 3 Baqing→Dingqing County.

Day 4 Dingqing→Leiqi Temple→Xiaoenda Site→Yiri Hotspring→Machala Cave.

Day 5 Chambaling Monastery→Kanuo Ruins→Chamdo Folk Handicraft Factory.

Day 6 Chamdo→Lancangjiang River→Chaya Temple→Bongda Grassland→Basu Temple.

Day 7 Basu→Ranwutso→Palong Tsangpo.

Day 8 Zamu Town→Tongmai→Maichangqing Hotspring→Yarlung Tsangpo Gorge→Mount Nanjiabawa→Mount Jialabailei→Yigong Lake→Mount Sejila.

Day 9 Bayi Town→Basong Lake→Niangpu Scenic Spot→Mount Mila→Lhasa.

Self-Guided Tours

Along the northern Sichuan-Tibet Road

Starting from Lhasa and ending at Yaan, the journey takes about 13 days, passing Dangxiong, Nakchu, Baqing, Dingqing, Chamdo, Tuoba, Jiangda, Dege, Xinluhai, Gangtse, and Kangding. Major scenic spots along the way include Yangpachen hot springs, Namtso, Nakchu grasslands, Tangula Mountain Range, North Tibetan grasslands, source of Lancangjiang River, Leiwuqi Temple, Chambaling Monastery, the Kanuo ruins, Mount Damala, Baili Temple, Tagong Temple, and Tagong Grassland.

Lhasa Region

Best Time to Travel

Summer is the best season to visit Lhasa; the temperature at this time is warm and not too humid. The whole city is covered with flowers and greenery. Shoton (Opera Festival), one of the most important Tibetan festivals, also falls in this season.

Shopping Tips

Barkhor Street in Lhasa is world famous for shopping, and visitors can find not only local Tibetan handicrafts but also arts and crafts from India, Nepal, and Bhutan.

A visit to the Lhasa Department Store, west of Potala Square, is a must. Central air-conditioning, elevators, and other modern facilities make the store a convenient center for shopping, relaxation, and recreation.

Potala Palace

Capping the Red Hill of Lhasa, Potala Palace was built more than 1,300 years ago. Rumor has it that the Tibetan king Songtsen Gampo, a pious adherent of Buddhism, often went to the top of a mountain near Lhasa to chant scriptures and pray. He named the mountain Potala, which is a transliteration of a Sanskrit word referring to the residence of Avalokitesvara, the Goddess of Mercy (*Guanyin* in Chinese).

In 641, after marrying Princess Wencheng of the Tang

Potala Palace (From Quanjing)

Dynasty, Songtsen Gampo built Potala Palace for her and their descendants. However, the original palace was destroyed by lightning and succeeding warfare during Landama's reign. It is said that the existing statues of Songtsen Gampo and Princess Wencheng were lucky enough to survive the disasters. In 1652, Potala was rebuilt by the fifth Dalai Lama.

Built at an altitude of 12,139 feet, the palace is about 1,312 feet long and 984 feet wide, occupying a total area of more than 1,399,307 square feet. Its 13-floor main building is 384 feet tall, making it the world's highest-altitude construction.

Potala Palace is composed of two sections for different purposes. The White Palace is a seven-floor building originally built in 1645. The wall of the palace was painted white to convey peace and quiet, hence the name. The Great East Hall (Cuoqingxia) on the fourth floor is the largest open space in the White Palace, occupying 7,718 square feet and supported by 38 grand pillars. This hall is also used for important religious and political events. The living quarters and offices of regents are on the fifth and sixth floors; the top floor consists of the East Chamber of Sunshine and the West Chamber of Sun-

Great Statue of Buddha in Potala Palace (From Quanjing)

Perhaps due to the severe natural environment and the resultant hard work for survival, Tibetans yearn for peace and happiness. They pray that the gods will love and protect them. Consequently, Tibetan Buddhism has become an extremely important part of their lives. The prayer wheel is an important prayer medium for Tibetan Buddhists. Prayer wheels may be large like barrels, with fixed axes so that people can rotate them, or small like the one in the picture, which can be carried in the hands. (From Colphoto)

shine. Because of the light in there all year round, the East Chamber and West Chamber were where the Dalai Lamas lived, worked, and studied.

The other section is the Red Palace, built in 1690. Emperor Kangxi of the Qing Dynasty once sent more than 100 workers to help with the construction. The Red Palace consists mainly of various chapels and stupas for different Dalai Lamas. With a height of 49 feet, covered by more than 6,614 pounds of gold foil, and decorated with thousands of pearls, gems, corals, ambers, and agates, the fifth Dalai Lama's stupa is regarded as the highest and the most luxurious. While the White Palace serves as a living space and political center for Dalai Lamas, the Red Palace is mostly a religious center for various rituals.

In December 1994, Potala Palace was listed by UNESCO as a World Heritage site.

Potala Palace closes earlier on weekends than on weekdays. Admission is free in the mornings for every Tibetan Buddhist festival.

Door decoration of a Tibetan temple (From Quanjing)

Dragons Pond

One of the most famous garden constructions in Lhasa, Dragons Pond is located behind Mount Potala. According to legend, the sixth Dalai Lama invited eight dragons from Medro Gongkar to live in the large pond at the center of the garden, so he could provide offerings for them, hence the name Dragons Pond.

The garden is cleverly laid out in the shape of an irregular polygon. It is about 2,000 feet long, with a maximum width of 994 feet and a minimum width of 67 feet. In the middle of the pond is a small, round island with a diameter of about 138 feet. The island is connected to the surrounding land by a five-arch stone bridge, which is 80 feet long and 11 feet wide. Both the island and the surrounding land are covered in luxuriant and verdant woods.

Dragons Pond has become the first large modern park in Lhasa. With facilities like the Children's Playground and the Resting Place, the park is now an excellent place to relax and have fun.

Jokhang Temple

Lying in the heart of Lhasa's old section, Jokhang Temple was built in the seventh century by Songtsen Gampon in honor of Princess Wencheng. It is a splendid example of Tubo-era construction and is the earliest example of timber construction in Tibet. As the first Tibetan temple built on level land, it introduced a new layout style for temple construction in Tibet.

The Golden Dharma Wheel on the roof of Jokhang Temple, which is one of the Eight Treasures of Buddhism, is a symbol of propitiousness. The two kylins flanking the wheel, one male and one female, are called "saint kylins" by Tibetans and symbolize luck. (From Jin Yongji)

Jokhang Temple is not just the site of important religious events. After the fifth Dalai Lama established the Gandanpozhang regime, he located his government offices here. (From Quanjing)

In front of the temple's main entrance stand three stone pillars, one of which bears an inscription, in both Tibetan and Chinese, of the treaty between Tang and Tubo signed in 823. Walking clockwise behind the main entrance, visitors step into a large, open courtyard, the site of the Monlam Festival (or Great Prayer Festival). During the ceremonies, thousands of monks gather here to pray for social stability and the happiness of all living creatures. Rites such as expelling ghosts and greeting bodhisattvas are also held. The walls of the Thousand Bodhisattvas Cloister, which encircles the courtyard, are painted with a thousand murals of these enlightened beings. As visitors make their way through the halls beside the courtyard, they encounter the famous Jokhang Hall hidden behind hundreds of butter-oil lanterns. The principal structure as well as the center of the temple, Jokhang Hall is a four-floor building with a huge chamber in the center where monks learn, recite, and chant scriptures. Tibetan Buddhists believe that Lhasa is the heart of the world and that the center of the universe is found here.

In December 1994, Jokhang Temple was listed by UNESCO as a World Heritage site.

You can reach Jokhang Temple by taking a bus and getting off at the Tibetan Hospital stop.

Barkhor Street

Barkhor, a circular street at the center of Old Lhasa, was created by pilgrims walking around Jokhang Temple throughout the centuries. Buddhist pilgrims walk or progress by body lengths clockwise along the street every day until dark. Most of Lhasa's transient population consists of these pilgrims, who process outside the four temple columns on which colorful scripture streamers are hung, a custom begun in the Tubo period (633–877) as a way to show respect.

Barkhor is a place where Tibetan culture, economy, religion, and arts converge and should not be missed. It is also a marketplace where shaggy nomads, traders, robed monks, and chanting pilgrims congregate. Clustered shops and stalls sell printed scriptures, cloth prayer flags, religious vessels, jewelry, Tibetan knives, ancient coins, and other Tibetan artifacts. Various merchandise from India and Nepal is also sold here.

Ramoche Temple

Situated about a third of a mile north of Jokhang Temple and covering a total area of 43,056 square feet,

Lama (From Quanjing)

Ramoche Temple is one of the places for Tibetan monks to study Mi Zong (another Buddhist sect). Although the temple was originally built in the middle of the seventh century, it fell into ruin and went through many reconstructions; at present only the Buddha hall on the first floor of its main building remains in its original state. Inside the hall, there are ten pillars engraved with patterns such as lotus flowers, coiling clouds, and jewelry, which are reminiscent of the Tubo Dynasty. The third floor of the main building was once the bedroom reserved for the Dalai Lama. The building's golden peak, with its Han-style upturned eaves, can be seen from any direction in Lhasa city. This temple is a wonderful example of the combination of Han and Tibetan architectural styles.

The construction of Ramoche was ordered and designed by Princess Wencheng, who brought many Han architects from Chang'an, the capital during the Tang Dynasty, to help with the construction. The whole process took about a year, ending in 646, the same year in which the construction of Jokhang was finished. The gate of Ramoche faces east, which is the direction of Chang'an, to reflect Princess Wencheng's longing for her homeland.

Reting Monastery

Built in 1057 by Dromptonpa, founder of the Kadampa Order of Tibetan Buddhism, Reting Monastery is located 18.7 miles north of Lhasa.

West of Reting is the famous Sacred Path. According to Tibetan legend, on July 15 of every Year of the Ram (Tibetan calendar), hundreds of thousands of goddesses descend from the heavens and gather at this spot to save mankind from the sea of miserable life. As a result, every time this religious festival comes around, pious disciples, no matter how far away they are, congregate to make offerings and pray for peace and prosperity.

Chakpori Hill

Rising up beside Potala Palace, the peak of Chakpori Hill is 12,221 feet

Many folk engravers and nomad artisans work at the foot of Chakpori Hill. They work piously and carefully carve the various shapes and statues of Buddha and other gods on the rocks. For these amateur craftspeople, this is an important way of making a living. (From Quanjing)

high. From atop the hill, you can see a panorama of the ancient city and the surrounding landscape. During the seventeenth century, to further the development of Tibetan medicine, a temple was built at the top of the hill, where lamas selected from other temples were brought to study traditional Tibetan medicine. Inside the temple is a large statue of the Buddhist Medicine King. Legend has it that this king is able to treat patients no matter what their diseases are or how difficult they are to cure. Consequently, the hill is also called Yaowang Shan, translated as "Medicine King Hill." On the southeastern slope is an extremely well-preserved grotto, which contains more than 70 engraved statues. The grotto is in the shape of an irregular rectangle with a large stone pillar at its center. The space between the pillar and the surrounding cave walls is so small that only one person can pass at a time. Nonetheless, many pilgrims enter the grotto and walk clockwise, demonstrating their piety.

On the southeastern side of Chakpori Hill is an extremely well-preserved grotto, which contains more than 70 engraved statues.

Drepung Monastery

Situated in the western suburb of Lhasa, Drepung Monastery is known as the most important monastery of Gelugpa in Tibetan Buddhism. Covering an enormous area of 239,234 square feet, the monastery in its heyday housed 7,700 monks. Seen from afar, the imposing white structure gives the appearance of a heap of rice, hence the name Drepung Monastery, which means "Monastery of Collecting Rice." The monastery was established in 1416, and with the support of plutocrats, it developed into the richest religious community of Gelugpa. In 1464, seven *zhacangs* (academies or schools) were set up in the monastery to teach classical sutras.

Situated at the center of the monastery is the great Coqen Hall, which is supported by 183 finely deco-

Drepung Monastery (From ImagineChina)

rated pillars. The second floor of the hall houses the most precious treasure in the monastery—a huge bronze statue of Qamba Buddha—while the third floor houses a dextro triton, another Buddhist treasure. (A dextro triton is a triton whose shell curves in the clockwise direction. Since dextro tritons are extremely rare in nature—about 1 in every 100,000—they are highly treasured by Tibetan Buddhists.) The walls of the hall are painted with extraordinary murals, making it one of the most famous sightseeing spots in Tibet.

A bus can take you only to the foot of the hill where Drepung Monastery is located. If you want to avoid the trouble of hill climbing, take a taxi, which will cost about 20 yuan.

Norbulingka

Norbulingka, also known as the Summer Palace in Lhasa, is located in the western suburb of Lhasa, at the bank of the Kyichu River, less than a half mile southwest of Potala Palace. The garden covers an area of about 900 acres, and the palace contains 374 rooms. It is the largest man-made garden in Tibet. Built in the eighteenth century, during the reign of the tenth Dalai Lama, the garden served as the place where the Dalai handled political affairs and religious activities. Today, in addition to being a destination for pilgrims, it is also a place for relaxation and recreation. In December 2001, UNESCO listed Norbulingka as a World Heritage site as an extension of Potala Palace.

You can get to Norbulingka by taking Bus No. 2 at the Tibetan Hospital stop.

Tibet Museum

The Tibet Museum is located in the southeastern corner of Norbulingka, in Lhasa. Covering a total area of 253,307 square feet, the museum is equipped with modern facilities to ensure a quality experience for visitors, as well as safety and the efficient administration of the museum itself.

The museum building is a pioneer institution in the history of Tibet. Designed by a Han Chinese architect from Sichuan Province, the complex is a wonderful combination of Chinese and Tibetan architectural styles. Upon entering the Prelude Hall, visitors' attention is immediately caught by the colorfully ornamented beams, pillars, lintels, banners, and wall hangings. As visitors make their way through the museum, they will notice that it is divided into two main sections. The first consists of two exhibition halls on the first floor,

Full-body prostration is a popular way for Tibetan Buddhists to show their piety. To perform it, Tibetan Buddhists have to first hold their palms together above their heads. Then, as they take the first and second steps, they lower their palms, still holding them together, first down to the front of their faces, then down to the front of their chests. As they take the third step, they hold their hands out to touch the ground with their palms. At this time, their knees bend until they lie on their faces and touch the ground with their foreheads. After that, they stand up, and the process starts over again. (From Quanjing)

featuring the splendid history of Tibet and its abundant natural resources. The other section is on the second floor and comprises five small exhibition halls displaying Tibetan religion, folk customs, treasures, and arts and crafts. The Tibet Museum houses a rich collection of prehistoric cultural artifacts including statues of the Buddha in different postures, imperial jade seals, gold albums, gifts granted by emperors, colorful tangkas, and various printed Sanskrit and Tibetan scriptures. Visitors can also examine a variety of folk arts such as unique Tibetan handicrafts, costumes, jewelry, and ornaments of gold, silver, and jade, in addition to fine Chinese pottery.

At present the Tibet Museum provides guide service in four languages: Tibetan, Mandarin, Japanese, and English.

Yangpachen Hot Springs

Although not as famous as other scenic spots such as Potala Palace in Tibet, Yangpachen attracts visitors for its unique hot springs. About 54 miles from Lhasa and covering an area of 15 square miles, Yangpachen is known for the abundant geothermal heat. First utilized in the 1970s, it was the earliest hot spring put into use in China. At an altitude of more than 14,000 feet, it is also the highest power plant generating geothermal heat in the world.

Yangpachen is at its most beautiful in the morning when the air is still cool, and the whole area is shrouded in mist, making it look like a fairyland.

Yangpachen was originally used as grazing land. Now indoor and outdoor pools have been constructed, and visitors can swim (at a cost of 40 to 100 yuan). Sometimes people are lucky enough to experience a snowfall while they are bathing. The water from the hot springs is rich in hydrogen sulfide, which is beneficial to the health. However, strenuous sports are not recommended since this could lead to breathing problems due to the thin atmosphere.

Ganden Monastery

Ganden Monastery is located on Wangbur Mountain, which is more than 12,792 feet high, in Tagtse County, 29 miles from Lhasa. Built in 1409 by Tsong Khapa, the founder of Gelugpa (a branch of Tibetan Buddhism known as the Yellow Hat Sect, as its disciples wear yellow hats), it is the largest Gelugpa monastery as well as one of the three great monasteries in Lhasa—the other two being Sera and Drepung. At the height of its power and splendor, the monastery covered an area of about 37 acres, almost three times as large as Potala Palace.

Clouds of mist at Yangpachen, surrounded by mountains covered with glistening snow, constitute one of the most amazing natural wonders at this Roof of the World. (From Quanjing)

The monastery comprises over 50 structures, among which Coqen Hall and Tri Thok Khang are the best known. Coqen Hall, which serves as the main assembly space, is large enough to hold over 3,000 lamas. Tri Thok Khang is one of the earliest Buddha halls in the Ganden Monastery and once served as the bedchamber of Tsong Khapa and other tripas. In 1419 Tsong Khapa passed away in this hall, and in the following year his disciples built a silver pagoda for him here. Later on, the thirteenth Dalai Lama covered the pagoda with pure gold. From then on, each time a tripa died, a silver pagoda would be built in his honor, so that by the time Tibet was liberated, 95 pagodas had been constructed. Besides these 95 holy stupas, the monastery also houses many other rare and well-preserved cultural relics.

> If you take the bus from Jokhang Temple Square at 7:00 a.m. for Ganden, you can return by the same bus at 2:00 p.m.

Namtso Lake

In its November 14, 2005, issue, Namtso Lake was ranked as one of the five most beautiful lakes in China by the Chinese edition of *National Geographic*. Its touching beauty should not be missed by any traveler who visits Tibet. *Namtso* is the Tibetan word for "heavenly lake." As one of the three holy lakes in Tibet, Namtso is famous for its high altitude (15,485 feet), vast area (757 square miles), and stunningly beautiful scenery.

A Mani stone left beside Namtso by Buddhists. (From Quanjing)

The second-largest saltwater lake in China (after Qinghai Lake), Namtso is the biggest lake in Tibet. It is also the highest-altitude saltwater lake in the world. The water here is crystal-clear blue. Cloudless skies merge with the surface of the lake at the horizon, creating a cohesive scenic vista. The soul of every visitor who has ever been here seems to be cleansed by the pure lake water.

Summer is the best time to visit Namtso Lake. Yaks, hares, and other wild animals leisurely look for food along the expansive lakeshore; countless migratory birds fly here to nest and feed their young; sometimes beautiful fish jump out of the water, seeking the warmth of the sunshine; herds of sheep and cows punctuate the landscape of the verdant

(From Jin Yongfi)

grassland, which stretches as far as the eyes can see; the dulcet tones of the herdsmen's songs resound through the valleys. At this time of year Namtso Lake is full of life and activity, and it is no wonder Tibetans regard Namtso Lake as the symbol of beauty and happiness. The lake is indeed a blessing from nature.

Besides its magnificent scenery, Namtso is also a well-known sacred Buddhist site. Zhaxi Temple is located on the Zhaxi peninsula. In every Tibetan Year of the Sheep, thousands of Buddhists come here to worship. As a part of their ritual, pilgrims walk clockwise around the lake in order to receive the blessings of the gods.

> There are no direct buses to Namtso Lake. The best way to get there is to hire a taxi or minibus from Lhasa.

Shannan Region

Best Time to Travel

As the cradle of Tibetan civilization and culture, the Shannan region is a good choice for traveling and sightseeing at any time of year.

Yarlung River Scenic Resort

Lying in the southern part of the Shannan region and covering an area of more than 3.5 square miles, Yarlung River Scenic Resort is at present the only major national scenic area in Tibet. Yarlung River is Tibetan for "river flowing from the upper reaches." Starting in Cuomei and flowing into the Yarlung Tsangpo River, it has a total length of 42 miles. Here visitors can enjoy snowy mountains, glaciers, pastures, river valleys, alpine plants, holy mountains and lakes, and historic sites, as well as experiencing simple and unsophisticated folk customs. Major cultural sights include Yumbu Lakhang, the earliest palace in Tibet; Samye Monastery, the first temple in Tibet; and Trandruk Monastery and the Graveyard of Tibetan Kings, both of which are on the list of major national cultural sites to be protected.

At the juncture of the Yarlung and Yarlung Tsangpo rivers lies the town of Zetang, seat of the government of the

Shannan Prefecture. This has been a holy land for Tibetans for centuries; it was here that the Tibetan ancestors explored their first piece of arable land and founded their first village.

Yamdrok Yumtso Lake

Yamdrok Yumtso (or Yamdrok-tso), one of the three holiest lakes in Tibet, lies at Nhagartse, about 62 miles southwest of Lhasa. According to legend, the lake was a fairy who descended to earth. Her husband followed and was transformed into Mount Kampala. Besides Kampala, Yamdrok Yumtso is also surrounded by Mount Nyinchenkhasa, Mount Chetungsu, and Mount Changsamlhamo. Befitting its mythical feminine origins, the turquoise blue lake is indescribably beautiful, prompting Tibetans to compare it to a fairyland. Because of its shape, the lake is also called Coral Lake of the Highlands.

Yamdrok *is Tibetan for "upper pasture," while* Yum *means "jade." With its numerous branches like those of coral, Yamdrok Yumtso is also called Coral Lake. The lake freezes up in mid-November every year, and the ice is often as thick as 18 inches. (From Jin Yongji)*

The charming lake produces abundant aquatic life. On the surrounding expansive pasture, animals and birds flourish. There are dozens of islets in the lake, on which flocks of birds roost. During the herding season, local herdsmen ferry their flocks of sheep across to these islets because there are no predators there, and they leave them to graze until the onset of winter.

The holy lake is also a pilgrimage site for Tibetans. Every summer, troops of pilgrims trek there to pray and receive blessings. Pilgrims believe that its water can make the old young again, grant the middle-aged a longer life, and make children smarter.

To get to Yamdrok Yumtso from Lhasa, you must trek up a long ascent winding through cliffs and valleys. Be aware that road conditions here are primitive.

The Samye Monastery is renowned for the characteristic style of its buildings and its vivid murals as well as other ancient relics stored within. (From Quanjing)

Samye Monastery

Begun in 767 by Trisong Detsen of the Tubo Kingdom and finished in 779, Samye Monastery is the first temple built in Tibet.

In the middle of the ninth century, with the prohibition of Buddhism by the Tubo government, Samye was closed for a time. It was not until the latter part of the tenth century, when Buddhism resumed its influence in Tibet, that the monastery became the central temple of the Red Sect of Tibetan Buddhism. Covering an area of about half a square mile and consisting of 108 halls, Samye acquired its fame as "a city of temple halls" due to its great scale. The entire structure of the temple is grandiose and complicated, replicating the universe as described in the sutras. The central world, Mount Meru, is represented by the majestic Wuzi Hall. The Sun and Moon chapels stand to the north and the south, just like the sun and the moon in the universe. Four larger halls and eight smaller halls are distributed around all sides of the central hall, symbolizing the four large continents and eight small ones. In the four corners lie the Red, White, Black, and Green pagodas, guarding the Dharma like the Heavenly Kings. A circular wall surrounds the temple as if marking the periphery of the world. The layout of Samye Monastery resembles the Mandala in Esoteric Buddhism.

Samye Monastery is located at the foot of Mount Haibu Rishen, north of the Yarlung Tsangpo River. You can travel there by bus from Lhasa to the Samye Ferry and cross the river by boat or bridge. Then take the special monastery bus. The mountaintop is also the best place from which to photograph a panoramic view of the monastery.

The Graveyard of Tibetan Kings

High atop Mure Mountain in Chonggye County of the Shannan Prefecture sits a large imperial graveyard with nine massifs. These variably sized earthen structures are the tombs of Tibetan kings who governed from the seventh to the ninth century. Originally of similar size and shape—high and square with flat tops—some of the tombs are now rounded or otherwise eroded. Here, in the Graveyard of Tibetan Kings, the largest preserved imperial graveyard in Tibet, the nine recognizable tombs stand as reminders of the rich history and lore of ancient Tibet.

Yarlung Tsangpo River is densely covered with reefs, making water transportation impossible. (From Liu Liwen)

Yarlung Tsangpo River

Yarlung Tsangpo River, usually just called "Tsangpo" (meaning "purifier"), originates from the Jima Yangzong glacier near Mount Kailash in the northern Himalayas. It then flows east for about 1,000 miles, at an average altitude of 13,123 feet, and is thus the highest of the major rivers in the world. The river drains a northern section of the Himalayas before it reaches its easternmost point and enters the gorge near Pe, Tibet. As the gorge bends around Mount Namcha Barwa (25,446 feet) and cuts its way through the eastern Himalayan range, the river drops from 9,843 feet near Pe to less than 1,000 feet at the end of the gorge, forming the famous Yarlung Tsangpo Canyon, considered the deepest in the world. After this passage, the river enters Arunachal Pradesh, India, and eventually becomes the Brahmaputra.

Qingpu Meditation Place

Located on the side of Narui Mountain, 5 miles to the northeast of Samye Monastery, Qingpu Meditation Place is a valley at an altitude of 14,108 feet. *Qing* in the name refers to the Qing Clan here, while *pu* means the upper part of a valley. Surrounded by mountains on three sides and facing the grand Yarlung Tsangpo River on the south, this is where many accomplished monks once stayed for meditation and contemplation. Rumor has it that there were for a time as many as 108 meditation caves and 108 celestial burial platforms (where bodies are exposed to birds of prey as a ritual) here. However, over time, most of them were buried or destroyed, and only about 40 of them are preserved today. With numerous sutras buried in the valley throughout history, the place is actually no less well known than Samye. The climate here is quite pleasant, with temperate summers and winters. As a result, it has become a favorite resort for pilgrims and travelers.

Mindroling Monastery

In the Zaqi District, to the east of the Zanang River in Zanang County, lies the Mindroling Monastery, covering a large area of nearly 23 acres. It is one of the six most famous Tibetan Buddhism monasteries of the Nyingma (or Red) Sect. The monastery was originally built in the late tenth century and has been renovated several times. The largest hall

Lamas dining before praying in Mindroling (From CFP)

in the monastery is called Guihuakang, and the main hall in the monastery is Lakhang Buddhist Hall.

Mindroling is well known for the study of astronomy, the calendar, medicine, and calligraphy. It is a tradition that some monks from the monastery will be sent to Potala Palace as teachers. In addition, the monastery is in charge of the compilation of the Tibetan calendar. Unlike the practice in many other monasteries, the monks in Mindroling may marry and have children. The succession of abbots in the monastery is not limited to the relationship of son and father; son-in-law and father-in-law relationships are also acceptable. Familiarity with this principle is useful in studying the origin, development, and decline of the Nyingma Sect.

Trandruk Monastery

Trandruk Monastery is justly famous throughout Tibet because the first Buddhist chapel was built there. This is also one of the earliest Buddhist monasteries in Tibet, founded at the same time as Jokhang and Ramoche in Lhasa. Trandruk lies about 3 miles south of Tsedang on the road to Yumbu Lakhang. Built during the reign of Songtsen Gampo (617–650), Trandruk later experienced large-scale reconstruction after it converted to Gelugpa. According to legend, the monastery could be built only after Songtsen Gampo turned into a roc and conquered an evil dragon. The name *trandruk* means "a roc conquering a dragon."

The main building in Trandruk is the Tshomchen, in which Padmasambhava is enshrined. The Tshomchen was built in the style of Tang Dynasty structures and adopted the characteristics of Nepalese and Indian architecture. The building has many chapels. In one of the chapels, a precious pearl Thangka, representing Chenrezi at rest, is housed. The Thangka, or scroll painting, is an elaborate and intricate depiction of Buddha's various forms and teachings, and is a distinctive art form in Tibetan Buddhism. The Thangka in Tshomchen is made up of 30,000 pearls and hundreds of other gems, such as diamonds, sapphires, turquoise, rubies, and amber. In Tibet, Thangkas are frequently the center of Buddhist religious ceremonies. Pilgrims throw money to the Thangka to show their respect.

Yumbu Lakang

Yumbu Lakang, reputed to be the first palace in Tibet history, is also one of the oldest buildings in Tibet. Lying 7.5 miles southwest of Tsedang, it perches on a small hill east of the Yarlung River. The soaring building is a legendary palace built in the second century by the Bon followers for the first Tibetan king Nyatri Tsenpo, who was said to have descended from Heaven. Later it became the summer palace of Songtsen Gampo and Princess Wencheng. Legend has it that in the fifth century, a Buddhist sutra fell from the sky onto the roof of Yumbu Lakang. Nobody could read the book. However, a sage predicted it would be interpreted between the seventh and eighth centuries, and the sutra was kept locked up in the palace.

Tibetan girls singing and dancing (From Imagine-China)

After Songtsen Gampo moved his capital to Lhasa, Yumbu Lakang became a chapel and was converted to a Gulugpa monastery during the reign of the fifth Dalai Lama. About a quarter mile northeast of the chapel is a spring that is said to be able to cure all diseases. Therefore, most pilgrims to Yumbu Lakang also come here and drink water from the spring.

Yumbu Lakang is about 6 miles from Tsedang. Visitors can get there by hiring a pedicab or taxi in Tsedang, for round-trip fees of about 40 yuan and 80 yuan, respectively. Conveniently, tourists can stop by Trandruk on their way to Yumbu Lakang.

Shigatse Region

Best Time to Travel

The best time to visit Shigatse is from May to July. There may be heavy rains in the south, but almost all parts of the region can be reached during these three months. Road travel in Shigatse is quite convenient.

Tashilhunpo Monastery

Tashilhunpo Monastery is located at the foot of Drolmari (Tara's Mountain), 1.2 miles west of Shigatse. Founded by the first Dalai Lama in 1447, the monastery's structure was expanded by the fourth and successive Panchen Lamas. Tashilhunpo covers an area of nearly 75 acres. The main structures in the monastery are the Maitreya Chapel, the Panchen Lama's Palace, and the Kelsang Temple. Tashilhunpo has been the seat of the Panchen Lama since the fourth Panchen Lama took charge of the monastery, which

Scenery in Shigatse. (From Quanjing)

now houses nearly 800 lamas. The monastery also retains the largest gilded bronze statue of Qamba Buddha in the world.

Palkhor Monastery

Palkhor Monastery, also called Palcho Monastery, is very different from other monasteries. It lies at the foot of Dzong Hill, about 143 miles south of Lhasa and 62 miles east of Shigatse. Built as a Tibetan monastery, its structural style is unique. The building houses monks from the Gelugpa, Sakyapa, and Kahdampa orders. Although they once quarreled and fought, the different orders eventually discovered a way to get along with each other. The monastery is the only one known to house monks from different orders in harmony. As a result, its structural style, enshrined deities, and murals are very special. Palkhor also features the Bodhi stupa, or *Kumbum* in Tibetan, which was built in 1412 and completed ten years later. Deemed the symbol of the monastery, the spectacular stupa consists of hundreds of chapels in layers, housing about 100,000 images of various iconic figures, including Buddhas, bodhisattvas, vajras, dharma kings, arhats, disciples, great leaders of different orders in Tibetan Buddhist history, and such outstanding figures in Tibetan history as Songtsen Gampo and

Trisong Detsen. Because of the great number of statues, it is also referred to as the Myriad Buddhas Stupa.

Gyangtse Dzong Fortress

Dzong Fortress lies atop Dzong Hill at the center of Gyangtse. In 1904, British troops invaded Tibet and occupied parts of Tibetan territory. They met with strong resistance in Gyangtse at the small hill, which was the seat of the local Dzong government. Brave and unyielding Gyangtse people used primitive weapons to fight British invaders equipped with modern guns. The Gyangtse defense lasted for eight months but finally failed. Tibetan warriors even threw stones from the hill, which constituted their last ammunition. They jumped off the cliffs, refusing to surrender. Emplacements in the ruins still overlook the valley. Four pillars erected by Qing ministers during the reign of Emperor Qianlong are well preserved.

The Tibetan word dzong *means "castle" or "fortress." It's also the original word used to refer to a county government of the Tibetan local regime. Built at the beginning of the fourteenth century, structures on Dzong Hill include the office of the Dzong chief (head of a county), Buddha halls, sutra halls, and various storehouses. (From Liu Liwen)*

Shalu Monastery

Shalu Monastery is located about 12.5 miles south of Shigatse. It was founded in 1040 by Chetsun Sherab Jungnay. The story of its founding involves Chetsun and his teacher, who suggested that Chetsun shoot an arrow and build a monastery where the arrow landed. The flying arrow hit a new bud, hence the Tibetan name *Shalu,* meaning "new bud."

The monastery is architecturally distinctive. In 1329, an earthquake destroyed it. In 1333, Buton rebuilt it under the patronage of the Chinese Mongolian emperor. Since many Chinese Han artisans participated in rebuilding the monastery, it incorporated the local Tibetan style along with the Chinese style of the Yuan Dynasty. This is the only monastery in Tibet that combines these styles.

Great statue of Shalu Monastery (From Colphoto)

Shalu Monastery possesses four religious treasures. One is a sutra board, which is 700 years old and cannot be reassembled if ever broken apart. A passage from a sutra is printed on the board, which is believed to bring good luck. The second treasure is a brass urn, which contains holy water that can cleanse away the 108 filths of human existence. The urn is usually sealed and covered with red cloth, and the water is changed every 12 years. The third treasure is a stone basin that was once Chetsun Sherab Jungnay's washbasin. The fourth treasure is a stone tablet on which the mantra *om mani Padme Hum* is written and four dagobas are carved. It was uncovered during the original construction of the monastery.

> Shalu Monastery is quite far from Shigatse, so visitors are advised to get there by taxi.

The art of Tangka is the primary art form of the Tibetan culture. (From ImagineChina)

Sakya Monastery

This monastery is a must-see for visitors to Tibet. The monastery lies 81 miles southwest of Shigatse. The Tibetan word *Sakya,* meaning "gray soil" because of the color of the local soil, is the central monastery of the Sakya Sect of Tibetan Buddhism. Its walls were painted in red, white, and gray stripes, which represent the Manjushri, Avalokiteshvara, and Vajrapani bodhi–sattvas, respectively. Because the monastery has an enormous collection of highly valuable art works, it is deemed the "Second Dunhuang." The Drum River divides it in two: the Northern Monastery and the Southern Monastery.

Established first, the Northern monastery was founded by Khon Konchog Gyalpo in 1073, from which the Sakya Sect arose that once ruled Tibet. Unfortunately, it is now in ruins due to its destruction during the Cultural Revolution (1966–1976). The ruins still reflect its splendor, however. The fifth Sakya throne holder, Drogon Chogyal Phakpa, known as Phakpa, built the Southern Monastery in 1268. Phakpa was the spiritual guide of Kublai Khan, a Mongolian Chinese emperor who granted Phakpa secular and religious authority over Tibet. After Phakpa, the Sakya Sect ruled for more than 100 years in Tibet.

The Southern Monastery is in better condition than the Northern. A typical Mongolian structure, the fortresslike monastery covers nearly 484,375 square feet, is surrounded by a moat, and has an outer wall and an inner wall. With fortifications and battlements on top, it has only one entrance on the east.

Sakya contains countless murals, mostly of the Yuan Dynasty. Of these, the murals of mandalas and former Sakya throne holders are the most outstanding. Among its collection of treasures are 3,000 pieces of palm-leaf sutras written in Tibetan, Chinese, Mongolian, and Sanskrit, which cover a wide range of knowledge. Other artifacts such as seals, crowns, robes, Buddhist vessels, and statues bestowed by emperors of the Yuan Dynasty are also on display there.

> There are few restaurants in Sakya County and hostels are poorly equipped. At present, there is still no electric power supply in the county.

Mount Qomolangma (Mount Everest)

The Tibetan name, *Qomolangma* means "goddess." At an altitude of 29,035 feet, it is the highest mountain in the world. Sometimes people mention it together with the North and South poles, referring to it as "the Third Pole of the Earth."

Addresses and Phone Numbers

Note: Although costs are low in hostels run by local Tibetans, sanitary conditions are usually substandard. Tourists are advised to carry their own sleeping bags and toiletries in case they need accommodations on their way to Mount Qomolangma.

Mount Qomolangma Hotel	About five minutes to the north of Tingri, which visitors must pass on their way to Qomolangma. Prices are very high at this hotel.	0892-8262775

Qomolangma is located in the midsection of the Himalayas, directly south of Tingri County in Shigatse. Originally this area was a vast ocean. It was not until the middle of the Miocene Epoch, when the Himalayan orogeny started, that the mountain gradually rose from the ocean bottom and finally became the highest peak on earth. Today, this mountain formation is still at work, which means Mount Qomolangma will keep getting higher and higher.

The Qomolangma region is dotted with five mountains higher than 26,250 feet and 38 mountains higher than 23,000 feet. The mountaintop is covered with ice and snow year-round, and in some places the ice can be more than 300 feet thick. Climate here is divided into the dry season and the wet season. During the dry season, the west-wind belt takes control and little or no precipitation can be expected on the north ridge of the mountain. But during the wet season, the southwest monsoon from the Indian Ocean brings a great deal of snow to this region.

As the apex of the world, Mount Qomolangma is also blessed with many natural wonders. When the sun shines on the mountain, the peak looks like a white pyramid miraculously transformed by the goddess. More often than not, the thick, freely moving clouds and banks of fog, appearing like flags waving from their mast, shroud the peak. This peculiar phenomenon is known as "Flag Cloud." An additional natural wonder found here is the ice of bright glaciers, which forms itself into various shapes such as bridges and pagodas. You can also find miles of efflorescent rock formations here, for example, stalagmites, stelae, and stone swords and pagodas. The Sherpas and hikers refer to this high-altitude splendor as "the Largest Park on the High Mountain."

As one of the national nature reserves in China, the Qomolangma region is home to numerous species of animals and plants, among which the snow leopard and sandalwood are two of the most precious.

The magnificent landscape and natural wonders of the Qomolangma region have long attracted mountain climbers and trekkers, explorers, and scientists from all over the world. Since the beginning of the nineteenth century, climbers from around the world have planned to climb this mountain. However, two weather conditions are required for climbing Qomolangma: the wind speed should be less than 65.6 feet per second at an altitude of 26,247 to 29,528 feet, and there should be very little or no precipitation. Only three months in the whole year meet these requirements: May (the best time for mountain climbing), September, and October.

At the foot of Mount Qomolangma lies Rongbuk Monastery, the highest temple in the world at 16,404 feet. About 16 miles from Qomolangma, this is the best place from which to appreciate the mountain scenery. Rongbuk Glacier in this area is also the largest among all the glaciers here.

(From Liu Liuen)

Inscription of the Tang Envoy to Hindu

This inscription appears on a cliff wall, which is about 50 feet wide and 13 feet high, in a valley about 3 miles north of Jilong County, in the Shigatse region. It was discovered in 1990. Experts in Tibetan history believe that in 657 Wang Xuance, envoy of the Tang Dynasty to Hindu, left this precious inscription when he traveled past this valley. The inscription is a record of his journey, and it is also the most ancient stone inscription discovered in Tibet up to this point.

Ngari Region

Best Time to Travel

The best time to visit Ngari is from May to July and from September to October. For the Sacred Mountain, April 15 in the Tibetan calendar is the most important festival. The most festive day in Pulan County is August 1, when you can see many unique folk costumes that are not on display at other times.

Shiquanhe

At an altitude of 14,108 feet, Shiquanhe (named after the Shiquan River) is the highest town in China as well as the political, economic, and cultural center of the Ngari region. Major natural resources here include minerals, among which gems, jade, and coal are dominant, as well as solar energy and geothermal heat. Economic resources here include wool, cashmere, and highland barley.

In recent years, with the help of the central government and Hebei and Shanxi provinces, the town has experienced great changes. The appearance of such amenities as computers, supermarkets, and public telephones makes Shiquanhe a modern town in this border area.

Thada Mound Forest

In Thada, there is a famous mound forest, which took shape in ancient times as a result of the formation of the Himalayas. Geologists confirmed that more than one million years ago, the area between Thada and Pulan was originally a vast lake. As a result of the mountain formation, the lake floor was constantly being eroded by running water. Later, when the water level declined and the lakebed rose up, erosion by wind and rain finally shaped it into its present configuration. Trees in the mound forest are in various shapes. Visitors who travel through the forest by car feel as if they are navigating around many giant feet.

To reach Thada from Shiquanhe by taxi costs 2,000 to 3,000 yuan for a round-trip. The journey takes about 12 hours. However, since taxis are not readily available, visitors may have to stay in Thada for a night. One thing to note is that the hostels in Thada are no more than earthen cottages built by local Tibetans, which are not very comfortable or sanitary.

With its numerous and regularly shaped tiers, the mound forest in the sunlight resembles an extraterrestrial landscape rather than a natural wonder. (From CFP)

Ruins of Guge Kingdom

Located in the Ngari Region, the Ruins of Guge Kingdom are the Old Summer Palace of Tibet. These ruins were once an imperial estate that fell into disrepair after the civil revolt and the invasion of the allied armies of eight foreign countries. The area also encountered civil strife and foreign attacks, which fragmented the once prosperous state. However, the legendary kingdom hasn't been totally lost, as much can be learned about it from its remains.

The greatest mystery about Guge is how a kingdom with such a splendid culture could vanish almost overnight. Its existence was scarcely known to the outside world for several centuries following its destruction, since no damage has been found that can be attributed to human activity. The kingdom's appearance is practically the same as it was on the day it was destroyed. (From Liu Liwen)

Established in about the tenth century, the Guge Kingdom played an important part in the economic and cultural development of Tibet. The kingdom advocated Buddhism, and many orders of this religion were founded here. The area also served as a major center for Tibet's foreign trade.

The Ruins of Guge Kingdom now extend around the sides of a mountain, which is about 984 feet high. Explorers have found more than 400 chambers and 800 caves here, as well as some fortresses, secret paths, pagodas, armories, granaries, and burial places. Except for some temples, the ceilings of all the chambers have collapsed, leaving only the walls. The ruins are surrounded by a city wall, and a fortress marks each of the corners. Palaces, temples, and local residences can be found from the mountaintop to the base, and only secret roads lead to the top, a layout designed to signify the supremacy of the king and ensure the safety of the palaces. Due to its great research value, the Ruins of Guge Kingdom have been listed in the first group of cultural sites of national importance under the protection of the state.

Perhaps the most interesting aspects of the ruins are the five temples and palaces—the White Temple, Red Temple, Samsara Temple, Imperial Palace, and Assembly Palace, which contain many inscriptions, statues, and murals. The most intact and valuable remaining artifacts are the murals, which are mainly pictures of Sakyamuni Buddha, kings, queens, princes, and other royal servants. In the sanctuary, pictures of the cultivation of male and female Esoteric Buddhas can be found. The colors and execution of these murals can be compared with those of the Mogao Caves in Dunhuang, Gansu. Most of the statues here are gold and silver Buddhist statues, among these the Silver Eyes of Guge is of the highest quality.

➡ Because of its remote location (11 miles from Thada), the Ruins of Guge Kingdom are not easily accessible. Taxis are available for hire; otherwise, visitors must wait by the road south of Thada for a military vehicle to give them a lift.

Tholing Monastery

The Guge Kingdom in Tibet experienced a brief period of prosperity, which lasted for about 700 years. Today two of its remaining glories are still accessible. One is its political center, the Ruins of Guge Kingdom, and the other is the religious center, the sublime Tholing Monastery.

The Tibetan word *Tholing* means "hovering in the sky forever," indicating the imposing position occupied by the monastery. Built by the second monarch of the Guge Kingdom in 996, it is the oldest Buddhist temple in the region. During its heyday, it was the center for the translation of Buddhist scriptures and the holding of religious ceremonies. The kingdom's dominant function in introducing Buddhism to the heart of Tibet also contributed much to this temple. In the mid-eleventh century, the prestigious lama Atisha was invited from India to give sermons here, which led to the revival of Buddhism in Tibet. In subsequent years, the monastery went through many changes and was finally recognized as a cultural site of national importance under the protection of the state on its one-thousandth anniversary.

In the Xiangquan Valley near Tholing, there is a long line of pagodas that extends as far as the eye can see. (From Liu Liwen)

The Tholing Monastery incorporates the craftwork of the architecture and Buddhist statues of neighboring India, Nepal, and Ladakh (the present), imitating the style of the archetypal Tibetan temple—the Samye Monastery. The many buildings here include halls, monks' residences, and pagodas, among which the Jiasha Hall, Red Hall, White Hall, and the 108 pagodas are the most interesting.

> Visitors are advised to bring flashlights with them if they want to see the murals in the Tholing halls, since the lights are dim there.

Donggar Grottoes

Located 25 miles north of Thada County, Donggar Frescoes are the largest remnants of the ancient Buddhist frescoes. About 25 miles northwest of the Guge Ruins, Donggar is a small village of ten or so households. The frescoes are scattered in the grottoes on the bluff north of the village. There are about 200 grottoes now, which spread throughout about a mile and a half and resemble honeycombs. Several of the grottoes with fine frescoes are clustered on the eastern U-shaped crag. Donggar Frescoes, which are grouped together in the three grottoes halfway up the mountain, are well preserved. Tibetan historic, religious, and cultural records do not mention when or how these frescoes were painted. But scientists believe that they are about 1,000 years old, and their discovery is significant in the field of archeology. The frescoes are mainly paintings of Buddha and bodhisattva figures, depictions of Buddhist stories, and various vignettes. The figures of heavenly maidens are especially vivid and well preserved.

> At present, Donggar Grottoes are not open to visitors. Tourists who wish to see them can apply to the Thada Culture Bureau.

Mount Kailash

Kailash means "snow mountain of the gods." The name originates from the year-round snow on its peak and its historical religious connections. The mountain is sometimes called "Mother of Iceberg," since it appears to be gazing at another mountain, Namcha Barwa, or "Father of Iceberg," in the far distance.

Mount Kailash, with an altitude over 21,655 feet, is the highest peak in the massive Gangdise mountain range. The peak looks like a pyramid piercing the sky. Seen from the south, the vertical ice trough and horizontal rock formation combine as the Buddhist symbol Swastika 卍, which represents the eternal power of Buddha. More often than not, clouds gather above the peak, so clear days are thought to be a blessing because local residents can get an unimpeded view.

Legend has it that a prestigious lama named Milarepa competed with Naro Bonchung, the leader of Bon, for supernatural power. Milarepa was triumphant, and thus the mountain came under the authority of Buddhism. However, the mountain is also said to be the gathering place of masses of gods, among which are the highest gods of Hinduism. It is no surprise that many pilgrims of different faiths visit here.

Walking around the mountain is a popular ritual, despite the length and rough terrain. According to the sayings of Buddhism, one circle around the mountain can atone for all the sins committed throughout a lifetime. Completing ten circles around the mountain will prevent eternal damnation in one's reincarnations for 500 years. In a Year of the Horse (when Sakyamuni, the founder of Buddhism, is said to have been born), worshippers get credit for 13 circles for every one completed. Naturally, these years draw the largest number of tourists.

> Most tourists will walk around Mount Kailash as a sign of respect for this sacred mountain.

Lake Manasarova (Mapam Yumco)

Lake Manasarova lies about 12.5 miles southeast of Mount Kailash. The name means "Invincible Jade Lake." It originates in a story that Buddhism won a victory against Bon in a religious match beside the lake. The lake is the same "Jade Pool of the Western Kingdom" described by the prestigious monk Xuanzang of the Tang Dynasty in his *Journey to the West*.

The altitude of Manasarova is about 15,000 feet, making it one of the highest fresh-

Pilgrims to Ngari feel respect for the sacred mountain and lake. Walking around them is a test of their faith. (From CFP)

water lakes in the world. The water is very transparent and bright. Hindu legend has it that the amrita designed by the great god Brahma can wash away all one's sins as well as any anxiety or improper thoughts. Many pilgrims bathe in the lake and take some water back as a gift to their relatives and friends.

The sacred lake is surrounded by four rivers: Maquan in the east, Shiquan in the north, Xiangquan in the west, and Kongque in the south. Named after the four divine animals in Buddhist legends—horse, lion, elephant, and peacock—these four rivers are also the respective sources of the other four famous rivers, the Ganges, the Indus, the Sutlej, and the Yarlung Tsangpo.

Walking around the lake for one circuit takes about four days. There are eight temples along the way, the two most notable being Jiwu and Chugu. Visitors may find lodging in these temples, but they should bring enough food for themselves.

Lhanag-Tso—the Ghost Lake

Lhanag-tso is a saltwater lake famous for its dark blue color. There is very little plant or animal life surrounding the lake, and this austere environment inspired the name Ghost Lake.

It is said that Lhanag-tso and Mapam Yumco (Lake Manasarova) were once a single lake. The middle part of the lake later sank, and a long hill divided it in two, becoming Mapam Yumco Lake and Lhanag-tso Lake. A long channel, Ganpa Chu, still connects the two lakes. Although the channel is usually dry, local people believe that one day water from Mapam Yumco Lake will flow into Lhanag-tso Lake and a red fish will swim into the lake. Then the water in the Ghost Lake will be as sweet as that in Mapam Yumco Lake.

Banggong Co Lake

Banggong Co Lake, which means "the long, narrow enchanting lake," is located on the route from Shiquanhe to Doima Township. It is also known as the "swan lake" of the border between China and Indian Kashmir. At an altitude of 13,914 feet, with a total length of more than 93 miles from west to east, the lake is narrower from south to north, with the narrowest point being 131 feet. The lake has an approximate area of 233 square miles. Its deepest point is 136 feet. The eastern part of the lake belongs to China, while the western part belongs to Indian Kashmir. Ice covers the lake for six months every year.

Bird Islet where thousands of gulls live, is located in the lake. The islet is small, about 984 feet long and 656 feet wide. Red willows cluster along the lake bank, creating a beautiful view. Gulls and their eggs can be seen everywhere—between rocks, in the grass, on the lake, and on the bank. There are also a small number of other birds and fowl, such as gray ducks that live on fish in the lake. When spring comes and warm air from the

With a length of about 93 miles from east to west, Banggong Co Lake is the longest lake in China. At its widest point, the lake is 9.3 miles wide, and at its narrowest is just 131 feet. (From CFP)

Bay of Bengal blows into the Ngari Plateau, groups of birds that have migrated from the cold plateau to the warmth of southern Asia the previous winter fly back to the islet. The months of May through September are the best season for observing birds. Herdsmen living on the lakefront often tell the story of dragons and monsters in the lake, which adds to its mysterious color.

Banggong Co Lake is located 6.2 miles north of the county seat of Rutog County and 84.5 miles northwest of Shiquanhe. Tourists can rent a car to go get there, and it takes three to four hours from Shiquanhe. Once at the lake, tourists can rent the small boats berthed at the lakeside to go to Bird Islet.

Nakchu Region

Best Time to Travel

The cold climate (the average annual temperature is below 32°F) and thin air in the Nakchu region make it uncomfortable for tourism most times of the year. Therefore, the best months to visit Nakchu are from June to September, when the temperature is relatively high.

Zhoima Canyon Scenic Area

Zhoima Canyon Scenic Area, discovered accidentally by an inspection team, is situated in Gulu Township, Nagqu County, 7 miles from the 109 highway and 143 miles from Lhasa. With an elevation of about 15,420 feet, Zhoima Canyon Scenic Area boasts lush forests, colorful and fragrant flowers, beautiful lakes and mountains, grotesque rocks, and caves.

Changtang Grassland

As one of the five biggest pastures in China, Changtang Grassland is surrounded by the Kunlun, Tanggula, Kangdese, and Nyainqentanglha mountains. It is a rich land as well as a paradise for wild animals and plants. On the

Beautiful prairie (From ImagineChina)

vast grassland, herds of yak, sheep, and many nomadic camps can be seen everywhere. The colorful long-standing nomadic culture is evident.

Mount Sangdankangsang

Among the many mountains on the Northern Tibetan Plateau, Sangdankangsang is the most famous because it is one of the 25 highest mountains in Tibet. Seen from the south, the mountain resembles a king sitting on his throne; seen from the west, a lion in the sky; seen from the east, a crystal pagoda; seen from the north, a silver tent. As the season changes, the mountain also takes on different colors: milky in summer, silver in winter, and white and shining bright in spring and autumn.

Qinghai-Tibet Highway is the fastest and easiest way to reach Mount Sangdankangsang.

Chamdo and Nyingchi Region

>>>

Best Time to Travel

May, June, and September are the golden months for visiting Chamdo, while any time from April through October is perfect for a visit to Nyingchi.

Chambaling Monastery

The monastery in Chamdo was founded in 1444 by one of Tsong Khapa's disciples and it has usually maintained a close relationship with past Chinese governments. It still has a brass seal granted to its abbot by Emperor Kangxi. Well preserved, Chambaling has hundreds of statues of Buddhas and great leaders, thousands of feet of murals, and magnificent Thangkas, which represent the highest artistic achievement in Chamdo. The most famous feature of the monastery is its religious dancing, which is performed with ferocious and living masks, elegant posture, and gorgeous costumes, against a backdrop of fantastic scenery.

Chambaling is about 20 minutes' walk from the old section of Chamdo.

Kanuo Ruins

Located in the village of Kanuo, 7.4 miles southeast from Chamdo, the ruins sit at an altitude of 10,171 feet. Discovered in 1977, they were first excavated between May and August 1978; an area of 19,375 square feet was unearthed. The remains of 26 houses were discovered, together with many cultural artifacts—mainly stone tools such as shovels, hoes, and cutters; tossing, cutting, and striking tools; scraping and grinding tools; axes; and stone digging tools. Adornments such as loops, beads, and bracelets as well as pottery, corn, and animal bones were also found. Archeologists' work shows that the ruins constitute New Stone Age sites, which date back 4,000 to 5,000 years, revealing that the ancient people were engaged in farming and livestock breeding, and that they used rough tools as early as more than 4,000 years ago.

Tourists can get to the Kanuo Ruins by taking the minibus to the Cement Factory. The cost to hire a taxi is about 100 yuan.

Sacred Mount Dola

Located 39 miles east of Basu County on the Sichuan-Tibet Road, Mount Dola is traditionally divided into the outer circle, middle circle, and inner circle. Walking around the mountain along the middle circle takes about four hours. Visitors can admire the celestial burial platforms as well as different kinds of stone inscriptions along the way. The inner circle is the major sightseeing route of Mount Dola. It takes visitors about two hours to complete the circcuit.

Visitors can view different kinds of stone inscriptions, Buddhist statues, and pagodas on their way around Mount Dola.

Bayi

At 9,842 feet high and 252 miles from Lhasa, Bayi is a burgeoning frontier town in southeastern Tibet. As the political, economic, and cultural center of the Nyingchi Prefecture, it resembles a garden spot, covered with green and flowering plants all year round. Traffic conditions here are excellent, and architectural styles are unique and various. The town is also blessed with comprehensive facilities for science, education, medicine, communication, commerce, and culture, as well as places for recreation and relaxation.

Motuo Nature Reserve

On the southeastern border of the Tibetan Plateau and in the great Yarlung Tsangpo Gorge lies an uninhabited place, which is the now-famous Motuo Nature Reserve. Although hunting is popular among local Tibetans, the numerous cliffs and waterfalls in the reserve make it almost impossible to access. Consequently, the primitive conditions in the reserve remain pristine.

In the Motuo Nature Reserve, there are more than 3,000 precious species of plants, among which more than 40 are named after Motuo. (From CFP)

Motuo is at present the last county without roads in China. Visitors who want to go there must take a bus and get off at Bomi, then walk to Motuo. Note that there are quite a few insects and leeches along the way, so come prepared.

Backward and secluded, Motuo is an isolated island on the plateau and appears to exist far removed from modern society. (From CFP)

During the Shoton Festival, Drepung Monastery hangs up a supersize image of Sakyamuni on Mount Gambo Utse to be worshipped by tens of thousands of pilgrims. The magnificent spectacle is the grandest event of Drepung Monastery in the year. (From Quanjing)

Tibet Style

Tibetan Buddhism

Any discussion of Tibetan Buddhism must bring up Songtsen Gampo, the first emperor of a unified Tibet. To consolidate his power, Songtsen Gampo married the Nepalese princess Khri b'Tsun and the Chinese princess Wencheng. When the princesses—both devout Buddhists—came to Tibet, they brought with them as dowries devotional images of Sakyamuni along with several sutras, and so it was that as Songtsen Gampo welcomed the two princesses into Tibet, he also welcomed Buddhism along with them. He converted to Buddhism, under the princesses' influence, and constructed the first Buddhist temples in Tibet, including the Jokhang Temple in Lhasa. In the middle of the eighth century, Buddhism again entered Tibet, this time from India. A distinctly Tibetan form of Buddhism emerged by the latter half of the tenth century, and by the thirteenth century the religion had spread outward to Mongolia. The religion flourished, spreading, factionalizing, and promoting the Buddhist faith throughout the area. As the religion grew in popularity, the lamas rose to political power in Tibet, resulting in a Buddhist theocracy unlike any other government in the world.

The Six-Character Mantra

Wherever you go in Tibet, the words you'll most often see and hear will be *Om mani padme hum.* These six syllables, known as the six-character mantra or the six-character enlightenment, form one of Tibetan Buddhism's most important invocations—as vital a part of Tibetan life as tsampa or ghee. The words may be recited or carved into surfaces as a prayer to Buddha for one's efforts to succeed—and so have become a symbol of Tibet and Tibetan Buddhism. Every Tibetan you ask is

Six-character mantra (From ImagineChina)

A praying elder (From Imagine-China)

likely to have a different interpretation of the mantra's meaning—as if as long as reciting it helps bring them an inner peace, the meaning were secondary.

Prayer Wheels

Men, women, children, and the elderly—you're likely to see all of them spinning prayer wheels in their hands. The tradition of prayer wheels arose from widespread illiteracy among the faithful. The wheels, each containing the text of a sutra, or Buddhist scripture, are spun day after day, year after year, as a way for revenants to complete their spiritual purification. Endlessly turning for countless revolutions, prayer wheels have passed from hand to hand and generation to generation to become one of the best-known symbols of Tibet.

Mani Stones and Five-Color Wind Horse Flags

Mani stones and five-color wind horse flags are the most prolific artistic manifestations in Tibet. On the Tibetan Plateau, travelers can see Mani stones of different forms and wind horse flags printed with scriptures everywhere. Mani stones are made of a vast number of slabstones on which figures of Buddha, mantras and portions of scripture are engraved. A certain number of slab stones are stacked, correlating with, for instance, the number of laps of a prayer wheel, or Chokhor, circumambulating the Mani stone. A five-color wind horse flag consists of flags of five colors—white, yellow, red, green and blue—which represent cloud, land, flame, river, and sky, respectively.

The Shoton Festival and Buddha Display

June 30 in the Tibetan calendar is the Shoton Festival, which is celebrated every year and is one of the traditional holidays in Tibet that has a long history. The Tibetan word *sho* means "yogurt" and *ton* means "eat." So the Shoton Festival is the festival when you eat yogurt. On that day, the Drepung Monastery hangs up a super-size image of Sakyamuni on Mount Gambo Utse to be worshipped by tens of thousands of pilgrims. The magnificent spectacle is the grandest annual event of Drepung Monastery.

Great Prayer Festival

In commemoration of Buddha Sakyamuni, Jokhang Temple holds the Great

Both Mani stones and five-color wind horse flags are artistic and religious sights in Tibet. (From CFP)

Tibetan opera (From ImagineChina)

features loud and clear high pitched voices, long end rhyme, and a chorus. As one of the few ethnic minority folk operas in China with a systematic structure, Tibetan opera plays a significant role in the history of Chinese drama.

Prayer Festival, or Monlam Chenmo, every year from January 4 to 25 in the Tibetan calendar. The grand events can be traced back to 1409, when Tsongkapa, founder of the Gelupa Sect of Tibetan Lamaism, held a prayer meeting in Lhasa. The tradition has been preserved and handed down from generation to generation. During the festival, Jokhang Temple holds the Geshe Degree test in the form of a debate. For Buddhist monks, this is an important day.

Cham Dance and Tibetan Opera

Each year on October 10 in the Tibetan calendar, Samye Monastery holds the Cham Dance ritual, also known as the "dancing God." Following completion of the Samye Monastery, Padma Sambhava organized a Cham Dance ritual to consecrate the monastery, dispel evil, and offer a sacrifice to the gods. This was the earliest form of the Cham Dance, which has been passed down from generation to generation to the present time.

A similar art form is the Tibetan opera. As one of the most popular performing arts in the Tibetan Plateau, it has a history of over 600 years and consists of two parts: the White Mask and the Blue Mask. Like many other folk operas, the Tibetan opera has narrative, music, dance, melody, and dialogue, as well as a unique and systematic performance procedure. When performing Tibetan opera, actors wear modeled masks. Drums and cymbals are the only instruments in the performance, which

Nagqu Horse Race Festival

People living in the special natural environment of the plateau rely heavily on horses in their daily activities, particularly when they are engaged in war. After so many generations, a deep emotional connection has emerged between Tibetan people and horses, which leads to the sanctification and spiritualization of horses and a belief that the horse has a decisive influence on destiny and the leaders of tribes. Therefore, a horse racing event was included in almost all Tibetan festivals that have been passed down. In ancient times when war was frequent, it was common to select leaders by means of a horse race and competition of military skill. Based on deep-rooted horse worship, many horse race festivals arose in the Tibetan region, of which Nagqu Horse Race Festival is the largest. In August, when the northern

Tibetan area is bathed in mild wind and bright sunshine, and beautiful flowers dot the expanses of grassland, herdsmen in flamboyant holiday costumes flock to the competition field days before the festival from every corner of northern Tibet, bringing with them tents and all kinds of food such as barley wine and yogurt. During the festival, colorful flags are flown over the racing field. When the race starts, riders lead their horses into the field, circle the area, and then walk to designated positions, where they mount their horses and wait for the starting signal, at which they whip the horses and dash at a full gallop to the finish line. In recent years, this traditional festival has evolved to include weight lifting, tug-of-war, singing of Tibetan Epic King Gesar, and other events in addition to the traditional events of the horse race, archery, and equestrian competition. At the same time, a large trade fair is also held.

Presenting Kha-btag (From CFP)

Equestrian competition is an important event at the festival, during which riders in special costumes display their extraordinary riding skills on the backs of fine galloping horses, while bending to pick up a trail of white Kha-btags from the racetrack and holding them overhead.

Kha-btag

Presenting the Kha-btag is the most widely seen demonstration of etiquette among the Tibetan people. It conveys the concepts of purity, sincerity, and faithfulness. Since ancient times, white has been considered by the Tibetan people as the color of purity and luck. Thus, most Kha-btags are white. The gestures used to present the Kha-btag vary from person to person. Generally, Kha-btag presenters hold the Kha-btag in both hands and raise it to the level of their shoulders, then bend over and extend it out toward the receiver so that the Kha-btag is at the same height as his head, which shows respect and most sincere blessing to the receiver. The receiver reaches out his hands to receive the Kha-btag in a reverent gesture. When presenting Kha-btags to distinguished guests or senior family members, one should hold the Kha-btag overhead, bend forward, and present it

The riders' impressive performance adds to splendor of the entire horse race festival. (From ImagineChina)

Thangka (From Colphoto)

in front of the receiver's seat or at his feet. For a peer or subordinate, the presenter can directly tie the Kha-btag around the receiver's neck.

Thangka

Thangka is a unique form of art in Tibetan culture dating back to the Tubo Period. The Tibetan word *Thangka* originally meant "seal" and later on it gradually came to mean the name of scrolled paintings. Most Thangka artworks highlight religious themes and can be divided into two major categories: Guotang, which is made of silk and satin as materials using embroidery, knitting, collage, or a layout printing technique; and Zhitang, which is painted on canvas using dyestuff. Based on the dyestuff used for the background, Zhitang can be further divided into golden Thangka, red Thangka, black Thangka, and colorful Thangka. There are many schools of Thangka art from different years and regions; the Miantang School is the dominant one in the Lhasa area.

Religious Taboos

Always circumambulate temples, Mani stones, shrines, and other religious objects clockwise. Do not walk around them in reverse. Likewise, prayer wheels may not be rotated counterclockwise, which is regarded as an offense. However, in contrast to this, prayer wheels in the Bonpo Religion *should* be rotated counterclockwise. Watch out for this when you are visiting a temple. If you have no idea what to do, just follow those around you. Don't touch any display of scripture, statues, murals, or ritual instruments in a temple. More important, do not step over them. When sleeping, be sure not to point your feet toward the shrine or the Buddha statue. When making the bed, do not turn the mattress over, as this is done only after people die.

Tibetan Costume

Tibetan Clothes

The most prominent features of Tibetan attire are long sleeves, loose bodices, off-center openings, lack of buttons, flamboyant colors, and supreme elegance. Most Tibetan robes in agricultural areas are made of Pulu. Also known as Tibetan wool, Pulu is woven wool and serves as the major material for the Tibetan robe and boots. Given the cold weather in Tibet, most people wear a leather robe, or *Chuba* in the Tibetan language. A chuba has loose sleeves to facilitate arm movement. It can be used for a number of interesting purposes: as clothing during the day, as bedding at night and as a pouch when it is fastened around the waist. According to historical records, Tibetan clothes in the eleventh century BCE had the basic earmarks of modern Tibetan attire, so they are a living record of the whole Tibetan civilization.

(From ImagineChina)

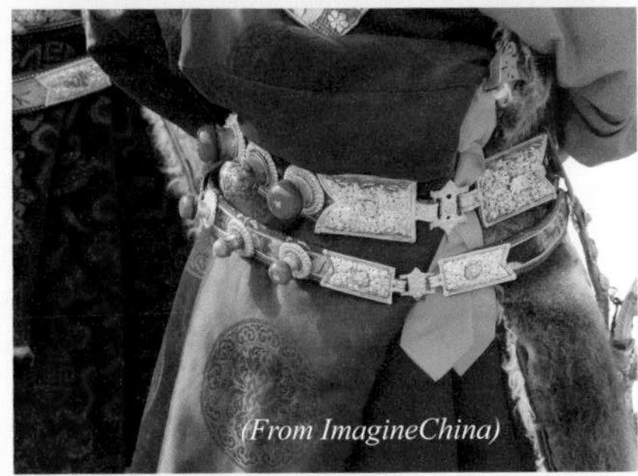
(From ImagineChina)

Belts and Boots

Basic features of Tibetan costumes make necessary a series of accessories. Belts are an indispensable accessory for the Tibetan costume. Without a belt, the loose-bodied robe hampers movement and makes people less graceful.

The Tibetan boot is also known as the Songba boot. The sole is made of cowhide and the upper is made of Pulu. Moistureproof, warm, waterproof, and wearable, it is perfect for Tibetan people. The Tibetan boot is mainly handmade and its fine workmanship makes it a specialty craft in Tibet.

Tibetan Hats

Tibetan hats can be divided into five types based on their use: the common hat, the official hat, the monk hat, the military hat and the artist hat. There are also winter hats and summer hats. The fox pelt hat is the most beautiful of all Tibetan hats as well as the most popular one among Tibetan people in winter and spring. It is 7.87 inches in height and has one of two different shapes: a round-top, tube-shaped hat and a cuspate-top, bag-shaped hat. The round top of the tube-shaped hat is usually made of overlapping silks and satins of different colors and resembles a beautiful flower in bloom. In summer, Tibetan people love to wear Jiaya, a kind of Tibetan hat with a wide brim that shields them from sunshine and rain. Beautiful and elegant, Jiaya feature the distinctive style of a local ethnic group.

Tibetan Knife

The Tibetan knife is an important instrument in the daily life of the local people. It is a practical tool used to cut meat and protect people from physical harm as well as serving as an ornament. Tibetan knives for men are sharp and are more primitive, while those for women are more delicate. The most famous Tibetan knives are the Gongbu knife made in Gongbu and the Lazi knife made in Rikaze, which has a beautiful sheath with silver ornaments and fine engraved patterns. Yet most Tibetan knives on sale on Borkhor Street nowadays are fake and are made in the hinterlands as opposed to the originals made in Tibet. Besides, the biggest problem

(From Quanjing)

for buyers of Tibetan knives is that knives may not be carried on planes and can only be delivered by mail.

The Kangba Costume

Chamdo is located in the migration corridor of ethnic groups along East Tibet, West Sichuan, and Northwest Yunnan. An abundance of ethnic customs and artifacts have been passed down over the centuries, and Kangba culture is one of the most typical ones.

The special geological territory where Kangba people live has given rise to a rich variety of florid and distinctive costumes in the Kangba area. The most remarkable feature of the Kangba costume is its luxurious ornamentation for both men and women. From top to toe, local people wear a large number of ornaments of various shapes, colors, and patterns that are made of gold, silver, agate, emerald, coral, and Turkish stone fashioned meticulously. Some of the ornaments are extremely valuable. Kangba men in the Chamdo region often wear ivory hair rings, red coral earrings, and necklaces of precious gems. They wear their hair in black and shining braids and pin them up on their head, which is called a hero knot. Most of them lift the skirts of their robes above the knees and bind the sleeves around the waist to show their wealth, dignity, and bravery. Women in Kangba wear red coral ornaments called *meiduo,* meaning "flower," which are inlaid in silver and bronze frames. They also comb their hair into small braids of different thicknesses and dress them up with fine coral and other ornaments. In addition, Kangba women have a particular liking for Bangdian, a kind of woolen fabric.

(From CFP)

Tibetan Cuisine

Clarified Butter

Clarified butter, or *ghee,* plays a crucial role in Tibetan cuisine. The butter is made from cow's or sheep's milk and purified using traditional methods that have changed little over the centuries: Tibetan women heat the milk slightly before pouring it into a wooden bucket and churning it vigorously until the oil and water in the milk separate and a yellow layer of buttery oil floats to the top. This is scooped out and poured into a leather bag in which it cools and congeals to form the ghee. Ghee is high in nutritional value—important for Tibetans, particularly herders and nomads, who rarely eat vegetables and fruits and must rely upon the ghee, along with meat, for their caloric intake. Ghee is used in many ways in Tibetan cuisine—most commonly it is stirred into yak butter tea and tsampa. As part of their New Year celebrations, Tibetans also use ghee when roasting nuts and gathia.

Highland Barley

Qingke highland barley—also known as *ke damai* and *yuanmai*—is one of the main ingredients in Tibetan tsampa. It is usually stir-fried and ground into flour, then mixed together with ghee and eaten or mixed together with peas to make tsampa. Barley tsampa, a staple of the traditional Tibetan diet, is now served to Chinese and foreign visitors staying at Lhasa's main hotels. On religious feast days, Tibetans sprinkle tsampa in the air as a sign of celebration.

Beef and Mutton

Beef, mutton, and dairy products are the staples of the Tibetan diet. In the herding regions, people rarely eat vegetables, sticking instead to a generally high-fat, high-protein diet. The high caloric content of beef and mutton helps people living in these high-altitude regions fight the cold. Some Tibetans eat raw meat; if you go to these herders' homes, you will see strips of wind-dried beef and mutton hanging indoors or inside their tents. If you are fortunate enough to be a guest of these people, your host may invite you to try some of the dried meat—a unique food available only in the altiplano regions. The dried meat is prepared in December of every year, when the temperature plummets below freezing. The beef and mutton are carved into strips, sometimes salted or treated with wild herbs, then hung in a cool, well-ventilated, shady spot where the wind will dry them while preserving the fresh taste. By spring of the next year, the meat is ready—a crispy, tasty delicacy.

Tibetan peasants collect highland barley. (From CFP)

Dairy

Yogurt and milk curd are the most popular dairy foods in Tibet. There are two types of yogurt: one is cheese, or *daxue* in the Tibetan language, which is made of milk from which ghee has been extracted; the other is *exue* which is made of unprocessed milk. As a milk product in which the sugar has been broken down, yogurt boasts a higher nutrition value and is easier to digest; thus, it is ideal for the elderly and children. Milk curd is made of the remnants of milk after ghee is extracted from it and it undergoes boiling and evaporation. It can be processed into milk cakes and milk biscuits. In heating milk, a thin layer of milk film can also be lifted from it. Like tofu sheets, milk film is both delicious and nutritional. Dairy products are important foods for Tibetan people. Wherever they go, they take them along. In Tibet, parents usually give children milk curd as a snack.

Sichuan

Geography at a Glance

Sichuan Province, also known as Chuan or Shu, is located in the southwest of China, at the mouth of the Changjiang River. Its eastern neighbor is Chongqing; Yunnan and Guizhou lie to the south. It is east of Tibet and south of Qinghai, Gansu, and Shaanxi. It covers an area of 185,329 square miles and has a population of 83,290,000 (2000 census).

Geographically speaking, Sichuan Province borders on Aba, Gangtse, and the eastern boundary of Liangshan Autonomous County. The province can be divided into two parts, Sichuan Basin in the east and the Western Sichuan Plateau. The average altitude of the Western Sichuan Plateau is more than 3,000 feet. The northern part of the plateau, covered with vast swamps and grasslands, is part of the Tibetan Plateau. The southern part of the plateau is in the northern Hengduan Mountains, where there are valleys of thick forest. This is the primary forest area in Sichuan. As for the Sichuan Basin, the altitude at the base ranges from 652 to 2,461 feet. Rivers in Sichuan belong to two major water systems, the Yellow River and the Changjiang River, and the drainage area is 3 percent of the province's entire area.

Sichuan Province's typical climate is subtropical. Due to the complicated landform and various seasonal winds, the climate differs a great deal between the east and the west. The eastern basin is located in a subtropical damp area; therefore, it has four distinct seasons and plenty of rain, with an annual average temperature between 57 and 66°F. The areas along the Changjiang River

(From ImagineChina company)

Bamboo Sea in Southern Sichuan (From ImagineChina company)

are relatively flat, which makes it difficult for the heat to diffuse, and as a result, these areas are generally hot and humid. In summer the temperatures in these areas can rise to above 100°F. Compared to the climate in the basin, the surrounding mountains remain relatively cool, and rainfall is plentiful.

Featured Cuisine

Little pigeon with shallot, fish-flavored chicken claws, crispy rice and pork slices, fish-flavored pork slices, kung pao chicken, little fried chicken, homemade trepang, sour-spicy tendon, jade-like lettuce with duck tongues, boiled beef, pork thighs cooked à la Su Dongpo, fish marinated with pickled Chinese cabbage, pickled vegetable and crucian (fish), long wonton, Lai tangyuan (stuffed dumplings made of glutinous rice flour), husband-and-wife beef slices, Zhong jiaozi, pearl meatballs, Grandma Chen's bean curd, fiery beef from Zigong, Northen Sichuan cool starch noodles, Sichuan hot pot.

Featured Commodities

Local Specialties

Song Dynasty–style Leshan pens, bamboo curtain drawings from Nanchong, fresh bamboo shoots from Chengdu and Ya'an, red kongfu tea from Yibin, starch vermicelli from Luzhou, board-cooked duck from Xichang.

Folk Handicrafts

Sichuan embroidery, Sichuan brocade, bamboo-shred biscuit ware, Zigong Gong fans, Anyue bamboo matting,

Notes 

❶ It's best to ride the cable car to the summit of Emei Mountain. Hiking up the mountain is time consuming and may cost tourists the marvelous but transient sunrise spectacle.

❷ The Leshan Giant Buddha can be fully seen only from a boat in the middle of the river. Boats are always available at the riverbank piers. The river flows so quickly that boats can stay in front of the Buddha for only a few minutes. Tourists are advised to prepare their cameras beforehand, so as not to miss the best shots.

Fushun straw matting, Chongqing and Chengdu bamboo weaving.

Transportation Tips

By Bus

Road transportation is the main way of traveling in Sichuan Province. All roads in the province center around Chengdu. The arterial roads include the Sichuan-Shaanxi Road, the Sichuan-Tibet Road, and the Chengdu-Chongqing Road. The Chengdu-Chongqing highway is the main artery between Sichuan Province and Chongqing. The Chengdu-Dujiangyan Highway, Chengdu-Mianyang Highway, Chengdu-Leshan-Emeishan Highway, Chengdu-Yaan Highway, and Neijiang-Zigong-Yibin Highway (among others) connect tourist sites in the province into an orderly network.

By Train

In Sichuan Province there are now five arterial railroads: Chengyu, Baocheng, Chengkun, Neikun, and Dacheng. Besides these, there are also nine tributary railroads: Sanwan, Xiaoli, Ziwei, Chengwen, Detian, Guangyue, Panzhihua, Guangwang, and Yigong. Baocheng Railroad is China's first electrified railway and the first one

POPULAR FESTIVALS

Chengdu Lantern Show

Held in the People's Park every year during the Spring Festival. Tourists can watch various types of performance art and acrobatics, and enjoy special food and snacks.

Zigong Lantern Show

Held every year from early February to early March. Thousands of artistic craft lanterns are displayed, and there is also a trade fair.

Dujiangyan Water-Releasing Ceremony

Held at the Qingming Festival every year at the Dujiangyan Dam, when the water is released. Folk dancing and singing are performed during the ceremony.

Mountain Circling Festival

Traditional festival of Kangding held on April 8 of the lunar calendar, the traditional birthday of the Buddha. On this day people from Kangding dress in their finest and bring the whole family and friends to climb Paoma Mountain and take part in the mountain circling.

Xinjin Dragon Boat Show

Held in the Nanhe River in Xinjin County every year. There are various events, including a dragon boat exhibition and race and a night journey on colorful boats.

Wangcongci Singing Fair

Held every year on May 15 of the lunar calendar in Pixian County. Various cultural, recreational, and sports events take place.

Gadeng Festival

In early lunar July every year, people gather on the lawn here for singing and dancing. There are also a trade fair and many local sports competitions, such as wrestling and horseback riding.

to connect Sichuan with other parts of the country.

By Plane

Chengdu is the hub for air travel in the southwest. There are also other airports in Sichuan, including Yibin, Xichang, Dazhou, and Luzhou. There are 102 operating flights, among which 96 are domestic and 6 are international or interregional ones for chartered flights.

By Water

Sichuan is one of the provinces that boasts highly developed water transportation. The Changjiang River runs through the province; seven other trunk streams (Jinsha River, Minjiang River, Tuojiang River, Jialing River, Beijiang River, Qujiang River, and Wujiang River), and more than 120 tributaries or small rivers are also connected, forming a natural network of water transportation. Now more than 120 counties and more than 1,400 villages can be reached by water. There is also water transportation between major industrial areas and important cities.

Recommended Routes

Featured Routes

Five-day tour: Customs of the Zang and Qiang ethnic groups

Day 1 Arrival in Chengdu. Lodging: Jinjiang Hotel.

Day 2 Chengdu→Hongyuan. Lodging: Hongyuan Hotel.

Day 3 Waqie→Tower Forest→Sika Raising Farms→The Moon Bay. Lodging: Hongyuan Hotel.

Day 4 Experience the customs of the Zang and Qiang minorities, including milking cows, making buttered tea, making zanba (roasted qingke barley flour), riding, fishing, tasting Tibetan food, viewing a colorful Tibetan clothing exhibition and Tibetan songs and dances. Lodging: Hongyuan Hotel.

Day 5 Hongyuan→Chengdu. End of tour.

Five-day tour: Bamboo Sea in the south of Sichuan

Day 1 Arrival in Chengdu. Lodging: Jinjiang Hotel.

Day 2 Chengdu→Yibin→Changning County→Wanli Town→Cuimen Pass (Jade Gate Pass)→Wangyan Pavilion (No-Words Pavilion)→Zhuzei Gate (Punish-the-Traitor Gate). Lodging: Bamboo Sea Mountain Villa.

Day 3 Wanli Town→Dragon Lake (Qinglong Lake)→Rainbow-Colored Waterfall→Luohun Stage→Heaven Treasure Stockaded Village→Fairy Lake→Fairy's Home Cave→36 Combat Strategies Carved on the Cliff→Ancient Plank Roads along the Cliff→Sanhe Area (the area where three worlds come together)→Long Jade Corridor. Lodging: Wanli Town.

Day 4 Bamboo Sea→Yibin→Chengdu. Lodging: Jinjiang Hotel.

Day 5 End of tour.

Seven-day tour: Northern Sichuan tourist sites

Day 1 Chengdu→Jiuzhai Valley. Lodging: Aba Jiulong Hotel.

Day 2 All-day tour of the Jiuzhai Valley (Ze ChaWa Valley→Rize Valley→Shuzheng Valley). Lodging: Aba Jiulong Hotel.

Day 3 Jiuzhai Valley→Huanglong→Maoxian County. Lodging: Maoxian County.

(From CFP)

Day 4 Maoxian County→Dujiangyan Dam→Chengdu. Lodging: Jinjiang Hotel.

Day 5 Chengdu→Wolong (Crouching Dragon) Nature Reserve→Balang Mountain→Rilong Town of Siguniang Mountains (Four Beauty Mountains) →Shuangqiao Valley (Twin Bridge Valley)→Yinyang Valley→Wuse Mountain (Five-colored Mountain)→Shajilin Plank Road along the Cliff→Nianyu Dam→Mount Lieren (Mount Hunter)→Niupengzi→Niuxin Mountain→Abi Mountain (Mountain of Mother)→Mount Yeren (Mount Savage). Lodging: Siguniang Mountain Hotel.

Day 6 Rilong Town of Siguniang Mountains →Changping Valley→Daguniang Mountain (First Beauty Mountain)→Erguniang Mountain (Second Beauty Mountain)→Sanguniang Mountain (Third Beauty Mountain)→Siguaniang Mountain (Fourth Beauty Mountain)→Kushu Shoal (Shoal of Withered Trees)→Tangbo Ancient Road→Leigu Rock→Tibetan Villages. Lodging: Siguniang Mountain Hotel.

Day 7 Siguaniang Mountains →Chengdu. End of tour.

Traditional Routes

One-day tour: Chengdu

Thatched Cottage of Du Fu→Wuhou Memorial Temple Wuhouci→Qingyang Palace→Wangjianglou Pavilion→Wenshu Monastery. End of tour.

Five-day tour: Siguniang Mountains (Four Beauty Mountains)

Day 1 Arrival in Chengdu.

Day 2 Route: Chengdu→Wolong Natural Reserve→Balang Mountain→Siguniang Mountains →Rilong Town.

Day 3 Shuangqiao Valley (Twin Bridge Valley)→Yinyang Valley→Wuse Mountain →Shajilin Plank Road along the Cliff→Nianyu Dam→Mount Lieren→Niupengzi →Niuxin Mountain→Abi Mountain→Mount Yeren.

Day 4 Changping Valley→Siguniang Mountains→Kushu Shoal →Tangbo Ancient Road→Leigu Rock→Tibetan Villages.

Day 5 Siguniang Mountains→Wolong Nature Reserve→Chengdu. End of tour.

Three-day tour: Emei Mountain and Leshan Mountain

Day 1 Arrival in Chengdu.

Day 2 Route: Chengdu→Leshan Giant Buddha→Lingyun Temple →Plank Roads along the Cliff→Emei Mountain.

Day 3 Route: Wannian Temple (Temple of Ten Thousand Years)→Qingyin Pavilion (Pavilion of Clear Ringing)→The Monkey World. End of tour.

Addresses and Phone Numbers

Jinjiang Hotel	80 South Renmin Road, Chengdu	028-85506666
Hexiang Mountain Villa (Flying Crane Mountain Villa) of Dujiangyan	Qingcheng Mountain, Dujiangyan, Chengdu	028-87288006
Xiongfei Holiday Hotel	193 Jiefang Road, Ziliujing District, Zigong	0813-2118888
Hualong Grand Hotel	58 Teichang Road, Nanchong	0817-2322111
Zhuhai Mountain Villa (Bamboo Sea Mountain Villa)	Zhuhai Town,Chang'an County,Yibin	0831-4918000
Emei Mountain Hotel	Baoguo Temple (Patriotic Dedication Temple)of Emei Mountain	0833-5590518
Hanyuan Hotel	20 Jiefang Road, Fulin Town, Hanyuan County, Ya'an	0835-4221070
Gongga Hotel	Moxi Town, Luding County, Gangtse	0836-3266666
Siguniang Mountain Hotel	Rilong Town, Xiaojin County, Aba	0837-2791578
Xingyu International Hotel	Zhangzha Town, Jiuzhaigou County, Aba	0837-7766888
Hongyuan Hotel	Hongyuan County	0837-2662586

Self-Guided Tours

Historic Sites of Jianmen Pass and Sichuan Road

Tourists drive from Chengdu to Guangyuan. Along the route are Deyang, Zitong, Jianmen Pass (Sword Gate Pass), and Jian Pavilion (Sword Pavilion). Main sites include Cuiyun Corridor (Jade Cloud Corridor), Huangze Temple in Guangyuan, Stone Carvings on the Thousand-Buddha Cliff, Bailong Lake (White Dragon Lake), Tangjiahe Natural Reserve, Pinglan Natural Reserve, Fule Mountain (Mountain of Wealth and Happiness) in Mianyang, Damiao Mountain (Great Temple Mountain) in Zitong, Fresco of Yuanjue Temple, and Pangtong Ancestral Temple in Deyang.

Adventure on the Prairie of Northern Sichuan

Tourists start from Chengdu. Along the way are Maoxian County, Songpan, Chuanzhu Temple, Galitai, Baozuo, Ruoergai, Hongyuan, Shuajing Temple, Shuama Temple (Temple Where the Horse Is Washed), and Miyaluo. Major sites include the beautiful scenery on the Minjiang River, the Relic of Diexi Earthquake, Chuanzhu Temple, the Grand Valley of Namo, Thermal Springs of Paojiangzha, the Flower Sea, and Dazha Temple.

Chengdu, Deyang, Ya'an Region

Best Time to Travel

Zigong has four distinct seasons, and, the area doesn't have hot summers or cold winters. The period between March and November is the finest time to visit. Spring is the best time to visit Chengdu. The rail and highway systems can take tourists anywhere in the province.

Shopping Tips

Hongqi Department Store is located on the Zongfu Road in Chengdu. One of the best choices for tourist shopping, the store sells various local specialties, well-known wines, water products, and mountain delicacies.

Chunxilu is located in the heart of Chengdu. It is the most representative, most prosperous, and busiest pedestrian street. Chunxilu is a must-see for tourists.

Royal Tomb of Wangjian

The tomb is located at the northwestern corner of the city, on Yongling Road, at Sandong Bridge. This is the tomb of the Sichuanese king Wangjian from the period of Five Dynasties and Ten Kingdoms, and historically it has been called Yongling, meaning "the tomb forever." With a full length of 77 feet, the tomb chamber is made up of 14 stone arches and is divided into three parts: front, middle, and back. The chambers are separated by wooden doors, and the middle chamber is where the king's coffin is found. On the eastern, western, and southern walls of the chamber, 24 musicians playing different instruments are carved into the walls, which is the only complete image of the imperial orchestra of the Tang Dynasty so far unearthed in China. Jade belts, silverware, iron pigs and bulls, and similar artifacts have been found here.

Wuhou Memorial Temple

Built at the end of Western Jin Dynasty, this is the memorial temple of Zhuge Liang, a master teacher in ancient China and the prime minister of Shu Kingdom (current Sichuan Province) in the period of Three Kingdoms. The title of "Wuxianghou" (*hou* is a high official rank in China, roughly equivalent to "duke" in English)

The city of Chengdu enjoys a temperate climate. It is never too hot in the summer nor too cold in the winter. (From Quanjiing)

was conferred upon him; thus, the temple is called Wuhou Memorial Temple. Its gate opens to the south. The entire area is divided into five parts: the main gate, secondary gate, Liubei Hall, Passage Hall, and Wuhou Memorial Temple. In front of the main gate is a hall of monuments. The western hall houses monuments from the Ming Dynasty, while the eastern hall houses the precious monument from the Tang Dynasty, which is just 12 inches tall. Pei Du, a famous prime minister in the Tang Dynasty, composed the monument's inscription; Liu Gongchuo, a well-known calligrapher (Liu Gongquan's elder brother), hand-wrote it. Then, Lujian, a first-class inscriber,

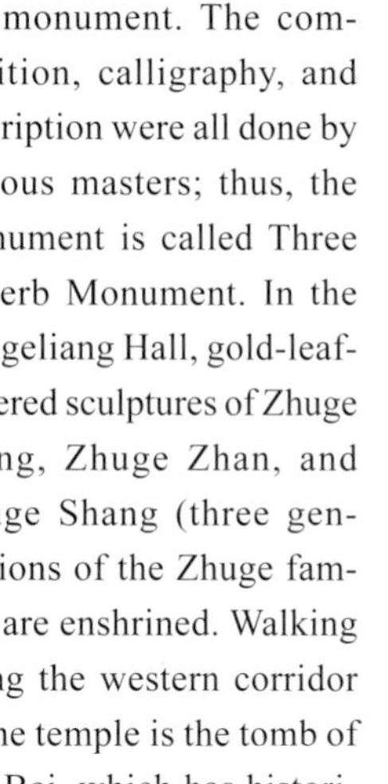

engraved the characters on the monument. The composition, calligraphy, and inscription were all done by famous masters; thus, the monument is called Three Superb Monument. In the Zhugeliang Hall, gold-leaf-covered sculptures of Zhuge Liang, Zhuge Zhan, and Zhuge Shang (three generations of the Zhuge family) are enshrined. Walking along the western corridor of the temple is the tomb of Liu Bei, which has historically been called Huiling.

The exhibition and display of cultural relics from the Three Kingdoms Period are worth seeing for those with a particular interest in that historical period.

This is the Passage Hall, which is next to Liubei Hall. The calligraphy that reads "Wuhou Memorial Temple" on the horizontal inscribed board was done by Guo Moruo, a famous scholar. The poetic antithetical couplet on the poles was composed and hand-written by Dong Biwu. Across from this hall is Zhuge Liang Hall. (From Quanjing)

One of Du Fu's poems reads: "How can I find thousands of mansions to shelter the homeless and bring a smile to their faces?" Visitors to the pavilion of the Shaoling Cottage monument find that the former residence of this great poet has only mud walls and a thatched roof. Reading his poem, one cannot help but be touched by the poet's great love for people.(From Quanjing)

Thatched Cottage of Du Fu

The Thatched Cottage of Du Fu is located in the western suburb of Chengdu, beside Huanhuaxi Brook. The famous poet Du Fu lived in the cottage for five years and composed more than 240 poems there. The cottage buildings are in the Qing Dynasty style. The unique garden architecture is called "blended" classical design. At the original site of the cottage, the six buildings, aligned along their centers, are the Screen Wall, the Front Gate, the Lobby, the Hall of Poem

History, the Simple Wooden Door, and the Gongbu Shrine. There are halls and other buidings, all of which are symmetrical. To the east of the Gongbu Shrine is the pavilion of the Shaoling Cottage monument. The lobby displays the Chinese painting *Full Views of Thatched Cottage of Du Fu* and a brief overview of Du Fu's life. In the middle of the Hall of Poem History stands a sculpture of Du Fu walking while composing a poem aloud; between the poles hang rubbings of Du Fu sculptures from all dynasties and poetic couplets commemorating him. In the exhibition halls on both sides, paintings based on Du Fu's poems and calligraphic works by modern artists are on display. Inside the Gongbu Shrine stands a colored sculpture of Du Fu. The sculptures of two other famous poets from the Song Dynasty, Huang Tingjian and Lu You, are also on display in the shrine; *Study in the Cottage (Cao Tang Shuwu)* and *Qia'ai Hangxuan* are on the left and right side, respectively. The shrine also houses ancient editions of Du Fu's works and versions translated into other languages.

Wenshu Monastery

Built in the Sui Dynasty, Wenshu Monastery is at 15 Wenshuyuan Street, in northwestern Chengdu. It is one of the Four Well-Known Gardens from the Qing Dynasty in western Sichuan. In 1681 Chan Master Cidu came here to practice Buddhism. When the monastery was rebuilt in 1697, it was called Wenshu Monastery. The monastery faces south. As a typical Qing Dynasty design, several buildings are centrally aligned, including Tianwang Temple, Three Dashi Temple (a temple of three bodhisattvas: Bodhisattva of Compassion, Bodhisattva of Ultimate Knowledge, and Bodhisattva of Universal Benevolence), the Great Buddha's Hall, and the Lecture Hall of Buddhist Laws. The bell tower houses a bronze bell that weighs almost a thousand pounds. Many famous Buddhist masters practiced at this monastery, including Cidu, Benyuan, Nenghai, and Kuanlin. Ancient treasures are also enshrined here, such as the skull of Tang Xuanzang, the White Jade Buddha from Burma, the Ink Dragon Painting from the Song Dynasty, a tapestry of Bodhisattva Wenshu, and rare sutras.

Heping Tower east of Wenshu Monastery. A tall iron tower, it measures 72 feet high. (From Quanjing)

> The vegetarian food at Wenshu Monastery is quite delicious. Tourists interested in gourmet food may want to sample it.

Wangjiang Pavilion Park

Wangjiang Pavilion (pavilion with a view over the river) is located outside the eastern gate of Chengdu, on the southern bank of the Jinjiang River. The park itself, covered with thick forests and bamboo, encompasses more than 32 acres. There are beautiful views of pavilions and lakes. The buildings include Chongli Pavilion, Zhuojin Pavilion (Brocade Wash Pavilion), Huanjian Pavilion, Wuyunx-

Wangjiang Pavilion, 128 feet high, has four floors. While the upper two floors are octagonal, the lower two floors are square, which is an innovative and significant design. (From ImagineChina)

ian Pavilion, Liubei Pond (Toppled-Cup Pond), and Quanxiang Pavilion (Fragrant Spring Pavilion). The park came into being through efforts in the Ming and Qing dynasties to commemorate the former residence of Tang Dynasty poetess Xue Tao. Xue loved bamboo, and more than 150 kinds of bamboo are planted here, giving the place its alternate name of Bamboo Garden of Chengdu. Wangjiang Pavilion is the largest building in the park. Built in 1889, it is now a landmark in the city.

Zhuojin Pavilion is to the west of Wangjiang Pavilion. In the Han Dynasty, brocade makers used to wash their products in the Jinjiang River, so the river was also called Zhuojin River (Brocade Wash River). This is how the Zhuojin Pavilion got its name. To the east of Wangjiang Pavilion is Yinshi Pavilion (Pavilion for Humming Verses), modeled after the Yinshi Pavilion in Bijifang, Xue Tao's residence in her last years. To the southwest of Yinshi Pavilion is an alley of loquat. It was built according to Wang Jian's poem to Xue Tao, which reads "lead a detached life amongst loquat flowers." After crossing the loquat alley, tourists come to several memorial buildings: Wuyunxian Pavilion, Quanxiang Pavilion, Qingyuan Room, and Huanjian Pavilion. The park includes a well from which Xue Tao took water to make writing paper, although this particular well was actually built in the Ming Dynasty by the principality of Sichuan to replicate the historic well.

Qingyang (Green Ram) Taoist Temple

Qingyang (Green Ram) Taoist Temple is located inside the western First Ring Road and is the largest Taoist temple in southwestern China. The Taoist classic *Essence of the Taoist Canon,* kept here, can be found only in China. The temple was first called Xuanzhong Guan in the Tang Dynasty. When soldiers in the Huangchao Uprising took the city of Chang'an in 880, Emperor Xi of the Tang Dynasty paid a visit to the temple. Later on, he gave an imperial order to change the temple's name to Qingyang ("Green Ram") Taoist Temple. The currently existing buildings in the temple were rebuilt during the Qing Dynasty and include Sanqing Hall, Doumu Hall, Hunyuan Hall, Lingzu Pavilion, Zijin Stage, Eight Trigram Pavilion, as well as a few others. In the temple are various sculptures and statues, and different kinds of animals and dragons are painted on the walls. In front of Sanqing Hall stands a pair of bronze rams carried here from Beijing under Emperor Yongzheng's rule in the Qing Dynasty. One of them, incorporating the characteristics of all 12 animals of the Chinese zodiac, is unique in design and has become an important cultural artifact for the study of Taoist culture.

Dujiangyan Dam

Dujiangyan Dam is located in the west of Guan County, Sichuan Province. It is an ancient irrigational wonder. It was built between 276 and 251 BCE by Prefecture Li Bing and his son. It is now the world's oldest and only dam whose levee works without a dam. It successfully solved the natural diversion and erosion problems with the river, making the western Sichuan Plain the "Heavenly Kingdom." Dujiangyan Dam is the gem of ancient irrigation. It is made up of three parts: Yuzui ("fish mouth" or "water-dividing mouth"), Feishayan (the "mud-and-sand funnel"), and Baopingkou ("treasure bottle neck," the water inlet). Yuzui is a levee built in the middle of the river to divide the Minjiang River into two parts: Neijiang (the inner river) and Waijiang (the outer river). With the mud-and-sand funnel in the middle of the levee, floods, mud, and sand flow into the outer river automatically, allowing active control over the flow of the inner river, thus ensuring the inner river's irrigational function and the outer river's flood protection. The water inlet controls the flow into the inner river. With its shape like a bottle neck, Baopingkou ("treasure bottle neck") is an apt name.

Dujiangyan Dam consists of three parts: Yuzui (fish mouth, the water-dividing mouth), Feishayan (the mud-and-sand funnel) and Baopingkou (treasure bottle neck, the water inlet). This is a picture of the bottle neck, which channels and controls the water flow. (From CFP)

Qingcheng Mountain

Qingcheng Mountain is located in the Dujiangyan Dam Scenic Area, near Chengdu, in Sichuan Province. Just 33 miles from downtown Chengdu, it is a well-known Taoist mountain with a covering of thick forest and many peaks with views in different directions. On the mountain it feels like spring throughout the year, which is why it is called Qingcheng (a "place that is evergreen"). Qingcheng Mountain includes Front Mountain and Back Mountain, along with 36 famous peaks. There are scenic spots such as Shangqing Palace, Jianfu Palace, Tianshi Cave, and Natural Paintings Pavilion. Jianfu Palace was built during the Tang Dynasty. With a long history and after much reconstruction, it now has only two halls and three courtyards. To the west of Jianfu Palace is the Natural Paintings Pavilion, built during the rule of Emperor Guangxu in the Qing Dynasty. Viewing the craggy rocks and swirling clouds from the pavilion, visitors feel as if they have walked into a painting, thus the pavilion's name. A mile or so from the Natural Paintings Pavilion is the main Taoist temple of Qingcheng, Tianshi Cave, in which Three Emperor Hall the Tang Dynasty stone carvings of the three emperors are enshrined. Leaving Tianshi Cave and crossing Fangning Bridge, visitors arrive at the Zushi Temple. Farther north is Chaoyang Cave, followed by Shangqing Palace high on the stone ledge. Shangqing Palace was built in the Jin Dynasty. Stone carvings can be found on the cliffs indicating "The Fifth Best Known Mountain under Heaven," "The First Peak of Qingcheng," and so forth. Near Tianshi cave are scenic spots such as Sandao ("tri-island") Rock, Xixin ("mind cleansing") Pond, and Yixiantian (a "glimpse of heaven"). On Back Mountain are four deep and dangerously steep valleys. The valleys are walled by steep cliffs, and contain plank roads, deep ponds, waterfalls, and many other amazing sights.

When climbing Back Mountain, tourists can try the *jampan* (similar to a sedan chair) for a unique experience.

Sichuan has many mountains. Jampans *or sedan chairs, were once the main method of transportation. Nowadays many sites provide the jampans for tourists so they can experience this local custom. (From Colphoto)*

Longxing Temple

Longxing Temple is located at the northwestern gate of the urban area of Pengzhou. It was allegedly built during the rule of Emperor Yixi of the Eastern Jin Dynasty and renamed Longxing Temple at the start of the Tang Dynasty. It covers an area of 376,736 square feet. Inside the temple is the newly built tallest tower in Southeast Asia at 268 feet. Main buildings in the temple include the Tianwang (Heavenly King) Temple, Dafo (Big Buddha) Temple, the Great Buddha's Hall, and the four-storied Cangjing Ge (Sutra Keeping Pavilion). Other buildings include Visitors' Hall, Ancestors' Hall, Buddhist Discipline Hall, Buddhist Abbot's Room, and Monks' Rooms. The overall layout is carefully designed and has an integrated classic style. The temple has been called "Sacred Land of the Seven Bodhisattvas" and is the largest temple in western Sichuan.

Longxing Temple encompasses not only buildings and statues, as in regular temples, but also the *Dazang Sutra* from the early Qing Dynasty, a gift from Japan; Buddhist relics and the *Sanskrit Palm Leaves Sutra,* a gift from the Sri Lankan king; and a jade Buddha from Burma, all of which are precious cultural artifacts. In the Underground Palace of the Ancient Tower in the temple, ten incomplete stone-carved bodhisattvas are kept, among which is the Sakyamuni Double-Body Sculpture, made by Liang Zhong in the Southern Dynasty (533). Most of these stone bodhisattvas were made in the early Tang Dynasty.

Baoguang Temple

Baoguang (Auspicious Light) Temple is located in northern Xindu County, a little more than 12 miles from Chengdu. It is one of the four great Buddhist monasteries in Southern China and also the Buddhist temple with the longest history, largest scale, and widest collection of cultural artifacts in Chengdu. It was built during the Eastern Han Dynasty. It is said that Emperor Xizong of the Tang Dynasty fled to Sichuan for the Huangchao Uprising. He saw auspicious light at the foot of Fugan Tower in the temple, and later a stone box containing 13 Buddhist relics was unearthed there. The temple was named Baoguang Temple, and because of the stone box found there, the tower was named Stainless Pure Tower of Buddhist Relics, or for short Baoguang Tower. The tower leans slightly to the west and has also been called the Oriental Leaning Tower, but the temple itself faces the south. In the Arhat Hall (Luohan Tang) of the temple, 577 arhat sculptures can be seen, each more than 6 feet tall. This is the oldest and largest arhat hall preserved in China.

Xiling Snow Mountain, two hours' car ride from Chengdu, has beautiful views and a temperate climate. China's largest alpine ski runs and grass ski runs are located here. (From CFP)

Manor of the Liu Family

Located in Changkou, Anren, Dayi County, southwest of Chengdu, this estate was the manor house of Liu Wencai, a landlord before China's Liberation. It's also the best-preserved manor house of feudal landlords in China. There are more than 350 rooms divided into two major parts, the old and new residences, together with 27 courtyards. The walls around the manor are about 20 feet tall. The whole area encompasses various landmarks, such as the Grand Lobby, the Counting House, the Employee Yard, the Rent-Collecting Yard, the granary, the Moon Appreciation Platform, the Palace for Ecstasy, Garden, and the orchard. It is the epitome of rural society in half-colonial, half-feudal China.

Xiling Snow Mountain

Xiling (Mount West) Snow Mountain is 59 miles from Chengdu. It covers an area of 186 square miles. Du Fu, the master poet of the Tang Dynasty, wrote, "In my window is framed the snow-capped peak of Mount West," and that is how the mountain got its name. Inside Xiling Snow Mountain Scenic Park, is Miaoji Ridge, with an altitude of 17,598 feet. It is the tallest peak on the mountain and is covered with snow all year round. Yinyang Boundary is not only a mountain peak but also the watershed between two drastically different climates. On one side of the boundary is sunshine and cloudless sky; on the other side is fog, mist, and haze. Hundreds of peaks are snowcapped and sunny throughout the year, and they can all be seen clearly in downtown Chengdu on a clear day. These spectacular mountains and waters, through years of nature's artful work, have evolved into beautiful scenery such as Nine Waterfalls and One Glimpse of Heaven, Flying Spring Cave, Leopard Roar Spring, Stone Forest, and Azalea Forest. The Grand Flying Waterfall in the valley of Shuanhe Village is a view well worth seeing. Water flows from a limestone cave about 4,600 feet high in the middle of Mount Baique and drops 1,181 feet with a thunderous sound.

Bifeng Valley

Bifeng (Green Peaks) Valley is 5 miles north of the city of Ya'an. The scenic park includes two valleys—one is 4.3 miles long and the other is 3.7 miles long—forming a V shape. The valleys range from 98 to 229 feet wide and from 2,296 to 6,467 feet in altitude. The relative height of the cliffs is from 328 to 656 feet. Both valleys are thickly forested and are as green as jade. The peaks take various shapes; the cliffs are high and the valleys deep, many with small creeks. Two of the mountains merge into one, making the valleys even more beautiful. The silvery sound of flowing water echoes in the valley, adding an artistic touch to the picture. Tourists are attracted by the serene natural beauty here.

The main body of Bifeng Valley Scenic Park has an altitude that ranges from 2,296 to 4,101 feet. Peaks mount on peaks, and clouds swirl around them; trees are thick with leaves, and animals can be seen everywhere; the valleys are quiet and deep, and stunning waterfalls and running springs add to the ambience. Green peaks and old temples, a bell tower, and the setting sun coalesce into an impressive picture. Bifeng Valley is a masterpiece of nature; with its simple, unsophisticated style and rich, mysterious atmosphere, Bifeng Valley gives tourists an unforgettable experience.

Gao Yi's Tomb

Gao Yi's Tomb is located in the village of Koubei, about one and a half miles from the city of Ya'an, and covers an area of more than 21,528 square feet. It is the tomb of Gao Yi, magistrate of Yizhou in the Han Dynasty, and Gao Shi, Gao Yi's younger brother. More than 1,700 years old, the tomb and stone carvings were erected during the Eastern Han Dynasty in 209. The scenic park now encompasses the tomb, monuments, walking paths, palaces, and wild animals. Its excellent architecture, sculptures, and calligraphy contribute to its fame as the best-preserved, most beautiful tomb from the Han Dynasty. The East Que (palace) and West Que are about 42 feet apart. Each of them has four parts: the pedestal, the body, the pavilion, and the roof. The main palace has 13 floors and is 19 feet tall, 5 feet wide, and about 3 feet thick. It is the greatest

A one-thousand-year-old tree in Houyan in the Bifeng Valley. (From Colphoto)

of all 37 remaining tombs from the Han Dynasty. As such, the tomb possesses great historical, artistic, and aesthetic value, and this site has always won praise from celebrities and experts, among them Zhao Mingcheng and Wang Xiangzhi (Song Dynasty), Yang Sheng'an (Ming Dynasty), He Shaoji, Huang Yunji, Kang Youwei (Qing Dynasty), and Lu Xun.

The statue of Guanyin in the Pilu Grotto (From ImagineChina)

Sanxingdui Museum

Sanxingdui Museum is located in the northeastern corner of the Sanxingdui Site, on the banks of the Yazi River in western Guanghan, a historic site. The museum re-creates the local landscape, historical sites, and pottery and sculpture of cultural significance. It merges ancient aesthetics with modern beauty to show the abundance of Sanxingdui culture and the richness of its history. The main indoor exhibition offers the Showcase of the Culture of the Ancient City, Ancient Sichuan, and the Ancient Kingdom. There are over 1,000 precious cultural artifacts that have been unearthed at the Sanxingdui Site, including pottery, jade, bone, gold, and bronze wares. Sanxingdui Site is the home of the ancient Sichuan people, and the Sanxingdui Museum is where modern people go to visit the past.

Bronze statue (From Quanjing)

Anyue Grottoes

Anyue is located in the hilly land in the central Sichuan Basin. The stone carvings in Anyue were begun in the Northern and Southern dynasties, and reached their peak in the Tang, Song, and the Five dynasties. With their great number and supreme artistic beauty, these carvings acquired the reputation as another treasury of ancient Chinese carvings. There are 129 grottoes containing more than 1,600 statues carved along the 1,640-foot-long cliff wall. The choice spot in the grottoes is a 75-foot-long statue of Sakyamuni lying on his side. The statue of Guanyin (Goddess of Mercy) in the Pilu Grotto is a sculptural masterpiece. With a lively expression and an elegant figure, it has been renowned as the "Oriental Venus." Since most of the stone carvings in Anyue were created during a period when the art of stone carving was at its peak, their artistic value is exceptionally great.

Visitors can reach Anyue Grottoes by taking Bus No. 6 at Guanghan.

Guangyuan, Mianyang Region

Best Time to Travel

The months between April and October are the finest time to visit Guangyuan.

Stone Carvings on the Cliff of Huangze Temple

Huangze Temple is located at the foot of Mount Wulong (known as Wushan Mountain today), on the west bank of Jialing River, in Guangyuan. It is a shrine in memory of Emperor Wu Zetian. On the cliffs around the temple are buildings from the Qing Dynasty including Dafo (Giant Buddha) Pavilion, Zetian Hall, Xiaonanhai, Lvzu Pavilion, and Wufo (Five Bodhisattvas) Pavilion. There are 50 grottoes, 1,203 sculptures, 6 sutra pillars, and 4 *Working Farmers* paintings. People began excavating these grottoes as early as the Northern Dynasty. The construction of the buildings reached its peak in the Tang Dynasty and declined during the Five Dynasties. The remaining sculptures are mainly from Tang Dynasty.

Sculptures on the Thousand-Buddha Cliff have a long history and different shapes. They are all carved with fine craftsmanship and display the artistic level of various dynasties. (From Colphoto)

Sculptures on the Thousand-Buddha Cliff in Guangyuan

The Thousand-Buddha Cliff is located on the east bank of Jialing River, 3.1 miles north of Guangyuan. The ancient plank road and Stone Chest Pavilion are located on the south side of the cliff. These are the largest mass grottoes in Sichuan, and their construction began during the Northern Wei Dynasty. The cliff is 147 feet high and over 656 feet long from north to south. Thirteen layers of grottoes, each overlapping the other, dot the steep cliff. At this time, a little more than 400 of the grottoes and over 7,000 sculptures are extant. The Thousand-Buddha Cliff is also called the Museum of Grotto Art.

Heming Mountain

Heming Mountain, also known as Dongshan (East) Mountain, is located about a quarter mile east of Jiange County. It is said that Zhang Daolin, the grandfather of the Taoist religion, learned about Taoism here. The mountain is home to great numbers of Taoist sculptures. Only one of them stands in the open air while the rest are in grottoes. The Sculpture of Celestial Worthy of Longevity is the most representative example. Built in 857, the 6-foot-tall statue shows the figure wearing Taoist boots and a wide gown, and bearing a solemn expression.

Cuiyun Corridor (Corridor of Jade-like Clouds)

Cuiyun Corridor refers to the tree-shaded roads along both sides of the Jianmen Shu Road (Road of Sword Gate in Sichuan). This ancient Shu Road from Jianmen

Pass (Sword Gate Pass) to Jiange County is more than 300 miles long and was once a green corridor made up of nearly 10,000 cypress trees. More than 8,000 of these ancient cypress trees remain, forming a rarely seen artificially planted roadside forest, which is a global wonder called the "Soul of Shu Roads."

Jianmen Pass

Jianmen Pass is located 28 miles south of Guanyuan. The east-west mountain range extends for more than 60 miles, with 72 peaks piercing the clouds. At the pass, cliffs on both sides face each other like the two pillars on either side of a gate, forming a pass strategically important but difficult to access. In the Three Kingdoms Period, General Jiang Wei of Kingdom Shu guarded this pass. The commander in chief of Kingdom Wei led 100,000 soldiers to attack Kingdom Shu, but they were stopped outside Jianmen Pass, unable to triumph over the enemy general and the difficult land-scape.

A beam at the midsection of the steep cliff, the plank road clings to the side of the cliff. (From Colphoto)

The Ancient Plank Road

The Ancient Plank Road, also known as Gedao Road or Zhange, is located in the Mingyue Valley (Valley of a Bright Moon) and Qingfeng Valley (Valley of Clear Wind), Chaotian County, 28 miles north of Guangyuan. The plank road, built to closely hug the steep cliff east of Jialing River, is a famous heritage site of the ancient Sichuan–Sha'anxi Shu roads. The road was first built in the early Qin Dynasty, and has been repaired often throughout successive dynasties.

> The plank road can no longer be walked on, but the posts used to hold it to the cliff still remain. This ancient plank road is a remnant of the famous Shu Roads between Sichuan and Shaanxi. Seen from afar, the road looks like a corridor in midair; therefore, it is also called Yunge ("Corridor Amid Clouds").

Douchuan Mountain

Douchuan Mountain is 15.5 miles north of Jiangyou, and 112 miles from Chengdu. The north-south mountain has an altitude of 3,740 feet. Its shape resembles a grain

Yunyan Temple, built in the Tang Dynasty, is found at Douchuan Mountain. The Western Hall of the temple houses a giant sutra pillar called Feitiancang. It is said to have been built according to the small wooden model recorded in Rules of Construction, *a book from the Song Dynasty. It is the only one of this size and age in the world. (From Quanjing)*

bin, wide at the top and narrow at the foot, giving it its name, which in Chinese is *Chuan*. Douchuan Mountain's extraordinary shape, with its three peaks rising sharply from the ground, looks as if it was cleaved by an axe. The mountain, covered by green trees, is serenely beautiful.

Baoen Temple (Temple Where a Favor Is Repaid)

Baoen Temple is located in Pingwu County, Sichuan Province. It is a well-preserved example from the Ming Dynasty. Construction began in 1440 and continued for six years. The design was based on a spiderweb and is highly resistant to earthquakes. Experts from around the world have referred to it as "shock resistant building mass with ingenuity."

Leshan Region

>>>

Best Time to Travel

The months between March and November are the finest time of year to tour Leshan Mountain Tourist Area. Tourists should be aware of the heavy rains in summer and autumn.

A monument of magnanimity and majesty, and this is the largest stone Buddha in the world. There is a saying: "The mountain is a Buddha, and the Buddha a mountain." (From Quanjing)

Leshan Giant Buddha

The Leshan Giant Buddha is located at the point where three rivers converge: the Minjiang River east of Leshan City, the Qingyi River, and the Dadu River. The sculpture depicts the seated Buddha Maitreya carved into the cliff of Qixia Peak, on Lingyun Mountain, right next to the water. The carving began in 713, the first year of the Tang Dynasty, and continued for more than 90 years.

The Buddha has a graceful posture and a solemn face, and it is carved into the cliff with its feet stepping into the river and its hands on its knees. The Buddha is 233 feet tall; the head is 49 feet long and 33 feet wide, the ear is 23 feet long, the nose is 18 feet long, the eyebrows are 10.8 feet long, the shoulders are 91 feet wide, the fingers are 27 feet long, and each foot measures 28 feet wide. More than 100 people at a time can sit around one of its feet. The hair is dressed into 1,021 buns. Seen from far away, these buns seem to be part of the head itself, but in fact they were studded onto it. At the bare part of each hair bun, clear studding seams can be seen, but there is no concrete of any kind sticking it to the head. Each bun is covered with two layers of mortar, and the inner layer is lime. Each layer is between a quarter inch and 1 inch thick. On the back of the right earlap is a small hole more than 9 inches deep, in which rotten wood has been discovered. A small hole has also been discovered below the nose, inside which were three pieces of wood laid in a triangle. This means the nose might also be made of wood and covered with lime. The Leshan Giant Buddha, the "Greatest Buddha in the World," is the largest ancient Chinese sculpture of Buddha Maitreya as well as the world's largest stone sculpture. It is a classic work combining religion, hydro-science, and techniques of traditional sculpture.

Emei Mountain

Emei Mountain is located in the city of Emeishan. The tourist area covers 59 square miles, and the tallest peak has an altitude of 10,167 feet. As a well-known Buddhist mountain, Emei has been given many honorable names, such as "Celestial Mountain, the Homeland of Buddhas" "the Kingdom of Plants," "the Paradise of Animals," "Geology Museum," and the like. It has often been said that Emei is the most beautiful mountain on earth. Throughout history, Emei Mountain has been one of the first choices of people who want to pray to the Buddha, to tour around, and to engage in scientific studies, as well as being a desirable spot to spend spare time. People have historically come here to burn joss sticks (a way to pray to the Buddha). Peaks and waterfalls take various intriguing shapes, both majestic and beautiful. Unforgettable scenic spots include Clear Sound of the Twin Bridge, Plank Roads in the Valley, Clear Water in Autumn Wind, Snow-Covered Fields, Morning Rain at the River Source, Home of the Nine Old Deities, Crescent in the Elephant Pond, and Auspicious Light on the Golden Peak. Since the second century, temples have been built in the mountain; this temple building culminated in the fifteenth century, with more than 100 temples. These temples are scattered everywhere on the mountain, some high up on the peaks, some deep down in the valleys. Every one of them takes advantage of its unique landscape, presenting an impressive scene. Renowned personages from all dynasties came here to compose poems and paintings, and the historic sites persisted through time. There is more beauty here than meets the eyes.

The Golden Peak of Emei Mountain rises sharply into the clouds. As a result of the high altitude, it is always cold at the top. The photo shows is Huazang Temple, covered with snow, on the mountaintop. (From Jin Yongji)

Thousand-Buddha Cliff in Jiajiang

The Thousand-Buddha Cliff is 1.86 miles west of Jiajiang County, Leshan. On a cliff on the left bank of Qingyi River, over 200 grottoes with more than 2,400 Buddhist sculptures are lined up; hence, the site is called Thousand-Buddha Cliff . The excavation and carving began in the Sui Dynasty, reached its peak in the Tang Dynasty, and continued to the Ming and Qing dynasties. The sculptures are arranged in picturesque disorder, some taking up a whole grotto each, some sharing the same grotto with hundreds of others. They also vary in size and position, but all are carved by fine hands, especially the Bodhisattva of the Sacred Land. They are a sample of the superb stone-carving technique in ancient China. Besides the sculptures, there are also inscriptions from all dynasties.

Jinkou Grand Valley of Dadu River

Jinkou Grand Valley starts at Wusi River in the west and continues to Jinkou River in the east, for a total length of 1.62 miles. Before entering Sichuan Province, the Dadu River flows through the last mountain range in the western Sichuan Basin—the Washan Mountains—forming the Jinkou Grand Valley. The deepest point of the valley is more than 8,530 feet. The cliffs of Jinkou Grand Valley rise sharply from the bottom and show hardly any trace of humans. Limestone from the Sinian Period, widely found in the valley, has assumed various formations as the result of water erosion and the force of gravity. The beauty of this valley matches that of the Three Gorges Valley.

Zigong Region

Best Time to Travel

Zigong has four distinct seasons, but the summers are not too hot and the winters are not too cold. The period between March and November is the best time to visit.

Xiqin Guild Hall

Xiqin Guild Hall is located on East Jiefang Road, Ziliujing District, in Zigong. It once enshrined Guandi (the God in Charge of Wealth), so it is also called Guandi Temple. The hall was built in 1736 by a group of businessmen from Shaanxi. In the main building, several pillars support the beams, above which is a multilayer roof with a unique appearance. This type of composite structure with numerous eaves is rarely seen in Ming and Qing Dynasty buildings.

> Xiqin Guild Hall houses a museum of the history of the salt industry of Zigong.

A pictorial explanation of salt production in the museum. (From Colphoto)

Haiguyan Well

Haiguyan Well is located in Changyantang, Da'an District, Zigong. The well is situated at an altitude of 11,200 feet and is 3,285.5 feet deep. It was dug in 1823, using the traditional Chinese method of impact excavation, and was the first of such wells to be deeper than 0.62 miles. It produces about 4,000 gallons of halogenous water and from 1.3 million to 2.1 million gallons of natural gas every day.

Giant Buddha in Rongxian County

The Giant Buddha in Rongxian County is a stone sculpture of Buddha Maitreya. Located in the eastern suburbs of Rongxian County, the Buddha was carved during the Tang Dynasty. The Buddha faces south and is 120 feet tall. It is the second-largest Buddha in China and the third-largest in the world. The Buddha, with its high bridged nose, thick lips, large eyes, and low brow, wears a U-shaped cassock and has an X-shaped belt with bands attached. Both of the Buddha's hands are on his knees, and his bare feet rest atop two lotus flowers. There is a folk saying: "Giant Buddha in Leshan is majestic, while Giant Buddha in Rongxian County is beautiful."

The recovered skeleton of Tianfu Emei Dinosaur and other dinosaurs in the Zigong Dinosaur Museum. (From Quanjing)

Zigong Dinosaur Museum

The Zigong Dinosaur Museum is located at the Dashanpu site where dinosaur fossils have been found, in the northeastern suburbs of Zigong. It is another on-site museum in China, as are the Banpo Relics and the Qin Terracotta Warriors. The site covers an area of about 62 acres and contains five exhibition halls. In the Fossils in Earth Hall, tourists can see fossils of dinosaur bones embedded in the ground rock. The Skeleton Hall exhibits skeletal remains of various dinosaurs. One of these, the skeleton of the Tianfu Emei Dinosaur, is nearly 33 feet tall. The museums archive 3 classes, 11 orders, and 15 families of dinosaurs, including stegosaurs, which lived in the Mid-Jurassic Period, the earliest among those discovered so far, and pterosaurs from the Late Triassic through the Cretaceous Period, which were discovered here for the first time.

For an extra fee, guide service is available in the museum.

Yibin Region

Best Time to Travel

Yibin has plenty of rainy nights and few sunny days. The period between March and November is the optimal time to visit.

Shopping Tips

Shibajian, a shopping street in the golden commercial zone downtown, is located in the center of Yibin. This street has more than 100 shops, making it the first choice for shopping and recreation.

Group of Temples in Zhenwu Mountain

These temples are located in Zhenwu Mountain, in the northwestern part of Yibin. The area was a famous Taoist holy land in the Ming and Qing dynasties. Back in the Song Dynasty, Zhenwu Mountain was called Xianlu Mountain. In 1573, the magistrate of Sichuan, Zeng Xinwu, asked Zhenwu (a Taoist master) to help his teacher. He built a Zhenwu shrine in the mountain, and many temples were built afterward. There are stone stairs from the foot to the top of the mountain. Imitating Taishan Mountain, people built three Chinese stone arches, naming them the First, Second, and Third Gate of Heaven. By the Qing Dynasty, there were already more than 20 buildings, making this a landmark Taoist mountain in southern Sichuan. Eight of those ancient buildings are still standing. Xuanzu Hall, built in 1574, is the main hall of Zhenwu Temple. Ruyi Arch, a stone-and-wooden arch built in the Qing Dynasty, is in front of the hall. In front of Zushi Hall, built in 1581, stands the stone Yexian Bridge (Bridge Where One Meets with a Deity). Doumu Hall, Sanfu Hall, Wenchang Hall, and many other temples, together with Xuanzu Hall, form a majestic temple group.

The existing temples in Zhenwu Mountain are mainly from the Ming Dynasty. They consist of various structures, such as halls, pavilions, corridors, ponds, and stages. Although most of the temples are Taoist, the group is actually a combination of Confucian, Buddhist, and Taoist constructions. (From Colphoto)

Cui Ping Mountain

Cui Ping (Jade Green Screen) Mountain, situated in the western part of Yibin, rises 1,663 feet above sea level. Lush woods on the mountain serve as a screen towering over the riverside, hence its name. It is the second-largest wooded city park in China. The Cui Ping Academy of Classical Learning was established in May 1959, and in 1963, the Zhao Yiman Memorial was built to commemorate this national hero in China's war of resistance against Japan.

The memorial covers an area of 33,583 square feet, and the building itself covers 5,888 square feet. There are three showrooms, displaying inscriptions from the Chinese Communist Party (CCP) and national leaders such as Zhu De, Dong Biwu, Song Qingling, and Chen Yi, and documents concerning Zhao Yiman's activities in the revolution and his feats in the armed struggles against Japanese invaders in northeastern China. This collection includes 171 artifacts related to Zhao, 706 pictures, and more than 200 inscriptions. A white marble statue of Zhao Yiman stands at the front of the memorial.

These bamboo carvings are exquisite. (From CFP)

Xingwen Stone Forest

Xingwen Stone Forest is located at the Shihaidong Village scenic park in Zhoujia, Xingwen County. It features karst geology, with various interesting rock formations aboveground and water-eroded caves underground. This impressive stone forest consists of several forms of stones, including sprout, chessboard, and pointed ridge. Scenic spots here are Greeting Stone, Couple Peak, Seven Maiden Peak, and Cui Ping Ancient Tower.

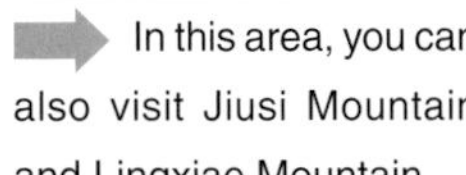

In this area, you can also visit Jiusi Mountain and Lingxiao Mountain.

Bamboo Sea in Southern Sichuan

Originally known as Wanlingjing, this natural bamboo forest is located at Wanling Mountain at the line between Changning County and Jiang'an County. The forest covers an area of 45 square miles at altitudes ranging from 1,969 to 3,281 feet. You can climb a peak to enjoy the green sea of numerous bamboos—there are 58 different kinds of bamboo and various other kinds of plants and animals found there. This bamboo forest is a famous Buddhist scenic area, as there are ancient Buddhist temples and grottoes throughout the forest.

The bamboo sea is indescribably green, and the cabins in the depths of the forest reveal infinite poetic flavor. (From CFP)

There are still more than 200 coffins in the Yi Bin cliff. (From CFP)

Matang Hanging Coffins of the Bo People

The coffins of the Bo people (an ancient coffin tribe prior to the Ming Dynasty) can be found in Matangba and Sumawan, where at least 265 remnants of these coffins hang anywhere from 33 to 164 feet above the ground, with the highest hanging 328 feet.

Coffins have been laid in the cliffs in three ways: According to the first, several holes have been cut into the cliff and spiles or stone spikes used to secure the coffins; in the second, large holes, either sidelong or erect, have been cut to put coffins in; in the third way, natural holes or cracks in the cliff were used to insert the coffins into. Academic circles still are not sure which tribe or tribes utilized this hanging coffin burial style.

> You can take a train from Yi Bin to Gong County, then transfer to a bus to Matangba and Sumawan.

Xijiashan Folk Residence

Xijiashan Folk Residence is in Bashang, Xijiashan, a little more than 12 miles southeast of Jiang'an. The residence was built in 1612 by a wealthy family named Xi; 108 rooms are still intact, comprising a total area of 55,391 square feet. This site is a traditional Chinese courtyard dwelling with four sides containing the living spaces. The front door, the hall in the middle, and the back parlor are aligned. Surrounding the house are traditional Chinese ponds and gardens. The residence was built in the Song and Ming Dynasty style of folk-house buildings. Xijiashan Folk Residence is commonly referred to as a relic of Chinese folk construction.

The decorations of the main buildings of Xijiashan Folk Residence are diverse in style. Flowers, landscapes, characters, and dramatic stories have been carved on doors and windows. (From Colphoto)

Nanchong, Guang'an, and Bazhong Region

Langzhong Grand Buddha

The Langzhong Grand Buddha is located in the Tang Dynasty Grand Buddha Temple on the side of Daxiang Mountain, which is opposite the Jialing River, which flows by southeastern Langzhong. One of the ten stone carvings of the Sitting Buddha in Sichuan is a sitting Maitreya Buddha, with a height of about 33 feet. At the back of the Buddha are 4,700 four-inch-high stone carvings of Buddha in an orderly arrangement and displaying exquisite technique. There are more than 30 tablet inscriptions from the Tang to the Qing dynasties, five stone statues, and one stone pillar of Buddhist scriptures at the site.

Zhanghuanhou Memorial Temple

Situated at West Street, Baoning, Langzhong, Zhanghuanhou Memorial Temple is also called Han Huan Hou Ci, meaning "temple in memory of Huanhou"—the official title of the famous general Zhang Fei in ancient China of the Han Dynasty. Those four characters are inscribed on a big wooden board hanging on the front gate of the temple. There is a stone carving of Zhang Fei's warhorse with Zenggong's inscriptions on it. Since Zhang Fei was killed in Langzhong, this site is the most cherished among all the temples erected in his memory.

Baba Temple

Originally known as Jiuzhao Ting ("Ever-Shining Pavilion"), the Baba Temple is on Panlong Mountain in Langzhong. During Emperor Kangxi's reign in the Qing Dynasty, the Islamic holy descendant Abdullah of Mecca came here to do Islamic missionary work. He was buried here, and people built the temple in order to memorialize him. Baba Temple has since become a pilgrimage site for Muslims.

Huaguang Tower

Huaguang Tower, also praised as the greatest tower of Langyuan, was built by Yuanying, king of Teng in the Tang Dynasty. With an area of 6,458 square feet, it is located at the ancient southeastern city of Langzhong, on the northern side of the Jialing River. It was originally built as Zhenjianglou Tower (South River-Calming Tower) in the Tang Dynasty, and the present tower was rebuilt in 1867. You can climb to the top of the tower to view the beautiful scenery of Langzhong.

Langzhong, an ancient town with beautiful natural scenery and many areas of cultural importance, has applied to be listed as a World Heritage site.

With a height of 118 feet, Huaguang Tower has four floors. The gateway on the first floor is where merchants and peddlers once gathered. (From Quanjing)

Former Residence of Zhude

Located at Zhujiadawan on the west side of Linlang Mountain in Ma'an, Yilong County, this old residence is an improved courtyard with three sides containing living space. Zhude's Memorial was built at the opposite side of the residence in 1982. The name of the memorial is an inscription by the former leader Deng Xiaoping; inside are many precious documents from Zhude's revolutionary life.

Former Residence of Deng Xiaoping

Located in the archway village of Guang'an's Xie Xing, the Former Residence of Deng Xiaoping comprises a common courtyard with three sides encompassing dwelling quarters unique to the eastern Sichuan farmhouse style. This residence is also called Deng's Old Courtyard. There are 17 rooms, all of which are made of wood with black tile roofing and the concave-convex craftsmanship adapted to a columnar structural system. This is where Mr. Deng spent his childhood. There are many pictures and photographs of Deng Xiaoping's life on display here.

Statue of Ksitigarbha Bodhisattva in the twenty-fifth grotto. (From Colphoto)

The inscription on the board in front of the Former Residence of Deng Xiaoping was written by former president Jiang Zeming. (From Colphoto)

Graves of the Anbing Family

Completed in 1223, the Graves of the Anbing Family are found in Shaoxun Village, Shuanghe County in the city of Huaying. Anbing was a *daxueshi* (a senior government official in control of official documents) in the Southern Song Dynasty and was also called Luguogong. The graves were discovered by local villagers in 1996 and constitute the largest and best-kept family grave sites from the Song Dynasty known in China.

Nankan Cliff Grottoes

Nankan cliff grottoes are situated at the back of Nankanpo Mountain in Bazhong County. They were built in the South-North Dynasty and later became a well-known grotto group. They reflected the style of carving done in the Prosperous Period of the Tang Dynasty.

Aba Region

Best Time to Travel

Autumn is the best season to visit Aba. The scenery of Jiuzhaigou and Siguniang Mountain is at its most beautiful from the middle to the end of October.

Monument Park for the Long March of the Red Army

This park is located at Yuanbao Mountain near Chuanzhusi, in Songpan County. It consists of a main monument, large-scale granite carvings, and a display room. Towering at the top of Yuanbao Mountain, the monument is 135 feet tall. The 48.5-foot-high bronze statue of a soldier has a gun in one hand and a bouquet of flowers in the other.

Siguniang Mountain (Mountain of Four Girls)

This mountain is situated at the border between Xiaojin County and Wen County. It consists of four adjoining peaks of the Hengduan (transversal) Mountain Range. According to the legends of the local Tibetan people, these four peaks were originally four beautiful sisters, hence the Chinese name Siguniang, meaning "four sisters." Steep and magnificent, the mountain is often referred to as "the Oriental Alps." The peaks rise 17,569, 17,894, 18,583, and 20,505 feet above sea level. Since the 24,790-foot-high Gongga Mountain is the "King of Sichuan's Mountains," Siguniang Mountain is honored as the "Queen of Sichuan's Mountains." The scenic area covers about 174 square miles and consists of Siguniang Mountain, Shuangqiao Gully, Changping Gully, and Haizi Gully.

Siguniang Mountain (From Jin Yongji)

Jiuzhaigou Scenic Resort

Jiuzhaigou (Nine-Village Valley) lies in the Jiuzhaigou County of the Aba Tibetan and Qiang Autonomous Prefecture in northwestern Sichuan Province. It is a source area of the Jialing River, which belongs to the Yangtze river system. Its altitude ranges from 6,562 to 14,108 feet above sea level. It has been said that the 118 lakes in the valley were fragments of a broken glass, which the god Dage intended to give to Goddess Semo as a gift. These beautiful lakes make Jiuzhaigou a modern-day fairyland.

This wonderland resort area was first discovered by timbermen in the 1970s. Since then, it has achieved fame throughout the world for its pristine and dreamlike scenery. Jiuzhaigou is justly renowned for its ancient and mysterious scenery, featuring snowcapped mountains, forest, grasslands, waterfalls, streams, and lakes. Covered with luxuriant primitive forests and dotted by more than a hundred lakes and ponds of various sizes, the valley is home to a great variety of plants and rare animals.

The rustic beauty of Jiuzhaigou is distributed across three valleys that form a Y shape. The water is so clear that the bottom is visible despite depths of several dozen feet. Waterfalls are a beautiful accent to the scenery in Jiuzhaigou, occurring between lakes at different levels so that the water flows down the tree-covered cliffs. The water actually oozes through tree trunks into the falls. Pastural sights like waving flags, ancient watermills, and carefree yaks all exist in harmony in this magical place. In 1999, Jiuzhaigou was added to the World Heritage List.

(From Jin Yongji)

Huanglong Scenic Resort

Huanglong (Yellow Dragon) Scenic Resort lies in Songpan County and covers an area of 7,535 square feet. Honored as the "Jade Pond in the World," it is famous for its unique scenery and primitive ecology.

Huanglong Valley is a calcified waterway between mountains over 4 miles long and 984 feet wide. There are more than 3,400 natural springwater ponds. Seen from a bird's-eye view, Huanglong is shaped like a giant dragon lifting off high into the air. The colorful ponds lie layer on layer, like scales on the body of the dragon. Huanglong Scenic Resort has a calcified landscape of golden sand, five karst waterfalls, four stalactitic water-eroded caves, and three ancient temples. The area can be divided into three parts: the lower part consisting of three waterfalls, the middle part with various colorful ponds, and the upper part which includes Huanglong Cave and Huanglong Back Temple. In the surrounding area, more than 10 mountains rising over 16,000 feet above sea level. It is indeed a great wonder of nature.

Danyun Valley is 11 miles from the main scenic area of Huanglong. It is one of the "five uniquenesses" in Huanglong, featuring a stark and beautiful valley landscape. In autumn, maple leaves here turn red throughout the valley. The Chinese word *danyun* means "red clouds." In every season, there are different attractions to enjoy.

On the way to Huanglong, some travelers may experience a reaction to the high altitude. Eating fruit and drinking water are good ways to counteract this, but you may also take an oxygen mask with you.

Wolong National Nature Reserve

Some 62 miles from Chengdu, Wolong

In the Huanglong Valley, the banks around the ponds are as limpid as the yellow jade; the water in the ponds is clear and bright. Various beautiful plants and flowers grow in profusion beside these ponds. (From Jin Yongji)

(Crouching Dragon) National Nature Reserve is located in Wenchuan County in Aba. This is one of the few panda habitats in the world, covering an area of about 772 square miles. With its high altitude and humid climate, it is suitable for growing the arrow bamboo and Huaju bamboo, the primary food of pandas. Besides pandas, there are many other rare animal species such as golden monkeys and snow leopards, in addition to endangered plant species such as the dove tree, the katsura tree, and the Bole tree. Because of these protected species, Wolong has been recognized as "the storehouse of animal and plant genes." The Panda Breeding Center in Hetaoping is the only panda research center in the world.

Panda Breeding Center (From CFP)

Gangtse Tour Region

Best Time to Travel

The most beautiful times of year in Gangtse are from April to May and from September to October.

Baili Temple

Baili Temple is in Shengkang Village, 8 miles from Gangtse County. The Tibetan word *baili* means "an auspicious islet in Qinggang Mountain." The lamasery was built in the Qing Dynasty, and it was once the seat of the Boba government of the Red Army. In 1909, the Living Buddha Geda came to take charge of Baili Temple. He edited many of the local Guozhuang lyrics, some of which are still sung. While the Living Buddha Geda was in charge, Baili Temple often housed orphans, waifs, and the persecuted.

Gongga Mountain

Known as the "King of Mountains in Sichuan," Gongga Mountain lies at the juncture of three counties—Luding, Kangding, and Jiulong—in Gangtse Tibetan Autonomous Prefecture. The Tibetan word *gong* means snow and *ga* means white, so the two characters together mean "pure white peak." Gongga Mountain, snowcovered throughout the year, is the highest peak of the Hengduan Mountain Range. Glaciers have been preserved here. The glacial waterfall in Hailuogou is the largest in China at 3,543 feet high and 3,609 feet wide. In the surrounding area are 71 glacial rivers. The drop in altitude from the main peak to the Dadu River Valley is 21,509 feet, resulting in the enormous diversity of plant and animal species and the variable climatic conditions. With Gongga Mountain at the center, the Gongga scenic area is more than 107,639 square feet in size, the largest in China.

> The best time of year for climbing Gongga is from May to June, when the temperature and amount of rainfall are moderate. Remember to choose a suitable route and be well prepared for weather changes.

Dege Sutra-Printing House

Dege Sutra-Printing House, also called Dege Auspicious and Wisdom-Gathering House, is located in Dege County. It was built in the seventh year of Emperor Yongzheng of the Qing Dynasty by Chokyi Tenpa Tsering (1687–1738), the twelfth headman and sixth dharmaraja of Dege. It is now a famous treasury of Tibetan culture and arts. The Dege block edition of the Great Scriptures, which was cut in the Qing Dynasty, is well known. The Printing House is the largest of the three big sutra-printing houses in the Tibetan regions of China (Lhasa sutra-printing House in Tibet, Lhapuleng House in Gansu, and Dege Parkhang in Sichuan).

Hailuogou Glacier Forest Park

Hailuogou Glacier Forest Park is located on the eastern side of Gongga Mountain in Luding County, 33 miles from the county seat. Hailuogou glaciers can be

The mountaintops in Hailuogou are covered with snow throughout the year. (From Quanjing)

as long as 9 or 10 miles. The park encompasses many geographic attractions, including ancient glaciers, enormous glacier cascades, virgin forests, wild animals, and hot springs. Classified as a modern glacier, those in Hailuogou came into being around 16 million years ago. They are rarely found either in low-latitude or low-altitude places. The lowest measurement in the glacier park is only 9,350 feet above sea level. With an elevation of 19,685 feet, Hailuogou has seven climatic zones, and its vegetation varies at different altitudes, making it a rare natural botanical garden. There are 4,800 plant species and 400 animal species in the forested area. There are also many varieties of flowers, the most familiar of which are azalea, magnolia, primrose, orchid, and rough gentian.

The terrain of Hailuogou is somewhat rough, and you should watch out for snow slides, mud-rock flows, and ice cracks.

"Warm the steep cliffs lapped by the water of Jinsha, Cold the iron chains spanning the Dadu River." (A line from the poem "The Long March" by Mao Zedong.) (From CFP)

Luding Bridge

Luding Bridge spans the Dadu River in Luding County. It was built in 1705, the forty-fourth year of Emperor Kangxi of the Qing Dynasty. Thirteen chains support the side posts as well as those for the bridge floor. The bridge measures 328 feet long and 9.5 feet wide. The towers at the two sides are ancient wooden buildings with a unique style. At the west end of the bridge, under the Kwanyin Pavilion, is a stone pillar on which the three characters denoting *Luding Qiao* were inscribed by Emperor Kangxi.

Liangshan Region

Xichang Satellite Launch Center

Xichang Satellite Launch Center is located in Mianning County in the Liangshan Prefecture, approximately 37 miles north of the city of Xichang, a one-hour drive. The center is an important aviation and aerospace base in China and is also the largest and most advanced in Asia. Since it began operating in 1984, it has successfully launched 17 satellites using Long March III, Long March IIE, and Long March IIIA carrier rockets.

Xichang Earthquake-Recording Pillar Forest

Located in Guangfu Temple in Lushan, south of Xichang, the Xichang Earthquake-Recording Pillar Forest contains more than 100 stone pillars. They have recorded several strong earthquakes that have taken place throughout history in places like Xichang, Mianning, Ganluo, and Ningnan.

At Huanglianguan, 18.5 miles south of Xichang, there is a naturally formed mound forest. (From Colphoto)

Situated in the fault zone between Anning River and Zemu River, Xichang is one of the major earthquake regions in southwest China. The strong earthquakes in this region provide scholars with useful information for research, and this center, together with Xi'an Pillar Forest in Shaanxi, Qufu Pillar Forest in Shandong, and Gaoxiong Pillar Forest in Taiwan, are known as the four largest pillar forests in China.

Mount Lushan

Mount Lushan sits on the south bank of Lake Qionghai, 3 miles south of Xichang. It rises 7,602 feet above sea level and 2,648 feet higher than Lake Qionghai. It is near the Lushui River (now Shengsha River), hence the name Mount Lushan. Moreover, as the mountain is shaped like a crouching frog, it is also referred to as Mount Washan (*wa* means "frog," while *shan* means "mountain"). Lake Qionghai is to the east of the mountain, Anning River to the west, Xichang to the north, and Mount Luojishan to the south.

The whole mountain is covered with coniferous and broadleaf evergreen forests. There are many very old trees on the mountain, among them, the Xichang Oak (Huangban) is a rare ancient species, which has been called a "living tree fossil." Other large ancient trees of the Han, Tang, and Ming dynasties are also worth a visit.

There are many ancient buildings on the mountain as well, including Guangfu Temple, Mengduan Memorial Temple, Sanjiao'an Temple (a temple with monks, nuns, and Taoists coexisting under the same roof), Zushi Dian (Taoist Founder Hall), Guanyin Ge (Avalokitesvara Pavilion), and Wangmu Dian (Heavenly Queen Palace). Guangfu Temple is the largest building complex on Mount Lushan. Well-preserved artifacts housed here include many fancy carvings, beautiful poems, and writings from many dynasties, as well as huge copper religious figures and incense burners.

Lake Qionghai

Lake Qionghai is the second-largest freshwater lake in Sichuan, located about 4 miles from downtown Xichang, with Mount Lushan to the southeast and Mount Luoji to the south. It covers

Sleeved copper trumpets are a requirement for many of the religious activities of Tibetan Buddhism. (From Quanjing)

an area of 12 square miles, extending at its longest 7 miles from north to south, and at its widest 3 miles from east to west. The average depth is about 46 feet, with the deepest point at 112 feet . The lake is situated on a fractured and subsided basin.

Litang Zang girls in beautiful native dress. (From Quanjing)

Lake Qionghai is famous for its picturesque and peaceful landscape. There are more than 40 kinds of fish in it. Surrounded by mountains, the lake contains a number of islands scattered throughout its crystal waters. The scenery changes with the season, surprising and delighting visitors to the area. In addition to the beautiful scenery, there are also many fascinating legends about the lake, making it even more mysterious and intriguing.

Scenic views of Lake Qionghai include those from Qionghai Park, Lotus Pond (Lianchi), Moon Bay (Yueliangwan), and Blue Dragon Temple (Qinglongsi).

Liangshan Yi Museum

Liangshan Yi Museum is on the north side of Mount Lushan, to the southeast of the city of Xichang. It was built and opened in 1985 as the first specifically clan-oriented museum. The museum is also the only one in the world that focuses on the clan system of the Yi people and its slave society. It is divided into four theme areas: Beautiful and Abundant Liangshan, the Long History of the Yi Ethnic Group, Slave Society before the Democratic Reform, and the Great Democratic Reform. In eight exhibition halls, more than 2,000 cultural relics and photographs are displayed, reflecting all aspects of the clan system of the Liangshan Yi ethnic group and their slave-owning society. These artifacts and other related information are extremely valuable for the study of the creation, development, and demise of this once endemic society.

Liangshan Yi lacquerware is variously colored in black, red, and yellow, with realistic designs taken from nature and daily life. (From Colphoto)

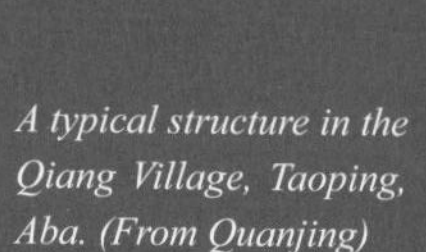

A typical structure in the Qiang Village, Taoping, Aba. (From Quanjing)

Sichuan Style

Stockaded Village of the Qiang Ethnic Group in Taoping

Located in the town of Taoping, Li County, Aba Autonomous Prefecture, the stockaded village of the Qiang ethnic group is the most intactly preserved existing architectural relic of the Qiang ethnic group, and a primitive Qiang village that persists in its extremely simple and unsophisticated customs and practices to the present day. The village is about 100 miles from Chengdu and 25 miles from Li County.

This stockaded village hugs close to the neighboring mountain, with the Zagunao River flowing before it. Viewed from a distance, visitors to the area can see the profusion of ocher-colored stone houses strewn upon the slope. The site was at one time called the "mysterious oriental old castle." At the topmost point of the village, there are two 9-floor fortified towers built up with rocks opposite the beacon tower on the other bank. Each household in the village reserves a roof beam hole for later inhabitants when they build their houses, creating a pattern in which households lean against each other and the flat tops of the towers are connected with planks. Thus, assorted passageways make it very convenient for people in the old stockaded village to come and go. The ancient Qiang villagers channeled spring water and built hidden ditches under their houses so that the waterway was connected to each household and they could get water by simply pulling back the slate cover. Walking around the village, you can hear the musical sound of underground water.

The stockaded village of the Qiang ethnic group in Taoping has its indigenous customs and practices. Qiang embroidery, Qiang song and dance, and Qiang-style food attract tourists to the historic site of the ancient Qiang ethnic group.

Daocheng

Daocheng County is located at the southwestern edge of Sichuan Province, south of Ganzi Tibetan Autonomous Prefecture. It is 108 miles long from south to north and 39 miles wide from east to west. In 1928, American botanist and explorer Joseph Lock arrived here; he published an article with related photos in *National Geographic* in July 1931. In December 1997, the provincial government approved Daocheng as a provincial-level nature reserve. In 2001, It became a national level reserve.

The largest landform created by glaciers in Qinghai-Tibet Plateau—Haizi Mountain Nature Reserve—lies north of Daocheng. The natural landscape here is original and primitive. There are open river valleys and plains in the middle area, with abundant grass and fresh flowers. In the south, there are mountains chains in various forms, with peaceful glens and turbulent waterfalls throughout.

Daocheng has everything that you may imagine as well as things beyond your imagination. (From Quanjing)

The heights of snow mountain Junior Gongga in Daocheng kiss the clouds. Junior Gongga is composed of the three snowy peaks of Xiannai ri, Yangmaiyong, and Xianuoduoji, respectively meaning "Buddha Guanyin," "Buddha Wenshu," and "Buddha Jingang." Natural features to be found here include glaciers, flourishing forests, and fertile meadows. Between the two peaks of Xiannai ri and Yangmaiyong, is a beautiful lake that shines and sparkles in the sun. It is as clear as a green jade emerald, inlaid among the snowy peaks like a crescent moon in the night sky, which conveys the feeling of being in a wonderland.

Litang

Litang enjoys the reputation of being the world's highest city, as well as the holy place in this snowy region and a pearl in the prairie. Located in the western part of Sichuan Province and the southern Ganzi Prefecture, it is 406 miles from the provincial capital Chengdu and 176 miles from the prefecture capital Kangding. While Tibetans account for 94 percent of Litang's total population, there are seven ethnic groups in the county, including Han, Hui, Yi, Tujia, Naxi, Miao, and Qiang. *Litang* is the Tibetan word "prairie as flat as a bronze mirror" and its name is derived from Maoya Prairie within its boundaries.

As a bright scenic spot along the Shangri-la tourisi route as viewed either from the geomorphic standpoint for its mountains and natural resources or on the basis of its historic development and folk customs and practices, Litang is one of the must-see tourist destinations of the Tibetan Region.

Kangding

Kangding, which was formerly called Dajianlu, is located at Horse Race Mountain in the northern end of Gongga Mountain in the western part of Sichuan Province. It is both the capital of Ganzi Tibetan Autonomous Prefecture and a century-old city on the plateau. The ancient city is surrounded by three mountains and two rivers. Zheduo River flows through the city, and various examples of architecture incorporating ethnic features spread out along the riverbank in a seemingly random yet orderly pattern.

Horse Race Mountain in Kangding is the famous divine mountain for local Tibetans, and it is called *Lamuze* in Tibetan, meaning "mountain of the fairy." Its name is derived from the annual horse race held here. The circular singing competition stadium built on top of the mountain is where villagers get together for entertainment. This is the origin of the line "strolling the mountain with horse race," which has made Horse Race Mountain in southern Kangding famous. Nowadays, many tourists to Kangding regard Horse Race Mountain as a major destination.

Tagong Temple in Kangding, which is also called the little Dazhao Temple, is one of the famous temples for the Saskya sect of Tibetan Buddhism. This is the mecca where Tibetans worship in the Kangba region. The Tibetan-style cameo, color engraving, frescoes and ghee products, as well as many ancient Buddha towers which are distinct from each other in form, embody the unique ethnic, religious, and cultural features to be enjoyed here.

Teahouse

You cannot be said to have been to Chengdu if you have not been to the teahouses. The teahouse is both a cultural institution in Chengdu and a lifestyle for the Chengdu people. As a place for cultural expression and entertainment, teahouses organize the sitting and singing of the Chuan Opera players, which also involves the Wei drum. In addition, some teahouses offer performances of the Sichuan dulcimer, storytelling, comic dialogues, and clapper talks. Teahouse patrons can drink tea

Kandding is full of the charm of the plateau ethnic groups. (From CFP)

while enjoying various kinds of folk art with local flair. In addition to recreation, teahouses are also important locations for social intercourse. In the old society, people in various trades would meet in teahouses to find out about market prices, negotiate business, and examine goods to execute business transactions. From that time to the present, teahouses have been a good place for Chengdu people to make friends and get together. The teahouse is a mirror that reflects social life in Chengdu, which in turn reflects the Chengdu people's transcendent attitude toward life.

Chengdu's teahouse culture grew out of the indigenous lifestyle and appeals to both refined and popular tastes. (From CFP)

Chuan Opera

The Chuan Opera is one of the important features of Sichuan culture. Throughout its development, the Chuan Opera has absorbed

Belching fire (From ImagineChina)

Changing facial makeup (From ImagineChina)

and combined melodies from Jiangsu, Jiangxi, Anhui, Hubei, Shaanxi and Gansu, evolving its own style that contains the five tunes of *Gaoqiang, Huqing, Kunqiang, Dengxi,* and *Tanxi.* Among other qualities, *Gaoqiang,* which is the primary singing form in Chuan Opera, is rich in the names of its songs, features pleasing vocal music, and exemplifies local character. The language of the Chuan Opera is vivid and lively, humorous and interesting, full of clear local color and the intense flavor of life, and enjoys broad popularity. There are several hundred types of opera that are commonly seen on stages, including singing parts, spoken parts, acting, and punch lines, and accompanied by instrumental music. This unique art form developed into a school of its own with such characteristics as changing facial makeup, belching fire, and the water sleeve.

Torch Festival of the Liangshan Yi Ethnic Group

The Torch Festival is the most primitive and distinctive cultural heritage of the Yi ethnic group. The Torch Festival is held each year on June 24 of the lunar calendar. During the festival, the Yi people dress in their festival clothes, assemble, drink liquor and sing songs, and walk through the fields while holding hand torches that form fire dragons

Young people of Yi, wearing traditional Yi costume, sing in the Torch Festival. (From Quanjing)

to symbolize the burning of pests to death, the provision of the hard-won fruits of their labor, and the celebration of the harvest.

The Torch Festival has a long history of over 1,000 years, from Han Dynasty and the Tang Dynasty. As the story goes, in ancient times, Sireabi, who was Hercules in heaven, was once defeated by Ertilaba, who was Hercules on earth. Sireabi then made mischief in heaven. God lashed out in a fury and spread pestilence to ruin the crops. As a result, there was no harvest, and the masses had no means by which live. Thereupon, the hero Ertilaba led the people to light torches to get rid of the pests and ultimately won a victory over God. To celebrate this victory, the people congregated on a plateau (the torch field nowadays) called Ridudisan and held a carnival for three days and three nights.

Since then, the Torch Festival has become a tradition among the Yi people. At festival time, *Amimi* (girls) who enjoy dressing up will tailor new clothes and colorful dresses, boys will tame horses and wrestle with each other, and *Ayi* (little boys) will use the roosters to seek food in the mountains. According to Yi tradition, the Torch Festival should last for three days. On the morning of the first day, men gather beside the river to butcher pigs, cattle, and lambs and to divide the meat; women remain at home, where they keep busy steaming buckwheat buns and grinding roasted qingke barley flour to prepare cooked food for the next two days. On the second day, people from various places in full costume swarm onto the torch field from tens or even hundreds of miles away. Activities on this day are many and varied and include traditional events such as horse racing, bull fighting, lamb fights, cock fights, wrestling, post climbing, shooting, lamb grabbing, a song contest, a dress contest, a beauty contest, the game in which an eagle chases chicks, the *Jilehe* dance, attacking the lover's fire, and playing with a torch. The activities are rich in primitive charm and local color. The third day continues the activities of the previous day. In the evening, people return to their villages and light torches made of fleabane stems or slender bamboo. With these, they conduct the holy torch farewell ceremony. They walk around their houses for three rotations, then walk toward the narrow passes in the field, gradually gathering together and shouting loudly along the way. Echoes from the mountain and the valley make the ceremony even jollier. Under the dark sky where masses of stars are twinkling, people gather on several main paths to form fire dragons that appear to float among the villages and across the vast sky. The scene as they twist and turn along the wandering mountain pass is spectacular. With the climactic jubilation of the Torch Festival, the people hope that the torch will baptize the mountains and the woodland to secure a harvest the next year, eliminate all kinds of diseases and ailments, and bring good luck forever.

The two counties of Butuo and Puge are where the ancient folk customs of the Torch

Festival are preserved most completely and typically. They are the focal point of the Liangshan Torch Festival and are called the "original place of the torch."

Sichuan Chafing Dish

The chafing dish is called *Dabianlu* in Guangdong, "pot" in Ningxia, "warm pot" in Jiangsu and Zhejiang, and "chafing dish in Sichuan. There are two stories about the origin of the chafing dish. One story says that the bronze tripod during the period of the Three Kingdoms—Wei, Shu Han, and

Wu—or during the time of Emperor Yang in the Sui Dynasty, was the origin of chafing dish; another story says that the chafing dish originated in the East Han Dynasty among the unearthed cultural relics. It is clear that the chafing dish has a history of over 1,900 years. The Sichuan chafing dish was recorded in *Ode of the Three Capitals* by Zuo Si, and it is at least 1,700 years old.

Nowadays, the Sichuan chafing dish is an ongoing innovation based on the supply of goods, pots, and tables, from dishware to gravy, materials, and patterns, as well as storefront and environment. Dishes based on balsam and sesame paste are usually used for the chafing dish in Sichuan. However, Sichuan people who love the chafing dish most use dry dish (*dish* means flavoring substance). In fact, Sichuan people generally use a balsam dish plus a dry dish, so that they can dip some food in the balsam dish (for example, mutton, sliced lotus root, or fish) and then dip some food in the dry dish (for example, duck intestine, cattle stomach, cattle aorta, or kidney), which makes the food even more delicious.

Sichuan chafing dish is both a gourmet food and a cooking method. Moreover, it is a major component of Sichuan food culture. The preparation of the gravy for the Sichuan chafing dish is very sophisticated, with the cooking liquor being made from fresh ingredients and flavorings. Whether for red gravy or white gravy, the raw ingredients used, such as chicken, fish, and great pastern bone, must be all very fresh. For example, sucking fish in the chafing dish is live fish butchered on the spot to cook and eat immediately. Live yellow eel is butchered and put into the pot along with the blood so that most of the nutritional value is preserved and the food is not only fresh and delicious, but also beneficial to health.

Shadow Play in Sichuan

Shadow play is also called "lamp shadow play" or "shadow theater." It is a form of comprehensive art based on the integration of the ancient and unique formative arts with the art of drama. It is also the precursor of traditional Chinese drama. Its artistic effect is achieved through lighting, shadow play, sound effects, and vocal music. The shadow players manipulated by the actors not only can appear on the stage as properties, but also are folk artworks with typical local features.

Shadow play became prevalent in the Yuan and Ming dynasties. Along with the population migration and cultural exchange, it spread across the country and gradually evolved into various schools with different styles—Shaanxi shadow play, Shanxi shadow play, Beijing shadow play, Sichuan shadow play, and so on. Most of the Sichuan shadow play retains the simple and unsophisticated charm of the stone carvings from the Han and Wei dynasties, which were very popular in the Qing Dynasty.

Shadow play is divided into the two schools of east and west. The eastern school is distributed mainly in eastern Sichuan and northern Sichuan. The form of the shadow players is mainly one of straight lines, and the carving is fine. The body is about 30 centimeters high and is made out of cow leather. As it was brought over from south of the Wei River in Shaanxi, local people call it "shadow from south of Wei." The western school is mainly distributed in Chengdu, Sichuan. The form of the shadow players was influenced by that of Beijing shadow plays, and they are about 60 centimeters high. The facial makeup in Sichuan shadow play is more ordinary compared with that of Shaanxi and Beijing, which is more exaggerated, with particular attention paid to individual characteristics. Importance is especially attached to the design of the character's eyes. If the entire face is carved in intaglio, the eyeballs and the eye region will be of incised inscription so that the eyes are bright and the artistic touch is of great significance.

In addition to history, myth, and legend, most of the operas in Sichuan shadow play are comedy; the forms of shadow players are often exaggerated, dynamic, and funny, with their facial makeup and costumes mostly imitating those of the Chuan Opera, full of local color.

A shadow screen must be set up in front of the stage in order to perform shadow play, with actors performing behind the screen.

In the past, lighting was created by using oil lamps and storm lanterns but in the present day, electric lights and fluorescent lamps are used. Shadow play performances consist of two parts: acting and singing. The two parts should coordinate with each other to make the play vivid, and the atmosphere and effects can be fully realized. (From ImagineChina)

Chengdu Snacks

Long Chao Shou

Long Chao Shou is a famous Chengdu snack. Mince is wrapped in a flour-based shell and then boiled. After adding light broth, red oil, and other flavorings, it can be enjoyed with bean curd. The snack is tender and delicious, and the broth is slightly hot. Chao Shou is the name of Chinese dumplings made by the Sichuan people and produced throughout China. Red oil Chao Shou is one of the best-known varieties.

Rice Balls with Sesame Sauce

Rice balls with sesame sauce have experienced a century's history. The boss Lai Yuanxin boiled and sold rice balls with sesame sauce along the streets of Chengdu starting in 1894. The shell of the rice balls with sesame sauce remains intact while boiling, the mince is not exposed and the soup does not become thick. While being eaten, the rice balls do not stick to the chopsticks or the teeth and do not feel oily. Nourishing and moist, tasty, and refreshing, this is the most popular snack in Chengdu. The present form of rice balls with sesame sauce has continued the good quality of the original, with white and clear color, soft shell, and tasty oil, as well as being rich in nutrition.

Dandan Noodles

Dandan noodles are a popular Chengdu snack. The flour is rolled into noodles; then the noodles are boiled in water, scooped out, and mixed with minced pork. The noodles are thin, slippery, and springy, while the thick gravy is savory, with a salty taste, and mildly hot. The spicy smell is immediately recognizable, and the noodles are very tasty. They are quite popular in Sichuan and often serve as snack food.

Ma Po Bean Curd

Ma Po Bean Curd is one dish that typifies the local flavor of Chinese tofu cuisine, and it has become a well-known feature of Sichuan cuisine around the world. The dish is broiled; the snow-white, soft bean curd is topped with browned ground beef and green garlic sprouts. Around the bean curd is drizzled a circle of bright red oil, like jade besetting amber. Its particular flavor is peppery, hot, warm, soft, tender, savory, and fresh.

Couple Beef

The characteristic flavors of couple beef is peppery, hot, and savory. It is said that in the 1930s, the couple Guo Chaohua in Chengdu made a living by selling beef along the streets. As the beef was fine and unique in taste, people loved it very much and that is how it got the name of "couple beef." Later on, it became available in stores; the ingredients were replaced by beef heart, tongue, stomach, head, and skin; and the quality was further improved. It has become one of the most well known Sichuan dishes.

(From Colphoto)

Chongqing

Geography at a Glance

Chongqing, or "Yu" for short, has become the fourth municipality directly under the Central Government of China since 1997. Its many other names include Jiangzhou, Bajun, Chuzhou, Yuzhou, and Gongzhou. In 1189, a Song Dynasty emperor was first appointed Prince Gong here, and later he came to power as the emperor–thus the city got the name Chonqing, meaning "double celebration." Chongqing covers an area of 31,776 square miles, stretching 292 miles from east to west and about 280 miles from north to south. It has a population of 31.14 million, of which Han are the majority; there are also more than 40 ethnic groups in the area, including the Tujia and Miao.

Chongqing lies in southwestern China, with the upper Yangtze River flowing through the territory. Adjoining central and western China, Chongqing shares its borders with many other provinces, among them Hubei, Hunan, Guizhou, Sichuan, and Shaanxi. Because the city lies between two rivers—the Jialing and the Yangtze—it is often known as "the city by the river"; it is also called "the city on the mountain" because of its hilly terrain. The average altitude of Chongqing is 1,312 feet above sea level.

Chongqing lies in the North Subtropical Zone (NSZ). The average annual temperature of the city is 64°F. In July and August the temperature usually hovers around 80 to 100°F, but it has been known to reach a high of 110—thus Chongqing is considered to be one of the "Three Furnaces" in the Yangtze drainage area (the other two are Wuhan and Nanjing). The city gets nearly 40 to 55 inches

(From ImagineChina)

Heaven Pit in Xiaozhai (From Imagine China)

of rain each year, much of which falls in the evening. There have been many beautiful poems written about the night rainfall of Bashan (Chongqing).

Chongqing has many old-fashioned and intriguing local customs and is well known for its art and native craft forms. The area's population—now about 30 million—is expanding as a result of the construction of the Three Gorges Project. The potential for development is enormous: In addition to supplying hydropower and flood control, the project is expected to open the region to international business investment.

Featured Cuisine

Cold zanba, Shancheng boiled rice dumplings, Jiuyuan steamed stuffed buns, flatiron-shaped cakes, Dandan noodles, cold noodles with shredded chicken, bridge chaoshou (a kind of Sichuan soup dumpling), lightly fried dumplings with chicken soup, diced rabbit with special flavor, beef with dried orange peel, chicken with dried orange peel, Mapo stewed bean curd with minced pork in pepper sauce, home-style boiled beef, sauteed diced chicken with peanuts, sauteed diced fresh scallops, twice-cooked pork, fried salted pork, Taibai chicken, duck with tea, and camphor-tree leaves.

Featured Commodities

Special Local Products

Fuling mustard, Wulong ramie, Chongqing chukar, cold zanba, Shancheng boiled rice dumplings, Yongchuan fer-

Notes 

❶ There are several types of sightseeing cruises for touring the gigantic Three Gorges Project. Tourists may want to take a luxury cruise, but second- and third-class accomodations are also available.

❷ Shennong jia consists of high mountains and dense forests and is relatively uninhabited, so to be safe, tourists should not travel there alone. The tourism bureau of Shennong jia can arrange different kinds of safari trips.

mented black beans, Jiangbei roast duck, Baishiyi dried salted duck, Dianjiang pickled cucumber, Cuiping silvery needle tea, Xi'nong Maojian tea, Old Sichuan sliced beef, Baoding delicate dried cabbage, Jiangjin sweet puffed rice, Hechuan sliced peaches.

Local Handicrafts

Rongchang china handicrafts, Rongchang folding fans, Dianjiang brown bamboo walking sticks, Jiangjin liquor, Tujia brocade, Longshui hardware and tools, Three Gorges ink-stone.

Transportation Tips

By Bus

There are several national highways radiating from Chongqing to Chengdu, Hanzhong, Guiyang, Wuhan, and Changsha, and one

(From Quanjing)

expressway, the Chongqing-Chengdu Expressway. Bus transportation within Chongqing covers Chongqing City, Wanxian, Fuling, and Qianjiang. It is a good idea to take public transportation between cities.

By Train

There are three electric railroad trunk lines: Chengdu-Chongqing, Sichuan–Guizhou, and Xiangfan-Chongqing, which are connected

POPULAR FESTIVALS

Xiushan Huadeng (Festive Lantern) Festival

The Xiushan Huadeng Festival is held from the 3rd day to the 15th day of the first lunar month each year. Entertainment at this festival includes the festive lantern dance, lantern burning ceremony, and other exciting activities.

Baishou (Swaying Arms) Festival of Tujia Ethnic Group

The Baishou Festival is held in Youyang County from the 3rd day to the 15th day of the first lunar month or in the third lunar month each year, where you can see Tujia dance performances.

Tongliang Dragon Dance with Lanterns

This event is held during the Spring Festival as well as other celebrations, including shows and competitions of the dragon dance.

Baoding Incense Fair

The Baoding Incense Fair is held from the middle of the first lunar month to the beginning of the third lunar month each year and most followers of Buddha go there on the 1st, 15th, and 19th of the second lunar month. The 19th is especially festive and the fair reaches a climax as people celebrate the birthday of Kwan-yin. Many followers of Buddha from around the country come here during the fair.

Peach Blossom Festival

The Peach Blossom Festival is held in the third lunar month in Hualong, Dazu County. People come here from all over the world to marvel at the beauty of the peach blossoms.

with the national network. Two local lines also cross Chongqing: the Dazhou-Wanxian line and the Chongqing-Huaihua line.

By Plane

There are two airports in Chongqing: Jiangbei International Airport and Wanzhou Wuqiao Airport, both of which have about 100 international and domestic airlines.

By Ship

As the Yangtze River crosses Chongqing, boat travel is very convenient. There are ports in Chongqing City, Fuling, Wanzhou, and Hechuan. Chongqing Passenger Port is in the East Yuzhong district and Chaotianmen (Gate toward the Sky) is near the confluence of the Yangtze and Jialing rivers. This is the best place to take a sightseeing boat trip for the Three Gorges. Buses going directly to the ports include No. 401, 418, 102,103, 128, 232, and 382.

Recommended Routes

Classical Routes

Seven-day tour of the Three Gorges Scenic area of the Yangtze River

Day 1 Arrival Chongqing. Lodging: Chongqing Guest House.

Day 2 Former Residence of Bai→Zhazi Cave→the Ancient town of Ciqikou→the Great Hall. Lodging: Chongqing Guest House.

Day 3 Chongqing→Fuling→Wujiang Gorge→Three Natural Stone Arc Bridges of Wulong→Xiannu Mountain. Lodging: A hotel on the Xiannu Mountain.

Day 4 Alp Meadow on Xiannu Mountain →Furong Cave in Wulong→Fuling. Lodging: Fuzhou Hotel.

Day 5 Fuling→Fengdu→Zhangfei Temple→Fengjie. Lodging: Baidi Hotel Heaven Pit in Fengjie→the Three Gorges of the Yangtze River→the Minor Three Gorges of the Daning River Lodging: Passenger ship.

Day 6 the Three Gorges of the Yangtze River passing the lock of the Three Gorges Dam). YichangLodging: Yichang.

Day 7 Three Gorges Dam. End of tour.

Five-day tour of West Chongqing

Day 1 Arrival in Chongqing. Lodging: Chongqing Guest House.

Day 2 Chongqing→Dazu Carvings→Chongqing. Lodging: Chongqing Guest House.

Day 3 Chongqing→Wulong→Three Natural Stone Arc Bridges→Xiannu Mountain. Lodging: A hotel on the Xiannu Mountain.

Day 4 Alp Meadow on Xiannu Mountain→Downtown Chongqing (Jiefangbei Shopping Plaza). Lodging: Chongqing Guest House.

Day 5 Former Residence of Bai→Zhazi Cave→the Ancient Town of Ciqikou. End of tour.

Traditional Routes

Two-day tour of Chongqing

Day 1 Arrival in Chongqing.

Day 2 Former Residence of Bai→Zhazi Cave→Ancient Town of Ciqikou→Chaotianmen Square. End of tour.

Six-day tour of Chongqing→Guang'an →Three Gorges of the Yangtze River.

Day 1 Arrival in Chongqing.

Day 2 Chongqing→Guang'an (the former residence of Deng Xiaoping and the ancestral grave of the Deng Family)→Chongqing.

Day 3 Ancient Town of Ciqikou→Former Residence of Bai→Zhazi Cave→Chaotianmen Square→Convergence of the Jialing and Yangtze rivers.

Day 4 Chongqing→Three Gorges of the Yangtze River.

Day 5 Baidi Town→Shennong River→Qutang Gorge→Wuxia Gorge→Xiling Gorge.

Day 6 End of tour.

Self-Guided Tours

Tour of Cultural Sites of Chongqing and Sichuan

Tour starts from Chongqing and ends in Chengdu. You will visit sites of Yongchuan, Dazu, Neijiang, Zigong, Yibin, Bamboo Sea, Leshan, and Meishan.

Main Scenic Spots: Dazu Carvings, Baoding Mountain, North Mountain Carvings, Bamboo Sea, Tianbao Village, Grand Buddha in Leshan, Wuhou Shrine, Wangjianglou, and other places of interest.

Tour of Chongqing→Three Gorges of the Yangtze River→Yichang→Zhangjiajie.

Tour starts from Chongqing and ends in Zhangjiajie, passing through the Three Gorges of the Yangtze River and Yichang City in Hubei Province.

Main Scenic Spots: Ghost City of Fengdu, Shibao Village, Zhang Fei Temple, Baidi Town, Big Three Gorges, Minor Three Gorges.

(From Quanjing)

Addresses and Phone Numbers

Chongqing International Grand Hotel	1 Tuanjie Road, Yangjiaping	023-68522000
Yongchuan Hengtong Hotel	129 Xidajie Road, Yongchuan	023-49863302
Yongchuan Hotel	22 Xidajie Road, Yongchuan	023-49869999
Baidi Hotel	Baidi, Fengjie County, Chongqing	023-56721445
Jiangshan Hotel	Lakefront of Longtan Lake in Simian Mountain, Jiangjin	023-47666228
Shennv Peak Guest House	210 Zhongshan First Road, Yuzhong District	023-63557818
Sanxia Hotel	1 Shannxi Road, Yuzhong District	023-63555555
Dazu Hotel	350 Longzhong Road, Longgang, Dazu County	023-43721888

Chongqing Region

>>>

Best Time to Travel

The best times to visit Chongqing are in spring and winter. Late spring and summer can be very hot and humid.

Shopping Routes

The shopping area of Jiefangbei ("Monument of Liberation") in the Yuzhong District includes a wide variety of stores, recreation centers, hotels, and other facilities. Good places to shop are the Chongqing Department Store, Daduhui Shopping Mall, and Carrefour Supermarket. Trolleybuses No. 401, 402, and 405 will take you there.

Pipashan (Loquat Mountain) Park

Pipashan Park, at 1,132 feet above sea level, is located on Loquat Mountain at Zhongshan Second Road in Yuzhong District. The highest spot in downtown Chongqing, it is a good place from which to view the whole city or the night scene. There are several sources for the name of the mountain. The first is the large number of loquat trees on the mountain; the second is that the shape of the mountain resembles a traditional Chinese musical instrument, the pi-pa (lute); and the third is that a beautiful mountain maiden once played the pi-pa every night to call her lover across the river.

Garden of Sweet-Scented Osmanthus (Gui Yuan)

Gui Yuan was originally the residence of General Zhang Zhizhong of the Kuomintang. It is located at No.65 Fourth Zhongshan Street in Yuzhong District. During the Chongqing Negotiation in August 1945, Mr. Zhang refurbished the residence as Mao Zedong's working and meeting place. The garden got its name because there are two sweet-scented Osmanthus trees there.

50 Zengjiayan Road

50 Zengjiayan Road, also known as the former residence of Zhou Enlai, is located on Zhongshan Fourth Road in the Yuzhong District, which borders the Jialing River. It was once the main office of the South China Bureau of the Communist Party in Chongqing. An interesting juxtaposition occurred here: On the right-hand side of Zhou Enlai's house was Dai Li, director of the Bureau of Investigation and Statistics of the Kuomintang; on the left-hand side of Mr. Zhou's residence was the local police station of the Kuomintang.

There is a bronze standing statue of Zhou Enlai at 50 Zengjiayan Road. This former home of Zhou Enlai witnessed the history of the Chinese revolution and is now a major cultural site under national protection. (From CFP)

Revolutionary Martyrs Memorial Park in Hongyan Village

The Hongyan Memorial is located on the banks of the Jialing River in Chongqing. It comprises four important buildings: 13 Hongyan Village, 50 Zengjiayan Road, the Garden of Gui, and the Former General Office of *Xinhua Daily*. These are the bases of the South China Bureau of the Communist Party of China. During the negotiation with the Kuomintang in 1945, Mao Zedong lived at No.13 Hongyan Village.

After the Japanese invaders seized Guangzhou and Wuhan in October 1938, the government of the Kuomintang moved to Chongqing. As representatives of the Communist Party of China, Zhou Enlai, Dong Biwu, Lin Boqu, Wu Yuzhang, Ye Jianying, Wang Ruofei, and Deng Yingchao came to Chongqing to establish the South China Bureau of the Communist Party of China. The former department and the office of the Eighth Route Army in Chongqing were both located in Hongyan Village.

This is the statue of Xiaoluobotou (nickname for a small boy who died in the camp, literally meaning "Little Radish Head") at the site SACO camp. (From Colphoto).

Jinyun Mountain Scenic Area

Jinyun Mountain Scenic Area is located along the banks of the Jialang River at Wentang Gorge in the Beibei District, 37 miles from downtown Chongqing. The area includes Jinyun Mountain, North Hot Spring, Fishing Town in Hechuan, and several other places of interest along the Jialing River. Jinyun Mountain, also called Minor Emei Mountain, is a wonderful place to watch the sunrise and marvel at the banks of clouds. On the mountain itself is a rare living fossil—the Dawn Redwood—the only extant speciman of the giant redwood species *Metasequoia*. There are perhaps only 1,000 living specimens of this ancient tree, which is native to central China. This species is known to have existed for 160 million years.

Jinyun Mountain has been a Buddhist holy site for more than 1,500 years, and many cultural artifacts can be found on the mountain.

Site of the Sino-American Cooperation Organization Concentration Camp

This site is located at Gele Mountain in northwestern Chongqing. The Sino-American Cooperation Organization (SACO) was built in 1942 and officially established in 1943. In name, it was a mutual intelligence-gathering organization directed at the Japanese invaders; in reality, it was a secret entity of the Kuomintang and a detention camp for members of the Chinese Communist Party (CCP). The organization was headed by Dai Li, director of the Kuomintang Bureau of Investigation and Statistics, and a U.S. Navy captain, Milton E. Miles. In November 1949,

The Exhibition Hall is in the former Residence of Bai and the Zhazi Cave Jail. Luo Guangbin and Yang Yiyan's book Hongyan (Red Rock) *explains more about this exhibit. (From Imagine-China)*

more than 300 supporters of revolution were massacred by the Kuomintang before they withdrew from Mainland China. After Chongqing was liberated, the People's Government built a martyrs' mausoleum and a memorial pillar. The actual site of SACO is now the present exhibition hall.

In addition to the Residence of Bai and Zhazi Cave, Songlin Po (Slope of Pine Trees) is a place worth visiting.

Jindao (Golden Knife) Gorge

Jindao Gorge, 2,707 feet above sea level, is on the southwestern side of Huaying Mountain in the Beibei district, 56 miles from downtown Chongqing. It is a magical setting with primeval scenery. According to legend, the gorge got its name from a golden knife that shone on it every night. The 3.8-mile-long gorge is divided into two parts: the upper gorge and the caves and ponds in the lower part.

Take the bus to the Beibei district, then transfer to Bus 270 to Huaying Mountain. You can also take a cable car at Tuanshanbao in Beibei to get to the mountain.

Furong (Lotus) Cave of Wulong

Discovered in May 1993, Furong Cave is located on the banks of the Furong River, 2.5 miles from Jiangkou in Wulong County. It has been called a world wonder and the "Underground Arts Palace and Museum of the Science of Caves." Many experts consider this large-scale limestone cave one of the best caves open to visitors in the world. The main cave is 8,858 feet long, ranges from 98 to 160 feet tall, and its Resplendent Lobby has 118,402 square feet of floor space.

Furong Cave of Wulong (From ImagineChina)

The Three Natural Stone Arch Bridges of Wulong

These limestone bridges are located 12.4 miles southeast of the county seat of Wulong, Chongqing. The Tianlong Bridge, Qinglong Bridge, and Heilong Bridge stretch across the enormous gorge of the Yangshui River in Wulong. The area's one gorge, two holes, three bridges, four caves, and five springs create a perfect natural setting for a traditional Chinese painting of mountains and waters.

Heaven Pit in Wulong (From Quanjing)

Fishing Town

Fishing Town, 1,312 feet above sea level, is located on Diaoyu (Fishing) Mountain along the south bank of the Jialing River, almost 4 miles from the town of Hechuan. It is bounded by the Qu, Rong, and Jialing rivers on three sides. An ancient well-preserved battleground during the Southern Song Dynasty, Fishing Town is called "the Oriental Mecca" by Europeans.

Simian (Four Sides) Mountain

A two-hour drive (about 87 miles) from Chongqing brings you to Simian Mountain, whose lush vegetation and luxuriant forest covers an area of about 93 square miles. The name refers to the way the mountain encircles the area on all sides. Wugongling, the highest peak, is to the south at 6,260 feet above sea level. Simian Mountain is naturally serene and slightly mysterious, with its clear, clean water and peaceful lakes. Besides the many streams and lakes in the area, there are hundreds of waterfalls in various configurations, and the sound of rushing water can be heard from miles away.

Jinfo (Golden Buddha) Mountain

Honored as one of the four most famous mountains in Sichuan and Chongqing, Jinfo Mountain is situated southeast of the city of Nanchuan in the Chongqing municipality. At 7,385 feet, Fengchuiling, the highest peak, is also the highest peak of the Dalou mountain range. When the sun shines on the mountain, the cliffs resemble a Buddha with a golden cassock, hence its name.

The largest carving on Baoding Mountain (From ImagineChina)

Dazu Carvings

Dazu County, 168 miles west of Chengdu, is located southeast of the Sichuan Basin. There are more than 60,000 Buddhist, Taoist, and Confucian rock carvings and at least 100,000 character inscriptions dotting the landscape around Dazu. Some carvings date back to the early Tang Dynasty (618–907). Many were carved during the Ming and Qing dynasties. In 1999, UNESCO gave it official status as a World Heritage site.

A mile and a quarter south of the county seat of Dazu, you will find the Beishan grotto carvings. The carvings of the Fowan area are the most famous.

Beishan (North Mountain) Carvings

North Mountain, originally called Longgang Mountain, is 1,837 feet above sea level. The carvings in this area date from 892, in the Tang Dynasty, to the Ming Dynasty. The Fowan carvings, famous for their exquisite artistry, are divided into the carvings of the southern part, which were completed in

Dafowan (Grand Buddha Bay) carvings on Baoding Mountain (From ImagineChina)

the later Tang Dynasty and Five Dynasties, and those of the northern part, which were produced mainly in the Northern and Southern Song dynasties. They are world-famous.

Baoding Mountain Carvings

The Baodingshan carvings, found at 1,732 feet above sea level, are about 9 miles northeast of Dazu. Baoding Mountain, like Emei Mountain, is a Buddhist sacred land where you can see more than 10,000 different Buddhist carvings on the cliff.

Baidi

The town of Baidi, 2.5 miles from Fengjie County, is on Baidi Mountain on the north side of the Yangtze River. Originally known as Ziyang, it is an ancient town of great historical interest. According to a local folktale, when construction of the town began, a column of white steam rose up from a well, like a white dragon flying up to heaven. The town was named Baidi, meaning "heavenly white dragon." The well is still in existence. During the Three Kingdoms Period (220–280), Emperor Liu Bei of the Shu Kingdom was disastrously defeated by the Wu Kingdom and retreated to Baidi. After a series of bloody defensive battles, the Shu people remained in the town. Liu fell fatally ill, and just before his death he confided his state affairs to his son Liu Chan, the future emperor of the Shu, and to his prime minister, Zhuge Liang. This incident later became known as "confiding to the orphan at Baidi."

Carvings of small underworld spirits in the Ghost City of Fengdu. (From CFP)

Ming (Famous) Mountain of Fengdu

Ming Mountain is on the northern bank of the Yangtze River, 107 miles from downtown Chongqing. During the first years of the Western Zhou Dynasty, Fengdu was the capital of the state of Ba. Many Buddhist temples are located throughout the area. In Fengdu (also known as Ghost City) you may be able to spot a number of realistic and well-executed spirit carvings.

Zhang Fei Temple of Yunyang

Opposite the town of Yunyang, Zhang Fei Temple is situated at the top of Feifeng (Flying Phoenix) Mountain, on the southern bank of the Yangtze River. It is 237 miles from the heart of downtown Chongqing. The temple was originally built in the later years of the kingdom of Shu Han (221–263) to commemorate General Zhang Fei, and has since been rebuilt many times. The magnificent temple covers a constructive area of 15,440 square miles, with 42,460 square miles of garden. Zhang Fei Temple is the only ancient site that

Shibaozhai (From ImagineChina)

would be completely submerged as a result of the Three Gorges Project, but it has been relocated to Yunyang County.

Shibaozhai (Precious Stone Fortress)

Shibaozhai is in Zhong County on the northern bank of the Yangtze River. It is 28 miles from the Zhong County seat. The original pagoda was built in the Qing Dynasty in 1750. The mountain is actually a 98-foot rectangular rock with sheer cliffs, and the pagoda, which is a 12-story, 184-foot wooden tower, leans against the cliff. The water level of the river will reach the gate of the pavilion in 2009, the projected completion date of the Three Gorges Project. At that time, Shibaozhai will be surrounded by water on four sides, but a dam is being built to protect the base of the pagoda.

Heaven Pit in Xiaozhai

There is a large, mysterious heaven pit in the village of Xiaozhai, in Fengjie County. Geologically the hole is called a karst funnel, which is formed through the collapse of a water-eroded cave or results from erosion by surface water. According to one story, it was formed by the impact of a meteorite several hundred million years ago. The largest of its kind in the world, the funnel is 2,172 feet in diameter at the top, 1,713 feet in diameter at the bottom, and 2,185 feet deep. There is a clear underground river flowing through the bottom of the Xiaozhai heaven pit.

Precipices surround the heaven pit in Xiaozhai, as if carved by an axe or knife. The pit is completely enclosed, so if you stand at the very bottom, it seems as if you're looking at the sky from the bottom of a well. (From ImagineChina)

Three Gorges (Sanxia) Scenic Area of the Yangtze River

The Three Gorges Scenic Area is located in East Chongqing and West Hubei Province. Comprising Qutang Gorge, Wuxia Gorge, and Xiling Gorge, the area starts from Baidi in Fengjie County in the west and ends at the Nanjin Pass in Yichang City in the east. These are the Three Big Gorges, with a total length of about 124 miles.

Qutang Gorge, only 5 miles long, is the shortest of the three. Famous for its sheer and spectacular precipices, it is also the narrowest among the three, with the widest point measuring only 328 feet across. Kuimen (Kui Gate) is the entrance to Qutang Gorge, and the mountains here are very steep.

The scenic Wuxia Gorge is 15.5 miles from Qutang Gorge and is about 25 miles long. Noted for its deep and serene scenes, Wuxia Gorge is full of unusual zigzag peaks, rising mists, and beautiful views. The famous Twelve Peaks, seen from both banks of the river, are the most spectacular.

Xiling Gorge, the longest of the three gorges, stretches from west to east for 47 miles from the mouth of the Xiangxi River at Zigui to Nanjin Pass near the city of Yichang in Hubei. This gorge is known for dangerous rapids and numerous shoals, the latter including the Qingtan, Kongling, and Xietan shoals. The Three Gorges Project is the largest hydropower station project in the world.

(From Quanjing)

(From Quanjing)

(From CFP)

(From Quanjing)

(From Quanjing)

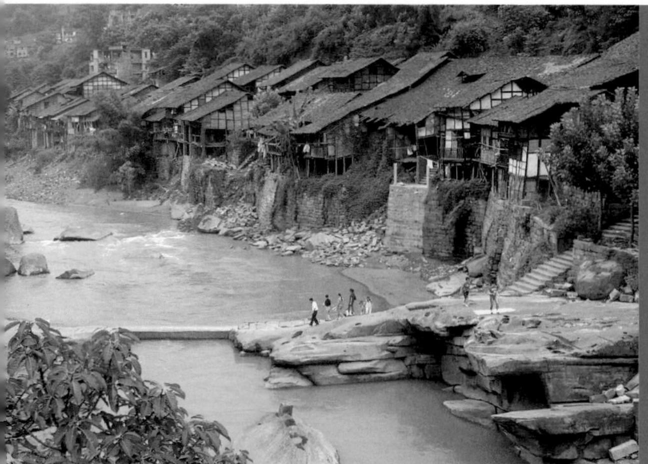

The ancient town of Zhongshan is located in a mountainous area, with the Sunxi River flowing from the south to the north. The buildings in the town are mainly two-story suspended bamboo structures. The first floors are stores, and the second floors are living spaces, which is the traditional style of Sichuan and Chongqing. (From CFP)

Chongqing Style

Zhongshan Old Town

Starting from the city of Jiangjin and traveling more than 310 miles south toward the scenic area of Simian Mountain, you arrive at Zhongshan beside the Sunxi River. With a history of over 1,000 years, Zhongshan is one of the ten oldest towns in the Chongqing area.

In close proximity to mountain and river, the old town has a touch of the watery region south of the lower reaches of the Yangtse River. Possibly because it is closed off from the hustle and bustle of the outside world, it boasts well-preserved construction techniques and an unsophisticated lifestyle that have been passed down from generation to generation. A 1.8-mile-long narrow lane is bordered by structures built in the Qing Dynasty, which remain in perfect condition. This, plus the flagstone road, gives the town its old and inviting appearance.

As you walk along the ancient roads paved with dark blue stones and along the crooked narrow lanes, the fragrance of herbs in the air and the ringing sounds from the blacksmith combine to create a harmonious and naturally artistic atmosphere. The old white-haired barber sitting under the overhang of the roof of his house is a peaceful scene, which like an oil painting, reveals the unique charm of the old town.

The historically and culturally significant town of Zhongshan, also called Sanhechang, is in the Simian Mountain area. Almost 5 miles long, the town is divided into several parts, and you'll notice that all the streets are paved with flagstones. (From Colphoto)

Business in the town include a pot factory, a spade factory, a silver shop, a blacksmith, a dye house, a pharmacy (nine generations old!), an ancient teahouse, and a tavern. There are also numerous old bridges, over 70 old temples, and 110-odd old villages.

Zhongshan was formerly known as Sanhechang. Three vigorous Chinese characters spelling *Sanhechang* are engraved on a stone wall along the road out of Zhongshan. The wall is about 1.8 miles long and dates back to the Guangxu period of the Qing Dynasty. Sanhechang was once a busy port and the commodity transportation and trade center of the mountain areas of the Sichuan and Guizhou provinces. A total of 82 inscribed characters from the South Song Dynasty have been preserved here, narrating the trip of Li Jiyong, Yu Zixian, and others by water.

The site of a large tomb from the Han Dynasty can also be found in the old town, along with Longdong (Dragon Cave) Reservoir, ideal for swimming and leisurely trips.

An elden living in the Old Town. (From ImagineChina)

To get to Zhongshan, travel from Caiyuanba in Chongqing to Jiangjin, where you transfer. The shuttle bus from Zhongshan stops operating at 5 p.m.

Ciqikou Old Town

When talking about ancient places in Chongqing, people always think of the old town of Ciqikou, which is really ancient. This old town is a flickering light in the hearts of many Chongqing people, just bright enough to cast a dreamy spell over their busy lives.

Established during the Zhenzong era of the Song Dynasty, the old town of Ciqikou developed into a commercial port that connected land and waterways during the Ming Dynasty and reached its peak of prosperity in the Republic of China era. It is acclaimed as a "miniature Chongqing." During the Anti-Japanese War, many renowned cultural figures

Typical old town arts stall (From CFP)

Buildings in the town reflect the distinctive character of houses in the eastern part of Sichuan Province. The slate road goes well with the houses along the way. Most houses are of bamboo and wood with beam-penetrated hollow walls or half-penetrated wooden walls. (From ImagineChina)

gathered here, including Guo Moruo, Xu Beihong, Feng Zikai, Fu Baoshi, Ba Jin, and Bing Xin. Mr. Ding Zhaozhong, a famous Chinese-American scientist, once pursued his studies in the old town. Hua Ziliang, a character in the novel *Red Rock*, also escaped from the enemy's control at the dock in the old town.

The old town is located on the outskirts of Chongqing. In the vicinity of the town is Ma'an Mountain, flanking which are Jinbi Mountain and Fenghuang Mountain. The three mountains stand apart, forming two deep valleys. Fenghuang Brook and Qingshui Brook zigzag out of the valleys. Turbulent Jialingjiang River flows through from the north. The famous Baolun Temple on Ma'an Mountain was built in the Tang Dynasty. Its magnificent palaces have been well preserved. It is said that Emperor Jianwen of the Ming Dynasty took refuge in the temple, thus it is also known as Longyin Temple. At its height, the temple housed more than 300 permanent monks.

There are high mountains, clear water, fresh air, a dense growth of trees, and well-preserved local ethnic character. The people who live here have an easy and peaceful life. Buildings in the town reflect the distinctive character of

The wide river and open land on both sides form an excellent natural harbor. (From ImagineChina)

houses in the eastern part of Sichuan Province. The slate road blends well with the roadside houses, most of which are bamboo and wood structures with beam-penetrated hollow walls or half-penetrated wooden walls and three deep rooms. In the richly ornamented buildings, windows and doors are decorated with elegant and fancy patterns. Typically, behind the house is a square yard, inhabited by rich merchants and eminent families.

To get to the old town, you can catch a bus in front of the Chongqing Grand Hotel.

Qingyun teahouse in the old town has its own folk music band. In Longyin Teahouse, a Sichuan Opera is performed from 2:00 to 5:00 p.m. on the 6th, 16th, and 26th of each month.

Chongqing Hot Pot

Chongqing now has three famous tourist attractions: eating hot pot, appreciating the night scene, and traveling around the Three Gorges. You can't visit Chongqing without sampling the hot pot. This culinary specialty is well known across the country, yet few people know that it actually originated on the banks of the Yangtse River, where it was popular among boatmen and boat trackers, and then spread to Chongqing. After that, Chongqing promoted it in every corner of the country.

The section of the Yangtse River from Yibin in Sichuan Province to Wushan Mountain in the Three Gorges is called Chuanjiang River, which is 621 miles long. Numerous boatmen and boat trackers made a living here. Given their poverty and constantly changing residence, they did not have permanent kitchens in which to make meals like farmers, nor did they have enough money to treat themselves in restaurants on shore like boat owners or rich merchants. Therefore, after working hard and docking their boats, they would select a few stones and scoop a few ladles of river water in a crock. Then they would gather firewood and make a fire. They added some cheap vegetables or even wild vegetables to the water and seasonings such as prickly ash and peppers, which were popular among Sichuan people. The dish, delicious and convenient, satisfied their hunger and warmed up the body, and thus became popular along the river.

On learning that boatmen were fond of hot pot, peddlers at the docks moved the cooking method ashore, improved the cookware and adjusted the ingredients. They carried the hot pot with a shoulder pole and started peddling, attracting laborers along the river. Not until the advent of the Republic of China did high-end and indoor hot pot restaurants appear in Chongqing. These restaurants gradually thrived and continue to enjoy great popularity.

Chongqing hot pot (From ImagineChina)

Yunnan

Geography at a Glance

Yunnan, also called Dian or Yun for short, is the southwesternmost province of China, with the Tropic of Cancer crossing its southern part. Yunnan adjoins Guizhou and Guangxi to the east, Sichuan and Tibet to the north, Myanmar (Burma) to the west, and Laos and Vietnam to the south. The province has an area of about 146,719 square miles, a national border that is 2,523 miles long, and a total population of about 42 million people (2000 census). There are 25 different ethnic groups in Yunnan, making it the most ethnically diverse province in China.

Within its borders, Yunnan also features diverse topography. Mountains cover 84 percent of the area. In the east lies the Yungui Plateau, with hilly landscapes. In the south are middle and low basins. In the west is the plateau valley area over the Hengduan Mountains. The highest point in Yunnan is Mount Kawagebo, the main peak of Taizi Snow Mountain in the Nu Mountains, which is 22,113 feet above sea level. By contrast, the lowest point is at the confluence of the Nanxi and Yuan rivers, which lies at only about 254 feet above sea level. Throughout the province are 672 rivers, which feature high discharge, great variation of high and low water levels, and precipitous banks, as well as rapids and shoals. With 37 lakes for a total area of 425 square miles, Yunnan also ranks among the five lake regions in China.

Located on a low-latitude plateau, Yunnan has an immensely diverse climate, which features two distinct dry and wet seasons, but not much difference among the four seasons otherwise; minor yearly temperature variations but a major daily range; and complicated horizontal topographical variations and distinct vertical heights.

(From ImagineChina)

The Three Towers of the Chongsheng Temple (From Jin Yongji)

Featured Cuisine

Chicken steamed in a pot (qiguoji), honey-basted ham (*mizhi huotui*), mashed fresh broad beans (*xiancandouni*), elephant trunk and chicken, ham slices (*sanjiaxiangbi*), stir-fried muntjac slices (*chaojiroupian*), braised jicong (*a special yunnan mushroom*) in brown sauce (*hongshao jicong*), steamed besugo (*qingzheng jinxianyu*), crossing-the-bridge rice noodles (*guoqiao mixian*), sixi sweet rice dumplings (*sixi tangyuan*), taishi pancake (*taishibing*), dudu steamed wheat dumplings (*dudu shaomai*), shepherd's-purse dumplings (*jicaijiao*), braised rice with ham and beans (*huotuidou menfan*), small-pot rice noodles (*xiaoguo mixian*), spicy pig's ears (*lu'erkuai*), and chicken barbecued with fragrant couchgrass (*xiangmaocao shaoji*) from the Dai ethnic group.

Featured Commodities

Herbal Medicines

Yunnan Baiyao (a traditional herbal medicine of Yunnan ethnic groups), sanqi, snow lotus, yunling, yungui, yunmuxiang, and many other local herbs.

Special Local Products

Pu'er tea, snow tea, Tibetan butter, flower teas, rice, jicong mushroom, rose elephant garlic, pine mushroom, small granular coffee, bamboo mushroom.

Local Handicrafts

Gejiu tin handicrafts, Dongchuan mottled copper handicrafts,

Notes 

❶ It can be very cold in Zhongdian County, so tourists are advised to bring heavy, warm sweaters and coats, hats, and gloves. It is recommended that they also bring high-calorie snacks to compensate for the loss of energy.

❷ Zhongdian County is located on a plateau. Tourists should avoid extreme physical activity, try to keep a steady, slow rhythm while hiking or walking, and be aware of shortness of breath because of the high altitude. Healthy people generally do not experience any effects other than feeling slightly short of breath.

POPULAR FESTIVALS

Huashan Festival

On the 3rd day of lunar January, the Miao people from the northeast and south of Yunnan celebrate this festival through traditional singing, performing the Lusheng Dance (accompanied by a tribal instrument), and climbing a flower-pole.

Sanduo Festival

On the 8th day of lunar February, the Naxi people celebrate their tribal heritage by joining hands in a circle and performing the Naxi group dance (Lili), horse racing, and picnicking.

Chahua Festival

On the 8th day of lunar February, the Yi people from Shuangjiang, Dayao, observe the end of summer with flowers, singing, and a performance of their tribal "Left-Foot Dance."

Daogan Festival

On the 8th and 9th days of lunar February, the Lisu people living in the mountains along the Nujiang River perform tribal rites of walking on burning charcoal, climbing a ladder of sharp blades, antiphonal singing, and traditional dances.

Sanyuejie Festival

From the 15th to the 21st day of lunar March, the Bai people in Dali celebrate their traditional festival with dancing and other folk performances.

Raosanling Festival

From the 23rd to the 25th day of lunar April, the Bai people in Dali hold religious ceremonies (visiting three holy places), go picnicking, and sing and dance to traditional music.

Munao Zongge Festival

On the 15th and 16th days of lunar May, this famous Jingpo festival is celebrated with their traditional dances, dancing around a pole, antiphonal singing, and offerings of rice wine.

Panwang Festival

On the 29th day of lunar May every year, the Yao people offer sacrifices to their ancestors, sing and dance, and hold a spectacular feast.

Torch Festival

From the 24th to the 26th day of lunar June, the Yi and Bai people from Lunan, Chuxiong, and Dali place torches throughout the villages, build bonfires, paint their faces colorfully, set off fireworks, and hold bullfights.

Water Splashing Festival

In mid-April (or late June or early July of the Dai calendar), the Dai hold dragon-boat races, water-splashing activities (symbolizing good luck and best wishes), singing and dancing, pouch tossing (between unmarried men and women as tokens of love), and fireworks displays.

(From ImagineChina)

Kunming ivory carving, Dali stone handicrafts, Dali straw hats, Dali carpets, Dali stone carvings.

Transportation Tips

By Bus

In Yunnan Province, there are seven national highways linking Sichuan, Guizhou, Guangxi, and Tibet, which also go to Myanmar (Burma), Laos, and Vietnam. For the self-guided tours, it is most economical to go into Yunnan by bus.

By Train

The major railways in Yunnan include the GuiKun line (Guiyang–Kunming), the ChengKun line (Chengdu–Kunming), and the NanKun line (Nanning–Kunming), all of which connect with rail networks in other cities and provinces. Tourists can reach Kunming by traveling south from Chengdu, Guiyang, Nanning, or any other city on the lines.

By Plane

Kunming Wujiaba International Airport is one of the five large Chinese international airports. The airport has six international routes, connecting to 47 Chinese cities. In addition, there are eight other airports across the province.

Recommended Routes

Featured Routes

Four-day artistic tour of terrace fields in Yuanyang

Day 1 Kunming→the former county seat of Yuanyang. Lodging: County Guesthouse.

Day 2 Visit terrace fields in Duoyi→Cloud sea and sunrise→Shengli village→Quanfuzhuang village→Ethnic village in Jingkou→Mushroom houses in Jingkou→Zhaizhonglin wood→Baoshanzhai village→Terrace fields in Bada→The county seat. Lodging: County Guesthouse.

Day 3 Yuanyang→Jianshui. Lodging: Lin'an Hotel.

Day 4 End of tour.

Five-day tour of Lijiang and Lugu Lake

Day 1 Take the night train to Lijiang. Lodging: The bus.

Day 2 Lijiang→Jade Dragon Snow Mountain→Yunshanping→Ganhaizi→Baishui River→Yushuizhai village→Dongba Park→Sifang Street→Yuquan Park. Lodging: Gucheng Hotel.

Day 3 Lijiang→Lugu Lake. Lodging: Households near the lake.

Day 4 Lugu Lake→Snake Island→Mosuo household visit→Ninglang. Lodging: Xiaoliangshan Hotel.

Day 5 End of tour

Traditional Routes

Six-day tour of Yunnan folk and scenery

Day 1 Arrival in Kunming.

Day 2 World Horticulture Expo (Horti-Expo) Garden→The Golden Temple→Shibo Jixin Banquet Dance.

Day 3 Western Hill→Longmen→Daguanlou Tower.

Day 4 Stone Forest→Dali→Erhai Lake→Nanzhao Folk Island.

Day 5 Three Pagodas of Dali→Ancient City of Dali→Street of Foreigners.

Day 6 Jade Dragon Snow Mountain→Yunshanping→Ganhaizi→Baishui River→Yushui Mountain Village→Dongba Park. End of tour.

Addresses and Phone Numbers

Kunming Hotel	52 East Dongfeng Road, Kunming	0871-3162063
Youth Hotel	141 Cuihu South Road, Kunming	0871-5175395 0871-5167131
Tuofeng Hotel	Jinbi Square, Jinbi Road, Kunming	0871-3640359
MCA Hotel	Wenxian Road, South Gate of Dali Ancient City, Dali	0872-2673666
Siji Hotel	55 Bo'ai Road, Dali Ancient City	0872-2670382
Jinhaiwan Hotel	In front of Cangshan, East to Erhai Lake, Dali	0872-2476166
Erhai Lake Hotel	212 South Renmin Road, Xiaguan	0872-2125225
Gucheng Hotel	Jishan Lane, Xinyi Street, Lijiang	0888-5189000
Lijiang Youth Hotel	44 Mishi Lane, Xinyi Street, Lijiang Ancient City	0888-5105403
Shangri Hotel	No. 10, Jishan Lane, Xinyi Street, Lijiang	0888-5180435
Nu's Granny Ding's Home	Zhongding Village, Binzhongluo, Nujiang River	0886-3581144
Shuyuan Restaurant	Intersection of North Jinghong Road and North Minzu Road, Xishuangbanna	0691-2123132
Guesthouse of Xishuang Banna Song and Dance Emsemble	58 Mengle Avenue, Xishuangbanna	0691-2122743

Thirteen-day tour amid the clouds

Day 1 Arrival in Kunming.

Day 2 World Horti-Expo Garden→Golden Temple→Shibo Jixin Banquet Dance.

Day 3 Stone Forest→Xishuangbanna.

Day 4 Daluo frontier trade→Single-Tree Forests→Boundary markers between China and Myanmar (Burma)→National Gate→Burmese Temple→Xiaomengla Market→Bajiao Pavilion.

Day 5 Menglun Botanical Garden→Lancang River scenery→Ganlanba Market→Menglun Botanical Garden→Dai village scenery.

Day 6 Tropical Rain Forest Park→Dai People Splashing Water→Bride-Snatching→Ethnic Singing and Dancing→Dali.

Day 7 Cangshan Mountain and Erhai Lake of Dali→Xiaoputuo→Guanyin Pavilion→Butterfly Spring Park→Three Pagodas of Chong Sheng Temple→Dali Ancient City→Street of Foreigners.

Day 8 Lijiang→Black Dragon Pool Park→Lijiang Ancient City→Sifang Street.

Day 9 Jade Dragon Snow Mountain→Yunshanping→Baishui River→Ganhaizi→Dongba Park.

Day 10 Lijiang→Tiger Leaping Gorge→The First Bend of the Yangtze River.

Day 11 Lijiang→Lugu Lake→Liwubi Island→Tusi Island.

Day 12 Kunming→Western Hill Longmen→Daguan Tower.

Day 13 End of tour.

Self-guided Tours

Tiger Leaping Gorge route

Starts from Daju and ends at Tiger Leaping Gorge. At Xindukou visitors can see Tiger Leaping Gorge and Bendi Bay in the distance, with the rushing Jinsha River below. After crossing the river, visitors ascend to the highway along a hill path and view the peak of Jade Dragon Snow Mountain after passing Shanbailian in a walnut garden and Xiashan Spring Hotel. Then they head for the Baishuitai of Shangri-la and reach Tiger Leaping Gorge.

Around Yunnan route

Starts and also ends in Kunming. Leave Kunming by coach for Dali to see the night view of the Ancient City of Dali, where tourists can lodge for the night. Then visit Erhai Lake and Cangshan on horseback. Along the route, pass the Lijiang and Baisha Murals, enjoy ancient music of the Naxi, and see Jade Dragon Snow Mountain. Then hike to Tiger Leaping Gorge and the first bend of the Yangtze River. Tourists can take a side trip to Lijiang for Lugu Lake to search for the villages of the Mosuo people or visit the three islands of Lugu Lake in a Zhucao boat before returning to Kunming.

"Among the 18 wonders in Yunnan, one can see houses built by piling logs up." This saying refers to the log cabin type of construction, known as "Muleng house." These houses are cool in summer and warm in winter, and also resist earthquakes. (From Quanjing)

Kunming, Qujing, Honghe Region

Best Time to Travel

Kunming's four seasons are all spring-like and suitable for tourism. Be aware that from May to October is the rainy season.

Shopping Tips

The Flower and Bird Market located on Yongdao Street in Kunming is the city's most popular market. All imaginable flowers, fish, birds, and local specialties are available.

To best experience the market life of Kunming, tourists can visit the Cultural and Commercial City, located near the Southwest Commercial Building on Qingnian Road in Kunming. Here, ethnic costumes, authentic antiques and reproductions, calligraphy, paintings, and foods of all kinds are abundantly available.

Kunming's largest flower market is located on Shangyi Street, where the scent of flowers permeates the air. The flowers and arrangements are inexpensive and come in special paper boxes.

Cuihu Park lies at the foot of Luofeng Mountain in the urban area of Kunming, opposite the entrance to Yunnan University. Though not very large, the park is known for the seagulls that come here every winter from Siberia, some of which rest in Cuihu Lake. (From ImagineChina)

Western Hill (Xishan)

Located alongside Dianchi Lake, 7,700 feet above sea level and extending over 25 miles, Western Hill is known for having the most beautiful scenery in Yunnan. Here ancient trees reach for the sky. The hill resembles a sleeping beauty lying on her back with bent legs by Dianchi Lake, so it is also called the Sleeping Beauty Hill.

On Western Hill, there are lush forests and a great variety of plants. An immense forested park and nature reserve is now open in the area. Western Hill is famous for its many ancient buildings, each with unique features hidden among the thick forests. These include Huating Temple (Huating Si), Taihua Temple (Taihua Si), Sanqing Pavilion (Sanqing Ge), and Longmen, among which Longmen ranks first. On the way there, tourists first pass Sanqing Pavilion, which is built among cliffs, like a pavilion suspended in the air. Overlooking Dianchi Lake and the urban area, tourists are treated to a magnificent and ever-changing view. Almost 1,000 feet above the water surface of Dianchi Lake, Longmen stands on a precipitous cliff.

The plank road up to Longmen is very narrow, allowing only two people at a time to pass.

Dianchi Lake

Dianchi Lake, a famous plateau lake, is the biggest lake in Yunnan Province and also the sixth-largest freshwater lake in China. Situated southwest of Kunming, 6,190 feet above sea level, it has a total area of over 115 square miles and is shaped like a crescent moon. As part of the Yangtze River system, the water in Dianchi Lake flows into Pudu River through Haikou and then into Jinsha River. Surrounding Dianchi Lake is Jinma Hill to the east, Biji Hill to the west, Snake Hill to the north, and Crane Hill to the south. The hills adjoin each other, forming a natural boundary around Kunming. The landscape consists of fertile soil and an abundant water supply convenient for irrigation and navigation. The climate is mild. The view of the lake is charming, with stretches of clear water dotted with sails and fishing boats.

Take Bus 24 then Bus 44 to Haigeng Park northeast of Dianchi Lake.

Yunnan Native Village

Located in the south of Kunming, the Yunnan Native Village concentrates the architectural styles, customs, culture, and art of all the ethnic groups in

Yunnan, making it a window for understanding the people of Yunnan. Currently, village camps for nine ethnic groups have been established, including Dai, Bai, Yi, Naxi, Mosuo, Jinuo, Lahu, Buyi, and Wa. Tourist attractions include the Hall of Ethnic Dances and Songs, and the Square of Ethnic Unity. Each village features a camp for the ethnic group, in conjunction with displays of their various cottages, production, methods of lifestyles, and religious customs. The Yunnan Native Museum, which exhibits the history and culture of all the ethnic groups in Yunnan, should not be missed.

Visitors can reach the village, which is 5.5 miles from the downtown area, by taking Bus No. 73 or 44, or by taxi.

Daguan Park

Daguan Park, also named Jinhuapu, is located southwest of Kunming's urban area, opposite Taihua Hill, with a lake in between. The park gets its name from the tower at its center, which is poetically portrayed as standing "by water against a long, long mountain range with clouds at the top." In front of the tower, there are three stone pavilions in the lake, set up to imitate the "Three Pools Mirroring the Moon" of West Lake, Hangzhou. Beyond the lake is a long bank, separating the park from Dianchi Lake. In the park itself, a rock garden, pavilions, towers, long alleys, flowers, and potted plants are all arranged in orderly patterns. It is a lovely and serene experience to wander in the formal gardens and view the lake and its pavilions.

*Daguan Tower is a three-story wooden structure in ancient Chinese style, built in 1828. Looking down from the top level, visitors enjoy the vast and splendid scenery (*daguan *in Chinese). An indigent scholar named Sun Ranwong, during the Qing Dynasty, composed a long couplet of 180 Chinese characters, which became a universal sensation and was called the longest couplet in Chinese.(From Quanjing)*

Take a taxi or Bus No.1, 4, or 5 from the downtown area to get to Daguan Park.

Besides the famous Daguan Tower, Daguan Park also boasts clear, rippling water, lotus ponds with jumping fish, pavilions, trees, long verandas, and gorgeous reflections in the water. (From Quanjing)

Qiongzhu Temple (Qiongzhu Si)

Located on Yu'an Mountain about 6 miles to the northwest of Kunming, Qiongzhu was the first Zen Buddhist temple in Yunnan under the influence of Central China. This well-known temple is hidden in a dense wood. According to historical research, it was originally built in the Yuan Dynasty and was rebuilt under the reign of Emperor Guangxu of the Qing Dynasty. The ancient temple fits into the topography of the mountain and consists of four levels and three courtyards of unique design. The biggest attraction is the 500 arhats (figures of enlightened Buddhas) molded in clay by master sculptor Li Guangxiu and his four students. The arhats all look as if they were alive, each with a characteristic serene appearance. It is no wonder that this marvelous sight has been called "a shining pearl in the treasury of oriental sculpture."

From downtown Kumming, take Bus No. 19 or 37 to the temple.

Taihe Palace

Taihe Palace, also called Tongwa Temple, sits at the top of Mount Mingfeng (Mount Parrot). The complex, where Taoism and Confucianism coexist, covers an area of 861,112 square feet, and includes over 20 ancient buildings. Among the major buildings are Gold Hall, Ancient Bronze Hall, and Zijin City. Bronze Hall is a square imitation wood structure with double eaves, gable-and-hip roof, and a pavilion. Gold Hall is made of bronze and shines golden in the sunlight. The hall is 22 feet high, 20 feet wide, and 20 feet deep. Inside, the round columns and carved checkered fans are all made of bronze, with a total weight of 13.75 million pounds. Larger than the one on Wudang Mountain in Hubei Province and more completely preserved than the one on the Wanshou in the Summer Palace of Beijing, Gold Hall is the largest and best preserved hall made of pure bronze in China. The hall's steps, floor, and railings are all decorated with delicate marble. Behind the hall there is a camellia and two purple royal palm trees, which are as thick as a man's embrace and are said to have been planted during the Ming Dynasty. At the Spring Festival every year, thousands of camellia flowers burst into fiery bloom, creating a spectacular seasonal display.

Taihe Palace. (From Quanjing)

Kunming World Horticulture Expo Garden

The World Horticulture Expo Garden is located in the Gold Hall scenic area in the northeast suburbs, about 4.5 miles from downtown Kunming. Built in 1999 in contemporary style blended with traditional Chinese ar-

One of the exhibits at the International Hall of the Kunming World Expo displays this set of Indian silverware, which is exquisitely made with elegant shapes and distinct ethnic features. (From CFP)

chitecture, the garden consists of five exposition halls, themed gardens, outdoor exhibits, and several plazas for special performances and displays. All of the gardens, horticulture, and modern buildings of various styles have been integrated into their surroundings and the effect is quite grand. More than 94 countries and international organizations have set up thematic exhibits in the International Outdoor Exposition Garden. Here, visitors can stroll through gardens and examine the different horticultural traditions from Asia, Europe, North America, and Australia.

Take Bus No. 10, 47, or 68 to Kunming World Horticulture Expo Garden.

Buddhist Scripture Tower of Dali Kingdom

Also called the Dizang Temple Scripture Tower, or Ancient Scripture Tower, it was built by Yuan Douguang, an official of the ancient Dali Kingdom (938–1254). The tower, which is 27 feet high and made of stone, consists of seven stories. The first story takes the shape of a drum on which are inscribed Buddhist scriptures: *Foding Zunsheng Baochuangji* in Chinese, and *Foshuo Banruo bo luomi duo Xinjing, Dayuezun fayuan*, and *Fa si hongshiyuan* in Sanskrit; on the second story are carved the *Four Heavenly Guardians* and *Tuoluonijing* in Sanskrit; on the four corners of the third story are images of four gods and that of Sakyamuni; on the fourth story are Buddhas, bodhisattvas, attendants, and heavenly eagles. On the seventh story, the tower becomes cylindrical, with small Buddhas carved all around the walls. A total of 292 Buddhas appear on the tower. The top of the tower is shaped like a gourd and is decorated with lotus petals. The entire tower, with its delicate carvings, exquisite lines, and vivid images, is regarded as some of the finest art in central Yunnan.

Museum of Yunnan Province

Located on West Jiangfeng Road in Kunming, the Museum of Yunnan Province is a seven-story building, flanked by three-story pagoda-like buildings. The museum stands 130 feet high, and its first three floors are exhibition halls with a total area of 25,800 square feet. The museum is home to more than 130,000 artifacts, among which are the relics of the Yuanmou people, dating back 1.7 million years, and the earliest bronze drum from the Mid-Spring and Autumn periods. On the third floor is an exhibition of Yunnan's paleontologic and dinosaur fossils, among which is a skull of the Lama ancient ape excavated in 1988 on the Butterfly Ridge in Wumao, Yuanmou County, Yunnan Province. The museum also has a large number of ancient paintings and writings. Among them are the *Xishan Xinglu Scroll* by Guoxi of the North Song Dynasty, the *Shanxi Fangdai Scroll* by Huang Gongwang of the Yuan Dynasty, the poem "Manuscript Sent to Monk Miaoxing of Chicken Foot Hill" by Xu Xiake of the Ming Dynasty, the *Wugaoshan Scroll* by Monk Dandang of the Ming Dynasty, and *Du Shaoling Riding a Horse* by Qiangfeng of the Qing Dynasty, as well as other rare and precious manuscripts.

Jingang Tower of Miaozhan Temple

Also called Chuanxin Tower, this landmark is located on Guandu Street about 6 miles east of Kunming. Built in the second year of Emperor Tianshun's reign during the Ming Dynasty, the tower is the oldest and also the only typical lama-style Buddhist tower made entirely of gravel in China. The square base is 16 feet high, with a perimeter of 34 feet. In the base there are square holes instead of doors for people to enter. Above the base there are five Buddhist towers in the Jingang style, giving the structure its name. The tower is elegant and charming, in appearance, and the main tower is harmoniously integrated with the four lesser towers. This is a unique example of Chinese lama design.

The Tanhua Temple is located to the east of Kunming. It consists of three courtyards. The temple includes the Ruiying Tower, which is 148 feet tall and is known as the foremost tower in Yunnan. Tourists can climb to the top for a panoramic view. (From Colphoto)

The unique Indigenous Nest Sculpture Gallery in the suburbs of Kunming is worth a visit. (From CFP)

Stone Forest (Shilin)

The stone forest is located in Shilin Yi Nationality Autonomous County, 53 miles from Kunming. This area was once beneath the ocean; about 200 million years ago, when the sea subsided, the stone forest, a karst landscape, was formed by erosion, sedimentation, collapse, fall, and the accumulation of limestone. Various unique and wonderful formations resulted from the process, including peaks, towers, columns, flowers, caves, and ledges all made of stone. This extraordinary sight is known as one of the wonders of the world in China. There are traces of Neolithic Age petroglyphs on the cliff sides. Within the stone forest are lakes and pools, along with three lesser stone forests. In the major stone forest, Lotus Peak is extremely perilous and hard to climb, but at the top, the stark beauty of the entire stone forest is fully in view. The smaller stone forests have their own style. The stone peaks are not so concentrated here, the ground is flatter, and meadows dot the landscape. Beside Stone Forest Lake is a graceful stone peak, which, according to a folktale, was the embodiment of a beautiful Sani girl named Ahshima.

The stone forest is a rare wonder, with a unique charm. While preserving the original features, the stone forest scenic area also incorporates some traditional Chinese garden art, which enhances its attraction. In late June the Yi people gather here for their Torch Festival, which celebrates summer with various ethnic games, food, and traditional lion and dragon dances.

The stone forest is an organic combination of culture, geology, ecology, and evolution, and displays a panoramic view of a karst landscape. In 2001, the stone forest became one of the first national geological parks in China. (From Colphoto)

> If driving, take the Kunshi highway, the major tourist highway in Yunnan Province. There are also express buses from Kunming's four bus stations.

Dadieshui Waterfall

Once called Dieshui Yanyun, or Flying Dragon Waterfall, this impressive site is located 14 miles southwest of Shilin Yi Nationality Autonomous County and 17 miles west of the stone forest. Here the Daying River rushes to the edge of the cliff and splashes over with a thundering sound, creating a magnificent scene.

The Dadieshui Waterfall is about 65 feet wide and falls more than 130 feet. The two sides of the waterfall descend like white silk ribbons. On sunny days, you can see rainbows here.

Dadieshui Waterfall descends to a deep pool, creating a permeating mist that can dampen your clothes within 100 paces. (From Jin Yongji)

Take a tour bus from Shilin Yi Nationality Autonomous County.

Lingzhi Forest

Located 6 miles to the north of the Lizijing stone forest, with an area of almost 5 square miles, Lingzhi Forest is so named because the stone columns here look like Lingzhi (tinder mushrooms). Because the stones here are all black and rugged, the place is also called Naigu (*Yi* for "black") Stone Forest. To the east is Baiyun Lake, and to the west is another stretch of stone forest. The main attractions are the Venue of Romance, the Terrace of Gods, Fengshang Wang, the Single-Stone-Forest, the Tail-Spreading Peacock, Gulin Yaochi, Valley and Waterfall, Mencius's Mother Teaching Son, the Tower and Cavern, and Ghost Valley.

Jiuxiang Scenic Area

This scenic area is located in the town of Jiuxiang Yi Nationality and Hui Nationality in Yiliang County, more than 43 miles from Kunming, with an area of 68 square miles.

Jiuxiang Scenic Area features limestone caverns and includes Diehong Bridge, Dasha Dam, Three-Footed Cave, Ahlulong, and Moon Lake. Here you will find underground streams and caverns, splashing waterfalls, and water passages flanked by steep cliffs. The combination of green water and blue sky create a feeling of tranquility and wonder. Vegetation of various kinds, including Yunnan and Huashan pine trees, cover the area with lush growth.

Take an express bus at Tour Street near the Kunming South Bus Station.

Jiuxiang Scenic Area is the site of China's enormous limestone cavern group, known as the Limestone Cavern Museum. (From Jin Yongji)

Colorful Sand Forest

Located at the foot of Wufeng Mountain, 11 miles southeast of Luliang County, is the Colorful Sand Forest with an area of 2.3 square miles, including a 0.4-square-mile reservoir. The Colorful Sand Forest was formed by erosion and the evaporation of water from sand, which left behind colorful sands and natural sculptures that glisten in the sunlight.

Nine-Dragon Waterfalls parallels Huangguoshu Waterfalls in scale, power, and view. In the river passage no wider than 2.5 miles, there are over 10 calcified shallows and ten levels of waterfalls, with unique appearance and much vegetation. (From Quanjing)

One-Thousand-Buddha Tower (Qianfo Tower)

One-Thousand-Buddha tower is located in the Dajie Temple of Luliang County; it is also called Dajie Temple Tower or Jinji Tower. The tower was built in the Yuan Dynasty and reconstructed in the Wanli period (1573–1620) of the Ming Dynasty. Hexagonal in overall shape, with seven levels, the tower is 58 feet high and comprises four parts: base, platform, body, and top. The base is a square Xumi seat made of stone with a niche on each side that once contained a figure of Buddha made of china, which is now missing. The platform is also square and made of stone. All seven levels are constructed with bricks. The top, a gourd shape made of stone, was once capped with a bronze pot. The tower houses at least 1,000 figures and paintings of Buddha.

Nine-Dragon Waterfalls

These falls have long been known as a wonder of South China. They are located on the Jiulong River, 14 miles north and slightly east of Luoping County. The naturally formed geological configuration and long-term erosion by the river have created a unique view of the Nine-Dragon Waterfalls. The ten levels of the falls vary in height and width, and each has a distinctive appearance. Some whisper, some roar, some spill like the Milky Way, and some look like fish sporting in the water, providing a source of endless delight. When the water level is high, the mighty, thundering waterfalls can be heard several miles away. In spring and winter the splashing water resembles broken jade, scattered, transparent, and shining.

The highest level, called Shenlong Waterfall, is 185 feet high and 360 feet wide. When water flow is abundant, it thunders over the precipice, creating a rising mist and shining ripples that fascinate onlookers.

Duoyi River

Flowing 25 miles southeast of Luoping County, from the mountains that face the village of Lazhe of the Buyi ethnic group, the Duoyi River basin encompasses ten clear springs, which converge in a green and pretty stream. Along the river's 7.5-mile course are over 50 calcified waterfall shallows of various sizes. It is rare to see so much calcified accumulation in a moderately tropical river valley at an altitude of 2,360 feet. Along its banks are many ancient trees, whose roots twist together and form a magnificent gallery of natural root sculpture. Picturesque villages with their traditional houses dot the landscape here.

*Luoping has a long history and beautiful scenery, with an abundance of tourist attractions. Rape flowers (*Brassica napus*, an old world herb of the mustard family) constitute its traditional industry. During February and March each year, this area becomes the largest natural garden in the world, with hundreds of thousands of square miles of waving golden and fragrant rape flowers, which attract bees and butterflies. (From Quanjing)*

Maotian Mountain

Located 4 miles from Chengjiang County and 35 miles from Kunming, this area contains a concentration of fossils of Chengjiang paleontologic creatures and has been called a sacred place for world paleontology. It became a National Geologic Garden in 2001. The excavation site winds around for 12.5 miles; it is 3 miles wide and more than 165 feet deep. The enclosed protected area covers 7 square miles, with a core area of almost half a square mile. So far, over 30 fossil sites have been discovered and some 30,000 fossils have been collected. Scientific studies have revealed fossils of 40 species and over 100 subcategories, covering all types of modern flora and fauna. Many animals that are now extinct have been excavated, exceeding the scope of present animal classification and advancing the history of vertebrates by 60 million years. Furthermore, these fossils also help verify the eruption of life in the Cambrian period about 530 million years ago.

Puzhehei Scenic Area

In the Yi language, *Puzhehei* means "lake full of fish and shrimp." Part of the karst area in southeastern Yunnan, the Puzhehei Scenic Area is a typically developed karst landscape, in the Puzhehei Basin of Qiubei County. The area includes 312 isolated peaks, 83 caverns, 54 natural lakes, 15 streams, and underground rivers whose total length amounts to 75 miles. The water in Puzhehei is extremely clear, with vis-

The costumes of the Yi nationality have varied styles. Both men's and women's jackets are characterized by right-hand buttons, tight fit, and embroidery on the sleeve, collar, and jacket sides. Over the jackets the people wear wool cloaks called Ca'erwa, *usually dyed black or natural wool color. Men wear pants of three different lengths, the longest being 6 feet and the shortest just covering the ankles. Women wear florid pleated skirts that drape to the ground, sewn with cloths of different colors and whose seams are covered by beautiful lacework. (From Imagine China)*

ibility that reaches 10 feet deep. The water system connects with three small lakes, including Xianrendong. The harmonious combination of peaks and waters results in a marvelous scenic destination for visitors. Each peak contains caverns through which clear water flows. The stalactites in the caverns exhibit unique and diverse shapes. In front of Moon Cave is a crescent pool, 100 feet long and 16 feet wide, with water the color of glaze. Around the lake area are reservoirs and dams, presided over by Dalong Mountain, which is surrounded by water on three sides. Mandarin Duck Island, Pearl Island, Gold Island, Sun Island, and Lotus Island, with their lush forests and wide meadows, dot the lake itself.

> There are buses to Qiubei from Kunming. However, it may be more economical to take a minitaxi from Qiubei County to Xianrendong.

Ahlu Ancient Cavern

Ahlu means a cavern with water and rocks. This cavern is located about a mile northwest of Luxi County and was the residence of the Ahlu branch, one of the "37 savage branches in Yunnan" in the Song and Yuan Dynasties. Ahlu Ancient Cavern consists of Luyuan Cave, Yuzhu Cave, and the Yusun River, extending over 2.5 miles. Luyuan Cave is a hall-style limestone cave, including rooms of varied sizes and shapes. Among them, Rosy Clouds Hall is over 33 feet wide, with magnificent colorful walls. The halls are linked by narrow passages like an underground maze. Connecting with Luyuan Cave, Yuzhu Cave contains many standing stone columns, one of which is 26 feet high, 12 inches in diameter, and hollow at the core, a rarity. The Yusun River flows underground through the cavern for more than 2,600 feet; it is about 10 feet deep

The Tuku houses in Chengzi Village, Yongning, Luxi County, are considered by researchers as extremely rare. The houses are walled structures of one or two stories, which at first glance might be seen as ancient barracks, with the higher ones being castles and the lower ones being blockhouses. The Tuku houses here differ from those in other regions in that here they are built in groups next to the hills, and all houses are connected to each other. The linked roofs serve both as a base for the villagers' activities but also as a platform to dry the grain. (From CFP)

and its water is clear to the bottom. Here, tourists might be able to spot the transparent fish, which has no eyes and whose skeletons and internal organs can easily be seen.

➡ There are express buses from Kunming to Ahlu Ancient Cavern. Tourists might want to first visit the stone forest and then this site.

Chaoyang Tower

Chaoyang Tower is the gate tower of the east gate of Jianshui, standing massively at the center of Jianshui County (at the east end of Jianzhong Road). Built during the Ming Dynasty, the tower is the landmark of Jianshui County.

During the Tang Dynasty, the Nanzhao Kingdom built the city of Huili here. The city had four gates: the east gate was called Yinghui Gate, the south, Fu'an Gate; the west, Qingyuan Gate; and the north, Yongzhen Gate. At the end of the Ming Dynasty, only the east gate survived the flames of war, and this gate is today's Chaoyang Tower. The tower is made of 48 enormous wooden columns and numerous tenons, covered by three layers of roof. It stands 80 feet tall, with five open rooms, three inner rooms, and four winding corridors. On the front side of the tower hangs a huge board inscribed "Safeguarding the Southeast," by Tuzhuo, the famous calligrapher of the Qing Dynasty. The inscription ranks among the four most famous in Yunnan from the Qing Dynasty; the structure and skill of each 6-foot character are of the highest quality. The tower doors bear exquisite wood carving, which is vivid, delicate, and elegant. On the east side of the tower there is an enormous bronze bell more than 6 feet high, whose resounding tones can be heard several miles away.

Chaoyang Tower, with a history of over 600 years, has gone through many wars and major earthquakes and still remains intact.

➡ Visitors can catch a train and get off at the Miandian station or take a tour bus.

In ancient times, Chaoyang Tower was already a famous attraction referred to as "the East Tower Bordering on Han." Today, as the premier tower in Yunnan, it is even more popular as a tourist destination. (From Quanjing)

Confucius Temple (Wenmiao)

Confucius Temple is located on the north side of Wenmiao Street in Jianshui County. Construction on it started in 1285, and it has a history of more than 700 years, during which it has been expanded and renovated many times. Now it covers an area of about 753,473 square feet, second only to the Confucius temples in Qufu and Beijing in terms of its scale, construction skill, and preservation. Jianshui Confucius Temple, which was built in accordance with the style and scale of the Qufu Confucius Temple,

There is plenty of rainfall in the Ailao Mountain area of Yunnan, where large terraced fields are cultivated. On cloudy and foggy days, large stretches of the fields are shrouded in mist, resembling ladders leading to heaven. (From ImagineChina)

is in traditional palace style and symmetrical from north to south along the central axis. It once comprised 37 different areas, including a pool, halls, principal rooms, three towers, five pavilions, five ancestral temples, and archways. At present, 31 of them have been carefully restored. The Jianshui Confucius Temple complex, which is situated toward the south, is 2,050 feet wide. The Dacheng Hall is flanked by the east and west Minglun halls, which embody the integration of the temple and Confucius's doctrines. In front of the temple gate is an oval pool called the Sea of Learning, at the center of which there is a small island with pavilions on it. To the east of the Chongsheng Temple are Two-Saint Temple and Cangsheng Temple. The former is in honor of the two scholars who lectured here for over ten years in the Hongwu period of the Ming Dynasty; the latter is for the commemoration of Cangjie, the ancient inventor of the Chinese characters.

> The route to Confucius Temple, which is open from 8 a.m. to 5 p.m. daily, is the same as that to Chaoyang Tower.

Zhu's Garden

Zhu's Garden includes the residence and ancestral temple built by the wealthy late Qing landlords Zhu Weiqing and his brother. Construction was started in the Guangxu period of the Qing Dynasty and was finished 30 years later, in the Xuantong period. Located on Jianxin Street within the ancient town of Jianshui, Zhu's Garden is a large-scale residential complex of the Qing style, long known as the Grand Showplace in South Yunnan. It covers over 118,000 square feet, with a building area of more than 43, 000 square feet. The main structures are arranged in a layout of

Zhu's Garden is delicate, elegant, and majestic. (From Colphoto)

"three lengthways and four breadthwise," characteristic of Jianshui's linked parallel residential construction units. The houses are also arranged symmetrically; the courtyards are linked together, creating 42 dooryards. The rooms and halls are laid out to produce an enormous and varied sense of space and labyrinthine perspective. At the front of the complex are three parlors flanked by girls' boudoirs. In front of these parlors is a garden naturally separated into eastern and western parts by a wall with carved windows. The garden is huge; to its front there is a lotus pool, shrubbery, and a plant nursery, with flowerbeds scattered here and there, which creates a lovely private garden.

Dual Dragon Bridge (Shuanglong Qiao)

Located 2 miles west of Jianshui, Dual Dragon Bridge is a huge stone arch bridge with three towers and 17 arches, spanning the juncture of the Nanpan River's two tributaries—the Lujiang River and the Tachong River. The bridge is named after the two rivers that wind around the area like two dragons. The construction of the bridge was started in the Qianlong period of the Qing Dynasty, when only three arches were built. The other 14 arches were added in the early Daoguang period. The whole bridge, consisting of tens of thousands of pieces of huge bluestone, is 485 feet long and 10 to 16 feet wide, broad and even on its surface. On the bridge are three towers, which are oddly shaped but laid out well, and at the base of these towers is the bridge passage. From the towers, there is a view of endless stretches of good land and thousands of peaceful households. The Jianshui Dual Dragon Bridge is of the largest scale and of the highest artistic value among the ancient bridges in Yunnan. It followed the traditional

The old well in Jianshui. (From ImagineChina)

construction style of the Chinese multiarch bridges and combined the science of bridge construction with the art of architecture. Embodying the supreme skills and intelligence of the people in southern Yunnan, it is a masterpiece of ancient bridge building and holds a significant position in the history of Chinese bridges.

Brush Pen Tower (Wenbi Tower)

Brush Pen Tower sits at the top of Baifo Mountain near the Baishui River, 2 miles south of Jianshui County. Brush Pen Tower was built here in the Renmian style in 1828. Its name comes from its appearance, which resembles a huge standing brush pen. The body of the tower is built of bluestone and stands 103 feet high, which equals the perimeter of its base.

It is said that in ancient times Lin'an contained no civilian officials, only warriors, and there were often armed conflicts between different villages. Local officials wanted a building that looked like the biggest brush pen in the world, representing learning, to house martial arts instruction. Since the establishment of the tower, many scholars have come here, and learning has prevailed. The town was renamed for education. Observed from the foot of the mountain, the tower looks like a fantastic pen. Seen from the plain, the pen shaft thrusts high, with the tip pointing to the sky and the tower body hidden in clouds and mist, resembling a rocket to be launched to the moon.

Swallow Cave (Yanzi Cave)

Swallow Cave is located in a hidden valley through which the Lujiang River flows, 18 miles east of Jianshui County. The cave is known for formations such as the Cave Wonder, Gathering Swallows, and Plaques Hanging on Stalactites. On the cliffs in and outside the cave are tens of thousands of white-bellied swallows. Every spring and summer, the swallows swarm into the cave, constantly twittering, which is how the cave got its name. There are, of course, huge numbers of bird's nests, which provide rare culinary treats here.

There are hundreds of stalactites in Swallow Cave. There are also large areas of curling stones that look just like jade, shining and transparent. Some take the form of fine hair, some needles, some tubes; some grow horizontally, others vertically. (From Colphoto)

Swallow Cave consists of the upper dry cave and the lower water cave. The dry cave has an enormous hall and terraces, which are naturally formed and can hold thousands of people. Along the cliffs are plank roads and towers. In the hall, stalactites hang low, set off in stone curtains; there are even cliff carvings and literary inscriptions in the cave. The thousands of plaques hanging on the stalactites over 165 feet above the river are a sight unique to Swallow Cave. Every year from August 8 to 10, the Bird's Nest Festival is held here.

Dali Region

Erhai Park

Erhai Park is located on Tuan Mountain about a mile to the northeast of Xiaguan, in Dali. The park was established in December 1976 on what was the deer farm of the Nanzhao king in the eighth century. The park covers an area of about a quarter of a square mile, with a lake area that is slightly larger. The area is lushly wooded, dotted with towers, corridors, and waterside pavilions. There are also various flowerbeds on display. The park has become the largest-scale comprehensive park with modern facilities in the city of Dali. It offers picturesque views throughout the year. In spring, tourists can enjoy various flowers and plants as well as Erhai Lake, while walking along the shore covered with willows. In summer, visitors can swim in the lake; in fall, they can enjoy the rippling view of Erhai Lake from the pavilion on Tuan Mountain or in the long allee. In winter, the attraction is the view of the 19 peaks of Cangshan Mountain in the distance.

Cangshan Mountain

Cangshan Mountain, also called Dian Cangshan Mountain or Lingjiu Mountain, belongs to the Yunling system of the Hengduan Range. It extends from Dengchuan in Eryuan County in the north to Tianshengqiao in the city of Xiaguan in the south, from the shore of the Erhai Lake in the east to the banks of the Yangbi River in the west. Extending more than 30 miles from north to south and about 15 miles from east to west, this mountain is truly magnificent.

Cangshan has 19 peaks, among which the highest is the 13,524-foot-high Malong peak. Known for its vistas of snow, clouds, and springs, Cangshan ranks first on the list of Dali's four famous attractions—

Erhai Lake subsumes the 18 brooks of Cangshan Mountain to the west, and its headwaters flow from the Luoshi River. At its east and west sides are the Yulonggou Pool and the Fengweijing Pool, whose waters are abundant and clear. Racoma (Gong fish) abound in the lake; fresh and tender, it is known as the best fish. (From Quanjing)

wind, flower, snow, and moon—due to the snow on the mountaintop, which does not melt even in summer. In the fine weather of March, the mountaintop appears shining and serene, the view crystal clear. Here lie several ice lakes surrounded by lush primeval forests. Cangshan also boasts 18 brooks, rich marble resources, and more than 3,000 types of plants.

There is a local saying: "Dali has beautiful scenery in March." The best time to visit Cangshan is in spring. Conveniently, there are express buses for Cangshan at each bus stop and major hotel in Dali.

Three Towers of Chongsheng Temple

Located at the foot of Yingyue Peak on Cangshan Mountain northwest of the old town of the Dali, these three towers form a triangle and constitute a major attraction in the area.

The tallest of the three, Qianxun Tower is 227 feet high and is a 16-story dense-eave structure typical of the Tang Dynasty architectural style. Looking up from the bottom, you get the sensation that the motionless tower might topple against the background of the moving clouds. The square foundation of the tower has two levels. The perimeter of the lower story is 110 feet, and it is surrounded by a stone railing, with a stone lion at each corner. The perimeter of the upper story is 69 feet; on its east face appear four stately and stylish characters meaning "Guard the Land Forever," inscribed by Mu Shijie, offspring of Mu Ying, Duke Qianguo. The three towers were once part of Chongsheng Temple. Now the temple is gone, but the towers remain. Inside the towers, some 600 cultural artifacts were discovered, including many from the Nanzhao and Dali periods, as well as Buddhist scriptures, small Buddhist figures and pagodas made of china, and print molds for Sanskrit scripture from the Song Dynasty.

The Three Towers are 8 miles from Xiaguan, capital city of the Dali Bai Nationality Autonomous Prefecture. Tourists may come here by bus, but it is also convenient to come on foot or by carriage from Dali Old Town.

Magnificent Door Eaves:

In the construction of Bai residential buildings, whether large or small, close attention is paid to the door overhangs, which even in common residences follow the palace style and are decorated with wood and stone carvings, colorful paintings, and clay sculptures. They look exquisite, delicate, and magnificent.

Openwork Carvings:

The skillful Dali Bai craftsmen are especially good at exquisite openwork carvings. They can carve three to five distinctly separate layers of landscapes, flowers, birds, insects, and fish on the side walls of the houses.

(From Quanjing)

Stone Walls:

"Dali has three treasures; stones are used to build walls which never fall." In Dali, the villagers not only build houses with regular stone blocks, but also build solid high walls with pebbles.

Coated Walls and Painted Eaves:

The Bai people usually use paint to draw an outline on their buildings; the central areas of the walls are also coated in white. The eave lines bear colorful paintings of varied width, which are often beautiful geometric designs, landscapes, flowers, birds, or calligraphy.

(From Quanjing)

The door overhangs are the most sophisticated part of the residences and what the Bai residents pay the closest attention to. They usually have layered arches and upward-pointed corners, and are decorated with exquisite wood carvings and colorful paintings. Both sides are often decorated with marble, which looks impressive and graceful. Wood carvings are used on the paneled door, horizontal planks, and hanging columns. Designs of various animals and plants, such as curling grass, flying dragons, bats, and rabbits are skillfully worked into the carvings. There are also many symbolic and interesting works, such as "Gold Lions Stepping on the Embroidered Ball," "Qilin Staring at Banana," "Red Phoenix Keeping a Peal," and "Peaceful Chrysanthemum."

Zhoucheng

Located along the Dian-Tibet Highway, 24 miles from Xiaguan, Zhoucheng is the largest natural village in Yunnan, covering an area of over 11.5 acres. Today, the town preserves all the traditional customs of the Bai people and is known for this. The slab roads interconnect like a web, and whispering spring water flows along the winding lanes, which creates an ancient, simple, and tranquil picture. The lanes are flanked by buildings of white walls and gray tiles, which reflect the traditional stone-wall civil construction of the Zhoucheng Bai people. It is commonplace that a Zhoucheng residential building usually has "three lanes and one screen wall" and "four walls and five dooryards." The ancient opera platform, construction of which started in 1895, is regarded as a masterpiece of the Zhoucheng Bai traditional architecture for its grand scale and exquisite execution. The platform is characterized by a single-eave, gable-and-hip roof and post-and-lintel construction. It is used for festival celebrations and the entertainment of the Zhoucheng residents. The Zhoucheng Bai people are generally adherents of Buddhism, and the town is home to Buddhist temples including Yingxiang Temple, Longquan Temple, and other, smaller temples. As in other Bai villages, the people here show traditional respect for the ancient feudal system. There are two Suzerain temples in the town. Here, the ancient and elegant bridal costumes are still worn for weddings. It is said that the bride still keeps the custom of wearing sunglasses to ward off misfortune.

Butterfly Spring

Butterfly Spring is located at the foot of Qunong Peak on Cangshan Mountain. It is a clear spring hidden amid ancient trees. The base area, which ranges from 22 to 33 feet wide, is paved with bluestone. The spring got its name from a pair of lovers who turned into butterflies after jumping together into the spring in their struggle against a feudal contract marriage.

Filtering through the sand layer between the rocks, the water in the Butterfly Spring is very clear, evidenced by the pool formed as the spring water emerges, which is free from pollution. In recent years, water from Butterfly Spring has gushed into three additional pools, making a total of four pools, which have become the most attractive view in Butterfly Spring Park. Every year

The beauty of Butterfly Spring lies in its greenery. Hehuan trees beside the spring bloom in early April every year. During the daytime, the petals open like butterflies; at night, they close and give off a delicate fragrance. Poets compare the butterflies to flying blooms and the blooms to still butterflies. It is a magnificent sight with butterflies and blooms mingling during the Butterfly Meet so that it is hard to tell them apart. (From Quanjing)

from March to May, butterflies as big as the palm of your hand and as small as a bee alight in the Hehuan trees beside the spring.

> Catch a tour bus at the west gate of Dali. About 15 miles from the downtown area, the trip to Butterfly Spring takes 30 minutes.

View of Cangshan Mountain (From ImagineChina)

Stone Bell Mountain Grottoes (Shizhongshan Grottoes)

The Stone Bell Mountain Grottoes, also called the Jianchuan Grottoes, are named after a huge, bell-shaped stone at the back of the temple. They are located 15 miles southwest of Jianchuan County. The grottoes consist of three areas—Stone Bell Temple, Lion Gate, and Shadeng Village. They are the largest and best preserved of Yunnan's grottoes, with great historical and cultural value. The carving of the grottoes was begun in the Nanzhao period over 1,000 years ago. The grottoes have been carved according to the shape of the mountain. Of the 17 grottoes, there are 8 in Stone Bell Temple, 3 in Lion Gate, and 6 in Shadeng Village. They extend for about 4 miles and contain 139 figures, which are delicate, vivid, and unique, carved in distinctive local styles.

Baoxiang Temple

Baoxiang Temple, also called Shibao Temple, is located on the cliffs behind Stone Bell Mountain at the top of Foding Hill. It was built by Gaolun, governor of Heqingtu in the Zhengtong period of the Ming Dynasty. At first it was a Taoist temple. Later on, as Buddhism prevailed, figures of Buddha were placed in most of the halls, except for the Jade Emperor Tower. Thus, the temple became a place where Taoism and Buddhism coexisted.

Facing east, the tiered towers cling to the twisted cliffs, looking precarious. Due to its uniqueness and

The old alley of Shaxi, in Jianchuan. (From CFP)

precipitous location, the temple is known as the Midair Temple of Yunnan. Along the pass, stone steps lead to the Temple Gate, then climb to Tianwang Hall and Daxiong Hall. Miler Hall and the Jade Emperor Tower were built seemingly suspended from the cliff and are inaccessible except by climbing from either side. The ninety-nine steps of the Heavenly Ladder lead to the Gold Top, where the Stone Pagoda, Shibao Spring, and Gold Top Temple stand. From here, visitors have a delightful bird's-eye view of the scenery below, recognized as the eight attractions of Baoxiang: Temple Hidden in Dense Wood, Stone Bridge and Gates, Birds Chattering in Deep Valley, Towers on Steep Cliffs, Waterfall Hanging High, Cliff in Sunset, Ancient Trees and Hanging Vines, and Red Leaves Like Flowers.

Dali Nanzhao Fengqing Island

Nanzhao Fengqing Island is located in the Cang-Er Scenic Area and is one of the three islands in Erhai Lake. It is totally surrounded by water, adjacent to Chicken Foot Mountain, the famous Buddhist sacred place, to the east, Shibao Mountain to the north, Dali to the south, and Cangshan Mountain and Erhai Lake to the west. It is often said that "the most beautiful scenery in Dali is in Cang-Er, and the most beautiful scenery in Cang-Er is in Shuanglang." Around the island, the water is clear and the sand white, making for hundreds of acres of beautiful scenery.

Nanzhao Palace, the main structure on the island, covers an area of more than 86,000 square feet. The architecture is based on the Tang Dynasty style and incorporates the styles of Nanzhao and Tufan, with an emphasis on the integration of different nationalities characteristic of the Nanzhao period. At the west of the island is Suzerain Square. Four bronze figures of the Suzerain stand within and without the enclosing walls. At the center is the bronze figure of the Central Suzerain, Duan Zongbang, head of the 500 lords, known as "King of Suzerains."

Visitors can reach this site by boat from the Erhai dock or by bus. The palace is open from 9 a.m. to 6 p.m.

Chicken Foot Mountain (Jizushan)

Chicken Foot Mountain, also called Jiuchong Yan, is located in Jizushan, 25 miles northwest of Binchuan County. It is 62 miles from Dali and covers an area of 11 square miles. It faces southeast, with three peaks in the front and one range at the back. It resembles a chicken foot, hence its name. With Wutai Mountain, Ermei Mountain, Putuo Mountain,

Fishing boats by the Dali River. (From Colphoto)

and Jiuhua Mountain, it is one of China's most famous Buddhist mountains, enjoying renown not only in China but throughout Southeast Asia. It is also a famous tourist attraction with its 40 immense hills, 30 steep peaks, 34 cliffs, 45 caves, and more than 100 springs and pools. From a distance, the mountain looks high and majestic; nearby, the primeval forest appears dense and tranquil, blotting out the sun. Towers, temples, and convents are scattered here and there among the high cliffs, forming a marvelous view of the combination of natural and human endeavor.

The largest and most famous temple on Chicken Foot Mountain is Zhusheng Temple, whose name was granted by Emperor Guangxu and means "good wishes for the limitless longevity of the Empress Dowager Cixi." The highest peak is Tianzhu, which is also called Four-Sight Peak because one can see in all four directions the four sights of sunrise, cloud, Erhai, and Jade Dragon Snow Mountain.

The Buddhist figures are an important component of Chicken Foot Mountain. They are carved with professional skill, using smooth lines and vivid images. In the temples and convents, the sculpture and allocation of the Buddhist figures follow rules and have religious significance. (From Colphoto)

Start from Dali and change buses at Binchuan County. There are many convenient buses shuttling between Binchuan and Xiaguan, and between Binchuan and Chicken Foot Mountain.

Jihong Bridge

Spanning the Lancang River at Yandong in Yongping County and Pingpo in the city of Baoshan, Jihong Bridge is the earliest ferry bridge on the Bonan Ancient Silk Road of Yunnan, and also one of China's earliest iron-chain bridges, occupying an important position in the history of bridge building. Jihong Bridge was built in 1681 and renovated during the Guangxu period (1875–1908) of the Qing Dynasty. It is 380 feet long, 12.5 feet wide, spans 185 feet across the river, and consists of 18 iron chains. Two of the chains serve as the railings on either side of the bridge and the rest as the deck, on which are two crisscrossing layers of planks. There are semicircular piers on each riverbank, onto which the chains are tightly fastened. The landscape is forbidding: On the west bank is a steep cliff; on the east bank is a perilous peak; below is the rushing water. At the two ends of the bridge are the bridgeheads. On the Putuo Cliff south of the bridge, inscriptions—"The First Bridge in the Southwest," "Perilous Cliff and Marvelous Ferry," "Natural Fortress," and "Chain-Lock at the South End of the World"—are carved into the rock.

Lijiang Region

Best Time to Travel

The Lijiang region is fairly high above sea level, with relatively low temperatures throughout the year and large temperature differences between day and night. The optimum tourist seasons are spring and summer.

Mu Mansion ranks first in Yunnan in terms of scale and grandeur, and fully embodies the Naxi people's open-minded absorption of various cultures. (From Quanjing)

Lijiang Mu Mansion (Lijiang Mufu)

Lijiang Mu Mansion is located in the southwest corner of the old town of Lijiang and is the showplace of its culture. It was once the official Mu residence, for the hereditary governor of Lijiang, who was also the head of the Naxi people. The governorship was passed down through the three dynasties of Yuan, Ming, and Qing for 470 years. In 1382, this massive palace complex was built. It faces east and comprises 162 rooms, including Consultation Hall, Hufa Hall, Guangbi Tower, Yuyin Tower, and the opera platform. On the wooden honorific archway in front of the gate are four inscribed characters: *Tian Yu Liu Fang,* meaning "go for schooling" in the Naxi language and expressing the admiration of the Naxi people for learning. A second archway, which is three stories high and made entirely of stone, is a masterpiece of China's stone architecture. Consultation Hall is stately, spacious, and magnificent, and once served as the administration center for the governor. Wangjuan Tower holds a collection of more than 2,000 years of cultural heritage, including thousands of Dongba scriptures, hundreds of Dazhang scriptures, poem collections of the six governors, and numerous paintings and calligraphy, all of which are treasures of learning. Yuyin Tower is where people received the imperial edicts and was the entertainment center for singing, dancing, and banqueting. Sanqing Hall resulted from the admiration of the Mus for Taoism. Furthermore, in the depths of the ancient cypress trees of Lion Mountain, there are sites where the Mus offered sacrifices to God, ancestors, and Nature. Lijiang Mu Mansion is famously known as the Forbidden City of Lijiang for its magnificence and grandeur.

Tourists can reach Mu Mansion by a 10-minute walk along the small river on the west side of Sifang Street in the Lijiang old town.

Jade Dragon Snow Mountain (Yulong Xuanshan)

Jade Dragon Snow Mountain is located 9 miles northwest of Lijiang Naxi Autonomous County on the east side of the Jinsha River. The main peak, Shanzidou, is 18,360 feet above sea level and remains snowcapped throughout the year. Thrusting skyward, the Yulong Twelve Peaks, aligned north to south, appear like a huge flying dragon, not only mighty but majestic.

Tourists are attracted here by the white sand and the emerald lake, the snowy peaks and the pine woods, the grassland and the livestock, the jade cliffs and the golden rivers. On the west side of the mountain is the overwhelming spectacle of Tiger Leaping Gorge and farther up is a treasureland of animals and plants. In late spring and early summer, the blooming flowers, lush woods, and diverse species of rare birds and animals become lively and add to the charm and fascination of the mountain terrain.

It is about an hour's ride from the Lijiang's old town by tour bus. A cableway is available on the mountain, and riding down this way offers a view of the Baishui River.

The perennially snowcapped Yulong Snow Mountain is a modern ocean glacier, the closest one to the equator in the Northern Hemisphere. (From Quanjing)

Yufeng Temple

Located at the southern foot of Yulong Snow Mountain, 10.5 miles from Lijiang's old town, Yufeng Temple is a Tibetan Buddhist temple and one of the 13 ancient Lama temples in northwestern Yunnan. It was expanded in 1756. Situated in a lush wood, the temple commands a graceful view, facing a plain in front and set against a snow range at the back. A clear spring flows around the temple all year, and behind it is Sisters Lake. Many ancient trees, such as camellia, yulan magnolia, ginkgo, and the hanxiao trees of Yunnan, have been planted around the temple.

Yufeng Temple is world-famous for its camellias, planted in the Yongle period of the Ming Dynasty (1403–1424) more than 600 years ago. The camellia tree is still lush and lively today. There used to be two camellia trees, one Shizitou and the other Zaotaohong, which were too closely planted and thus have intertwined, forming a wall of flowers 10 feet high and 13 feet long. The flowers of the Shizitou are as big as dishes and as pretty as roses, and they grow as double blossoms. The flowers of

The Black Dragon Pool, reflecting the distant Yulong Snow Mountain, presents a charming and serene view. (From CFP)

the Zaotaohong bloom individually and are dark red in color. They are in bud during the solar period of Xiaoshu (Slight Heat, falling between the 6th and 8th of July) every year, start to bloom on Lichun (beginning of spring, 3rd to 5th of February) of the next year, and fade by Lixia (beginning of summer, 5th to 7th of May). The blooming period spans more than 100 days and seven solar terms, and contains over 20 continuous phases, with each phase producing thousands of flowers. Altogether, over 20,000 flowers bloom every year. Therefore, the tree is often referred to as the "king of camellias."

Black Dragon Pool (Heilongtan)

The Black Dragon Pool, also called Jade Spring (Yuquan), is located at the foot of Elephant Mountain. Clear spring water gushes into it, reflecting both Yulong Snow Mountain and Elephant Mountain. There are hanging willows, lush green grass, an assortment of blooming flowers, as well as towers and pavilions scattered among the thick woods, which makes the area resemble a beautiful gem on the Northwestern Yunnan Plateau. The crescent-shaped pool covers an area of nearly 293,500 square feet, with a pavilion in the middle. On the other side of the pavilion and the pool is the outlet of a pearl spring. The outlet of the Black Dragon Pool was at one time the Jiuyan Hole (meaning "nine dragons governing the water") and a tower was built there. Now the tower has been transformed into a stone bridge with five arches, called the Yudai (Jade Belt) Bridge. The water in the pool is as clear as jade, cool in summer and warm in winter, and is good for the complexion. In the freezing-cold weather of winter, dense mists float above the entire pool, making it feel warm as in spring.

The area around Black Dragon Pool is now known as Black Dragon Park and includes four sections: Jade River, Dragon Pool, Qing Brook, and the Woods. The recently constructed Dongba Cultural Institution, Dongba Cultural Museum, and Dongba Cultural Hall are also located in the park.

> The stunning reflection of Yulong Snow Mountain is a major attraction of Black Dragon Pool.

Dabaoji Palace

The Dabaoji Palace, built in 1582 during the Ming Dynasty, is located 9 miles north of Lijiang Naxi Autonomous County. The palace is multi-eaved, with a gable-and-hip roof, and a square front consisting of three rooms. The palace is home to 12 murals from the

The White Sand Murals had their origin in the combination of Han and Tibetan paintings. They have absorbed the characteristics of various religions, cultures, and artistic schools, and formed a unique style. (From Quanjing)

Hongwu and the Wanli periods, covering a total area of 660 square feet. These murals cover 55 walls; the largest one contains 100 Buddhas and it is likewise the largest among Lijiang's well-preserved extant murals. In another painting, Dacheng Buddhas, Taoist figures, and Tibetan Buddhas mingle, reflecting both the absorption of various painting schools and a unique painting style. Bold strokes, rich colors, and precise proportions blend with the features of the Dongba paintings in their unconstrained representation, sharply contrasting colors, even lines, and concise strokes. Besides figures from the three religions, there are also life scenes such as playing music, dancing, carpentry, weaving, iron forging, cutting firewood, fishing, and slaughtering livestock. A painting based on a story in the Pumenping scripture depicts images of officials, yamen workers, executioners, travelers, and criminals, which truly reflect the social life of the Ming Dynasty.

Tiger Leaping Gorge (Hutiaoxia)

The Jinsha (Gold Sand) River suddenly changes its direction to the north at the town of Shigu (Stone Drum), and after about 25 miles rushes to Qiaotou, Zhongdian County, then hacks out a valley between Yulong Snow Mountain and Haba Snow Mountain. This is called Tiger Leaping Gorge, which is 5,900 feet above sea level and consists of upper, middle, and lower sections. Standing on the gorge gives visitors an overwhelming sensation of the extreme landscape—sheer cliffs, billowing waves at the bottom of the valley, and whistling winds all around. It is said that in ancient times, there was a tiger that could jump across the gorge with just one pause on a midriver rock. That is how the gorge was named. The perils of Tiger Leaping Gorge are world famous. On both sides of the gorge are high mountains—to the east is Yulong Snow Mountain, with its peak thrusting into the clouds and its foot at the riverbed; to the west is Haba Snow Mountain, which is perennially snowcapped and steep at the base. The water coursing through the gorge is itself perilous, as huge rocks often break off from the steep cliffs and tumble into the gorge as a result of weathering, so the gorge is now littered with reefs and dangerous shallows. From the upper gorge to the lower gorge is a drop of 558 feet, with rapid currents and thundering waterfalls shaking the valley. All of this makes for a marvelous river spectacle rarely seen elsewhere.

> You can start out from Lijiang or Shangri-la; however, it is more convenient to reach the gorge by chartered bus from Lijiang.

First Bend of the Yangtze River

After rushing down the Qinghai-Tibetan Plateau, the upper reaches of the 3,100-mile Yangtze River suddenly change direction to the north between Shigu (Stone Drum) and Qiaotou, Zhongdian County, and form a huge V-shaped bend, which is known as "the first bend of the Yangtze River." Owing to the bend, the Jinsha River, which would otherwise flow out of China, returns and remains within China's borders. The Jinsha River is thus jokingly called a "patriotic" river.

At the bend, the river surging from the north becomes peaceful and quiet, like a plateau lake, with reflections of mountains coalescing into a picturesque and relaxing aspect. Here at Shasongbi, the Yangtze River becomes clear and still, with groves of willows on both banks and 38 square miles of golden rape flower blooming on the plain and reflected in the water. The top of the hill behind the village of Shasongbi commands a panoramic view of the first bend of the Yangtze River.

Lugu Lake Scenic Area

Located on the border between Ninglang Yi Autonomous County and Yanyuan County of Sichuan, Lugu Lake Scenic Area is like a clear gem inlaid among the mountains of northwest Yunnan. The lake is endowed with not only marvelous natural beauty but also unique features. It perfectly integrates natural sights with cultural spectacles, particularly the culture and customs of the Moso people, which lends it special and rich connotations and makes it an irreplaceable representative of cultural heritage in China. Lugu Lake is called Mother Lake by the Moso people and is an important part of the Lijiang Yulong Scenic Area. Covering a water surface area of 20 square miles, the lake is 8,562 feet above sea level; the average depth is 130 feet and it is transparent to 36 feet. Surrounding the lake are green hills, lush forests, towering trees, and gurgling rivers. There are three islands in the lake itself, which make for a charming view on the clear and peaceful water. Near the lake are the villages of the Moso people with their houses of wood and garden courtyards.

There are two routes to this scenic area: starting in Kunming, for a distance of 395 miles, and starting in Lijiang, a frequent route, for a distance of 135 miles.

The view of the bend is picturesque. Historical artifacts found here and the ancient ferries along the banks create an overwhelming sense of history, as if from an old Naxi tale. (From Quanjing)

The Scenic Area of the Three Parallel Rivers

Located in the Zonggu region of the Hengduan Range in northwestern Yunnan Province, three rivers—the Jinsha, the Lancang, and the Nu—run parallel to one another from north to south for over 250 miles within Deqin County. This unusual landscape, with its torrential currents and numerous dangerous rapids and shallows, makes for a unique geographical spectacle.

(From ImagineChina)

The Jinsha River, in the upper reaches of the Yangtze River from the mouth of the Batang River in Yushu County, Qinhai Province, to the city of Yibin in Sichuan Province, is 1,435 miles long. It suddenly changes its course northward at Shigu and cuts into the plateau, forming the famous Tiger Leaping Gorge. The river has rapid currents and high cliffs on both sides; the river valley is more than 9,840 feet deep, 1,970 feet deeper than the Grand Canyon in the Colorado Plateau. The two headwaters of the Lancang River, Zhaqu and Jiqu, originate on Tanggula Mountain in Qinhai Province and meet in Changdu in the Tibet Autonomous Region. The river runs from east to south in western of Yunnan and exits China from the southern Xishuang-banna Dai Autonomous Prefecture, where it is called the Meigong River. The upper and middle reaches of the Lancang run through the Hengduan Range in deep valleys between high cliff banks, and with many stony shallows. Along the river, there are geological phenomena formed by the collision of the European-Asian Plate and the Indian Plate.

The Nu River originates at the south foot of Tanggula Mountain at the border between Qinhai and Tibet, and then runs across the east of the Tibet Autonomous Region into Yunnan Province, where it turns south into Burma at the Nu River in Lisu Autonomous Prefecture, Baoshan area, and the Dehong Dai and Jingpo Autonomous Prefecture, where it is called the Sarwen River. The Nu River runs between Nu Mountain and Gaoligong Mountain, in a deep valley with rapid currents.

The scenic area consists of high mountains and snowy peaks, rushing rivers, snow-laden forests, and changeable weather. Meanwhile, where the Tibetan, Naxi, and Lisu people live together, there are also colorful national customs and practices. The area presents a comprehensive view of snowy mountains, valleys, grasslands, lakes, primitive forests, and ethnicity. As a scenic spot with both natural and cultural sites, the Three Parallel Rivers Scenic Area has been designated as a UNESCO World Heritage site since July 2003.

(From Quanjing)

(From Colphoto)

(From Quanjing)

(From Quanjing)

Diqing Region

Best Time to Travel

The average altitude of over 9,840 feet above sea level in the Diqing area may produce high-altitude sickness. The optimum tourist months are May, June, September, and November. If you have trouble breathing the thin air, remember to walk slowly and accustom your body to the altitude.

Diqing is a place where many religions and beliefs coexist in peace. Everywhere there are temples, monks, Mani piles (stone piles made by the Tibetan people as a way to practice their religion, Tibetan Buddhism) and white towers. At the same time, in the area where the Lisu and the Pumi peoples live in close community, you can find believers in Christianity, the Dongma cult, Islam, and Taoism, creating a truly ecumenical flavor. (From CFP)

Central Town Hall

The central town hall, generally known as the Tibetan Scripture Chamber (called *Ruibaxikang* in Tibetan), is located at the foot of Big Tortoise (or Dagui) Mountain in southeastern Shangri-la County. An architectural complex combining Han and Tibetan styles, it is a center for Tibetan official discussions, assemblies, and religious activities, and is also available for holding weddings, funerals, or banquets. The hall was built in 1724 and underwent several cycles of destruction and renovation. The principal three-story building was rebuilt in 1983, with the four Buddha Warrior Attendants painted on the side walls. At the center of the hall is a tall, thick central column, which the local Tibetan people regard as extremely sacred and bind with cypress branches and hada (kha-btags) to show their reverence. Chaoyang Tower at the top of Big Tortoise Mountain is the highest point of the central town, commanding a panoramic view of the entire town.

In April 1936, the Second Regiment of the Red Army led by Helong passed through the central town and used the hall as the command center. The hall is now a museum in honor of the Long March of the Red Army. The late Banchan E'erdeni Quejijianzan inscribed the sign for the museum.

Guihua Temple

Guihua Temple, also called *Gedansongzanlin* in Tibetan, is 3 miles from Shangri-la County. The temple was built in 1679, the first Tibetan Buddhist temple in Yunnan. It covers a large area with solid, thick walls and gates. It faces the south, and is a five-story tower building of the Tibetan style. At the center and the highest point of the temple are Zhaseng and Jikang, the two primary temples, which are also two of the Thirteen Temples in the Kang area constructed under the decree of the Fifth Dalai and Emperor Kangxi of the Qing Dynasty. The main hall is paneled with copper tiles, with animal heads and flying eaves on each roof corner, reflecting the architectural style of the Han ethnic group. The main hall can hold 1,600 people. At the front of the main hall is the bronze figure of the Fifth Dalai Lama; at the back are the bronze figures of Buddha Maitreya and the Seventh Dalai Lama. The temple is also equipped with various murals and exquisite wood carvings. The bell rings in the morning, at noon, and in the evening, and can be heard 3 miles away.

Natural Bridge (Tianshengqiao)

Located 6 miles to the east of Shangri-la County, the Natural Bridge is a naturally formed limestone bridge formed by the erosion of the underground limestone caves by the Shudugang River flowing westward. The bridge is 10,830 feet above sea level, 230 feet high, 33 feet wide, and 165 feet long, with a straight and even surface, as if man-made. It is often referred to as "the first bridge on the earth." Tourists can climb onto the bridge via the stone steps on the rock walls and experience the perilous wonder of the sharply profiled cliffs. The cliffs are densely populated with mini-caverns, in which many plateau birds such as rock doves and red-beaked ravens make their homes. Beside the bridge there is a wooded granite slope, where several warm springs gush water throughout the year, with a median temperature of 85°F. As the springs are distributed among stalactites, they contain large quantities of minerals such as sulfur, calcium, germanium, and iron. Three miles to the southeast of the bridge are also widely scattered steaming warm springs, which are collectively called

Guihua Temple (From Jin Yongji)

Xiagei Warm Springs. The geothermal energy here is bountiful. The mouths of some of these springs lie in swampland, some are under rocks, some in caves, and some even on the tops of rocks. All of them produce year-round, presenting a marvelous spectacle.

Start from Shangri-la County and proceed 6 miles on the highway from Zhongdian to Sanba. Go another 3 miles to Xiagei Warm Springs.

Girls of the Bai ethnic group are skillful at weaving straw hats and dance the straw hat dance, which is light and graceful, lithe and demure. It is said that "the dance is charming but the dancer is even more." (From Colphoto)

White Water Terrace (Baishui Terrace)

Baishui Terrace is located on the hill at Dixiangbowan village in the Sanba area, 64 miles to the southeast of Shangri-la County. This is a spectacular karst landscape formed by the white sediment of calcium carbonate in spring water. It covers an area of about 1 square mile, and is 7,800 feet above sea level. The terrace descends along the incline of the hillside and is the largest of its kind in China. In the Naxi language, the terrace is called *Baduanbapaiduan.* Baishui Terrace incorporates varied shapes, with its layered rocks resembling moonlight on earth, similar to terraced fields in formation. Beside the terrace there is a crescent spring gushing with clear water, where it is said that fairies used to bathe. Below the spring is a stone formation, which is white in color and resembles the shape of a pregnant woman. This is where local people gather to worship the god of reproduction.

At the foot of Shangbai Peak opposite Baishui Terrace, there is a limestone cave, which was once a place for worshipping the Dragon God. Later, Ahmingshiluo, the second saint of the Dongba cult of the Naxi ethnic group, had a religious experience here; thus, the place has been called Ahmingmingka, or "Ahming Divine Cave."

Take the express bus from Shangri-la County to reach Baishui Terrace.

A view of Baishui Terrace (From ImagineChina)

Bitahai Lake

Bitahai Lake is located in the mountains 16 miles to the east of Shangri-la County. In Tibetan, Bitahai is *Bitadecuo,* meaning "carpet of cattle hair." Bitahai Lake has long been known as the pearl of the plateau, situated as it is 11,700 feet above sea level and the highest lake in Yunnan. In folklore, this is the "poisonous lake" mentioned in the biography of King Gesar, and the mid-lake island is where King Gesar sealed up the devils. Bitahai Lake is formed by water trickling down from the surrounding mountains. It is clear and quiet. On the island, a winding path leads to a serene and scenic spot where there is lush green grass, fragrant flowers, and singing birds. The beautiful view is reminiscent of a fairyland. In early summer, the rhododendrons bloom like a beautiful wreath encircling the lake and the island. When the fermented flowers fall into the lake, they are eaten by the fish, who then become intoxicated and float upside down on the surface of the water. Tourists and locals alike can reap a good harvest by picking up the fish without much effort.

Because of a lack of pollution, the supply of fish in Bitahai Lake is healthy and abundant. Among them, there is a very rare and prehistoric species, the Bita multilipped fish, which indeed has three lips and dates to about 2.5 million years ago. In winter, Bitahai Lake looks as clear as glass. (From Quanjing)

> Take a chartered bus. After getting off by the lake, a 4-mile horseback ride takes you directly to the lake.

Shangri-la Valley Group

The Shangri-la Valley Group is located in northwestern Shangri-la County. Here, the valleys are of various widths, ranging from about 260 feet to only 30 feet. Lush forests, fragrant wildflowers, and clear, pure streams make up the landscape. Shrouded in mists and clouds, the grouped valleys look like landscape paintings, as beautiful as a fairyland. On the cliffs of Bixiang Valley there are old stone carvings, petroglyphs, and cliff paintings, which add the color of a mysterious human culture to the place. The Shangri-la valleys are well known for their mystery and beauty; their average height is 9,840 feet above sea level. Here you will also find the largest limestone cave in Zhongdian, the Chitu Immortal Cave; on the cliff at the cave entrance is a naturally formed imprint of a footstep, complete with all five toes. There is also a spring, called Han (Calling) Spring, whose mouth is hidden deep inside the cave. At a loud call at the entrance, water gushes out of the cave, which tastes

Diqing handicrafts are especially beautiful as well as practical. Even the daily utensils are richly decorated. (From Colphoto)

sweet and, according to legend, cures diseases. The Hongshan, the Bula, and the Bisang gold mines have been mined since the Ming and Qing dynasties. The alluvial gold produced here and in neighboring Benzilan is called "Tibetan gold." In the Ming Dynasty, the local Tibetan governor Mu donated 600 tons of gold to the construction of the Shisanling Ming Tombs.

Chartered bus is the most convenient way to reach the valleys.

Meili and Taizi Snow Mountains

Meili and Taizi Snow Mountains are located on the Yunnan-Tibetan border, west of Deqin County, and are connected to each other from north to south. They are linked to the Ahdonggeni Mountain in Tibet to the north, and to the Biluo Snow Mountain to the south, all of which are geologically of the fold-fault type. Meili Snow Mountain, meaning "medicine mountain," is the famous medicine bank of Yunnan, with a large crop of worm grass, snow lotus, fritillaria, and other sources of herbal medicines. The peaks are all higher than 16,400 feet; the main peak, Shuolacengguimianbu, is 17,157 feet above sea level. Taizi Snow Mountain has 13 peaks higher than 19,685 feet, and its main peak, Kagebo, is 22,113 feet high, the highest in Yunnan and a sacred place for Tibetan Buddhism. In late autumn and early winter each year, flocks of pilgrims come from thousands of miles away to worship at the foot of Kagebo Peak.

As Meili and Taizi Snow Mountains are extremely steep and rugged, with complicated topography, Kagebo remains the only unconquered peak in the world.

The mystery of the Meili Snow Mountain virgin territory attracts more and more Chinese and foreign tourists to visit and explore. (From Quanjing)

Baoshan, Dehong Region

>>>

Baoshan Lying Buddha Temple

Located at the foot of Yunyan Mountain 10 miles north of the city of Baoshan, Baoshan Lying Buddha Temple is world famous for its Reclining Buddha, the largest in China. Construction of the temple began in 716 in the Tang Dynasty. The Buddha is magnificent, with its exquisite configuration and enormous size. The temple contains figures of the 500 Luohan (arhats or teachers), the eight Jingang (Buddha's guardian warriors), the four Tianshen (Celestial Gods), and the two generals named Heng and Ha, each with unique charm. The hall of the temple is quite unusual as it is built to integrate perfectly with the natural cave.

There are express buses from the downtown area of Baoshan or you can hire a taxi to the temple.

Taibao Mountain Park

This park is located at the foot of Taibao Mountain, with forests covering 90 percent of its area. The park features natural mountain forests and well-preserved broadleaf woods native to the semitropical climate. On the mountaintop is the second-largest Wuhou Temple in the southwest region; behind the mountain are various pillars, stone inscriptions, and stone carvings dating from ancient to modern times.

From the downtown area of Baoshan, the park is a 20-minute walk.

Tengchong Volcano Group

These volcanoes are located along the world-famous Alps-Himalayan geological configuration belt, particularly on the line where the European-Asian Plate and the Indian Plate converge. The entire area of Tengchong County has active crustal movement, and there are 97 dormant volcanoes, among which 23 have intact cones.

Tengchong has the densest and the most spectacular volcano group in China. (From Colphoto)

Take the express tour bus or chartered bus from Tengchong County.

Tengchong Geothermal Springs

Located 12 miles from Tengchong County and covering an area of 3.5 square miles, the Tengchong hot springs are a well-known scenic area, also known as the "heat sea" due to its extremely rich geothermal resources. Scattered everywhere in the area are many different steam springs, hot springs, and warm springs, such as the Toad Mouth Fountain, the Lion Head Spring, and the Pool of Beauties.

Guoshang Cemetery

Located on Xiao Tuanshan Mountain at the southern corner of Tengchong County and to the south of the Dieshui River waterfalls, Guoshang Cemetery was completed in July 1945. It was built by Li Genyuan in honor of the victory in the Sino-Japanese War and those who died in the war to reclaim Tengchong. As China's largest cemetery in honor of Sino-Japanese War martyrs, it covers an area of over 538,000 square feet. More than 8,000 Chinese soldiers sacrificed their lives in that war.

Take a bus in Tenchong County and get off at Mazhan. The cemetery is less than a mile away.

The Tower Wrapped by Trees (Shubaota)

This tower can be found on the east side of the middle section of the pedestrian street on Friendship Road in the town of Mangshi. More than 200 years old, this is an incredible natural spectacle of trees growing completely around a tower. According to historical records, the tower was built by Fangyuzhu, the seventeenth Tusi (local lord) of Mangshi in honor of a victory.

Fly from Kunming to Mangshi, then take a taxi from the airport to the tower.

An ancient courtyard in Heshun. (From Colphoto)

Heshun

Located 2.5 miles southwest of Tengchong County, the town of Heshun has more than 1,300 households and a population of 6,000, among whom 80 percent are returning Chinese and their families. Heshun is China's earliest border trade town and is known for its extraordinary beauty and cultural traditions. The movie industry has filmed here for many years because of the well-preserved architecture and the magnificent scenery. This is truly one of the most delightful small villages to visit and take in the local history, crafts, and ethnic food.

In Heshun are ancient pavilions, platforms, elegant bridges, and gentle streams everywhere. (From Colphoto)

Bodhi Temple

Bodhi Temple is located on the west side of the middle section of Xinan Road in the city of Luxi. The temple, dedicated to the worship of Hinayana, is well known throughout Southeast Asia. Construction of the temple began in 1677, in the Qing Dynasty. The main hall gracefully combines the Dai, Han, and Sanskrit architectural styles. There are also artistic and cultural artifacts of the Dai people from the last 300 to 400 years, including murals, cut-paper artwork, and tens of thousands of rolls of Buddhist scriptures.

A 10-minute walk from the Tower Wrapped by Trees will get you here. On the 8th, 15th, 23rd, and 30th of each month in the lunar calendar, the nearby Dai people bathe and worship at Bodhi Temple with articles of respect and tribute.

Wanding Bridge

Located on the border between China and Burma, and over 65 feet long and 16 feet wide, Wanding Bridge, though not an exceptional landmark, was the only international land passage in southwestern China during the Sino-Japanese War. At that time, thousands of vehicles transporting war materials to assist China crossed the stone bridge every day.

The city of Wanding is more than 520 miles from Kunming. Tourists can take the bus from the stations in Kunming, or first fly to Mangshi and then travel here by bus.

Jiele Golden Tower

Located in the village of Jiele in the suburbs of Ruili, Jiele Golden Tower is the oldest Buddhist structure and Buddhist activity center in Ruili. The body of the tower was originally built with earth and surrounded by smaller towers. The present tower was rebuilt in 1980 with bricks. The main tower is 120 feet high and surrounded by 16 towers that successively decrease in size. All the towers are gold in color.

The street feast in Munaozongge (From CFP)

Take a bus or minibus from downtown Ruili to reach the tower.

Huihuan Dai Village

Located 30 miles southwest of Wanding, Huihuan Dai Village is known for its beauty and tranquility. Among the 80 households, 98 percent are of Dai ethnicity. Overlooking the village from the distant hills, visitors can see the many simple yet elegant Dai bamboo houses laid out symmetrically.

Take a bus or minibus from downtown Wanding to reach the village.

Manglin Banyan Trees

These four magnificent trees grow in a line along the Kunrui Highway near Mingling Village, Jiele, Ruili. The biggest is 120 feet high, 20 feet in diameter, with eight root masses hugging the ground, and shading an area of 64,580 square feet.

From the thick stems of the banyan trees, fibrous roots grow downward into the soil and become stemlike columns, forming the unique view of "a wood made of one single tree." (From Colphoto)

Ruili River—Daying River Scenic Area

Located in the western part of Yunnan Province, the Ruili River—Daying River Scenic Area consists of three separate sections comprising 60 scenic spots. The area adjoins the Burmese landscape, where Dai, Jingpo, and De'ang people intermix across the border. The Ruili River, called the Nanmao River in ancient times, flows in China for 33 miles and ranges from 330 to 650 feet wide, with slow currents. The fertile drainage area is a land with abundant rice, produce, and fish.

Take a bus from Tengchong through Yingjiang; the trip to the scenic area takes 5 or 6 hours.

Ruili Nongdao

Ruili Nongdao is located 19 miles from the downtown area of Ruili. It is actually not an island but one of the most remote areas in southwestern China. The whole area is 38 square miles, with Dai, Jingpo, Han, and other native inhabitants. Nongdao is surrounded by Burma on three sides, with unique, exotic touches. From here, tourists can see the scenery of Nankan in northern Burma across the Ruili River.

Take a bus along the Ruili-Nongdao highway.

Xishuangbanna Region

Best Time to Travel

Xishuangbanna is part of the rain forest climate. There is no winter here, and the summer is very long. Thanks to the lush forests in the region, it is never too hot here, even in deepest summer. The optimum tourist season is between October and June.

Nationality Garden

The Nationality Garden is located on the banks of the Liusha River less than a mile south of Jinghong, about 2.5 miles from Xishuangbanna Airport and covering an area of 12 square miles. It epitomizes the Xishuangbanna ethnic traditions. The garden consists of the north garden and the south garden containing tropical fruit trees, rare plants and flowers, and several tourist paths. From these, one can view the six small, elegant rail-pattern bamboo houses that demonstrate the customs of the Dai, Hani, Lahu, Bulang, Jinuo, and Yao peoples who have lived in Xishuangbanna since ancient times. The garden also contains the magnificent Xishuangbanna Liberation Monument and several colorful squares. The garden has recently been developed into a comprehensive theme park featuring the multinational customs centering around the Dai people and the tropical landscape.

The Dai people believe in Hinayana; in the Xishuangbanna Dai villages there are many Buddhist pagodas, which form a harmonious and mysterious Buddhist view integrated into the tropical landscape. (From ImagineChina)

The Xishuangbanna Nationality Garden was once a tropical orchard. In the orchard, there are various tropical fruit trees arranged in separate areas, including the Lichi trees, which look like huge umbrellas. Near the back of the orchard, there is a bamboo grove and a clear pool that reflects the surrounding bamboo, presenting a lovely, fairyland scene.

In the Wild Elephant Valley, there was once an elephant pool where wild elephants often bathed and drank water. (From CFP)

> The Nationality Garden is open from 7:00 a.m. to 9:00 p.m. Tourists can take Bus 1 from Jinghong. The shows are scheduled at 9:00 a.m. and 3:00 p.m.

Mangefo Temple

The Mangefo Temple is located next to the village of Mange and on the north bank of the Lancang River, about 1 mile north of Jinghong. In the Dai language, the temple is called *Wamange,* meaning "central temple." The whole complex looks grand, golden, and brilliant. Encircled by Dai bamboo houses and broadleaf trees such as puti, mango, and pinang, the temple is of a typical southern Chinese Hinayana style. Construction of the temple began in 1164, in the Southern Song Dynasty. The main temple is supported by sixteen 26-foot-high and 15-inch-thick round mahogony columns. The beam framework is a tenoned *dougong* structure. There are 16 small, exquisitely carved figures of white elephants on each of the eaves. No nails or rivets were used in the entire complex. At the center of the hall is the figure of Sakyamuni, sitting with crossed legs, 13.5 feet high, encircled by several long, narrow red flags with yellow edges; on the flags there are skillfully embroidered mascots, Buddhist stories, and fairy tales. On the roof and the surrounding walls there are paintings of golden dragons, white elephants, peacocks, and fairies; on the beams hang many pieces of glass, which reflect the incoming sunlight and look shiny and brilliant. In the past, the temple also stored many Dai scriptures, which were the cultural and artistic fruits of the Dai people.

Ganlanba Flatland

The Ganlanba Flatland, also called *Menghanmu* or *Menghanmanting* in the Dai language (*han* means "curling up"), is located about 25 miles down the Lancang River to the south of Jinghong. The Ganlanba Flatland covers an area of 19 square miles and is 1,740 feet above sea level, which is the lowest among the 23 flatlands (*Bazi*) in Xishuangbanna. It is also the hottest place in the region. A great variety of tropical fruits grow in the area, creating a market for fresh and candied fruits. Natural, simple, and tranquil, the Ganlanba Flatland has long enjoyed the graceful appellation of "peacock's tail plume" (meaning "the most beautiful place in Xishuang ban-na")—on the flatland are widely scattered beautiful and rich Dai villages, which look like the shiny spots on a peacock's tail plume. Huanyuanzhai and Huanguozhai are two of the largest villages. Here, tourists can see typical Burmese Buddhist temples and traditional Dai bamboo houses. Around the villages are the Tiedaomu trees, which thrive on being cut repeatedly. In order to protect the local forest resources, the Dai people, who pay great attention to environmental protection, plant these "cut trees" around their villages for firewood.

➡ Take a bus from Jinghong (a 45-minute ride), or arrive by boat to enjoy the beautiful scenery along the river.

Sanchahe Scenic Area

The Sanchahe Scenic Area, also called Wild Elephant Valley, in Xishuangbanna, is located in the Mengyang Nature Preserve, about 31 miles north of Jinghong. It is a tropical valley forest covering an area of 540 square miles and is noted for the great variety of butterflies to be found there. The scenic area features ravines, dense forest, and many rare plants. It provides a safe habitat for wild animals such as the Asian elephants and is the only place in Xishuangbanna that offers the combination of wild elephants, birds, native plants, and tourist adventures.

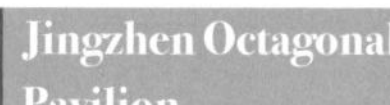

Jingzhen Octagonal Pavilion

The Jingzhen Octagonal Pavilion is located on Jingzhen Hill 9 miles west of the town of Menghai. The pavilion is 51 feet high, 28 feet wide and consists of the base, the body, and the top. The top is the most interesting part: an octagonal wooden structure, with multiple eaves that look as if they are covered with fish scales. The whole pavilion is exquisitely beautiful and is among the best examples of Dai Buddhist architecture. On the 15th and 30th of each month of the Dai calendar, the Buddhas in the Jingzhen area meet in the pavilion to hear eminent monks preach and discuss religious issues. The pavilion is also where major daily routines are conducted and where the ceremonies for the promotion of monks to Buddhas are held.

It is said that Jingzhen Octagonal Pavilion was built in memory of Sakyamuni, and its shape followed the style of the Jinsitai hat, Kazhonghan, worn by Buddha. (From CFP)

➡ Take the bus from Menghai County directly to the pavilion.

In Yunnan Province, the Bai ethnic group has a population of more than 1.3 million, accounting for about 85 percent of all Bai people in China. Most of the Bai people live in Dali Bai Autonomous Prefecture. (From Jin Yongji)

Yunan Style

Puerh Tea

Puerh tea, also known as Dianqing tea, is the best black tea. It took its name from Puerh County, its original transportation and sales center. It has a history of over 1,700 years. In ancient times, Puerh tea was used as medicine to help warm the stomach, generate saliva, refresh the spleen, and neutralize alcohol. Thanks to its distinctive processing technique, its fragrance is intense and lasting, and the tea liquor is dark orange. Puerh tea can be purchased as bulk tea and block. It is exported to over 10 countries and regions including Hong Kong, Macao, Japan, Malaysia, Singapore, the United States, and France.

Three-Course Tea of the Bai Ethnic Group

The three-course tea of the Bai ethnic group refers to the bitter tea, sweet tea, and aftertaste tea, which imply suffering, happiness, and enlightenment in one life, respectively. It is said that the three-course tea originated

The three- course tea show (From CFP)

during the early Tang Dynasty, when Buddhism thrived in Dali, thus facilitating the development of tea culture. As the first course, bitter tea, also known as grilled tea or Baidou tea, is, naturally, bitter in taste; sweet tea is refreshing and invigorating; the aftertaste tea contains such ingredients as pepper and so conveys a delicate aroma that lingers. From Song and Yuan Dynasties to Ming and Qing Dynasties, grilled tea became more and more popular among the Bai people. While sweet tea was served to guests, the three-course tea was for weddings and holidays. For thousands of years, tea has indisputably been the national drink of China. As the most well known tea of the Bai ethnic group, the three-course tea is a brilliant pearl in China's tea culture.

Dali Straw Hat

Weaving common straw into fine straw hats is a technique handed down for generations by women of the Bai ethnic group in Dali, Yunnan Province. With the traditional and primitive beauty of the Yunnan style, the Dali straw hat is very practical and cost effective. It incorporates a rich variety of patterns and is appealing to tourists both at home and abroad.

Bars in Lijiang

The numerous bars are among the most prominent features of Lijiang. Each with its special name, all these bars likewise have their distinctive flavors. Before the night sets in completely, strings of red lanterns light up in front of the bars. These lanterns, reflected in the nearby clear running water, create a scene of unspeakable beauty. Most bars in Lijiang are two-story structures with a wooden floor, stairs, and windows and hand-made tablecloths that lend an antique flavor and a quiet, simple, and elegant atmosphere to the bars. Sitting at a window on the second floor, sipping a mellow Fenghuaxueyue beer (a local brand in Dali), appreciating the beautiful scene of the old town bathed in misty rain, and enjoying the melodious ancient Naxi music of unknown origin, it is easy to become intoxicated with it all. The bars are peaceful; people drink, chat, browse online, and read, and everyone becomes immersed in their own world. The word *leisure* is defined by the bars of Lijiang.

Bar in Lijang (From CFP)

Mosuo girl (From CFP)

The Mosuo People

The Mosuo people like to call themselves Na or Tari. A nomadic nationality in ancient times, today's Mosuo people at Lugu Lake still preserve the traditions of the original matrilineal clan society. In a matrilineal family, all siblings and children of the mother's sisters are considered children of a single mother. The elders of a family include only the grandmother and her siblings. The Mosuo people call men of this generation *Apu* and women *Ayi.* The parents' generation includes only the mother and her siblings. They call mother *Aba* and her brothers *Awu.* The peer generation includes only siblings and children of the mother's sisters. They call the older ones *Amu,* the younger brothers *Geri,* and the younger sisters *Guomi.* Children call their father *Ada, Abo* or *Awu.* All family members live in harmony and regard it as a disgrace to hoard money and divide the family. They work together and solve problems through discussion. Democracy prevails in the family and the opinions of the majority are valued. They care for their children and give particular care and respect to the elderly, the weak, the sick, and the disabled. There are few conflicts and disputes between the mother-in-law and the daughter-in-law or among sisters-in-law. Over a long period of time, a system of conventions and ethical standards have come into being among the matrilineal families of the Mosuo people.

An ancient Naxi music show (From ImagineChina)

Ancient Naxi Music

A kind of classical music widespread among the Naxi ethnic group, ancient Naxi music has been acclaimed as a musical artifact. It amazingly integrates into its melody the ritual music of Taoism, the ceremonial music of Confucianism, and even the Cipai and Qupai music of the Tang, Song, and Yuan Dynasties to form its distinctive clear and airy style. It consists of Baishaxi music, Dongjing music and Huangjing music (now lost) and has an old and strict tradition. Students could learn the music only from their teacher or father, who gave oral instructions based on Gongchi notations. The students recited the notations based on a paragraph or a piece of music and at the same time they learned to play an instrument until they commanded all the necessary skills. In this way, the ancient music was passed down from generation to generation. Dongjing music is solemn and pure. It reflects a primitive simplicity and the elegance of Jiangnan music as well as the Naxi ethnic style and thus sounds mysterious, distant, and aloof. Over 20 pieces of Dongjing music have been preserved, including Langtaosha, Shanpoyang, and Shuilongyin. Baishaxi music tells an emotional story that is sad, inspiring, sorrowful, sentimental, and moving. The composition as a whole comprises an overture, a letter, the beautiful cloud, and the crying princess. Ancient Naxi music can be traced back to the Tang Dynasty. Its instrumentation follows ancient and traditional styles and includes the Sugudu and curved-neck lute. Ancient music, ancient musical instruments and the longevity of musicians are called the "three treasures of ancient Naxi music."

Batik

Batik is a traditional folk textile craft in China. It has a long history and utilizes the characteristic of wax that it does not dissolve in water and thus can protect the original color of the fabric. The craftsman first dips a wax spatula into the molten wax to paint patterns on white flax, which is then soaked it in crude indigo. Then he removes the wax, and the cloth reveals either a white pattern on a blue background or a blue pattern on a white background. When soaked, the wax, which serves as dye-resisting agent, inevitably cracks, thus producing a rippled effect on the cloth.

Water-Splashing Festival (From Jin Yongji)

In Yunan Province, batik is popular mainly among the Miao and Bai people. Most patterns are derived from the local mountains, rivers, and scenic spots and feature a unique style.

Bamboo Houses of the Dai People

The traditional Dai bamboo houses are of three styles: the Payasangmudi (after the inventor of the bamboo house), the Mahasati, and the Henmen. The Dai villages of Xishuangbanna are usually located by a river. From the distance, the bamboo houses look half-hidden in green bamboo woods; up close, they look orderly, pretty, and elegant.

These rail-pattern constructions are mainly made of bamboo, including the columns, beams, rafters, doors, and walls. In some places, even the roof tiles are made of bamboo poles cut in half. The houses have two levels: the upper story, supported by wooden poles, is the living quarters; the lower story is for raising poultry and domestic animals as well as storing odds and ends.

Climbing the steps of the wooden ladder, one comes to the outdoor corridor and balcony on the upper story. The simple balcony is a good place to enjoy the cool breezes or do needlework and crafts. Rooms on the upper story are separated into the bedroom and the living room. The living room is at the outer part and is very wide; at its center is a large bamboo mat, on which people eat, rest, or receive guests. There is also a stove in the living room. The bedroom is separated from the living room by walls made of thick bamboo strips or wood planks. Here, family members of different generations sleep on mats. Outsiders are not allowed to enter the bedroom.

The Dai bamboo houses not only have a beautiful appearance but are sturdy, with a practical layout. Especially in summer, the houses stay cool, which is necessary in the rainy and hot climate of Xishuangbanna.

Food of the Dai Ethnic Group

The Dai are the most hospitable of people. They are overjoyed if you pay a visit to their bamboo home. After setting a cup of fragrant tea on the small, round bamboo table, the host will chat with you, while Bilang, the hostess,

The traditional Dai bamboo houses (From CFP)

is busy in the kitchen preparing the meal. After a while, a full and hearty meal will be brought to the table.

Fragrant Bamboo Rice

Fragrant bamboo rice is also known as bamboo tube rice. To make it, put glutinous rice into a fragrant bamboo tube, immerse the tube in water for 15 minutes, and then roast it over a fire. When it is done, tap to soften the tube so that the bamboo film on the inner wall of the tube sticks to the rice. Cut the tube with a knife to reveal the soft, fine, and fragrant bamboo rice.

Roast Pork

Roast pork is a famous dish of the Dai ethnic group. To make it, they slaughter a half-year-old Dehong small-ear pig, gut it, and stuff it with seasoning, then sew it up with a bamboo split, and roast it over a slow fire. When the pork turns dark yellow and the juices are released, they use a sharp knife to cut the hide open, add some wet straw ash, and continue to roast it. When the pork smells delicious, they slice and serve it.

Cooked Chicken and Sour Bamboo Shoots

To make this dish, put salted bamboo shoots and chicken into a pot and cook them till the chicken is well done. Put pepper, ginger and Chinese onion into a pan with hot oil, and stir-fry them. Then add the salted bamboo shoots and chicken to the pan and stir-fry again. The dish is sour, spicy, tasty, and refreshing.

Citronella-Flavored Roast Fish

To make this dish, you don't need to remove the fish scales. Just cut the fish away from its backbone and gut it. Stuff it with Chinese onion, pepper, salt, and other seasonings, bind the fish with citronella, rub it with an appropriate amount of lard, and roast it till done.

Dongba Culture

Dongba culture is an important part of the culture of the Naxi ethnic group. Dongba culture—that is, ancient Naxi culture—got its name from the Dongba religion where it has been preserved. With a history of over 1,000 years, Dongba culture consists mainly of Dongba characters, scripture, painting, music, dance, ritual instruments, and all varieties of sacrificial rites.

Dongba Characters

Dongba characters are a kind of picto-phonetic system consisting of more than 1,400 characters. Acclaimed as the only picto-phonetic to be completely preserved in the world, it is a valuable cultural artifact for all of human society.

Dongba Scripture

Dongba scripture refers to sutras written with Dongba characters. There are now approximately 40,000 Dongba scriptures collected and preserved in the libraries and museums of Lijiang, Kunming, Nanjing, Beijing, Taiwan, the United States, the United Kingdom, Germany, and France. Rich in content, Dongba scriptures are precious historical records for the study of the ancient philosophy, religion, customs, society, history, literature, and art of the Naxi ethnic group.

Dongba dance

Dongba dance notation written with Dongba characters is one of the earliest such systems in the world. Dongba dance is a kind of reli-

A Naxi ethnic minority man performs a traditional dance in front of Naxi's Dongba pictographic characters. (From ImagineChina)

gious dance that Dongba flamen performed during Dongba religious rituals based on the type of ritual. It was rooted in the social life of the ancient Naxi people. Many of its movements, simulating those of various animals, are quite vivid.

The style and character of Dongba dance, featuring primitive touch and strict standards for movements, are unique among all types of dances in the Lijiang area and in the dance culture of the ethnic groups of Yunnan and other areas.

Dongba Painting

Dongba has a long history and is an artistic relic of the Naxi ethnic group with distinctive features. When preparing for rituals, Naxi people painted all kinds of Buddha, gods, human beings, objects, animals, plants, ghosts, and evil spirits, worshipped, and offered sacrifices to them. All of these paintings that served religious purposes are collectively referred to as Dongba painting.

List of Festivals

Ethnic Group	Festival	Major Activities	Time
Yi ethnic group	Torch Festival	Torch-playing, wrestling, bullfighting	June 24
	Flower Arrangement Festival	Flower arrangement, antiphonal singing	February 8
	Costume Contest Festival	Song and dance, costume contest	March 28
	Tiger Festival	Tiaohusheng, tiger dance	January 8–15
Bai ethnic group	Dali Sanyuejie Festival	Trade fair, horse racing, song and dance	March 15–21
	Raosanling	Sacrificial ritual, seedling planting	April 23–25
	Seedling Planting Festival	Sacrificial ritual, seedling planting, antiphonal singing	Mangzhong (Grain in ear)
	Torch Festival	Torch setting, dragon boat race, performance of Daben song	June 25
Dai ethnic group	Water-Splashing Festival	Dragon boat race, water splashing, song and dance	Mid-April (solar calendar)
	Farewell-to-Dragon Festival	Sacrificial ritual, song and dance	January (solar calendar)
Hani ethnic group	Amatu	Sacrificial ritual, song and dance, street feast	Dragon day of February

	Girls' Festival	Swing playing, song and dance	February 4
	Dragon Sacrificial Day	Cowhide drum, Bawu, four-string guitar	February 2
Miao ethnic group	Flower Mountain Festival	Climbing flower pole, Lusheng, song and dance	January
Lisu ethnic group	Bath Festival	Bathe in hot spring, singing competition	January 2
	Knife Pole Festival	Climbing knife pole, treading fire, dropping bag	February 8
Naxi ethnic group	Mila Festival	Picnic, horse racing, farm tool trade	February 8
Lagu ethnic group	Zhaku Festival	Elephant foot–shaped drum dance, antiphonal singing	Late Mar or early Apr (Dai calendar)
Va ethnic group	Lamu Drum Festival	Sacrificial ritual, song and dance	"Gerui Month" in Va calendar
Bulang ethnic group	Gangyong Festival	Sacrificial ritual, song and dance	April and September
Derung ethnic group	Kaquewa Festival	Sacrificial ritual, cattle slaughtering, song and dance	December or January
Jingpo ethnic group	Munaozongge	Sacrificial ritual, song and dance	January
Nu ethnic group	New Year Festival	Memorial ceremony for ancestors, land sacrificial ritual, drama	Dec to Jan 10 of next year
Pumi ethnic group	Mountain Trip Festival	Mountain trip, song and dance	May 5
Tibetan ethnic group	Hua'er Hui	Antiphonal singing	June 14
Hui ethnic group	Corban Festival	Group sacrificial ritual, livestock slaughtering	October (Hui calendar)
	Ramadan Festival	Chapel, scripture chanting, song and dance	June
Jino ethnic group	Temaoke Festival	Song and dance, visit to stockade village, top whirling	January (Jino calendar)
Yao ethnic group	Panwang Festival	Sacrificial ritual, song and dance	May 29
	Ganba Festival	Copper-drum dance	late December
Zhuang ethnic group	Longduan Festival	Drama, sideshow, song and dance	June
Buyei ethnic group	June 6th Festival	Trade fair, performance of folk song and dance	June 6
Deang ethnic group	Water-splashing Festival	Water splashing, song and dance	Seven days after Qingming Festival
Mongol ethnic group	Luban Festival	Sacrificial ritual, song and dance	April 2

Guizhou

Geography at a Glance

Guizhou Province, also called Qian or Gui for short, with its capital in Guiyang, is located in southwestern China, adjoining Sichuan Province and Chongqing Municipality to the north, Yunan Province to the west, Guangxi Province to the south, and Hunan Province to the east. Guizhou includes nine regions, prefectures, and cities, including Guiyang, Liupanshui, Southeast Guizhou, Anshun, Tongren, and Bijie, which in turn govern 10 county-level cities, 67 counties (including 11 ethnic autonomous counties), 7 municipal districts, and 2 special regions. Guizhou extends about 370 miles from east to west, and about 316 miles from north to south, with a total population of more than 37,480,000. Guizhou covers an area of over 440,300 square miles, 89 percent of which is mountainous, with 11 percent hills, basins, river valleys, and plains. The topography declines from west to east, forming three slopes from the central part to the northern, eastern, and southern parts, with an average altitude of about 3,600 feet. There are many mountains in Guizhou: the Wuling Mountains in the northeast, the Miao Range in the middle-south, the Wumeng Mountains in the west, and the Dalou Mountains in the north. There are also many rivers in Guizhou, including the Nanpan, Beipan, Hongshui, and Duliu rivers in the south, and the Wujiang, Chishui, Qingshui, Hongzhou, and Wuyang rivers in the north.

Guizhou has a subtropical humid monsoon climate. All seasons feel pretty much like spring. The annual temperature averages 60°F and the annual rainfall averages 50 inches.

Guizhou's unique natural scenery, fascinat-

(From ImagineChina)

Around half the Miao population lives in Guizhou. The rest of the people are found in Hunan, Yunan and other regions. (From ImagineChina)

ing national customs, interesting history and culture, and pleasant climate form a unique, primitive, unsophisticated, and mysterious setting that is attracting increasingly more tourists, both domestic and international.

Featured Cuisine

Shibing dog-meat soup, Shibing sour-soup fish, Shibing green-bean jelly, Weining buckwheat cake, Bijie rice dumplings, Suiyang macaroni, Zunyi bean noodles, Zunyi mutton jelly, Zhenfeng glutinous rice, Xingyi roast duck, Shuabatou, Shu's Kangzi noodles, pickled radish, Huajiang dog meat, Huajiang fried rice noodles, Dushan salt pickles, Zhenningbo candy, Ma'an noodles, braised wild rabbit, aged Dao dish, cold Zhe'ergen in sauce, stir-fried eel in chili sauce, spicy fish with crispy skin, bowl cake, hot pot rice, pomegranate rolls, Siwawa, Yipin package.

Feature Commodities

Herbal Medicine

Tianma, Duzhong, Wuzhuyu.

Special Local Products

Maotai liquor, Dong liquor, Dujun Maojian tea, Guiding Yunwu tea.

Local Handicrafts

Anshun batik, Yuping flutes, Huangpin silverware, Huangping clay whistles, Anshun local opera masks, Dafang lac-

Notes 

Guizhou's topography rises and falls drastically and is quite complex. Consequently, it is common to experience climate variation to the extent that "the four seasons coexist on a single mountain and the weather is different just ten li away." The daily sunshine in Guizhou amounts to an average of only three to four hours, and the province also has the most cloudy days a year in China. It is said that in Guizhou "sunny days never last over three days."

POPULAR FESTIVALS

Sisters' Festival

Also called Sisters' Meal Festival. Held on the 15th day of either the second or third lunar month every year in different regions.

March 3rd Festival

On the 3rd day of the third lunar month every year, the Buyi people sing to each other on platforms and blow leaf whistles until the sun sets and the moon rises.

April 8th Festival

Celebrated by the Miao, Buyi, Dong, Zhuang, Yi, Tujia, Gelao, and other minor nationalities in Guizhou, west Hunan, and north Guangxi in memory of an ancient dedicated Miao cacique who was buried on the 8th day of the fourth lunar month in Penshuichi area.

Tongxiang Lantern Festival

The Lantern Festival in Tongxiang, Jinping, features lanterns (including exquisitely made, almost lifelike dragon lanterns) and riddles.

Dragon Boat Festival

On the 24th day of the fifth lunar month every year, the Miao people hold dragon boat races starting from Shibingping Village, through Longtang and Rongshan, and ending in Shidong.

June 6th Festival

On the 6th day of the sixth lunar month every year, the Buyi people gather by the Huaxi River and sing and dance to express their gratitude in memory of a Buyi girl who is said to have created the beautiful landscape.

Chabai Song Festival

A traditional festival of the Buyi people in southwest Guizhou, held from the 21st to the 23rd day of the sixth lunar month every year in Chabai Village in west Guizhou.

Gu Festival

Also called the Lagu Festival, the Gu festival is a grand traditional festival of sacrifice. The periodic cycles vary: In different regions, the festival is held once every other year. The festival usually occurs between late September and early November of the lunar calendar.

Torch Festival

From the 24th to the 26th day of lunar June, the Yi and Bai people from Lunan, Chuxiong, and Dali scatter torches, ignite fire gates, paint colorful faces, set off fireworks, and conduct bullfights.

Miao New Year

The grandest and most representative festival of the Leishan Miao people, who observe lunar October as the beginning of the New Year.

Dong New Year

Celebrated from late October to November in the lunar calendar. Before the festival, people clean their houses and slaughter livestock. During the festival, all the Dong people dress in their festive best and perform the Lusheng Dance and the Cangtang Song and Dance, and hold bullfights.

(From ImagineChina)

querware, Songtao Miao brocade, Southeast Guizhou Miao cut paper, Miao silverware, Zhunyi Tongcao Pictures, Zunyi silk fabrics, Bonamo dust-pan pictures, Xiongjing carvings, Buyi carpets, Lusheng flutes, Anshun knives.

Transportation Tips

By Bus

The highways in Guizhou center around Guiyang. Four national roads (Xiang-Qian, Qian-Gui, Dian-Qian, and Chuan-Qian) and three superhighways (Guiyang-Anshun-Huangguoshu, Guiyang-Zunyi, Guiyang-Bijie) radiate out from Guiyang.

By Train

Transportation out of Guizhou depends mainly on the railroads. The three major tourist regions (southwest Guizhou, southeast Guizhou, and central Guizhou) are all near the railroads. Four main lines (Gui-Kun, Chuan-Qian, Qian-Gui, and Xiang-Qian) meet in Guiyang and provide service for the entire province.

By Plane

Guiyang's Longdongbao airport is located 6 miles from the downtown area in the eastern suburbs and offers direct flights to more than ten provincial capitals in China. Recently, Tongren opened an auxiliary tourist airport.

Recommended Routes

Featured Routes

Three-day floating tour on the Maling River

Day 1 Yixing→Huangguoshu Waterfalls. Lodging: Huangguoshu Hotel.

Day 2 Floating on the Maling River→Maling River Grand Canyon. Lodging: Panjiang Hotel.

Day 3 Wedding Customs Museum→Wanfeng Wood→Miao Villages. End of tour.

Six-day tour of Guiyang and Kaili

Day 1 Arrive in Guiyang, Jiaxiu Tower→Hongfu Temple. Lodging: Baidun Hotel.

Day 2 Guiyang→Guiding→Kaili→Ganhaizi→Tonggu Village. Lodging: Rongjiang Hotel.

Day 3 People's Village Museum→House on Stilts. Lodging: Rongjiang Hotel.

Day 4 Kaili→Rongjiang→Shanglangde Long-Skirt Miao Village. Lodging: Rongjiang Hotel.

Day 5 Rongjiang→Congjiang→Zhaoxing→Drum Tower→Fengyu Bridge. Lodging: Zhaoxing Ecological Hotel.

Day 6 End of the tour

Four-day tour of revolutionary artifacts and Huangguoshu

Day 1 Hongfeng Lake→Natural Miao Village. Lodging: Xinglong Vacation Village.

Day 2 Huangguoshu Waterfalls→Tianxing Scenic Area. Lodging: Huangguoshu Hotel.

Day 3 Xifeng concentration camp→Site of Zunyi Conference→General Political Department of the Red Army→Red Army Cemetery→Former Residence of Mao Zedong. Lodging: Zunyi Hotel.

Day 4 Qianling Mountain→Hongfu Temple→Jiaxiu Tower. End of tour.

Traditional Routes

Ten-day tour of Guizhou

Day 1 Arrive in Guiyang.

Day 2 Jiaxiu Tower→Hongfu Temple.

Addresses and Phone Numbers

Baidun Hotel	18 Yan'an East Road, Guiyang	0851-5827888
Guiyang Restaurant	66 Beijing Road, Guiyang	0851-6823888
Zunyi Hotel	3 Shilong Road, Zunyi	0852-8224902
Huangguoshu Hotel	Inside the Huangguoshu Scenic Spot	0853-3592110
Tianpu Grand Hotel	Daili Center, Guihuang East Road, Anshun City	0853-3516888
Ganglong Grand Hotel	134 Hebin Road, Duyun City	0854-8222898
Mingcheng Hotel	In front of the county government of Zhenyuan County	0855-5726018
Rongjiang Hotel	47 Guzhou Middle Road, Rongjiang	0855-6624188
Zhongshan Hotel	46 Zhongshan West Road, Liupanshui City	0858-8223285
Lijiang Youth Hotel	4 Panjiang West Road, Xingyi City	0859-3223524

Day 3 Kaili Nationality Customs Museum.

Day 4 Anjiang Iron→Chain Bridge→Huangping Feiyun Cliff→Zhenyuan.

Day 5 Yanghe→Zhuge Gorge→Longwang Gorge→West Gorge→Shuilian Cave→Peacock Lieping→Sandieshui→Qinglong Cave Ancient Architectural Complex.

Day 6 Kaili→Taijiang Fanpai Wooden-Drum Dance→People's Museum.

Day 7 Langdeshang Village→Matang.

Day 8 Kaili→Guiyang→Qianling Mountain.

Day 9 Guizhou Provincial Museum→Huaxi.

Day 10 Departure from Guizhou.

Four-day tour on Fanjing Mountain

Day 1 Arrive at Fanjing Mountain.

Day 2 Heiwanhe Waterfalls→Guimenguan→Yu'ao→Jindao Gorge→Zhenguo Temple→Golden Summit→Mushroom Rock→Jiuhuang Cave.

Day 3 Fanjing Mountain.

Day 4 Tongren→Yuping→departure from Yuping at end of the tour.

Six-day tour of Guiyang, Huangguoshu and Shanmu River

Day 1 Arrive in Guiyang.

Day 2 Huangguoshu→Dragon Palace→Tianxing Bridge.

Day 3 Zhenyuan→Qinglong Cave Ancient Architectural Complex.

Day 4 Shibing→Floating on Shanmu River.

Day 5 Yuntai Mountain.

Day 6 End of tour.

Self-Guided Tours

Miao-Dong ethnic customs route

Start from Kaili and end in Huangguoshu, covering the Leishan Natural Customs Museum, Langde, 1,000-household Miao Village, Leigong Mountain National Forest Park, Tonggu (town of Majing farmers' paintings), Kala (Danzhai bird cages), Rongjiang's Dong customs in Sanbao Dong Village,

Basha (the last hunting tribe in China), Zhaoxing Dong Village in Liping, Longli Ancient Town in Jingping, Sanmentang Ancestral Halls in Tianzhu, Fanpai Wooden Drum Dance in Taijiang, Jianhe Hot Springs, Museum of Fossils, and the Huangguoshu Waterfalls.

Miao and Shui customs route

Starts from Leishan, covering Lusheng manufacturing in Paika, town of bronze drums in Zhang'ao, Datang New Bridge, Yongle cuisine street, Shui Customs Village in Dadi, and Leigong Mountain or Liping and Congjiang.

Guiyang, Anshun Region

Best Time to Travel

Guiyang's four seasons all feel like spring, without wind or sand storms, and are all suitable for tourism.

Shopping Tips

Guiyang's Shangxi Commercial Street is the largest wholesale market and distribution center for small commodities of all qualities in Guizhou Province. Shopping here is both economical and convenient. Note that there are two entrances and exits.

The flower and bird market is strongly recommended. Here tourists can find flowers, birds, rare stones, antiques, calligraphy, paintings, medicinal herbs, old books, architectural salvage, Miao embroidery, wax prints, and masks, as well as pets such as dogs and cats.

The Jiaxiu Tower presents a comprehensive view of the surrounding water and mountains. The name Jiaxiu *means "batches and batches of best talents" in Chinese and is the principal landmark of Guiyang. (From CFP)*

Jiaxiu Tower

Jiaxiu Tower, considered the symbol of the city of Guiyang, is built on Aotouji Rock in the Hanbi Pool. In the twenty-fifth year of the Wanli period of the Ming Dynasty (1597), Jiang Dongzhi, governor of Guizhou, had the tower built here and named it "Jiaxiu." Later, the Fuyu Bridge connecting the north and south banks was built at the tower's foot. Then, the square Hanbi Pavilion was built on the bridge. Jiaxiu Tower is three stories tall and has three-eaves, with four corners and a pointed top. It is about 65 feet high, supported by 12 stone columns, and surrounded by a white stone railing with carved designs. The Fuyu Bridge is almost 300 feet long, with nine arches, thus the site is called "Nine Eyes on the Sandbar." However, only seven of the nine arches are visible; two were buried during road construction.

Jiaxiu Tower is located to the west of Guiyang's Wuhong Bridge. From the tower, tourists can enjoy

Minibuses 68, 76, and 108, and Buses 8, 11, and 14 all pass the Jiaxiu Tower. Tourists should try to visit at night to enjoy the spectacular view of the illuminated tower reflected in the water.

the view of the surrounding mountains. Nearby is the Guanfeng Terrace; in the distance is the green Qianling Mountain, flanked by many peaks, including Xixia, Fufeng, Xiangbao, and Nanyue. Jiaxiu Tower also bears many inscriptions by refined scholars, which make the tower a major cultural site. With a history of over 400 years, Jiaxiu Tower stands as a living witness to the history of Guiyang.

Qianling Park

Qianling Park is located northwest of Guiyang city, about 9 miles from the downtown area. It is famous for Qianling Mountain, which has long been called "the first mountain in South Guizhou." It consists of a series of hills linked together, including Xiangwang Ridge, Tan Hill, White Elephant Hill, and Daluo Ridge, and it covers an area of a little more than a square mile. Very tall ancient trees abound throughout the park, together with over 1,500 kinds of plants, including more than 1,000 medicinal plants. There are also widely distributed springs and rocks, as well as groups of Luo monkeys and birds that have their habitats here. Hongfu Temple, Qilin Cave at the mountain's foot, and the cliff inscriptions on the mountain are all important cultural sites under provincial protection. During the war, the patriots General Zhang Xueliang and General Yang Hucheng were placed under house arrest in Qilin Cave. Along the winding path leading to Hongfu Temple, tourists will notice the inscriptions on the steep cliffs. In front of the mountain are Qinlin Cave, Xiangshi Cave, Shifo Cave, Xibo Pool, and "Tiger" Cliff, as well as several pillars. Behind the mountain, the Monument to Martyrs in the Liberation of Guizhou stands among green cypress and bamboo. Kanzhu Pavilion at the mountaintop offers a panoramic view of the city of Guiyang. At the foot of the mountain sits Qianling Lake. Qianling

There are many rhesus monkeys living along Jiuqu Path in the park. One yuan buys a packet of food to feed them, but be aware that these are still wild animals and might bite.

Due to long-time direct contact, the rhesus monkeys in the Qianling Park have become unusually tame. (From CFP)

Park also includes a zoo in the quiet valley and relics of the fourth ice age on the mountaintop.

Wenchang Pavilion

Wenchang Pavilion is located near the semicircular enclosure at the east city gate of Guiyang, facing the west and covering an area of 13,000 square feet. Construction of the tower began in 1609, and it was renovated in 1669. Further renovation and reconstruction were also done in the Yongzheng, Qianlong, Jiaqing, and Daoguang periods of the Qing Dynasty. The pavilion is a pagoda-shaped structure with three stories and nine facets. The halls on the sides and the back rooms connected with them in front form a Chinese traditional rectangular courtyard. The main tower is about 65 feet high and almost 38 feet wide and deep. The pavilion is three-eaved, with nine uneven corners and a pointed top. The windows and column surfaces are covered with colorful paintings. The carvings on the sparrow braces differ considerably from those of northern architecture. The pavilion is of unique local style and its nine-sided construction is rare in China.

The mostly gray Wenchang Pavilion is 65 feet high. Its exquisitely carved doors and windows and gently upturned corners represent the distinctive Ming architectural style. It is also the only asymmetrical ancient wooden pavilion in China. (From CFP)

Huaxi Park

Huaxi Park is located on the riverbank 10.5 miles from the southern suburb of Guiyang. It was originally built in 1938 and was expanded after 1949; it now covers an area of over 133 acres. Huaxi Park, formerly known as Huacaolao, has many tourist attractions, including Chess Pavilion, Cypress Ridge, Biyunwo, Feiyun Pavilion, Fanghe Islet, and Baibu Pavilion, which all center around the four hills of Lin, Phoenix, Turtle, and Snake. Lin Hill is the high spot in Huaxi Park, and it features many towering rocks as well as a cave at the side, called Feiyunxiu. The cave crosses the Huaxi riverbed and from inside you can hear

From the very beginning, Wenchang Pavilion was dedicated to cultivating the local intellectual tradition and advocating Confucianism in Guiyang. Numerous Guizhou scholars left their footsteps in its long corridor. (From CFP)

The Ten-li river bank (From CFP)

the river gurgling. Outside the cave, Feiyun Pavilion sits on the cliff. From here, Fanghe Bridge can be seen below. The top of Lin Hill commands a full view of the beautiful scenery of Huaxi Park. At the center of Huaxi, Turtle Hill and Snake Hill stand opposite each other, with waterfalls pouring down between. Across Ping Bridge is the highly obscured Biyunwo, which is very steep, with several villas built among the green woods. Baibu Bridge was built by pieces of stone that were placed in the water. Golden Avenue is the most attractive spot in Huaxi Park, with a hill on the left and the river on the right. In the fall, the avenue is covered with golden leaves that have fallen. Xuaxi is a kingdom of hills, a world of pavilions, and also a place where streams and rivers meet.

Tianhe Pool

This spectacular pool is a karst depression 165 feet in diameter and 230 feet deep. It is located in the town of Shiban, Huaxi District, Guiyang City, 15 miles from downtown Guiyang, and covers an area of almost 6 square miles. It is a typical karst landscape of thin and bare carbonate rock. This scenic area offers four main tourist activities: viewing the waterfall in the calcified shallows, the Xiangbagou Water Culture, boating in the water cave, and touring the dry cave. The waterfall in the calcified shallows of the Tianhe Pool is the widest one of its kind in China. The section of the river below the waterfall is called Xiangbagou and it encompasses many limestone caves of curious form, including Meishui, Huanshazhou, Wanjiyuan, and Xiannuchurong. Beside the waterfall is Wolong (Lying Dragon) Lake. The long spine of the dragon, which is actually a 100-step stone bridge, floats in the lake. Longtan Cave consists of both a water cave and a dry cave. The water cave is about 3,280 feet long and over 265 feet at its widest and 65 feet at its narrowest. The cave offers spectacular views of stalactites, stalagmites, and stone columns. The three-level dry cave contains a natural stone bridge, the Naihe Bridge, which links two cliffs inside the cave; below the bridge is an apparently bottomless, dark pool. Tianhe Pool, combining various unusual and interesting geological formations is without question an extraordinary tourist destination.

Baihua Lake

Baihua Lake, 14 miles from downtown Guiyang, contains more than 100 large and small islands. Because the landscape here resembles that of Guilin, the lake is known as "Little Guilin." The island groups in the lake naturally divide it into three parts: the middle lake, the south lake, and the north lake. Three small villages on the islands are home to scores of households. Their fishing boats add to the picturesque view. The scenic Baihua Lake area includes more than 50 attractions, among which 23 are now open, including the Distant View of the Pine Wood, Two Monkeys Guarding the Field, Crab Islets and Snail Islands, Guanyin Cave, Baihua's Double Narrow Places, Green Peaks, Golden Toad Playing with Water, Pretty Single Peak, Extraordinary Rocks, Ancient Barrack and Castle, and Bird Island. Tourists can row a boat in the lake and enjoy the beauty of the landscape, including many different plants and animals.

Tourists can reach Baihua Lake by taking a suburban bus to Zhuchang at Shanlin Road.

Ancient Town of Qingyan

The ancient town of Qingyan is located in the southern suburb of Guiyang, about 18 miles from the downtown area. It is one of the well-known ancient cultural towns in Guizhou. The town has a long history. In 1378 the town of Qingyanbu was officially established. From 1624 to 1627 Banlingui, who then controlled the eight Fan and the twelve Si, built an earth castle at Sizhiba Slope about 6 miles from the town of Qingyanbu. The castle was known in Chinese as Wangcheng, meaning "military castle" or "barracks." That was the forerunner of today's town of Qingyan and also accounted for the origin of Qingyan's strange nickname Sizhiba ("four handles").Through hundreds of years of changes, the town was renovated and expanded many times. The

Stone-plate houses face the green hill both at back and in front. Except for the wooden purlins and rafters, everything is built with stone, making the houses stately, solid, warm in winter, cool in summer, moistureproof, and fireproof. (From CFP)

Guizhou abounds in bamboo. Bamboo weaving in the ancient town of Qingyan has a long history and has become an important local industry. (From CFP)

original earthen castle developed into stone walls and stone streets. Qingyan has over 100 cultural attractions. Within the town are 37 Ming and Qing structures, including nine temples, eight joss houses, five pavilions, three caves, two ancestral halls, one palace, and one courtyard. These structures are all decorated with paintings and carvings as well as upturned corners and multiple eaves. Though time-worn, their charm remains. The stone carvings in the Ciyuan Temple and the wood carvings in the Shoufo Temple are artistic masterpieces exclusive to Guizhou. The layout of the town of Qingyan follows the Ming and Qing style. The Entrance Gate, the Waist Gate, and the old stone and wooden counters have all been well preserved, adding to the feeling of antiquity. The ancient town is also a gathering place for many cultures. Here Confucianism, Buddhism, Taoism, Roman Catholicism, Christianity, and the cultures of several ethnic minorities all merge into each other, forming the unique culture characteristic of the ancient town of Qingyan.

> No admission is charged to enter the town, but there is a fee to visit the old houses. Qingyan's bean curd and rose candies are local specialties.

Zhenshan Village

Zhenshan Village is located on a peninsula in the central part of the Huaxi Reservoir. It is 13 miles from Guiyang, surrounded by water on three sides and a hill on the other side; it is situated opposite Banbian Hill and Li Village, with a body of water between. The three landmarks form a triangle and make an impressive sight. By water, the village lies about 3 miles from Huaxi Park in the southeast and about 2 miles from Tianhe Pool in the northwest. Zhenshan Village has a history of more than 400 years, having been an important military fortress during the Ming Dynasty and then the principal home of the Buyi people since the mid-Qing Dynasty. It is a stone castle consisting of gate towers, walls, houses, and paths. Scenic spots including the Village Fort, Martial Temple, the stone-plate residences, and the stone steps and lanes are all well preserved. On the hill to the right south of Zhenshan Village are the tombs of the historical figure Li Renyu as well as those of his two sons, General Dewu and General Zhenwu.

Kaiyang Nanjiang Grand Canyon

The Kaiyang Nanjiang Grand Canyon, located over 37 miles from Guiyang, includes diverse limestone valleys and waterfall groups, presenting an extraordinary spectacle. The canyon is

Red Maple Lake in Guiyang has long been known as the "Pearl of the Plateau."Fascinating scenery abounds here in all seasons. Tourists may rent a wooden boat and linger amid the beautiful scenery. (From CFP)

almost 25 miles long and plunges 1,300 feet at the deepest point. It is a typical canyon landscape of low and medium hills. In the canyon, there are over 80 natural sights and more than 40 waterfalls. On the cliffs live many rare animals, such as the Tibetan Qiu monkeys and rhesus monkeys. Schools of fish swim through the water while Mandarin ducks patrol the surface; egrets can be spotted overhead. These combine to give the canyon the appellation of "Shangri-la in Guizhou."

Red Maple Lake

Red Maple Lake is located in the suburbs of the town of Qing, 21 miles from Guiyang. The lake covers a total area of 22 square miles, with a water volume of more than 2 billion square feet. The deepest point reaches hundreds of feet, and it is the deepest of the man-made lakes on the Guizhou plateau. The lake is 1.25 miles from east to west, and 15.5 miles from north to south. The lake is totally encircled by maple trees that turn red in fall, giving the lake its name. It consists of four parts: the middle, north, south, and back lakes. The north lake is known for its islands, among

In Guizhou many ethnic minorities live together, each with its unique customs and charm. The Dong girls are particularly attractive in their festive costumes. (From CFP)

which the most prominent are Bird Island, Snake Island, and Turtle Island, all named according to their shapes. On the lakeshore are cultural sites including the ancient tombs of the West Han Dynasty and the barracks of the Miao King from the Ming Dynasty. The south lake is known for caves, in which there are remarkable stalactites. Jiangjun Cave, in particular, is almost 2,000 feet long and contains three interior lakes. The middle lake is located between the north and the south lakes and is known for its picturesque stones and peaks. The back lake is heavily vegetated. Red Maple Lake encompasses over 100 islands and is known as the "Pearl of the Plateau." Included in this scenic spot are the Dong and Miao villages, which observe their own unique customs.

Many buses from Hebin Park in Guiyang go directly to the Red Maple scenic area. Be careful of the steep stairs at the drum towers in the Dong village.

Anshun Confucius Temple

Also called Fuxue Palace, this particular temple is located at Hongxuebai northeast of Anshun. Construction began in the first year of the Hongwu period of the Ming Dynasty (1368), and 22 structures survive. In front of the temple there is a screen wall. Inside the entrance are Li Gate and Yi Path, between which stands a stone pillar called the Dismounting Pillar. Three of the original four sections of the temple are generally well preserved. There is also a museum of wax printing at the temple.

Anshun Dragon Palace

Anshun Dragon Palace, located almost 17 miles to the southwest of downtown Anshun and 18.5 miles from the Huangguoshu Waterfalls, covers an area of about 3 square miles. A typical karst landscape, the area is particularly known for its caves and hidden lake.

The dragon palace is almost 2 miles long and consists of five sections of limestone caves linked by a hidden lake. The lake is more than 90 feet deep and almost 100 feet wide, and its narrowest place allows only one small boat to pass through. The first section extends from the Palace Gate to Clamshell Rock, on whose surface are many holes of various sizes that serve as nests for the swallows that fly in and out of the nearby cave. The second section extends from Clamshell Rock to Colored Fish Pool, the third from Colored Fish Pool to Green Fish Pool, and the fourth from Green Fish Pool to Maple Cave, where there is a constantly swirling pool measuring almost 400 feet in diameter near Qingshui Cave. The fifth section extends from the swirling pool to Guanyin Cave and then to Xiaocaihua Lake.

It is said that "the Sichuan people fear no hot pepper, the Hunan people overcome all hot pepper, but the Guizhou people are afraid that hot pepper is not hot enough." In the culture of the Guizhou people, hot pepper is indispensable. (From CFP)

Anshun Dragon Palace is known for its three records among Chinese caves: the longest length, the highest waterfall, and the lowest natural radioactivity. (From Quanjing)

In front of the dragon palace is a small mountain lake, covering an area of over 107,639 square feet. More than 140 feet deep, it is also called the Heavenly Pool or Dragon Pool. Anshun Dragon Palace incorporates more than 20 dry limestone caves, including Bamboo Cave, Skylight Cave, Night Cat Cave, and Tiger Den Cave. The dragon palace's majesty lies in the integration of its mountains, woods, springs, caves, lakes, rivers, and waterfalls. Near the entrance are attractions such as the Longmen Waterfall, the Bangyan Swallows, the Huayu Fairyland, the Yunshan Stone Forest, the Wolong Pool, and the Bashang Bridge. Longmen Waterfall at the entrance is about 80 feet wide and more than 110 feet high and is created by the water from a mountain lake pouring down through sinkholes. It is called the "White Dragon out of the Den" by the local people. The name Longmen, meaning "dragon's gate," derives from the water falling down the stone walls. Longmen Waterfall ranks first among underground waterfalls in China.

Guizhou is the most comprehensive area of karst landscape in China. It is said that "whatever exists in the world's limestone caves exists in Guizhou's caves, too."

Huajiang Grand Canyon

This awe-inspiring place is located in southwestern Guanling Buyi Autonomous County, with its center not more than 2 miles from Huajiang. The canyon is 3,280 feet deep, nearly 2 miles wide, and almost 50 miles long, covering an area of 115 square miles. The canyon lies along the Beipan River, ranging from Guangzhao in the north to the mouth of the Sancha River and consists of five sections: Sanjiangkou, Bangui, Xiagua, Shanggua, and fossils. The canyon features picturesque cliffs and the rushing and surging Huajiang River at its bottom, as well as sights including the Panjiang stone inscriptions, the Huajiang Iron-Chain Bridge, and the Panjiang Bridge. In the village of Niujiangjin are six Niujiangjin murals, and on the cliff at the village of Xiagua near the river there are Mayanjiao murals. In Hanyuan Cave, about 6 miles from Xiagua, are inscriptions of ancient poems and murals of the sun, clouds, dragons, and turtles. The famous Chinese TV series *Xiyouji* (*Journey to the West*) selected several scenic spots here for shooting.

Huangguoshu Waterfalls

The Huangguoshu Waterfalls Scenic Area is a major national scenic spot in China, with the Grand Falls as its central attraction and more than 10 other waterfalls of different forms. It features a subtropical karst landscape and vegetation and figures prominently in the customs of the Buyi people and the Miao people. It is located in the Zhenning Buyi and Miao Autonomous County, 28 miles to the southwest of Anshun (which is the tourist center in west Guizhou) and 93 miles from Guizhou's capital, Guiyang, covering an area of about 170 square miles. The majority of the falls are concentrated above Dabang Cave, and the Baishui, Baling, and Erwang rivers at the boundary between Zhenning County and Guanling County. The major attractions of this scenic area are the impressive and spectacular Grand Falls, the Shizhai section, the Tianxingqiao section, the Dishuitan Falls section, the Balinghe Valley historical section, and the Langgong section. At the periphery are separate sights such as the Guanjiao Falls, Rhinoceros Cave, and Guanyin Cave. The Huangguoshu Waterfalls are the largest in China and also one of the most spectacular waterfall sites in the world.

The great traveler and geographer Xu Xiake of the Ming Dynasty gave vivid descriptions of the Huangguoshu Waterfalls in his famous Travel Notes: "A stream hangs down from the sky; and it falls like tens of thousands of pieces of white silk ribbons. In the stream spreads a stone lotus leaf with three openings at the verge. Overflowing the leaf, water plunges down like numerous flying silk fabrics covering the cliff hollows like gates; the drop of the fall can't even be measured by zhang (roughly 11 feet). The flying water droplets look just like ground pearls and broken jades, and also like rising mists, forming a really spectacular view. The majesty of the waterfall even exceeds what is depicted in the verse lines 'A pearl curtain that can't be pulled up; a piece of white silk that hangs in the distance.'"

The Grand Falls are more than 240 feet high and 265 feet wide, the form varying with the seasons. In the winter, the falls are charming and pretty, gently pouring down; in the summer and fall, with much more water flowing, their thrilling power is strong enough to shake the earth. Sometimes the splashing water droplets and mists reach as high as hundreds of meters, enveloping the vicinity in a flying drizzle—as a line of poetry says, "The silver rain falls on the golden street." Behind the waterfall is a water-curtain cave, which is the most awe-inspiring sight in this scenic spot. In the 440-foot-long cave

(From CFP)

(From CFP)

(From Quanjing)

(From Quanjing)

are six cave windows, five halls, three springs, and one waterfall. Walking through the cave, tourists can watch the plunging water through the windows. At sunset, visitors are occasionally treated to the sight of the distant misty clouds and pink sky on the mountaintop, which long ago inspired the name "Sunset from the Water-Curtain Cave." The Grand Falls plunge into the 60-foot-deep Rhinoceros Pool, which resembles a round mirror made of green glass. Early on sunny mornings, the light refracted through the splashing water droplets produces flashing rainbows. As an ancient line of verse says, "The rainbow in the air has the blue sky as its background, while rainbows on the Rhinoceros Pool are projected against the snow-white waterfall." The site derives its name, "Mountain Rainbows Set against White Snow," from this poetic line. It is believed that there are rhinoceroses guarding treasure in the pool. Many ancient trees and twining vines grow on the cliffs around the pool. Red and black phoenix butterflies, wild foxes and rabbits, and apes and monkeys all call this place home. The valley through which the waterfalls flow consists of a series of connected shallows, called *Dieshui* (Fallen Water). Beyond the Rhinoceros Pool are Sandao Shoal, Horse-Hoof Pool, Fallen Bull Cave, Youyu Well, Wanba, Huayu Pool, and Maoshui Pool, each contributing to the beautiful landscape view.

(From C[illegible])

(From ImagineChina)

(From CFP)

Tianxing Bridge Scenic Area

Located 20 miles from the Huangguoshu Waterfalls, the Tianxing Bridge Scenic Area is an integration of mountain, water, woods, and caves. The Tianxing landscape is situated across the Sancha River and consists mostly of stone forest in water, covering a very small area. Its main attractions include Bubujing ("one sight after another"), Yixianshui ("a narrow water passage"), Konglingshi (Kongling stone), Tianxingzhaoying ("stars in water reflection"), Changbiaoxia (Changbiao valley), Ceshenyan ("sideways rock"), Waishushi (Waishu stone), Yanyangteng ("vines of mandarin ducks"), Panlongtu ("picture of coiling dragons"), Meinurong ("banyan beauties"), Xiangbishi ("Elephant-trunk stone"), and Tianxinglou ("star tower"). The magnificent landscape of the Tianxing Bridge Scenic Area has been described as "an endless stretch of potted scenery carved in stone with wind-knives and water-swords" and "an extraordinary ancient painting painted on silk with root-pen and vine-ink." Located in the middle of the Tianxing Bridge Scenic Area is Tianxing Cave, which is a typical limestone cave with main halls and side halls supported by four huge stone columns more than 65 feet tall. The main sights in the cave include Grape Hall and rock formations resembling the Great Wall and Miao's terraced fields as well as birds, insects, fish, animals, flowers, trees, and fruits and vegetables. About a half mile from the Tianxing Cave is the small stone forest section. Above the stone forest is a funnel-shaped waterfall, called Yinlianzhuitan ("silver silk falling into a pool"). The falls split at the upper part of the stone forest into two flanking branches, which meet again at the lower part, thus encircling the stone forest. On the water surface are scattered stones of various forms.

Among the Miao silver ornaments, the earrings are available in most styles and are available in four types: pendants, rings, hooks, and wheels. The picture shows a wheel earring worn by a Miao woman.(From CFP)

The Tianxing Bridge Waterfall is mighty, magnificent, and fascinating. (From Quanjing)

There are express buses from Huangguoshu to the Tianxing Bridge. There are also cableways available in the scenic area.

Southwest Guizhou Region

Best Time to Travel

The annual average temperature in southwest Guizhou is 60°F. It is warm and damp all year round. All four seasons are suitable for tourism.

Malinghe Valley Scenic Area

The Malinghe Valley Scenic Area, a major national scenic area located in Xingyi, Guizhou Province, covers a total area of almost 175 square miles. Its unique and precipitous landscape is known for the valley, the waterfalls, and the calcium carbonate stalactites. It consists of three sections: the Malinghe Valley, Wanfeng Lake, and the Wanfeng Woods. The Malinghe Valley is the most characteristic of the area. It is a canyon some 46 miles long, ranging from 160 to almost 500 feet wide in places, and from 390 to 920 feet deep. Inside the valley are flying waterfalls, hanging green bamboo, interconnected limestone caves, and the remarkable spectacle of "one hundred pictures, waterfalls, curtains, and springs." The "one hundred pictures" refers to the highly picturesque cliffs flanking the valley that cuts deep into the earth, the "one hundred waterfalls" to the 56 waterfalls of varied size, the "one hundred curtains" to the more than 100 rarely explored water-curtain caves, and the "one hundred springs" to the more than 120 springs, including Xixin Spring, the Cheliang hot spring, Tianyan Spring, Heavenly Pool, and Terrestrial Pool. Many Chinese and foreign tourists enjoy making their way down the valley.

Different from the usual canyon configuration, the Malinghe Valley is essentially a grand cleavage in the Earth, where the roaring waterfalls are gathered into impressive groups. Its unusual appearance has led some observers to proclaim it "the most beautiful scar on Earth." (From Quanjing)

At the Master Station in Guiyang, take a coach to Xingyi.

Liu's Manor

Liu's Manor is located in the village of Xiawutun, to the south of Xingyi. It is China's largest village-fortress and was once the residence of Liu Xianshi (eminent civil and military governor of Guizhou) and Liu Xian-qian (guerilla commander and supervisor of border issues in Guizhou and Yunnan), both of whom served in the early KMT administration. Liu's ancestral hall, drawing room, gun turrets, and Zhongyi temple (as well as some western-style features) remain, covering a total area of about 430,556 square feet. In addition, many remains and relics of the late Qing and the early KMT period can be seen in the manor. They have significant value for studying the warlord history of Guizhou and were incorporated into the Guizhou Nationality Wedding Customs Museum in October 1989.

Take the T1166 train at Kunming Station at night and arrive at Xingyi County the next morning.

Southeast Guizhou Region

Best Time to Travel

Ethnic groups are most concentrated in the southeast portion of Guizhou Province. They observe more than 130 festivals in a year, which occur mainly from March to July, according to the lunar calendar.

Qinglongdong Temple

Qinglongdong Temple was built in the middle of the Ming Dynasty, with a long history of nearly 500 years. It is located at the foot of the Zhonghe Mountain near the Wuyang River to the east of the old town of Zhenyuan, covering an area of 97 acres. It consists of 36 separate features divided among six areas: Qinglongdong (Black Dragon Cave), Ziyang Shuyan (Ziyang Academy), Zhongchanyuan (Middle Buddha Hall), Wanshougong (Longevity Palace), Zhushengqiao (Zhusheng Bridge), and Xiangluyan (Censer Rock). Lesser features include pavilions, platforms, storied buildings, temples, joss houses, and ancestral and other halls. Qinglongdong, known as "Southwest Suspending Temple," is an integration of Confucianism, Taoism, Buddhism and the buildings, bridges, and pathways representing a perfect combination of the Han building culture of Jiangnan (the region south of the Yangtze River) and the mountainous region building culture of the southwest ethnic groups. On the stone arch at the gateway in front of Longevity Palace are two precious brick carvings, which are extremely tiny but depict a panorama of three Qinglongdong building complexes that cover nearly 107,639 square feet. The proportion is about 1:8,000. These carvings are rare national treasures.

The stone columns of the gate of Qinglongdong Temple are engraved with a couplet: "As the literary place is near a stream, two rivers encircle the old temple; as the censers stand opposite, smoke from numerous household kitchens permeates the woods." (From CFP)

In addition to Qinglongdong, tourists may want to visit the old town of Zhenyuan, where walking in the street feels like being in a mountainous landscape painting from the Song, Yuan, or Ming Dynasty.

In the Chong'an River area of southeast Guizhou, the local residents "start laboring at sunrise and lie down to sleep at sunset." To this day, they power their mills by waterwheels. (From CFP)

Wuyang River

The Wuyang River, also named Wushui or Wuxi, has its headwaters at the foot of Duoding Mountain in Wong'an County. After it converges with the Qingshui River at Qianyang (where its name becomes the Yuanjiang River), it then flows into Dongting Lake. The total length is about 250 miles. This waterway was once the artery between the ancient southwest border areas and the middle and lower reaches of the Yangtze River, which bears the name "Gold Waterway." Today, the Wuyang River draws many Chinese and foreign tourists with its primitive and beautiful natural attractions, such as Jinjijiaotianmen (Golden Cock Crowing to the Heavenly Gate), Yuanyangwan (Mandarin Duck Bend), Sandieshui (Three-Level Waterway), and Kongquekaiping (Tail-Spreading Peacock).

Taking the bus at Anshun, Guiyang, or Shuicheng, tourists can arrive at the three gorges of the Wuyang River. It is about a three-hour ride.

Censer Mountain

Censer Mountain, at an altitude of more than 3,940 feet, is located a little more than 9 miles to the west of the city of Kaili. Surrounded by steep cliffs of three levels, it is flat at the top and concave at the waist, like a censer, lending the mountain its name. Many ancient trees grow on the mountain, which is enveloped in mists and clouds. The oldest and grandest Miao festival of Chiguzang ("eating bull's purtenance"), also called Ciniu ("stabbing bulls") or Gusheji ("drum sacrifice"), is held here. It is a very solemn Miao ceremony, at which sacrifices are dedicated to Miao ancestors. It is the Miao people's belief that the spirits of their ancestors reside inside a large drum made of bull's hide, and that the drum is also the bond and symbol of blood lineage.

Take a mini-bus at the Kaiyunsi Bus Station in Kaili for Longchang and Yudong, or take Bus No. 38 on the suburban route and get off at Huzhang.

It is not easy to climb Censer Mountain. A climbing festival is held here in June every year, but be prepared to spend five hours on the trip up and back down the mountain.

Yuntai Mountain

Yuntai Mountain, meaning "cloud platform," is one of many attractions in the Wuyang River state-level scenic area. It is 8 miles north of Shibing County and covers an area of about 77 square miles. It consists of peaks including Yuntaishan, Waiyingtai, Jiaodingshan, and Daotiannao. The main peak, Tuanchangyan, is 3,500 feet high and is sharply steep on all sides and singularly thrusts halfway into the clouds, its top like a platform enveloped in the mists. Other attractions here include the well-preserved Guogong Temple, Xugong Hall, and many cliff inscriptions.

Zengchong Drum Tower

Zengchong Drum Tower, the oldest drum tower built by the Dong people in Cong-

There is no fixed staircase between ground level and the second floor in the Zengchong Drum Tower. Fixed staircases start from the second floor up. On the roof of the fifth floor hangs a wooden drum commanded by the head elder. Under the eaves of the fourth and fifth floors are inserted some wooden brackets called Ruyi Dougong, which are both supporting and ornamental. (From Quanjing)

With both temple and garden, Feiyunya's special charm is drawing more and more tourists. (From CFP)

jiang County, is considered an architectural treasure and is an outstanding expression of the Dong culture. Built in 1672, the Zengchong Drum Tower is located in the village of Zengchong, in Congjiang County. Covering an area of 1,000 square feet, the tower is 85 feet high, with 13 levels of eaves and a 22-level top. The top of the tower commands a full view of the near and distant buildings and landscape. Inside the tower is a fir structure supported by four thick main columns (called "golden columns"), each of which is 50 feet high and 2.5 feet in diameter at the base. The corners of the lime-coated tile ridges curve upward and bear clay figures of birds and animals. The walls inside the eaves are painted with various designs, including phoenix, fish, and shrimp. Areas below the eaves are decorated with delicate wooden carvings. Remarkably, the tower is connected by fir tenons without a single nail or rivet.

To mark civic and cultural activities, the big drum in the tower is beaten to summon all of the villagers into the drum-tower hall to listen to the head elder. At other times, the hall serves as a place for public amusements.

> To get here, take one of the buses from Congjiang.

Feiyunya Scenic Area

The Feiyunya Scenic Area is one of the many such spots in the Wuyang River area. It is located on Dongpo Mountain, about 7.5 miles from Huangping County. It is called Feiyunya ("rock with flying clouds") because it features a suspended rock that resembles flying clouds. Feiyunya, for many years a major attraction in Guizhou, has always been Guizhou's natural protection from outsiders. It is also where the Guizhou Nationality Festivals Museum is located. Below are Chengtan, a clear pool, and a deep valley. To one side is a waterfall and in front stand clustered peaks, on which sit the Shengguo and Dicui pavilions. Beside the Chengtan pool is the Yuetan Temple Residence, as well as some structures built during the Qing Dynasty, including Qingfeng Pavilion, Daguan Hall, Guanpu Platform, Youyun Pavilion, Qingxin Hall, and Yangyun Pavilion. All of these make the Feiyunya area more splendid and colorful. It is said that the Feiyunya rock is the most frequently mentioned site of its kind in historical records and bears the most literary inscriptions. It is no wonder that on the stone arch east of the bridge the Qing scholar E'ertai inscribed "The First Attraction in South Guizhou." With both temple and garden, Feiyunya's special charm draws many tourists.

> Take a coach or express tour bus from Guiyang, Zhenyuan, Shibing, and other places to Feiyunya.

Langde Village

Langde is a Miao village 18 miles from the downtown area of Kaili and about 4 miles from the county. It is a gem on the eastern tour route of Guizhou, having acquired the title "Home of Chinese Folk Arts" awarded by the Chinese Ministry of Culture. As the first village museum in China, it is also the only open-air museum of ethnic customs. Langde consists of Upper Langde Village and Lower Langde Village. In the upper village, which is an ethnic village museum, houses on stilts sit among lush trees along the hills. The Wangfeng River, on which dozens of waterwheels turn day and night, passes by the village. Wine plays an extremely important part in the local customs and culture. Langde's wine culture permeates every aspect and constitutes an institution unto itself. When guests approach the village entrance, the Miao people greet them with traditional songs and rice wine, the so-called "toasting songs" and "blocking wine." There are many other wine rituals. Once inside the village, guests are ushered to Tongguping to watch the dance of "stepping on bronze drums." All the roads in the Langde are paved with arrow-shaped stone bars. Along the roads are over 40 small bridges. Cattle and fish are the two kinds of animals most essential to the village. Cattle worship is as solemn as ancestor worship. Images of cattle are common in the local folk art, including wax prints, cross-stitch works, and silk fabrics. The fish motif is utilized throughout the village, in such implements as carpenter's ink markers, various handles, shoulder pole ends, embroidered hats, and wooden combs. Fish also play an integral part in some major festivals, such as the Chixin ("eating new rice") Festival. The diverse customs of Langde exhibited in the ethnic village museum, have drawn more than 500,000 tourists and researchers over the past decade.

The Dong women wear richly ornamented hair buns. In Liping, they wear silver crests with fish, butterfly, or coin-shaped emblems, sometimes holding feathers of various colors. (From CFP)

Diping Fengyu Bridge of Liping

The Diping Fengyu Bridge, also called the Dipinghua Bridge, is located near Diping, 68 miles to the south of Liping County, in Gui-

The wooden Fengyu Bridge, famous for its covered corridor, towers, and wayside benches, serves not only as a passage but also as a resting place and a shelter, hence its name which means "wind and rain." (From Quanjing)

zhou Province. Spanning the Nanjiang River, the bridge is 166 feet long and 15 feet wide. A stone pier stands in the middle of the river, and the body of the bridge is a wooden corridor flanked by benches. On the bridge there are three towers, one bigger and two smaller. The bigger tower stands in the middle, which is of palace style with five levels of eaves and four pointed corners, about 16 feet high, and with a gourd-shaped top. The two smaller towers at each side are both about 10 feet high, with three levels of double eaves and double-inclined roofs. In between the towers and also on the ridges of the towers are clay figures of upside-down turtles, three dragons competing for a pearl, and two phoenix facing the sun. Also painted on the middle tower are four black dragons, as well as pictures of Dong women spinning, weaving, embroidering, and singing Caigetang songs, as well as images of bullfighting and historical figures. The roof features colorful designs of dragons, phoenix, white cranes, and rhinoceroses. The structure of the entire bridge is highly ingenious, being made without using a single nail or rivet. With its superb construction and exquisite craftsmanship, the bridge embodies the Dong people's workmanship and indigenous construction style. The bridge is on the list of major cultural relics to be protected in Guizhou Province.

The only access to Liping is by road, and the buses to Rongjiang are available only in the morning.

Liping Tiansheng Bridge

The Liping Tiansheng Bridge, also called Zisheng Qiao or Tianran Qiao (meaning "a natural bridge"), is located near Gaotun in Liping County. The bridge measures 387 feet at its widest spot, 340 feet long, and 110 feet high. A clear, fish-filled river about 200 feet wide flows under the bridge, and a lush woodland, home to more than ten kinds of rare birds, grows nearby. Tourists to Liping rarely skip this famous attraction.

The Miao and Shui women in Guizhou excel at embroidery. These exquisite insoles are their handiwork. (From CFP)

Zunyi, Tongren, Bijie Region

Best Time to Travel

Any month of the year is fine for travel to Zunyi, but May to October is the best time to visit the Chishui Scenic Area.

The Buyi people live mainly in the two Miao-Buyi Autonomous Prefectures in south and southeast Guizhou. (From ImagineChina)

Zunyi Conference Site

The Zunyi Conference Site is located at 80 Hongqi Road (the former Ziyin Road) in the old town of Zunyi, formerly known as Pipaqiao. The conference site is a two-story brick-and-wood building, which faces the south and combines Eastern and Western construction styles. The gable-and-hip roof features a "tiger window." Around the building are the so-called Baosha corridors. The site is composed of the main building and the courtyard. The main building is encircled by winding corridors and is equipped with shutter-shaped doors and windows. At both the east and west ends are winding staircases with wooden fences. The entire building is 56 feet deep, 84 feet wide, and 40 feet high and covers an area of 5,680 square feet. The front gate of the building faces the street and was once flanked by eight storefronts. At the entrance hall is a huge brick archway bearing colorful embedded characters: *Weilu* in the front and *Shendu* at the back. Through the archway is a small yard; to its south is a side door leading to

The Zunyi Conference was convened at a critical moment for the Chinese Red Army, during which the CCP made the first independent application of the basic principles of Marxism to solve the major issues of the Chinese revolutionary war. (From CFP)

an interior square courtyard, and to its north is the main building. The building, considered the grandest of all in Zunyi in the 1930s, was the private residence of Bai Huizhang, commander of the second division of the 25th Corps of the former Guizhou troops.

Tourists should be aware of Zunyi's poor road conditions, winding mountainous roads, and often late buses.

Tomb of Yang Can

The Tomb of Yan Can is located at Huangfenzui, Yong'an, Longping, Zunyi County, Guizhou Province. It has a flat roof and two chambers built of white sandstone bars, covering an area of 540 square feet. The two chambers are parallel, the southern chamber holding Yang Can and the northern his wife. Both chambers consist of a door, a front compartment, and a back compartment, and the two are connected by an aisle. On the back wall of the southern chamber is an eye-catching painting called *Gongshitu* ("Picture of Paying Tributes"), which reveals the connections between the central government and the ethnic minorities of the border areas at that time.

Loushan Pass

Loushan Pass, also called Lou Pass or Taiping Pass, is located on Dalou Mountain in Zunyi County, at an altitude of 5,170 feet. Because the pass sits at the border between Zunyi and Tongzi, commanding the route both to Sichuang in the north and to Guizhou and Guangxi in the south, it has always been a strategic point.

In front of the entrance to the Loushan Pass stands a huge screen-like pillar, on which is engraved Mao Zedong's poem "Yi Qin E—Loushan Pass." About a mile from the pass is a cave complex consisting of Zhencang Cave and Guanyin Cave. Within the Loushan Pass Scenic Area are attractions including the Tongzi people in Tianmen Cave, Paleolithic cultural artifacts on Ma'an Mountain, Tongzi Little West Lake, where General Zhang Xueliang was imprisoned, and the Hailongtun ancient pass and ancient battlefield relics. Loushan Pass, with its towering peaks and precipitous cliffs as well as the winding Chuan-Qian highway, is considered the most perilous landscape in northern Guizhou.

Express buses run from Zunyi to the Loushan Pass.

An autumn view of the Miao household. (From CFP)

Even the cloth bags used to carry their babies are made with superb craftsmanship by the Miao women. (From CFP)

Hailongtun Fortress

Hailongtun Fortress, known as Longyantun during the Song and Yuan dynasties, is located east of Longyan Mountain in Taiping, Zunyi County, about 12 miles from the city of Zunyi. The fortress is situated on top of mountains surrounded by steep cliffs and flanked by streams, with only one narrow path at the back of the mountain leading to it, where it is said a single armed man can stop an army. Ancestors of Bozhou Tusi (chieftain) Yang Yinglong took advantage of the topography by building a 3-mile complex of earthen walls and intersecting circular enclosures as well as tall buildings, warehouses, and water prisons. The fortress area consists of nine passes, including Bronze Column, Iron Column, Flying Dragon, Fly Phoenix, Chaotian, and Wan'an; they are connected by walls extending more than 3 miles along the mountain. As China's only extant ancient military fortress, with its grand scale and well-preserved walls and facilities, Hailongtun has become an important resource for studying the Tusi (official title for local chieftains among some ethnic groups in the old days) system and the many passes in the southwestern region.

Chishui River Scenic Area

The Chishui River Scenic Area, located in the north of Guizhou Province adjoining three counties in south Sichuan, is known as the Gate of North Guizhou. It covers an area of 1,900 square miles, including waterfalls, bamboo forests, spiny tree ferns, the Danxia landscape, and rain forests. It also holds the history, culture, and historical artifacts of the Long March, thus constituting a tourist attraction that combines ecology with education and culture. There are 352 streams of various sizes, more than 790 pools, lakes and reservoirs, and numerous waterfalls, which gives Chishui City the appellation "A City with Thousands of Waterfalls." The Shizhangdong Grand Waterfall, 262 feet wide and 250 feet high, is considered the number one tourist attraction in South Sichuan and North Guizhou. Its roar is audible for almost a quarter of a mile. Nearby are vast camellia woods and stretches of azaleas and spiny tree ferns. The Danxia landscape in the Chishui River Scenic Area boasts many unique sites, including Danxiachibi, Guzhaifengji ("Isolated and Narrow Ridges"), Qishanyishi ("Extraordinary Mountains and Rocks"), Yan-

The ample rainfall of the Yungui Plateau helps produce high-quality tea with a strong fragrance and special flavor. Among the most famous brands are Dunyun Maojian, Zunyi Maofeng, Guiyang Yangmaofeng, and Leishan Yinqiucha. In early spring, the tea gardens are filled with busy tea-leaf pickers. (From ImagineChina)

The spiny tree fern may be the only existing ligneous (woody) fern, considered a "living fossil" useful for studying paleontology. The stem stands gracefully upright, with many elegantly spreading fronds at the top. (From Quanjing)

Express buses run from the Chishui Bus Station to Shizhangdong. Be sure to use an umbrella or wear a raincoat while viewing the waterfall to avoid getting soaked.

langdongxue ("Rock Corridors and Caves"), and the Danxia Valley. The spiny tree ferns are another interesting sight in this scenic spot, covering an area of 12 square miles. As the only surviving primitive forest of tree ferns at the same latitude around the globe, the area is called by scientists "the Alsophila spinulosa Kingdom by the Chishui River," the city of Chishui has a history of more than 900 years and contains cultural sites such as stone walls and gates, temples and palaces, and numerous exquisite stone carvings. Historical attractions include many memorial sites of the Chinese Red Army's four passes of the Chishui River.

Nine-Dragon Cave

Nine-Dragon Cave is located on the hillside of Guanyin Mountain along the banks of Malong Creek, 10.5 miles east of Tongren. The cave has the higher Liulong ("Six Dragons") Mountain at its back and the pretty Jinjiang River in front. It is said that on Liulong Mountain there were six yellow dragons that invited the three black dragons in the Jinjiang River to meet in the cave. However, both groups wanted to take the cave as their own and started fighting with each other. At dawn, they coiled to rest on a huge colorful column in the depths of the cave but got trapped forever. There is a creek at the foot of the mountain, where people used to swear at the nine dragons because of their noisy fighting. That is how Jiulongpanzhu ("Nine Dragons Coiling around a Column") and the Malong ("Swearing at Dragons") Creek received their names. Nine-Dragon Cave is 230 feet wide, ranges from 100 to 230 feet high, and is 1.4 miles long, covering a total area of 366,000 square miles. There are seven halls in the cave, three of which are open to tourists.

Take a bus to Jiulongdong, or take a boat along the Jinjiang River.

Fanjing Mountain

Fanjing Mountain is located at the border area of Jiangkou, Yinjiang, and Songtao counties. It covers an area of 219 square miles and is the tallest mountain in the Wuling Range, at 8,440 feet. It was called Sanshangu in ancient times, and later Jiulong Mountain or Yuejing Mountain. Since the Ming Dynasty, it has been called Fanjing Mountain. Its main attractions include Laojingding ("Old Golden Gop"), Jingding ("Golden Top"), Jiulong ("Nine Dragons") Pool, Baiyun ("White Clouds") Temple, and Tianxian ("Fairy") Bridge. The Fanjing Mountain boasts abundant green vegetation and clear water. A series of creeks, known as Ninety-nine Creeks, merges into eleven main streams including the Heiwan River and the Macao River, which in turn form waterfalls. Since the Wanli period of the Ming Dynasty (1573–1620), temples and roads have been built on Fanjing Mountain, which has since become a famous Buddhist mountain equal to the distant Emei Mountain, Wutai Mountain, Putuo Mountain, and Jiuhua Mountain. There are 48 temples and convents on Fanjing Mountain, including Cheng'en Temple, Baoguo Temple, Sakyamuni Hall, and Maitreya Hall. All these make the mountain a sacred place to Buddhists. Over the past several hundred years, an unbroken stream of pilgrims has visited the mountain. Yan Yinlang, Zhao Puchu, and Qigong, among others, left inscriptions here. The Fanjing Mountain is included in the UNESCO International Man and Biosphere Reserve Network.

The nearest railroad station to Fanjing Mountain is at Yuping. From Yuping and Tongren, there is only a narrow road leading to the mountain.

Tourists may lodge at the guesthouse or the temples on the mountaintop in order to watch the cloud sea at sunrise.

For the sake of environmental protection, there is no cableway in the scenic spot. Climbing the more than 7,800 steps presents a significant physical challenge.

It is said that the Mushroom Rock is the essence and symbol of Fanjing Mountain. The huge rock, whose square top is perched upon a thinner rock column, suggests a mushroom. Athough the rock appears likely to collapse at a slight touch, it has stood here at the mountaintop for tens of thousands of years. (From Quanjing)

Dafang Yangchang Natural Bridge

In the town of Yangchang, about 8 miles south in Dafang County in Guizhou, is a natural limestone bridge formed by an enormous mountainous cavern. As measured by geologists, its scale surpasses the Guinness-recorded Gaotun Natural Bridge in Liping, Guizhou. According to experts, the bridge, called Qingxu Cave by the local people, measures 585 feet tall and 346 feet high. Near the bridge, karst landscape features, including stone forests, stalactites, and stone caves, may be seen everywhere. The Dafang County administration is taking active measures to apply for a Guinness World Record for the Dafang Yangchang Natural Bridge and has started to widen the highway from the county to the bridge to facilitate increasing tourism.

Zhijin Cave

Zhijin Cave, originally known as Daji Cave, is the most spectacular limestone cave discovered to date in China. It is located in Zhijin County, Guizhou Province, and has a length of 7.5 miles and an area of more than 27 square miles. The cave contains stalactites, stalagmites, and stone curtains of various shapes and formations; there are also intermittent pools and underground lakes. Also present are more than 120 forms of mineral accumulation and crystals, which are of much scientific value for the study of China's ancient geography and meteorology. Zhijin Cave is divided into many attractions, including Wangyuelou ("Moon Watching Tower"), Talin ("Pagoda Forest"), Nantianmen ("South Heavenly Gate"), Wanshoushang ("Longevity Mountain"), Wangshanhu ("Mountain Watching Lake"), Guanghanggong ("Guanghan Palace"), Xuexianggong ("Xuexiang Palace"), Lingxiaogong ("Lingxiao Palace"), Tiandu Square, and Yinyugong ("Silver Rain Palace").

Zhijin cave (From Colphoto)

Bai-li (One-Hundred-li)

This lovely and extraordinarily beautiful place extends from Jinpo in Qianxi County to Pudi in Dafang County in Guizhou Province. The altitude ranges from 3,600 to 6,950 feet, and the place covers an area of 70 square miles. As the woods extend over 164,000 feet (100 li), they are known as "One-Hundred-li Azalea." Among the most famous sections are the Huangping Ten-li Azalea, Jinpo Section One, Jinpo Section Two, Duizuiyan, and Huadiyan. Blooming between spring and summer, the flowers range from magena to blood red in a wide variety of dark to light shades. (Note: One li roughly equals 1,640 feet.)

Southeast Guizhou has long had the reputation as "the sea of songs and dances." All the ethnic groups here are known as good singers and dancers. Among their colorful dances are the Miao people's Wooden Drum Dance, the solemn Drum-Treading Dance, the simple and lively Lusheng Dance, and the Dong people's Duoye Dance. (From CFP)

Guizhou Style

Ethnic Customs of Southeast Guizhou

Many ethnic groups live in beautiful and rich southeast Guizhou, including the Miao, Dong, Han, Shi, Yao, Zhuang, Buyi, Tujia, and Mulao. Here, the festival ceremonies and amusements, the remarkable folk crafts, and the folk residences that preserve the Tang and Song styles are all distinctive tourist attractions. More than 200 festivals occur every year, including the Miao people's Lusheng Festival, Climbing Festival, Sisters' Festival, Siyuba (April 8) Festival, Chixin ("Eating New Rice") Festival, Dragon Boat Festival, and New Year; the Dong people's New Year, Niren ("Clay Figurine") Festival, Wrestling Festival, Linwang Festival, Sanyuesan (March 3) Song Festival, and Ershiping Song Festival; the Shui people's Duan Festival; and the Yao people's Panwang Festival. All of these festivals showcase the customs and cultures of Southeast Guizhou. Among them, the Chixin Festival is one of the grandest and most solemn festivals of the Miao people, held at the spring equinox. On the first day, guests in festive costumes arrive with gifts and a fighting bull. The second day includes activities such as bullfighting, horse races, and Lusheng dances. The Lusheng Contest on August 15, which is held once every two years, is a popular festival in the Dong region of southern Guizhou. On that day, all ethnic groups near Luoxiang in Congjiang gather at Luoxiang to participate in the grand activity.

The festive costumes of Miao women at the Sisters' Festival in Taijing in southeast Guizhou. (From CFP)

Qian Xiang Handicraft

Hand-Stitching Work

A very ancient craft, Guizhou hand-stitching work has by now enjoyed a long history of more than 500 years. It is a type of embroidery and the techniques used can be categorized into clear stitch and blind stitch. In this craft, different designs can be woven with silk and cotton threads according to the pattern formed by the crossed warp and filling threads of the base cloth. As a result, not only the Miao girls but also girls of the Bouyei, Shui, Dong, and Gelao ethnic groups enjoy this craft very much. Ordinary cotton threads seem to come alive in their skillful hands, and are turned into beautiful flowers, birds, fish and insects or into lovely cows, sheep, cats, and dogs. Nowadays, hand-stitching work has assimilated many modern elements and is being used not only for clothing, but on shawls, bags, and hats. Therefore, it is a great favorite of tourists.

Embroidery

Embroidery is widely used on the national costumes of ethnic groups. Almost every woman in the family here can embroider, and they generally use paper-cut designs as their patterns instead of drawing them on the base cloth. Miao embroidery includes dozens of needle techniques, including plain stitch, split thread stitch, patched stitch, Chinese knot stitch, coiled stitch, plaited stitch, and thread stitch. All these embroidery techniques feature simplicity, elegance, smoothness, and bright color. Embroidery is strongly decorative and its designs have distinct features in different regions.

Miao Silver Ornaments

Miao women's festive attire includes a variety of silver decorations. Categorized

The Tang'an Village in Liping County is the only existing Dong ecological museum in China. From houses on stilts to pathways paved with stone slabs, the primitive Dong features are well preserved. (From CFP company)

according to where they wear the decorations, there are head ornaments, breast ornaments, and back ornaments. Most of the Miao silver ornaments have kept their original appeal. Many reflect Miao beliefs and customs in specific stages of their social and historical development. Silver ornaments from the southeast of Guizhou and the west of Hunan are second to none in terms of craftsmanship. The level of craftsmanship ranges from relatively basic styles to very delicate skillful work. The former includes necklaces, neckbands, and bracelets made in eastern Guizhou including Huangping, Lushan, and Taijiang. Silver jewelry of this kind generally is not elaborately manufactured, but requires a large quantity of silver to make. The purpose of wearing this kind of jewelry is to show off the affluence of the wearer. The more skillful work is very delicately made. The most renowned of this kind include silver flowers, waist lace, feathers, coronal, Lohan, and bells made along the coasts of Qingshui Jiang and Wuyanghe in eastern Guizhou Province, and silver chains, flowers, earrings, neckerchiefs, and silver coronals used for sacrificial ceremonies made in western Hunan Province and northeastern Guizhou Province. The silver coronal made in eastern Guizhou Province is the cream of all silver craftwork. A great variety of silver decorations are welded on a coronal that is not so big, including silver flowers, bells, birds, butterflies, and stickers and weighing about 30 to 40 liangs (equal to 50 grams). Each of these decorations is a work of art.

Di Opera in Anshun

Anshun Di Opera is circulated mainly among the Han villages in the Anshun region. However, as Anshun is a multinational region with people from Han, Miao, and Bouyei ethnic groups living together, different cultures among these ethnic groups intermix. As a result, Di Opera has become widely popular across the whole Anshun area. Reputed as the embodiment of Chinese drama, Anshun Di Opera enjoys great visual and research value. Di Opera used to be called Tiao Shen and was performed to worship the deities and drive away evil. Now it has evolved into a major form of entertainment for the peasants in their leisure time. Whether in a courtyard or in any other spacious place, Di Opera can be performed as long as there is an audience available; no special stage needs to be built. This is what constitutes Di Opera today.

It is worth mentioning that in Di Opera, there are no female performers. Even the female roles in the opera are acted by male performers. (From Colphoto)

When Di Opera is being performed, the players wear tilted-front style long gowns and long trousers in green, blue, and white, with green-colored cloth waistbands, cloth shoes, and four flags on their backs. They also wear a great variety of masks, such as those of ferocious warriors with their eyes glowering, those of brave warriors with flying beards, those of aged warriors with wrinkles on their foreheads, and those of female warriors with smiling, pretty eyes. All the masks are skillfully engraved with vivid facial expressions. Talking and singing play a major part in the performance; dancing appears only when necessary. The actors speak when they are narrating and begin to sing when they are expressing their emotions. Their voices are simple, unsophisticated, heated, and powerful, displaying very distinctive regional features. In this kind of opera, the music is always the same for all roles. Di Opera mainly tells about some famous stories from Chinese history—for example, about Yue Fei's fighting against Jin invaders, the Romance of Three Kingdoms, the Romance of the Sui and Tang Dynasties, and the Yang's Saga. More than

30 traditional plays have been kept up till now, and generally the performance of the traditional plays lasts for several days.

Nuo Culture

Nuo was in ancient times a ritual to greet the deities and dispel ghosts. However, with the passage of time, it became more of a performance for entertainment, with people's working life and some legends beginning to be presented as part of the Nuo ritual. In some places, it even took the form of a kind of drama with very simple and unsophisticated characteristics; this was called Nuo drama. As a kind of historical and cultural phenomenon, Nuo involves a great variety of fields of study, including anthropology, history, philosophy, theology, ethnology, folklore, and literature.

Mask of a ferocious warrior with eyes glowering (From Imagine-China)

Wujiang River Basin (covering the counties of Shiqian, Sinan, Yinjiang, Dejiang, and Yanhe), which lies in the eastern part of Guizhou Province, is a center and a reserve for China's ancient Nuo culture. Inhabitants here include 27 ethnic groups and more than 400 Nuo troupes. Nuo activities here have a distinctive local flavor and are characterized by their lack of sophistication and primitive simplicity. These activities generally cover various aspects of people's daily customs including dispelling misfortune, avoiding disasters, getting rid of evil, augury, curing diseases, praying for children, praying for long life, praying for wealth, and receiving good luck. All these activities are called *Wujiang Nuo* or *Tongren Nuo* culture in the academic community. Nuo activities in the Tongren region are generally held during the slack season for farming, after the autumn harvest each year to the spring ploughing of the next year. A Nuo activity can last seven days and nights at most and a minimum of three days and nights. It usually includes several performing formats like Nuo ritual, Nuo drama, Nuo dancing, and Nuo performance. The performers wear masks while performing. They sing, narrate, jump, somersault, spring, and play at acrobatic fighting in order to express their wishes of sacrifice to their ancestors, praying for blessing and dispelling the evils. The overall performance creates a kind of mysterious and horrible atmosphere that affects the audience greatly. Anshun Di Opera is just one variety of Tongren Nuo culture. The masks used in Tongren Nuo drama have become coveted works of art both at home and abroad.

They sing, narrate, jump, somersault, spring and play acrobatic fighting in order to express their wishes of sacrifice to their ancestors, praying for blessing and dispelling the evils. (From Colphoto)

Xinjiang Uygur Autonomous Region

Geography at a Glance

Xinjiang Uygur Autonomous Region, generally known as Xinjiang, is located in Northwest China, covering an area of 617,632 square miles, about 16.7 percent of the nation's total area. It is the largest in land area among China's provincial regions, with a population of 19.25 million (2000 census). It is a region with the longest border line among the provincial regions, about 3,355 miles.

Xinjiang is situated in the hinterland of Eurasia. It is an important part of the world-famous Silk Road. Xinjiang is surrounded by such lofty mountains as Aertain, Kala Kunlun, Kunlun, and Aerjin. The Tianshan range cuts the whole region into two parts: South Xinjiang and North Xinjiang; the area around Turpan and Hami is called East Xinjiang.

Xinjiang has a typical continental climate, with little rainfall and relatively low moisture. The winters and summers are long; springs and autumns are short. It has a long period of daylight and a huge variation in temperature between daytime and evening. Sometimes the difference is more than 68°F. The saying goes: "In the morning you have to wear fur coats but in the afternoon you have to wear shirts; you can eat watermelons around the stove." North of Tianshan is the frigid-temperate zone and south of the mountain is the warm-temperate zone.

(From Quanjing)

Uygur group's conventional caps (From ImagineChina)

Featured Cuisine

Grape fish, Xinjiang ravioli, mutton kebabs, roasted steamed stuffed bun, flavored mutton chop, roasted sheep, hand-catching rice, Xinjiang noodle, chicken with potato, finger mutton, beef with caladium, stuffed haggis, oil-fried wheaten food, Kuche noodles, crystal noodle soup, Xinjiang chili noodle, grape snow-cock flavored snack, Uygurian barley powder, Uygurian braised moxa, braised sheep sweetbreads.

Featured Commodities

Herbal Medicines:

Ferula, licorice, root of codonopsis pilosula, safflower, snow Saussurea, Xinjiang caladium.

Special Local Products:

Shanshan white grape wine, Jinghe beer flower, Kashi Uygurian hand drums, Kashi Uygurian weather drums, Xinjiang horses.

Local Handicrafts:

Wall rugs, flowered hats, cashmere shirts, Yingjisha knives, Hetian jade stone, Aheqi felt, Hetian carpets, Yining saddles.

Fruits and Delicacies:

Grapes, figs, Badan apricots, mulberries, peaches, pistachios, sea buckthorn, Jiashi sweet melons, Hami melons, Yecheng megranates, Korla pears, Yining apples, Aksu walnuts, Atushi figs, Kuche white apricots.

Notes 

❶ There is a time difference of 2 to 2.5 hours between Xinjiang and Beijing. Urumqi time is 2 hours behind Beijing time, but the rest of the region is on Beijing time. In summer the sun rises at 6:30 or 7:00 a.m. and sets at 10 p.m. Office and business hours are from 10:00 a.m. to 1:00 p.m. and from 4:00 to 7:30 p.m..

❷ In Xinjiang it is considered impolite to stare at the local Uygurian people or their belongings.

Transportation Tips

By Bus

At the boundary of South Xinjiang and Tibet Autonomous Region, the famous Xin-Zang Road (or Qiangtang Road) starts from Yechang County, across the Kunlun range all the way to the Shiquan River and Pulan in the Ali area in Tibet. Travelers often call traveling along this road "traveling to Ali." It is a very long and hard journey, but views along the road may be the most beautiful in the world. It is very expensive to travel along the road. There is no public transportation, and you need to hire a local vehicle and driver. Military vehicles can usually complete the trip in three or four days.

Snow Saussurea is beautiful in shape and considered sacred. Local people believe that if you can drink the dew on top of its leaves, you will be cured of illness and evil things, and thus prolong your life. (From CFP)

By Train

Xinjiang has three important railroads: Lanxin line (from Lanzhou to Urumqi), South Xinjiang line, and the west part of

POPULAR FESTIVALS

The Grape Holiday in Xinjiang

Held annually from August 20 to 26 in Turpan City to celebrate the grape harvest. There are performances of merchant camel caravans, and ethnic dance and song contests.

Laylatul-Bara'ah

Held on August 15 of the Islamic calendar, which is one month from Ramadan. During the day people will fast. Every family makes fried pancakes in advance, so local people also call this day the Holiday of Fried Pancakes. Many families go to their ancestors' tombs to pay respects and take fried pancakes to give them to beggars or to present them to relatives and friends. In the evening people traverse the graveyards until the followiing morning.

Eid al Fitr

Also known as the Festival of Fast-breaking. September of the Islamic calendar is Ramadan, and people eat only before sunrise and after sunset. The daily fasting lasts until after the day of Eid al Fitr, when people have three days of celebration.

Eid ul Adha

Also known as the Festival of Sacrifice. It is held on December 10 of the Islamic calendar, or 70 days after Eid al Fitr. During the holiday Muslims bathe and wear formal clothes to go to the mosques. They also visit relatives and friends, butcher sheep to treat guests, and take part in many kinds of entertainment.

Lanxin line (from Urumqi to Ala Mountain). The famous Euroasia Second Continental Bridge runs through Xinjiang, leaving China at Ala Mountain and ending in the Harbor of Rotterdam in the Netherlands.

By Air

Xinjiang is the most remote area in China; the quickest way in and out of Xinjiang is by air. More than 10 important cities north and south of Tianshan form an air transportation network of Urumqi. Korla has planes flying to many large cities in the country. In Xinjiang there are flights to more than 30 important cities in mainland China.

Recommended Routes

Feature Routes

Six-day tour of ethnic customs on Yining Prairie

Day 1 Arrival in Urumqi. Lodging: Yindu Hotel.

Day 2 Urumqi→Sayram Lake→Yining-Nalati Prairie→Bayanbulak→Nalati-Urumuqi. Lodging: Yindu Hotel.

Day 3 Urumqi→Shihezi→Karamay→Boertala Mongolia Autonomous Prefecture →Tuoli→Sayram Lake→Yining. Lodging: Yili Hotel.

Day 4 Yining→Nalati→Bayanbulak. Lodging: Bayanbulak.

Day 5 Bayanbulak→Nalati. Lodging: Nalati.

Day 6 Nalati→Urumqi. End of tour.

Six-day ecological tour of Kanasi

Day 1 Arrive at Urumqi. Lodging: Yindu Hotel.

Day 2 Urumqi→Buerjin. Lodging: Buerjin.

Day 3 Buerjin→Aletai Prairie→Moon Bay→Lying Dragon Deep Pool→Kanasi Lake. Lodging: cabins.

Day 4 Kanasi Lake→Buerjin. Lodging: Buerjin.

Day 5 Buerjin→Karamay→Urumqi. Lodging: Yindu Hotel.

Day 6 End of tour.

Traditional Routes

Seventeen-day tour of Xinjiang

Day 1 Arrival in Urumqi.

Day 2 Urumqi→Tianshan Mountain Tianchi→Urumqi.

Day 3 Urumqi→Aletai (visit the second largest desert in China—the Guertonggute Desert, Aerte Mountain, Five-Color Bay, Fire-Burning Mountain, and the Gobi Desert.

Day 4 Aletai→Buerjin→Kanasi Lake (visit Keermuqi Stone Statues Tombs, ancient rock drawings, aerolites, Erqisi River, Moon Bay, Lying Dragon Deep Pool, and the Sacred Spring).

Day 5 Kanasi Lake→Karamay (visit the Ghost Town).

Day 6 Karamay→Sayram Lake.

Day 7 Sayram Lake→Fruit Valley→Huoerguosi→Yining (visit Old City of Huiyuan).

Day 8 Yining→Nalati→Gongnaisi Forestry Center→Bayanbulak Prairie.

Day 9 Bayanbulak Prairie→Swan Lake→Kaidu River→Kuche.

Day 10 Kuche→Aksu.

Day 11 Aksu→Kashi (visit Apak Hoja Tomb, carriage ride to East Bridge, and visit Id Kah Mosque).

Day 12 Kashi→Pamir Highland.

Day 13 Tashkurgan County→Hongqilafu Port→Kashi.

Day 14 Kashi→Hetian (visit White Jade River, carpet factories, silk factories, walnut trees, and a thousand miles of the grape corridor)→Luntai.

Day 15 Hetian Luntai (travel through Takla Makan Desert and view Euphrates Poplar, the "hero tree in the desert").

Day 16 Luntai→Bosten Lake→Korla.

Day 17 Turpan→Karez Well→Old City of Jiaohe→Flaming Mountain→Grape Valley→Bezeklik Thousand Buddha Caves →Asitana Tombs→Old City of Gaochang →Sugong Minaret→Urumqi.

Self-Guided Tours

Tour of Pamir Highland

Start from Tashkurgan Tajik Prefecture and end in Urumqi. On the way are Kalakuli riverside, Kashi City, Aksu, Kuche County, Big Dragon Pool, Small Dragon Pool, Nalatidaban, Qiaoerma, Nileke County, Yining City, and Fruit Valley. Major scenic spots include the Stone City, Gonggeer Mountain, Mushitage Summit, Id Kah Mosque, Apak Hoja Tomb, local bazaar, Kizil Thousand-Buddha Grottos, Thousand-Tear Spring, Kizilgaha Beacon Tower, Tianshan Mountain, Bayanbulak Prairie, Nalati Mountain, Yilianhabierga, Tangbulake Prairie, Yining Mosque, Yili Bridge, and Sayram Lake.

Tour of Lop Nor

Start from Urumqi, end in Urumqi. On the way are Camp No. 1 of Kuluketage Mountain, Yadan, Camp No. 2 of Tianshan, Kandier, Turpan, and Urumqi mountains. Major scenic spots include a forest of pillars in the center of Lop Nor Lake, the Tomb of Yu Chunshun, the Old City of Jiaohe, the Flaming Mountain, Grape Valley, Karez Wells, and Ten-Thousand Buddha Hall.

Addresses and Phone Numbers

Yindu Hotel	No. 179, Western Xihong Road, Urumqi	0991-4536688
Royal Hotel	98 Changjiang Road, Urumqi	0991-5855555
Shihezi Hotel	4 East Ring Road, Shihezi	0993-2012587
Garden Hotel of Changji	272 Ningbian East Road, Changji	0994-2363333
Turpan Hotel	2 Youth Road, Turpan	0995-8569100
Bosten Hotel	92 People's West Road, Korla	0996-2022007
Seman Hotel of Kashi	337 Seman Road, Kashi	0998-2582129
Yili Hotel	8 Yingbin Road, Yining	0999-8023126
Hami Hotel	4 Yingbin Road, Hami	0902-2233140
Golden Bridge Hotel of Aletai	No. 2, Cultural Road,Altay	0906-2127566
Boertala Hotel	208 Culture Road, Bole	0909-2313871

Urumqi, Changji Region

Best Time to Travel

It is best to tour scenic spots around Urumqi from July to September. From December to February tourist areas such as the Tianchi have winter sports activities.

Shopping Tips

Erdaoqiao Market in Urumqi has the most ethnic features. Tourists can enjoy all kinds of ethnic handicrafts, souvenirs, music, and clothes, and soak up the local flavor and languages of various ethnic groups.

The Red Mountain

The mountaintop of the Red Mountain looks like a tiger. The cliffs and the violet sand rocks, which appear red in the sunlight, were formed about 2.5 billion years ago. Rising high into the sky in the center of Urumqi City, the mountain has steep cliffs. At sunrise and sunset, the sunlight shines on the cliff, turning everything on the mountain red. The mountain extends east to west, and the summit is almost 3,000 feet above sea level. After many years of forestation, the Red Mountain has been developed into the Red Mountain Garden. At the summit you can get a good view of the whole city. The ruggedness of the mountain and the many legends about it have made it a sacred place, and the Red Mountain has become the symbol of Urumqi.

Museum of Xinjiang Uygur Autonomous

Planned and built in 1953, this museum is on the northwest road in Urumqi. As the storage and research center of cultural artifacts in Xinjiang, it is a large museum decorated with local native architectural styles. The exhibition hall covers an area of 84,000 square feet and houses more than 50,000 historical and ethnic artifacts, along with mementos of the revolution. At present the museum has five basic exhibitions: (1) Ancient Historical Relics, which reflects periods of Xinjiang's historical development. The relics here include well-preserved pottery, fine jade articles, clay figures

Viewing Urumqi from the top of Red Mountain, you can see rows upon rows of buildings . In the distance snow-covered mountains rise loftily into the sky. (From Quanjing)

View of the Red Mountain Garden (From CFP)

of various images, colorful fabric, rare wooden tablets, diversified stoneware, bronzeware, and ironware; (2) Ethnic Customs, which shows visually the customs of different ethnic groups in Xinjiang through architectural art, farming tools, clothes, articles for daily use, and cultural items; (3) Exhibition of Ancient Bodies, where as many as 21 mummies are displayed. Among them are the perfectly preserved "Beauty of Loulan," which is more than 3,800 years old; the Hami female body, which has the European characteristics of the handsome male body in Qumo; the 2,500-year-old mummy of Subeixi; and the mummy of Zhang Xiong, General of the Left Guards in Gaochang in the Tang Dynasty. Also included in the exhibition are the restored ancient tombs and dried, well-preserved articles of food and clothing; (4) Revolutionary Relics and Historical Materials, which gives the history of revolutionaries who gave their lives for the peaceful liberation of Xinjiang; and (5) Saving China's Ancient Machines. Here you can see models of large ancient machines such as Lu Ban's wooden carriages and horses, made more than 1,000 years ago, and Zhuge Liang's wooden oxen and gliding horse. The museum has published several books such as Unearthed Cultural Relics in Xinjiang and The Silk Road.

Tianchi Lake (Heavenly Lake) on Tianshan

Tianchi, also known as "Yao Chi" in ancient times, was a sacred bathing spa for immortals . Situated at the foot of the ice-covered Bogda Peak about 62 miles east of Urumqi, it has an altitude of 6,234 feet. Surrounding the lake are snowy mountains, spruces, and glass-like green water, forming a beautiful landscape. Bogda Peak, with its year-round snow-covered summit, is 12,664 feet above sea level, making it rich in glacial resources. After the snow and ice melt, beautiful ice rivers, ice valleys, ice bridges, ice mushrooms, and ice fountains are formed. Tianchi has three sections: the major lake, the eastern Black Dragon Pool, and the western Jade Beauty Pool. Fifteen hundred feet or so east of the major lake, the Black Dragon Pool is said to be the place where Queen Mother used to bathe, wash, and dress. It is also called "The Gully of Washing and Dressing" or "The Bathing Basin for Immortals." Below the pool is a high cliff, where you can see 3,000-foot waterfalls. The western Jade Beauty Pool is said to be the place where Queen Mother used to wash her feet. The pool looks like a full moon, and the water is clear and deep. On the side of the pool hangs a waterfall, flying all the way down to the ground just like the Milky Way. Such beautiful scenery has attracted many poets and calligraphers who have left poems in praise of the lake over the centuries.

The South Mountain Tourist Area

Situated at the northern foot of Kelawucheng Mountain, a branch range of the North Tianshan, about 37 miles from downtown Urumqi. In this area there are ten large and small valleys running east to west. The area is not only a good natural pasture but also a natural scenic spot where people can spend their summer holidays. Locally the area is known as the South Mountain Pasture. Major scenic spots are scattered in several valleys running north to south in the front of the mountain. From west to east they are West Poplar Valley, Gangou Chrysanthemum Platform, East Poplar Valley, Water-West Valley, Zhaobishan Mountain, Miaoer Valley, and Daxi Valley, covering a total area of 46 square miles. The most famous is the West Poplar Valley, which is around 47 miles from downtown Urumqi. It is situated in the valley between middle and low mountainous regions with an altitude of 7,000 feet, and the annual precipitation measures about 20–23 inches. In the valley you can see snow-covered hills, craggy mountains, tall spruces, and green grass everywhere.

Tianchi Lake has three sections: the major lake, the eastern Black Dragon Pool, and the western Jade Beauty Pool. (From Quanjing)

Shuimogou Valley

Shuimo Valley, three miles northeast of Urumqi, is divided by the Shuimogou River. On both sides of the valley are dancing trees and spurting springs, strewn with ancient temples and pavilions. In 1760, the Kashi girl Apak Hoja bathed in the hot springs of Shuimogou Valley, leaving her legend behind. The hot springs of Shuimogou have been famous ever since. The springs maintain a temperature of 82-86°F year-round; the water contains kalium, natrium, magnesium, zinc, niter, and niton, all of which are helpful in the treatment of arthritis and skin diseases, and can also be drunk as mineral water. Shuimogou Hot Springs, Tangshan Hot Springs in Nanjing, and Huaqingchi Hot Springs in Lintong are the three hot springs in China nearest to cities. As early as the Qing Dynasty, this place has drawn tourists from all

Inside the Old City of Beiting the southern, western, and northern city walls still remain, and the moat around the city has survived the wars. The grand city walls that once reflected on the moat are now in ruins. (From CFP)

over China. There is now an amusement park and recreation area in the outskirts of the valley.

Take Bus 3, 34, or 104 to the site.

The Old City of Beiting

The Old City of Beiting is situated in the town of Beiting, about 7.5 miles north of Jimusaer County. In 640 Tang Taizong set up the Prefecture of Tingzhou in the city; in 702 Wu Zetian established Anxi's Military Viceroy's Office, having jurisdiction over four counties, namely, Jinman, Luntai, Pulei (later called Houting), and Xihai. It was a very important city in the Northern Tang Dynasty; in the Song Dynasty Tingzhou was the site of the Gaochang Uygurian king's court; in theYuan Dynasty Bieshibali Marshall's Mansion was constructed here, and the city remained an important one in the Western Regions. In the fifteenth century, Beiting was destroyed by warfare, and as a result the city is in ruins. The old city has two city walls, the inner wall and the outer wall, looking like the Chinese Character 回 (Hui, meaning "return"). The outer wall has a perimeter of 15,092 feet and is roughly rectangular in shape. The inner wall has a perimeter of about 9,843 feet. Both walls are protected by moats, and the river courses can still be seen today. Inside the Old City many precious cultural relics have been unearthed. Xu Song, archaeologist in the Qing Dynasty, once researched the Tang Dynasty pillars in Jinman City. He concluded that the Old City was the site of Anxi's Military Viceroy's Office in Beiting. After 1949 archaeologists unearthed the bronze official stamp on which is engraved "The Stamp of Pulei Prefecture," bronze lions, earthen animals, Kai Yuan Tong Bao (coins in Tang Dynasty), and many bricks and eave tiles.

Turpan Region

Best Time to Travel

The scenery of Turpan is at its peak from April to October. Grapes are ripe from August to September. During that time tourists not only can enjoy beautiful scenery but also savor delicious grapes and wine.

Sugong Minerat

Sugong Minaret is also known as Imin Minaret. An ancient Islamic minaret with novel structures, it is the largest minaret in Xinjiang and the only Islamic-style minaret among China's more than 100 famous towers. Sugong Minaret is built on an open space about 6,562 feet southeast of Turpan. South of the minaret are the ruins of the Old City of Anle. Sugong Minaret is a huge round minaret built with grayish yellow bricks. It is 144 feet tall, with a base perimeter of 33 feet. The body of the minaret is simple and lively, decreasing in perimeter from bottom to top, with 14 geometrical patterns drawn on the outside. At the center of the minaret is a 72-step staircase, serving as the central column reinforcing the body of the minaret. In Turpan, where wood is rare, this minaret is a prime example of the Islamic style of Uygurian architects. At the entrance of the minaret there are two incised stone pillars with inscriptions in Uygur on one pillar and in Chinese on the other. Sugong Minaret was built in 1778 by the second son of Iminhezhuo, king of Turpan, to commemorate his father's achievements in the unification of China and to show loyalty to the emperor of the Qing Dynasty. There is an observation platform from which much of the area can be seen.

The surface of Sugong Minaret is made of bricks with all kinds of patterns and figures. There is no cornerstone, nor are there supporting wood materials. The top of the minaret is vaulted. (From Quanjing)

Grape Valley

Grape Valley, under the jurisdiction of Grape Town, Turpan, is situated 6 miles from downtown Turpan. It is a valley on the west side of the Flaming Mountain, 5 miles long from south to north. On the west bank of the valley there are steep cliffs that make a natural barrier. The valley is intertwined with grapevines. All around are elegant birch trees, flowers, grasses, and fruit trees. On the gentle slopes farmhouses are scattered. Although it is extremely hot at the foot of the Flaming Mountain, Grape Valley always has a cool breeze. There is an impressive variety of fruit, nut, and shade trees: Peach, apricot, apple, pomegranate, pear, fig, walnut, elms, poplars, willows, and Japanese pagoda trees are seen everywhere in the valley. The valley also produces many fruits and melons and vegetables. Three ethnic groups are native to the valley: the Uygurian, Hui, and Mandarin. The valley has a total population of more than 6,000. There is about 1.5 square miles of cultivated farm land. With 237,000 square feet of vineyards, the valley is worthy of the name, "Home of Grapes." The many varieties of grapes grown here contribute to the fame of its grapes, wine, and raisin harvest.

Fresh grapes are available here during the harvest season. On August 30 every year, a grape festival is held in the valley.

Yarhotto (Ancient City of Jiaohe)

Yarhotto is situated on a 98-foot-high plateau in Yarnaz Valley, about 8 miles west of Turpan. Originally the capital of the state of South Chechi, one of the thirty-six states in the West Regions, this city was built by local Turpan people in the eighth century and later was destroyed in wars. Yarhotto covers an area of about 85,000 square miles, which comprises temples, houses, and government offices. After entering the south gate there is a main road about 1,200 feet long and 33 feet wide, leading directly to the largest temple to the north of the center of the city. On top of the stupa in front of the temple, you can get a panoramic view of the whole city. There are many other temples in the city and an impressive two-story building with the first floor built underground. According to research it is probably the seat of Anxi's Military Viceroy's Office in the Tang Dynasty. The Ancient City of Jiaohe distinguishes itself from other ancient cities due to three features: First, it has only two city gates, the South Gate and the East Gate. The South Gate deteriorated long ago, leaving a huge breach. The East Gate, cut by the cliff, is today nonexistent. Second, the city faces cliffs on three sides, so there was no need for city walls commonly seen in other ancient cities. Third, all the buildings are built with mud and earth, and wood was rarely used.

Flaming Mountain

Flaming Mountain is located on the north edge of Turpan Basin at the foot of Tianshan Mountain. In ancient books it was called "Mountain of Red Rocks." In Uygur it is called *Keziletage,* meaning "Red Mountain." Under the blazing sun the red sandstone rocks glow and hot air curls up like smoke as though

*The Ancient City of Jiaohe is so named because it was built at the conjunction of two rivers (*Jiaohe *in Chinese means "two rivers join together"). The remaining structures in the city were all built in or after the Tang Dynasty. (From Jin Yongjin)*

Legends tell of the Flaming Mountain as a mountain spurting out fire. Because the Flaming Mountain in Turpan is situated in an inland basin and the heat stays in the basin and does not rise easily, it is always very hot there. (From ImagineChina)

the rocks were on fire. The mountain is 322 feet long and 30 feet wide, with an average height of 1,640 feet. The highest peak is near Tuyu Valley in Shanshan County, with an altitude of 2,729 feet above sea level. Flaming Mountain is desolate and is said to be the hottest place in China. In July 1965 the record high temperature was 120°F, with the temperature on the sand hills reaching 180°F.When summer comes, the sun and the movement of hot air make the red mountain look like a flying dragon. As a result of tectonic crustal movements and river erosion, there are many valleys in the middle of the mountain, the major ones being Grape Valley, Peach Valley, Wood Valley, Tuyu Valley, Lianmuqin Valley, and Subo Valley. Trees in the valleys form canopies, rivers murmur, and fruits and melons give off their fragrance, forming a beautiful scene, which is quite different from the hot and desolate Flaming Mountain.

The complicated terrain of Flaming Mountain makes it easy for people to get lost. If you travel alone, do not go too far into the mountain, and we suggest that you hire a local guide for your safety and enjoyment in the dangerous environment.

Bezeklik Thousand-Buddha Caves

Located in Wood Valley in Flaming Mountain, about 30 miles northeast from downtown Turpan. Once known as "Ningrong Caves," they are the earliest caves from the Gaochang period. From the Tang Dynasty through the Yuan Dynasty, caves were continuously built. Until the thirteenth century the caves served as a sacred space for Buddhists in the Turpan area. The remaining caves are mostly expanded or rebuilt from the Xizhou Uygurian period. There are now 77 numbered caves with a total area of more 13,000 square feet, in which there are more than than 40 examples of mural paintings. At the back of Cave 33 there is the mural of "Mourning Disciples and Mourning Monks," the figures still vivid and distinct. There are rare images of the ancient stringed musical instrument, the Xiaohulei, in the mural of "Musicians" in Cave 16. From these paintings people can still see the different appearances of kings, queens, and common people of all walks of life in the ancient Uygurian era, and also the scenes of everyday life. There are also inscriptions in ancient

Uygurian, Chinese, and Persian, which are helpful in the study of ethnic languages and histories, especially the Uygurian language and history.

A little more than 9 miles south of Bezeklik is the Ancient City of Gaochang. Tourists can visit Bezeklik on their way to the Ancient City of Gaochang.

The Ancient City of Gaochang (Kharakhoja)

The Ancient City of Gaochang is situated on the north bank of Aiding Lake, south of the Flaming Mountain more than 25 miles east of Turpan, with an altitude of 164 feet below sea level. It is also called *Yiduhucheng* in Uygurian, meaning "king's city." It used to be the capital of the state of Gaochang, covering a total area of around 4,960 acres, all built with rammed earth. Built in the first century BCE by garrison troops in theWest Han Dynasty, the city has an extremely long history. Once the largest international bazaar and religious center in the West region and one of the printing centers in Asia, it was destroyed in wars in the thirteenth century. The ancient city is grand and magnificent, rectangular in shape and divided into the outer city, the inner city, and a palace complex. The base of the outer walls is 39 feet wide, and the walls are 38 feet high. The whole city has nine gates, with three gates in the south and two on each of the other three corners. At the southwest and southeast corners of the outer city there are the remains of two temples. The site at the southwest corner covers an area of about 108,000 square feet and comprises an arched gate, a courtyard, a lecture hall, a library of sutras, a main hall, and dormitories for monks. In the southeast temple there is a polygonal pagoda and a sacred cave, which is the only place where mural paintings are well preserved. In the north of the inner city there is an unusual square castle, called by local people "Khan's castle." In the palace complex in the north many terraces, each about 13 feet high, are still visible.

The Ancient City of Gaochang is the largest site of ancient cities found in the West region. Legends say that Monk Tang (Xuanzang) preached here. The picture shows donkey-drawn carriages in the Ancient City of Gaochang. (From CFP)

The Ancient City of Gaochang covers a large area with many sightseeing places. Tourists can visit the city in donkey-drawn carriages.

In the middle of the back wall of No. 216 tomb of Asitana Ancient Tombs, there is a group of six mural paintings. From left to right they are tilted jugs, a clay figure, a gold figure, a stone figure, and an earthenware moneybox with no words or paintings on it. The paintings are visual adages. (From CFP)

Ancient Tombs of Asitana

The Ancient Tombs of Asitana are a large group of ancient tombs about 25 miles southeast of Turpan, with an average altitude of 82 feet below sea level and an area of about 4 square miles. The tombs are all chamber tombs with sloping passages, all of which are in the shape of the Chinese character *Jia,* meaning "no. one" or "armor." In front of the chamber is a sloping passage over 33 feet long. The end of the passage is connected to the chamber, which is usually more than 6 feet high in an area of about 43 square feet. The top of the chamber is flat or vaulted. The bodies were placed on the brick beds or simple wooden beds at the back of the chamber. Around the bodies are miniature pavilions, terraces, towers, horses, carriages, honor guards, musical instruments, chess, brushes, ink, grapes, melons, and other fruits. On the back walls of some of the chambers are painted scenes of people, birds, animals, flowers, grasses, mountains, and rivers. More than 10,000 artifacts have been excavated from the tombs and include documents; inscriptions; paintings; clay figures; articles made of pottery, wood, gold, or stone; ancient coins; silk; cotton; and wool articles. The Chinese mummy, which compares in beauty with Egyptian mummies, is also here. The Ancient Tombs of Asitana are a sequestered place where inhabitants of the old city of Gaochang sought peace and quiet after death. Officials, aristocrats, generals, and common folk alike, their graves are all piled together in this arid place, which is about 6 miles in circumference. The Ancient Tombs of Asitana are known worldwide as "the living historical documents of Gaochang."

Karez Wells

Karez Wells are among "the Three Grand Projects in Ancient China," the other two being the Great Wall and Jinghang Grand Canal. In ancient times they were known as the "Well Channel" or the underground canal. Karez Wells are made up of vertical wells, underground channels, ground channels, and small reservoirs. It is an underground channel construction created by farmers to conserve water and irrigate the land. Karez Wells draw underground river water out of the ground, enabling the appearance of many

To construct a Karez Well, it is necessary to dig vertical shafts in the ground at specific intervals, and then an underground channel is dug to connect the bases of these vertical wells. (From ImagineChina)

oases in the dry Turpan area, which was once known as "Fiery State" and "Depot of Wind." In Xinjiang there are about more than 1,600 Karez Wells, mainly in Turpan Basin, Hami, and Hetian, but the majority of these wells are in Turpan. If interconnected, the channels would run 3,000 miles. Turpan is strewn with Karez Wells, which are marvels of ingenious design and intricate construction.

Aiding Lake

Aiding Lake lies at the north foot of Jueluotage Mountain, a little to the south in the hinterland of Turpan Basin. Moon-shaped and calm, Uygurian people also call it *Aiding Kule,* meaning "moonlight lake" or "moon lake." The lake is about 509 feet below sea level, second only to the Dead Sea in Jordan. Aiding Lake is an inland freshwater lake, a product of orogenic or folding movements of the Himalayas. Hard sand clay and salt pan can be found around the lake, and the surrounding area is extremely dry and desolate. Sterile saline swamps encompass the lake basin, and the resulting salt pan on the surface is unique, forming a primitive picture.

Hami Region

Best Time to Travel

The best time to tour Hami is from May to October, when the weather is warm and pleasant and there is a lot of sunlight. You can observe both the planting and the harvesting of local fruits and vegetables..

Tombs of Hami Kings

Also called Mausoleum of Hami Kings, these tombs are in Oleaster Well of Huicheng in the west suburbs of Hami. Covering an area of more than 23 acres, this site has been the mausoleum of local Uygurian feudal for more than 233 years. The Uygurian people call it *Aletongleke,* meaning "the place of gold." In 1709 the family of the King of Hami, Edubeila, was buried here along with later generations of royal family members. The architecture comprises the big tomb, the small tomb, and Id Kah Temple. The big

Kazak herdsmen in Balishen county with their flocks and tents. (From Quanjing)

tomb holds the remains of King Boxier, the seventh Islamic king, his wife, and concubine. The structure combines Buddhist style, with rectangular and round shapes, and Islamic style, with a round top and a rectangular base. The impressive tomb is 584 feet high, covering an area of more than 16,000 square feet. The small tomb is south of the big tomb. Originally there were five wooden pavilion-like tombs, but only the east and the west ones remain, both being tombs of Uygurian kings. Based on the Islamic-style vaults and incorporating Chinese-style octagonal spires and Mongolian helmet-top wooden structures, the east and west wooden tombs are spectacular examples of Islamic mausoleum construction in Xinjiang.

Id Kah Mosque is on the left side of the big tomb and was built during the Uygurian King Edubeila's reign. It now covers an area of about 25,000 square feet and can hold 5,000 worshippers. The ceiling of the mosque is supported by 108 carved wooden columns. The four walls are decorated by patterns of flowers and grasses and verses from the Koran in ancient languages. It is the largest mosque in the Hami area.

The four corners of the Big Tomb of Hami Kings have round columns with ceramic veneers. Square in shape with the vault at the center, the whole building is made of green glazed bricks and ceramic bricks with blue and green flower patterns against a white background, making the tomb very beautiful not only in structure but also in color. (From Quanjing)

> There are two Id Kah Mosques in Xinjiang, one in Hami, the other in Kashi. The Id Kah Mosque is open to the public only on Eid al Fitr and Eid ul Adha when Muslims are allowed to worship there.

Gaisi Mazar (Tomb of Gaisi)

Also known as Tomb of the Saint and the Green Tomb, the Tomb of Gaisi is situated on a mesa southwest of Dayingmen in Hami. It is the burial place of Gaisi, an Arab missionary in the early Tang Dynasty. Gaisi had traveled to China to promote cultural exchanges between China and foreign countries. He died in China due to fatigue on the way. The tomb is 72 feet long from east to west and 39 feet wide from south to north, with a height of 49 feet. The tomb is rectangular at the base, the top is round and vaulted, covered by green glazed bricks. The veranda is supported by 24 wooden columns, with flying eaves at the four corners. The magnificent tomb is a combination of Arabic-style and Chinese-style architecture. On the top of the mesa are silks, satins, and rugs presented by pilgrims from all over the world. On the walls are glass frames and brocaded curtains. Inside the hall there are lections of the Koran on the white wall. As the body of an outstanding

Islamic sage is buried here, the place has become an important holy site for Islamic pilgrims.

Wubao Ancient Tombs

Situated about 46 miles southwest of Hami, covering an area of about 1,930 square feet, these tombs were built in the later Neolithic period, about 2,900 to 3,200 years ago. With such a low altitude, it is very dry here with almost no rainfall at all. Since they were discovered in 1978, the tombs have been excavated three times and 113 tombs have been restored. The tombs are arranged in order densely. The three ancient bodies unearthed here still have intact clothes, their flesh is still elastic, their eyebrows remain, their eyes are not sunken, and they have golden hair. They are of great interest to historians, archeologists, and tourists.

Hami Tianshan Scenic Spot

This lovely area is on the north slope of East Tianshan Mountain. It spreads to the Valley of Cold Air in the east, the Pond of Pine Trees in the west, the Temple of Tianshan in the south, and to the Hill of Sounding Sands in the north, with a total area of 46 square miles. It is about 43 miles from the city of Hami. In the scenic area there are not only lofty mountains, immense forests, and dynamic prairies stretching to the horizon but also the desertlike Hill of Sounding Sands, which is one of the four famous hills of its kind in China. The ingenious arrangements of Nature have turned the place into a colorful picture, making this a prime vista for tourists.

Prairies, wheel tracks, tree shadows, blue sky, and sunset present a serene portrait of Hami countryside. (From Quanjing)

Near Balishen Lake at the north foot of Tianshan in Hami, there are about 20 ancient beacon towers. They played an important role in military vigils and mail delivery on the Silk Road. (From Quanjing)

Hetian Region

Best Time to Travel

From March to April flowers blossom during the warmth of spring. It is when Hetian is most beautiful.

Yuetegan Site

This ancient site is situated in the village of Yuetegan of the town of Bageqi, Hetian County, 8 miles from Hetian, covering about 4 square miles. The entire area points to an important tribal site in ancient Hetian, but at present no traces of buildings can be seen at the site, and the contours of the city are not clear. At the northeastern corner of the site there is an exposed cultural layer, where pottery fragments are scattered. All of the unearthed cultural ruins have been from this layer, which is more than 16 feet deep. Christian gold pieces, crosses, and a gold medal have also been found, which indicates that Christian missionaries were once in the area.

There are no railroads in Hetian. Airplanes or long-distance buses are the only public transportation options in the area.

Uygurian family silk businesses in Hetian are prosperous. Even the old can use traditional handmade tools adeptly. (From Colphoto)

In the shadowed Grape Corridor, life takes on a poetic beauty. (From Jin Yongji)

Ancient City of Malikewate

Located about 15.5 miles southwest of the city of Hetian, these ruins stretch 32,808 feet from south to north and 6,552 feet from east to west. Built 1,500–1,600 years ago, the city contains not only ancient tombs but also groups of ancient architecture. At the back of the sand hill on the west side of the site are three eroded and mysterious caves.

Grape Road of a Thousand Miles

This is not really a road but a grape corridor built on the sides of channels by Uygurian farmers to protect farmlands and fight erosion from wind and sand. With a total length of more than 4,856 feet, equivalent to the distance from Beijing to Changsha, the Grape Road is an interesting and picturesque area.

Talimu River

Talimu River, also called the Reinless Horse, is the longest inland river in China, with a total length of 3.5 miles. It is a convergence of Akusu River, Yeerqiang River and Hetian River, covering a drainage area of about 1,354 miles. The river empties into Taitema Lake. The rate of flow of Talimu River varies from season to season. When the snow and ice begin to melt in summer, causing the rate of flow to increase dramatically, the river is like a reinless horse, galloping on the ancient deserts and prairies.

On the river is a concrete bridge, with a total length of slightly less than a mile. There are many irrigation facilities built by the hard work of a wide diversity of people, which have turned the deserts into farmlands. The two sides of Talimu River have become prosperous with fruitful orchards, fertile land, and rice fields.

In the river basin there is the only forest reserve of primitive Euphrates poplar in the world. The poplar trees here account for one-tenth of the total number in the world. Situated in the hinterland of Takla Makan Desert south of Luntai, with an area of about 1,274 square miles, the reserve has become a natural barrier of the Talimu River.

Euphrates poplar is the only tree in the desert hinterland of Central Asia. Practically indestructible, the tree is resistant to heat, cold, wind, sand, alkali, and draught, and will grow in infertile soil or sand. Part of the willow family, it is one of the oldest and most primitive trees in the world. The shape of its leaves changes in the process of growing. The Euphrates poplar blossoms in May, and the seeds ripen in August, when the ice melts and rivers overflow. At that point the seeds float along with the water and burgeon very quickly on wet lands. Patches of young trees help change the structure of soil by stabilizing and elevating river banks and forcing overflowing water

(From Jiang Yuhui)

to change course and irrigate other patches of young trees.

Although Euphrates poplars live in inland arid areas, they are not dry plants by nature. They need two kinds of water: surface water to help their seeds sprout, and underground water to help them grow. The always changing Talimu River properly meets the demand and reinforces their particular growth pattern. If underground water is rich, the trees grow vigorously. They can reach as high as 98 feet or more. Local people call them "Three Thousand Years," meaning "for one thousand years they do not perish, for one thousand years they do not fall, for one thousand years they do not decay." For thousands of years the trees have formed a great green wall about 1,000 miles long running east to west between the Takla Makan Desert and the Kuluke Desert. They help protect the surrounding ecological environment and stabilize the invading sands of Takla Makan Desert, creating living space for people. As a result the Xinjiang people call Talimu River the "mother river." Zhang Qian, Xuan Zang, Marco Polo, Xu Xuake, and Sven Hedin all traveled through the river basin of Talimu River and saw the Euphrates poplars.

According to ancient records, Euphrates poplar groves were so thick that it was almost impossible for people to walk through. Many wild animals, such as red deer, wolves, camels, and Xinjiang tigers lived in the forest. This "Green Corridor" was important on the famous Silk Road and also a strategic path connecting the hinterland and Xinjiang. Its importance in missionary work and trade made it the junction of such ancient cultures as China, India, Persia (Iran), and Greece.

Euphrates poplars are not only a protector of desert ecology but also a legendary natural sight and spiritual treasure.

(From ImagineChina)

(From Quanjing)

Aksu Region

Best Time to Travel

It is cool year-round in Aksu, and from August to September the area takes on the trappings of a summer resort.

Kizil Thousand-Buddha Grottos

Found in the cliffs on the northern bank of Muzhati River in Kizil, Baicheng County, Aksu, and Xinjiang, the grottos are among the four famous ones in China. The grottoes were first built in the later Han Dynasty, and construction work continued for more than 500 years, reaching its height in the sixth and seventh centuries. The grottos are distributed in the Guxi, Gunei, Gudong, and Houshan areas, stretching for nearly two miles. In the 236 caves that have been numbered, there are rare buildings, sculptures, and mural paintings, the murals covering an area of about 108,000 square feet . Most of the murals depict stories about Jataka and the missionary work of Hinayana. Unique in design, the figures are painted with iron wire outlining water colors, producing vivid characters.

Near Kizil Thousand-Buddha Grottoes there is a mineral spring.

The murals of Kizil Thousand-Buddhist Caves. (From Colphoto)

Kizil Gaha Grottoes

Kizil Gaha Grottoes are situated about 7 miles west of Kuche City. In Uygurian *kizil* means "girl" while *gaha* means "living place." Originally there was a Han beacon tower not far away from the grottos in which the daughter of a king of that time had lived. Thus the grottos were called Kizil Gaha. There are many magnificent murals, most of them depicting Buddhas, such as Sakyanumi, his disciples, officials in heaven, musicians, flights to heaven, patrons, Jataka, and Buddhist stories.

Subashi Buddhist Temple

Also called the Grand Zhaoguli Temple, the Subashi Buddhist Temple is situated on the south foot of Molana Queerdage Mountain, 14

The east part of the Subashi Buddhist Temple is built into the side of the mountains. Inside the temple stupas and houses are all made of mud bricks. From the ruins of towers and other buildings people can imagine the wondrousness of the temple in those days. (From CFP)

miles northeast of Keche. Built in the Wei and Jin periods, this is the largest temple site discovered so far in Xinjiang. The temple is divided into the east part and the west part, with a total area of almost 46 acres. The east part backs into the mountains. The temple is centered around stupas, and in the temple there are ruins of temples, monks' dormitories, caves, stupas, and halls. Cultural relics unearthed include articles of bronze, iron, pottery, and wood; murals; and clay figures. In addition to the other excavated relics, wood chips and scraps of paper, on which words are written in ancient ethnic languages, have also been found.

Eshiding Mazar (Tomb)

Also known as the tomb of Molana Hezhuo, this tomb is between the new city and the old city of Kuche County. "Molana" means the offspring of saints. According to legends, Eshiding was an ancestor of Islam coming from the West, who came to Kuche to preach Islam during the time of Emperor Lizong of the Song Dynasty (1224–1264). In the mausoleum there is a temple complex, which comprises the temple gate, the temple proper, the door of the coffin chamber, and the chamber itself, all decorated with green glazed bricks. The temple is typical of Islamic style architectures, beautiful and impressive. Below the west eave of the temple is a plaque on which is written "Saint from the Holy Land," inscribed by Li Fan in 1881.

Landscape of Aksu-kashi (From CFP)

Kashi Region

Best Time to Travel

Kashi is the most remote city in Xinjiang, but there is decent and convenient transportation to and within the area. March to November is the best time to visit.

Id Kah Mosque

Id Kah Mosque, in the center of Kashi City, is an impressive Islamic structure more than 500 years old. The mosque comprises the worship hall, preaching hall, gate towers, water pools, and other auxiliary buildings. It is 459 feet long from south to north, 394 feet from east to west, with a total area of around 180,883 square feet. The ruler of Kashgar, Shakesimierzha, built a mosque here in 1442. After many restorations and repairs in later dynasties it developed into its present shape and size. The main hall of the mosque is more than 525 feet long and 53 feet wide. The eaves are extensive, with more than 100 patterned wooden columns supporting the ceiling, which displays many fine wood carvings and colorful patterns of flowers. The gate of the mosque is made of yellow bricks with plaster in the cracks. On both sides of the gate are round brick columns half embedded in the walls, each about 59 feet high. On the tops of the columns are little towers; at dawn every morning the imam calls the faithful to worship. There is a pool surrounded by pottery jugs in the tree-shaded court for worshippers to bathe their hands and feet before and after prayers.

In front of Id Kah Mosque devout Muslims flood into the mosque. The worship hall in the mosque can hold 4,000 people. (From Quanjing)

Women are not allowed to enter the mosque. Tourists must remove their socks and shoes before entering the mosque. If visitors want to take photos, they must ask the permission of the imam . Take care not to disturb the worshippers or call attention to yourself. It's a good idea to arrive at the Id Kah Square before 7 a.m. so that you can choose a place to take photos at the top of the shopping mall at the right of the square.

Apak Hoja Tomb

Also called Xiang Fei Tomb, this is the mausoleum of an Islamic saint's family. It was first built around 1640, about 3 miles northeast of Kashi. It is said that there may be at least 72 people from five generations of the same family. From the first generation is Yusuf Hoja, the famous Islamic mis-

The main building of Apak Hoja Tomb , in which there are 58 large and small graves, is in typical Islamic-style architecture. (From Quanjing)

sionary. After he died his eldest son, Apak Hoja, took over his father's mission work and was buried here after his death. Because he was more famous than his father, people began to call the mausoleum "Apak Hoja Mazar" (mausoleum of Apak Hoja). The tomb is made up of a group of impressive buildings. The mausoleum is the largest of the group at 85 feet high, with its base 128 feet long. The top is round, with a diameter of 56 feet. The outside of the mausoleum is covered with green glazed bricks. The hall of the tomb is wide and tall, without any supporting columns, and inside the tomb is a platform about half a man's height, decorated with white glazed bricks with orchid patterns, on which the graves are arranged. The large chapel is in the west of the tomb where religious services are held. The small chapel and the gate tower are the two outer structures containing extremely fine murals and brick-carved patterns. Among the descendents of Apak Hoja, there was a certain Yiparhan, granddaughter of Apak Hoja, who was a favorite concubine of a Qing Dynasty emperor, Qian Long. Because Yiparhan often wore perfume of oleaster flowers, people called her "Xiang Fei" (the Fragrant Concubine). After she died she was buried in the Eastern Royal Tombs of Qing Dynasty in Zunhua County of Hebei Province. To commemorate Xiang Fei, Uygurians later called the place "Xiang Fei Tomb."

> There is no bus from downtown Kashi City. Tourists will need to take a taxi.

Three Buddha Caves

Called Tuokuziwujila Buddha Caves by local people, these caves are on the cliffs of the riverbanks of Qiakemake River in the village of Takuti, about 9 miles southwest of Atushi. The caves comprise the east cave, the central cave, and the west cave, all built in the Han Dynasty. The three caves are parallel to each other; each of them is more than 6 feet high and more than 3 feet wide. The entrances are rectangular like doorframes, and each cave has both front and back chambers. The front chamber is about 13 feet long and about 8 feet high. The back chamber is half the size of the front one. Mural paintings in the central cave have not been preserved. There was once a Buddha sculpture in the middle of the back chamber, but it has been destroyed. Inside the west cave the stone texture has been exposed and the walls are densely covered by chisel marks. Inside the east cave precious murals and ceilings have been preserved intact. More than 70 Buddhist figures, different in size, are scattered throughout. At the top of the ceilings is a lotus, around which are painted 20-inch-high sitting Buddha figures. The figures are different in shape and appear lifelike. In the back chamber there is a painting of a standing Buddha, whose upper body is naked, with the right hand at the waist and the left hand drooping. Its robe is unique, with the lower body decorated by horizontal strokes of green, blue, and red, rare in Buddhist figure paintings. According to initial research, the caves are at least 1,800 years old and may be the earliest Buddhist cave ruins in western China after Buddhism was introduced into China in the Han Dynasty, with a history of at least 1,800 years.

Mahmud Kashighari Mazar

On the mesa near Cheshixia Zular in Wupar, Shufu County, 28 miles southwest of Kashi, there is a simple adobe mausoleum among the green trees. This is the tomb of Mahmud Kashighari (1008–1105), a famous Uygurian linguist. After many years of study, he compiled the first Turk dictionary in Arabic in 1076. The dictionary included a rich variety of words, with precise structure and distinct entries, which can be called an encyclopedia of the Turk people. To the east of the mausoleum is a mosque, in which Muslim tourists and local villagers can worship. To the north of the mausoleum is a room holding cultural relics, the Turk dictionary, and various books and materials about Mahmud Kashighari's life and deeds. In front of the mausoleum there is a spring, beside which there is a small grove of ancient poplar trees, creating a lovely and serene resting spot.

An old man in Kashi (From ImagineChina)

Xinjiang is a multicultural area with distinct ethnic customs and practices. The picture shows Uzbeks playing native musical instruments. (From ImagineChina)

In the south suburb of Kashi is the mausoleum of another Uygurian scholar from the mid-eleventh century, Yusuf Has Hacib. His epic poem, Kutadgu Bilig, written in ancient Uygurian, has been translated into many languages.

Pamir Ice Peak

Once called the Ridge of Shallot, Pamir Ice Peak is now known as "the Ridge of the World." Since 1870 Pamir has been the homeland and pasturing area of Chinese Tajiks and Kirks.

The mountains on Pamir are spectacular. There are many famous ice peaks in the Tianshan range, such as the highest snow mountain in the east, Bogda Ice Peak, and the snow-covered Mushitage Mountain. With an altitude of 24,757 feet, the mountain is called the Father of Ice Peaks.

Mushitage Mountain is famous for hiking and mountain-climbing. At the foot of the mountain there are strange hills and stones, flowers and grasses, fountains, hot springs, lakes, and pastures everywhere. Ruins of ancient cultural relics such as the Stone City and the Castle of the Princess are scattered among the towering ice peaks. Tourists can enjoy the beautiful view of several sunrises and sunsets in a single day, hear local legends about the ice peaks, and learn about ethnic customs.

Tourists should be aware that they can hire camels only from the Office of Mountain-Climbing to go from Subashi Crossing to Mushitage Mountain. However, it is much less expensive to hire donkeys from local Kirks.

Bayin'guoleng Region

Best Time to Travel

May to early June is the optimal time to visit the swan protection area.

Iron Gate Pass

Iron Gate Pass, in the rugged Kuluketage Mountain, is about 5 miles north of Korla City. More than 2,000 years ago the Silk Road ran from here along the Peacock River into an 18.5-mile-long valley and was a strategic passage on the ancient Silk Road. There has been a pass here since the Jin Dynasty. Because of the difficulty of access, it is called Iron Gate Pass and is among the 26 famous passes in ancient China. In the past Iron Gate Pass has seen many battles and skirmishes to control the area; ruins of passing armies can still be found at mountainsides near the pass. Today, dams and reservoirs have been built at Iron Gate Valley. Part of the rough area of the Silk Road has been submerged in large stretches of water, and the new hydroelectric power station carries electricity to many different places. In the valley trees are green, flowers are blooming; and pavilions, terraces, and towers are scattered everywhere. Opposite the pass on the Ridge of the Princess stand the tombs of Tayier and his lover. Iron Gate Pass has seen centuries of history. In 60 BCE Prince Rizhuof Xiongnu

Mushitage Mountain is covered by clouds and fogs all year, making it difficult to photograph . (From CFP)

led 12,000 soldiers out of the pass to surrender to the Han Dynasty, which led to the unification of the south and north of the Tianshan Mountain. Ever since people of different ethnicities in the Western regions have been liberated from the slave system of Xiongnu, and the Western regions have officially fallen under Han Dynasty's jurisdiction. Iron Gate Pass is a historical monument of national reconciliation.

Bayanbulak Swan Protection Area

Bayanbulak Swan Protection Area is located in a basin in Zhuletusi Mountain on Bayanbulak Prairie, at 6,500-8,000 feet above the sea level. The swan reserve is a highland lake with an area of more than 116 square miles. Around the lake there stretches snow ridges and towering ice peaks, forming the natural barriers of the lake.

Bayanbulak Swan Protection Area is a nature preserve for swans. (From CFP)

Spring water, rivulets, and melting snow all converge into the lake. At the lakeside the grass is lush and the air is cool and moist. When spring comes, ice and snow melt, and everything comes back to life. Large flocks of swans fly across lofty and precipitous peaks from India and the south of Africa to Swan Lake to mate and raise their young. The water, sunlight, clouds, and swans form a beautiful picture. According to research, there are more than just whooper swans, tundra swans, and mute swans here. Ten or more different species of rare birds, such as gray geese, bar-headed geese, white-headed snipes, terns, eagles, and vultures also make this spot their resting or mating ground. Inside the protection area observation towers are built especially for tourists to watch the life cycle of the swans and other water birds.

From May to June is the time when swans mate, hatch eggs, and nestlings are born. During this time the lake is filled with wild birds and is a paradise for birdwatchers. Be aware that the swans are a protected species and should not be disturbed.

On the Bayanbulak Prairie surrounded by mountains, there are thousands of acres of green grass. Herds of cows and sheep are seen everywhere. Snowy mountains and ice peaks loom on the horizon. Together they form a spectacular natural landscape. (From Quanjing)

Every April more than ten kinds of rare birds fly from the south to Swan Lake. They migrate in September. Some swans and other water birds remain, and tourists can see them year-round. On the clear surface the white shadows of swans, set off by the snowy mountains and ice peaks, make a lovely scene. (From ImagineChina)

Lop Nor

Lop Nor is a lake in the northeast of Ruoqiang County with an altitude of 2,600 feet and covering an area of more than 1,158 square miles. It is famous for being at the communication center of the ancient Silk Road to the east of Talimu Basin. In ancient times the rivers of Tianshan, Kunlun, and Aerjin mountain ranges fed incessantly into the low areas of Lop, forming Lop Nor. As a result of its special geographical location, the area often changes. In the fourth century the once water-rich Loulan, west of Lop Nor, began to enact laws to limit the use of water. Toward the end of the Qing Dynasty when the water of Lop Nor swelled, the lake was 80–90 miles long from east to west, 2 or 3 miles long from south to north. In 1921 the Talimu River changed course to run east into Lop Nor. By the 1950s the lake covered an area of more than 772 square miles. Due to the influence and interference of human economic activities, the lower reaches of the Talimu and Peacock rivers dried up in the 1960s, cutting off the source of Lop Nor. Because the lake is landbound with no outlet, in 1972 the lake finally dried up, and the base of the lake became white, salty ground. Trees around the lake withered and died. The lower reaches of the Talimu and Peacock rivers are now sandy, salty marshes. In 1964 China staged its first nuclear bomb here; since then the lake has become a nuclear test site.

Loulan Ruins

This ancient site is about 4,5 miles west of Lop Nor in Ruoqiang County, on the south bank of the Peacock River. The ruins are scattered in Yadan on the west bank of Lop Nor. The kingdom of Loulan once was one of the 36 kingdoms in the Western regions in the Western Han Dynasty. In early days, the city of Loulan was the political, economic, and cultural center of the kingdom. To its east is Dunhuang, to the northwest are Yanqi and Weili, and to the southwest are Ruoqiang and Quwei. The ancient Silk Road is divided into the south road and the north road here in Loulan. As a communication center in the hinterland, Loulan has played a very important role in cultural exchanges between the East and the West. The once-prosperous kingdom, including the city of Loulan, suddenly disappeared in the desert around the fourth and fifth centuries. Even today no one knows the reason for its sudden disappearance. However, the Ancient City of Luntai, the ruins of Quwei, ancient tomb groups, mummies, and ancient rock drawings attract the attention of people all over the world. Cultural relics unearthed in Loulan have astonished the world. Among them is the precious handwritten copy of Stratagems of the Warring States in the Jin Dynasty. Archaeologists have also excavated a female mummy in Loulan (the Beauty of Loulan), which is about 3,800 years old. Other artifacts include fine brocades from the Han Dynasty, Five-Zhu coins of the Han Dynasty, money of the Guishuang kingdom, money from the Tang Dynasty, and broken tablets in Chinese and Qulu.

The remaining city walls in the east and west of the city of Loulan are about 13 feet high and 26 feet wide. The walls were tamped out of loess; the fences in residential areas were made by bundling reeds together or weaving wickers and applying clay to them. The houses were all made of wood, and the columns made of Euphrates poplars. All of the doors and windows of the houses can still be clearly seen. (From CFP)

Loulan Ruins are designated as a national relic protection zone. Tourists can not go there alone but must contact in advance local travel agencies and relics protections offices.

Bosten Lake

Bosten Lake was called the West Sea in ancient times. In the Tang Dynasty it was called the Sea of Fishes. It got its present name in mid-Qin Dynasty. Situated in Bohu County southeast of the Yanqi Basin, it is the largest inland freshwater lake in China. *Bosten* means "standing" in Mogolian because three mountains stand high into the sky in the lake center. Bosten Lake is about 9 miles from Bohu County, with an altitude of nearly 3,500 feet. It is 34 miles long from east to west and 15.5 miles wide from south to north, roughly rectangular in shape. The big lake covers an area of 381 square miles; the small lake has a total area of about 93 square miles. The lake is rich in reeds. With more than 15 square miles of reeds, the lake is one of the four largest reed areas in China. The wetlands with reeds, snowy mountains, lake water, oases, deserts, rare birds, and animals form a colorful landscape.

In the Aerjin nature reserve in Bayinguoleng, wild animals lend a solemn and stirring color to the sunset in the distance. (From Quanjing)

Golden Beach Resort

Golden Beach Resort is 14 miles south of National Highway 314 in Wushitala Town, Heshuo County, Bayinguoleng Mongolia Autonomous Prefecture, Xinjiang. It is 224 miles from Urumqi. Situated on the northeast bank of Bosten Lake, the resort has a beautiful white sand beach, and the lake water is crystal clear and pure. With a shoreline of more than a mile long and about 525 feet wide, the beach is a perfect resort, known locally as "Hawaii in Xinjiang." Tourists can see Bosten Lake stretching to the horizon.

Tourist facilities in Golden Beach Resort are first rate. There are many kinds of recreational activities, such as fishing, rowing, diving, aquatic parachuting, swimming, aquatic sports, archery, tennis, horse racing, and beach volleyball.

Yili Region

Best Time to Travel

July to September is the best time to tour Yili. During that time the fields are green, the flowers are blooming, and all kinds of fruits, vegetables, and melons are available in the markets.

Shopping Tips

Huoerguosi Port, about 12 miles west of Huocheng in Yili, is a place worth visiting. Connecting China and Kazakhstan, the port is very active in trade. If you have time and want to buy authentic foreign goods, this is the place to go. Huoerguosi Port, Hongqilafu in Kashi, and Alataw Pass are three open ports of Xinjiang. However, tourists need a border permit to go to Huoerguosi.

Grand Uygurian Temple in Yining

The Grand Uygurian Temple in Yining is situated on the East Xinhua Road in Yining. Construction of the temple was started in 1760 and finished in 1781. The temple was originally known as Ninggu Temple, and later as Phoenix Temple, Grand Temple in Shanxi, Grand Temple in Shangan, and Kengkeng Temple. It has always been the place where Muslims hold religious services. Originally the temple had an area of about 65,000 square feet, but after more than 200 years of wind and rain, it has shrunk to about 30,000 square feet. The Grand Uygurian Temple in Yining is typical of the style of classical halls in Central China. There is also an Arabic-Islamic-style element, making it impressive yet plain. In the 1911 Revolution, the temple

The view of the evening sun setting over the long river is radiant and magnificent. (From CFP)

was an important place for revolutionaries in Yining to gather. After 1911, patriotic Uygurian people built a private elementary school inside the temple to promote the new culture.

Yining, the capital of Yili, has no railroads. There is a local airport in the city, which has daily flights. The flights take about an hour and a half. There are buses going from Yining to other parts of Yili prefecture, but it takes more than 12 hours to go to Urumqi.

Blessed with a favorable climate, Yili has many beautiful scenic spots. (From Jing Yongji)

Fiery Dragon Cave

Fiery Dragon Cave is situated on the hills 12 miles northwest of the city of Yining. As underground coals burn year-round, the place is rich in terrestrial heat. Hot air often erupts out of the ground, thus the name of Fiery Dragon Cave. Mineral-rich hot water flows out of the cracks in rocks, making this place a veritable health spa for curing chronic diseases, such as skin diseases and rheumatoid arthritis. In 1972 the hospital of Fiery Dragon Cave was established in the town of Bayandai, where the cave is located. The buildings of the treatment area are built according to the distribution of hot air in caves and geysers. On the walls inside the cave there are epigraphs in different languages from many successive periods. Some people have even canonized the cave, tying cloth prayer strips of different colors at the entrance of the cave.

Sudan Waisi Han Mazar

In the town of Mazar on the north side of Aburele Mountain east of Yining County, there is a mausoleum covering about 17 acres. There stands an ancient Chinese pavilion-like structure, which is Sudan Waisi Han Mazar. *Sudan* is the transliteration of Arabic words, meaning “emperor” or “king.” *Waisi* is the offspring of Genghis Khan, and *Mazar* means the mausoleum of feudal aristocrats among Islamic followers. Facing south, Waisi Han Mazar is erect and tall. The first, second, and third tiers are rectangular, with drooping eaves in the four corners. The fourth tier is hexagonal, with rising eaves in the four corners. The mausoleum is a classical pavilion-like structure with Chinese ethnical features among the many famous Islamic mausoleums in Xinjiang. The hexagonal top of the mausoleum is covered with colored glazed tiles. Constructed of wood and earth, the mausoleum has 12 columns supporting the eaves at the base, with a vaulted top. The windows on both sides are round and latticed. At the center of the windows there are Arabic poems. Around the pavilion there are many old trees, some more than 100 years old. About 66 feet northwest of Waisi Han Mazar is an earthen tomb, said to be the tomb of Waisi's mother. At the west side inside the wall, there is a grand mosque, adding a religious atmosphere to this historic site.

Huiyuan Bell Tower

Huiyuan Bell Tower stands at the center of the ancient city of Huiyuan, which was one of the "Nine Cities of Yili" built in the Qing Dynasty. Situated to the southeast of Huocheng County in Yili Kazak Autonomous Prefecture, the city is divided into the new section and the old one. The old city was built near the north bank of Yili River in 1763 but suffered severe flooding. In 1871, when Russia invaded Yili, the old city was demolished. In 1882, when Yili was reoccupied by Qin troops, another new city was built about 46 miles north of the old one. Among the "Nine Cities of Yili" the ancient city of Huiyuan is the most intact one with a perimeter of about 4 miles. At the center of the city a three-tier bell tower was built in 1897. With flying eaves and painted columns, the tower is magnificent and remains intact today. It is said that the tower is a replica of the Drum Tower in Beijing.

God-Blessed Temple

God-blessed Temple is set on the river side of the Hongnahai River at the foot of Tianshan Mountain, northwest of Zhaosu County, covering an area of about 21,500 square feet. It is the only Mongolian lamaist temple that has been preserved relatively intact in Xinjiang. The large temple has a quiet and solemn atmosphere. First built in the late

Green prairies, blue rivers, white glaciers, and the immense Tianshan form the very beautiful natural scenery in Xinjiang. (From Quanjing)

The ingenious design and superb technique of Kazak handicrafts show the intelligence and skills of the Kazak nationality. (From CFP)

Qing Dynasty, the buildings have been severely damaged due to lack of repair and adverse climate. At present only eight buildings remain. Inside the temple ancient trees rise high into the sky; pines and firs block out the sun. Looking along the axis, eight buildings are placed symmetrically, and along this same axis are the shining wall, the main gate, the front hall, the main hall, the back hall, the left and right halls, the side hall, and an octagonal two-story, double-eaved pavilion. The Grand Hall is the main structure of God-blessed Temple. The hall is 56 feet wide, with seven bays, square at the base, with steep tops. The flying eaves in the four corners are like dragons stretching their heads into the sea. The square wooden blocks between the tops of columns and the crossbeams are supported by layers of horizontal beams. This gold-plated building, richly decorated, looks natural and peaceful, yet sumptuous. The eaves of the hall are supported by giant columns, on which are painted rare birds and animals, such as phoenixes, lions, tigers, and kylins all in different postures. On the facing wall of the Grand Hall are mural paintings in traditional Chinese style, such as two dragons teasing a ball, Jiang Ziya fishing, and Su Wu shepherding sheep.

> Most of the exquisitely embroidered curtains and flags in the hall are from Tibet.

Site of General of Yili□s Mansion

Historically many towns have been built in Yili to guard the border and promote trade, as geographically Yili has been an important pass connecting the hinterland and Central Asia. To enhance administration in Yili area, Emperor Qianlong of the Qing Dynasty appointed a general of Yili, built the city of Huiyuan, and later built around it eight satellite cities—Huining, Suiding, Guangren, Ningyuan, Zhande, Gongchen, Xi, and Taerqi. Together they are called the "Nine Cities of Yili." The Yili general's mansion was built in the city of Huiyuan, which had once been a military and political center in western China, and the mansion, with its main gate, halls, corridors, and general's pavilion, retains a lingering charm. At the center of the ancient city of Huiyuan is a tall and impressive bell tower. From the top of the tower, visitors can have a panoramic view of the whole city.

Tuheilutiemuerhan Mazar (Mausoleum of King Tuheilutiemuer)

This impressive vaulted mausoleum is situated in the east suburb of Alimale, northeast of Huocheng County. Tuheilutiemuerhan, a legendary king of Chagatai Khanate, is the

Fine Kazak handicrafts are purely handmade by skilled craftsmen. (From CFP)

seventh-generation descendent of Genghis Khan. In 1346 the 16-year-old Tuheilutiemuerhan was king of Mengwuersitan. He embraced Islam at the age of 18. In 1352 he forced the 160,000 Mongolians under his rule to convert to Islam, thus promoting the spread of Islam in Xinjiang. In March 1360, he waged a war to unify the Hezhong area. He succeeded in temporarily unifying Chagatai Khanate. In 1363 Tuheilutiemuerhan died and was buried here. The main gate of the burial hall of the mausoleum faces east; the front walls are covered with 26 kinds of glazed bricks of violet, blue, and white, on which are carved various geometrical patterns. The uppermost part of the gate is covered with blue glazed bricks, with embedded eulogies in Arabic. The whole structure is both immense and simple, magnificent and graceful. Inside the hall there are no supporting columns, with four empty walls, and there are stairs leading to the top level. Tuheilutiemuerhan Mazar is the oldest Islamic-style architecture in Xinjiang. Parallel to the mausoleum is a vaulted mausoleum, smaller in size, said to be the mausoleum of the younger sister of Tuheilutiemuerhan. Tuheilutiemuerhan Mazar has become a place for many Muslims to worship.

Fruit Valley Scenic Spot

This area got its name from the many wild apples growing in the valley. The view is pleasant and unique. For a long time it has been considered a tourist resort in Xinjiang, with a reputation as the most beautiful sight in Yili. The valley runs 17 miles through North Tianshan Mountain. Once a strategic section of the northern Silk Road connecting China with Central Asia and Europe, it is still an important part of Urumqi-Yili Main Road. When Genghis Khan began to conquer the west, he ordered hills to be chiseled, roads made, and bridges built. The mountain roads are twisting and rough south of Pine Head, but they are the most difficult part of the valley. A waterfall pours from the mountains down into the valley, like white silk hanging in the sky, looking very spectacular. In Fruit Valley the climate is cool, and the view is very beautiful, with lofty mountains,

Scenery of Fruit Valley in Yili (From ImagineChina)

Snow Mountains, glaciers, primitive forests, prairies, rivers, and lakes form the beautiful scenery of Kanasi Lake. (From Jin Yongji)

flourishing trees, colorful flowers, spurting wells, and plunging waterfalls. When Lin Zexu was banished to Xinjiang, he could not help but marvel at the beauty of Fruit Valley when flowers blossomed in summer. He said: "It is like being in the valley of ten thousand flowers."

> To go from Yiling to Fruit Valley, tourists can take buses first to Reed Valley and walk from there.

Huoerguosi Port

Huoerguosi Port is in Huocheng County, bordering Alamutu Prefecture in Kazakhstan. It is 56 miles from Yining, the capital city of Yili Kazak Autonomous Prefecture and more than 400 miles from Urumqi. The "New Silk Road" freeway, begun in August 2006, connects Xinjiang with the port and so far has the largest amount of traffic in West China. There is an enormous market for Chinese and Kazak inhabitants of border areas to trade at the port, with its 6,500 residents and a daily floating population of around ten thousand. The port imports and exports 500,000 tons of goods a year on average. Huoerguosi Port is in the middle of the second Eurasia Continental Bridge. It is richly endowed with diversity in geography, ethnicity, languages, and customs. Transit trade through the port with Europe has the advantage of shorter distances, lower expenses, and shorter turnover time. With the deepening of China's reform and the implementation of the strategy of developing the West, Huoerguosi will become an important corridor linking China's six eastern provinces with the rest of the world.

Kanasi Lake

Kanasi Lake is a highland lake in the forests of the Aertai Mountain and is situated in Buerjin County, more than 164 miles northwest of Aletai. *Kanasi* means "lake in the valley"in Mongolian. With an altitude of 4,508 feet above sea level, the lake covers an area of about 18 square miles. The total area of the nature reserve around it is more than 2,000 square miles. Surrounding the lake are lofty snow-covered peaks, but on the lakeside green trees grow surrounded by colorful butterflies. In the lake area there are many lovely trees of Siberian origin, such as larches, cedars, spruces, and firs, in addition to hundreds of birch trees. Known trees include 798 species of 298 genera, belonging to 83 families. Also in the lake area there are 39 types of animals, 117 types of fish, and 4 types of reptiles. In the lake there are 7 different kinds of fish and more than 300 kinds of insects. It is the only complete preserve of animals and plants of south Siberian origin. In the lake there is a particular kind of large fish, the Hucho taimen, which local people call "lake monster." Kanasi Lake can also change its color several times a day, sometimes green, sometimes blue, sometimes gray, and sometimes milky white. Near craggy cliffs on the east bank of Kanasi Lake there are sarsen stones (a hard sandstone) hundreds of feet long. Besides the T-shaped scratches made by glaciers, there are rock paintings, petroglyphs, and carvings made by ancient nomads.

> Tourists need to have a border permit to visit Kanasi Lake. It is easy to obtain one, but you must remember to bring photos and secure identification. Tourists can stay for the night in the vacation villas by the lake, but it might prove more exciting and interesting to stay in the nearby village yurts.

The red fox, living on Nalati Prairie in Yili, with its fiery coat, adds lively color to the long, wide, green prairie. (From CFP)

Yili River

This famous river irrigates farmlands in the northwest. It originates from the western part of the Tianshan range in Xinjiang, running more than 249 miles inside China and covering a total drainage area of about 138 acres. It has the largest amount of water among all rivers in Xinjiang, with its runoff about one-fifth of the total. In the upper reaches are the Tekesi, Gongnaisi, and Kashi rivers. The Tekesi, originating from the north side of Hantenggeli Peak, is the major source of water in the upper reaches of Yili. The river runs west to Yining. After the Kashi joins , the river runs onto the wide plains in the valley. The resulting riverbed is extremely wide due to

Sheep are the livestock of choice in Xinjiang. Yili, with its wide and fertile Yili riverbed, provides sheep with ample, lush grass in north Xinjiang, making it a famous sheep-raising area in China. (From CFP)

Ice- or snow-covered mountains and peaks, vast prairies and plains, and scattered herds and flocks create a poetic scenery that arouses people's yearnings and imagination. (From Quanjing)

the confluence of so many tributaries. After joining the Huoerguosi River, the Yili flows into the territory of Kazakhstan and finally into the lake of Baerkashi. The middle and lower reaches of the Yili River are stable and slow, making the area from Yama Ferry to the borderline inside China open to steamships. Near Yining, the riverbed is more than a half-mile wide. There are many beaches, cays, and isles, where the scenery is beautiful and the air is cool. The large riverside park is a wonderful place for recreation.

> Sunset over the Yili River is a lovely view. Since there is a two-hour time difference between Xinjiang and Beijing, the best time to watch sunset is from 8 to 9 p.m.

Sayram Lake

Sayram Lake is in the mountain basin in the western part of Tianshan in the city of Bole, Xinjiang. In Mongolian it is called *Sayramzhuoer,* meaning "the lake on the ridge of mountains." The lake is about 19 miles from east to west, and 12 miles from south to north, covering an area of 176 square miles. With an altitude of 6,801 feet, it is one of the highland lakes in Xinjiang. Sayram Lake, together with the hilly countries and forests around it, has become a famous tourist attraction.

Every year when winter comes, snow falls down onto the surface of the lake, and the water freezes. Surrounded by ice mountains and snow fields, the slightly oval lake adds a trace of spring to them. When summer comes, flowers blossom and grass spreads on the lakeside. The far-flung prairies are dotted with tents; smoke from kitchen chimneys wave in the wind; flocks and herds graze in large numbers. The picturesque Sayram Lake is the largest base of aquatic products in the prefecture. Every July on the lakeside prairie people celebrate Nadamu, making the lake even more beautiful. When the natural scenery mingles with the happy atmosphere of the holiday, there are many beautiful things to enjoy.

On the lakeside there are prairie cabins, which offer tourists a taste of nomadic life. However, modern conveniences are rare here.

Ghost Town

Ghost Town is situated on the Gobi Desert east of Zhungeer Basin, about 62 miles from Karamay, with an altitude of 1,148 feet in an area of about 39 square miles. Due to its peculiar wind-eroded features the city is also called the Town of Wind. Whenever the wind blows, yellow sand flies all over the landscape. Flying sand and stones rage in the town, making sad and shrill sounds, just like the crying of ghosts and the howling of wolves, causing some people to tremble with fear. In Mongolian it is called *Sulumuhake,* and in Kazak it is *Shayitankeerxi,* both meaning "a ghost-haunted place." But when the sun rises the next morning, Ghost Town becomes quiet and peaceful in the sunshine, looking extremely beautiful and totally different from the scary atmosphere in the night. In Ghost Town there is a strange-looking hill that appears to be the ruins of an ancient castle. On the left side of the hill stand two huge rocks, one big, one small, both looking like old castles and gate towers. The hill changes daily: When the morning sun shines, it looks like a warrior wrapped by rays of morning sunshine; when the sun rises higher, it looks like an old grandfather wearing a bamboo hat. Due to diastrophism or tectonic distortion, the surface of Ghost Town is strange and abrupt. Rich in petroleum and natural asphalt, the place is a gold mine for economic and tourist-related development.

Listening to the sound of wind and birds in the night in Ghost Town is a thrilling experience.

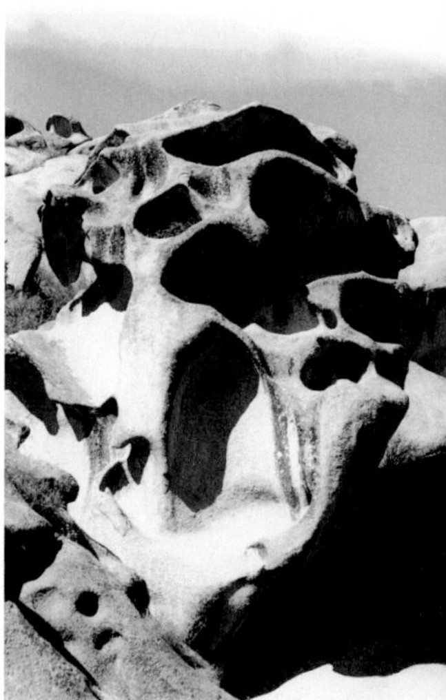

Valley of Strange Rocks is a mountainous place, made of granite. Years of wind and water have made the otherwise common rocks into bizarre shapes. (From CFP)

Valley of Strange Rocks

Also known as the Ravine of Strange Rocks, this site is in the mountainous area, about 30 miles northeast of downtown Bole. Covering an area of about 38 square miles, the valley is home to a rare group of enormous rocks, famous for their often bizarre shapes. Some of them look like peacocks spreading their tails to display their fine feathers; some like elephants drinking water; some like ancient castles, pavilions, or Buddhist caves. The strange yet beautiful scenery was formed by thousands of years of wind and water erosion and earthquakes. Tourists visit and reflect on the extraordinary creativity of nature.

Marxirp is a very popular folk drama of the Uygur people as well as their favorite recreational activity. (From ImagineChina)

Xinjiang Style

Dolan Dance

Dolan dance originated from Maigaiti County on the western edge of Taklimakan Desert, which was called Dolan in ancient times. Until now, Uygur people still insist that they are Dolan people, who are famous for Dolan dance.

Ancient Uygurs living in the Tarim Basin used to have a high level of music and dance. Dolan dance evolved by absorbing the merits of these ancient arts. Most Dolan dances reflect hunting activities of ancient people in primeval forests to demonstrate their wisdom and bravery in the fight against dangers from nature. This is where the Dolan dance differs from other large-scale folk dances. Almost all Dolan people of all ages can perform the dance. The movement and posture of Dolan dance is natural, unrestrained, and vigorous. With a clear style, it excites and inspires people. People tend to dance all night until the singer's voice cracks, the musician's finger bleeds, and the dancer passes out. The festive atmosphere remains in the participant's memory forever.

Performance of Aken

For nomadic Kazakstan people on the grassland, horses are an integral part of their lives; so are their songs, which have a distinctive style. Every summer, Kazakstan people (those that can sing songs and compose poetry) will stage an Aken concert on the picturesque meadow. The loud and sonorous voice of singers and the beautiful melody of

Performance of Aken (From CFP)

Chasing girl (From CFP)

tambouras echo on the grassland day and night. Spontaneous composition is the most brilliant talent of Aken singers and musicians. Most of them can compose songs instantly to express their feelings about what they see. Lyrics of Aken songs are an accurate reflection of the generous character of Kazakstan people and the development of the grassland near Tianshan Mountain.

Chasing Girl

"Chasing girl" is a popular recreational activity of the Kazakstan people, as well as a means for them to express their love to each other. In the activity, a young man and a young woman ride their horses for a distance. On their way, no matter how often the young man tells or plays jokes or expresses his love for the girl, the girl may not get mad at him. Upon arriving at the end point, the young man will turn around and dash back, while the girl will chase and whip him. The embarrassed appearance of the young people often provokes the loud laughter of the audience. If the girl shows mercy to the young man or even makes glances at him, it is very likely that she is in love with him.

Sheep Grabbing

Sheep grabbing is a competitive sport event on horseback that requires bravery, a strong mind, and wit. Kazakstan people hold the event to pray for blessing. Participants are divided into two teams. After a prayer ritual, the event master will slaughter a two-year-old white lamb, cut off its head and trotters, fasten its esophagus, and place it on the open grassland. When the competition starts, all riders will rush to the lamb and scramble for it in a crowd. The final winner will get the spoil and dash out of the competition field to the applause of all. He will also roast the lamb on the spot and invite everyone to share it. The meat is named "meat of fortune."

Kashi Grand Bazaar

The bazaar is the window and guide to the oasis civilization. Its principal function, of course, is economic exchange. In Uygur, bazaar means "trade fair," which is very popular in areas densely inhabited by Uygur people. The Grand Bazaar at the east gate of Kashi is the largest international trade market in the northwestern area of China. Kashi was a famous historic and cultural city as well as commodity trade center on the ancient Silk Road. At that time, merchants from Xi'an, whether they traveled along the southern or northern routes of Tianshan Mountain, met there. With a history of over 2000 years, Grand Bazaar is known as the largest trade fair in Asia. It now includes over 5000 stands with more than 100,000 visitors and nearly 10,000 commodities traded every day.

Xinjiang Hand-Drum

Xinjiang Hand-Drum, or Dapu in Uygur, is the most common percussion instrument in Uygur music. It is round, 25–40 inches in diameter and 9–12 inches in height. With its frame made of mulberry wood or satin walnut and decorated with patterns, gems, and colorful jade, the drum is very beautiful and flamboyant. In the frame are many small copper plates and iron rings. One side of the drum is covered by sheep or donkey hide. The performer hits the

Xinjiang Hand-Drum (From CFP)

drum alternately with both hands. Generally, musicians hit the center of the drum with their right hands to make the "dong" sound as the ictus and hit the drum's edge with their left hands to make the "da" sound as the off beat. Hitting the drum edge with both hands produces uninterrupted sounds.

Marxirp

Marxirp is a very popular folk drama of the Uygur people as well as their favorite recreational activity. It is a form of recreational art that integrates song and dance. Marxirp has no limit to the number of participants and is usually held on holidays or in the evening, when people gather together for singing, dancing, playing different kinds of musical instruments. and performing acrobatics and magic. Everyone can step on the stage to perform his program. The content, form, and scale of Marxirp vary from area to area. In Kashi and Yili areas, for example, there are different kinds of Marxirps: Marxirp held alternately by people in the same neighborhoods, seasonal outdoor trips to regional Marxirps, and Marxirps for girls and women. Marxirp has a long history. According to historical records, the ancient Turki hosted evening parties and feasts in the winter, called Suoerqiuke and Suhediti.

Atlas silk (From CFP)

Atlas Silk

In Uygur, atlas means bandhnu. Using the ancient Chinese bandhnu craft, it is a silk-making technique with a long history of over 2000 years. Atlas silk is tender, light, and elegant and has very flamboyant colors and a rich variety of patterns. In Xinjiang Uygur Autonomous Region, particularly in the southern part of Xinjiang, the silk is popular among local people. The atlas silk workshop in Jiya, Luopu County produces high quality products using the most ancient production techniques.

Food

Nang

Nang is a type of round pancake that can be preserved for a long period of time. Like Mantou in north China, cooked rice in south China, and bread in the west, nang is the principal food in families of people native to the Xinjiang Uygur Autonomous Region. Local people can live without vegetables, but never without nang, which is an evidence of the importance of the food in the daily life of the Uygur people. Roasted nang has a history of over 2000 years. Archaeologists have unearthed nang in ancient burial mounds. There are currently dozens of types of nang. The most common one, about 12–13 inches in diameter, is thin and crispy. Another type of nang, as large as a bowl, is thick and soft. Depending on its ingredients, Nang can also be divided into fat nang, wowo nang, sesame nang, meat nang, and sliced nang. People eat different nangs on different occasions. Wowo nang, sliced nang, and fat nang, for example, are the most common food in daily lives, while the stuffed meat nang is the most popular type among local people. Roasted nang, with yellow surface and delicious and crispy taste, is also favored by many.

Grabbed Rice

Grabbed rice, or bonuo in Uygur, is a delicious dish with a unique local flavor. Uygur, Ozbek, and other ethnic groups often feast on this with their guests. Ingredients of grabbed rice include fresh mutton, carrot, onion, vegetable oil, mutton fat, and rice. Cooked rice is a great appeal for one's eyes, nose, and appetite. During festivals and on the occasion of weddings or funerals, grabbed rice is an indispensable dish served in Uygur families. Some families have now introduced the Han practice of using spoons at meals.

Roast Mutton

Roast mutton in Turpan is as famous as Beijing roast duck. To make roast mutton, people need to slaughter, skin, and gut a wether of high grade, remove its trotters, insert through it a stick with a long embedded iron nail, and put it in a sealed pit to roast it.

Xinjiang Pasta

Xinjiang pasta is made by pulling rather than rolling or pressing dough. Both stir-fried noodle and mixed noodle in Xinjiang are made of it.

Kebab

Kebab is a kind of snack with unique flavor. Well-made kebab is golden yellow and shiny with fat. It is tender, slightly spicy, delicious, and free of sheepy odor or too much grease.

Oily Pyramid

Just as its name implies, oily pyramid is a kind of pyramid-shaped wheat. It is one of the favorite foods of Uygur people. Oily pyramid is white and shiny with fat. The wheat sheet is as thin as paper and there are many layers. It is oily yet not too greasy, soft and savory yet not sticky.

Thin-Skin Stuffed Bun

Thin-skin stuffed bun is also known as *Piteermanda* in Uygur, meaning "stuffed bun made of unleavened dough." It features thin skin, tender meat, and oily stuffing. With a flavor of onion, it is very tasty.

Rice-filled lungs and rice-filled sausages both are made of guts of sheep. They are chewy, savory, and have unique flavor.

Nang (From CFP)

Qinghai

Geography at a Glance

Qinghai Province ("Qing" for short) is in northwest China and situated in the northeast part of the Tibetan Plateau at the headwaters of three rivers: the Yangtze, the Yellow, and the Lancang. Qinghai has an area of 278,881 square miles and a total population of 5,180,000 (2000 census). The earliest inhabitants in Qinghai were the Qiang people, but now Qinghai has become a multicultural area. Major ethnic groups include Tibetan, Hui, Tu, Sara, Mongolian, and Kazak. The major religions are Tibetan Buddhism and Islam.

Sitting on the "roof of the world," Qinghai's altitude ranges from 9,842 feet to 22,507 feet above sea level. Most of the summits of major mountain ranges are more than 14,000 feet high. In the southwest there is the rugged Tanggula Mountain; in the north and the northeast there are the Aerjin and Qilian Mountains. Kunlun Mountain, with an average altitude of 18,000 feet, is the major part of the Qinghai mountain range. In Qinghai there are numerous rivers and more than 2,000 large and small lakes, covering a total area of 5,276 square miles.

Because Qinghai is in the highlands and away from the coast, it has a cold and dry climate. Temperature and rainfall vary from area to area. Winters are cold and long; summers are cool but short.

(From Quanjing)

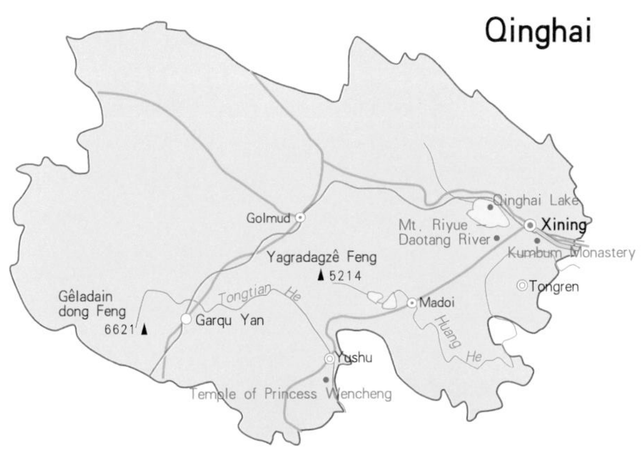

Wedding of the Tu ethnic group in Qinghai (From ImagineChina)

Featured Cuisine

Mutton kebabs, mutton sweetbreads, rangpier, wheat kernel rice, ma shi'er, handmade slices of wheat flour, cold jelly, cold noodle, ox tendon, crystal noodle soup, sheep tendon with ginseng, sweetbread soup, sweet unstrained spirits, ghee glutinous rice cake, beef jerky, dried fish.

Featured Commodities

Special Local Products

Strong Huangyuan vinegar, Huzhu wine, barley wine, black sheepskin, Huhuang fish, gem stones, and jade.

Local Handicrafts

Kha-btags, Tibetan pulu, Tibetan horse boots, plaited yak tails, silver ornaments, fur clothes, rugs and textiles.

Transportation Tips

By Bus

The road network in Qinghai Province is centered around the city of Xining. There are no direct routes between many smaller places. The coaches are mainly medium-sized microbuses and large tourist buses, which are often poorly equipped. If tourists want to take a self-guided car tour of Qinghai, they should be aware of some areas with frozen ground, such as Kekexili. In summer the roads turn to mud and can trap cars easily.

Notes 

❶ In places where prefecture or county governments are situated, Mandarin Chinese is spoken. On the prairies and in Tibet, the majority of Mongolian and Tibetan herdsmen speak their own languages and dialects. It is a good idea to hire a multilingual tour guide for these outlying areas.

❷ Be aware that the high altitude in some areas of Qinghai may cause breathing difficulties and "mountain sickness."

❸ Tourists should carry cold remedies, inhalers, and extra-warm clothing for traveling in this mountainous area.

By Train

There are trains every day from Xining to other cities in the country. It is also convenient to take trains from Xining to other places in Qinghai Province.

By Plane

There are not many flighs in Qinghai Province, but Xining has direct flights to Beijing, Shanghai, Xi'an, Guangzhou, Urumqi, Chengdu, Shenyang, and Lhasa. Geermu City has flights to Xining, Xi'an, and Lhasa.

Recommended Routes

Classical Routes

11-day tour of Tibetan Horse Race in Yushu

Held in the vast Jiegu pastureland between July 25 and August 1 each year, this Yushu

POPULAR FESTIVALS

The Festival of Happiness

In mid-June, flowers blossom on the prairies, the sheep are fat, and the milk is fresh. At this time the Festival of Happiness, a traditional pageant, takes place. People put on new clothes, bring food, and set up tents on the prairies or in the forests. There are also other activities such as horse racing and traditional antiphonal singing.

Dragon Boat Festival

During this holiday the Tibetan people do not do farm work. It is a time to buy new clothes, picnic in the woods or the fields, and gather together to drink and sing in antiphonal style. The favorite food during this festival is cold noodles.

Horse Racing In Qinghai

Held in summer and autumn.

Holiday of Singing and Dancing on the Prairie

Held in summer and autumn.

Eid ul Adha

Held on December 10 of the Islamic calendar. There is an 11-day difference between the Gregorian calendar and the Islamic calendar,so it's best to check with your tour guide for the correct day.

Ramadan

Celebrated on October 1 of the Islamic calendar.

Nadam Fair

Held from July to August.

Fasting and Happy Days

The 8th and 29th or 30th every month of the lunar calendar; the first half month of January (lunar month), when Sakyamuni defeated opponents in debates; February 7 or 15 of the traditional lunar calendar, the birthday of Sakyamuni; March 15 of the traditional Chinese calendar, when Sakyamuni first preached Esoteric Buddhism; April 15, the day when Sakynamuni's mother became pregnant; October 25, when Tsongkapa (a Buddhist master living from 1357 to 1419) died.

horse race is the most celebrated Tibetan festival in Qinghai.

Day 1 Arrival in Xining. Add a full stop. Lodging: Qinghai Hotel.

Day 2 Xining→Ta'er Temple→Sun-Moon Mountain→Qinghai Lake. Lodging: tent hostel

Day 3 Qinghai Lake→Maduo County. Lodging: rest house of Maduo.

Day 4 Maduo County (headstream of the Yellow River)→Yushu. Lodging: Yushu Hotel.

Day 5-7 Yushu Horse Race. Lodging: Yushu Hotel.

Day 8 Jiegu Temple→Xinzhai Sutra Stone Heap→Temple of Wencheng Princess → Celestial Burial Platform. Lodging: Yushu Hotel.

Day 9-10 Yushu→Xining. Lodging: Qinghai Hotel.

Day 11 Leave Xining.

10-day tour of mysterious Qinghai-Tibet Plateau

Day 1 Arrival in Xining.

Day 2 Ta'er Temple→Sun-Moon Mountain→Visiting Tibetan families. Lodging: Chaka Hotel.

Day 3 Qinghai Lake→Birds Heaven Island. Lodging: Birds Heaven Island Hotel.

Day 4 Chaka Salt Lake→Gobi. Lodging: Goermu Hotel.

Day 5 Snowy Mountains→The highest bridge across the Yangtze River. Lodging: tent.

Day 6 Hot Well→Snowy Mountains along Tanggula mountain range. Lodging: Dongxiong Hotel.

Day 7 Yangba Well→Lhasa. Lodging: Kailasi Hotel.

Day 8 Potala Palace→Dazhao Temple→Luobulinka→Bajiao Street. Lodging: Kailasi Hotel.

Day 9 Sela Temple→Zhebang Temple. Lodging: Kailasi Hotel.

Day 10 Leave Lhasa.

Traditional Routes

8-day tour of Qinghai

Day 1 Arrival in Xining.

Day 2 Ta'er Temple→North Zen Temple.

Day 3 Sun-Moon Mountain→Visiting Tibetan families→Sandy Island.

Day 4 Qinghai Lake→Birds Heaven Island.

Day 5 Treasure Coast pastureland → mosque.

Day 6 Kanbula Forest→Wind-eroded landform in Danxia→Nun's Temple.

Day 7 Visiting Tu community.

Day 8 Leave Xining.

Regong art (From CFP)

Addresses and Phone Numbers 

Qinghai Hotel	158 Huanghe Road, Xining	0971-6144888-31/24/48
Huaqiao Building	30 North Street, Xining	0971-8231888
Beifu Hotel	40 Wusi Street, Xining	0971-6155666
Xiadu Holiday Inn	19 Xinning Road, Xining	0971-6128777-6288/6298
People Hotel	2 Dongda Street, Xining	0971-8225951
Jianyin Hotel	55 West Street, Xining	0971-8261886
Goermu Hotel	43 Kunlun Road, Goermu	0979-8424298
Zongge Hotel	57 Yingbin Road, Huangzhong	0971-2236761
Yushu Hotel	10 Mingzhu Road Jiegu Town, Yushu	0976-8822999

4-day tour of Qinghai

Day 1 Arrival in Xining.

Day 2 Ta'er Temple→Sun-Moon Mountain→Qinghai Lake.

Day 3 Birds Heaven Island→Treasure Coast Pastureland in Haiyan.

Day 4 Wild animal safari from Xining.

Once part of the sea, Chaka Salt Lake sits on the largest plateau of the world, the Tibetan Plateau. (From CFP)

Self-Guided Tours

Going on a pilgrimage

Start from Xining, Qinghai and end in Xiahe, Gansu. Along the route are Tibetan Buddhist temples as well as other scenic sights, including North Zen Temple, Ta'er Temple, Ancient City of Gui De, Yuhuang Mansion, Kanbula National Park, Nanzong Temple, Nun's Temple, former residence of 10th Panchan lama, Jiezi Mosque, Camel Spring, Longwu Temple, Wutun Temple, Guomari Temple, and Laboleng Temple.

A drive on the "roof of the world"

One can make an adventurous drive along the 1,200-mile route from Xining to Lhasa. Views along this route are world famous and should not be missed. Recommended sights include Ta'er Temple, Sun-Moon Mountain, Qinghai Lake, Chaka Salt Lake, Shell Mountain, Charhan Salt Lake, glaciers, Kekexili, headstream of Yangtze River, and Potala Palace.

Xining, Huangnan Region

Best Time to Travel

The cool summer in Xining is a perfect time to visit; June through September is usually the prime tourist season.

Shopping Tips

Among the various local specialties, the best ones are spiced dried beef, cashmere sweaters, and wild oat wine.

Guchengtai Market, Commercial Lane Market, and Dongtian Market are the finest markets in the city. Local specialties are also available in the Hualian supermarket.

Ta'er Temple

Located in the suburban area southwest of Xining City, Ta'er Temple is the religious center of northwest China. It is among the six largest temples of Lamaism, and also the birthplace of Zonggeba, founder of Shamanism. It is in his honor that the temple was built in 1569. The buildings are a combination of cultural works of both Hans and Tibetan. The most famous artworks in the temple are ghee flower, murals, and barbola (delicate flowers and other decorative clay oranaments).

The Lama pagodas in Ta'er Temple are quite different in style from other Buddhist pagodas commonly seen in China. (From Liu Liwen)

The main shrine in Ta'er Temple is the Grand Golden Temple. After a generous donation from a local lord in 1711, the temple was re-decorated with gold-plated tiles and has been known since as the Grand Golden Temple. The most impressive building in the temple is a hall with 108 sculptured pillars and thousands of small golden Buddha on the walls. A wondrous and magical moment in this hall occurs when more than 2,000 lamas chant sutra together. Check with your travel guide for the time when this will take place. The five huge cauldrons in the kitchen used for cooking tea and rice during religious events are 5–8.5 feet in diameter.

> Take a direct bus from the bus terminal at Xiguan Avenue to Ta'er Temple.

Dongguan Mosque

Dongguan Mosque is one of the largest mosques in China and also the religious and academic center of Islam in northwest China. It has a 600-year-long history and covers more than 310,000 square feet. The buildings in the mosque show both Chinese tradition and Islamic features.

The grand moment of worship in Dongguan Mosque (From Colphoto)

Dongguan Mosque has long been an important site of Islamic worship. During religious activities, the number of worshippers can reach 20,000.

> Tourists can take bus 12, 2, or 23 directly to Dongguan Mosque.

Longwu Temple

Longwu temple is located in Longwu Town, Tongren County, Huangnan Tibetan Autonomous Prefecture, 116 miles south of Xining. One of the most ancient temples of Tibetan Buddhism, it was built in 1301 and decorated with various artworks and cultural relics, including two tablets favored by Chinese emperors of the seventeenth century. Covering more than 18,000 square feet, the hall for sutra chanting is supported by 18 enormous pillars and 146 shorter ones. Enshrined are numerous lifelike Buddha figures. In northwest China, the area, position, and influence of Longwu Temple is exceeded only by Laboleng Temple and Ta'er Temple.

> In January, March, September, and October of the lunar calendar, there are great and solemn Buddhist rituals held in Longwu Temple.

Huangshui River

Also called the Xining River, Huangshui is a tributary of the Yellow River and flows northwest through Xining. In early summer each year, the water from the melted snow in the mountains runs into the river and creates one of Xining's most impressive views, the "summer surge."

North Zen Temple (Beichan Si)

North Zen Temple is also called North Mountain Temple, because it is

A Buddhist figure in Longwu Temple (From Imagine-China)

Pilgrims (From Imagine-China)

built against cliffs of the 7,874-foot Tulou Mountain. As the second largest "hanging temple" of China, the buildings are supported by wooden and stone racks and stand at the very edge of the abyss. Another feature of the temple are the grottos carved into the cliffs, which are linked by trestles, alleys, and bridges. The frescos and sculptures in these grottos tell stories of myths, legends, and sages. From the top of the temple, you can also get a magnificent birds-eye view of Xining.

Taxis will take you directly to North Zen Temple.

Treasure Valley (Baoku Xia)

Treasure Valley Natural Park is located in northwest Datong County, 43 miles from Xining. Covering an area of 12 square miles with altitudes between 9,409 and 13, 895 feet, the area features sandstone hoodoos, or stone forests, and valleys. The eccentrically shaped rocks are given names according to their shapes–Camel, Hare, Phoenix, and the like. It is also a natural vivarium, with beautiful wildflowers, precious herbs, and rare animals.

Potion Coast Hot Well (Yaoshuitan Wenquan)

Located in valleys 25 miles south of Xining with a temperature between 68 and 100°F, the greenish water has a strong smell of sulphur and feels soapy. Scientific analysis shows that it contains many microelements, and drinking or bathing in the water can be beneficial to health. A new state-of-the-art sanatorium has been built beside the well, welcoming tens of thousands of guests each year.

Wutun Temple (Wutun Si)

Located in Wutun Village, Tongren County, Wutun Temple is renowned for its wide collection of Rebgong artwork, many of which have a long history and great artistic value. The frescos, barbolas, colored paintings, and sculptures in the temple are true to life and beautifully crafted.

Wutun is on the way from Xining to Longwu; visitors can take a bus from Xining Coach Terminal. From Longwu, tourists have a choice of a minibus or three-wheeler.

Great statue of Wutun Temple (From CFP)

Haidong (East Qinghai) Region

Best Time to Travel

May to September are the best months for visiting this section of Qinghai.

Qutan Temple enjoyed the emperors' favor and superior position during the Ming Dynasty. (From CFP)

Qutan Temple

Qutan Temple is located south of Xining. Bearing Sakyamuni's family name, the temple was built in 1392 by the famous Sanluo Lama and redecorated in 1782. Situated in a square fort, it covers about 107,000 square feet with the usual three sections.

Qutan Temple is more than a temple. It is a museum of various artworks and cultural relics, among which the 4,306-square-foot fresco is the most precious.

Take a bus to Qutan Temple from Xining to Lanzhou, Gansu, and get off at Nianbo, Ledu County.

Ancient Cemetery in Liuwan (Liuwan Gumu)

Located in Liuwan Village, 9 miles east of Ledu County, this ancient cemetery covers a total area of more than one million square feet and is one of the largest primitive cemeteries in China. The tombs can be traced from 3,900 to 4,500 years ago and are of different cultures. The cemetery has 1,700 tombs and 30,000 excavated shards, most of which are painted potteries. The common figures on the potteries are frog figures and circles, and sometimes human faces and bodies.

"Rolling-swing" is a typical game of the Tu people, demonstrating both speed and beauty. (From Liu Liwen)

Five Peaks Mountain (Wufeng Shan)

Five Peaks Mountain is 25 miles northeast of Xining. Viewed from a distance, the five peaks in the area resemble the shape of a hand. It is famous for its woods, caves, and springs, among which Dragon Palace Spring provides not only soothing scenery but also high-quality spring water. Five Peaks Temple, built in Qing Dynasty, is located near the Dragon Palace Spring. The painted halls and pavilions of the temple are astonishingly beautiful.

Five Peaks Mountain is also a place for local folk-song contests. In early summer each year, area singers gather here and participate in a grand celebration of local culture.

Tu Folk Village

As the only autonomous county of Tus in China, Huzhu County is a large Tu community where their living habits and customs are well preserved. The Folk Village in Huzhu gives tourists a chance to experience Tu history, culture, residents, artwork, and customs. They are also able to visit local families, taste ethnic food, and enjoy local games and shows.

Huzhu County is 25 miles north of Xining. Visitors can take a bus at Xining Coach Terminal.

North Mountain National Park (Beishan Guojia Senlin Gongyuan)

North Mountain National Park is located in the northwest part of Huzhu Tu Autonomous County. The park features lush vegetation, various wild animals, and well-preserved primitive ecology. There may be more than 1,000 different plants, covering 60 percent of the entire area. The park is an ideal spot for rare flowers and animals. Besides incredible natural scenery, North Mountain National Park also features Tu folk cultures and customs.

Mengda Natural Park

It is a short 12-mile drive from Xunhua Autonomous County to Mengda Natural Park. The park covers an area of 3,475 square miles, with altitudes ranging from 5,840 to 13,714 feet above sea level. Influenced by monsoons from both sides of the area, and with plenty of rainfall and moist weather, the park has about 600 plant varieties and 100 species of wildflowers. It is also a preserve for various wild animals.

Another feature of Mengda Natural Park is its strange stones and soothing waters. Stones of various shapes are named "frog," "echoing wall," "five young disciples," and the like. The 8,000-foot-high "sky pond" halfway up the mountain is an especially inviting view.

Take the bus from Xining Coach Terminal to Xuhua County.

Sky Pond of Mengda Natural Park (From CFP)

Qinghai Lake

(From Liu Liwei)

Qinghai Lake, or "Azure Sea," this area has also been called "West Sea," "Fresh Water," "Fresh Sea," or "Fairy Sea." As the largest inland saltwater lake in China, it is 124 miles from Xining and is 10,500 feet above sea level.

Nearly 30 rivers flow into the lake, which is surrounded by mountains. All the way from the mountains' lower slope to the coast of the lake are vast grasslands. With moderate weather, the area is an ideal place for herds of grazing livestock.

(From Quanjing)

Each year in May and June, more than 100,000 different kinds of birds migrate and nest in Birds Heaven Island. Tourists need to be very careful not to disturb the colorful nests and eggs. The island became a nature preserve in 1975, and the environment is ecologically sound, keeping this area safe for birds and tourists alike.

(From Liu Liwen)

(From CFP)

(From Quanjing)

Accommodation Tips

Note: Qinghai Lake has an extremely high salt content. We recommend washing carefully after visiting here.

Birds Heaven Hotel	About an hour from Heimahe, this hotel is near the coast and Birds Heaven Island.
Tent Hostel	Hostels near Qinghai Lake provide tourists with hot water and simple food.

North Qinghai Region

Best Time to Travel

May to September are the best months for visiting the north section of Qinghai. For birdwatchers at Qinghai Lake, May to June are the optimal months.

Atom City

This is the place where China's first atomic and hydrogen bombs were born. Built in 1958 as a nuclear weapon base, it was transferred to local government in 1987. After a series of environment protective measures were taken, the base was renamed "Western Sea Town" in 1993. There is a monument designating China's first nuclear weapons base as well as the fallout landfill pit.

Sun-Moon Mountain (Riyue Shan)

Sun-Moon Mountain, once called Red Mountain because of its color, is east of Qinghai Lake. Historically it was a border defense fortress between the Tang Dynasty and middle Asian countries. The mountain is 16,000 feet high. Sun-Moon Mountain is now a watershed for the water system in Qinghai and also a dividing line between the agricultural and herding areas.

There is no direct bus from Xining to this mountain. Visitors are advised to contact a travel agency and join a one-day tour of Qinghai Lake, which will cover this sight.

Border stones laid in 734 in Sun-Moon Mountain (From CFP)

Scenery of the Reversing River (From CFP)

Reversing River

The Reversing River originates from the west foot of Sun-Moon Mountain and flows westward into Qinghai Lake. The total length is 25 miles. A small town sharing the same name is located beside the mouth of the river.

There are many beautiful myths about the river and why, unlike most rivers in China, it flows west. Before the upheaval of Tibetan Plateau, Qinghai Lake was once a vast sea. Over thousands of years the sea dried up, but the Reversing River remains faithful to its birthplace.

Qilian Mountain (Qilian Shan)

Qilian Mountain is famous for its glaciers. The average altitude of the mountain is 13,000 to 16,000 feet. On a clear summer day, the snow line halfway up the mountain can be seen. Medicinal herbs can be found in the snow-covered area, and since there is no clear division between seasons, local people say that "it snows in June in Qilian."

The natural park of Qilian Mountain is an impressive sight. The primitive forests are home to many different varieties of trees, shrubs, and wild animals.

The impressive view of glaciers and grasslands in Qilian Mountain (From ImagineChina)

West Qinghai Region

Best Time to Travel

Summer is the optimal time for tourists. It is always windy and quite cool in spring and autumn.

Qiandam Basin (Chaidamu Pendi)

Hidden in 13,000-foot-high mountains, Qiandam is the highest basin in China. There are more than 5,000 more saltwater lakes in the basin, the largest of which is Qinghai Lake. The weather is dry and cold, and the soil is highly salinized. Only a few desert plants can survive the harsh environment. Although practically lifeless, the area is rich in mineral resources such as salt, crude oil, natural gas, and coal. The mysterious Yadan landforms at the bottom of the basin attracts adventurers from all over the world.

Desert and Yadan landforms in Qiandam Basin (From CFP)

Tianjun Mountain

Tianjun Mountain or White Mountain is located on the eastern edge of Qiandam Basin, about 12 miles from Tianqun County. The summit is more than 13,000 feet high. The mountain is most famous for its stone forests on the south slope of the main peak. The colors of the stone forests range from gray to brown, white, and even pink. Tianjun Mountain is also an area inhabited by wild animals.

A pilgrim on the Qinghai-Tibet Road (From CFP)

Twin Lakes

There are two connected lakes here: Keluke, a freshwater lake, and Tuosu, a saltwater lake. Both lakes are famous for clear water, grassland, herds, and many species of bird, as well as Monkey Mountain nearby.

Kunlun Mountain

Kunlun Mountain is located in southwest Qinghai, neighboring Pamirs. The mountain chain is 1,553 miles long with an average altitude of 18,000–19,700 feet; the total area is close to 200,000 square miles, creating a magnificent wild area for viewing glaciers, snowy mountains, and animals. The highest point of Kunlun Mountain is Mount Bugedaban at 22,500 feet. In Chinese myth, Kunlun is the residence of the West Queen, a deity of eternal life and beauty.

Nachitai Spring

Nachitai Spring, near the north bank of the Kunlun River, is 57 miles southwest

Lying across middle Asia, Kunlun Mountain is known as the "backbone of Asia." (From CFP)

of Ge'ermu City. Although buried in a world of ice, Nachitai Spring is one of the rare warm-water springs in Qinghai. The silent spring that flows year-round offers tourists a scene of warmth and hope.

The water of Nachitai is said to be the West Queen's "drink of everlasting life." The water, with various microelements, minerals, and no pollution, is indeed a drink of health and beauty.

Nanbaxian Yadan Landforms

Nanbaxian is located in northwest Qinghaiand, the location of one of the most famous wind-eroded landforms in the world. Yadan, in local language, means "wind-eroded dirt piles." Nanbaxian covers a total area of 81,000 square miles, and has an altitude of 10,695 feet above sea level. It is the largest area with Yadan landforms in China.

Ge'ermu City

Located on the south edge of Qiandam Basin, Ge'ermu City is the second largest city in Qinghai. The city was built originally as a relay station during the construction of Qingzang Highway, and now it is a relay station for tourists on their way to Tibet and Xinjiang. The majority of people who live in Ge'ermu come from inland and work in the power plants and the gas and oil industry.

Charhan Salt Lake

Charhan Salt Lake is located in the southern part of Qiandam Basin, at an altitude of 8,759 feet, in a 2,239-square-mile area. Due to the blazing heat there, the lake is partly covered by a 10- to 13-foot-thick salt layer. The layer's carrying capacity is so huge that highways, railroads, and even factories are built on it. There are several salt atolls in Charhan Salt Lake, forming small lagoons in the lake.

The famous Salt Bridge, about 37 miles north of the downtown area, is 20 feet long, spanning the entire lake. Built completely of salt, the bridge is straight, flat, and smooth.

In the Salt Lake area, summers are extremely dry and hot with hardly any rainfall. Visitors should avoid too much exposure to the sun in this area.

Chaka Salt Lake

Chaka Salt Lake is located in south Wulan County. In the local language, Chaka means "sea of salt." Covering a total area of 39 square miles and with rich salt resources, the lake has been the source of salt extraction for more than 3,000 years. The lake is also famous for its extraordinary mirages.

The only way to visit the Chaka Salt Lake is to join a tour group, which will take buses to Chaka, Wulan, or Delingha to reach Chaka, 186 miles from Xining. Food and accommodation are available in the Salt Lake area.

Dulan International Hunting Land

Located in south Dulan County, Dulan is the first hunting land open to foreign tourists in this area. With a total area of about 50 square miles and 17 square miles of actual hunting area, the land is rich in wild animals. The hunters should be accompanied by expert guides. Hunters can enjoy local or Western food in the camp, and they can also choose to stay in Mongolian-style hotels or yurts.

Zhaling Lake and Eling Lake

Located in Maduo County, Zhaling Lake and Eling Lake are the two largest freshwater lakes near the upper Yellow River. Surrounded by grassland and rolling mountains, the views of the lakes are spectacular and many local legends abound.

There are no special buses to Zhaling and Eling Lakes, but visitors can hire taxis from Xining or Maduo County. Be aware that the road is not in good condition.

Headstream of Yangtze River

The Yangtze River, the largest river in China and the third largest in the world, is revered as the birt hplace of Chinese civilization and is the lifeblood fueling China's socio-economic development. The Yangtze River begins in Tangula Mountain in south Qinghai;

Extraordinary view of Chaka Salt Lake (From CFP)

There are 20 mountains almost 20,000 feet high along the mountain chains of Tanggula, all of which are covered with glaciers. (From CFP)

the actual source of the Yangtze comes from huge glaciers. In summer days, the immense glaciers and ever-expanding grasslands provide an irresistible view for tourists.

Headstream of Huanghe River

The Yellow River, the second largest river in China, has a total length of 3,395 miles. It begins in northern China in the Kunlun Mountains in Qinghai, south of the Gobi Desert. The sources of the river are numerous springs, marsh lands, and pools. The headwaters of Yellow River, known since 821, are now a natural preserve, famous not only for its primitive scenery but also for its environmental significance.

> ➡ The best season to visit the headwaters of yellow River is from June to September.

Headstream of Lancang River

The Lancangjiang River starts in the snowy mountains of the southeast Tibetan Plateau. The headstream of the river is 17,677 feet, and it flows all the way through the southeast part of China. The area is famous for its magnificent views of huge glaciers, vast marshlands, and mysterious valleys.

Longyang Valley Hydraulic Power Station

Longyang Valley Hydraulic Power Station is located about 91 miles south of Xining. With a total length of 25 miles and width of 5.5 miles, Longyang Valley is surrounded by mountain ranges and plateaus. The primary dam of the power station is

Beautiful scenery of Longyang Valley Reservoir (From CFP)

584 feet high and 3,740 feet long, its bottom width 262 feet, its top width 49 feet. It is the largest hydroelectric power station on the mainstream of Yellow River and is a perfect combination of beautiful natural scenery and grand human endeavor.

For the sake of safety, tourists must visit Longyang Valley Hydraulic Power Station by a designated route. Special buses are available in Longyangxia.

Temple of Princess Wencheng

With a history of more than 1,300 years, the Temple of Princess Wencheng is built in Yushu, southeast of Qinghai-Tibet Plateau. In 641 the princess married the Lord of Tibet. When she passed by Yushu, she loved the place so much that she made a brief stay. She taught local citizens farming and weaving.

Built against the cliffs of the Beina Valley, the temple is a typical Tibetan-style building. It is 31 feet tall, with 3 stories and covers an area of 6,458 square feet. The temple is famous for the figure of Princess Wencheng and numerous sutra lines carved on the nearby cliffs.

Jia'ang Sutra Stone Heap

Jia'ang Sutra Stone Heap in Xinzhai Village of Yushu County in south Qinghai is 528 miles south of Xining. The mound is the largest of its kind and is called *doben* in local language, which means "100,000 sutra stones."

The stone heap can be traced back hundreds of years and is now more than 328 feet long and 131 feet wide. It allegedly has 2 billion sutra stones, each of which is carved with sutra lines or religious figures. The oldest sutra stones are deeply buried in the mound, and new ones are being placed year by year. Now every family in the village has generations of sculptors.

Sutra Stone Heap is a living history of Tibetan Buddhism. (From CFP)

A legend has it that when Princess Wencheng was married to Songzanganbu, the local Buddhists, for the purpose of showing their respect to her, made an offering of a butter flower in front of a Buddha brought from Chang'an by the Princess. (From CFP)

Qinghai Style

Three Peerless Art Forms at Ta'er Monastery

Butter flower, mural art, and raised embroidery are known as "three peerless art forms" at Ta'er Monastery. The butter flower is not the flower of a plant, but a sculpture made from yak butter mixed with various colors. It became a convention and later was spread to Ta'er Monastery in 1594. The mural art refers to the murals of various kinds on walls, curtains, doors, and pillars with styles characteristic of both Tibetan and Hindu art. Painted with natural mineral pigments, all of them look so bright and colorful that it is hard to imagine that they have been there for centuries. Raised embroidery is one of the Tibetan art forms originated by Ta'er Monastery. Colorful silks and satins were cut into various shapes which then were filled with wool and cotton. Buddha, Buddhist stories, landscapes, flowers, and birds and animals were painted on the curtains. It is really a special religious artwork with fine workmanship, unconventional design, and vivid images.

Regong Art

Regong art is a unique artistic form combining Tibetan culture with central plains culture. It is an important school of Tibetan Buddhism art with a long history of more than 700 years. It has extensive influence and enjoys a great reputation in the southwest and northwest area of China as well as in some places of Southeast Asia. Regong art mainly centralizes in the areas of Nianduhu, Guomari, Gashari, Wutunshang, and Wutunxia. Its contents include painting, sculpture, raised embroidery, design, architectural ornament, and woodcut painting. Regong artworks are exact and vivid in model making, elegant and careful in the brushwork, and dazzlingly beautiful in colors. They are rich in decoration. With full display of the sense of rhythm and movement as well as the solidity of the lines, it has the beauty of entirety. Regong art is of high visual, artistic, and monetary value.

Gansu

Geography at a Glance

Gansu Province ("Gan" means "Long") is situated in northwest China, at the very geographical center of China, on the upper reaches of the Yellow River at the juncture of the Loess Plateau, Qinghai Tibet Plateau, and Inner Mongolia Plateau. A long thin region from northwest to southeast with altitudes above 3,300 feet, the area is divided into 14 districts at prefecture level, covers about 150,580 square miles, and has a total population of 25.61 million (2000 census). Lanzhou, its political, economic, and cultural center, is the capital of Gansu. From southeast to northwest, its subtropical moist climate gradually changes to temperate dry climate. The annual average temperature range is 32–57°F, and the annual average precipitation is between 12 and 20 inches.

River valleys at the upper reaches of Jin and Wei are the birthplaces of the Chinese nation and the cradle of the ancient Chinese civilization. Fuxi, the Chinese nation's primogenitor credited with the creation of Chinese characters and calendars, was born here. Primitive agriculture first appeared here around 3,000

(From Quanjing)

The picture is the exterior of Mogao Caves (From CFP)

years ago. During the Han dynasty, Emperor Wu constructed the corridor to the West via the Silk Road. The four great inventions of China—production technology, silk, china, and ironware—arose in this era. Astronomy, mathematics, Western and Indian religions, precious stones, spices, and cotton were introduced to China through this region.

Featured Cuisine

Longxi preserved ham, lily peach, hundred-year-old chicken, bangzi smoked chicken, gaosan soy-sauce cooked pork, jincheng assorted cold cuts, braised algae, hotbed chives and chicken, backed and roasted mutton, roasted suckling pig, tangwang boiled mutton, chenchun hot starch noodles, Dunhuang cold noodles, soy-soup, jiangshui noodles, niangpizi, hand-pulled noodles with beef, beef crisp cake, longlife noodles, rice, fried cold bean jelly, fried rice cake.

Featured Commodities

Herbal Medicines

Licorice, herbal teas, and many specific Chinese herbal remedies.

Special Local Products

Lanzhou dark melon seeds, peppercorns, hemp shoes, carpet, Gansu dark lambskin, Sanbei lambskin, rice.

Local Handicrafts

Bronze horses, inkstone, Lanzhou carved gourds, carved scree, Jiuquan luminous cup, carved lacquer, inkstone, broadswords,

Notes 

❶ There are many wild and untraveled areas in Gannan. The Tibetan mastiff, the Zangao, is known to roam this area. We recommend that you hire a local guide and stay within the beaten paths.

❷ The altitude of Gannan area is generally above 6,500 feet. Be aware that the high altitude and thin atmosphere can cause "altitude sickness" (shortness of breath, headache, nausea, confusion) and come prepared.

❸ The weather of Gannan changes quickly; remember to take layered clothing, sunblock, sunglasses, and warm sweaters.

cut-paper folk art, musical instruments, flutes.

Fruits and Delicacies

White melon, melon, pear, apple, watermelon, apricot, apple-pear.

Transportation Tips

By Bus

There are four national highways through Lanzhou, seven bus stations, five provincial highways, and 50 county highways. Travel by bus is the most convenient.

By Train

Lanzhou is the biggest transportation hut of the northwest, where four main railways

A grassland in Gansu (From CFP)

(Longhai, Lanxin, Lanqing, and Baolan) meet. It is also an import station of the second Asia-Europe continental bridge, which starts from Lianyungang in the east and ends at the port of Rotterdam of Holland.

POPULAR FESTIVALS

Flower Festival of Lotus Mountain

Held at Lotus Mountain from the 1st day to 5th day of the first lunar month. To herald the beginning of spring, local people climb the mountain, picnic, sing and dance, and prepare local food and drink.

The Monlam Summons Ceremony

Also known as the Great Prayer Festival. Held at La Bo Leng Temple of Xiahe County, end of February to the first week in March. This important religious festival combines pilgrimages, sermons, grand ceremonies with new prayer flags, and special foods.

Xiahe La Bo Leng Temple Grand Summons Ceremony

Held at Xiahe La Bo Leng Temple from the 4th day to 17th day of the first lunar month and the 29th day of the sixth lunar month to 15th day of the seventh lunar month. The activities center around Buddhist prayers, sermons, religious rites, singing, and dancing.

Spring Flower Festival

Held at the Dongfanghong Square in Lanzhou around the time of the Lantern Festival.

Fuxi Fulture Festival

Held in Fuxi Temple on June 13 to exhibit folk culture.

International Gliding Festival

Held at the base of Jayuguan in July. Gliding performances and contests, local food, and fireworks are featured.

July Shuofa Festival

Held at Xiahe La Bo Leng Temple from the 29th day of the sixth lunar month to the 15th day of the seventh lunar month. Special lectures and sermons, temple rites, dancing, and singing take place.

Lanzhou Station is located at the foot of Gaolan Mountain, and more than 50 trains pass by everyday.

By Plane

Lanzhou Zhongzhou Airport runs nearly 30 flights to Bejing, Shanghai, Guangzhou, Shenzhen, Chengdu, Xi'an, Nanjing, Hangzhou, Dunhuang, and Jiayuguan.There are flights to Hong Kong every Tuesday. The airport is about 43 miles from downtown; there are shuttle buses and taxis available.

Recommended Routes

Featured routes

7-day tour of the northwest

Day 1 Arrive at Lanzhou. Lodging: Ganlan Hotel.

Day 2 White Pagoda Mountain (Baita Mountain)→Waterwheel Park (Shuiche Yuan) →Zhongshan Bridge→Sculpture of the Mother Yellow River. Lodging: Ganlan Hotel.

Day 3 Lanzhou→Xiahe→La Po Leng Temple→Sanke Grasslands. Lodging: La Po Leng Hotel.

Day 4 Xiahe→Linxia Hui Autonomous Prefecture→Lanzhou→Jiayuguan. Lodging:train.

Day 5 Jiayuguan (western part of the Great Wall of Ming Dynasty)→Dunhuang. Lodging: Dunhuang Hotel.

Day 6 Echoing-Sand Mountain→Crescent Lake→Mogao Grottoes. Lodging: Mogao Hotel.

Day 7 End of tour.

7-day tour of folk and religion culture

Day 1 Lanzhou→Linxia Hui Autonomous Prefecture→Binlingsi Caves→Liujiaxia reservoir→Red Park. Lodging: Linxia Hotel.

Day 2 Linxia Hui Autonomous Prefecture →Xia River→La Po Leng Temple→Gongtang Pagoda. Lodging: La Po Leng Hotel.

Day 3 Xia River→Sanke Grasslands→ Langmu Temple. Lodging: Langmu Temple.

Day 4 Ruoergei→Maerkang. Lodging: Maerkang.

Day 5 Maerkang→Danba (visiting military watchtowers and local residences)→ Kangding. Lodging: Kangding Hotel.

Day 6 1-day tour of Kangding (Paoma Mountain→Tashan Grasslands→Xindu Bridge). Lodging: Kangding Hotel.

Day 7 End of tour.

4-day ancestor tour

Day 1 Arrive at Lanzhou. Lodging: Ganlan Hotel.

Day 2 Lanzhou→Tianshui→Fuxi Temple →Yuquan Guan. Lodging: Maiji Hotel.

Day 3 TianShui→Maiji Mountain→ Maijishan Grottoes. Lodging: Maiji Hotel.

Day 4 Tour of Tianshui.

Traditional Routes

6-day tour of Dunhuang

Day 1 Arriving at Dunhuang.

Day 2 Echoing-Sand Mountain→Crescent Lake→Folk Museum→Leiyin Temple.

Day 3 Mogao Grottoes→The Art of Grottoes Exhibit Center→Cangjing Caves Cultural Relic Exhibition Hall→Replica of Ancient City of Song Dynasty.

Day 4 Invisible Sleeping Buddha→West

Thousand Buddha Caves→Yang Pass→Yumen Pass→Great Wall of Han Dynasty.

Day 5 Yulin Cave→Suoyang City.

Day 6 Jiayuguan→Xuanbi Great Wall.

6-day tour of Tianshui

Day 1 Tianshui.

Day 2 Maiji Mountain→Stone Gate→hot spring.

Day 3 Jingtu Temple→Xianren Cliff→Plum Garden, Forest Park.

Day 4 Nanguo Temple→Fuxi Temple→Yuquan Guan→Xingguo Temple in Qin'an→Dadi Bay.

Day 5 Gangu Giant Statue Mountain→Jiangwei Grave→Wushan Water Curtain Cave Grottoes→Wushan Hot Spring.

Day 6 Cingshui Cliff→The Grave of Zhaochong→Cingshui Hot Spring→Zhangchuan Guanshan Red Deer Natural Scenic Spot.

1-day tour of Air-Space City

Dingxin Airport→Exhibition Hall of Astronautic Base History→Shenzhou Spacecraft Launching Base→Launching Tower→Dongfeng Martyrs' Cemetery.

Self-Guided Tours

Roof of the world—Qinghai-Tibet Altiplano

From Lanzhou to Lantou via Xining, Kokonor Lake, Chaka, Geermu, Tanghla Moutain, Anduo, Naqu, Dangxiong, Nianqing Tangula, Linzhou, Lhasa, Zedang, Yangzhuoyong Lake, Jiangmu, Rikaze, and Yangbajing.

Tour of Silk Road

Lanzhou to Xi'an via Tianshui, Pingliang, Baoji. Main scenic spots: Yellow River Iron Bridge, Yellow River Waterwheel, Sculpture of the Mother Yellow River, White Pagoda Mountain, Yuquan Guan, Fuxi Temple, Maiji Mountain, Kongtong Mountain, Dayan Pagoda, Forest of Steles, terra-cotta warriors and horses, Huaqing Pond, Banpo site.

Addresses and Phone Numbers

Linxia Hotel	9 Hongyuan Road, Linxia	0930-6232100
Ganlan Hotel	266 Pingliang Road, Lanzhou	0931-8464747
Tianma Hotel	West Cross, Wuwei, Gansu	0935-2215170
Zhangye Hotel	56 County Government Street, Zhangye	0936-8212601
Dunhuang Hotel	14 Yangguan East Road, Dunhuang	0937-8822538
Jiuquan Hotel	33 Jiefang Road, Jiuquan	0937-2612554
Dunhuang Fly Sky Hotel	22 Echoing-Mountain Road, Dunhuang	0937-8822726
Jiayuguan Hotel	1 Xinhua North Road, Jiayuguan	0937-6226983
Maiji Hotel	West side of Tianshui Railway station square	0938-4920000
La Po Leng Hotel	West side of La Po Leng Temple, Xiahe county	0942-7121849

Lanzhou, Linxia Region

Best Time to Travel

The climate of Lanzhou is the typical monsoon climate: dry with great temperature variation from morning to evening. The summers are cool but pleasant, and the lodgings in major cities make winter a good time to visit.

Shopping Tips

Zhangye Street is the major shopping area in Lanzhou. There are more than 20 malls and 360 different shops offering services, products, and food for every need.

Railway New Village is located at the intersection of West Democracy Road and Gaolan Road, the main business district. It is one of the largest trade markets.

Located downtown in Laocheng district, Nanguan–Xiguan Business District is the biggest commercial district of Lanzhou. There are more than ten large-scale shopping malls.

White Pagoda Mountain (Baita Mountain)

White Pagoda Mountain lies in the center of Lanzhou on the north side of the Yellow River. With a height of 5,577 feet, its undulating and perilous mountain ranges are impregnable ramparts embracing the city. There is indeed a White Pagoda on the summit. The first bridge over the Yellow River, built before the White Pagoda Mountain in 1385 (Ming Dynasty), was originally a float bridge and renovated as an iron bridge in 1907 (Qing Dynasty). The bridge is about 755 feet long and 23 feet wide.

The White Pagoda Temple at the summit is also named "Lama Temple," built in the architectural style of the Lamaism of Tibet and Nepal. The original pagoda, destroyed later, was first built to commemorate a monk who came to pay respects to Genghis Klan but died of illness in Lanzhou on his way to Mongolia. The pagoda was rebuilt by the eunuch Liuyongcheng, who guarded Gansu in the Ming Dynasty. In 1715 it was enlarged by provincial governor Chuoqi and renamed Cien Temple. Founded on a round base, the pagoda is octagonal, with seven

Situated on the Loess Plateau, Lanzhou is narrow from north to south and wide from west to east. It is about 25 miles long and 300–1500 feet wide. The Yellow River flows through the city from west to east. (From Liu Liwen)

The bronze galloping horse of the Han Dynasty in the Gansu Provincial Museum (From CFP)

stories and upturned carved roof corners in dragon-head shape on each tier. The outside of the pagoda is pure white. Baita Mountain has been developed into a travel resort that attracts thousands of people.

Take Bus 13, 15, or 112 to the site.

Five-Spring Mountain

Situated on the north of the Gaolan Mountains, Five-Spring Mountain is 5,249 feet above sea level. Legend has it that a general from the Western Han Dynasty, Huo Qubing, stabbed his sword into the ground after finding no water for his horse or himself. Five springs erupted from that spot and are still flowing today. When you pass the west side of Wenchang Temple, you will see the first spring, Ganlu (meaning sweet dew or timely rain). At the north side of Wenchang Temple is the second spring, Juyue, in the shape of a well. On Middle Autumn Day, the shadow of the moon reflects in the spring just like someone holding the moon in her hands. The third spring is Mozi in the Mozi Cave under the Kuangguan Pavillion. The fourth one is Meng. It is said that if people use the water from this spring to make Meng Tea, the flavor will be extraordinary. The fifth spring is the round Hui.The natural beauty of the five springs is enhanced by verdant groves, and the temples (Mani, Chunqing, Wenchang, and Dizang) make it a famous religious destination.

At the summit of Five-Spring Mountain, travelers have a panoramic view of Lanzhou.

The Gansu Provincial Museum

Located at the north side of Xijin West Road of Qilihe District in Lanzhou, this museum is a comprehensive collection of provincial and national artifacts. Occupying more than 700,000 square feet and in beautiful surroundings, the museum, built in 1935, is in the shape of Chinese character 山 meaning "mountain." It has five floors in the middle, and three floors on both sides linked by corridors with thirteen exhibition halls and a lecture hall. The museum holds abundant and distinctive collections of more than 140,000 rare cultural relics. Three of the most valuable exhibits are color-painted pottery, exhibits of the Silk Road of the Han and Tang dynasties, and the Buddhism displays. The bronze galloping horse and the fossils of a Stegodon (primitive elephant) from the Yellow River are especially famous. There are also collections of Han Dynasty wooden blocks, once used to relay information and news, and many cultural relics of the New Stone Age.

Liujiaxia Power Station

Liujiaxia Power Station, in the upper reaches of the

Yellow River, Yongjing County, about 28 miles west of Lanzhou, is one of the seven planned series of power stations along the Yellow River. The water-storage capacity is tremendous (more than one billion gallons) and the water area covers about one million square feet, stretching 34 miles from southwest to northeast. The dam across it is 482 feet high and 2,756 feet long. The right side of the dam is the spillway which is 2,297 feet long and 262 feet wide. In addition to providing hydroelectric power, farmland irrigation, and flood control, there are many natural scenic areas and places of cultural interest along the reservoir, such as Sanxia Everglades conservation zone, the fossils of dinosaurs' footprints from the Cretaceous Period, Bami Mountain, the primeval forest of Baolong Mountain, an ancient fortress, a beacon tower, portions of the Great Wall, and several ethnic tribal communities.

Sleeping Buddha statue in Bingling Thousand Buddha Caves (From CFP)

Bingling Thousand Buddha Caves

Located on the Small Jishi Hill, the caves are about 22 miles west of Yongjing County in Lanzhou. ("Bingling" means "ten thousand Buddhas" in Tibetan.) The caves date back to 420 (Western Jin Dynasty) and are famous for their fine stone sculptures. Stretching about 6,561 feet on the west cliff in Dasi Gully, there are 183 niches, 694 stone statues, 82 clay sculptures, and nearly 10,000 square feet of

Located in the Yellow River canyon of Yongjing County, Liujiaxia is not only a large-scale major water-control project but also a holiday resort. (From CFP)

frescoes and murals. Cave 169, made during the Northern Dynasties, is the most imposing and delicate one. It holds the clay sculptures of West Qin and occupies 2,153 square feet. On its north wall there are epigraphs from 420, the earliest ones in the history of China's cave art. These stone sculptures represent the social situations and customs of the Northern Dynasties and are well worth a visit.

> Liujiaxia Power Station and Bingling Thousand Buddha Caves can be toured in one day. Note that the water line is too low in winter for sightseeing boats to get to Bingling Temple from the power station.

Lu Tusi Yamun

Lu Tusi Yamun, in Liancheng in the west of Yongdeng County, used to have the offices of the local ethnic minority chief (Tusi) in the Qing and Ming dynasties. Yamun was first established in 1378 (Ming Dynasty) and restored in 1818. Imitating Beijing's building, Tusi Yamun was originally a brick masonry construction. Leaning against the Bijia Mountain and facing the Datong River, Lu Tusi Yamun occupies nearly 38,000 square feet and is richly ornamented; people often refer to it as "small summer palace."

Jingtai Tulin Canyon

Located in Jingtai County, Lanzhou City, Jingtai Tulin Canyon covers an area of about 23 acres. Tulin is composed of gigantic yellow, bronze-colored, reddish brown, and russet rocks that form a canyon. The average height is between 10 and 80 feet, the highest one reaching almost 89 feet. Most of these rocks are shaped like columns or peaks.

> Tulin has high value as a natural resource of exploration and development. Its primitive beauty is well worth a visit.

Tianshui Region

Best Time to Travel

September to November is the optimal time for visiting Tianshui. July is the hottest month, January the coldest. The average temperature of Tianshui is 53°F.

Fuxi Temple

Fuxi Temple, also known as Taihao Temple, is located in Xiguan, Tianshui. It is said that Fuxi, one of the three human

The door of Xiantian temple, which is the main part of Fuxi temple, is chiseled and carved with delicate touches. (From CFP)

primogenitors, was born here. Established in 1490 (Ming Dynasty) and rebuilt in 1524, the complex occupies about 65,000 square feet and is the largest group of buildings for offering sacrifices to Fuxi. Legends say that the ninth day of the first lunar month is the actual birthday of Fuxi, and many pilgrims come here to pay their respect to Fuxi on this day.

> The 15th day of the first lunar month and the 13th day of the fifth lunar month are Fuxi culture festivals.

Maijishan Grottoes

Maiji ("shaped like wheat sheaves") Mountain, located on the south side of Beidao Township and 31 miles southeast of Tianshui, is an isolated peak of the West Qinling Mountains. There are 194 grottoes containing 7,200 statues and some 14,000 square feet of frescoes from ten dynasties (from the Later Qin to the Qing Dynasty). These grottoes belong to one of China's four famous grottoes, the other three being Dunhuang Mogao Grottoes, Datong Yungang Grottoes, and Longmen Grottoes. Maiji Mountain is small, less than

Xianrenya Grotto in Maiji Mountain (From CFP)

500 feet high, but with cliff pavilions, Mo caves, Moya niches, and corridors. The grottoes have various shapes and contain important materials for the study of culture exchange between China and Western countries and the development of Gansu's architectonics.

Most of the grottoes hold clay sculptures and frescoes rather than statues because the quality of rocks is too soft for carving. The clay sculptures are mainly Buddhas, bodhisattva, disciples, and various gods. The sculptures of different dynasties have their own particular styles, which systematically reflect the development of China's clay sculpture.

> Photography is prohibited in Maijishan Grottoes.

Dadiwan Site

Dadiwan Site is located in the gentle hillsides on the south bank of Qingshui River in Qinan County, Tianshui City. The earliest site dates from 7,800 years ago, and the most recent site dates from 4,800 years ago. The long cultural span and large scale are rare in China's archaeological history. Dadiwan Site occupies almost 92 acres,with 242 house sites, 357 ash pits, 79 graves, and various other Neolithic relics that indicate a pottery-making culture.More than 8,000 shards, decorations, and household utensils made of bone, stone, china, or mussel shell have been excavated along with 17,000 animal bones. The house sites of Dadiwan are broad in scale and complicated in structure. There are frescoes on some of the unearthed floors in the shape of human or animals, which are the earliest primitive floor frescoes in China. Dadiwan provides extraordinary and rare materials for the study of China's art history.

> Dadiwan is famous for its temples, floor frescoes, and colored pottery.

The Big Buddha statue in Daxiang Mountain Cave (From Colphoto)

Water Curtain Cave Grottoes

Water Curtain Cave Grottoes are located in the canyon 15.5 miles northeast of Wushan County, Tianshui. With peak after peak rising ever higher and stretching far into the distance, winding paths leading to secluded spots, and rushing springs in caves, these grottoes seem like a fairyland.

Water Curtain Cave Grottoes were established in the Late Qin Dynasty and rebuilt in North Wei, North Zhou, Sui, Tang, Five, Song, and Yuan dynasties. The prime scenic areas are Xiansheng Pond, Water Curtain Cave, Lashao Temple, Thousand Buddha Cave, and Sanqing Cave. Located on the east side cliff of Shifu Mountain, Water Curtain Cave is about 164 feet long, 98 feet wide, and 65.5 feet deep. Facing Water Curtain Cave, Lashao Temple was established in 559 and contains a great amount of grotto artworks from the North Zhou Dynasty to the Yuan Dynasty. There are three relief carvings on the steep cliff showing Bodhisattva with Lotus surrounded by many little Buddha sculptures of Song Dynasty in niches.

Daxiang Mountain Cave

Daxiang Mountain, once called Wenqi Mountain, is located in the outskirts of Gangu County, Tianshui. The famous Giant Buddha was carved into the side of the mountain and might date back to the Northern Wei Dynasty, about 1,500 years ago. The statue is about 74 feet tall and 34 feet around the waist. With a kind and pleasant countenance, the Buddha statue is sitting in the lotus position. The cave has a dome with sculptures on two sides. Leaning against the mountain, a long corridor was built on the two sides of Big Statue Cave. There are 22 Buddha niches on the corridor. The distinctions of the Big Statue are the large-scale niches with domes and the caves for Buddhist priests to meditate.

Pingliang, Qingyang Region

>>>

Best Time to Travel

Pingliang has pleasant weather and four distinct seasons. The average temperature is about 49°F.

Kongtong Mountain

Kongtong Mountain, at about 7,000 feet above sea level, is located in Pingliang, Gansu Province. It played an important communication role on the ancient Silk Road and is also one of the birthplaces of Taoism in China during the Qin and Han dynasties. The mountain is dotted with more than 40 temples, the biggest one being Taihe Temple. The main temples are Zhenwu, Yuhuang, Laojun, Sanguan, Taibai, Zushi, and Yaowang, most of which were built during the Ming Dynasty. The bronze statue of the Zhenwu Emperor is enshrined in the Zhenwu Temple. Representations of Lao-Tse, Yinxi, and Xujia are in Laojun Temple. There is a Ming Dynasty drawing of Lao-tse on the wall, and various Taoist goddesses are enshrined in Offspring Temple.

There are many buses between Tianshui and Liangping, all of which take 6 to 8 hours. Travelers can visit Kongtong Mountain when they visit Tianshui.

Kongtong Mountain is the birthplace of Chinese Taoism. Legend tells that Emperor Xuanyuan came here to ask Taoism's Guang Zicheng for the way of cultivating morality. The first Emperor of Qin Dynasty also came here after he unified China. (From Quanjing)

Chongxin Ancient Chinese Scholar Tree

This giant tree is in the village of Guanhe, Tongcheng Township, Chongxin County. About 2,700 years old, the trunk is 6.5 feet high, the girth is 33 feet around, and the crown is 112 feet wide from east to west and 122 feet long from north to south. There are six branches. The girth of the biggest branch is 16 feet and the smallest is about 10 feet. Its big roots are exposed like curling dragons. It is thick with leaves and looks like a green hill. Five Dragons Mountain, Tangmao Mountain, and Cherry Ditch form a delightful contrast around the ancient tree.

Wangmu Temple Cave

Wangmu Temple is located at the juncture of the Jing and Ne rivers in Jingchuan County, 46 miles northeast of Pingliang City. Wangmu Mountain is also known as Guizhong Mountain. It is said that Emperor Mu of the Zhou Dynasty and Emperor Wu of the Han Dynasty both visited here. The goddess of Taoism, Hsi Wangmu (Queen of the Western Heaven), once held a banquet in the mountain at Yaochi (abode of fairy mother goddess). Many of the buildings on the mountain were built in 1522 (Ming Dynasty), but most were destroyed by war in the Qing Dynasty. Remaining are Wangmugong Cave, an ancient clock, and stone tablets.

Wangmugong was excavated in the Northern Wei Dynasty and is probably 1,500 years old. Square in shape, it has a 39-foot pillar in the center. There are Buddha statues and carvings on the pillar, and the three sides of the cave hold some magnificent murals.

> The 20th day of the third lunar month is the date of a grand celebration and family gathering at Wangmu.

Southern Cave Temple was carved into the red sandstone on the north bank of the Jing River. (From Colphoto)

Southern Cave Temple

Southern Cave Temple is located in Jiangjia village, about 5 miles east of Jingchuan County. It was excavated by prefectural governor Xi Kangsheng in 510 (Northern Wei Dynasty). Today there are five niches: No. 1 east cave and No. 2 west cave are well preserved.

The east cave is the main part of Southern Cave Temple, 42 feet high, 56 feet wide, and 46 feet deep. In the shape of a rectangle, it occupies 2,583 square feet of space. The style of each of the seven statues of Buddha is unique, showing the right hand up and drooping the left in the gesture of giving lectures. They are each 6.5 feet tall and display the level of carving art at that time.

On the two sides of the west cave are 16 Arhats, 8 bodhisattvas, and 6 warriors. In the middle are 3 bodhisattvas, all of which are in the style of the Tang and Late Qing dynasties.

Jingchuan Hot Spring

Jingchuan Hot Spring is located in Hejia Ping, 4.5 miles east of Jingchuan County on the south bank of the Jing River. Leaning against the mountain and facing the river, it is extremely picturesque and has a long history and splendid cultural background. It is said that Hsi Wangmu, Queen Mother of the West and goddess of immortality, often visited here. Its natural scenery is more beautiful than any fairyland, and the mineral-rich water is said to contain many healthful qualities. The spring's water retains a pleasantly warm temperature all year, and bathing in the spring can activate blood circulation and may cure many diseases.

> Jingchuan Hot Spring is close to national highway 312.

North Cave Temple

North Cave Temple is located at the juncture of the Pu and Ru rivers, 15.5 miles northwest of the Xifeng district of Qingyang, at the foot of

Fuzhong Mountain. It is said that North Cave Temple was established by prefectural governor Xi Kangsheng in 509 (Northern Wei Dynasty) and rebuilt in the following dynasty. It is the biggest cave temple in the eastern area of Gansu with a total of 296 niches for religious figures.

The group of caves was dug from the cliff which is about 66 feet high and nearly 394 feet wide. All the niches are triptyches holding 2,126 extant sculptures, among which those from the Northern Wei and Tang dynasties are the most delicate.

The Cave Dwellings in East Gansu Province

The landform of Qingyang is a typical loess plateau in east Gansu. The local residents keep the traditional lifestyle that is distinctive of the loess plateau's cultural landscape.

East Gansu is also one of the birthplaces of the Chinese nation. The great amount of relics from the Zhou Dynasty proves that the appearance of Zhou culture is closely connected with this land. According to historical data, tribal ancestors of the Zhou Dynasty lived here. The cave dwellings were dug into the cliff horizontally from the ground. Using slopes of ditches or cliffs, people established their cave homes. There are several types of cave dwellings, such as "bright cave," and "dark cave." The dark cave dwellings can be divided into "under the ground" and "half bright and half dark." There is a small population of farm families still living in a portion of these caves; many of the underground dwellings join aboveground houses. The caves are warm in winter, cool in summer, and dry and protected from the harshest elements by virtue of their location. This fascinating culture was discovered and explored in 1987; those who want more information should refer to the benchmark book on the subject, *Chinese Landscapes: The Village as Place* by R. G. Knapp for a more in-depth study.

Be sure not to miss the Lantern Festival where the amazing "Gaoxinzi" performance is staged.

The picture is the exterior of North Cave Temple. (From Colphoto)

Wuwei Region

Best Time to Travel

June to September are the best months to visit. Hot in summer and cold in winter, the temperature varies greatly from morning to evening. Be sure to layer clothing and pack extra sweaters and warm coats and hats.

Temple of Literature (Wen Miao)

The Temple of Literature is in northeast Wuwei. A group of buildings imitating the style of imperial palaces and thus creating a place for intellectuals to pay respect to Confucius, the temple was built in 1439 (Ming Dynasty) and enlarged in the following dynasty. Facing south, the Temple of Literature now occupies about 16,146 square feet. Two groups of ancient buildings stand in the east and west of the temple complex. The Holy Temple and the Wenchang Temple are the best preserved of the extant buildings.

The layout of Dacheng temple is a square. There are many ancient steles in it. (From Colphoto)

There is a collection of stone tablets in the Temple of Literature. One of them, the Tablet of West Xia, was initiated by Emperor Li Qianshun of West Xia Dynasty in 1049. The tablet is 8 feet high, 3 feet wide, and about 12 inches thick, with essay inscriptions on both sides. The main text is written in the official language of the

Pan Pond and Lingxing Door are in front of Dacheng Temple. The bridge over Pan Pond is known as Zhuangyuan Bridge (Number One Scholar Bridge). (From CFP)

The Bell Tower of Dayun Temple (From CFP)

Western Xia Dynasty, The back of the tablet contains lettered sentences in the style of Xiaozhuan. The epitaph relates the process of building and rebuilding of the Huguosi pagoda in both Han characters and Western Xia characters, and has great value in the study of the Western Xia language.

Copper Bell of Dayun Temple

The bell is located in Dayun Temple in the northeast of Wuwei. Dayun Temple, originally built by Zhang Tianxi in 363 and then renovated in 690 (Tang Dynasty), is one of the most famous ancient buildings in northwest China.

The extant Old Bell Tower in Dayun Temple was rebuilt in the Qing Dynasty and is still magnificent after 200 years. In 1927 an earthquake in Wuwei destroyed many local residences and temples, but the Old Bell Tower was untouched. It is 25.5 feet high and built on a 1,345-square-foot base surrounded by corridors. A large bell about 8 feet tall and 4 inches thick hangs in the tower, and the diameter of its mouth is about 5 feet. Three layers of pictures are carved on the exterior of the bell. The first layer depicts flying asparas (female divinities); the second, ghosts; and the third, dragons and the emperor. The bell was probably cast in the Tang Dynasty or earlier. Cast with alloy, it is one of China's six famous bells. Stentorian and magnificent, the bell can be heard miles away.

Leitai

Leitai, located outside the north gate of Wuwei, is a four-sided stereobate 28 feet high, 348 feet long from south to north, and 197 feet wide from east to west. Built in the Ming Dynasty, the extant buildings are Sanxing Temple, Leizu Temple, Triones Temple, and Southern Dipper Temple. In 1969 a large brick tomb of the late Eastern Han Dynasty was found under Leitai. There are three rooms in the tomb. The tomb door faces east, and the distance from the door to back room is more than a mile. There are 221 relics of different materials, such as gold, silver, bronze, iron, jade, bone, stone, and china, among which are 99 delicate bronze chariots and warriors. The world-famous bronze galloping horse is 26 inches high, 17.5 inches long, and weighs nearly 16 pounds. It is sculpted with its right rear hoof treading on a flying bird. The bronze galloping horse is so well-made that it is known worldwide as the "champion of ancient art." It is now the symbol of Wuwei City.

Leitai Han Tomb is one of the most famous spots in Wuwei. It takes a little less than one hour to visit the complex.

The inner construction of Leitai Han tomb (From Colphoto)

Haizang Temple

Haizang Temple is 1.5 miles northeast of Wuwei. The temple, hidden deep in the lush forest and surrounded by springs, looks as if it is floating in the ocean. The original construction date is not known, but it was rebuilt in the Ming and Qing dynasties. The temple faces south with a three-floor wooden pailou (archway) outside the red temple wall with the inscription "Buddha's forest of Haizang." At sunrise, a thread of mist rises from the east side of the archway, twisting elusively among poplars and willows. The marvelous scene is called "Haizang willows in mist" or "chilly mist at sunrise." Entering the door, you can see two immense temples. You can see a spectacular panorama of the entire Haizang Temple complex from the top of Lingjuntai. There is also a divine spring which is said to connect with the well of the Potala Palace in Tibet.

Wuwei was named "Liang state" in ancient times. From the Tang Dynasty to the Song Dynasty, Wuwei was part of Tibet and Xixia. The picture shows a colorfully painted wooden figure excavated from Wuwei. (From CFP)

Desert Park

Desert Park is located 12 miles east of Wuwei, at the edge of the Tennger Desert. It is the first desert park in China with both desert and oasis. The park occupies an enormous 86 million square feet and contains 20 species of cedar, totaling 5,000,000 plants. In the park, there are not only groups of Chinese ashes, toons, willows, and shiny-leaved yellowhorns, but also endangered desert species such as caper and holly. There are also playgrounds, observation platforms, and pavilions. Walking in the park, tourists can enjoy the clear water, abundant trees, and pavilions that are partly hidden and partly visible in the forest. Outside the park an old portion of the Great Wall meanders through the desert.

Wuwei Hundred Towers Temple was established in 1246 (Yuan Dynasty). The following year, the religious chief of Tibet Saban and the Xixia emperor Kuoban held a meeting here, which established the Yuan central government's administration of Tibet. (From CFP)

Zhangye Region

Best Time to Travel

June to September are the optimal months for travel in this section. The climate is dry, and the average temperature is 43°F.

Longevity Temple Wooden Pagoda

Longevity Temple Wooden Pagoda is located on South Street in Zhangye, on the campus of the Zhangye middle school. It was built in Northern Zhou Dynasty and rebuilt in the following dynasties. It has a history of 1,000 years, combining the architectural skills of woodwork, ironwork, and brushwork. The extant half-wooden pagoda was rebuilt in 1926 and is one of the "five elements pagodas" in Zhangye. The octagonal pagoda is 107 feet high with nine layers. Each layer has eight angles, on which dragons with precious pearls in their mouths are carved; wind-bells hang from the eaves.

Longevity Wooden Pagoda has different doors and windows in different layers. In the first layer, the doors face east and west. In the second layer, the windows face north and south. In the third layer, there are four doors and one window. The sixth layer has a door but no window, and the seventh has a window but no door. (From CFP)

Big Buddha Temple (Dafo Temple)

Big Buddha Temple is located in the northeast of Zhangye City. Because it contains the biggest indoor sleeping Buddha in China, it is also known as "Sleeping Buddha Temple." It is the only extant Buddhist temple of the Western Xia Dangxian ethnic group. Established in 1098 (Western Xia Dynasty), it was rebuilt in the Qing Dynasty. The buildings in the complex are the Big Buddha Temple, Sutra Pavilion, and Pagoda of Soil. The Sutra Pavilion holds a collection of 6,000 volumes of sutras, which were donated by Emperor Yingzong of the Ming Dynasty.

Shandan Army Horse-Breeding Farm

The Shandan Army Horse-Breeding Farm (Damaying Farm) in the Qilian Mountains is located 34 miles south of Shandan County, Zhangye. It is the oldest and largest horse-breeding farm in Asia. The land is flat and the grass luxurious, an ideal place for horse breeding. In the Western Han Dynasty, the local Mongolian horses were crossbred with the fine horses of the Western regions, producing the world-famous Shandan horses. The Shandan farm

The charming scene of the Shandan Army Horse-breeding Farm attracts many travelers. More than 30 films have been shot here, making this farm a popular film site. (From Colphoto)

gradually became the horse-breeding base for the royal family.

The Shandan Army Horse-Breeding Farm offers horseback riding, camping, racing, and horsemanship performances. Tourists can also enjoy the beautiful scenery.

The Ancient Great Wall of New Heyi

The Ancient Great Wall of New Heyi, 12 miles northeast of Shandan County, is the best preserved section of the ancient Great Wall. Known as the "outdoor museum," it consists of the Great Wall of the Han Dynasty and the Great Wall of the Ming Dynasty. The 61-mile length of the Han Dynasty section dates back to more than 2,000 years ago. The wall was replaced by entrenchments that are still distinct. The Great Wall of Ming Dynasty section dates back 400 years and is parallel to the Han Dynasty wall.

The Horse's Hoof Temple

This is located in Yugu Minority Autonomous County in Zhangye. Legend says that the horse from heaven once left a hoof print here. The hoof print has been kept in the temple as a talisman protecting the temple.

There are 5,382 square feet of frescoes on the four walls and partitions of the second floor of the Big Buddha Temple, which depict the stories and tenets of Buddhism. (From Colphoto)

Jiuquan, Jiayuguan Region

Best Time to Travel

May to October are the best months to travel to Jiuquan. In Jiuquan, winter is severe and long, but summer is pleasant and mild. Spring and autumn are short. Temperatures vary greatly from morning to evening. The climate is dry with little rain.

Jiuquan Park

Jiuquan Park, also known as Quanhu Park, is located in the area about a mile east of Jiuquan City. Named after the Jiu spring, the parkland has a 2,000-year history. The park combines a classical garden, a natural lake, and cultural entertainment. The spring is also called "golden spring" because legend says that there is gold in the spring. In 121 (Han Dynasty), General Huo Qubin defeated the Han, and Emperor Wu gave him a cup of wine. Huo Qubin insisted that the victory was made by the whole army, so he put the wine into the spring and shared it with his soldiers. There are also several famous stone tablets in Jiuquan Park.

Jiuquan Museum

Jiuquan Museum is located at 56 East Street in Jiuquan, not far from the west side of Jiuquan Park. It was established in October 1979 and is a comprehensive museum combining the collection and protection of relics, research, and education. More than 300 kinds of relics with a total of above 6,000 pieces are exhibited in the museum. The relics come from New Stone Age, Han Dynasty, Wei Dynasty, Jin Dynasty, Northern and Southern Dynasty, Sui Dynasty, and Tang Dynasty. There are three main exhibits: Jiuquan historical relics, Jiuquan topography, and ancient agricultural development. The museum also assumes the protection and research work of more than 260 ancient graves and ancient architecture sites.

Dingjiazha Mural Tomb

Located in Dingjiazha and Xigou of Guoyuan County, Jiuquan, Dingjiazha Mural Tomb is the earliest well-preserved mural tomb of the Wei and Jin dynasties. It is known as the "precious gallery underground" or "museum underground." The murals, straightforward and realistic in style, depict the affectionate Xi Wangmu (Queen Mother of the West in ancient Chinese legend), flying horses, deer, and elegant yurens (yurens are creatures in ancient Chinese legend with the heads of human beings and the bodies of birds).

In the Qing Dynasty, Zuo Zongtang was authorized to administer military affairs in Xinjiang Province. He planted 26,400 willows on the way from Changwu to Huining. People call these trees "Zuogong Willows." (From Colphoto)

Because this tomb was robbed many years ago, the only remaining funerary objects are some copper coins, a foot of bronze horse, and pieces of gold and fragmentary china, but the frescoes in the tomb are well preserved because of the dry climate.

Jiuquan Satellite Launch Center

Located in the depths of Badan Jaran Desert, 130 miles east of Jiuquan, this facility was built in 1958. It is the earliest and largest satellite launch center in China, and also a launching site for all types of launch vehicles, sounding rockets, and geophysical rockets. The center itself is an advanced complex with every imaginable high-tech instrument and facility. Visitors may tour the launching site, the command and control center, the No. 2 Changzheng (long Manch) launch vehicle, the test center, an exhibit hall of the launch center's history, the martyrs' cemetery, and the Dongfeng Reservoir.

Ten people at a time can tour the launch center.

A rocket launch (From CFP)

Jiayuguan Pass

Located in Jiayuguan, Gansu Province, Jiayuguan Pass is the middle part of the Hexi corridor as well as the western end of the Great Wall of the Ming Dynasty. It was built at the foot of Jiayu Mountain and is well known as the "impregnable pass under Heaven."

Begun in 1372 (Ming Dynasty), the pass is more than 600 years old. It became an important strategic outpost for its dangerously steep position at the narrowest ravine between Qilian Mountain and Jiayu Mountain. Constructed withi an inner city, outer city, and moat, and connected with the Great Wall, it forms a multitier defensive work. There are 14 buildings on Jiayuguan Pass, such as the archer's tower, the watch tower, the garret, and the strobe tower. The general office, pavilion of the well, and Wenchang pavilion are found in the inner city. Outside the east door is the Emperor Guan Temple with its decorative archway and theater. With perfect layout and immense buildings, Jiayuguan Pass is a necessary sightseeing stop.

The Great Wall Museum

This famous museum, on the west side of Xinhua North road in Jiayuguan, was established in 1988 and officially opened to the public in October 1989. In China, it is the first ad hoc museum that systematically tells about the culture of the Great Wall. The Great Wall Museum occupies about 133,000 square feet, and the exhibit area is just about 19,000 square feet. There are eight exhibition halls. The main building is in the form of a beacon tower. The exhibition halls consist of the Great Wall of the Spring and Autumn periods and the Warring States Period; the Great Wall of the Qin and Han Dynasties; the Great Wall of the North Wei, Sui, Tang, Liao, and Jin Dynasties; and the Great Wall of the Ming Dynasty. The Great Wall's construction history of 3,000 years from the Warring States Period to the Ming Dynasty is condensed in the form of charts, models, letters, and colored pictures. Modern instruments depict the magnificence of the ancient Great Wall.

There is a single brick on the eave of the door in the Xiwen tower. It is said that it was the only one left because artisans calculated exactly for the materials. (From Quanjing)

Tickets to the Great Wall Museum and Jiayuguan Great Wall are readily available.

Xuanbi Great Wall

The Xuanbi Great Wall is located on the the north slope of Black Mountain on the north side of Shiguan Gorge, five miles north of Jiayuguan. It is a part of Jiayuguan's army defense system and was built by the regional governor, Li Han, in 1540 (Ming Dynasty). The original length was almost a mile and is now less than half of that. The wall was constructed of stones and clay. There are two mounds at the ends of the Great Wall. This wall hangs in the air and covers the Shiguang Gorge. It is as immense as the Great Wall of Beijing.

Xincheng Mural Tomb of Wei and Jin Dynasty

Located in Xincheng County 7 miles northeast of Jiayuguan and Dingjiazha. There are 1,400 groups of brick tombs of Wei and Jin Dynasties (220–419), most of which were built with painted bricks. The Xincheng Mural Tomb is known as "the biggest underground gallery in the world." Here, frescoes describe the life of working people, servants, and masters, and exhibit an art style earlier than that of the Dunhuang Mogao Grottoes. Using the technique of realistic representation, the paintings represent politics, economy, military affairs, nationality, science and technology, and local customs.

No.1 Mound of the Great Wall

Also called "Taolai River Mound" or "Tou Mound," this site is located in the cliff more than 80 miles from the north bank of the Tailai River and 4 miles south of Jiayuguan. It is the first mound of the west end of the Great Wall, across the river from Qilian Mountain. The mound was built by regional governor, Li Han, from 1539 to 1540 (Ming Dynasty). The area on the west side of the mound is broad and convenient for watching the enemy. The original mound's length, height, and width are all 46 feet, built

The Xuanbi Great Wall is made of clay outside, stone and sand inside, and was solidified by ramming or pounding. The government began rebuilding a collapsed part of the wall in 1987, and the section is now open to travelers. (From CFP)

in the shape of pyramid. Part of the wall of the mound has been destroyed by wind and rain. Standing against the wall, the extant mound is in a dangerously steep position. In recent years, the Jiayuguan government rebuilt the wall on the north side of the first mound, which is 98 feet long and imitates the ancient Great Wall. There are also guardrails to protect the mound.

Jiayuguan Gliding Base

Located in the civil aviation airport 7 miles northeast of Jiayuguan city. With air currents perfect for glide, it is one of the three best gliding bases in the world. (The other two are in Australia and North Africa, respectively.) The high altitude and clear sky help produce air currents that can last up to 10 hours a day. The visibility can reach from 18 to 30 miles, and the up currents often ascend to more than 13,000 feet. The base has every kind of instrument for gliding, and professional gliders can complete their training and receive licenses here.

Dunhuang Region

Best Time to Travel

May to October is the best time of year to travel to Dunhuang. Because it is located in the hinterland and rimmed by high mountains, the climate is relatively dry. The temperature varies drastically from morning to evening, and we recommend that tourists dress in layers, bring an extra sweater or light coat, and sunglasses.

The Old City of Dunhuang

The old city of Dunhuang, also called "Dunhuang Movie City," is 12 miles northwest of Dunhaung. It occupies more than 130,000 square feet. Built as the set for the movie *Dunhuang,* cooperatively filmed by China and Japan, it replicates the ancient Shaozhou city.

In the style of the West region, the city has three doors facing east, west, and south, named after the five main streets of the Northern Song Dynasty, dotted with temples, warehouses, shops, hotels, and residences in the old style. The old city of Dunhuang also reproduces the scenery of Dunhuang in the Tang and Song Dynasties. Because of its scenery and facilities, it has become the most popular movie set in western China.

There are many souvenirs available, such as tapestries, rugs and carved camels.

Echoing-Sand Mountain (Mingsha Mountain)

Echoing-Sand Mountain, also called "Shensha Mountain" or "Shajiao Mountain," is 3 miles from Dunhuang. From west to east, the mountain extends over 25 miles from Mogao Grottoes to the Danghe reservoir at the foot of Sleeping Mountain. The mountain stretches more than 12 miles from north to south. The highest peak is 5,627 feet above sea level. According to legends, the sand produces musical sounds even in sunny days without wind.

The mountain appears like a golden dragon winding its way over the horizon, which is a wonderful spectacle.

> If you plan to travel to Echoing-Sand Mountain in the summer, evening is the best time, when the visitor can avoid the scorching sands.

Crystal-clear Crescent Lake is beautiful and full of mysteries. (From ImagineChina)

Crescent Lake

Crescent Lake nestles in the embrace of Mingsha Shan (Mount Echoing Sand), shaped like a new moon. It is one of the eight famous scenic areas of Dunhuang.

There are schools of fish in the lake and carpets of lush green grass on the bank. Legend says that the fish, called "iron-back fish," can cure many diseases, and that the grass, called "seven-star grass," can hasten childbirth and restore virility and potency. There is an old saying that people can live a long and fruitful life by eating the fish and grass, and the lake is also called "Medicine Lake." Crescent Lake is about 984 feet long and 164 feet wide. Even after thousands of years of drifting sand, the clean lake has never been covered by the sand. On the rim of the lake, white poplars grow

The camel team coming back from Echoing-Sand Mountain raises yellow sand all over the sky. The scene reproduces the trade caravans of the Silk Road in ancient times. (From Liu Liwen)

tall and erect, the sweet smell of narrow-leaved oleasters greets visitors, and clusters of reeds sway in the breeze. To the south of the lake, there are groups of old buildings such as the Temple of Goodness, Palace of Dragon King, Cave of the Medicine King, Jade Spring Building, and Thunder Temple. Crescent Lake has dreamlike mysteries and miraculous legends passed on for thousands of years, making this area a popular scenic spot.

West Thousand Buddha Caves

West Thousand Buddha Caves (west of Mogao Caves) are situated on a cliff at the north side of the Dang River, about 21 miles northwest of Dunhuang. There are 22 extant caves of Northern Wei, Western Wei, Northern Zhou, Sui, Tang, Five Kingdoms, and Song Dynasties, in which there are almost 10,000 square feet of murals and 53 painted statues. Among these caves, the first three were excavated in the Tang Dynasty, the next five from the Wei Dynasty, and the sixteenth from the late Tang Dynasty. Because of river erosion, the cliff collapsed, and only a few caves remain.

The structure, frescoes, and sculptures of these caves, with an artistic style similar to Mogao Caves, are important contributions to Dunhuang art. In the nine well-preserved caves, most have altars in the middle with statues of Buddha in the niches excavated around them. On the wall, there are pictures of Xianjie Buddhas, sitting Buddhas saying dharma, and Buddha's nirvana. Under the pictures of Buddha on the altars and walls, warrior attendants are evident. On the south wall in a cave of Northern Wei, there are Zijing pictures on the west side and pictures of Laoducha fighting against Shengbian on the east side. These are the earliest pictures about this topic extant in the Dunhuang caves.

The caves lie along the road from Dunhuang to Yangguan Pass.

Big Fangpan City

Big Fangpan City is also known as Hecang City and is located in the Gobi Desert 56 miles northwest of downtown Dunhuang. Built squarely with rammed earth bricks as a depository for grain and fodder in the Han Dynasty, it is the only structure of its kind in Gansu. Now there are only a few foundations remain-

Big Fangpan City site. The walls and houses are made of clay but still keep their shape, despite hundreds of years of incessant wind and sand. (From Colphoto)

Countless trade caravans have gone through Yumenguan Pass, giving rise to legends and folk tales. In the place where spring winds cannot reach, the silent, crumbing Great Wall of the Han Dynasty has remained intact for 2,000 years. (From Colphoto)

ing, 492 feet long and 180 feet wide.

A 3-foot-high natural platform lies north of the city, on which there was once an grain storehouse, 433 feet long and 56 feet wide. Two walls separate the storehouse into three rooms with doors facing south. Many parts of the walls have collapsed. The thickness of the walls is about 5 feet, and the highest of the remaining walls is about 25 feet. Two rows of triangular vent holes were cut symmetrically on the south and north walls, three up and five down. The storehouse is encircled by another wall, which has only east and north parts. At each corner there is a mound, the southwest one being 23 feet high. Many scholars believe this city is the "Hecang City" recorded in ancient tracts. The Shule River is to the north of the city. It was once used to transport grain and fodder for soldiers and horses guarding Yumen Pass.

Site of Yumen Pass

The site of Yumen Pass is on the Gobi Desert 50 miles northwest of Dunhuang. Legend says that the jades of Hezhen in the West were imported to central China from there. The pass was built in the West Han Dynasty as the major passageway between the West and the East, also a necessary part of the south Silk Road.

The walls in the square pass are well preserved: 79 feet long, 87 feet wide, and 32 feet high and built entirely from yellow clay, covering 6,814 square feet. There are gates on the west wall and the north wall.

Site of Yangguan Pass

Yangguan Pass is on "Gudong Beach," 43 miles southwest of Dunhuang. It was built in 114 BCE (Han Dynasty) on the south side of Yumen Pass. In the

Yardang means "steep hill" in Uigur. The Yardang land formations in northwest Dunhuang are called "Ghost City." When strong winds blow, air currents dash against the sandstones, producing horrifying and eerie voices. (From CFP)

old days, south was called "Yang," thus "Yangguan." Yangguan Pass is the passageway to the West as well as a strategic point on the south Silk Road. In the Western Han Dynasty, it was regarded as an important military past. Since the Song Dynasty, Yangguan has been gradually buried by merciless desert winds and sands, leaving only a beacon tower standing on Dundun Hill at the north side of the Pass. Nearby, there are some intermittent castle foundations no more than 2 feet high, and that is the original location of the Yangguan Pass. On Dundun Hill, where the beacon tower stands, a long corridor of inscriptions has been erected. People can appreciate the poems and calligraphy, or visit the original site of Yangguan Pass, taking in the oasis, desert, and snow-capped mountains.

> The Yangguan Pass and Yumen Pass are included in the one-day tour of Dunhuang.

Dunhuang Yardang Land Formations

Yardang Land Formations is located 112 miles northwest of Dunhuang City. The geographical conditions have formed continuous groups of these formations, which cover about 154 square miles and are precious geological heritage.

The typical formation is a wind-eroded mound or hillocks found near Lop Nor. These large tracts of hillocks rise from a flat sandstone layer. Anxi County, commonly called "wind storehouse of the world," lies on a narrow corridor between two mountains. Its altitude is just 3,839 feet above sea level, and its terrain is low and flat. When air currents blow in, they funnel through this narrow corridor and produce strong horizontal winds, something like blowing air through a thin pipeline. Thousands of years of this wind combined with the blazing sun have changed the flat sandstone layer into all kinds of forms. The magnificent sights attract many visitors.

> It takes two hours to drive to Yardang Land Formations from Dunhuang. There are ATVs for rent at the scenic spots.

Yulin Grottoes

Yulin Grottoes, also known as "ten thousand Buddha gorge," is located along the Yulin River, 46.5 miles southwest of Anxi County. It is renowned for the large number of elms planted there. The 42 caves on both sides of the river trace back to the Tang, Five, Song, Western Xia, and Yuan Dynasties. Inside these caves, murals cover an area of about 60,000 square feet,and there are also 10,826 remnants of Buddha paintings. The oldest cave, quite different from the center-columned caves in the Northern Wei Dynasty, dates back to the early Tang Dynasty, and has the artistic style of early Yulin Grottoes. Cave 25 contains very well-preserved murals; the paintings are incomparable. Caves that date back to the Western Xia and Yuan Dynasties are also worth a visit, especially the six remnants of murals entitled "Journey to the West" found in caves of the Western Xia Dynasty.

Yulin Grottoes is similar to Mogao Cave in its contents, artistic styles, and painting techniques. After the period of Five Dynasties (907–960), art forms in Mogao Cave underwent a gradual decline; however, the murals of Yulin Grottoes are fascinating and well worth a visit.

The Ruins of the City of Suoyang

Named for the perennial plant Cynomorium (Suoyang), famed for its enhancement of male virility and potency, Suoyang, also known as Kuyu City, is 43 miles east of Anxi County to the west of the Hexi Corridor. In ancient times, the Shule River flowed through the city, which was founded in the Han Dynasty and prospered in the Tang Dynasty; thus, the architecture here follows the styles of Tang Dynasty. In the southeast, there is a temple, constructed in Yuan Dynasty. One big tower in the temple is 48 feet high, and several smaller temples are arranged in a straight line. Suoyang was initially situated on the Silk Road and played an important role in politics, economy, culture, and military affairs of the time. Constructed with an outer city and an inner city, a mound in the northwest is 59 feet high, from which you can discern the ruins of a lookout tower and arena. There is also an ancient defense system consisting of warhorses and an extensive farmland irrigation system.

The ruins of Suoyang (From CFP)

Mogao Caves

Mogao Caves, also known as "thousand Buddha caves," is located on the eastern slope of Mingsha Mountain (Echoing-Sand Mountain), 15.5 southeast of Dunhuang. Mogao Caves contains a large treasury of Buddhist art and well-preserved relics. In 1987, the cave was listed as a UNESCO World Heritage site.

According to records of the Tang Dynasty, Mogao Caves was founded in 366 and enlarged in the following dynasties. After thousands of years, it was enlarged to 5,512 feet long from south to north with more than 700 caves. There are 492 caves with statues and frescoes, 2,415 colorfully painted statues, almost 500,000 square feet of frescoes, five wooden eaves, thousands of lotus stone pillars and flowered floor tiles, and about 52,400 documents (two out of three are preserved).

The typical cave structure of the Sui and Tang Dynasties was flat and square, covered by an arched roof with a niche at back. From the late Tang Dynasty to the Song and Yuan Dynasties, the frescoes and niches had been replaced by altars in the middle of the caves, so that a whole rock cliff was reserved for large-scale frescoes. Painted statues are the typical art of Dunhuang, and most of the statues are the three-body combinations of one Buddha and two bodhisattvas; some of them are Anan, JiaYe, the Ten Great Disciples and arhats, deities, and Buddha's warrior attendants. The bodies were depicted as sturdy in the former Northern Wei Dynasty and gradually became slender. From Sui and Tang Dynasty, groups of painted statues with seven to nine

(From Colphoto)

bodies appeared. The style became more and more elegant and magnificent. The frescoes are the most eye-catching part of Mogao Caves, showing the outstanding creativity of the artists and their excellent achievements. They reflect the history of Chinese people from different stratums, including their work lives, social activities, science and technologies, music and dancing, cultures and customs of various ethnic groups, dresses, and adornments. In 1900, a cave of Buddhist scriptures was found in the corridor of the sixteenth cave, where about 50,000 relics of the fourth to the fourteenth century were found, including posthumous papers, embroideries, silk pictures, and paper pictures. Many of the papers are handwritten copies in Chinese, but there are also many other languages represented, such as old Tibetan, Sanskrit, Huihu, Yutian, and Guizi .

Dunhuang art is extensive and profound, and offers a treasury of art combining architecture, sculpture, and fresco in one. The relics and artwork in the caves attract many scholars from various countries.

(From CFP)

(From Quanjing)

(From CFP)

Notes

Dunhuang is about two hours behind Beijing. There are always hotels open, even if you arrive at midnight.

The ruins of Qiaowan (From Colphoto)

Gannan (South Gansu) Region

Best Time to Travel

Late spring and summer (from May to August) are the optimal times to travel in the south of Gansu. The place is quite beautiful during this period. If you come here in February and March, you might be able to participate in the Prayer Festival.

Pavilion of Buddha Milarepa

The Pavilion of Buddha Milarepa was originally founded in 1777. It was rebuilt in May 1988, and its reconstruction was completed four years later in 1992. The pavilion is a nine-story temple devoted to Buddha Milarepa, revered by many Buddhist groups in Xizang. In addition to more than 1,700 Buddha sculptures, there are excellently painted murals.

➡ Visitors must remove their shoes at the entrance to the pavilion.

Langmu Temple

Langmu Temple is situated in Langmu Temple Village, 56 miles south of Luqu City. At the side of Bailong (white dragon) River, this temple is in the common boundary of Gansu Provice and Sichuan Province. *Langmu* means "goddess" in the Xizang dialect. The rock in the cave looks like a beautiful maiden, who was thought by the local people to be a goddess.

➡ It is cold at night in Langmu Temple all year.

Bowbeam of Labrang Temple (From Colphoto)

Gate and decorations of Labrang Temple (From Colphoto)

The Ruins of Qiaowan

The city of Qiaowan, by the Shule River, is situated on the right side of Ganxin Road, 53 miles northeast of Anxi County and located in the common boundary of Jiayu Pass, Qilian Mountain, Menggu, and Xinjiang Province. Founded in 1732, Qiaowan was initially a military beachhead. Hui people rebelled against the government in 1862, and the city was evacuated. From east to west, it is 1,010 feet long and 400 feet long from north to south. There are also ruins of ancient buildings. Museums in Qiaowan display various exhibits of wild desert animals, mummies, and over 80 valuable cultural relics, among which is a replica of an ivory Buddha.

Prayer wheels in Labrang Temple are arranged in a line as long as two miles. It will take more than an hour to view each prayer wheel. (From CFP)

Labrang Temple

Labrang Temple, backed by Phoenix Mountain and fronted by Mountain Dragon, is about a half-mile west of Xiahe County. The temple, first founded in 1710, is now the biggest religious and cultural center in Gansu, Qingzang, and Sichuan provinces. Six academies are within the temple, making it the largest Lama university in the world.

On the 4th day to the 15th day of January and on the 29th day of Lunan to the 15th day of July, a prayer festival is held.

Gontang Pagodas

Situated in the southwest corner of Labrang Temple, which was founded in 1805, and originally named as "Golden Tower for Extrication." The existing pagodas were built in February 1991 on the site of the original pagodas. The five-story tower is 103 feet high, in the middle of which stand four adjoining Buddha palaces. Wooden Buddha sculptures and more than 20,000 volumes of sutra are be found there.

Lake Dazong

Lake Dazong is about 6 miles from Wangxia Road in Xiahe County and sits some 10,000 feet above sea level. Around the lake, there are many rugged rock mountains and lush pine trees. It covers an area of nearly 400,000 square feet, stretching 1,148 feet from north to south and 328 feet from east to west. Situated in an open coastal area, the lake is surrounded by fertile meadows on one side and mountains on the other three sides.

Lake Dazong is regarded as a "divine lake" by local people. Every June, pilgrims from all over the country come here to pray for happiness and good luck.

The best place to have beef noodle is at the street side stall, where you will watch the cook stretch the big chunk of dough into springy noodles with a flourish and hear the sound of noodles slapping against the noodle board and wheat flour. It is an amazing skill. (From ImagineChina)

GanSu

Lanzhou Beef Noodle

As the most famous local food in Lanzhou, Lanzhou beef noodle is also called beef noodle with clear soup. It is characterized by five features: first is its soup (clearness), second is its whiteness (white radish), third is its redness (red pepper oil), fourth is its greenness (coriander), and fifth is its yellowness (bright yellow noodle). In terms of thickness, the noodle can be divided into several types such as extra wide, wide, narrow, extra narrow, fine as hair, leek leaf, and buck wheat leaf. The soup is clear and refreshing, the beef is tender, and the noodles are pliant and smooth.

Only when you taste beef noodle in Lanzhou can you be considered to have visited Lanzhou.

Saozi Noodle

Saozi noodle is the famous traditional wheat food in Lanzhou. According to legend, it evolved from the "longevity noodle" of the Tang Dynasty, prepared for the elders and children on their birthdays and for guests on festive occasions. It was served with the promise of "living a long life with fortune." When eating Saozi noodle, you eat the noodles first with chopsticks, then the Saozi with a spoon. The spicy and hot soup with long and thin noodles of pliant texture make Saozi noodle a nutritious dish suitable for both the old and the young.

Gansu Hua'er Folk Song Competition

Since ancient times, Gansu has been a province inhabited by various ethnic groups. Among the 45 ethnic minorities are the Dongxiang, Yugu, and Bao'an, the three ethnic groups native to Gansu Province. The Han, Hui, and Tibetans are the largest ethnic groups in present–day Gansu. Each nationality in Gansu has different customs

Luminescent cup (From ImagineChina)

regarding wedding, funeral, holiday, diet, attire, residence, etiquette, and cultural events. As these social events are held in different times at different locations, they form a scenario of successive festive activities on a grand scale. As an event popular among various nationalities in Gansu, the Hua'er folk song competition in Lianhua Mountain of Linxia is well-known throughout China. Located in an area bordering Kangle County of Linxia and Lintan and Zhuoni Counties of Gannan, Lianhua Mountain is the cradle of the northwestern folk song style called *Hua'er*. From 1st to 6th of Lunar June every year, Hua'er folk singers from nearby places assemble in Lianhua Mountain and participate in the singing competition. The folk singers improvise their songs and compete without any constraint, presenting songs of great interest. Most of the Hua'er are short love songs.

Luminescent Cup

"From cups of jade that glow with wine of grapes at night, drinking to pipa songs, we are summoned to fight." This line from "Starting for the Front" brought the luminescent cup great renown. The luminescent cup is also called Yangguan Jade cup, carved out of Qilianshan's black jade, yellow jade, and green jade through more than 30 procedures. It has a unique shape and a bright and clear quality. It's so smooth that it feels like water drops. It's so colorful that it looks like jade crystal. The luminescent cup is mainly used to hold liquor. It won't crack when you pour either cold liquor or heated liquor into it. The most amazing feature is that the cup gives off a dazzling glow when you put wine into it in the moonlight.

Qingyang Paper-cut

Paper-cut is China's traditional folk art form with a long history and unique style, deeply loved by people both at home and abroad. Qingyang paper-cut is of an ancient and simple style, with a sense of natural vigor and a pattern of sophisticated design. It not only reflects the Chinese ancestral totem culture, but also represents the essence of pre-Qin culture. The Chinese contemporary literary figure, Mr. Guo Moruo, praised it as "the art of skillful use of scissors exceeds that of the god, and the beauty from the common masses never perishes." So Qingyang paper-cut is also referred to as the "living fossil" of ancient culture. Qingyang paper-cut falls into two categories: colorful and single color. In terms of technique, there are three kinds: cutting, carving, and smoking flower.

Qingyang paper-cut. (From CFP)

Famous Qin Opera performers (From CFP)

Among these, smoking flower is unique to Qingyang paper-cut, an innovation based on the paper-cut: put the pattern of the paper-cut on a sheet of white paper, spray water on it, smoke it with kerosene lamp, then take off the paper-cut and the whole design stays on the white sheet of paper. It's vivid and charged with emotion.

West Qin Opera

Qin Opera used to be popular in the central part of Sha'anxi and most of the northwestern region. After 1949 and upon the instruction from Premier Zhou Enlai, the July 1 Opera Troupe was organized in Zhangye of the Hexi region. Most of the actors of this troupe were famous Qin opera performers at the time. As time went by, the local flavor was added to their performance and a regional branch of Qin opera gradually came into being known as West Qin Opera. In the 1970s, West Qin Opera was very popular among the people living in Hexi region. However, except in some remote areas, the popularity of West Qin Opera seems to have declined recently.

Leather-silhouette show in Zhangye (From CFP)

Leather-Silhouette Show

Leather-silhouette show can only be found in China. As a unique folk art form, the show uses the leather which is hard to preserve. That's why there are not many stage props left from the old times. Leather-silhouette show can be dated back to as early as West Han Dynasty up to Northern Song Dynasty. The material used is cow hide or donkey skin, which is carved into various vivid opera figures enjoyed by the audience. The stage props have the characteristics of simple design and exaggerated lines.

Silk Road

The ancient Silk Road generally refers to the deserts and oasis from Chang'an (present day Xi'an) to the eastern coast of Mediterranean. Gansu is situated in the golden portion of the ancient silk road, which stretches its way throughout Gansu covering a distance of 1,000 miles. Nowadays, thousands of tourists from every part of the world are still attracted by the myriad cultural antiques, historical artifacts, splendid natural scenery, and colorful local customs.

The Silk Road is like a colorful ribbon, connecting the civilizations of ancient Asia, Europe, and Africa. It was via the Silk Road that the techniques of raising silk worm and weaving silk as well as a great variety of silk products, tea, and porcelain were

The caravan on the Silk Road (From CFP)

brought to the other countries in the world. Therefore, the influence of the Silk Road upon the social and economic development of countries in the world can't be underestimated. Meanwhile, the Chinese and foreign merchants introduced into China beautiful horses, grapes, India's Buddhism, new music, sugar making, new medicines, West Asia's musical instruments, the making of gold and silver ware, astronomy, mathematics, cotton, tobacco, and sweet potato, enriching ancient China's civilization.

Three Unique Aspects of Longyuan

The three unique aspects of Longyuan refer to traditional delicacies in Gansu Province. They appeal to tourists and local residents by their special colors and particular tastes.

Ham and Preserved Meat

They are said to have a history of 300 years. They are famous for their choice material, refined ingredients, and meticulous processing. The lean meat, which is rich in color, does not taste dry; the fatty meat, which is as crystal as agate, does not taste oily.

Gold Coin Meat

Also called butterfly meat and corn meat. It's the traditional treasured delicacy of western Gansu. Its material is donkey penis with a red bright color and great taste. It appeals not only to the eyes but also to the taste buds. It contains plenty of protein and useful elements such as calcium, iron, and phosphorous. It can improve the health and fortify the kidney.

Longxi Roast Chicken Mix

It's made of chicken, egg, starch, spinach, and various seasonings. The brown soup and green powder with both chicken and egg is suitable for all seasons. In hot summer, it can be served cold to refresh your appetite, reduce the heat, and alleviate fever. In cold winter, it can be served hot to give a fresh and strong flavor. It tastes best when served with liquor. When a patient just recovers from illness, roast chicken mix can facilitate his/her recovery with great efficiency. So it is good for everyone.

Ningxia Hui Autonomous Region

Geography at a Glance

"Ning" is the colloquial term for the Ningxia Hui Autonomous Region. It is situated in northwest China and bordered by Gansu to the south, Shanxi to the east, and the Inner Mongolia Autonomous Region to the north, and it covers a total area of 25,637 square miles and has a population of 5.62 million (2000 census).

Ningxia is situated in the middle reaches of the Yellow River, a transitional zone from Loess Plateau to Mongolian Plateau. The landform features mountainous regions and plateaus, which comprises 75 percent of the total area: Helan mountainous region, Ningxia plain, Ordos Plateau, Loess Plateau, and Liupan Mountain. The main rivers in Ningxia are the Yellow, Qingshui, Kushui, Jing, Hulu, Hongliu, and Zuli.

It has a temperate continental climate with long, cold winters and short, hot summers. There is always plenty of sunshine, so the atmosphere is often dry and windy. The average annual temperature is 41–50°F, and the annual rainfall averages from 8 to 28 inches.

A unique landscape, quaint local customs and habits, and ancient history add up to make Ningxia an interesting tourist area for those wishing to discover a rich and diverse region.

(From Quanjing)

Ningxia Hui Autonomous Region

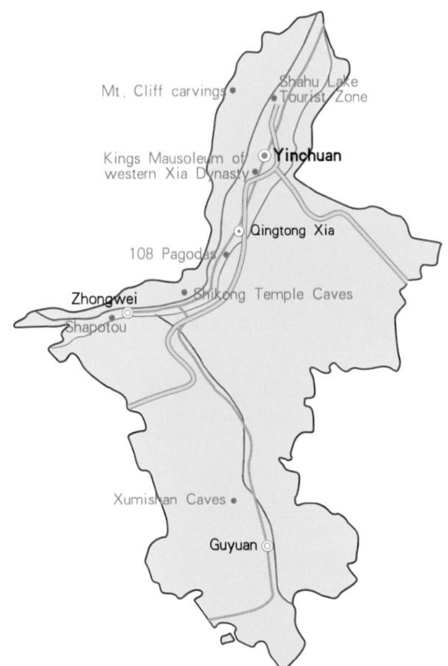

Featured Cuisine

Cooked mutton chop, boiled mutton, steamed carp, crispy fried mutton chop, instant-boiled mutton, noodles with cooked mutton, spicy chicken, stir-fried dough sheets with mutton, braised mutton with membranous milk vetch, cooked mutton with medlar, Malan noodle, roast sheep banquet.

Featured Commodities

Herbal Medicines

Ningxia medlar, Yanchi licorice, starwort root, fritillary bulb, peach seed, almond, upright ladybell root, plantain seed, pepperweed seed, sweet wormwood herb, folium artemisia argyi, peony root, white peony root, Chinese wolfberry root-bark, leonurus heterophyllus sweets.

Special Local Products

Jacquard blankets, lingwu charcoal, Tan-sheep wool, Yinchuan wine, Guyuan buckwheat, Guyuan fern, Taixi coal.

Local Handicrafts

Helan stone, Ningxia carpets, Qingtongxia woven willow, Shizui Mountain pottery, Yinchuan tan-sheep brand jacquard blankets, snuff pots, folding screens.

Scenery of Shahu Lake (From ImagineChina)

Notes 

❶ Dining and accommodation in Ningxia are quite inexpensive. Fast food and restaurants can be found everywhere. Local food is often quite spicy, somewhat like Sichuan cuisine.

❷ Restaurants run by Hui people are very clean. The food supplied there is popular with customers, especially cooked beef and mutton. Hui people make use of fragrant incense, which creates a comfortable atmosphere in restaurants and homes.

❸ Ningxia is the home of Chinese Muslims. As always, be respectful of the unique local customs and habits of the different ethnic groups.

POPULAR FESTIVALS

Ashura Commemoration

Ashura is held in the Hui area on the 10th day of the first Islamic month (end of January) to commemorate the martyrdom of the grandson of the Prophet Mohammed.

Shengji Festival

Shengji Festival is held on the 12th day of the third Islamic month. The imam delivers a well-attended sermon.

Dengxiao Festival

Everyone goes to mosque on Dengxiao Festival, which is held on the 27th day of the seventh Islamic month.

Kaizhai Festival

Kaizhai festival is the traditional holiday for the Hui ethnic group. It is held on the 1st day of the tenth Islamic month. At this time, everyone goes to the mosque and visits relatives. Many people take part in contests and horse races.

Guerbang Festival

The most important Hui festival is Guerbang, which is on the 10th day (70 days after Kaizhai) of the twelfth Islamic month according to the Islamic calendar. People attend mosques, visit relatives, and sacrifice sheep and other livestock.

Transportation Tips

By Bus

A transportation network has been built leading from Yinchuan, Zhongning, and Guyuan to all parts of the area. There are seven national highways and six provincial highways.

By Train

Baolan railroad runs from the northeast of Ningxia to the southwest. It starts from Baotou in the east, connects with the Jingbao line, and ends in Lanzhou in the west, where there are connections with the Lanxin, Lanqing, and Longhai lines.

By Plane

Yinchuan Hedong Airport, located in the southeast of the city, is the only airport in Ningxia. From here you can fly to nearly all of the major cities of China. In Qinghai, there are some areas with frozen ground, such as Kekexili. In summer the roads turn to mud and can trap cars easily.

Recommended Routes

Classical Routes

Eight-day tour of Ningxia

Day 1 Arrival in Yinchuan. Lodging: Ningxia Hotel.

Day 2 Yinchuan→Zhongwei (visiting Qingtongxia Tower 108 along the road). Lodging: Zhonngwei Hotel.

Day 3 Zhongwei→South Changtan (boat ride on the Yellow River). Lodging: Zhongwei Hotel.

Day 4 Zhongwei→Tengger Desert. Lodging: desert tents.

Day 5 Walking through the Tengger Desert. Lodging: desert tents.

Day 6 Tengger Desert→Yinyan Road→Zhongwei. Lodging: Zhongwei Hotel.

Day 7 Zhongwei→Yinchuan→Mausoleums of Western Xia Kingdom→Shahu Lake. Lodging: Ningxia Hotel.

Day 8 End of tour.

Six-day tour of Badan Jilin desert

Day 1 Arrival in Yinchuan. Lodging: Ningxia Hotel.

Day 2 Yinchuan→Jiukeshu (Nine Trees). Lodging: tents.

Day 3 Hike through Badan Jilin Desert. Lodging: tents.

Day 4 Badan Jilin Desert. Lodging: tents.

Day 5 Return to Yinchuan. Lodging: Ningxia Hotel.

Day 6 End of tour.

Traditional Routes

Six-day tour of Saishang Jiangnan

Day 1 Arrival in Yinchuan.

Day 2 Mausoleums of Western Xia Kingdom→Western Movie Studio→Helan Mountain.

Day 3 Yinchuan→Shahu Lake→Nanguan Muslim Mosque→Chengtiansi Pagoda

Day 4 Yinchuan→Zhongwei→Shapotou.

Day 5 Zhongwei→Guyuan→Sanying Village→Xumi Mountain→Yinchuan.

Day 6 End of tour.

Eleven-day tour from Ningxia, Kongtong Mountain to Baoji

Day 1 Arrival in Yinchuan.

Day 2 Mausoleum in Western Xia Kingdom →China West Film Studio→Helan Mountain→Shahu Lake.

Day 3 West Tower→North Tower→Yuhuang Pavilion→Nanguan Muslim Mosque→Qingtongxia Tower 108→Zhongwei.

Day 4 Shapotou→Tengger Desert.

Day 5 Zhongwei→Tongxi→Guyuan.

Day 6 Guyuan→Pingliang in Gansu.

Day 7 One day tour of Kongtong Mountain.

Day 8 Pingliang→Baoji.

Day 9 One-day tour of Taibai Mountain.

Day 10 Panxi Angling stage→Mausoleum of King of Fire.

Day 11 End of tour.

Four-day tour of Ningxia

Day 1 Western Xia Museum→Shahu Lake →Western Movie Studio→Helan Mountain.

Day 2 Mausoleums of Western Xia Kingdom→Great Wall of Ming Dynasty→Qingtongxia Tower 108→Gao Temple.

Day 3 Jingheyuan Scenic Park.

Day 4 Guyuan Museum→Grottoes of Xumi Mountain→Wuzhong farmers' market→Mosque. End of tour.

Self-Guided Tours

Peripheral area of Ningxia and Inner Mongolia

The tour starts from Yinchuan and ends in Ordos. During the drive, you will pass Helan Mountain, Shizui Mountain, Ba Yan Nao Er League, Baotou, and other sites. You will also see the Yellow River Bridge, Xiangsha Bay, Mausoleum of Genghis Khan, Ordos Grand Canyon, and Green Mountain.

Western Xia's culture tour

The tour starts from and ends inYinchuan. You will pass through Wuliji Sumu, Ejinaqi, and Lashanzuoqi. Major sites here include

Addresses and Phone Numbers

Helan Mountain Hotel	1 Sufang Road, New Downtown, Yinchuan	0951-2077075
Ningxia International Hotel	365 East Bejing Road, Yinchuan	0951-6728688
Kaida Hotel	256 South Qinghe Street, Yinchuan	0951-6021698
Yinchuan Hotel	No. 28, Southern Yuxingge Street, Yinchuan Ciy	0951-6037666
Green Mountain Hotel	81West Chaoyang Street, Shizui Mountain City	0952-2012926
Hongyan Hotel	Xinsheng Street, Wuzhong	0953-2018348
Zhongwei Hotel	33 West Avenue, Zhongwei	0955-7012609
Guyuan Hotel	94 Government Street, Guyuan	0954-2023750
Tour Hotel of Jingyuan	2 Baiquan Road, Jingyuan County, Guyuan	0954-5011941

Mausoleum in Western Xia Dynasty, Murals of Helan Mountain, Ming Dynasty Great Wall at Sanguan Pass, Black City, Red City, Green City, Juyan Cultural Relic, Mongolia King Palace, Divine Tree, Ghost Trees, Oriental Spaceflight Center, South Temple, North Temple, Moon Lake, Yanfu Temple, Yuhuang Pavilion, Bell Tower, Najiahu Mosque, and Haibao Pagoda.

Traditional goat skin rafts are used to cross the Yellow River. (From Colphoto)

Yinchuan, Shizui Region

Best Time to Travel

The best time to visit Yinchuan is from May to October. Although it is rarely rainy in Yinchuan, water resources here are abundant due to the "oasis effect." Because the climate is generally dry and windy, often with blowing sand, it would be best to carry wind-proof and sand-proof articles. It's better not to wear contact lenses.

Shopping Tips

Yinchuan Department Store is situated in 2 West Liberation Street. It is the first department store since the establishment of the Ningxia Hui Autonomous Region. Customers can buy many good-quality products at a fair price. Xinhua Shopping Center is in the busiest downtown area of Yinchuan City on Xinhua Avenue. It's an ideal place for shopping and finding bargains.

Yuhuang Pavilion

Yuhuang Pavilion is located at the crossroads between East Liberation Street and Yuhuang Pavilion Street in Yinchuan. It was built in Ming Dynasty and called Yuhuang Pavilion in honor of the Emperor of Yuhuang (Jade Emperor). This group of structures is built on a rectangular rammed-earth platform 121 feet long, 92 feet wide, and 26 feet tall. The center of the platform has a south-facing hall under a double gable-and-hipped roof, linked in the south to another hall featuring a curved-canopy roof. An exquisite portico under a curved-canopy roof is built into the facade of the main hall. Each floor of the building has red-lacquered doors, and the latticed windows are covered with richly embroidered panes. The balcony, surrounded by red-painted balustrades, provides an outstanding view of the surrounding landscape.

Chengtiansi Pagoda

Built in 1050, the octagonal Chengtiansi Pagoda graces the Chengtian Temple in the southwest corner of Yinchuan. According to history books, after the death of Li Yuanhao, the founding king of the Western Xia Kingdom, his mother conscripted tens of thousands of soldiers for the construction of the Chengtian Temple and its pagoda as a token of her wish for the longevity of Li Liang, the child king who had just been enthroned.

There are extraordinary vaulted pavilions on both sides of the gate of the Nanguan Muslim Mosque. (From Quanjing)

Haibao Pagoda

Also known as the Black Pagoda, the Haibao Pagoda stands in the courtyard of the Haibao Temple in the northern suburbs of Yinchuan. It is said that the pagoda was rebuilt by the king of the Daxia Kingdom in 407. The unique eleven-story pagoda is 177 feet tall and is well worth a visit.

> Haibao Pagoda is in a remote area, so you can get there only by taxi, which will cost you about seven RMB.

Nanguan Muslim Mosque

Nanguan Muslim Mosque is located on the periphery of the old city in Yinchuan. It was built in the Ming Dynasty and rebuilt in 1980. The mosque consists of a series of structures in Arabian style. The main building of the Nanguan Muslim Mosque is about 85 feet tall. The great hall upstairs is large enough to hold 1,300 worshippers. The middle section of the main building is topped with one large and four small green-painted domes.

> A local guide can explain native traditions and make sure you can participate in the traditional festivals of the Hui ethnic group.

Twin Pagodas at Baisikou

This pair of identical octagonal brick pagodas is about 31 miles northwest of Yinchuan. Standing 328 feet apart, these pagodas are the only remaining structures of what was once the summer

The relics of mausoleums of Western Xia Kingdom are also called "pyramids of China." (From ImagineChina)

Zhenbeibao (Northern Garrison Post), about 19 miles west of Yinchuan City. In the Ming Dynasty, it was built as a castle stationed with garrison troops in defense of Yinchuan. Founded by Zhang Xianliang, a contemporary Chinese novelist, it is now a film studio for a number of award-winning western Chinese movies.

resort of Emperor Li Yuanhao of the Western Xia. There are various seated and standing Buddha sculptures in the west pagoda.

Mausoleums of Western Xia Kingdom

These mausoleums on the eastern side of the Helan Mountain, 15.5 miles west of Yinchuan City, include nine tombs that house the imperial family and 140 tombs of dukes and ministers. The Western Xia mausoleums are not only unique in structure but also in size. Each one covers an area of more than 23 acres, stretching from north to south and from west to east.

Western Xia Museum

Western Xia Museum is located in the western suburbs of Yinchuan. Established in 1998, the museum covers an area of 57,048 square feet. Many treasures, arts, and sculptures, which tell the story of the rise and fall of Western Xia Kingdom, are exhibited in the museum.

Western Movie Studio

Also known as "Oriental Hollywood," the Western Movie Studio is located in

Helan Mountain

Helan Mountain is situated at the border of Ningxia and Inner Mongolia. The average altitude of Helan Mountain is 6,562 feet, and its highest peak is 11,000 feet high. The eastern side of the mountain stretches from Baisikou in the north to Sanguankou in the south. The mountain top overlooks more than 98,425 feet of scenic views from south to north, and 13,000 feet from east to west. The spectacular scenery of Helan Mountain is well worth a visit.

> Hikers can start from Suyukou to the main peak, where you can get a bird's-eye view of the beautiful mountain forests.

Wudang Temple

Wudang Temple, on the eastern side of Helan Mountain, is 3 miles from Shizuishan City. It covers an area of 129,167 square feet. The complex dates from around 1300, and many of the buildings were rebuilt in Qing Dynasty. The complex consists of 72 temples, 39 bridges, 36 nunneries, and 12 pavilions. The famous bells and drums in the North

Temple strike the hours, calling the monks to prayer and song. In 1994, the Wudang Temple complex was listed as a World Cultural Heritage Site.

A major Taoist ceremony takes place on the 8th day of the fourth lunar month. Tourists come from all around the world to watch these ceremonies and listen to the chanting of the monks.

Shahu Lake

Shahu Lake is situated in Pingluo County, about 35 miles from Yinchuan City. Encompassing nearly 65,000 square feet of lakes and rivers, 32,000 square feet of desert, and 12,917 square feet of bulrushes and wetland, Shahu Lake is a rare natural habitat for more than a dozen kinds of birds, such as white cranes, black cranes, and swans.

Pingluo Yuhuang Pavilion

Pingluo Yuhuang Pavilion is located at the junction of North Street and Fumin Street in Pingluo County. Built in the Ming Dynasty and reconstructed several times, the entire complex covers more than nine acres and is now the largest temple in Ningxia.

Pingluo Yuhuang Pavilion is the largest one among the preserved temples. (From CFP)

Wuzhong Region

Best Time to Travel

May to September are the best months for visiting this region of Qinghai.

All 108 towers are arranged in twelve rows. (From Quanjing)

One-Hundred-and-Eight Tower

The unique 108 Tower complex was built on the west bank of Qingtongxia Reservoir, 37 miles south of Yinchuan City. These 108 towers are a holy site for Buddhists, who hold the view that there are 108 kinds of troubles in people's lives. In order to avoid them, believers wear a string of 108 prayer beads and read the sutra 108 times. The highest tower is 11 feet tall, and all the others are 8 feet.

Near the tower groups, there is the Qingtongxia Birds Gorge, which is called the "Heaven of birds."

Niushou Mountain

Niushou Mountain is situated about 12 miles southwest of Wuzhong City. With an altitude of 5,820 feet, it is 29,527 feet wide and 95,114 feet long.. There are 45 temples scattered on and around the mountain, and these sites are generally categorized into the eastern section and western section. The scenery of the mountain with bamboo forests and misty mountain peaks is spectacular.

Many tourists and pilgrims come here on the 15th day of the third lunar month and the 15th day of the seventh lunar month.

Great Mosque

Also known as "Tongxin Mosque," the Great Mosque in the old city of Tongxin County. It was built in the end of Yuan Dynasty and the beginning of Ming Dynasty. It is the most famous mosque in the southern mountainous area of Ningxia. Many well-known Muslim scholars have visited and preached at this mosque, making it one of the most famous in Ningxia. The great hall in the mosque can accommodate more than 1,000 worhippers at a time.

Zhongwei Gaomiao Temple

Zhongwei Gaomiao Temple is located in the northern part of Zhongwei City. Originally built during the Yongle Era of the Ming Dynasty (1403–1424), it has gone through several reconstructions and is now a large-scale ancient architectural site. With its 270 towers and countless pavilions, the temple complex (around 163,000 square feet in area) integrates Tao, Buddhist, and Confucian beliefs.

The religious service hall can be divided into front palace and back palace. On the right of the religious service hall is the Awakening Building. (From Colphoto)

Zhongwei Gaomiao Temple is famous for its unique and exquisite architecture. (From CFP)

Shapotou Region

<<<

Desert Tour

Sandy beaches, dunes, and the Tengger Desert are the major tourist attractions in Ningxia. Located about 14 miles west of Zhongwei county city, this area is the site of the Shapotou Desert Experimental Research Station, which specializes in dune stabilization methods. For an exciting tour, a local guide can arrange a camel ride through the desert.

Yellow River Rafting is a newly developed tourism program. It is not only an adventure but also an enjoyment for you. (From ImagineChina)

Yellow River Tour

The Yellow River is a newly developed tourist attraction in Wuzhong City. You can visit the Yellow River Bridge, Yinchuan Hedong Airport, Castles of Hecheng City, Ming Dynasty Great Wall, Shuidonggou Relics, Tomb Group of Han Dynasty, Ganlu Temple, and many other interesting sites. Ancient relics alongside modern architecture create spectacular scenic areas. Boat rides are very popular and are readily available.

Guyuan Region

Sumeru Mount Grottoes

There are 100 grottoes on Mount Sumeru at the eastern foot of Xumi Mountain, northwest of Guyuan County in Ningxia. First built in North Wei Dynasty, and rebuilt throughout many subsequent dynasties, these grottoes contain exquisite sculptures of Western Zhou culture. So far, more than 20 grottoes have been preserved with incomparable treasures. The largest sculpture, about 85 feet tall, is that of Sakyamuni, which was carved in 849. There are also tablet inscriptions from various dynasties in the grottoes.

On the eastern edge of Sumeru Mount, there are grotto groups dating from the South and North dynasties (420–589). (From Colphoto)

> During the peak season, there are special tours to the many local attractions.

Liupan Mountain

Also known as the ancient winding path of Long Mountain, Liupan Mountain is situated in the south of Ningxia, in the triangle zone created by Xi'an, Yinchuan, and Lanzhou. With its long history and important location, Liupan Mountain continues to be admired for its resplendent cultural heritage. It is located on the Silk Road, and was the operating base for military operations. The Liupan Mountain Nature Reserve was established here in 1982 with the objective of protecting the forest lands and indigenous flora and fauna.

Shaanxi

Geography at a Glance

"Shaan" or "Qin" is the colloquial term for Shaanxi, a province located in the very heart of China. Boasting a population of 3,650,000 (2000 census) in an area of more than 73,000 square miles, Shaanxi is one of the cultural cradles of the Chinese nation.

Shaanxi has a varied terrain. In the north are plateaus; the center has plains; and in the south are mountainous areas, which include the Qinling and Daba ranges. The Qinling range is the major watershed of the Yellow and Yangtze River valleys. Tributaries of the Yellow River—the Wuding, Jinghe, Jialing, and Hanshui rivers—flow past the Loess Plateau and carry large quantities of mud and silt with them as they empty into the Yellow River.

Shaanxi Province has a continental monsoon climate, with great differences between the areas north and south of the Qinling range. The climate is temperate and semiarid in the north, subtropical and humid in the south. The average annual temperature is 44–61°F, and the annual rainfall averages from 16 to 40 inches.

Shaanxi is a base area of the new Chinese democratic revolution and a place with unique folk customs. The clamorous Shaanxi opera—a joyous clattering of gongs, drums, and traditional Chinese vocals, the exquisite cut-paper art, and the peasants' paintings full of rich life attract more and more tourists' attention from home and abroad.

(From Quanjing)

Terra-cotta warriors and horses exhibited at Emperor Qins Terra-cotta Warriors and Horses Museum in Xi'an. (From ImagineChina)

You can go to the east peak of Hua Mountain to watch the sunrise. (From CFP)

Featured Cuisine

Calabash chicken, cured mutton, steamed bread dipped in mutton soup, steamed pork with royal fern, abalone soup, fried quail, stewed turtle with gastraodia tuber, pork joint, variegated cabbage, hairlike seaweed, layered cake, dried persimmon, Biangbiang noodle, Shaanxi specialty noodle, sweet rice wine, fire pot, cold noodle, baked cake, braised noodle, bread stuffed with meat, dumpling banquet, dumplings with soy sauce, Qishan noodles, Jiasan guantang dumplings, fried cake, fried chitlings, steamed glutinous rice with honey.

Featured Commodities

Herbal Medicines

Schisandra chinensis (Clematis), magnolia bark, Qinba yam, licorice, musk, many special plants and herbs.

Special Local Products

Phoenix wine, Shaanxi green tea, thick wine, milled foxtail millet, Yang County black rice, Dukang wine.

Local Handicrafts

Tang tricolor pottery replicas, cut-paper art, Yaozhou carved celadon, Xi'an cloisonné, Mumashao mask, Fengxiang clay sculpture, clay whistles, Hu County folk art, Xi'an dyeing, Lantian jade sculpture.

Notes 

Shaanxi's staple food is flour-based, especially oat flour and buckwheat flour noodles combined with plentiful ingredients like chicken, pork and vegetables. Travelers in this province will find themselves well fed.

POPULAR FESTIVALS

Festival for Fathers-in-law

On the sixth day of the sixth lunar month, men in south Shaanxi will go with their wives and children to the houses of their fathers-in-law to celebrate this festival.

Xi'an Cultural Festival

The festival is celebrated in Xi'an from September 9th through the 15th. It features a display of Shaanxi folk arts, such as gong and drum, large-scale fireworks, and dance and music performances.

Lintong Megranate Festival

The megranate (something like a pomegranate) is the star of this festival. Here you can find tips on planting and harvesting the fruit, flower displays, and contests, in addition to Qing Dynasty artifacts.

Xi'an Terra-cotta Warriors and Horses and Megranate Festival

Held in Lintong in the middle of September for one week, the main activities include visiting the Terra-cotta Warriors and Horses, tours of Huaqing Hot Spring, visiting megranate gardens, and the torch ceremony at Beach Tower on Li Mountain.

Transportation Tips

By Bus

Shaanxi Province is constructing a highway transportation network comprised of ten national highways with Xi'an at the core. There are highways radiating from Xi'an to Tongchuan, Huashan, Tongguan, Xianyang, and Baoji.

By Train

Shaanxi is the railway terminus for China's northwest, southwest, and southeast. It is a transportation hub in the northwestern region linking all provinces and territories.

(From CFP)

By Plane

There are five cities in Shaanxi Province with airports: Xi'an, Yulin, Yan'an, Ankang, and Hanzhong. The Xianyang International Airport is the largest airport in northwest China, and it is also the fourth largest airport in China.

Recommended Routes

Classical Routes

Six-day tour of Yan'an

Day 1 Arrival in Xi'an. Lodging: Hyatt Hotel.

Day 2 Xi'an→Huangdi Mausoleum→Xuanyuan Temple. Lodging: Yan'an Hotel.

Day 3 Zao Yuan Revolutionary Site Date Garden→Pagoda Mountain→Yangjialing Village→Revolutionary Museum of China→Xi'an. Lodging: Hyatt Hotel.

Day 4 Xi'an→Lingtong→Terra-cotta Warriors and Horses→Huaqing Hot Spring→Mausoleum of the first Qin emperor. Lodging: Kaiyue Hotel.

Day 5 Great Wild Goose Pagoda→Forest of Pillars→City Wall of Ming Dynasty. Lodging: Meiyuan Hotel.

Day 6 End of tour.

Six-day tour of the hometown of Sima Qian

Day 1 Arrival in Xi'an. Lodging: Hyatt Hotel.

Day 2 Forest of Pillars→Great Wild Goose Pagoda→City Wall of Ming Dynasty→Bell-and-Drum Square. Lodging: Hyatt Hotel.

Day 3 Terra-cotta Warriors and Horses→Huaqing Hot Spring→Mausoleum of the first Qin emperor→Historical street. Lodging: Hyatt Hotel.

Day 4 Xi'an→Hancheng City. Lodging: Hotel of Hancheng City.

Day 5 Temple of Sima Qian→Puzhao Temple→Dangjia Village→Longmen regions of Yellow River. Lodging: Hotel of Hancheng City.

Day 6 End of tour.

Four-day tour of Cultural Artifacts of Three Kingdoms in Hanzhong

Day 1 Arrivale in Hanzhong. Lodging: Hanzhong Hotel.

Day 2 Hanzhong→Mian County→Machao Temple→Hanzhong. Lodging: Hanzhong Hotel.

Day 3 Hanzhong→Plank Road built along a cliff in Shimen→Shimen Reservoir→Zhangliang Temple. Lodging: Zhangliang Temple.

Day 4 End of tour.

Traditional Routes

Five-day tour of Shaanxi

Day 1 Arrival in Xi'an.

Day 2 Xi'an→Lintong→Terra-cotta Warriors and Horses→Huaqing Hot Spring→Mausoleum of the first Qin emperor→Huashan Mountain.

Day 3 One-day tour of Hua Mountain.

Day 4 Great Wild Goose Pagoda→Forest of Pillars→City Wall of Ming Dynasty.

Day 5 End of tour.

Seven-day tour from Xi'an, Yan'an to Hukou Waterfalls

Day 1 Arrival in Xi'an.

Day 2 Great Wild Goose Pagoda→City Wall of Ming Dynasty→Museum of Forest of Pillars→Historical street.

Day 3 Xi'an→Yan'an.

Day 4 Yangjialing Village→Revolutionary Museum of China→Pagoda Mountain→ZaoYuan Revolutionary Site→Hukou Waterfalls.

Day 5 Hukou→Xi'an.

Day 6 Terra-cotta Warriors and Horses→Huaqing Hot Spring→Mausoleum of the first Qin emperor.

Day 7 End of tour.

Self-Guided Tours

Tour of Loess Plateau

Start from Xi'an and end in Taiyuan. During the tour, you will pass Tongchuan, Luochuan, Yichuan, Nanniwan, Yan'an, Suide, Wubao, Liulin, Lishi, and Xinghua. The main tourist sites include Huangdi Mausoleum, Xuanyuan Temple, Hukou Waterfalls, Nanniwan, Pagoda Mountain, Wutai Mountain, Zao Yuan Revolutionary Site Date Garden, Wangjiaping Village, Yangjialing Village, apricot blossom village, Tianlong Mountain, and Jin Temple.

Tour of three provinces in west China

Start from Xi'an and end in Lanzhou. During the tour, you will pass Lintong, Yan'an,

Shaanxi History Museum is a grand complex of buildings imitating the architecture style of the Tang Dynasty. There are more than 375,000 cultural relics from China's long history, drawing visitors from all over the world. (From Quanjing)

Zhidan, Qingtongxia, Zhongwei, Yinchuan, and Lanzhou. The main tourist sites include Terra-cotta Warriors and Horses, Huaqing Hot Spring, Mausoleum of the first Qin emperor, Forest of Pillars, Great Wild Goose Pagoda, Qingtongxia Reservoir, Zhongwei Gao Temple, Shapotou section, Mausoleum of Western Xia Kingdom, Western Movie Studio, Sha Lake, Wuquan Mountain, Baita Mountain, Mother River, Ancient Mill Wheel, and Iron Bridge across the Yellow River.

Addresses and Phone Numbers

Hyatt Hotel	8 East Avenue, Xi'an	029-87231234
Shangde Masion	155 South-West Road Shangde Road, Xi'an	029-87445566
Meiyuan Hotel	8 Heping Road, Xi'an	029-87522827
Zhiyuan Hotel	111 Qingnian Road, Xi'an	029-87688333
Qinbao Hotel	West Weiyang Road, Xianyang	0910-3313388
Yaran Hotel	Zhongxin Street, Pagoda District, Yan'an	0911-2113122
Yulin Hotel	4 South Hubin Road, Yulin	0912-3681000
Hancheng Hotel	Western Section of the Taishi-Taifu Road, New Urban Area of Hancheng City	0913-5212600
Hanzhong Hotel	34 Jianguo Road, Hanzhong	0916-2522701
Zhangliang Temple Hotel	Liuhou Village, Liuba County, Hanzhong	0916-3966004
Duke Hotel	1 Baoyan Road, Baoji	0917-3469002
Xinmao Hotel	North Changhong Road, New City District, Tongchuan	0919-3181888

Xi'an Region

Best Time to Travel

From March to May and from September to November are the optimal travel months. The average temperature in winter hovers near 30°F, so remember to bring along heavy sweaters, a coat, and a hat. Be aware that the high tourist season in Xi'an is May or October, and all popular sites may be crowded.

Shopping Tips

Kangfulu Wholesale Market, on West Dongchangle Road in Xi'an, is the largest market in northwest China. You can find everything from leather to clothes, commodities, fresh meat, groceries, and local specialties here. The Minsheng Department Store at 103 Jiefang Road, Xi'an is the biggest shopping center in northwest China and has brand-name clothing, furniture, jewelry, perfumes, and other goods. The curio market on Zhuque Road, in the southern suburbs of the city, sells antiques and artworks.

The Small Wild Goose Pagoda has survived more than seventy earthquakes. Built on a compacted earthen cone, it is said that cracks in the pagoda have been closed by quakes that came later. (From Quanjing)

Big Wild Goose Pagoda

Big Wild Goose Pagoda is situated about 2.5 miles south of Xi'an in the southern suburbs. Also known as Ci'en Temple Pagoda, it was first built with local mud in 652 for Xuanzang, a Buddhist scholar, by the emperor to house Sanskrit scriptures from India. The pagoda soon collapsed but was rebuilt in 701. Built on top of a high mound, the pagoda is 210 feet tall and seems to rise into the sky like a wild goose taking flight.

Take buses 5, 19, 22, 24, 501, or 606 to go to the pagoda.

Small Wild Goose Pagoda

Small Wild Goose Pagoda is situated in Jianfu Temple just south of the downtown area. It is a little more than a mile from Big Wild Goose Pagoda and called Small Wild Goose Pagoda for its lesser height. At 114 feet, the brick structure is graceful and more elaborate than its sister pagoda. A giant iron bell (11 feet tall, weighing about 22,000 pounds) is situated inside the Jianfu Temple and is considered one of the eight cultural relics of Xi'an.

Shaanxi History Museum

Shaanxi History Museum is located to the northwest of Big Wild Goose Pagoda on East Xiaozhai Street. Opened in 1991, the museum comprises three large exhibition halls (arranged in historical progression) and is the first large-scale national museum with central air-conditioning, state-of-the art lighting, and modern security equipment in China. Shaanxi is considered the birthplace of Chinese culture, and the museum holds exhibits and artifacts from all 13 dynasties whose capitals were in the province.

Xi'an City Wall

This battlement, built from 1370 to 1378, is one of the best-preserved ancient walls in China. Surrounded by a moat, it has a circumference of about 8 miles and is 40 feet high, 59 feet wide at the base, and 49 feet wide at the top. There are 98 ramparts placed equidistantly on the wall; within each are sentry buildings. Originally, the interior of the wall was constructed of rammed earth, the exterior of brick; the wall has been restored three times, the latest in 1983.

> A circular park with beautiful trees and many flowers has been built (1983) along the high wall and the moat. You can rent a bike and ride around the wall.

Forest of Pillars

This museum holds more than 3,200 stone tablets, of which 1,700 are on display. One of the oldest pillars has the Confucian canon engraved on its sides and dates from 837; there are other historical tablets, such as the "Nestorian Pillar," which documents an early Christian sect (781), and there is also a marvelous collection of Buddhist scriptures, stone animals, and tomb bas-reliefs. Founded in 1087, it is located in a former Confucian temple on Sanxue Street, Xi'an.

> Rubbings are available in the Forest of Pillars. You can buy replicas of rubbings along with other souvenirs at the gift shop.

Bell Tower

Bell Tower, first built in 1384, is situated in the very heart of Xi'an. The huge bell in this tower used to toll the hour in ancient times. The two-story structure commands a fine view of the city.

> There are displays of cultural artifacts in the Bell Tower.

Drum Tower

In ancient China, these towers held large drums, which were struck on the hour to tell time for the townspeople. This tower, built in 1370, is the largest preserved drum tower in the country. The enormous original drum suffered ravages of time and wars but was replicated in

The square base of Bell Tower is made by bricks and is 118 feet high. (From Quanjing)

1996. Drum Tower, located south of Beiyuan Gate on West Avenue, is 108 feet high. Built on a rectangular base spanning West Avenue, the tower resembles a town gate.

Great Mosque of Xi'an

The Great Mosque of Xi'an is one of the largest and best preserved mosques in China. Built in 742, it has the striking features of Chinese pavilions, with painted beams and engraved ridgepoles mixed with traditional Muslim architecture. There are five courtyards with stone arches and stelae, two of which hold calligraphy from ancient masters, and several exquisite gardens. The mosque is northwest of the Drum Tower on Huajue Lane.

Take Bus 18, 43, 45, 203, 221, or 618, and get off at the Bell Tower stop. You can walk to the Great Mosque of Xi'an from there.

Sites of the Xi'an Incident

There are several buildings here that relate to the Xi'an Incident in December 1936 when Nationalist general Chiang Kai-shek was forced to give up his civil war against the CCP and join forces with Zhang Xueliang, forming a united front against the Japanese. The Xi'an Incident Memorial Museum was built on the former site of the residence of Zhang Xueliang.

Huaqing Hot Springs are famous for the love story of Emperor Xuanzong and his concubine, Yang Yuhuan. (From Quanjing)

Banpo Museum

The Banpo Museum is located in the eastern outskirts of Xi'an City. Comprising exhibition halls and the excavations of the Banpo prehistoric site, the museum covers an area of more than twelve acres and contains residential, pottery-making, and burial sections. Artifacts include remnants of houses, agricultural and residential tools, and various tombs. Banpo Site is a typical Neolithic matriarchal clan community of the Yangshao culture dating back about 6,000 years.

Li Mountain

Li Mountain is located south of Lintong County. There is a hillside pavilion built in memory of the Xi'an Incident. Walk west to the peak of the mountain and the Wanzhao Pavilion, where you can see Huaqing Pool quite clearly. Laojun Hall is on the third peak. Legend has it that Emperor Xuanzong saw Laojun two times here, so it was also called Jiangsheng Pavilion or Chaoyuan Pavilion.

The entrance of Li Mountain is about 650 feet east of the gate of Huaqing Hot Spring.

Huaqing Hot Spring

Situated at the northern foot of Li Mountian, 22 miles east of Xi'an City, Huaqing Hot Spring is famous for the love story of Emperor Xuanzong and his concubine Yang Yuhuan in the Tang Dynasty. Its long history and spectacular location make this site a must-see for visitors. In addition to excellent spa facilities there are various pavilions for dance and song performances. You can also participate in a traditional Chinese tea ceremony.

You can get to Huaqing Hot Spring by a designated tour bus at Nanmen Bus Station, Liberation Hotel, and Xi'an Train Station.

Xingjiao Temple

The Xingjiao Temple is located on the Shaoling Plateau, about 13 miles southeast of Xi'an. The iconic monk Xuanzang traveled from India along the Silk Road and collected and translated Buddhist scriptures and sutras. The temple was built in 664, and one of the pagodas contain his ashes. The 30-foot Reclining Buddha, carved from precious camphor wood, is in the back hall; the other halls and courtyards contain pillars and exhibits of ancient sutras.

Dagoba of Xuanzang in the Xingjiao Temple. (From Colphoto)

Site of Lantian Ape Man

Lantian County is located southeast of Xi'an, and is one of the cradles of the Chinese civilization. According to archaeologists, the fossilized remains date to the earliest Stone Age. The main cultural relics of Lantian Ape Man are stone implements, among which the stone axes are quite remarkable. Designated as a UNESCO World Heritage site in 1987, the site houses a large number of stone artifacts and cranial remains which are the earliest records of Homo erectus in northeast Asia and possibly the most primitive specimens in the world.

Gongshu Hall

Also known as "Ten Thousand Buddha Hall," Gongshu Hall is located in Qinan, Huxian County. Built in Yongle Era (1403–1424) of the Ming Dynasty, Gongshu Hall includes three exquisite wooden rooms with hundreds of Buddha sculptures. The architectural detail here should not be missed.

Mausoleum of the First Qin Emperor

This vast mausoleum is situated about 3 miles east of Lintong County. It was built from 246 BCE to 208 BCE by Qin Shi Huang, the first emperor of China. The world-famous Museum of Terra-cotta Warriors and Horses forms only part of the tomb, which is divided into three sections. No.1 Pit is the largest and contains the more than 6,000 life-size terra-cotta figures.

 Take Bus 306 or 307 to the site.

The Terra-cotta Warriors and Horses Museum is one of the most sensational archeological discoveries of all time. It was designated by UNESCO as a World Cultural Heritage site in 1987. (From Quanjing)

Xianyang Museum

Located on Zhongshan Street, in Xianyang City, the Xianyang Museum is a famous local history museum. Originally a Confucian temple, it was opened to the public in 1962 after reconstruction and expansion. Featuring nine exhibition halls and a corridor of pillars, the cultural artifacts in the Xianyang Museum focus on the Qin and Han dynasties.

Shun Mausoleum

Shun Mausoleum is south of Chenjia, 11 miles northeast of Xianyang. It is the mausoleum of the Empress Wu Zetian's mother, who died in 670. Wu Zetian was enthroned in 690, and she renamed her mother's tomb as "Shun Mausoleum."

Mausoleum of Western Han Emperor Liu Qi

The Mausoleum of the Western Han Emperor, Liu Qi, is located at Zhangjiawan, about 12 miles north of Xi'an, Shaanxi Province. The south burial pits were first discovered in May 1990 and comprise twenty-four small pits of varying sizes. There are more than 400 excavated painted pottery figures, weapons, and utensils.

Mao Mausoleum

The tomb of Emperor Wu, Mao Mausoleum is located about 25 miles from Xi'an. This mausoleum is called "the Chinese pyramid" since it is not only the largest but also holds the richest burial contents of all the mausoleums of emperors constructed during the Western Han Dynasty. Surrounded by the city wall, the cemetery is itself square. Around Mao Mausoleum, there are more than 20 tombs relating to Emperor Wu, most of which are tombs of imperial wives, ministers, and nobles.

Tomb of Huo Qubing

The Tomb of Huo Qubing lies 3,200 feet northeast of Mao Mausoleum. The base of the tomb stretches 344 feet from south to north, and 240 feet from east to west. The tomb itself is 82 feet high. There are 16 stone carvings in front of the tomb, which comprise the best-preserved example of the art of stone carving in the Han Dynasty. The astounding "Horse Treads on the Hun" is the main statue in front of the tomb.

Tomb of Yang Yuhuan

Tomb of Yang Yuhuan is located on the hillside of Mawei, about 8 miles west of Xingping. The Tomb of Yang Yuhuan is in a small cemetery, on whose gate is written "Tomb of Imperial Concubine Yang Yuhuan." The tomb itself is 10 feet high.

> There is a pavilion behind the tomb of Yang Yuhuan. The statue of Yang Yuhuan stands beside the pavilion.

The Tomb of Yang Yuhuan is 10 feet high, small but elegant. (From Colphoto)

Zhao Mausoleum

Located on Jiuzong Mountain, about 14 miles northeast of Liquan County, Zhao Mausoleum was first built in 636. Zhao Mausoleum is the tomb of Li Shimin, Emperor Taizong of the Tang Dynasty, and is the largest among the 18 mausoleums of the Tang Dynasty. It covers a total area of more than 7 square miles and has more than 180 satellite tombs.

Geodetic Origin of China

In 1975, on the basis of analyzing volumes of materials, the Chinese government concluded that the geodetic origin of China is located in Shijisi Village. The main structure has seven stories and is 82 feet tall. The top of the structure is a semi-dome, from which you can observe the stars and planets.

> Four expressways stretch across the city, making travel very convenient in Xianyang.

The perimeter of the pedestal of Chongwen Pagoda is 236 feet; the donors' names are carved around the base. In 1980, three copper statues were found on the top of Chongwen Pagoda. (From Colphoto)

Chongwen Pagoda

The pagoda, south of Jingyang County in Xianyang, was built in 1593. The octagonal green brick pagoda, 273 feet high, has 13 stories. Inside the pagoda a flight of brick steps wind along the walls to the top from where you can lean over the balustrades and enjoy the view.

The Big Buddha Temple

The Big Buddha Temple is about 6 miles west of Bing County, Xianyang. It was built in 628. There is a 79-foot-high Sitting Buddha in the cave of the Big Buddha Temple, and there are 107 grottoes in the temple.

Qian Mausoleum

The Qian Mausoleum occupies a prominent site on the summit of Liangshan Hill, some 4 miles from Qian County and 47 miles from Xi'an City. The tomb is shared by Emperor Gao Zong and his Empress Wu Zetian, the only female empress in Chinese history. Built in 684, the mausoleum once had inner and outer walls, four gates facing each direction, and countless halls and pavilions, creating a very secure tomb. It seems to have been the only mausoleum to escape the unwelcome attentions of tomb robbers over the centuries. The site covers a total area of some 23 acres; the stone carvings around the outside of the mausoleum are the only remaining original features. On the southeast side of the mausoleum, there are 17 additional satellite tombs.

You can travel by bus from Xianyang to Qian County, and then you can travel by farm vehicles to Qian Mausoleum for an interesting local experience. There are also special tour buses from Xi'an Train Station.

The Tomb of Princess Yongtai

The Tomb of Princess Yongtai is located north of Qian County. It stretches 900 feet from south to north, and 722 feet from east to west. Built to the same specifications as those of an empress' tomb, this one is famous not only for the quality of the many items found in it but also for the extremely fine wall paintings. The mural of fifteen maids of honor is well worth the visit. There is a pair of Mandarin ducks carved on top of the coffin, which symbolizes the love between Princess Yongtai and her husband.

The Tomb of Crown Prince Zhanghuai

Nearly 2 miles southeast of the Qian Mausoleum, the tomb of Crown Prince Zhanghuai consists of a paved path, arches, a patio, and two chambers. Covering some 4, 300 square feet, fifty well-preserved murals decorate the walls. The most interesting of these are known as "Hunting," "Polo," "Meeting of the Guests," and "Catching Bugs by a Bird."

The design of the Qian Mausoleum replicates the ancient city of Chang'an (Xi'an). Two ornamental octagonal columns mark the entrance. Qian Mausoleum is the only imperial mausoleum shared by two emperors. (From Quanjing)

Da Yu Temple was originally built in the Yuan Dynasty, and it has been rebuilt twice: in the Wanli period of the Ming Dynasty, and in the Jiaqing period of the Qing Dynasty. (From Colphoto)

Da Yu Temple

First founded in 1301, Da Yu Temple is located in the village of Zhouyuan, Hancheng. It was built in memory of Da Yu, an ancient hero who conquered a disastrous flood. The temple includes the main palace and a side palace. In the main palace, there are shrines and pavilions. The statue of King Yu holds pride of place in the center of the shrine.

Architecture of Dangjia

The village of Dangjia is located in Xizhuang County, some 6 miles northeast of Hancheng. It is a living reminder of an ancient agricultural community. The town was built in the early fourteenth century and, today, more than 1,400 villagers still live and work there. The superior style of the local houses in Dangjia and the fine carving decoration all attract tourists.

> If you want to experience the ancient Chinese culture and life in Dangjia, you can arrange a stay in the village for a few days.

Dragon Gate

Dragon Gate is located almost 19 miles north of Hancheng. Cliffs on both sides of the Yellow River stand face to face like a gate. It is said that only a dragon could get over the gate, and legend has it that the gate was created by Da Yu, so it is also called Yu Gate.

> You can take a powerboat ride under the bridge and enjoy the beautiful scenery along the Yellow River.

Sima Qian Temple

Lying on the escarpment of the south slope in Zhichuan County, 6 miles south of Hancheng, Sima Qian Temple was originally built in 310. Built in honor of Sima Qian (145–90 BCE), the temple complex leans against the side of the mountain. The temple was divided into two parts: the front yard and the back yard. In the front yard, there is a sitting statue of Sima Qian from the Northern Song Dynasty. In the back yard, the round brick tomb has inscriptions, the Eight Diagrams, and lovely flower carvings. Above the tomb an old cypress spreads its dense branches like a vigorous dragon, which reflects the Sima Qian's noble-minded personality and outstanding achievements as a historian and scholar.

> There are 59 stone pillars around the statue of Sima Qian, on which his life experiences and achievements are inscribed.

Cangjie Temple

Located in Shiguan, northeast of Baishui County, the temple was built more than 2,000 years ago in honor of Cangjie, the person who is believed to have created the earliest written characters. The temple is unique in that two opera towers were built next to its front gate. Sixteen ancient stone pillars remain in the temple, among which the "Cangjie Pillar" is the most precious.

Fengtuyi Storage

Fengtuyi Storage is located in Chaoyi, 10.5 miles east of Dali County in Shaanxi. Built in 1885, the building was originally constructed to store local grain. The architectural design was quite scientific, and wheat, rice, and other grains lasted for many years.

> Wheat stored in Fengtuyi Storage is known to have lasted as long as ten years.

Site of the Yaozhou Kiln

The site of the Yaozhou Kiln is located in the town of Huangbao, Tongchuan, Shaanxi Province. The Yaozhou Kiln was one of the six famous kilns in ancient China. Begun in the Tang Dynasty, and developed in the Five Dynasties, the kiln reached its peak in the Northern Song and Jin Dynasties, and closed at the end of the Yuan Dynasty. The Yaozhou Kiln, known as "Ten-li Kiln," has a history of firing pottery for more than 800 years, leaving behind a rich cultural heritage. More than 3 million pieces of various kinds of cultural relics and 200 workshops have been excavated near this kiln.

> Yaozhou Kiln Museum is now the largest museum for remains of ancient pottery in China.

Nearly 200 structures stand on Medicine King Mountain. Medicine King Palace is the main complex here. It is 74 feet high, 79 feet wide, and more than 187 feet in length. The statue of Sun Simiao is located within the palace. (From Colphoto)

Medicine King Mountain

Medicine King Mountain is located less than one mile east of Yao County. Here is the residence of Sun Simiao, a famous clinician of the Tang Dynasty, known and revered as the "king of medicine." The mountain was originally called "Wutai" for the five small mountains, but was renamed as Medicine King Mountain in Sun's honor. The Medicine King Palace was built in the Ming Dynasty, and boasts many fine statues, carvings, and stone pillars with elaborate inscriptions.

> There are many stone pillars in Jingying Temple on the hillside of Medicine King Mountain.

Mount Hua

Situated in Huayin County, Mount Hua is some 75 miles east of Xi'an City in Shaanxi Province. It is one of the five most famous mountains of China. Hua was historically the location of several influential Taoist monasteries and was known as a center for the practice of traditional Chinese martial arts. Hua Mountain is famous for its majestic crags, steep paths, and beautiful scenery; it is said to be the most precipitous mountain in the world.

> Tourists to the mountain are advised to bring their own food and drink.

Yan'an Region

Best Time to Travel

July, August, and September are the best months for visiting Yan'an. Having a temperate continental monsoon climate, Yan'an is an ideal place to travel through. This modern city is an economic and tourism center.

There are more than 10,000 Buddha statues on Qingliang Mountain. (From Colphoto)

Yan'an Pagoda

Yan'an Pagoda is located on Jialing Mountain on the banks of the Yan River. Originally built in the Dali period of Tang Dynasty (766–779), the pagoda was rebuilt in the Qingli Era (1041–1048) of the Song Dynasty. The octagonal brick pagoda on the hill's summit is 144 feet high. You can walk up to the top of the pagoda and get a great bird's-eye view of Yan'an City and environs. An enormous new *Ping'an Bell* (Safety Bell) and *Taiping Drum* (Peace Drum) are also at the top. If you ring the bell or beat the drum, legend says that this will bring you good health and happiness. Be sure to see the carved stone inscriptions in Chinese calligraphy by ancient scholars.

You may have to get in line to ascend the pagoda, as it is very narrow. Be sure to bring a camera!

Yan'an is of great historical importance to the Chinese revolutionary movement. Yan'an Pagoda Hill is a must to be explored if you want to really enjoy yourself in this remarkable city. (From CFP)

Qingliang Hill

Qingliang Hill, northeast of Yan'an City, faces Pagoda Mountain and Fenghuang (Phoenix) Mountain. Qingliang Hill is famous for its grotto art and is certainly worth a visit.

Many media buildings were located here before the People's Republic of China such as *Liberation Daily*, Xinhua News Agency, and the Xinhua Broadcasting Station.

Yan'an Revolutionary Memorial Hall

Yan'an Revolutionary Memorial Hall was built in 1950 in Wangjiaping, northwest of Yan'an. There is a well-known plaque by Guo Muoruo hanging in the center of the exhibition hall. The newly built memorial hall covers an area of 53,518 square feet, and the exhibit halls are about 34,000 square feet. Many relics, exhibits, special programs, and literature on the revolution are housed here.

Zaoyuan Revolutionary Site

Zaoyuan Revolutionary Site is located about 4.5 miles northwest of Yan'an. In 1940, the CCP Central Committee built cave houses here; Mao Zedong, Zhang Wentian, and Liu Shaoqi were stationed here for some 13 years after the famous Long March. Mao's house, consisting of five of these cave houses, has been preserved in its entirety. Zaoyuan, also known as Jujube Garden, also has lovely traditional Chinese gardens.

North of Zaoyuan, there is an aqueduct built by local residents, soldiers, and revolutionary cadres. Called "Happiness Aqueduct," it is still in use.

Site of the former offices of the CCP Central Committee–Yangjialing

This well-known revolutionary complex is located in Yangjialing, 1.5 miles northwest of Yan'an. Visitors can view the rooms where Chairman Mao, Premier Zhou, and others once lived. Hundreds of relics and historical documents are exhibited here. Yangjialing has become a popular tourist attraction not only because of its historical significance but also because it symbolizes the spirit of liberation during hard times.

The plaque on which is written "Yan'an Revolutionary Memorial Hall" by Guo Muoruo hangs in the center of the main exhibition hall. In front of the hall, there is a statue of Mao Zedong, which is about 16.5 feet tall. (From Colphoto)

Fenghuang (Phoenix) Mountain Revolutionary Site

Fenghuang Mountain Revolutionary Site is located on Fenghuang Mountain in Yan'an. It covers an area of 10,760 square feet. In January 1937, the former offices of the CCP Central Committee moved from Bao'an to Fenghuang Mountain. Many historical meetings took place here. Mao Zedong once stayed here, and this is where he met Dr. Norman Bethune, known as Bai Qiuen, a Canadian humanitarian and surgeon who went to China to help in their war with Japan. Many other revolutionary figures, such as Zhu De and Liu Bocheng, also lived here.

Wang Jiaping Revolutionary Site

Wang Jiaping Revolutionary Site is located about 2.5

miles northwest of Yan'an City. From January 1937 to March 1947, it served as the headquarters of the secretariat of the CCP and the Eighth Route Army, in addition to housing many revolutionary figures. In 1968, west of Wang Jiaping Revolutionary Site, the Yan'an Revolutionary Memorial Hall was built.

> Take train no. 3 at Yan'an Train Station or bus no. 8 on the east side of the Yan River Bridge to these sites.

Nan Niwan

Nan Niwan is located 28 miles southeast of Yan'an City. In the spring of 1941, the Eighth Route Army garrisoned this section and changed the former deserted area into an agriculturally rich land. Nan Niwan is not only famous for its historical significance, but also for its spirit during the process of development.

> The main tourist attractions of Nan Niwan include the former home of Mao Zedong, site of Brigade 359, a rest home for cadre leaders, site of former government of Nan Niwan, and the PLA Artillery School.

Nan Niwan, not a deserted area anymore, has become rich and beautiful. (From Colphoto)

You can find Huangdi tombs in many provinces, such as Gansu, He'nan, and Hebei. However, according to the ancient artifacts, Huangdi Mausoleum is most probably in Shaanxi. (From Colphoto)

Wayaobao Revolutionary Sites

Wayaobao Revolutionary Sites in Zichang County include more than 20 cave houses, the site of the Wayaobao meeting, and living spaces of Mao Zedong, Zhou Enlai and Liu Shaoqi. In December 1935, facing a Japanese invasion, the Wayaobao meeting marked the turning point when Mao's political line changed from land revolution to the anti-Japanese war.

Grottoes of Zhong Mountain

Located in Zhong Mountain, a little more than 9 miles west of Zichang County in Shaanxi, the famed grottoes were first excavated in 1067. The Zhong Mountain grottoes have a longer history than the "Four Great Grottoes of China" and they are replete with beautiful and valuable murals, inscriptions, and pillars.

Huangdi Mausoleum

Huangdi Mausoleum is hidden inside the dense evergreen cypresses on Mount Qiao (Bridge), less than one mile north of Huangling County in Shaanxi. Here, amid more than 8,000 ancient cypresses, is the tomb of Huangdi, known as the initiator of Chinese civilization. Huangdi was a great tribal leader of the last primitive society in ancient China. He revered the virtue of the yellow earth as the source of food and clothing, hence people call him Huangdi, the Yellow Emperor. This mausoleum is the symbol of Chinese civilization and center of great cultural activity.

Buses start from Xi'an or Yan'an to Huangling County. Every Qingming (Pure Brightness) Festival and Tomb-Sweeping Day, thousands of Chinese come here to pay homage to Huangdi.

Xuanyuan Temple

Xuanyuan Temple is also named Huangdi Temple. It is located in the east of Qiao Mountain of Huangling County and was built in the Han Dynasty. The main structures inside the temple are the Temple Gate, Chengxin Kiosk, Pillar Pavilion, and the Great Hall. Among more than ten ancient cypresses in the courtyard, don't miss the cypress planted by Huangdi himself. It is nearly 6 feet high and is the oldest cypress in the world.

Yulin Region

Best Time to Travel

The best season to tour Yulin is in the autumn. Night and day temperatures differ greatly; spring brings wind and dust and summers are rainy. Remember to bring sweaters and rain gear.

Hongshi Valley (Valley of Red Rocks)

Hongshi Valley, also called Xiongshi Valley, is about 3 miles north of Yulin, in the Yuxi River Valley at the foot of Hongkou Mountain right next to the Great Wall. With its red cliffs and rocks, Hongshi Valley is such a beautiful sight that many people claim it is the most scenic spot of the entire Great Wall. The cliffs of the northern section of the valley are dotted with natural lakes and waterfalls; on the southern section, there are grottoes, which were excavated during the Song and Ming Dynasties. Of those grottoes, 33 are still there today. There are a great number of inscriptions on the cliffs, with over 160 big or small stone tablets or pillars, forming a forest of stone tablets on which various schools of calligraphy show their beauty.

There are many inscriptions on the cliffs of Hongshi Valley, the largest of which has a diameter of almost 20 feet. These inscriptions have won Hongshi Valley the name of "Artistic Treasure House in the Open Air." (From Colphoto)

Take bus no. 3 from Yulin City to Hongshi Valley.

Zhenbei Beacon Tower

Zhenbei Beacon Tower is located on top of Hong Mountain, some 3 miles north of Yulin City. Built in 1607, it is the largest military watch tower on the Great Wall, built by the local magistrate of the Ming Dynasty, Tu Zongjun. Known

Zhenbei Beacon Tower has a square echelon shape with four floors. The total height is 99 feet. Every floor is built by bricks and there are 6.6-foot-tall buttresses and watch towers at the corners of each floor. (From CFP)

locally as "the first beacon tower of the great wall," it is the largest and most majestic Ming relic on the Great Wall.

Erlang Mountain

Erlang Mountain, popularly known as Xishan (Western Mountain), is located at the confluence of the Kuye and Qin rivers, just west of Shenmu County. Erlang Mountain is almost as steep and dangerous as Hua Mountain and is often referred to as "the Smaller Hua Mountain." Besides the majestic and beautiful natural scenery, ancient buildings also dot the mountain. On the 3,281-foot-long mountain ridge, more than 100 temples, halls, and pavilions are located in picturesque variety, each taking advantage of its unique geographic surroundings.

Hongjiannao Tourist Park

Hongjiannao Tourist Park is located in the heartland of Shenfu District and Dongsheng Coalfield, in the northwest of Shenmu County. Hongjiannao Lake covers an area of 21 square miles, making it the largest inland lake in Shaanxi Province and the largest desert freshwater lake in China. The lake surface is wide and beautiful, and its color and form changes with the seasons and the time of day. The park is located in a naturally pristine environment, providing an ideal habitat for migratory birds.

> In summer the lake is open for swimming; in winter, it becomes a perfect natural skating rink.

The Remnants of Tongwan

The remnants of the city of Tongwan are located in the village of Baichengzi, Hongdunjian Town, 36 miles north of Jinbian County. These are the only well-preserved remnants of the capital of the ancient northern kingdoms.

Li Zicheng's Xanadu

Li Zicheng's Xanadu is located in the Panlong Mountain, north of Mizhi County. It is a continuation of a Zhenwu Temple built earlier in the mountain. After the failure of Li Zicheng's attempt to take over Beijing, the Mizhi people gave the place its original name, Zhenwu Master Temple, and put up a statue of Zhenwu Master. This is how the Xanadu has been preserved.

The Xanadu is still there as are the stone lions. Li Zicheng's name has been written into history, leaving only endless memory and pity. (From Colphoto)

Baoji Region

Best Time to Travel

The city of Baoji (Precious Rooster) has an annual average temperature of 46–56°F, making any season the best time to visit. The high tourist time is late spring and summer.

Baoji Bronze Ware Museum

Baoji Bronze Ware Museum is the only thematic museum with bronze ware as its main focus. Located on the west side of South Gongyuan Road of Baoji, the museum opened to the public on September 8, 1998. More than 50,000 artifacts are exhibited here, many of which date to 56 BCE. The strikingly contemporary building is designed to show the sublimity, dignity, and majesty of its ancient bronze wares.

Tiantai Mountain

Tiantai Mountain is located on both sides of the highest peak in Qinling mountain range, 19 miles south of Baoji City. It covers an area of around 46 square miles. Tiantai Mountain is famous for its abrupt peaks, swirling clouds, and heavenly views. More than 150 scenic spots are included in this tourist area, among which over 50 are major scenic spots.

There are tourist buses and city buses from Baoji to Tiantai Mountain.

The Tomb of Yandi

The Tomb of Yandi is located on top of Changyang Mountain, a bit more than 4 miles south of Baoji City. Shennong Yandi and Huangdi are both honored as "primogenitors of Chinese civilization." The tomb comprises halls, pavilions, and stunning courtyards; there is a spectacular lake in front of the temple complex which reflects the beauty of the architecture and surrounding grounds.

Angling Rock (Diaoyu Tai)

Angling Rock is located on the Panxi River, 10.5 miles southeast of Baoji City. Jiang Ziya, a famous strategist in the Western Zhou Dynasty, once lived here as a hermit. The lake, circled by lush woods, has a clear, shining surface. There is a huge rock, about 16 feet high, next to the river. On the stone are two parallel smooth areas. Legend has it that they mark the place where Jiang Ziya kneeled on the rock to fish.

The Angling Rock on Panxi River of Baoji. Legend has it that Jiang Ziya fished with a straight fishhook and finally met with Emperor Wenwang. (From Colphoto)

Famen Temple

Famen Temple is located in the town of Famen, 6 miles north of Fufeng County. Built in the late Eastern Han Dynasty as a dagoba to house Buddhist relics, the temple was later constructed for the dagoba. The underground palace in Famen Temple is 70 feet long and covers an area of about 343 square feet. It is the largest underground palace for Buddhist relics so far discovered in China.

Take a bus at the Xi'an Train Station directly to Famen Temple.

Taibai Mountain

Taibai Mountain is located on the spot where Mei County, Taibai County, and Zhouzhi County join. It is about 62 miles southwest of Xi'an and is the highest part of Qinling mountain range. Baxian Tai, the highest peak of Taibai Mountain, has an altitude of 12,359 feet, making it the tallest mountain in East China. "The Snow-Capped Taibai Mountain in June" is one of the famous "Eight Scenes in the Guanzhong Basin." Taibai Mountain has a very unique geological structure, and it is home to various animals and plants, including rare and endangered flora and fauna. The Fourth Ice Age endowed Taibai Mountain with the wonder of "the Tri-Ponds of Taibai." Through the years, the water in the ponds is always crystal clear; if seen on a sunny day, it glows with rainbow colors.

The sea of cloud in Taibai Mountain (From ImagineChina)

The best time to visit Taibai Mountain is from April to October. A tour can take 2 to 5 days with different choices of routes.

Famen Temple (From Colphoto)

The dance called Ansai Waist Drum raises a hurricane of yellow soil, demonstrating the simplicity and heroic spirit of peasants on the Loess Plateau in northwest China. (From Colphoto)

Shaanxi Style

Folk Customs and Practices

Wooden-horse Ladle with Facial Make-up

People in the central Shaanxi plain and southern Shaanxi used to have the custom of hanging wooden-horse ladles with virtuous-looking color patterns of facial make-up in the house to keep the house safe and drive away evil spirits. Whenever the family encountered troubles, such as lack of descendants or occurrence of accidents, they would invite folk artisans to draw a virtuous-looking color pattern of facial make-up on the wooden-horse ladle and then hang it on the door frame or in the corridor. It is of the same meaning as other Chinese folk customs, for example, pasting spring festival scrolls and changing peach wood charms hung on the gate during lunar New Year, inserting calamus swords during the dragon boat festival, and hanging the portrait of Zhong Kui.

Ansai Waist Drum

Ansai Waist Drum is a unique art form of large-scale folk dance with over 2,000 years of history. Ansai Waist Drum performance can be played by several people or over 1,000 people simultaneously. The audience is often intoxicated by its great momentum and consummate expressive force.

Wooden-horse ladle with facial make-up (From CFP)

Shaanxi Opera

If you stay in Xi'an for some while, you will be impressed by forthrightness, simplicity, and enterprise of its people. The local people use large bowls for dining, and roar at the top of their voices while they act in a local opera. This high and vehement, intensive and pressing voice is Shaanxi Opera. It is said that Emperor Li Longji, also called Xuanzong of the Tang Dynasty, established a theatre to train opera actors who sang both court melody and folk songs. The musician Li Guinian, who was originally a folk artist in Shaanxi, composed *Opera of King Qin Breaking up the Battle Array,* which is probably the earliest music of Shaanxi Opera.

Shaanxi Opera is famous for its extremely high voice. It is joked that "to sing Shaanxi Opera, first, the stage has to be firm to avoid collapse due to the shake; second, the actor has to be fit to avoid collapse due to the physical demands; and third, the audience has to be bold to avoid being frightened to death."

Local Color in Northwest China

Culinary culture in Xi'an brims over with the intense local color of Northwest China. It is a great pleasure to taste the typical local dishes of Xi'an. From crumbled unleavened bread soaked in lamb stew, which is the favorite of people in Xi'an, to "Xi'an dumpling banquet," which is famous at home and abroad, the dishes have typical local features. In addition, there are other local dishes such as

(From ImagineChina)

Crumbled unleavened bread soaked in lamb stew (From Imagine-China)

"Biang-biang noodle," cold noodle, stir-fried rice noodle fish, paste pancakes, and "one thousand layer" flaky pastry.

Crumbled Unleavened Bread Soaked in Lamb Stew

It seems that your visit to Xi'an has no meaning if you do not eat crumbled unleavened bread soaked in lamb or beef stew. This local dish is substantial with bread that is made of stiff unfermented flour and large lumps of lamb or beef stew. The most magnificent thing is that the large bowl, which is also called the "sea bowl," can contain 0.7 to 0.9 pounds of food.

There is a legend about crumbled unleavened bread soaked in lamb or beef stew. Once, there was a general in the Tang Dynasty who was stranded in Xi'an suburb while he was fighting a war. It was extremely cold and the soldiers felt tired and hungry, so they butchered a lamb, made soup, and soaked their solid food in it. Unexpectedly, the soldiers' appetite was stimulated and they felt warm. As their morale was greatly boosted, they won the war. Since then, crumbled unleavened bread soaked in lamb stew became well known.

Biang-biang Noodle

In the alleys of Xi'an, you will hear some children who are saying the following doggerel: A point flies to the sky while the Yellow River bends with both ends, the Chinese character of Ba opens its mouth wide while the Chinese character Yan walks in. It twists to the left and to the right; it stretches to the left and to the right. The King Ma comes into the middle; the Chinese character Xin is its bottom component while the Chinese character Yue is its side component. Two thieves stand beside it, riding the vehicle to go anywhere.

The doggerel talks about how to write the Chinese character, "Biang." Biang-biang noodle is Xi'an's typical food. The breadth of one piece of noodle can reach two or three inches, and the length is about 3.28 feet. It can be as thick as a coin or as thin as the cicada wing. A piece of noodle may use up to 0.3 pounds flour, so for people whose appetite is small, one piece of noodle is enough for a meal while for Xi'an people with big appetites, one pound is no problem at all.

Beijing

Geography at a Glance

As the capital city of the People's Republic of China, Beijing, or "Jing" for short, is the center of the nation's politics, culture, transportation, and travel, and also a center for international commerce. The recorded history of Beijing can date back more than 3,000 years and as a capital more than 800 years. Divided into 16 districts and 2 counties, it covers an area of 6,486.5 square miles, stretching 99 miles from east to west and about 112 miles north to south. It has a population of 13,819 million (census 2000).

Beijing lies in the northwest of the North China Plain with the Bohai Sea located 93 miles to the southeast. The southeastern part of the city is a plain, while the city's west, north, and northeast are bordered by the mountains of Taihangshan, Jundushan, and Yanshan. This section of the city is called Beijing Bay because it looks like a bay bordered by land on three sides.

Beijing lies in the North Temperate Zone. The continental monsoon climate here makes it dry, windy, and sandy in spring, and hot and rainy in summer. Autumn is the best season of the year with blue skies and crisp, mild temperatures. Winter, on the other hand, is cold and dry with little snow. Spring and autumn are much shorter than summer and winter, but temperate weather usually lasts for 180 days. The average annual temperature in the main part of the city is 50 to 68°F. The average monthly temperature is 23.5°F in January and 79°F in July. The annual precipitation is measured at 25.6 inches, 75 percent of which falls in summer.

(From Quanjing)

The Temple of Heaven is an unrivalled masterpiece of construction. (From CFP)

Beijing has always been seen as a key area in China for its location, outstanding scenery, fertile soil, and abundant products.

Featured Cuisine

Beijing roast duck, pancakes with tuckahoe filling, Wangzhihe fermented soybean cheese, braised pork shoulder with soy sauce of Tianfu, North County smoked pork feet, gourd-shaped chicken with stuffing, mung bean milk, sticky rice cake slices, pudding-like arrowroot cake, chestnut cake, Quansuzhai's vegetarian dishes, Beijing pickled cucumber, Liubiju's pickled vegetable, bean-flour balls soup, deep-fried bean curd with sauce, sweetbread soup, tadpole-shaped mung-bean jelly, ear-shaped twists with sugar, baked wheat cakes with sugar, bread rings, rolling donkey, sticky rice balls, pea flour cake, grilled lamb pancake, Jingdong meat pie, fried dough drops.

Featured Commodities

Special Local Products

Xinghai brand two-stringed Beijing fiddle, chrysanthemum liquor, vintage cinnamon liquor, lotus liquor, Wangmazi's scissors, Yidege's ink-stick, Daiyuexuan's writing brushes and eight-treasure inkpad.

Local Handicrafts

Beijing snuff bottles, Beijing court lanterns, Beijing lacquerware, Beijing silk flowers, Beijing appliqué, Beijing

Notes 

❶ There are numerous one-way streets and cloverleaf junctions in Beijing. Drivers new to the city are advised to pay special attention to road signs.

❷ Since 1983, a flag-raising ceremony is held every morning in the Tian'anmen Square. It is worth a visit when a grand flag-raising ceremony is held.

sculpture, Beijing cloisonné, Beijing dough figurines.

Fruits and Delicacies

Beijing flowering crab, Miyun golden-silk jujube, Beijing ya-pear, millstone persimmon, Beijing crispy sugar, white gourd with lotus root powder cake, and pear-shaped potato cake.

Transportation Tips

By Bus

There are 12 national highways extending from Beijing to Shenyang, Tianjin, Ha'erbin, Guangzhou, Zhuhai, Nanjing, Fuzhou, and Kunming, and 6 main expressways surrounding the city: Badaling Expressway, Capital Airport Expressway, Beijing-Shenyang Expressway, Bejing-Tianjin-Tanggu Expressway, and Beijing-Zhangjiakou Expressway.

(From Colphoto)

Twelve long-distance bus stations in Beijing operate buses everyday.

By Train

Beijing is the rail hub of the nation with four train stations: Beijing Main, Beijing West, Beijing South , and Beijing North. Beijing Main Station runs routes from Beijing to Shanghai, Ha'erbin, Xi'an, and other cities; Beijing West is located in East Lianhuachi Road (East Lotus Pond Road) and runs trips from Beijing to Guangzhou and stations along the Longhai line; Beijing South is also called Yongdingmen (Gate of Eternal Safety) Station and

POPULAR FESTIVALS

Spring Festival Temple Fair

Various temple fairs are held in Beijing from the 30th day of the twelfth lunar month to the 6th day of the first lunar month. These fairs offer local food, snacks, and folk performances, which offer great entertainment and insight into the lives of Beijing natives.

Daguanyuan (Grand View Garden) Temple Fair

This spring festival temple fair features a variety of performances.

YanQing Ice and Snow Tourism Festival

Ice sculptures and ice lanterns in various shapes are shown in Longqing Gorge, Yanqing County, from January 15th to February 26th each year.

Peach Blossom Festival

Beijing Botanical Garden holds a peach blossom festival each April.

Cherry Blossom Festival

The Yuyuantan Park Cherry Blossom Festival is held in early April, during which visitors can marvel at the beautiful cherry blossoms and participate in various activities.

Peony Festival

The exhibition of blooming peonies is held in Jingshan Park from mid-April to mid-May.

Mid-Autumn Moon Festival Party

Extravagant parties are held to celebrate this festival in Suzhou Street of the Summer Palace and Yuetan Park on the 15th day of the eighth lunar month.

runs mainly short trips; and Beijing North is also known as Xizhimen (the Western Gate) Station and runs short trips to the suburbs, Inner Mongolia, and Hebei Province.

By Plane

Capital International Airport lies in Shunyi District, some 18 miles from downtown Beijing. A shuttle service operated by the civil aviation authority runs once every hour from the airport to locations such as the Xidan Civil Aviation Building, the Art Museum, Beijing Main Railway Station, and Gongzhufen (Princess Tomb) at a cost of 16 yuan per person. The trip takes about one hour. The shuttles starting from the Xidan Civil Aviation Building run for a longer time and stop at the Beijing Main Railway Station, Chaoyangmen (Gate Facing Toward the Sun), the Dong Sishitiao Station, Gongti (Workers' Stadium), and Sanyuanqiao (Sanyuan Bridge). Taxis are available for approximately 120–130 yuan to the city (not including suburbs). The 10-yuan airport expressway taxi toll is the passenger's responsibility.

Recommended Routes

Classical Routes

Three-day tour of the Great Wall in Beijing

Day 1 Badaling Great Wall→Shuiguan Great Wall.

Day 2 Juyong Pass→Simatai Great Wall.

Day 3 Jinshanling Great Wall.

Three-day tour of former residences in Beijing

Day 1 Former residence of Lu Xun→Former residence of Mao Dun→Former residence of Xu Beihong→Lao She.

Day 2 Gongwang Mansion (Prince Gong's Mansion)→Former residence of Song Qingling→Former residence of Mei Lanfang→Former residence of Guo Moruo.

Day 3 Former residence of Queen Wan Rong→Former residence of Soong May-ling and Chiang Kai-shek.

Traditional Routes

Six-day tour of Beijing

Day 1 Tiantan→Wangfujing Shopping Street.

Day 2 Tian'anmen Square→Monument of the People's Hero→Memorial Hall→Palace Museum→Jingshan Mountain→Beihai (North Sea)

Day 3 Badaling and Shuiguan Great Wall→The Thirteen Tombs→Asia Games Village exterior view and the blueprint for the 2008 Beijing Olympics.

Day 4 Huangchenggen (Imperial City Wall) Relics Park→China Century Monument.

Day 5 Summer Palace→Xiang Mountain (Fragrant Hills, Incense Mountains).

(From Colphoto)

Addresses and Phone Numbers

The Peninsula Beijing	8 Goldfish Lane, Dongcheng District	010-65128899
Great Wall Sheraton	10 North Dongsanhuan Road	010-65905566
Beijing Hotel	33 East Chang'an Avenue	010-65137766
Hotel Beijing Hilton	1 Dongfang Road, North Dongsanhuan Road	010-64662288
Beijing Friendship Hotel	1 South Zhongguancun Street	010-68498888
Hotel Kunlun	2 South Xinyuan Road, Chaoyang District	010-65903388
Diaoyutai State Guesthouse	2 Fucheng Road, Haidian District	010-58591188
Grand Hotel Beijing	35 East Chang'an Avenue	010-65137788
Beijing International Hotel	9 Jianguomennei DaJie	010-65126688
Hotel Nikko New Century Beijing	6 Southern Road Capital Stadium, Haidian District	010-68492001
Hongluoshan Vacation Resort	Hongluo Mountain, Huairou	010-60681595

Day 6 Gongwang Mansion (Prince Gong's Mansion) →Siheyuan (four-side enclosed courtyards) →Hutong (alley).

Self-Guided Tours

Hutong

The Hutong tour offers insight into the traditional Beijing culture and its customs. Take Bus 102 and get off at the Jiaozi Hutong stop, then walk south about half a mile; you will see the Fayuan Temple at the Xizhuan Alley. Next, take Bus 102 and change to Bus 13 at the Xisi stop; get off at Shitiao stop. Here you will see the Former Duan Qirui Government Building at the Ping'an Dadao (Peace Street) across the road. You can also take Bus 13 to the Guozijian stop (Imperial College); the alley with an archway at the west side of the road is Chengxian Street; the second largest Kong Temple in China is located on the east side of this street. When you walk out of the east end of the Chengxian Street, you will see the Xilou Alley across the road and the Bailin (Cypress Forest) Temple along the alley. There is a sal tree among the well-known ancient trees planted in Bailin Temple, which was once ranked as one of the largest trees in Beijing. All these sites are free of charge except the Fayuan Temple.

Clay figurine rabbit gods on display for sale at a taoist temple in Beijing. (From CFP)

Self-guided tour in the outskirts of Beijing

Drive north along the Beijing-Changping Expressway and after passing through Badaling and Kangzhuang, you will enter Huailai County in Hebei Province, which is 62 miles from Beijing. Forty-three miles are on an expressway; the remaining miles are via regular roads. At the foot of Yan Mountain and to the south of the Guanting Reservoir, there is a strip of natural desert, known as Tianmo.

Beijing Region

Best Time to Travel

Autumn is the best season to visit Beijing. It is dry and windy with lots of blowing sand in spring, hot and rainy in summer, and cold and dry with little snow in winter. Autumn in Beijing is clear, crisp, and pleasant.

Shopping Tips

Dongdan Silver Street is where stylish shops and contemporary and fashionable brands can be found.

Xidan Shopping Street is located between Xuanwumen (Gate of Military Declaration) and Xinjiekou Huokou. The northern part of it is the busiest commercial area with modern shopping places such as the Xidan Shopping Center and the Chung-Yo Department Store and other stores featuring well-known brands.

Wangfujing Street is nationally well-known for leisurely strolling and shopping.

Tian'anmen Square

Tian'anmen Square is located in the center of the city, stretching a half mile from north to south and less than a quarter of a mile from east to west. As one of the largest city squares in the world, it occupies an area of about 108 acres, spacious enough to accommodate nearly one million people. When this area was ruled by feudal kings, ordinary people were not allowed to step into this forbidden square. Throughout history, this famous place has been rebuilt many times.

Visitors who want to watch the flag raising ceremony should look for the electronic display in front of the Tian'anmen Gate, showing the time for raising and lowering the national flags.

Great Hall of the People

West of the Square is the Great Hall of the People, home of the Chinese legislature and the venue for official ceremonial activities and Communist Party meetings. It was built in ten months from the end of Oc-

To the north of the Tian'anmen Square is the Tian'anmen Gate. Built in 1417, it was first named the Cheng Tian Men and served as the front gate of the Forbidden City in the Ming and Qing dynasties. In 1651, it was rebuilt and renamed Tian'anmen. Now it is honored as the emblem of national unity. (From Quanjing)

tober 1958 to the beginning of September 1959: 1,102 feet long from north to south, 676 feet wide from east to west, and 153 feet tall at its highest point.

National Museum

The National Museum of China flanks the eastern side of Tian'anmen Square. It was created in February 2003 out of two separate museums: the Museum of the Chinese Revolution in the northern wing, and the National Museum of Chinese History in the southern wing. There are more than 4,500 items on display, including various objects, documents, drawings, photos, models, and sculptures, which cover the development of Chinese modern history.

Palace Museum

The Palace Museum, also known as the Forbidden City (literally "Purple Forbidden City"), is situated at the heart of the city, serving as the imperial palace during the Ming and the Qing dynasties. It is listed by UNESCO as the largest collection of preserved ancient wooden structures in the world and was declared a World Heritage Site in December 1987. Measuring 3,153 feet from north to south and 2,740 feet from east to west, it has over

There are 13,844 dragons in Taihe Dian (the Hall of Supreme Harmony). (From Quanjing)

890 buildings with more than 9,000 rooms.

Beihai (North Sea) Park

Northwest of the Forbidden City, the Beihai Park consists of the Beihai Lake and the Qionghua Island, both of which date back almost one thousand years. The park used to be the imperial garden of the Liao, Jin, Yuan, Ming, and Qing dynasties. Since 1925, it has been open to the public.

Yonghegong Temple

The Yonghe Temple (the Palace of Peace and Harmony Lama Temple), located in the east of Beixinqiao Beijie Road (which is to the northeast of the Palace Museum), is the largest and best preserved lama monastery in Beijing. Construction on the Yonghegong Temple started in 1694. It originally served as an official residence of Prince Yong (Yin Zhen), a son of the Kangxi Emperor and himself the future Yongzheng Emperor. The Yonghegong Temple is arranged along a north-south central axis, which has a length of about 1,312 feet.The building and the artworks of the temple combine Han, Manchu, Mongolian, and Tibetan styles.

The Pavilion of Ten Thousand Happinesses contains an 59-foot-tall statue of the

A mysterious touch of religion and imaginative art make the Yonghegong Temple irresistibly attractive. (From Quanjing)

This is the opera house in Prince Gong's Mansion. Visitors can sit at the tables in the house when they watch the opera performance here. (From Quanjing)

Maitreya Buddha carved from a single piece of white sandalwood.

> The statue is included in the *Guinness Book of Records* in 1990. Take subway line 2 or Bus 13, 62, 116, or 807.

Jingshan Park

Jingshan Park is located on the central point of the north- south axis of Beijing. To the north are the Bell and Drum Towers, to the south the Shenwu Gate of the Forbidden City, and to the west lies Beihai Park. It was first developed during the Jin Dynasty and became the imperial garden, named Qingshan (the Green Hill) in the Yuan Dynasty. In 1655 (during the time of Emperor Shunzhi of Qing Dynasty), Qingshan was renamed Jingshan. In 1749 (during the time of Emperor Qianlong of Qing Dynasty), it was enlarged and rebuilt into an elegant imperial garden.

Former Residence of Soong Ching Ling

The former residence of Soong Ching Ling is situated at No. 46 North River Street in the Rear Lake area. The arrangement of the house is kept exactly as they were before she died on May 29, 1981, at 8:18 p.m. Even the calendar and clock in the house are fixed at the precise time of death.

Gongwang Mansion and Garden

Prince Gong's Residence, also known as Cuijinyuan Garden, is located at West Qianhai Street. It is the most intact of Qing Dynasty's mansions preserved in Beijing and has a siheyuan (four-sided enclosed courtyard) with the largest contained area in the world. There are winding corridors that interconnect in addition to various pavilions and terraces. This mansion originally belonged to He Shen, the highest official in the reign of Qianlong.

> The scenery here is as beautiful and serene as that of the Rongguo Mansion and Daguanyuan Garden described in *Dream of the Red Mansion*, the masterwork of Cao Xueqin. Legend has it that Prince Gong's Mansion was the residence of Jia Baoyu (the main character in *Dream of the Red Mansion*). Take Bus 13, 103, 107, or 111.

Summer Palace

The Summer Palace is located in the Haidian District, about 7 miles northwest of downtown Beijing. It is the

Two major parts in the Summer Palace are the Longevity Hill (196.8 feet high) and Kunming Lake. There are over 2,000 magnificent buildings in the form of mansions, pavilions, and gardens. (From ImagineChina)

largest ancient garden preserved in China, built in the Qing Dynasty in 1750 as the Garden of Clear Ripples (Qingyi Yuan) to celebrate the birthday of the emperor's mother. In 1860 it was ransacked by British and French forces, but rebuilt in 1886 by the Empress Dowager Cixi who diverted the funds meant for the Chinese navy in order to finance the garden's construction. It was christened Yiheyuan in 1888; in 1900 it was again damaged by an eight-nation allied invasion but reconstructed in 1902 to it current status.

Xiangshan (Fragrant Hills) Park

Located in the west suburb of Beijing and on the eastern side of the Western Hills, Xiangshan Park is an ancient forest garden. It was built by Emperor Dading (during the Jin Dynasty) as the Xiangshan Temple and served as the royal hunting ground. It was also a scenic spot and a summer retreat for the royal families during the Yuan, Ming, and Qing dynasties.

Temple of the Azure Clouds (Biyun Si)

Situated on the northern side of the Western Hills, the Temple of the Azure Clouds was originally known as the Nunnery of the Azure Clouds. The temple was built by Emperor Zhishun during the Yuan Dynasty and expanded in the Ming and Qing dynasties. The front gate toward the east and the magnificent temple buildings were built along the sloping hills. Here are famous tourist attractions such as the Sun Yat-sen Memorial Hall, the Hall of 500 Arhats, and the Vajra Throne Tower. Hanging above the front gate of the Sun Yat-sen Memorial Hall is a red wooden plaque with gold-engraved words written by his wife, Soong Ching Ling. The Vajra Throne Tower is the highest building in the Temple of Azure Clouds.

Temple of Recumbent Buddha (Wofo Si)

The Temple of Recumbent Buddha is located at the foot of the Mountain of Longevity and Peace (Shou Shan). First built in the seventh century, it has been renovated and expanded many times. The Recumbent Buddha's Hall is the most important hall in the temple. The recumbent Buddha inside the hall is the statue of Sakyamuni, which is about 17 feet long and weighs 119,048 pounds. With his head in the west and his feet in the east, the Buddha is in a sleeping position. It was said that this pose is that of Sakyamuni when he attained nirvana.

Five Pagoda Temple (Wuta Si)

Still holding its original name of Zhenjue Temple, this site is located at No. 24, the Village of Five Pagoda Temple (Wutasi Cun) of Baishi Bridge outside Xizhi Gate in the Haidian District. It is the first museum specializing in the stone-carved artworks of Beijing. It was built on the original site of the Zhenjue Temple, which was constructed during the reign of Yongle in the Ming Dynasty (1403–1424).

Longevity Temple (Wanshou Si)

Located on the western side of Guangyuan Zha in Changhe, the Longevity Temple is a famous ancient temple in western Beijing. Built in the Tang Dynasty, its original name was Juse Temple. Renovated in 1577, the temple was renamed as Wanshou Temple. It was once known as the "Small Forbidden City in Western Beijing."

Great Bell Temple (Dazhong Si)

Located between Jimen Li and Shuangyushu in the Haidian District, the Great Bell Temple was built in 1733 with the name of Juesheng Temple (Temple of Awakening).

China Millennium Monument

The China Millennium Monument stands to the south of the Yuyuantan Park and to the west of the Military Museum and the Central Television Complex, opposite to the West Beijing Railway Station, occupying a 376,737-square-foot area. It serves not only as China's commemorative building to welcome the year 2000 but also symbolizes the country's splendid 5,000-year civilization.

Lugou Bridge

The Lugou Bridge is located in Fengtai, 9 miles to the southwest of Beijing. The bridge, the oldest stone arch bridge preserved in Beijing, straddles the Yongding River. Construction of the original bridge on this site began in June 1189. The Lugou Bridge is about 874 feet long and 31 feet wide. The stone lions in different shapes and poses, and standing on each pillar, are the most intriguing. According to an ancient book, *Book of Conghai*, there should be 627 lions on the bridge; at this time there are 501.

World Park

Located at Dabaotai of Huaxiang Township in the Fengtai District, the World Park opened in October

The ground in the middle of the Lugou Bridge is well preserved. (From Jin Yongji)

1993. It covers an area of 8,251 square feet and boasts 100 world-famous man-made and natural attractions from nearly 50 countries throughout the world, and it is considered to be one of the largest-scale micro-landscape parks in Asia. The layout is modeled after the five continents and four oceans. It contains miniature replicas of architecture from many different cultural backgrounds, including the Eiffel Tower, the Arc of Triumph, the White House, the World Trade Center, the Red Square, the Great Temple of Abu Simbel, and the Katsura Detached Palace, and others.

Dabaotai Western Han Dynasty Tomb Museum

Located in the Fengtai District, Dabaotai Western Han Dynasty Tomb Museum is a unique tomb museum. It was built more than 2,000 years ago on the site of the underground palace of Liu Jian (73 BCE–45 BCE), who was the Guangyang Feudal Prince in the Western Han Dynasty. It covers an area of more than 190,000 squre feet. Its main exhibitions include the original site of the underground palace, unearthed cultural artifacts, and an exhibition of Chinese mausoleums for the emperors in different dynasties. This museum is the only large-scale Han Tomb preserved at its original site in China.

Dabaotai Western Han Dynasty Tomb Museum (From Colphoto)

Stone slabs carved with the full text of the Tripitaka (From CFP)

Site of Beijing Man at Zhoukoudian

The home of Beijing Man is located on the Longgu Mountain in Zhoukoudian of the Fangshan District, almost 30 miles southwest of the central city, where the fossils of Beijing Man and Hilltop Caveman were found. There are eight sites of ancient people, 118 animal fossils, and more than 100,000 pieces of stone tools, considered to confirm the existence of humans in Beijing 500,000 years ago.

Take Bus 917 at Tianqiao bus terminal, and then change to a special-line bus at Fangshan.

Cloud Dwelling Temple (Yunju Si)

The Yunju Temple is located at the foot of Baidai Mountain in the southwest of the Fangshan District. Built in the late Sui and early Tang Dynasties, the temple is now lauded as Beijing's answer to Dunhuang because of its collection of 14,000 stone slabs carved with the full text of the Tripitaka (including sutra-pitaka, vinaya-pitaka, and abhidharma-pitaka). Through the renovation of successive dynasties, it now has five courtyards and six palaces with side halls, palaces for emperors, and monks' rooms. Two pagodas facing south and north respectively stand opposite each other. The cliffside sculptures of Buddhist figures from the Tang Dynasty rank among the best in the world.

The torii at the entrance to Changling Tomb in Thirteen Tombs of Ming Dynasty (From CFP)

Stone Flower Cave (Shihua Dong)

The Stone Flower Cave, formerly known as Qianzhen Cave, is located at the foot of Danan Mountain in Nancheying Village of Hebeixiang Township in the Fangshan District. The temple and relief carvings in the cave were done in 1446, during the Ming Dynasty. On the southern cliff of the cave entrance are carved ten Buddhist figures. This multilayered, water-eroded cave has been appraised by experts to be as beautiful and as large as the Ludi Cave in Guilin, which ranks as the best in North China.

The delicate stalactites in the Stone Flower Cave are all in the shape of flowers. (From Colphoto)

Silver Fox Cave (Yinhu Dong)

Located at the village of Xiayingshui of Fozizhuang Township in the Fangshan District, the Silver Fox Cave is the major spot in the scenic areas of water-eroded caves in the west suburbs of Beijing. It is named after the large, rare fox-sized white crystal in the cave. The cave itself is believed to be more than 3 miles long and partitioned with major caves, branch caves, river caves, and dry caves.

China Aviation Museum

Located at the foot of fascinating Da Tang Hill (Datang Shan) in Xiaotangshan Township of ChangPing County and to the north of Asian Games Village and Xuefu District, south of Thirteen Tombs, the China Aviation Museum covers an area of 5,704,867 square feet. The first aviation museum open to public in Chinese history, it is also the only aviation theme park in China.

Thirteen Tombs of the Ming Dynasty

This tomb complex is located to the south of Tianshou Mountain (Longevity of Heaven) in Changping County. Built over 200 years ago to hold the tombs of 13 Ming Dynasty emperors, this complex is the largest area of Ming Dynasty tombs.

Juyongguan Pass (Juyong Guan)

Located in Changping County, Juyongguan Pass is the most famous pass of the Great Wall, which had great strategic significance for the security of northwest Beijing in ancient times. It has two entrances, one at the south and one at the north. The south one is called "Nan Pass" and the north one is called "Badaling." The whole pass is located in the 11-mile-long Guangou Valley. Once there were lush flowers and trees around the pass like layers of green waves; thus, Juyongguan means "Juyong Green Layers."

Great Wall at Badaling

Located at Yanqing County, Badaling is the north pass of the area of Juyongguan Pass. It was built in 1505 and now is the best preserved section of the Great Wall of the Ming Dynasty. Averaging 25 feet high and 13 feet thick, this section of the Great Wall was built with giant stone slabs and specially made bricks, and comprises watch towers, embrasures, and drainage system.

Great Wall at Mutianyu

Located in Huairou County, the Mutianyu section of the

The Great Wall is the greatest piece of military construction of ancient China, extending for more than 3,728 miles from Shanhaiguan Pass in the east to Jiayuguan Pass in the west. (From ImagineChina)

Great Wall is connected with Juyongguan Pass in the west and Gubeikou Gateway in the east. Eight and a half miles to the northeast is where General Xu Da defeated the Yuan troops, and a barrier was built to prevent them from attacking again. In 1404, an official pass was constructed here. This section of the Wall runs 7,382 feet in length and holds 22 watch towers, among which the highest is 1,772 feet tall.

Great Wall at Simatai

Located at the Gubeikou Township in the northeast of Miyun County, the 62-foot-long wall is famous for its ruggedness and strategic significance. It is separated into the eastern and western parts by the Simatai Reservoir. There are 35 watch towers on this section of the wall. Originally built in the early years of the Emperor of Hongwu during the Ming Dynasty, and later strengthened by General Qi Jiguang and General Tan Lun, this section of the Great Wall is the only one to retain the original features of the Great Wall of the Ming Dynasty. UNESCO has designated Simatai Great Wall as one of the World Cultural Heritage sites.

The Peking Opera actor is performing the classical repertoire at the China Peking Opera Art Festival. (From ImagineChina)

Beijing Style

Quadrangles and Alleys

More than 1,000 years of history have given Beijing a great number of historic artifacts and sites. Reflecting the day-to-day life of ordinary citizens, the four-sided enclosed courtyards, also called quadrangles, and alleys of the city tell more.

The quadrangle is the traditional style of houses in Beijing. At the center of the quadrangle is a medium-sized yard for outdoor activities. The central room, built and decorated better than other rooms, is warm in winter and cool in summer. It is usually the room for elders and superiors while the side room is for children. Women live in the inner room, and guests and male servants live in the outer rooms. This structure is in accordance with the rites and customs of ancient China. The quadrangle features a symmetrical layout, majestic grandeur, and spaciousness, all in line with Chinese conventions, offering the residents a sense of tranquility and comfort.

Alleys run through the city in profusion, most of which were built in the Yuan, Ming, and Qing Dynasties. These alleys have seen much history and the cultural activities of many lives, famous and obscure alike.

A new "tour of alleys" is available giving the tourist a glimpse into ancient buildings and traditions.

Recommended routes for visiting quadrangles and alleys:

Take a pedicab to the Clock Tower for a bird's-eye view of the ancient city and the

(From ImagineChina)

new city in the distance. Take another pedicab to the Yinding Bridge to stroll through the ancient alleys and visit the quadrangles. Then onto the Gongwang Mansion, a reminder of noble Chinese life, for tea and a taste of local food. After a visit to the primary schools and nursery schools nearby, return by pedicab. This tour will give you a look at the gap between the elite and the common people, along with the cultural history of alleys and quadrangles.

Peking Opera

Peking Opera is the national opera of China, with a history of more than 200 years. It came into being and thrived during the Qing Dynasty. There are about 1,000 operas in the repertoire, but only several hundred of them are the most frequently performed. The main roles in Peking Opera are broadly divided into the male role ("sheng"), the female role ("dan"), the painted-face role ("jing"), and the comic role ("chou"). The music is unique, and tourists should make the time to attend a performance.

Teahouses

Beijing was once the capital of five dynasties throughout Chinese history and was also the center of Chinese tea culture. During the Qing Dynasty (1644-1911), Manchu aristocrats spent much of their time in teahouses. Later, teahouses were frequently visited by bureaucrats and politicians. Contemporary teahouses in Beijing are usually elegantly decorated with old-fashioned square tables for eight people, calligraphy, and paintings by celebrated artists on the walls. Waitresses generally wear the traditional cheongsam. While drinking tea and tasting refreshments, you can enjoy Peking Opera at the same time. You can also play chess in teahouses. The best

(From ImagineChina)

teahouses in Beijing include Wufu Teahouse and Laoshe Teahouse.

Liyuan Theater

Liyuan Theater is the primary opera house in Beijing, co-owned by the Beijing Qianmen Hotel and Beijing Opera Theater. It puts on a play every night by famous Peking Opera performers.

Bars in Beijing

Bars in Beijing are not only places for entertainment but also cultural places. Sanli Tun Street and Shishahai Street are two areas representing the bar scene in Beijing. South Sanli Tun Street came into being earlier because of its proximity to the embassies, but the bars on North Sanli Tun Street are more famous.

Shishahai is a large picturesque pool in Beijing, with beautiful scenery and vibrant culture. Quite a number of bars have been opened in this area, making this a lively and entertaining street.

(From ImagineChina)

The 29th Olympic Games in Beijing

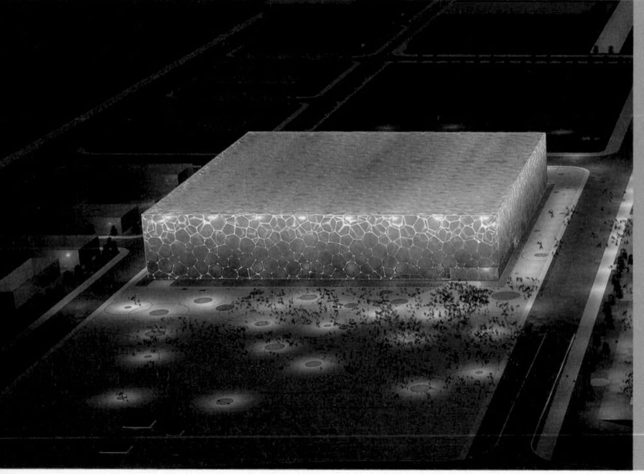

National Swimming Center (From BOCOG)

ONE WORLD ONE DREAM

The Olympic Torch Relay

The plans accepted by the IOC for the Olympic torch relay were announced on April 26, 2007, in Beijing. The relay, "Journey of Harmony," will take about four months, carrying the torch 85,100 miles—the longest distance of any Olympic torch relay to date. Beginning on March 25, 2008, in Olympia, Greece and arriving in Beijing on July 31, the torch will visit various cities and villages on the Silk Road, symbolizing links between China and the rest of the world. A total of 21,880 torch bearers will be selected from around the world by various organizations and entities.

There are plans to carry the flame to the top of Mount Everest. In June 2007, construction began on a 67-mile-long "highway" running up the Tibetan side of the mountain. There have been some concerns about the effects of the road on the fragile Himalayan terrain. The scheduled route also includes a stop in Taipei just before heading for Hong Kong, but this plan has not yet been finalized.

The Olympic Torch logo is based on traditional scrolls and uses a traditional Chinese design known as the "Cloud of Promise" (祥云). The torch is designed to remain lit in 40-mile-an-hour winds, and in rain of up to 2 inches an hour.

(From ImagineChina)

Olympic Park

The Olympic Park, built for the 2008 Olympic Games, is a new integrated sports and culture center in Beijing. The construction of the park broke the tradition that Beijing's development should only stretch south on the axes of the Forbidden City. Its construction in the north of Beijing formed a new development center in the city, and we can see a new side of Beijing in the twenty-first century. Guided by the slogan of the 2008 Olympic Games "Scientific Olympics, Green Olympics, Humanist Olympics," the Olympic Park lake is the largest man-made lake in the world and is fed entirely by recycled water. The plan is that the lake will cover an area of some 1,500 acres; 143,000 pounds of water will be needed every day just for the north area. Olympic Park will be a first-class sports establishment, a multifunctional public center that will hold sports matches and cultural activities not just for the 2008 Olympics but for many years to come.

National Stadium (From BOCOG)

National Stadium

Built to the south of the Olympic Park, this structure has been referred to as "the nest." It can hold upwards of 100,000 people. All parts of the gymnasium intermesh and support each other, forming a grid, which, with its interwoven girders, looks very much like a bird's nest. This grey steel network is covered with transparent film, which will allow events to proceed in spite of rain or extremely hot weather. The Nest also has a bowl-shaped reviewing platform. Here, traditional Chinese fretwork, the grain of chinaware, and the earthy red color of China's ancient rocks have been combined with the most advanced steel structure. The landscape outside the nest grid rises above the structure, and a subsidiary building is underground. A 2,000-seat warm-up area sits beside the Nest.

National Aquatic Sports Center

The shallow, blue, cubic building west of the National Stadium is the National Aquatic Sports Center, also known as "Water Cube." The construction area is about 753 square feet, and it will hold 6,000 permanent and 11,000 temporary seats. Like the Nest, the entire building is covered with transparent film. The blue film is surprisingly soft but substantial; it can insulate well, and is also easy to mend. If the film is broken by a starting gun, the damage will be shown on a monitor, and a piece of tape will repair it. The film is also easy to clean: dust can't adhere to it and any fog or condensation from the swimming pools will dissipate immediately.

(From BOCOG)

Competition Sites for the Olympic Games in Beijing >>>

Location	Address	Game Functions
The National Stadium *	Olympic Park	Athletics, Soccer
The National Aquatic Sports Center	Olympic Park	Swimming, Diving, Synchronized Swimming
The National Gymnasium	Olympic Park	Artistic Gymnastics, Trampoline Gymnastics, Handball
Beijing Shooting Range Hall	Number A3, Futiansi, Shijingshan District, Beijing	All shooting events in the Summer Olympic Games and the Handicapped Olympic Games
Wukesong Indoor Stadium	Wukesong Cultural and Sports Center	Basketball
Laoshan Velodrom	Westside of the GASC Cycling and Fencing Management Center Training Base in Laoshan, Shijingshan District, Beijing	Track Cycling
Olympic Rowing—Canoeing Park	Chaobai River, Mapuo Township, Shunyi County, Beijing	Rowing, Canoeing (flat-water racing), Canoeing (slalom racing)
The China Agricultural University Gymnasium	East Section of China Agricultural University	Wrestling
Peking University Gymnasium	Peking University	Table Tennis
Gymnasium of Beijing Science and Technology University	Beijing Science and Technology University	Judo, Taekwondo
Beijing University of Technology Gymnasium	Beijing University of Technology	Badminton, Rhythmic Gymnastics
Olympic Sports Center Stadium	South of the Olympic Games Center	Modern Pentathlon (athletics and equestrian)
Olympic Sports Center Gymnasium	Olympic Games Center	Handball
The Workers' Stadium	Workers' Stadium Road, Chaoyang District	Soccer

* **Post-game Functions:** International or domestic sports competitions, culture, or entertainment activities.

Location	Address	Game Functions
The Workers' Indoor Arena	Workers' Stadium Road	Boxing
Capital Indoor Statium	Baishiqiao, Haidian District	Volleyball
Fengtai Softball Field	Fengtai Sports Center	Softball
Yingdong Natatorium	Olympic Sports Center	Water Polo, Modern Pentathlon (swimming)
Laoshan Mountain Bike Course	Laoshan, Shijingshan District	Mountain Biking, Cycling
Beijing Shooting Range, Clay Target Field	South Section of Xiangshan Road	Trap Shooting
Gymnasium of Beijing Institute of Technology	Beijing Institute of Technology	Volleyball competition
Gymnasium of Beihang University	Beihang University	Weight-lifting
Fencing Hall of the National Conference Center	National Conference Center	Preliminary and final fencing contests
Hockey Field of the Olympic Forest Park	Olympic Forest Park	Hockey competition
Archery field of the Olympic Forest Park	Olympic Forest Park	Archery competition
Volleyball field of the Olympic Forest Park	Olympic Forest Park	Volleyball competition
Wukesong Baseball Field	Wukesong Culture and Sports Center	Baseball competition
Beach Volleyball Ground	Zhaoyang Park	Beach volleyball competition
Small-wheeled Bike Competition Ranch	Laoshan Mountain of the Shijingshan District	Small-wheeled bike competition
Triathlon Venue	Shisanling Reservoir	Triathlon
Urban Road Cycling Course	To be decided	Road-cycling competition

Tianjin

Geography at a Glance

Tianjin, or "Jin" for short, is the largest open coastal city in North China. In the north, it is next to Yan Mountain and in the east the Bohai Sea. Having a coastline of around 95 miles, it boasts a vast expanse of coastland. Abounding in fishing, mining, open water, and travel resources, it is known as the "Pearl of the Bohai Sea." The city covers an area of 4,247 square miles with a population of 10 million (2000 census).

Tianjin has three distinct terrains: mountains, uplands, and plains. Hundreds of small tributaries converge into the North and South Canals, the Yongding, Daqing, Ziya, and Chaobai Rivers, and the Ji Canal.

Tianjin has a warm temperate continental monsoon climate. The annual average temperature is 55°F. The hottest month is July, during which the average temperature can reach nearly 80°F. January is the coldest month, its average temperature hovering at 24°F. The yearly average rainfall is 20 to 27 inches.

(From CFP)

Featured Cuisine

18th Street twisted dough sticks (mahua), steamed buns with filling (goubuli baozi), fried rice cakes (erduoyan), stewed chicken, stewed duck, stewed pork elbow, stewed pork, stewed sea cucumber, stewed gluten, stewed fish, fried fish slices, braised shrimp meat, fried fish bone, stewed fish maw, braised gluten, fried shrimp meat, crab roe in egg custard, sea cucumber, steamed pork.

Typical Yangliuqing New Year painting (From Colphoto)

Featured Commodities

Special Local Products

Shawo carrot, weiqing carrot, preserved vegetable, Duliu vinegar, Xiaozhan rice, Panshan persimmon, Baodi red-skinned garlic, Hongzhong sauce, Tianjin leeka, yellow-skinned shallots.

Local Handicrafts

Yangliuqing New Year paintings, Zhang's colored clay figurines, Fengchuan carpets, Wei's kites, paper cutting, black pottery, violet pottery, cloisonné, brick-carvings.

Fruits and Delicacies

Sweet chestnut, walnuts, persimmon, pears, dates.

Transportation Tips

By Bus

Tianjin has three major highways: Beijing-Tianjin-Tanggu Highway, Beijing-Shenyang Highway, and Beijing-Shanghai Highway. The Beijing-Tianjin-Tanggu Highway is the best one and runs through many provinces and cities in China, serving as an important transportation link between Beijing and Tianjin.

By Train

Tianjin is at the junction of Jingshan, Jinpu, and Jinji lines, connecting to Beijing, Shanhaiguan Pass, Jinan, Ji County, and Bazhou. There are four train stations in Tianjin, Tianjin Main, Tianjin West, Tianjin South, and Tianjin North. Trains from Tianjin Main station connect to more than forty cities in China, including Beijing, Shijiazhuang, Guangzhou, Xi'an, Shanghai, Nanjing, Hangzhou, Ha'erbin, Manzhouli, and Kowloon.

Notes 

❶ The streets in Tianjin can be confusing for tourists, but your guide or local information center can show you the way.

❷ People from Tianjin are often typified as eloquent and loquacious. Tianjin natives are referred to as *weizuizi,* which translates roughly as "the Tianjin mouth."

❸ Things are much less expensive in Tianjin than in Beijing. Many people from Beijing shop and dine here.

By Plane

Located in Zhangguizhuang of Dongli District, Tianjin Binhai International Airport is 8 miles from the city proper. More than 30 international and domestic airlines have flights to and out of this airport. There are regular shuttle buses to Binhai International Airport from the ticket offices in Tianjin, which will also deliver your tickets for free. Shuttle buses also run every hour from 7 to 10 a.m. and from 1 to 4 p.m. from Tianjin to Beijing Capital International Airport.

Dagukou Fort Barbette (From Colphoto)

By Ship

Tianjin Port (Tianjin Gang) is located at the western shore of the Bohai Sea, which is the main departure point for going to Beijing by water. Its domestic sea routes are to Yantai,

POPULAR FESTIVALS

Dragon Heads-Raising Day

The Dragon Heads-Raising Day falls on the 2nd day of the second lunar month. People make pancakes of wheat flour, fried eggs, and bean sprouts (which are considered to be the whiskers of the dragon). Needlework is forbidden on this day.

Royal Performance at the Matsu Temple (Tianhou Temple)

Held on the 23rd day of the third lunar month, the concert is named after the Emperor Kangxi, who came to Tianjin to watch the performance and bestowed a royal flag.

Drum Dance Performance

Eight teenagers divided into two groups perform stories from Outlaws of the Marsh.

Dharma Drum Performance

Originally Buddhist music, it comprises a dozen of sets of melodies with Laoxihe and Yaotonggu as the most commonly used ones.

Five Tigers Shouldering the Box Performance

The stories and costumes are all from the Beijing Opera The Five Tigers of Ba's.

Chonggelao Performance

It starts during the reign of the Emperor Daoguang (1821–1850) of the Qing Dynasty. Also named "Higher and Higher," the show looks somewhat like Dieluohan, a performance in which a performer stands in place while a second performer stands on his shoulders, and the procedure repeats until no more performers are able to climb without losing balance.

Eighth Day of the Twelfth Lunar Month

The custom on this day is to make the laba congee. Its major ingredients include sticky rice, mung beans, and jequirities. The name *laba* means the eighth day of the twelfth lunar month.

Dalian, and Longkou; international routes are to Inchon in Korea and Honshu in Japan.

Recommended Routes

Featured Routes

One-day tour of Western-style buildings

Five Avenues→N. Jiefang Road→Huayuan Road→Matsu Temple (Tianhou Temple).

One-day folk culture tour

Tianjin History Museum→Shi Family Residence→Yangliuqing→Matsu Temple (Tianhou Temple)→Ancient Culture Street (Guwenhua Street),

One-day museum tour

Zhou Enlai-Deng Yingchao Memorial Hall→Memorial Hall of the Ping-Jin Campaign→Tianjin Science and Technology Museum→Tianjin Nature Museum→Tianjin Art Museum.

One-day tour of cultural relics

Temple of Great Compassion (Dabeiyuan)→Guangdong Guild Hall→Confucius Temple (Wen Miao)→Lu Zu Hall→Yinbing Shi→Matsu Temple (Tianhou Temple).

Three-day tour by water

Day 1 Haihe River→Bohai Sea.

Day 2 Jinhe River→Weijin River.

Day 3 North Canal (Bei Yunhe)→Ziya River (Yangliuqing).

Classical Routes

Two-day tour of Tianjin suburbs

Day 1 Dule Temple→Ji County.

Day 2 Pan Mountain→Huangya Pass.

Two-day downtown tour

Day 1 Tianta Lake (Tianta Hu)→Pinglu Golden Street (Pinglu Jinjie)→Water Park→Italian-style Street.

Day 2 Ancient Culture Street→Guyi Jie→Drum Tower Walking Street→Five Avenues→South Market Food Street.

Three-day tour of the coastal area

Day 1 Beach Holiday Resort.

Day 2 New Foreign Goods Market→Dagukou Fort Barbette.

Day 3 Northern Port (Bei Tang)→Tianjin Port→Donkey and House River (Luju He).

One-day cultural relics tour

Dule Temple→Matsu Temple (Tianhou Temple)→Five Avenues→Great Wall at Huangya Pass.

Addresses and Phone Numbers

Sheraton Tianjin Hotel	Zi Jin Shan Road, He Xi District	022-23343388
Friendship Hotel	Nanjing Road, He Ping District	022-23310372
Yuanyang Hotel	5 Yuanyang Plaza, He Bei District	022-24205518
Tianbo Hotel	11 Liujing Road, He Dong District	022-85580888
Jinxi Hotel	2 Sanma Road, Nan Kai District	022-27351688
Yongyang Hotel	16 Yongyang Dongdao, Yangcun, Wuqing District	022-29341219
Jiuzhou Hotel	27 Dongting Road, Development District	022-25326668

Tianjin Region

Best Time to Travel

Any season is suitable for a trip to Tianjin, especially summer. Many people come here from Beijing to spend their summer vacations.

Shopping Tips

The Antique Market at Shenyang Road is the largest market in Tianjin, filled with shops selling porcelain, furniture, clocks, watches, paintings, souvenirs, and the "four treasures of the study." These are the traditional Wen Fang Si Bao, or brush pen, inkstick, paper, and inkstone, indispensable tools for calligraphy. Travelers interested in collecting might just find what they're looking for.

The Fashion Street in the northeast of Nan Kai District is an ideal place for shopping. The Quanye Bazaar (Quanye Chang) and the China Great Theater are also in this area.

The Ancient Culture Theater outside the Eastern Gate in the northeast corner of Nan Kai District, west shore of the Haihe River, is a famous commercial pedestrian street in Tianjin. There are over 80 stores specializing in calligraphy tools, celebrity paintings, traditional opera costumes, and antiques, including traditional clay figurines and Chinese New Year paintings.

Guangdong Guild Hall

The Guangdong Guild Hall on Nanmenli Street, Nankai District, was built in 1907, under the reign of Emperor Guang Xu of the Qing Dynasty and co-funded by Guangdong businessmen. It became the Tianjin Museum of Drama in 1986 and is the largest and most exquisitely decorated and preserved Qing guild hall in Tianjin. The whole complex comprises 125 buildings, including a porch hall, a grand hall, side halls, a theater, a crossing courtyard, and sets of apartments. Among them, the north-facing theater with its vast internal space is a must-see, constructed as it is with wonderful workmanship. It is a rarity to see such a well-preserved area in China's ancient buildings.

The stage in the theater building is 33 feet high and 36 feet wide. The tier is double-floored with the box seats upstairs and extra seats downstairs, and can accommodate 700 people. (From CFP)

Zhou Enlai-Deng Yingchao Memorial Hall

The memorial hall dedicated to Zhou Enlai and Deng Yingchao is located to the north of the Park-on-the-Lake in the southwest of downtown Tianjin, once the site of the eastern building of Nankai High School. Originally built in 1904, the construction was devastated by an earthquake in 1976 and rebuilt in 1977. It holds more than 8,000 items, including objects, literature, and photographs.

Temple of Great Compassion (Dabei Yuan)

The Temple of Great Compassion is an enormous and well-preserved Buddhist temple in Tianjin. Located at 26 Tianwei Road, Hebei

District, it has a western and an eastern yard. The eastern yard, known as the Old Temple, was built in 1858 during the Qing Dynasty; the western yard, or New Temple, was built in 1940 and contains the main building of the whole temple, the Maravira Hall. A guild bronze Sakyamuni Buddha statue is enshrined there.

Shi Family Mansion

Located at 47 Guyi Street, Yangliuqing of Xiqing District, the Shi Family Mansion, also called Zunmei Hall, is the former residence of Shi Yuanshi, the son of Shi Wancheng from Shi family, one of the eight eminent families in Tianjin in the Qing Dynasty. With a length of 328 feet and a width of 230 feet, it comprises 12 courtyards and 278 rooms. The building was built in the first year (1875) under the reign of Guangxu during Qing Dynasty.

> Take the bus from the Development District at the Tianjin (Main) Railway Station to Yangliuqing, or take Bus 153 at the Tianjin West Railway Station to Yangliuqing. It's a 15-minute walk from there to the site.

Dagukou Fort Barbette

Dagukou Fort Barbette is located at the estuary of East Dagu River in Tanggu District. Five of these battlements were set up in the Ming Dynasty for the safety of Beijing. Three were located at the northern shore while the other two on the southern side. They are respectively named "Dignity," "Garrison," "Sea," and "Gate "and "Height." Among them only the square-shaped one named "Sea" at the southern shore is preserved and in good condition.

Tianjin Beach Holiday Resort

The resort is located at the Gaosha Ling beach of Tanggu District, west shore of Bohai Sea and near the Haifang Road. About 31 miles from the downtown area, it claims the best natural and geographical location: the water is warm, the beach flat, and the sand soft. It is also rich in geothermal energy resources. The largest bathing beach in China, it can accommodate 50,000 people.

Dule Temple (Dule Si)

Dule Temple, also called the Big Buddha Temple , is located at West Drum Tower Road in Ji County. First built in 636 and rebuilt in 984, it is one of the earliest wood constructions preserved in China. The Sanmon gate of the temple is three jian wide and two jian long (the area inside any four columns is called jian), ranking as the earliest tiger-hall style Sanmon gate in China.

Scenery of Shi Family Mansion (From CFP)

Pan Mountain

Pan Mountain in Ji County enjoys a reputation as the "First Mountain in Jingdong." Its major landscapes are called Five Peaks and Eight Stones. Because the mountain was once literally filled with temples (which were destroyed later but have now been rebuilt), Pan Mountain is also known as the Eastern Wutai Mountain. The sculptures on the rocks around the Temple of Thousands of Statues (Qianxiang Si) are the only linear carving works preserved in Tianjin.

Train 4457 runs to Ji County's South Railway Station from Beijing South Station every morning, and then take the bus to Pan Mountain. Tour bus 18 from the Gate of Military Declaration (Xuanwu Men) of Beijing goes straight to Pan Mountain.

Dule Temple has a central pavilion dedicated to Guanyin (Goddess of Mercy). It is the highest of all the double-floored pavilions preserved in China. The statue of Guanyin is 52 feet tall, one of the largest clay statues in China. (From Quanjing)

Great Wall at Huangya Pass

Also known as Small Yanmen Pass, this wall is located about 18 miles north of Ji County. This 9,925-foot-long great wall with its 52 battle platforms and 14 watch towers guarding east Beijing is a relatively complete ancient military defense system. It was built under the reign of Yongle during the Ming Dynasty (in the early fifteenth century). Connecting the Widow Platform (Guafu Lou) in the east and Wangmaoding Mountain in the west, it is famous for its ruggedness, beautiful scenery, and impressive design.

Take the bus at Northeast End Long-Distance Bus Station in downtown Tianjin to Xinglong; get off in Ji County (about a 3-hour ride). There is an ancient Great Wall Museum in the south of the Huangya Pass.

The Yangliuqing New Year paintings are characterized by the combination of block print and colored hand drawing. (From CFP)

Tianjin Style

Yangliuqing New Year Painting

As many scholars and painters lived in the ancient town Yangliuqing 9 miles west of Tianjin during the Ming and Qing Dynasties, New Year painting gradually developed into a business which now has over 300 years of history. Yangliuqing New Year painting is flamboyant in color and full of exaggeration, showing liveliness and happiness with intense local features. Yangliuqing New Year painting first emerged in the Ming Dynasty and gradually became mature in the middle of Qing Dynasty. “Enjoying the New Year While Having a Surplus” is the most famous traditional New Year painting in Yangliuqing. In recent years, Yangliuqing New Year painting has explored contemporary life. It it now appreciated by people around the world.

Clay Figurine Zhang

“Clay figurine Zhang” first referred to the famous clay figurine artist Zhang Mingshan in Tianjin in Qing Dynasty. Later on, it was also used to refer to the clay figurine works of Zhang Mingshan and his disciples, which became a famous old brand of clay figurine. As the story goes, Zhang Mingshan inherited his father’s business and soon the student surpassed

Painted clay figurine Zhang (From CFP)

the teacher. He had a unique skill, which was to make clay figurines in his sleeves without any mistake. He was praised by people like a legend. Painted clay figurine Zhang attaches importance to realism. It has precise proportion, is vivid and subtle, and wide in material selection. The works are well known at home and abroad and have won international awards.

Nanshi Food Street

Nanshi Food Street is located in Nanshi, the bustling old commercial center in Tianjin, where not only gourmet cuisines and tasty snacks from across the country are sold, but also the architecture has a unique style. The entire food street is like a palace that looks simple and solemn. It is currently the largest contemporary market engaged in special food brands and local products. There are the traditional cuisines from Sichuan, Shandong, Guangdong, Hunan, Jiangsu and Zhejiang; the folk snacks with sweet, salty, dry, and watery tastes; Italian and Russian-style food and snacks; food from mountain villages; seasonal seafood; simple village meals; and gourmet cuisine. With its unique charm as a scenic spot in Tianjin, Nanshi Food Street has attracted many tourists.

Tianjin's Snacks

Goubuli Steamed Stuffed Bun

One of the three unique snacks in Tianjin is Goubuli steamed stuffed bun. Its title is originated from a tale which says that its founder Gao Guiyou, whose nickname given by his parents was Goubuli, used to be an apprentice in a steamed stuffed bun shop. He later opened his own steamed stuffed bun shop after his apprenticeship ended. The steamed stuffed bun in his shop was delicate and looked nice, tasty but not oily. As time passed, people began to call it Goubuli steamed stuffed bun. There are three branch stores of Goubuli steamed stuffed bun in Tianjin and the headquarters store is located on Shandong Road not far away from Binjiang Road. Goubuli steamed stuffed bun is now famous at home and abroad. Everyone, from state heads to common people, wants to have a taste of it.

Erduoyan Fried Glutinous Cakes

Tianjin Erduoyan Fried Glutinous Cakes were first created in Emperor Guangxu's period of the Qing Dynasty. The first shopkeeper, Liu Manchun, opened a fried glutinous cakes store in Erduoyan Lane on the bustling Beimengwai Street in Tianjin. The shop was very particular about the selection of material and the application of fire, and the fried glutinous cakes that it produced were golden yellow in color, with crisp skin and glutinous inside, and the stuffing was sweet and unique in taste. It developed a school of its own and people called it Erduoyan Fried Glutinous Cake.

Goubuli steamed stuffed bun (From CFP)

Hemp Flowers on 18th Street

Guifaxiang hemp flowers with assorted stuffing on 18th Street in Tianjin are one of the three unique snacks in Tianjin. Its founders, the brothers Fan Guicai and Fan Guilin, opened a hemp flower store on 18th Street and Dagunan Road in 1950. The material selection and production method are very special. The hemp flowers are not only crisp and tasty, but can also stay firm for several months.

Pasted Bun and Cooked Fish

Pasted bun and cooked fish is a common dish and snack in Tianjin. Tianjin is rich in aquatic products, and therefore, Tianjin people love eating fish with the bun that is the staple food in households. Pasted bun and cooked fish are not produced separately; instead, they are cooked in one pot. The fish should be small and fresh. When the cauldron is warmed, the fish is cooled in the bottom while the bun is pasted around the upper part of the cauldron. Duration and temperature are very important and the slow fire should make the seasoning emit fragrance.

Home to Folk Art Forms

In its history, the city of Tianjin was gradually built up with the constant migration of people from outside. These people from other places brought the entertainment forms of their hometown to Tianjin, which allowed various folk art forms to develop and evolve in Tianjin.

Storytelling in Beijing Dialect with Drum Accompaniment

Storytelling in Beijing dialect with drum accompaniment was the most important folk

(From CFP)

art form in Tianjin, which evolved from clapper talks with drum accompaniment in rural areas in Hebei. It was introduced to Tianjin at the end of the nineteenth century. Folk artists from Hebei mostly use Hebei dialect while they performed on the streets. Later generations changed the original spoken parts and singing parts into Beijing dialect through constant adjustments. As a result, it was called storytelling in Beijing dialect with drum accompaniment. It is perfect in form, and there have been many famous artists and various kinds of schools.

Tianjin Cross Talk

For the origin of cross talk, there has always been the saying of "born in Beijing while fostered in Tianjin." During Emperor Guangxu's period in Qing Dynasty, Beijing had hard times and artists could hardly make a living, so cross talk artists came to Tianjin in search of a livelihood. Thus, cross talk had a deep foundation in Tianjin. During this period, many famous cross talk artists were born. Ma Sanli (1914–2003) was a cross talk artist most loved by the Tianjin people. His cross talk seemed to have a magic force. His famous sentence "Amuse you" has become the tag of countrymen.

Hebei

Geography at a Glance

The name *Hebei* means "north of the Yellow River," Hebei, or "Ji" for short, borders Liaoning, Inner Mongolia, Shanxi, Henan, Shandong, and the Bohai Sea on the east. Hebei completely surrounds Beijing and Tianjin municipalities, covering an area of 733,359 square miles and having a population of 67,440,000 (2000 census). The 54 ethnic groups here include Han, Hui, Manchu, Mongol, and Korean. Its capital, Shijiazhuang is its center of politics, economy, culture, and transportation.

Nearly 5,000 years ago, the three ancestors of the Chinese people—Emperor Huang, Emperor Yan, and Chiyou—combined forces and established the Chinese culture in the Hebei area. Another name for Hebei is "Yanzhao," after the state of Yan and state of Zhao, which existed here during the Warring States Period of early Chinese history. Since Beijing became the capital of the Jin, Yuan, Ming, and Qing dynasties, Hebei served as a critical place guarding the safety of the capital.

The terrain of the province is higher in the northwest and lower in the southeast with its mountains rising 3,281-4,900 feet above sea level. Hebei has a continental monsoon climate and four distinct seasons. The average temperature in January is 32 to 55°F, and the annual precipitation is 14 to 32 inches.

Featured Cuisine

Yutu steamed chicken in lotus-leaf packets, Nansha sweet cake with fillings, buckwheat

(From Quanjing)

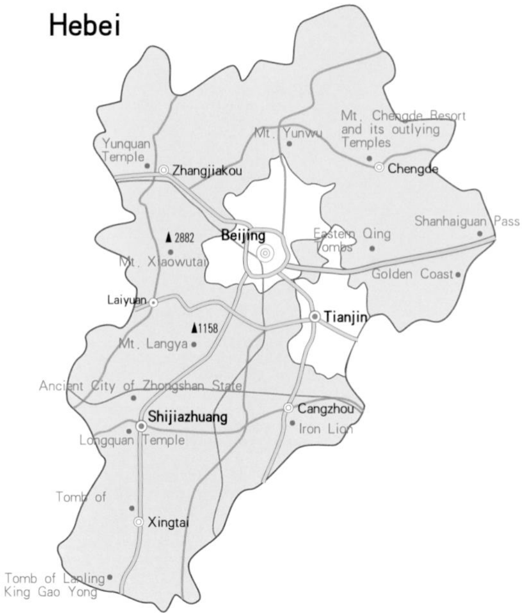

Hammer Peak (From Quanjing)

steamed bread, Jinzhou salted donkey meat, Chaigoubao smoked meat, Gaidao fried pork with bamboo shoots, Baoding Muslim-style stewed chicken, Paxiang mushrooms, Guoba roast dough cake, Xingtai fried dough twists, Baiyunzhang steamed bun with stuffing, Dingzhou sweet potato vermicelli, Handan sheet jelly, Gaobeidian beancurd noodle, Gaocheng imperial noodle, Raoyang golden silk noodle.

Featured Commodities

Special Local Products

Fern vegetable, jellyfish, sea crab, shrimp, sea pearl, Bashang mushroom, Chengde almond, Xuanhua wine, Shexian spicy berry, Handan Congtai liquor, Xushui Liuling liquor, Hengshui liquor, Changli soft–shelled turtle, Hebei chili pepper, Taihang Mountain rabbit.

Local Handicrafts

Shell carvings, Wuqiang Chinese New Year–themed watercolor paintings, Weixian paper-cut, Baiyangdian reed-braided basketry, Tangshan porcelain, Quyang stone carving, Gaocheng imperial lanterns, Cizhou porcelain, Ding porcelain.

Notes 

❶ Bashang Prairie has a highland climate with a high temperature in summer of 75°F. The evening temperatures vary drastically from those during the day. A coat or sweater comes in handy at night, so be prepared to bring layers of clothing. Sunblock lotion is useful to protect skin from the strong summer sun.

❷ Horseback riding is popular here. Wear jeans or riding clothes for comfort.

❸ Fireworks are permitted and readily available at tourist areas.

Transportation Tips

By Bus

The highways extending from Beijing to every province pass through Hebei, and there are nearly 24,845 miles of highways within Hebei. Four expressways run through Hebei, including the three from Beijing to Shanghai, Shijiazhuang, and Shenyang, and one to Taiyuan in the west and Huanghua in the east. There are ten national highways running to Northeast China, Inner Mongolia, Shandong, Shanxi, and Henan.

By Train

Hebei surrounds Beijing, so trains from Beijing to South China pass through Hebei. There are 15 important rail lines running through Hebei, including Jingguang (Beijing-Guangzhou) Jingshan (Beijing-Shanhai Pass), Jinpu (Tianjin-Pukou), Jingqin (Beijing-Qinhuangdao), Jingbao (Beijing-Baotou), Jingyuan (Beijing-Yuanping), Shitai (Shijiazhuang-Taiyuan), and Shide (Shijiazhuang-Dezhou) lines. The Shijiazhuang station is the railroad hub of the North China Plain. Special travel and tourist trains run from Beijing to Chengde, Qinhuangdao, Beidaihe, Yesanpo, and other scenic areas.

Pinju Opera (From ImagineChina)

By Plane

Shijiazhuang Airport has flights to 27 domestic cities including Beijing, Zhengzhou, Changsha, Guangzhou, Nanjing, and Shanghai, as well as seasonal flights from Chengde and Qinhuangdao to Beijing. The Shanhai Pass Airport in Qinhuangdao has 15 airlines to domestic cities including Beijing, Shanghai, and Guangzhou. Tourists to Hebei can also travel through the Capital International Airport of Beijing and Tianjin International Airport.

POPULAR FESTIVALS

Folk Fairs

Large-scale folk fairs are held in Hebei during the Spring Festivals. You can watch many native dances and performances, including lion dances, Yangge dance, running-donkey dances, folk lanterns, and others. Fireworks are always beautiful and exciting to watch at the fairs.

Wanquan She Huo

A large folk fair is held in Wanquan County during the Spring Festival, featuring ethnic and folk-art performances.

Dragon-Worship Festival (Longpai Hui)

Fanzhuang Village, Zhao County of Shijiazhuang, hosts this festival on the second day of the second lunar month. This is the time when people clean the temple and hang lanterns to celebrate the day.

By Water

There are a number of ports along the Bohai Sea, including Qinhuangdao, Tianjin, and Jingtang. Huanghua Port is currently under construction.

Recommended Routes

Featured Routes

6-day tour of royal palaces and gardens

Day 1 Arrival in Chengde. Lodging: Ligong Hotel.

Day 2 Mountain Summer Vacation Chengde →Puning Temple→Xumifu Temple→ Putuozong Temple. Lodging: Ligong Hotel.

Day 3 Shuxiang Temple→Bangchui Mountain→Pule Temple→Anyuan Temple →Puren Temple. Lodging: Ligong Hotel.

Day 4 Arhat Mountain→Hammer Peak →Jiguan Peak→Mulan Hunting Site. Lodging: Ligong Hotel.

Day 5 Kuixing Pavilion→Twin Pagoda Mountain→Chaoyang Cave. Lodging Ligong Hotel.

Day 6 End of tour.

4-day leisure tour of Chengde

Day 1 Arrival in Chengde. Lodging: Ligong Hotel.

Day 2 Puning Temple→Junior Potala Palace→Bangchui Mountain. Lodging: Ligong Hotel.

Day 3 Mountain Summer Resort of Chengde. Lodging: Ligong Hotel.

Day 4 End of tour.

3-day tour of Baiyangdian

Day 1 Arrival in Baoding. Lodging: local folk residences in Baiyangdian.

Day 2 Zhili Provincial Governor's Office→ Ancient Lotus Pond→Yaowang Temple. Lodging: local folk residences in Baiyangdian.

Day 3 Mancheng Han Tombs→Baiyangdian →Western Qing Tombs. End of tour.

5-day seaside tour

Day 1 Arrival in Beidaihe. Lodging: Youzheng Hotel.

Day 2 Shanhai Pass Great Wall→The First Pass→Old Dragon's Head→Mengjiangnu Temple→Jiaoshan section of the Great Wall. Lodging: Youzheng Hotel.

Day 3 Wild Animal Zoo→Nandaihe Beach →Bohai Sea. Lodging: Youzheng Hotel.

Day 4 Pegion's Nest→Tiger Rock→Beach. Lodging: Youzheng Hotel.

Day 5 End of tour.

Traditional Routes

3-day tour of the Zhao culture in Handan

Day 1 Arrival in Handan

Day 2 Ruins of the Zhao Capital→King of Zhao's City→Congtai Platform→ Lin Xiangru Returning Lane→Learning Walking Bridge.

Day 3 Ruins of the Santai Platforms→porcelain kilns of the Song Dynasty→Xiangtang Grottoes→Luxian Temple→Goddess Nuwa's Palace. End of tour.

8-day tour of Yan and Zhao

Day 1 Arrival in Shijiazhuang, visit the Pilu Temple.

Day 2 Xibaipo→Longxing Temple→ Rongguo Mansion.

Day 3 Cangyan Mountain→Baodu Stockaded Village.

Addresses and Phone Numbers

Hebei Hotel	10 Zhanqian Street, Shijiazhuang	0311-87898111
Shijiazhuang Hotel	Not far from Hebei Museum at 306 East Zhongshan Road, Shijiazhuang	0311-86049986
Baoding Hotel	733 West Yuhua Road, Baoding	0312-2082588
Yunshan Hotel	2 Banbishan Road, Chengde	0314-2055788
Shanzhuang Hotel	11 Lizhengmen Avenue, Chengde	0314-2095522
Qiwanglou Hotel	1North of East Bifengmen Road, Mountain Summer Resort, Chengde	0314-2022196
Menggubao Hotel	Wanshu Garden, Mountain Summer Resort, Chengde	0314-2272200
Youzheng Hotel	East of the Qinhuangdao Railway Station	0335-3855369
International Hotel	303 Wenhua Road, Qinhuangdao	0335-3083083

Day 4 Site of the Tunnel Warfare in Ranzhuang Village→Baiyangdian.

Day 5 Western Qing Tombs→Zhili Provincial Governor's Office→Ancient Lotus Pond.

Day 6 Mancheng Han Tombs→Zhaozhou Bridge→Bailin Temple.

Day 7 Hebei Musuem→Beidaihe→ Shanhai Pass.

Day 8 End of tour.

Self-Guided Tours

Self-drive tour in Hebei

Starting from Baoding and ending at Zhangjiakou, the journey covers Baoding, Shijiazhuang, Handan, Hengshui, Cangzhou, Tangshan, Qinhuangdao, Chengde, and finally Zhangjiakou. Major sights on the journey include: Lotus Pond, Ranzhuang Village, Baiyangdian, Yesanpo, Western Qing Tombs, Xumi Pagoda in Kaiyuan Temple, Pilu Temple, Cangyan Mountain, Longxing Temple, Zhaozhou Bridge, Congtai Platform, Learning Walking Bridge, Goddess Nuwa's Palace, Eastern Qing Tombs, Beidaihe, Shanhai Pass, Old Dragon's Head, Mengjiangnu's Temple, Nandaihe, Jade Island, Mountain Summer Resort of Chengde, Eight Outer Temples, Puning Temple, Shuxiang Temple, Pule Temple, Anyuan Temple, Puren Temple, Hammer Peak, Twin Pagoda Mountain, Mulan Hunting Ground, etc.

Site of the Second Plenary Session of the Seventh Central Committee meeting of the Chinese Communist Party at Xibaipo (From Colphoto)

Shijiazhuang Region

Best Time to Travel

Lying east of the Taihang Mountains, Shijiazhuang enjoys a climate characterized by four distinct seasons. With temperatures remaining high throughout summer while varying greatly from north to south in winter, autumn is undoubtedly the best season for tourism in this region.

Pilu Temple (Pilu Si)

Situated in the village of Shangjing in the western suburbs of Shijiazhuang, Pilu Temple is an ancient temple of the Linji sect of Buddhism in China famous for its well-preserved ancient frescos. It was first built in the eighth century. Pilu Palace, the major structure in the temple, houses an area of 1,398 square feet of bright-colored frescos, among which those on the four walls are the most splendid. Arranged into three rows, these frescos portray more than 500 Confucian, Buddhist, and Taoist figures in a unique and vivid manner, which makes the drawings very rare and valuable among ancient frescos in China.

You can reach the temple by taking buses from Shijiazhuang to Jingxing, Pingshan, or Xibaipo and getting off in Shangjing Village.

Former Office Site of the CCCCP at Xibaipo

Located in Pingshan, east of the Taihang mountains, Xibaipo was the office site of the Central Committee of Chinese Communist Party (CCCCP) as well as the People's Liberation Army PLA headquarters from May 26, 1948, to March 23, 1949, a period which is crucial to the final victory of the CCP.

Cangyan Mountain (Cangyan Shan)

Located in Cangyanshan in the south of Jingxing County, 31 miles from Shijiazhuang, the Cangyan Mountain covers an area of 24 square miles. Thanks to its splendid natural scenes, it has been a famous attraction since ancient times.

Built across a deep ravine, Qiaolou Hall is definitely a unique structure in China. (From CFP)

Major sights here include Fuqing Temple, Qiaolou Hall, Princess Memorial Temple, Cangshan Academy, and Wanxian Hall.

Fuqing Temple (Fuqing Si)

First built in the Sui Dynasty, the temple was originally named Xingshan. It was renovated and renamed Fuqing by Emperor Zhenzong of the Song Dynasty in 1014. Rumor has it that Princess Nanyang once lived here as a nun. She was the daughter of Yang Guang, a notorious tyrant in the Sui Dynasty.

Longxing Temple (Longxing Si)

Located in Zhengding County, Shijiazhuang, Longxing Temple is one of the largest and best preserved temples in China. It was first built in 586. On the central axis of the temple is the Hall of Heavenly Kings (Tianwang Dian), Hall of Manicheanism (Moni Dian), Mituo Hall (Mituo Dian), the Altar (Jie Tan), and Dabei Pavilion (Dabei Ge). Dabei Pavillion, also called Foxiang Pavilion or Tianning Pavilion, houses a 69-foot-high copper Buddha statue which is the treasure of the temple. Apart from this, the frescos and statues in the Hall of Manicheanism are well worth seeing, too.

Four Pagodas in Zhengding

The four pagodas in Zhengding County are: Lingxiao Pagoda (Lingxiao Ta) in Tianning Temple, which was built in 860; Hua Pagoda (Hua Ta) in Guanghui Temple, which was first built around the end of the eighth century and later renovated in the Jin Dynasty; Xumi Pagoda (Xumi Ta) in Kaiyuan Temple; and the smallest of the four, Chengling Pagoda (Chengling Ta) in Linji Temple, which, though built in 867, was also reconstructed in the Jin Dynasty.

Zhaozhou Bridge (Zhaozhou Qiao)

Anji Bridge is another name for the Zhaozhou Bridge, which spans over the Jiaohe River of Zhao County, Shijiazhuang. Zhaozhou Bridge was built in the flourishing period of the Sui Dynasty (605–616). It is the longest and oldest one-arch stone bridge still preserved in the world. The bridge is 165 feet long and the arch is 31 feet wide. The bridge is very solid, and has a magnificent appearance. On two sides of the big arch four holes were dug in a line, the effect of which lightens the weight of the bridge, economizes the use of stone, and makes it possible to extend the bridge. The railings and the pillars of the bridge are carved with dragons, ani-

Color statue in the Hall of Manicheanism in Longxing Temple (From Colphoto)

A similar but smaller bridge built in the Jin Dynasty spans the Qingshui River in the west of Zhao County.

Zhaozhou Bridge is designed to facilitate transportation both on and under the bridge. It is a pioneering design in the history of bridge construction. (From Quanjing)

mals, flowers, and bamboo, among which the dragons are the most elegant.

Zhangshiyan Scenic Area

The scenic area is located in the mid-section of the main range of the Taihang Mountains, southwest of Zanhuang County, Shijiazhuang. It covers an area of 46 square miles. The main peak, named Huangyannao, is 5,818 feet high. Strange stones, deep caves, and small streams are scattered around the scenic area. The mountains are steep and magnificent. Flowers bloom and birds sing in spring. The area is surrounded with mist, and streams flow gently in summer. The mountains are filled with red leaves in August and covered with white snow in winter.

Buses to Zhangshiyan are available at the Shijiazhuang West Bus Terminal.

Zhaozhou Dharani Sutra Pagoda

Located in Zhao County, this is the highest among all the dharani sutra pagodas in China. (A *dharani* is a type of ritual speech similar to a mantra. The terms *dharani* and *mantra* may even be seen as synonyms, although they normally are used in distinct contexts. The Japanese Buddhist philosopher drew a distinction between dharani and mantra and used this as the basis of his theory of language. Mantra is restricted to esoteric Buddhist practice whereas dharani is found in both esoteric and exoteric ritual.) The 58-foot-high pagoda was built in 1038. Since it was made of granite, it's also called "stone pagoda" by the local people.

Handan Region

Best Time to Travel

The climate of Handan is similar to that of Shijiazhuang, thus spring and autumn are the best seasons for tourism.

Congtai Platform

Located at the mid-section of Zhonghua Avenue in Handan, the platform is said to be the place where King Wuling (325–299 BCE) of the state of Zhao viewed military drills. King Wuling is a famous king in Chinese history who was open-minded enough to learn from the neighboring ethnic groups and finally made his own state powerful enough to defend itself.

The 43-foot-high Jusheng Pavilion on Congtai Platform, which was built in 1534. (From Quanjing)

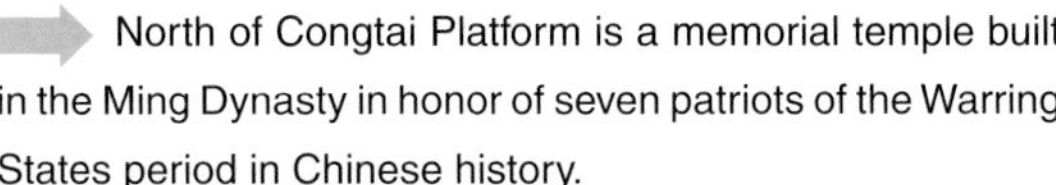

North of Congtai Platform is a memorial temple built in the Ming Dynasty in honor of seven patriots of the Warring States period in Chinese history.

Learning Walking Bridge (Xuebu Qiao)

Located at Beiguan Street in Handan, the bridge was built in 1617. It was so named due to a fable recorded *in Zhuangzi*. The fable goes like this: In Shouling of the Yan State, a lad heard that the people in Handan walked elegantly, so he went there to learn their style of walking. The result, however, was that he not only failed to learn the style, but also forgot how to walk. Finally, he had to crawl back to Shouling. The moral of the fable is that, when learning about the strengths of others, people should combine them with their own abilities instead of imitating others blindly and, therefore, failing miserably.

Learning Walking Bridge (From Quanjing)

Xiangtangshan Grottoes

Located on Gus Mountain in Handan, Xiangtangshan Grottoes is divided into north and south sections which are 49 feet apart. The construction of the grottoes started around 550. At present 16 grottoes remain, with a collection of more than 400 statues on the cliff, more than 3400 smaller statues, and many carved sutras and inscriptions.

LuxianTemple (Luxian Ci)

North of Handan City, the temple was built first in the Song Dynasty and later renovated in the Ming and Qing Dynasties in memory of Lu Chunyang, founder of the Quanzhen Sect of Taoism. According to legend, Lu Chunyang once had a dream in which he worked as an official for 31 years. Then he woke up and found that the 31-year dream was so short that the rice he steamed before falling asleep was still not ready yet. This incident made Lu realize that wealth and honor are just like dreams. From then on, he abandoned the idea of seeking wealth and honor for Taoism and finally became the founder of the Quanzhen Sect.

Goddess Nuwa's Pavilion (Wahuang Ge) in Goddess Nuwa's Palace is unique among Chinese structures in that it was fastened to a cliffside with eight iron chains.

The Zhu's Manor

Located in Jiaocun, Wu'an 12 miles southwest of Handan, this is a well-preserved manor built in the first few years of the twentieth century. Composed of 14 Chinese quadrangles (siheyuan) with more than 400 rooms, it is a large-scale and grand construction in the typical style of northern China.

Goddess Nuwa's Palace (Wahuang Gong)

Located on the mountainside of the Phoenix Mountain (Fenghuang Shan), northwest of Shexian County, Nuwa's Palace is said to be the place where the goddess Nuwa melted stones to repair the sky and created human beings with earth. (According to Chinese myths, the sky was once broken and about to collapse. It was the goddess Nuwa who repaired the sky and saved the world. Nuwa was also the creator of human beings in Chinese myths.) The palace is the largest and earliest structure that honors Nuwa in ancient China. It was built between 550 and 560.

Baoding Region

Best Time to Travel

Summer is the best season for tourism here. Visitors can use Baiyangdian as a summer resort, or appreciate lotuses in the Ancient Lotus Pond.

Shopping Tips

Special local products and handicrafts are available at reasonable prices in the craftwork shop east of the gate of the Zhili Provincial Governor's Office.

Ancient Lotus Pond (Gu Lianhua Chi)

Located in the center of Baoding City, the pond was built in 761 and originally named Aromatic Snow Garden (Xiang Xue Yuan). With the pond as its principal part, the whole garden consists of different kinds of structures, such as platforms, pavilions, and winding cloisters. Its dazzling beauty earns it a great reputation as the "Penglai in the City." (Penglai is a mountain well-known for its beauty in Chinese myths. Supposedly, everything on the mountain seems white, while its palaces are made of gold and platinum, and jewelry grows on trees. The fruits on the mountain are said to be the elixir of life. Because of this, Qin Shi Huang, the first emperor in Chinese history, made several unsuccessful attempts to find the island.) The garden also houses the only well-preserved and complete collection of translated Buddhist sutras in China.

The Lotus Pond is surrounded by different kinds of structures. (From CFP)

Zhili Provincial Governor's Office

Baoding used to be the provincial capital of Hebei and the original governor's office was built in the first year of the reign of Emperor Hongwu during the Ming Dynasty (1368). The governor of Zhili Province lived here in the eighth year of the reign of Yongzheng during the Qing Dynasty. Baoding served as the military and political center of the province under the leadership of 59 governors for a total of 66 terms. Comprised of several well-preserved ancient buildings, the office faces south and covers an area of 215,278 square feet.

Zhongshan Emperor Jing Tomb (Zhongshan Jingwang Mu)

Located halfway up the hill less than one mile west of Mancheng County, this tomb complex holds the tomb of Liu Sheng and his wife Douwan. Liu Sheng was the first emperor of Zhongshan State, Western Han Dynasty. Traditionally, the husband and wife were buried in separate tombs but in the same mausoleum. More than 4,200 articles have been excavated from these two tombs; the bronze artifacts, such as the Changxin Palatial Lantern, are the best examples.

Baiyangdian Lake is home to many kinds of fish, shrimp, and aquatic vegetables, such as lotus root and water chestnut, all of which constitute an ideal environment for flocks of ducks. (From Colphoto)

Baiyangdian Lake

Located in central Hebei and about 28 miles downstream from Baoding, Baiyangdian is the largest inland freshwater lake in northern China. As a flood-control area for the Daqing River, the entire system comprises 36 island villages, and 62 lakeside villages with a total population of 200,000. The flood control project contains 3,700 dikes and nearly one hundred dams. With a total area of 141 square miles, Baiyangdian plays an important role in balancing the ecosystem. The lake and its wetlands supplies large amounts of freshwater fish and aquatic products such as reed mats.

Site of the Tunnel Warfare in Ranzhuang Village

The Tunnel Warfare Museum is in the village of Ranzhuang in Qingyuan County, 19 miles from Baoding City. Commemorating the War of Resistance against the Japanese (1937–1945), the tunnels were preserved and rebuilt in 1959 when the museum was opened to the public. The tunnels run for nearly ten miles, with the crossroad in the village as its center. There are four main stems to the east, west, south, and north, with 11 lateral lines from east to west and 13 lateral lines from south to north. Every house in Ranzhuang Village has a tunnel entrance, and many of the tunnels also connect to other villages.

Yesanpo Scenic Area (Wild Three Parts of Slopes)

Located in the northwest of Laishui County, it is named after the three obvious levels of terrain. The whole area is divided into seven parts with more than 60 scenic spots. On the lowest slope is a wide beach along the Juma River where people enjoy swimming and sunbathing.

Yesanpo is close to the Fangshan District of Beijing. Take Bus No. 8 from Beijing to the scenic area.

Western Qing Tombs

At the foot of Yongning Mountain in Yi County is the Western Qing Tomb complex. This is one of two tomb systems for Qing Dynasty emperors. Of the ten emperors in the Qing Dynasty (1644–1911), four of them had their tombs built in the Western Qing Tombs. In addition there are ten tombs for six empresses and four princes and princesses. It covers an area of 309 square miles and has a perimeter of 62 miles. There are more than 1,000 rooms in the construction.

The construction of the Qi Gate in the tombs is unique. (From ImagineChina)

Stone Pillar Inscribed with the Book of Morals in Longxing Temple

The stone pillar is in the south end of the relics of Longxing Temple in the southeast of Yi County. It is the only well-preserved pillar from the Tang Dynasty inscribed with *The Book of Morals*. Built in 738, the octagonal pillar is made of white marble, 14 feet high and 3 feet across, with each face 15–16.5 inches wide. All 81 chapters of *The Book of Morals* of Laozi are inscribed on each face.

Kaiyuan Temple Pagoda

Kaiyuan Temple Pagoda, also known as the Watch Tower (Liaodi Ta) is located on the south side of the South Gate of Dingzhou County. The construction of Kaiyuan Temple Pagoda was from 1001 to 1055 during the Northern Song Dynasty. As Dingzhou City was on the border between the Song Empire and the Liao Kingdom, the Kaiyuan Temple Pagoda was used as a watch tower by the Song soldiers. Octangular in shape, it has 13 stories and is about 276 feet high, making it the tallest existing brick-and-wood pagoda in China.

The Imperial Examination Hall in Ding County (Dingzhou Gongyuan)

Located in Caochang Alley, East Zhongshan Road in Dingzhou, Dingzhou Gongyuan was first built in the third year of Emperor Qianlong's reign (1738) and expanded in the 14th year of Emperor Daoguang (1834). It is the only well-preserved imperial examination hall in North China. Taking the shape of a square, the complex covers an area of 237,989 square feet and the hall itself covers more than 16,650 square feet.

The South Gate of Dingzhou City, Urn City (Wengcheng) and Moon City (Yuecheng) are well worth visiting.

Northern Mount Temple

The Northern Mount Temple is located in Quyang County, 68 miles southwest of Baoding. In China, there are five famous mountains: Northern Mount Heng, Southern

Mount Heng, Eastern Mount Tai, Western Mount Hua, and Middle Mount Song.

Until 1660, the Northern Mount was in Quyang, and the temple for the Northern Mount God was built here. (After 1660, the Qing Dynasty emperor renamed another mountain as the Northern Mount.) Built between 500 and 512, Deningzhi Hall is its main building.

Hall of a Thousand Buddhas

Located on the Yellow Mountain in Quyang County, 50 miles southwest of Baoding City, the hall holds the earliest recorded stone-sculpture Buddhas in China. The stone itself is unique, a kind of granite dating back 3 billion years. The granite is extremely hard and difficult to polish, yet every Buddha figure and stone tablet in the hall is shiny and lustrous.

Best Time to Travel

The summer months of June, July, and August are perfect for outdoor recreation and the resorts; December and January are ideal for skiing and other winter sports.

The Mountain Summer Resort of Chengde

The Mountain Summer Resort of Chengde, also known as Chengde Palace or Rehe Palace, is found in a long narrow ravine by the west shore of the Wulie River, to the north of the city proper. The mountain resort was built in 1703; after 89 years of painstaking efforts through the Kangxi, Yongzheng, and Qianlong reigns, it grew into the world's largest classical imperial garden. It occupies a total area of more than 1,380 acres. In 1994, the unique cultural and natural value of Chengde's Summer Mountain Resort and the surrounding temples were confirmed when UNESCO listed the resort and the mountains as a World Cultural Heritage site.

Most of the buildings in the Mountain Summer Resort of Chengde, such as the Jinshan Pavilion, blend into the landscape in South China. (From Quanjing)

One of the four pagodas of the Dacheng Pavilion in the Puning Temple (From ImagineChina)

Puning Temple

Located by the Wulie River, north of the Summer Mountain Resort, the Puning Temple (commonly called the Big Buddha Temple) is a Qing Dynasty Buddhist temple complex built in 1755, during the reign of the Qianlong Emperor. The front half of the temple follows the layout of the Buddhist monasteries of the Han people, while the back half is based on mandala, the Tibetan Buddhist concept of the world. The world's tallest wooden figure of Kwan-yin (73 feet) should not be missed.

Fairs are held in the Puning Temple from the 25th day to the 27th day of the twelfth lunar month and from the 8th day to the 15th day of the first lunar month.

The main construction in the Xumifusi Temple of the Eight Outer Temples is composed of three circles of minor buildings surrounding three circles of major halls. (From Jin Yongji)

Pule Temple

Located on the eastern shore of the Wulie River, the temple was built in the 31st year of Emperor Qianlong's reign (1766) in order to receive annual tributes from defeated Mongol and Uigur tribes. Built in the same architectural style as the Puning Temple, the Pule Temple is famous for its sexually explicit sculptures and serene pavilions.

Take Bus No.10 to Puning and Pule temples.

Anyuan Temple

Located on the east bank of the Wulie River, Anyuan Temple was built in 1764. It is also known as the Ili Temple because it resembles the Guerzha Temple on the northern bank of the Ili River. The main building of the temple is the 86-foot-high Pudu Hall. The construction in the temple is a combination of Han and Mongol styles.

Hammer Peak

Located to the east of downtown Chengde, this mountain is named after its shape. The top, or upper part is 49 feet wide, while the lower part is 35 feet wide. With its raised base under the "hammer," the peak has a total height of 126 feet. From a pavilion named "Hammer Peak in the Glow of Sunset" to the west of Lake Ruyi in the Mountain Summer Resort, visitors can get a good view of Hammer Peak.

Twin Pagoda Mountain

Located in the Forest Park, about six miles to the southwest of Chengde, the mountain is 131 feet high and 65 feet across. There are two cliff summits with pagoda-like structures. The scenic spots are beautiful with brooks, forests, and valleys.

Eight Outer Temples

The Eight Outer Temples refers to a group of Lama temples situated on the east and north of the Mountain Summer Resort of Chengde. Built by the Qing court, these temples are strategically placed to duplicate the orientation of "stars surrounding the moon," representing the relationship between the ethnic groups and the imperial court, a symbol of national unity.

> There are many buses from the Mountain Summer Resort to the Eight Outer Temples.

Great Wall at Jinshanling

At the northeast end of Beijing City, there is a 6.5-mile section of the Great Wall called the Jinshanling Great Wall, so named because it is built on the Jinshan mountains. This part of the wall was initially built from

The total length of the Wall at Jinshanling is about 6.5 miles. The walls are especially thick and firm because the flat terrain presented defense difficulties. (From Jin Yongji)

1368 to 1389 in the Ming Dynasty; in 1567 or 1570 General Qi Jiguang was in charge of rebuilding that part of the Wall. The great number of watch towers and battle platforms makes it second only to Badaling in its complexity and quality of construction.

Scenery of Mulan Hunting Ground (From CFP)

Mulan Hunting Ground

Once a royal hunting ground in the Qing Dynasty, the Mulan Hunting Ground is famous for its natural grassland and well-stocked hunting safaris. It is located in Weichang County, Chengde. Tourists are welcome to visit Mongolian and Han communities where their culture and customs exist side-by-side. Hiking, hunting, and nature walks are favorite activities.

Tangshan Region

Best Time to Travel

In general, the Tangshan climate is moderate; January is the coldest month and July is the warmest (average 77°F). The most rainfall is in the summer months of July and August.

Eastern Qing Tombs

At the foot of Changrui Mountain about 80 miles from the heart of Beijing, you will find the Eastern Qing Tombs, the largest and most complete complex of imperial tombs in China. Built during the Qing Dynasty (mid-seventeenth century), the complex holds 15 tombs for five emperors, 14 empresses, and 136 concubines. There are dozens of magnificent structures such as the Stone Arch in the north end and the Spirit Path (Shendao). Bridges, gates, and underground chambers filled with Buddhist art and inscriptions are well worth a visit.

The construction of the tombs followed strict rules: the tomb roofs of emperors and empresses were built of yellow-glaze tiles, and those of the imperial concubines are red. The complex is a World Heritage site.

The underground palace in the Eastern Qing Tombs seems mysterious under dim lights. (From Quanjing)

Former Residence of Li Dazhao

The former residence of Li Dazhao is situated in the village of Daheituo of Leting County, Hebei Province. Li, one of the founders of the Chinese Communist Party (CCP), was born here in 1889. The brick and wood residence was built in 1881 and features a level roof and front, middle, and back yards. The western half of the residence serves as the exhibition area, depicting Li's revolutionary deeds.

Qinhuangdao Region

Best Time to Travel

June, July, and August are the best time to visit summer resorts and beaches. From mid-March to late May and from early September to mid-October bird watching and hiking are popular activities; from November through February are prime winter sports seasons.

Shopping Tips

The street outside the Lianfeng Mountain Park is the best place to shop for ethnic and folk art, inexpensive pearls, and fresh seafood.

Beidaihe Beach

The Beidaihe Beach Resort stretches about six miles from east to west from the Langya Mountain Bridge to the mouth of the Nandaihe river. The beach itself is covered with fine yellow sand; the water is calm, an ideal environment for swimming and sunbathing.

Pigeon Nest Park is the best place for viewing the sunrise above the sea in Beidaihe (From ImagineChina)

This beach can get very crowded in busy tourist seasons.

Shanhai Pass

Shanhai Pass, 9.3 miles from Qinhuangdao, was built in 1381 as a military stronghold during the Ming Dynasty. Situated between the Yan Mountains and the Bohai Sea, it is often referred to as "the Great Pass under the Heaven." The brick and earthen walls of the pass are 46 feet high, 22 feet wide, and almost 2.5 miles in circumference. The pass is connected with the Great Wall.

On the east gate of the city wall stands a tower hung with a horizontal inscribed board reading "The First Pass under the Heaven." The Great Wall Museum is about an eighth of a mile (660 feet) south of the tower.

Old Dragon's Head

Three miles south of the Shanhai Pass, Laolongtou stretches into the sea like

The Great Wall at Laolongtou stretches 2,211 feet, a bit less than a half mile. The Great Wall has often been compared to a huge dragon, and Laolongtou looks like the head of the dragon drinking water from the sea. (From ImagineChina)

a peninsula. With its strategic position and majestic military barriers, Laolongtou is the place where the Great Wall meets the sea.

Mengjiangnu Temple

Four miles east of Shanhai Pass, the temple of Mengjiangnu commemorates one of China's best known love stories. When Mengjiangnu discovered that her husband had died while being forced to build the Great Wall, she stayed by the wall and wept for days and nights and caused a 249-foot section of the wall to collapse. The temple is built of brick with 108 stairs in front; the pillars in front of the temple hall hold famous love poems.

Nandaihe Beach

Located about 12 miles southeast of Funing County, Nandaihe is connected to Beidaihe by a bridge. The long, 11-mile coastline is an ideal environment of sea, sand, and sun.

> Of the two beaches here, the one with paid admission is probably the cleaner and less crowded.

Emerald Island (Feicui Dao)

Emerald Island, named after its lush greenery and golden sand beach, is located along the Golden Coast in Changli County. The rolling sand hills and bird sanctuaries on the island make it an optimal place to enjoy bird watching and other outdoor activities.

Nandaihe Beach (From CFP)

Initiated in 1987, the China Wuqiao International Acrobatics Art Festival is named after Wuqiao, the world-renowned home of acrobatics. It is held once every two years in Shijiazhuang, the capital city of Hebei Province. (From CFP)

Hebei Style

Pingju Opera

Pingju is a popular local opera of northern China. It evolved by combining the traditional forms of musical performing arts, such as Hebei Bangzi and Beijing Opera, with the ballad of Lotus Rhyme and the Bengbeng play. Pingju is performed to the accompaniment of Banhu as well as the same striking instruments as those of Beijing Opera, and includes different forms such as Jianban, Dadiao, Anban, and Liushuiban. Pingju is good at depicting modern life and many excellent traditional plays have been passed down, among which there are *Young Son-in-law* and *Liu Qiaoer*.

Hebei Folk Song

Produced by working people, folk songs are generally created and spread orally and are polished and completed as they spread. The famous Hebei folk song, *Back to My Parents' Home*, is composed by Hebei people on the basis of their careful observation of daily life. Another traditional repertoire, *Little Shepherd Boy*, is a folk playlet which tells a story of a rural girl and a shepherd boy asking directions by means of singing and dancing.

Wuqiao Acrobatics

Wuqiao deserves its reputation for brilliant acrobatics. Enjoying a long history of over 2,000 years, Wuqiao is the birthplace of Chinese acrobatics and has been praised as the "home" and "cradle" of acrobatics. Performers from Wuqiao can be found in all Chinese acrobatic troupes, as well as in acrobatic troupes in 28 foreign countries around the world. As a result some say that "without the land of Wuqiao and the people who call it home, there would be no acrobatic troupes."

Shanxi

Geography at a Glance

The one-character abbreviation for Shanxi is "Jin." Famous for its coal, Shanxi is also one of the birthplaces of the Chinese civilization. Shanxi is situated in the central area of the Loess Plateau, through which the middle reach of the Yellow River flows. The entire area is surrounded by four mountain ranges: the Taihang mountains in the east, Lüliang in the west, Zhongtiao in the north, and Hengshan in the south. The Yellow River cuts through the southwest part of Shanxi province. Shanxi has a total area of over 57,915 square miles and has a population of around 32.97 million (2000 census).

Shanxi has a continental monsoon climate and four distinct seasons. Winter in Shanxi is cold and dry, and summer is warm and wet. The average temperature in spring is generally higher than in fall; the average annual rainfall is 16 to 24 inches, most of which is concentrated in autumn. The average temperature ranges from 39°F to around 57°F.

The Yellow River forms part of Shanxi's southeast border, and many mountain ranges are part of the landscape. A rich legacy of history, culture, and beautiful scenery make Shanxi an excellent tourist destination.

(From Quanjing)

Featured Cuisine

Qingheyuan tounao (a kind of stew); Zitui's steamed cake and Taiyuan fried pork with bamboo shoots; fried cake and oat wowo (a kind of steamed food) in Datong; turtle, Wenxi's boiled cake, and Wu's Hongdong smoked pork; Ruicheng sesame chips and preserved vegetables; Pingyao beef and Taigu cake; Jinnan cake.

Featured Commodities

Herbal Medicines

Florists chrysanthemum in Taiyuan; astragalus membranaceus bunge from Hengshan Mountain; bulbus lily in Pinglu cornu cervi parvum in Yushe.

Special Local Products

Daixian spices; Mengxian peppers; Shouyang tea; Zuoquan nuts; Zhuyeqing wine; Baozi wine; Yuping wine; Shanxi vinegar.

Local Handicrafts

Wutaishan ink stone; fine clay ink stone; Datong ceramics and corn-skin weavings; Fushan paper-cut; Xin Jiang sculpture; Daixian wood crafts; Hongshan ceramics and glass; Datong bronze pot.

Notes

❶ Shanxi dialect differs greatly from that of Putonghua, but there will be no problem in communication if you use Putonghua. Bus travel is the best way to get around in Shanxi. In more remote areas, you can flag down a local bus at the roadside.

❷ A guide is a necessity for touring in Shanxi.

❸ From Taiyuan Train Station to Jin Ancestral Temple, take bus 8. Tianlong Mountain, which is near Jin Temple, is well worth a visit.

❹ Transportaion in major cities is convenient, safe, and inexpensive.

❺ Temperatures vary greatly between morning and evening. Also be aware that the climate is quite different in the south and north parts of Shanxi.

Transportation Tips

By Bus

Most scenic spots are connected by highways and buses. Rented buses for groups are available to Wutai Mountains, Hanging Temple, and Yingxian Wooden Pagoda.

By Train

Shanxi has connections to Xi'an in the west, Beijing in the north, and Guangzhou in the south.

By Plane

Taiyuan Wusu is the main airport in Shanxi. It is about 9 miles south of the city, connected by buses or taxis. From here you can fly to Beijing, Shanghai, Guangzhou, Tianjin, Qingdao, Kunming, and all other major provinces.

See the Self-Guided Tour section. The Shanxi highway system goes to all major areas.

Recommended Routes

Featured Routes

Two-day tour on Shanxi merchant culture

Day 1 Pingyao ancient city→mansion of Wang family→"Ri Sheng Chang" old site. Lodging: Pingyao Hotel.

Day 2 Qiao family mansion→Qu family mansion→Cao family mansion. Lodging: Electricity Building.

Three-day tour of Wutaishan

Day 1 Zunsheng Temple→Foguang Temple→Xiantong temple→Tayuan temple

POPULAR FESTIVALS

Reception of Happiness

Several days after the Spring Festival (first day of a lunar year).

Sending Away Misfortunes

The 5th day after the Spring Festival; people throw old clothes over their walls to get rid of bad luck.

Festival for the God of Grains

The 10th day after the Spring Festival; ceremonies for the grain and planting gods are held on the day.

Festival for a Full Barn

The 23rd day after the Spring Festival; special foods are served for the day.

Festival of Dragon Head

According to the legend, the 2nd day of the second lunar month is the day when the dragon raised his head. Ceremonies are held for a year of good weather.

Peach Party in Ruicheng

The 3rd day of the third lunar month is the birthday of the Holy Mother (mother of the founder of Jin). Legend says that these peaches might extend life 3,000 years.

Fair at Jin Ancestral Temple

On the 2nd day of the seventh lunar month, there will be a fair at Jin Ancestral Temple.

Kitchen God Day

The 23rd or 24th day of the twelfth lunar month is the day in honor of the Kitchen God.

→Luohou temple→Buddha's Top. Lodging: Yunfeng Hotel.

Day 2 Dailuo Peak→Bishan Temple→Nanshan Temple→Zhenhai Temple. Lodging: Yunfeng Hotel.

Day 3 Cuishifeng Peak→Nanchan Temple→Longquan Temple→Lodging: Yunfeng Hotel.

Five-day tour to Yellow River

Day 1 Linfen Yao Temple→Hongdong Sunshine Tree. Lodging: Linfen Hotel.

Day 2 Hukou Waterfalls. Lodging: Jizhou Hotel.

Day 3 Yuncheng Guanyu Temple→Yongji Pujiu Temple→Yongle Palace. Lodging: Yuncheng Hotel.

Day 4 The iron bulls by the Yellow River→Ruicheng Dayu ferry. Lodging: Yuncheng Hotel.

Day 5 Departure.

Traditional Routes

Eight-day tour in Shanxi

Day 1 Yuncheng→Yongle Palace→Guanyu Temple→Pujiu Temple.

Day 2 Linfen→Guangsheng Temple→Susan Prison→Hongdong Sunshine Tree.

Day 3 Jixian County→Hukou waterfalls→Dongyue Temple→Xiao Xi Tian→Pingyao.

Day 4 Shuanglin Temple→Pingyao ancient city→ "Ri Sheng Chang" old site→Qiao family mansion in Qixian.

Day 5 Wutaishan→Buddha's Top→Xiantong Temple→Tayuan Temple→Wanfoge building.

Day 6 The Dayluo Peak→Bishan Temple→Jifu Temple→Puhua Temple→Shuxiang Temple→Longquan Temple→Nanshan Temple.

Day 7 Datong→Yingxian County Wooden Pagoda→Hanging Temple.

Day 8 Yungang Grottoes→Jiulong Wall→Huayan Temple.

Three-day tour of ancient buildings in North Shanxi

Day 1 Temples on Wutaishan→Yingxian County Wooden Pagoda.

Day 2 Datong Yungang Grottoes→Jiulong Wall.

Day 3 Huayan Temple→Hengshan.

Three-day tour of Hukou Waterfalls

Day 1 Linfen→Guangsheng Temple→Susan Prison→Hongdong Sunshine Tree.

Day 2 Jixian County Hukou Waterfalls.

Day 3 Hukou→Pingyao→Qixian County→Taiyuan.

The Chang family complex was built in the Confucian architectural style. (From CFP)

Addresses and Phone Numbers

Pingshuo Hotel	The living quarter in Pingshuo	0349-2052396/99
Yunfeng Hotel	Taihuai town, Wutaishan area	0350-6548131
The Electricity Building	39 Yingze East Street, Taiyuan (984 feet west to the train station)	0351-4052941
Yangquan Hotel	119 North Avenue, Yangquan	0353-2024800
Pingyao Hotel	Pingyao (the old residence for Hou Dianyuan, a famous Shanxi merchant)	0354-5683782
Chanye Hotel	10 Yingxiong Road, Changye	0355-2188001
Linfen Hotel	7 Jiefang Road, Linfen	0357-2086888
Jiaocheng Tianning Hotel	7 Tianning Street, Jiaocheng	0358-3532000
Ruicheng Hotel	8 East Yongle Street, Ruicheng	0359-3030611
Yuncheng Hotel	376 East Hongqi Road, Yuncheng	0359-2020508

Two-day tour at Ningwu

Day 1 Tianchi Lake→Ice Cave→Mouth of Fenhe River.

Day 2 Luyashan.

Wutaishan (From Colphoto)

Three-day tour of Pangquangou Valley and North Wudangshan

Day 1 Pangquangou Valley→Gushu Pagoda→Green Twilight→Shiny Mountain Top.

Day 2 Longquan Waterfalls→Blessed Heaven Gate→North Wudangshan.

Day 3 The Immortal's Direction→Tortured Swines.

Two-day tour on Manghe River

Day 1 Yangcheng→ancient Prime Minister's residence→Confucian temple.

Day 2 Manghe River nature reserve→Turtle Pool→waterfalls cave→Monkey Mountain.

Self-Guided Tours

Wutaishan

For the best view of the Wutaishan sunrise, take the 5 p.m. train from Taiyuan to Taihuai. There are also tour minibuses to Wutaishan, but they leave at 3 a.m. Be sure to dress warmly, as the mountain air is cold.

Taiyuan Region

Best Time to Travel

May through October are the best months to visit. Winters here are sunny, dry, and cold. Summers are cooler here than in Beijing and Tianjin. It's sunny but very windy in spring, so remember to take sunglasses and a hat or scarf. If you wear contact lenses, be aware that there is a lot of blowing sand.

Shopping Tips

Zhonglou Street is a traditional shopping mall in Taiyuan.

Qiaotou Street, east of Zhonglou Street, sells costumes and related items.

Liuxiang Street is a new shopping area in Taiyuan. There are a lot of new stores and opportunities to find bargains.

Chongshan Temple

Chongshan Temple, once named White Horse Monastery, is on Huangmiaoxiang, south section of Wuyi Road, Taiyuan. Built during the transition from Sui Dynasty to Tang Dynasty, the temple was once a summer palace for Yang Guang, the last emperor of Sui Dynasty. In 1381, Zhu Wang, the third son of Zhu Yuanzhang (the first emperor of Ming Dynasty), enlarged the temple in honor of his mother, Queen Ma, and renamed it Chongshan (temple for appreciating kindliness). The monastery burned in the nineteenth century, and only a fraction of its original buildings were saved and restored. Be sure to visit the "three splendid treasures": original sutras from five ancient dynasties; the "gem paintings"; and the three Ming Dynasty mud statues of Bodhisattvas, including a magnificent Kwan-yin.

Chongshan Temple mural: The King Sudhodana Summons. (From Colphoto)

The Shanxi Buddhist Association is located in the rear of the Shanxi Provincial Museum.

The twin pagodas are extraordinarily beautiful. Each is 13 stories tall (nearly 180 feet) and are octagonal in shape. (From Colphoto)

Twin Pagoda Temple

Another name for Twin Pagoda Temple is Yongzuo Temple. In the village of Haozhuang southeast of Taiyuan, this temple complex is Taiyuan's landmark building. Built in 1608, the towers are both 13 stories tall and built completely of brick and stone. Be sure to visit the collection of pillars on which writings and calligraphy from early dynasties are found.

The peonies and clove flowers are said to have been planted in the Ming Dynasty and are justly famous for their beauty and scent. On the 18th day of the sixth lunar month, legend says that you can get rid of bad luck by climbing the twin pagodas.

Jin Ancestral Temple

Jin Ancestral Temple is located at the foot of Xuanwengshan, which is about 15.5 miles southwest of Taiyuan. The temple is a Chinese garden of classical style. Many of its parts have been designated as national treasures. The cypress from the Zhou Dynasty, the Elixir Spring, and the Maiden Sculpture of the Song Dynasty are three most valuable cultural relics in Jin Temple. The Hall of the Holy Mother (mother of the founder of Jin) was built in a grand style with 43 painted sculptures. South of the Hall of the Holy Mother is the octagonal Elixir Pavilion. The Zhou Cypress covers the left side of the Hall of the Holy Mother.

Take the No. 8 bus or the sightseeing bus directly to Jin Temple.

Tianlong Mountain Grottoes

Tianlong Mountain Grottoes are about halfway up Tianlongshan Mountain, which is 25 miles southwest of Taiyuan. There are 21 grottoes with more than 1,500 sculptures and 1,144 reliefs, murals, and paintings from the East Wei, the North Qi, Sui, Tang, and Five Dynasties. The famous 26-foot-high Maitreya Buddha in the ninth grotto is the best preserved figure.

You can take one of many buses from Jin Temple to Tianlongshan Mountain. The trip is about 20 minutes long.

Wutaishan Mountains

Northeast of Wutai County, the Wutaishan range consists of five mountains: East Tai, West Tai, South Tai, North Tai, and Central Tai. With a height of 10,033 feet, North Tai is the highest and is known as the "Pillar of North China." Wutaishan is a sacred place for Buddhism. Built during the reign of Emperor Ming of Han Dynasty, Wutaishan is the only place where Han Buddhism and Lama Buddhism co-exist. The Grand White Pagoda of Sarira, 178 feet high, is the landmark of Wutaishan. People call Xiantong Temple, Tayuan Temple, Shuxiang Temple, Luohou Temple, and Buddha's Top "the five major sites of sacredness." On the north side of Taihuai is Xiantong Temple, on the south is Tayuan Temple. Luohou

Temples of Wutaishan Mountains (From CFP)

The white marble gate of Longquan Temple is covered with reliefs, including 89 dragons, 20 lions, and countless plants and animals. (From ImagineChina)

Temple lies to the east of Tayuan Temple, Shuxiang Temple is about 328 feet southwest. Buddha's Top is on top of Vulture's Peak.

> To visit the Wutaishan range, first go to Wutaishan station by train, then take a bus to Taihuai. Cabs are available to scenic areas on Wutaishan.

Longquan Temple

Three miles south of Taihuai, Longquan Temple is situated about halfway up Jiulonggang Mountain. Its 160 buildings are built into the side of the mountain. There is a spring beside the temple called Longquan Spring (Dragon Spring), after which the temple was named. Built in the Song Dynasty and rebuilt during the Republic of China era, the temple also served as the ancestral temple for generals of the Yang family. A memorial pagoda was erected for the monk Puji in the temple.

Nanchan Temple

Nanchan Temple is in Lijiazhuang, which is 13 miles west of Wutai County. With an area of more than 44,000 square feet, the temple complex comprises 30 buildings. The complex faces south, and the gate, the Hall of Dragon King, the Hall of Kuanyin, and the Hall of Great Buddha form a quadrangle. The main hall, the oldest wooden structure, was constructed during the reign of Emperor De of the Tang Dynasty in 782. There are 17 exquisite Tang Dynasty sculptures set on a raised platform 27.5 feet long, 21 feet wide, and about 2 feet tall. The style of these sculptures is identical with that of the Mogao Grottoes at Dunhuang.

> Summers in Wutaishan are usually very wet and quite chilly. Visitors need to bring raincoats, hats, and warm sweaters.

Foguang Temple

Foguang Temple is situated about 20 miles northeast of Wutai County, on Foguangshan Mountain. The temple has more than 120 separate buildings filled with Tang Dynasty relics. According to records, it was built during the reign of Emperor Xiaowen of the North Wei Dynasty (477–99).

Chang Family Mansion

The Chang Family Mansion is located at the village of Chewang in Dongyang, which is a little more than 9 miles from the Yuci District, Jinzhong. It was built by the Changs, who were successful merchants during the Qing Dynasty. The mansion compound covers an area of more than 7 million square feet, comprising at least 40 buildings. Formal gardens and beautiful decorations make a worthwhile visit.

Aoshen Building was built particularly for stage plays and performances. It is one of the four most famous buildings in Shanxi. (From Colphoto)

Houtu Temple

These ancient buildings on Miaodi Street, Jiexiu, reflect Taoist style. There is no official date when the temple was built, but most of the present buildings are relics of both Ming and Qing dynasties. Built to celebrate the Land God, the temple has over a thousand Taoist sculptures and artworks.

Ancient Fortress in Zhangbi Village

The ancient military fortress on Mianshan Mountain is 6 miles southeast of the village of Zhangbi in Longfeng township, Jiexiu. The architecture is unique: an open fortress with underground tunnels. According to records, the troops of Weichi Gong, the famous Tang general, once billeted here. The fortress was designed to conform to the contour of Mianshan. There is a 3-mile-long tunnel, which connects every corner of the fortress.

Forbidden City is the most famous among Chinese royal residences, but the Qiao Family Mansion is the best of civilian ones. (From Quanjing)

Wang Family Mansion

Seven miles from the center of the county, this family compound is built on Huangtuqiu Hill, in the village of Jingsheng, Lingshi County. The complex was built in the Qing Dynasty; because the Wang family was one of the four most influential families in this area, the buildings were constantly renewed and restored. Today's mansion consists of three parts, among which the Xiaoyi Shrine is well worth a visit. The buildings in this family compound are home to well-preserved sculptures, paintings, and ancient calligraphy.

Qiao Family Mansion

Located in the village of Qiaojiabao, Dongguan, Qi County, this mansion was once the residence of the famous merchant Qiao Zhiyong in the Qing Dynasty. There are 19 courtyards and 313 rooms, designed according to the Chinese character "囍" (double happiness).

> The train to Pingyao and Yuncheng passes through Qi County.

Qu Family Mansion

This large family mansion is on East Avenue in Qi County. It belongs to Qu Yuanzhen, the famous financier of the Qing Dynasty, and his offspring. There are 8 large courtyards, 19 small yards, and 240 rooms in the main house.

Local people compare the Qiao residence to the Forbidden City in Beijing. (From Jin Yongji)

Ancient Pingyao City

The ancient Pingyao city is located in the center of Shanxi province, 56 miles from the capital, Taiyuan. The city was originally built during King Xuan's reign in the West Zhou Dynasty (827–782 BCE) with rammed earth construction. In the Ming Dynasty (1370 CE), the ancient city was strengthened with bricks and stones for military purposes.

It usually takes about four hours to walk around Pingyao on the walls, but bicycles and rickshaws are available to rent. You can visit most of the ancient civil buildings in the city for a fee, which you must negotiate with the owner of the house.

The wall itself is 33 feet high, and more than 20,000 feet long with towers at each of the four corners. In addition, there are six gates with suspension bridges and a moat, which surrounds the city.

Rishengchang Exchange Shop

China's first private financial institution to provide currency exchange and savings accounts, the Rishengchang Exchange Shop is located at "the busiest financial street of the Qing Dynasty"—West Street in Pingyao. Created in around 1824, this early bank offered traveling merchants an alternative to the heavy silver coin used throughout the Qing Dynasty. During its one-hundred-year history, its bank branches provided safe and secure means of transferring funds throughout China and to banks in Europe, the United States, and Southeast Asia.

Zhenguo Temple

About 7 miles northeast of Pingyao is the Zhenguo, built in 963 CE. The bell on one of the towers was cast in the Qin Dynasty, making it an extremely rare relic of that era. The Hall of Ten Thousand Buddhas has gone through many renovations, but it has kept the original architectural style of the Five Dynasties (907–960 CE).

Wanfodian Hall in Zhenguo (From Colphoto)

Shuanglin Temple

Once the site of the central capital for the Liao Dynasty, Shuanglin was originally called Zhongdu Temple (central capital temple). It was renamed in the Song Dynasty because Sakyamuni, the founder of Bud-

Buddhist sculptures of Shuanglin. (From Quanjing)

dhism, achieved his nirvana in a place called Shuanglin. About 4 miles southeast from Pingyao, this temple complex consists of ten halls and 2,052 painted figures in the temple.

The glass eyes of Buddha sculptures are said to be able to move as viewers change positions.

White Pagoda

This white pagoda was built in the Puci Temple during the Jin Dynasty (272 BCE). The original name for the temple complex was Wubian, and when it was restored in the Song Dynasty, it was renamed. The pagoda is 7 stories tall (164 feet); all the other buildings in the complex are from the Qing Dynasty.

The Cao mansion was built in simple but imposing style and resembles a fortress. (From Colphoto)

Cao Family Mansion

Just about 3 miles southwest of Taigu is the mansion of the Cao family, successful merchants during the Ming and Qing dynasties. The buildings were constructed in the design of the Chinese character meaning longevity. People refer to the mansion as the three "mores"—more happiness, longer life, more offspring. It has 277 rooms from three different periods: Ming, Qing, and the Republic of China. Today it is a museum.

Kong Xiangxi Mansion

Kong Xiangxi is close to the Taigu Normal Insititution. It's the largest and best preserved mansion with middle Qing style in Taigu. Built in the Qing Dynasty, it was once the mansion for Meng Guangyu, a minor Taigu official. All rooms of the mansion are connected with Chinese-style doors, and the walls are interspersed with beautiful windows.

North Wudangshan Mountains

The North Wudangshan Mountains are about 19 miles southeast from Fangshan County, Lüliang Region. It was once called Longwangshan Mountains. During the Ming Dynasty, when the Xuantian Hall was renewed, the mountains were renamed as "Wudang" according to Taoist classics. The mountains are grand, strange, steep, and beautiful. The peak of the mountains is 6,506 feet high, which

On the 3rd day of the third lunar month, a traditional fair is held in the mountains. Buses from Taiyuan to Xinzhou can take you there.

is about 984 feet higher than the Wudangshan peak. Beautiful trees and plants make it a favorable place to visit.

Xuanzhong Temple

Xuanzhong (or Yongning) Temple is in Shibishan, 6 miles northwest of Jiaocheng County. It was the cradle of Sukhavati, a Buddhist sect, and is now the home of the Pure Land Buddhists. According to a slate in the temple, it was built in the fifth century. Tanluan, Daochuo, and Shandao once researched Sukhavati philosophy here about 1,200 years ago.

Datong, Shuozhou Region

Best Time to Travel

Spring and summer are the best times to visit Datong. Winters here are very cold, but summers are pleasantly cool.

Shopping Tips

Daxi Street and Sipailou Xiaonan Street are the busiest in Datong. In the evening there are street vendors, selling inexpensive goods and food.

Huayan Temple

Huayan was constructed according to the classical Hua Yan Jing architectural style during the Liao Dynasty. The paintings, murals, and sculptures in the temple are representative of the Liao Dynasty's artistic achievement.

Legend says that you can avoid illness by visiting Huayan on the 8th day of the Spring Festival.

Bojia library hall in Huayan Temple is the same style as Huayan Temple: precise, strong, and simple. The building has refined decorations and paintings. There are 38 exquisite wooden storage rooms for books, which are all built into walls. (From CFP)

Mist, clouds, waves, and cliffs typify this scenic area. (From Colphoto)

Jiulong Wall

Jiulong Wall is on East Street of Datong. Built between 1368 and 1398 in the Ming Dynasty, it is about 350 years older than Beijing's Jiulong Wall. The wall is 149 feet long, 26 feet high, and almost 7 feet thick. Nine flying glass dragons are set on the wall symmetrically, and beautiful decorations make the wall surface a magnificent sight.

Shanhua Temple

A complex of well-preserved Liao Dynasty buildings, Shanhua was originally built in the Kaiyuan period, Tang dynasty (713–41 BCE). It was renamed the Great Pu'en Temple. In 1122, the temple was destoyed in wars but was rebuilt from 1123 to 1149, and again renamed as Shanhua. The temple is grand in style. Many culture relics are kept here, especially the 24 Heavenly Kings sculptures from the Jin dynasty. They are China's treasures.

Take Bus 4 from Datong train station to the temple.

Yungang Grottoes

Yungang Grottoes is located at the south side of Wuzhou Mountain, which is about 10 miles west of Datong.

Sculptures of different eras in the Yungang grottoes reflect the way Buddhism merged into Chinese culture. (From Quanjing)

The summit of Wuzhou is called Yungang, giving the grottoes their name. The grottoes runs from east to west for about a half mile; the 252 grottoes and more than 51,000 sculptures make Yungang one of the three largest grotto series in China and a precious treasure for the world. Sponsored by Tanyao, a famous monk of that time, the construction of these grottoes began in 453 BCE and continued for nearly 50 years. More than 40,000 men joined the project. In 2001, UNESCO listed Yungang Grottoes as a World Heritage Cultural Site.

A good time to visit the grottoes is at sunset when the beauty of the grottoes are reflected in the setting sun. The site itself closes at 6 p.m.

Hengshan Scenic Site

The Hengshan mountain range is 6 miles south of Hunyuan county and 38.5 miles from Datong. Hengshan has two peaks and five scenic parks: Tianfengling, Cuipingshan, Qianfoling, Hotspring, and Hunyuan. The area around Longshan is a nature reserve.

There are buses from Datong to Hunyuan County, which is not far away from Hengshan. The distance between Hengshan gate to the parking lot is about 3 miles, and the summit is only an hour or so from the lot. You can choose from hiking, taking a cable car, or riding horseback. There are quite a few hotels, convenient to the area.

The Hanging Temple

This amazing cluster of buildings is located in the valley between Tianfengling and Cuipingshan, about 3 miles from Hunyuan. The temple was originally built in the sixth century (late Northern Wei period). During its 1,400 years, it has been rebuilt for four times. It now consists of more than 40 buildings scattered along the side of the mountain seemingly in defiance of gravity. The entire temple complex is attached to the mountain by beams, boards, and thin pillars, and the buildings are interconnected by a maze of passageways.

Chongfu Temple

Chongfu Temple, on East Street in Shuocheng District, was built in 665 during the Tang Dynasty by the Eguo Duke Weichi Jingde by imperial order. There are five well-arranged courtyards, and the connected buildings include the Bell and Drum Towers, the Thousand-Buddha Pavilion, Underground Treasure Hall, and the main Amitabha Buddha Hall. There sits Amitabha Buddha with a Kwan-yin on the left and two Bodhisattvas on the right. The Thousand-Buddha Pavilion was once a storage hall for sacred scriptures; during its renovation in the Ming Dynasty, 1,000 statues were placed there but have been lost or destroyed. The large temple is situated in an extremely scenic spot with tall cypresses; inside the buildings urals, paintings, sculptures, glasswork, and windows are well preserved.

The temple faces eastward. There are over 40 building units in the temple. (From ImagineChina)

Wooden Pagoda in Yingxian County

The Wooden Pagoda in Yingxian County, about 44 miles south of Datong, is a marvelous feat of mortise-and-tenon construction. The oldest and tallest wooden structure in China, the pagoda is about 220 feet tall and 98 feet wide at the base. There are nine stories all together, but only five can be seen from the outside; four other short stories are hidden inside the structure. The 36-foot statue of Sakyamuni on the first floor is an impressive sight, and the tiny wind bells placed under each eave give the whole area a mystical ambience.

You can visit both the Hanging Temple and the Wooden Pagoda in one trip.

The Wooden Pagoda was built with no nails and is an architectural wonder. (From Colphoto)

Guangyun Hall at the Yao Temple (From Colphoto)

Linfen Region

Best Time to Travel

April to October is the best time to visit Linfen. In general, springs are windy and cool; summers are short and wet; autumns are short but mild; winters are long, arid, and cold. If you are prone to respiratory problems, remember to take your inhaler or medication with you.

Yao Temple

About 2.5 miles south of Linfen, the Yao Temple is built in memory of the Emperor Yao, a legendary leader of patriarchial clans in primitive China. According to the legend, almost 1,400 years ago Yao declared Pingyang (today's Linfen) the capital of China, and this temple was erected in his memory. The original temple was first built in the Jin Dynasty and rebuilt several times. Several buildings and a few spectacular gates remain. Be sure to visit the Wufeng Building, Guangyun Hall, Pavilion of Yao's Well, and the Sleeping Palace, and make a side trip to the Yao Mausoleum 25 miles to the northeast.

Linfen is often called "the city of flowers and fruit." In late spring and summer, flowers of many different trees mingle together, creating beautiful views and perfuming the air.

Huozhou Yamen

The ancient residence (yamen) of an early governor of Huozhou is on East Street of Huozhou. Built in the Tang Dynasty by Weichi Gong, it is the only ancient provincial yamen preserved today. Over the centuries, natural disasters and wars reduced its original area from 414,410 square feet to 201,285 square feet. The remaining gate, the second gate, the archway, and the first and second halls were built during the Yuan, Ming, and Qing Dynasties.

Hukou Waterfalls

Hukou (mouth of the teapot) Waterfall, 28 miles west of Jixian County, is the only yellow waterfall in the world and the second largest waterfall in China. The Yellow River suddenly narrows, and the turbulent yellow-hued water plunges almost 100 feet to a rocky riverbed. In June, the Hukou International Waterfall Festival lasts for the whole month with cultural side trips in addition to the spectacular sightseeing opportunities at the falls.

The best time to view the Hukou waterfall is late spring (April–May) and autumn (September–November). In spring, both sides of the river are covered with peach flowers blossoms. In winter, the waterfalls often freeze, then melt in early spring, creating a tumultous and deafening roar and a sight not to be missed.

Dingcun Village

Dingcun is 2.5 miles south of Xiangfen County. The village comprises about 40 dwellings laid out in a quadrangle and includes main halls, workshops, towers, and archways. The dwellings date from 1593 to as recent as the Republic of China era (1912 to 1949). Seven of the couryards were turned into the Dingcun Museum of Folk Customs, which holds thousands of artifacts and several exhibits on primitive Dingcun culture and folklore. The architectural pattern, layout, and artistic decoration are fine examples from the Ming and Qing Dynasties.

Hukou *means "teapot spout," vividly describing the shape of the waterfalls. (From ImagineChina)*

The sculptures from the Ming Dynasty have retained their colors and are still lustrous after centuries of erosion. (From Colphoto)

Xiao Xi Tian

The original name for Xiao Xi Tian was Qianfo Nunnery (Thousand-Buddha Nunnery). Two thirds of a mile to the northwest of the Xixian area, the nunnery was first built in 1634. It got its present name because another temple in the county is called Da Xi Tian. Besides an agreeable physical environment, the nunnery is also famous for its preservation of color paintings from the Ming Dynasty.

The Tong Tian Bridge leads directly to Xiao Xi Tian.

The Ancient Sunshine Tree

This ancient Sunshine Tree (Erythrina variegata), or Ancient Scholar's Tree, is on the grounds of the Guangji Temple, a little more than a mile north of Hongdong County. The land around the tree is now a park in memory of ancient immigrants. According to the Ming Dynasty records, when the imperial order of immigration was issued, a temporary office was set up under the tree. Immigrants gathered here and then dispersed to every corner of Shanxi province. When they set out, they were reluctant to leave their homes and looked back to the great Chinese Scholar Tree with its storks' nests. For this reason the tree and the nest on the tree became the symbol of leaving one's birthplace against one's own will. Every year at the Qing Ming Festival, storks come here in large numbers and perch on the tree.

Susan Prison

The prison was built in Hongdong County during the Zhengde period of the Ming Dynasty (1396). Once known as the Prison of the Ming Dynasty, it was renamed Susan Prison after a female prisoner who became the heroine in the Beijing opera *Yutangchun*. Damaged during the cultural revolution (1966–76), the prison was rebuilt in 1984 to the original specifications. It has much historical value for the research of China's feudal criminal institutions. With two gates and double walls, the prison is also divided into two separate parts: one for ordinary prisoners, and the other for those who will be executed.

The Susan exhibit at the prison explains and depicts the miscarriage of justice.

The prison where the heroine Susan was kept. (From Colphoto)

Guangsheng Temple

This ancient temple is located at Huoshan, which is 10.5 miles northeast of Hongdong County. The temple was first built in 147 and called Julushe. In the Tang Dynasty in 769, Guo Ziyi, the king of Fenyang, repaired and enlarged the temple and named it Guangsheng Temple. The temple consisits of four parts: the upper temple, the lower temple, and the two water god temples. Stones and slates in the upper temple are valuable research materials for studying the evolution of Buddhism. The well-preserved Flying Rainbow Pagoda is the largest in China; in addition to the river god murals, the only large-scale frescoes of the traditional Chinese operas are also found here.

Li Shimin, the first emperor of Tang dynasty, wrote a famous poem for the temple: The Ode to Guangsheng Temple. (From CFP)

Dongyue Temple

This temple complex and folk custom museum is located a short distance from the Chaoyangmen subway entrance at 141 Chaoyangmen Outer Street. Built in the early thirteenth century, the main temple enshrines Huang Feihu, the emperor of Dongyue, in addition to many Taoist figures, plaques, and pillars. The complex comprises three large courtyards, 76 sacred offices, extraordinary archways and gates, the north China school of Taoism, 89 excavated pillars, and about 200 halls or rooms; the whole area covers more than 100,000 square feet. The temple offers a series of programs for praying for good fortune, and the museum hosts folk customs exhibitions throughout the year. On the 28th of the third lunar month, a temple fair takes place, and various folk custom exhibitions are held at the Spring Festival, the Dragon Boat Festival, the Moon Festival, and the Double Ninth Festival. At the back of the palace is the Hell Hall, which houses many figures of good and bad luck deities.

Feiyun Building of Dongyue Temple was built of wood. (From CFP)

Yuncheng Region

Xiezhou Guanyu's Temple

The Xiezhou city of Yuncheng is the hometown of Guanyu, a historical figure known to every Chinese. Built in 589 to honor Guanyu, a hero of the Three Kingdoms period, this temple is regarded as the largest ceremonial temple for Guanyu.

 Take Bus 11 from Yuncheng to the temple.

The Chunqiu Building is the main building in Guanyu's Temple. (From Colphoto)

The Wulaofeng Scenic Park

Wulaofeng Scenic Park is about 12 miles east of Yongji County. The park is built at the foot of the Wulaofeng Mountains and the ancient town of Puzhou, and presents many scenic spots like the Yellow River shoreline, Wangguanyu Valley, Dragonhead Mountain, and Yunxian Pavilion. From this location, you can see and visit 36 peaks, 12 caves, 9 waterfalls, and 64 temples. The highest point, Yuepingliang Peak, is about 7,000 feet above sea level. The Wulaofeng mountain range was called the East Huanshan mountains in the past but is now commonly known as the Mountain of Five Old Men.

Pujiu Temple

About 7.5 miles northwest of Yongji, the Pujiu Temple was established during the reign of Wu Zetian, a Tang Dynasty (684–704) queen. This temple and surrounding area is the setting for the famous novel *The West Chamber*. Rebuilt in 1986, the Yingying Pagoda is one of the only four echo buildings in China; the clear echoes and strange sound effects are justly famous.

Stork Tower

The Stork Tower (Guanquelou) is on the east bank of the Yellow River southeast of Yongji. It was built during the Northern Zhou Dynasty (557–81). Completed in 580, the tower inspired many famous poets and writers and was one of four ancient Chinese towers. Destroyed in the Yuan Dynasty, the present 242-foot Stork Tower was rebuilt in 1997 by the Yongji government.

The Yellow River Iron Bulls

Eight gigantic cast-iron bulls are set on the banks of the

The eight iron bulls were cast in prone position; each bull is 11 feet long, 5 feet tall, and weighs more than 70 tons. (From Colphoto)

The mural in Sanqing Hall Chao Yuan Tu. Height: 14 feet. Length: 308 feet. It depicts eight emperors and queens meeting the Yuanshi Tianzun god. (From ImagineChina)

ancient path of the Yellow River, about 9 miles west of Yongji. They were forged in 724 to anchor the Pujin float bridge, a vital connection between Shaanxi and Shanxi. The bridge was destroyed during the Yuan Dynasty, but the iron bulls survive.

Houtu Shrine

Located 25 miles southwest of Wanrong county, the Houtu Shrine is the oldest of its kind in China. Before the Ming Dynasty, emperors came here to hold sacrifice ceremonies for the Goddess of Houtu (the Earth Goddess).

The stone relief outside the Houtu Shrine (From Colphoto)

Yongle Palace

Known for its murals, Yongle Palace is about 2 miles north of Ruicheng County. In the 1950s, the entire palace was renovated and now includes the original gateway with lobby, the Dragon and Tiger Hall, Sanqing Hall, and others. Yongle Palace is composed of a large group of Taoist temples and a cluster of representative structures from the Yuan Dynasty. Hundreds of murals cover an area of more than 10,000 square feet and are well preserved within all the halls. These paintings show the finest artistic tradition of the Tang and Song Dynasties, and also reflect the characteristics of the Yuan Dynasty.

> The splendid murals hold pride of place in Yongle Palace.

Dayu Ferry

The Dayu Ferry can be seen 3 miles southeast of Ruicheng County. According to legend, Dayu, the great ancient leader, once crossed the river here, and the cypress tree was the place where he often rested.

A scene from an old play in ancient Pingyao (From ImagineChina)

Shanxi Style

Delicacies of Shanxi

Shanxi wheat-based food is famous throughout the whole world. The local delicacies enjoy a very high reputation. It is known to all that Shanxi people like to eat vinegar and their first greeting when meeting each other is always "Have you eaten?" Shanxi food has a long history and a variety of names, which exemplifies the importance of wheat-based food in the life of the Shanxi people. There are a lot of varieties. Every common housewife can cook with flour of wheat, sorghum, beans, buckwheat, and naked oats. It is recorded that there are 280 kinds of wheat-based food in Shanxi. The Shanxi people love the food so deeply that it is not only a food allaying hunger but also a "spiritual food" containing profound feelings and philosophy.

In the past, Shanxi people seldom ate vegetables but had salt and vinegar to go with their meals. As a result, they had a great physiological demand for water and consequently formed a custom of eating food served in soup. The first greeting of Changzhi inhabitants when meeting their neighbors is always "Have you drunk?" Among the everyday recipes of Shanxi people, the varieties of food served in soup is greater than all others. A saying popular in Shanxi goes like this: "Drink some soup before having your meal and you will never be hurt." It is reasonable from the perspective of nutritional science. It is also a habit of Shanxi natives to drink

Noodle masters are staging noodle slicing. (From Colphoto)

Mature vinegar (From CFP)

some soup after eating noodles because they believe an ancient maxim that "the original soup is helpful to digest the food." When you have the chance to visit Shanxi and have drunk and eaten to your heart's content, the host will offer you a bowl of noodle soup so as to "digest the food with the original soup."

There are various kinds of local snacks in Shanxi due to its different climate, soil texture, and living conditions. These delicacies are now gradually appearing in the restaurants and hotels of which the most famous are wantuo, buckwheat helao, poached egg in rice wine soup, mutton and bread pieces in soup, Jinyang yiguosu, Wenxi steamed cake, Linyi pickled yugua, Pingyao beef, fried meat, braised mutton, mutton entrails, braised toufu of Gaoping, Youcha, beanstarch jelly, toufu of northern style, maoerduo, and shaomei.

Mature Vinegar

Shanxi mature vinegar is widely known throughout the country. The vinegar made in Taiyuan is not only liked by Shanxi natives, but also popular in the whole country. The history of Shanxi vinegar can be dated back to the Spring and Autumn Period. Since then, the vinegar technology of Shanxi has been developed. It was in the Qing Dynasty that Shanxi mature vinegar and Taiyuna special vinegar were produced and became well known nationally. The grain sorghum is the base of Shanxi vinegar. It takes a year to produce mature vinegar. Among all the varieties of Shanxi mature vinegar, the Donghu brand made in Qingxu is the most famous. Among all the varieties of Taiyuan special vinegar, those made by Yiyuanqing Vinegar Workshop are the most famous.

Fen Liquor

Fen Liquor, one of the eight famous liquors of China, is made in Xinghuacun of Fenyang, Shanxi province. According to the tablet inscription of Xinghuacun, Fen Liquor was originated during the Northern and Southern Dynasties and has a history of more than 1500 years. Fen Liquor is glittering, lustrous, aromatic, and soft with a lingering aftertaste. It can be preserved a long time—the longer, the better. Fen Liquor is made from high-quality sorghum by adding special yeast and mixing mature wine preserved for a

The old well gloriette in Xinhuacun (From Colphoto)

(From CFP)

long time. It has curative effects for many diseases. *The County Annals of Fenyang* says that "the water from the well beside Shenming Pavilion seems better than that of Xiehuang." Fushan, a patriot living in the dynastic change period of the Ming and Qing Dynasties, wrote an inscription for the well. According to the experiments made by the local people, the water never spills over when it is boiled; the iron kettle used to heat the water never rusts; and the clothes washed with the water are very clean. Fen Liquor won a First-class Gold Medal in the Panama Pacific International Exposition in 1916. It has won various praises and honors dozens of times in the past 50 years. Presently Fen Liquor is being sold in more than 40 countries and regions of the world. The vintage wine enjoys a great fame throughout the world.

Pingyao Beef

Pingyao beef is made in Pingyao County of Shanxi and gained its fame more than 200 years ago. The Pingyao beef is bright and ruddy in color and tastes soft, aromatic, and delicious. It contains very little moisture and can be stored for a long time. Even in torrid seasons it can be preserved for half a month. Pingyao beef is the pickled meat of old cattle. The older the cattle are, the more aromatic the beef is. It is a unique meat product of Shanxi.

Folk Art

Folk Gong and Drum

Shanxi is one of the birthplaces of the Chinese drum culture. Shanxi gong and drum, praised as "the first drum of China," features a joyous rhythm, sonorous timbre, great momentum, and magnificent images. It exemplifies the strong character of descendants of Yan Di and Huang Di and the pristine nature of Loess Plateau.

There are great varieties of drumming styles in Shanxi including Qing gong and drum, beating and blowing gong and drum, drum dance, gong and drum scripture, and temple gong and drum.

There are many kinds of gongs and drums in Shanxi. The gongs include plate-shaped gong, bamboo-hat-shaped coin and cup-shaped bell. The small one is just 2.7 inches in diameter while the big one is 54.6 inches in diameter. The varieties of drums are even more, including drums with one side covered with leather (such as bangu, fisherman's drum, octagonal drum, fan drum, and tile drum) and drums with wooden shelves (such as rattle drum, xiangu, flower drum, waist drum, shugu, tuogu, tanggu, war drum, pinggu, serial drums, tonggu, handle drum, dungu and vehicle drum). The beating methods differ according to the different kinds of drums. Shanxi drums can also be classified as Taiyuan gong and drum, flower drum, turning-around drum, and fan drum as well as the famous awe-inspiring gong and drum according to the rhythm and performance mode.

Land Boat Dance

Land Boat Dance is a kind of folk performance that simulates a boat sailing in water. This kind of folk dance is popular in festivals throughout Shanxi Province.

The "land boat" is a wooden frame made in accordance with the appearance of a real boat. It is covered with seablue cotton cloth decorated with paintings of waves. The body of the boat is decorated with red ribbons and paper flowers, and sometimes with colorful lamps, bright mirrors, or other ornaments.

Generally there is only one boater, but sometimes there can also be two or three or even seven boaters sharing a boat. When dancing the Land Boat Dance, one of the performers acts as the helmsman who paddles in the front. The boaters usually walk in quick short steps in order that the boat can go forward stably as if it is heaving with the waves.

When performing the Land Boat Dance, it is common that a helmsman leads multiple boats. But in some cases, two helmsmen can paddle only one boat or one boat leads many boats with no helmsman. When they are going forward, they will perform a series of skills and tricks for which they have been trained. It is really an attraction to all people.

(From ImagineChina)

The Inner Mongolia Autonomous Region

Geography at a Glance

The Inner Mongolia Autonomous Region is on the northern border of China. The territory runs from northeast to southwest with an area of about 425,000 square miles and a population of more than 23.75 million (2000 census). Inner Mongolia was the first autonomous region in China and is the third largest province.

Generally, the region lies on a plateau, and most of the land is above 3,300 feet in altitude. Lakes dot the whole region, and thousands of rivers or tributaries cut across it. The Yellow, Argun, Nen, and West Liao Rivers are the four biggest water systems in the region. The northern part is the main body of this autonomous region while the eastern part, bordered by the Daxing'anling Mountains, is a huge grassland. The western part is desert.

There are four distinct seasons in Inner Mongolia. The summer is short and hot; the winter is long, cold, and arid; and the spring and fall are temperate. The annual rainfall is between 3 and 18 inches.

Featured Cuisine

Milkskin, white food, whole lamb feast, lamb fat cake, roasted lamb, boiled mutton pieces, roasted mutton, barbeque, horse-milk wine, cheese, yogurt, milk tea, camel feet, Hada cake.

(From ImagineChina)

Nei Mongol (Inner Mongolia) Autonomous Region

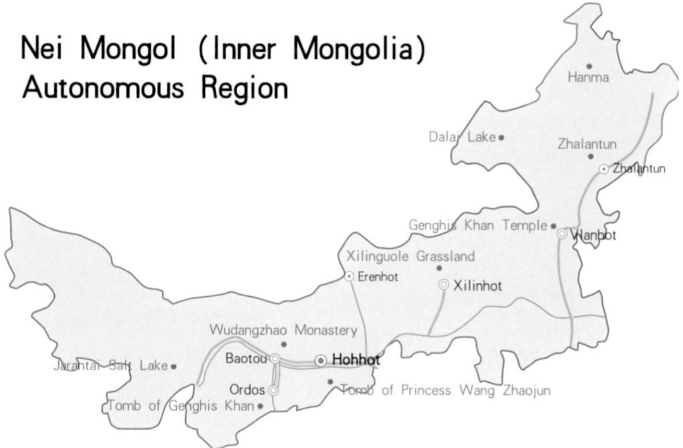

Shopping Tips

Herbal Medicines

Liquorice, huang chi (milk vetch), red bark root of peony, Chinese ephedra, ballon-flower root, plantago seed, other local herbal remedies.

Special Local Products

Deer tail, Yellow River carp, Balin colored stone, Chinese medical stone.

Local Handicrafts

Mongolian bowls, Mongolian knives, bronze locks, horse head stringed instruments, Balin stone sculptures, Mongolian carpets, carved Mongolian horn.

Transportation Tips

By Bus

Probably not the best option for Western visitors. Only buses from Beijing to Hohhot are recommended.

By Train

Railroads connect the autonomous region to all of its neighboring provinces, making travel convenient and pleasant.

By Plane

Major airlines connect to Hohhot, Baotou, Xilinhot, Chifeng, Tongliao, Ulanhot, and Hailaer.

Notes 

❶ The best time to visit the grassland is summer, from June to August. The temperatures between day and night change drastically, and the weather can be capricious. Extra clothes, warm sweaters, and rain gear are suggested, although summer days can be quite sunny and warm.

❷ No weapons are allowed on any vehicles, in any town throughout China.

❸ In Inner Mongolia, the host shows his respect by drinking toasts to you. Refusal to drink is regarded as bad manners.

Recommended Routes

Special Routes

Eleven-day tour to track Genghis Khan's footprints

Day 1 Hohhot. Lodging: Inner Mongolia Hotel.

Day 2 Hohhot→Gegentala Grassland. Lodging: Mongolian tent.

Day 3 Watching the sunrise in grassland→ Hohhot→museum→Zhaojun's Tomb→ Wuta Temple→Baotou. Lodging: Qingshan Hotel.

Day 4 Baotou→Sounding Sand Slope→Genghis Khan Tomb. Lodging: Qingshan Hotel.

Day 5 Wu Dang Zhao→ruins of Great Wall in the Spring and Autumn period→Hohhot. Lodging: Inner Mongolia Hotel.

Day 6 Hohhot→entering Mongolia→ Ulan Bator. Lodging: Ulan Bator

Day 7 Ulan Bator→Bayan Gobi Desert. Lodging: Bayan Gobi.

Day 8 Bayan Gobi→Khalaholin→ruins of the ancient Mongolian capital→Erdun Zhao →108 pagodas. Lodging: Mongolian tent.

Day 9 Khalaholin→Ulan Bator→Suho Bator Square→Capitol Building→National Opera Theater→Central Museum→ Dangan Temple. Lodging: Ulan Bator.

Day 10 Ulan Bator→Hohhot. Lodging: Inner Mongolia Hotel.

Day 11 Departure from Hohhot. End of tour.

Seven-day tour on the border grassland.

Day 1 Arrival at Hulun Buir. Lodging: Hailaer Hotel.

POPULAR FESTIVALS

Genghis Khan Ceremony

The 21st day on the third lunar month (around March 21) is the most important ceremony at the mausoleum. There are three other festivals held at this tomb, which contains mementos, clothing, and murals depicting the life of Genghis Kahn.

The Aobao Meeting

The traditional ceremonial meeting of Ewenki people who gather and pray for good weather, good harvest, and good fortune. Today's Aobao (Mongolian for "stone mound") Meeting is now a festival with song and dance performances, sports, commercial venues, and a special time to get together with friends and relatives. The festival is held on the fourth to the sixth lunar month (April to June).

Nadamu Meeting

In July or August, the Nadamu (games and entertainment) Meeting takes place. Traditional Mongolian games, wrestling, extreme horseback riding, archery, and ethnic dancing and singing are highlights.

Zhongyuan Festival

This festival commemorates ancestors.

The Bonfire Festival

On June 18 in Oroqen territory. On that day, the Oroqen dress in their finest to sing and dance around a bonfire.

Scenery of Inner Morgolia grassland. (From ImagineChina)

Day 2 Hulun Buir→Bayan Tsagann grassland→Xini River forest farm. Lodging: tents.

Day 3 the Xini River forest farm→Bayanhot. Lodging: tents.

Day 4 Bayanhot→Manchuria. Lodging: Friendship Hotel.

Day 5 Manchuria→Hulun Buir→Lodging: Hailaer Hotel.

Day 6 Japanese Bunkers→Xishan Park→Hall of Ethic Customs. Lodging: Hailaer Hotel.

Day 7 End of tour.

Traditional Routes

Four-day tour of Inner Mongolia grassland

Day 1 Arrival at Hohhot.

Day 2 Hohhot→Gegentala grassland or Xilamuren grassland.

Day 3 Watching the sunrise in grassland→Hohhot→Zhaojun's Tomb→Wuta Temple-Dazhao.

Day 4 End of tour.

Six-day tour of the Inner Mongolian folk culture

Day 1 Arrival at Hohhot.

Day 2 Hohhot→Gegentala grassland or Xilamuren grassland.

Day 3 Watching sunrise in grassland→Baotou→Hasuhai Lake→Mei Dai Zhao.

Day 4 Wu Dang Zhao→ruins of Great Wall from the Spring and Autumn period→Yellow River bridge→Sounding Sand Slope.

Day 5 Genghis Khan tomb→Hohhot.

Day 6 Zhaojun's tomb→Dazhao→White Pagoda→museum. End of tour.

Self-Guided Tours

Mongolia and the Yellow River

Start from Hohhot to Zhongwei in Ningxia Province. Pass Baotou, Wuyuan, Linhe, Chengkou, Wuhai, Shizuishan, Yinchuan, Qingtongxia, Zhongning. Main scenic sites: Inner Mongolia grassland, Zhoajun Tomb, Five Pagoda Temple, Inner Mongolia Museum, emperor's tomb of West Xia Dynasty, 108 pagodas in Qingtongxia, Shapotou scenic area, High Temple, Nanguan

Mosque, ruins of Ming Great Wall, Haibao Pagoda, Chengtian Temple Pagoda, Islam mosque.

The Inner Mongolia and Shanxi Tour

Starting from Hohhot to Pingyao, pass Baotou, Erdos, Datong, Yuanping, Xinzhou, Taiyuan, and Qixian county. Main scenic sites include: Inner Monglian grassland, Zhaojun Tomb, Five Pagoda Temple, Inner Mongolian Museum, Sounding Sand, Genghis Khan Tomb, Wu Dang Zhao, ruins of Zhao Great Wall, Yungang Grottoes, Jiulong Wall, Huayan Temple, Wutaishan Mountains, Yingxian Wooden Pagoda, Jin Ancestral Temple, Pingyao ancient city, Mingqing Street, "Ri Sheng Chang" old site, mansion of Qiao family.

Hohhot Section

Best Time to Travel

July to September is the best time to visit Hohhot. The famous Nadamu Meeting is held during this period; spring is also an excellent time to plan tours in this area.

Shopping Tips

Local and ethnic goods, pottery, clothing, and the like can be easily bought at street fairs. There are also several large department stores such as the New Century Plaza, Tianyuan Department Store, and Mandula Trade Building.

The eight-story Five Pagoda Temple (From CFP)

Addresses and Phone Numbers

The Inner Mongolia Hotel	31 West Ulan Tsabu Street, Hohhot	0471-6938888
Zhaojun Hotel	69 Xinhua Avenue, Hohhot	0471-6668888
Qingshan Hotel	1 Yingbing Road, Qingshan District, Baotou	0472-3331199
Damao Islam Hotel	Fuqiang Road, Baotou	0472-5161278
Jinlong Hotel	5 Hulun Street, Erlianhot	0479-2225999
Manchuria International Hotel	35 Erdao Street, Manchuria	0470-6248188
Manchuria Friendship Hotel	26 Yidao Street, Manchuria	0470-6248888
Manchuria Xinyuan Hotel	4 Sandao Street, Manchuria	0470-6235217
Hailaer Hotel	East Xin'an Street, Hailaer District	0470-8358114
Hailaer Buir Hotel	Central Avenue, Hailaer District	0470-8358388

Five Pagoda Temple

This temple was originally part of the Cideng Temple (built in 1727) and the five towers are all that remain. Each pagoda is about 50 feet tall. There are three relief inscriptions on the back wall of the base, one of which is the only Mongolian astrological chart in the world.

Take Bus 1, 26, 27, or 52 to the temple.

Xi Li Tu Zhao

Located at North Stone Street in Hohhot, Xi Li Tu Zhao is the largest surviving lama temple in the city. Known in Chinese as Yanshou Temple, it was built from 1567 to 1619 in Chinese style except the main hall, which reflects Tibetan style.

Dazhao

Dazhao (also known as Silver Buddha Temple) was built by Mongolian chieftain Alatan Khan in 1580. There is an 8.5-foot solid silver Buddha in the temple, and it is the earliest lama temple in the Inner Mongolia region.

The antique market near Dazhao is worth a visit.

Zhaojun's Tomb

Six miles south of the Dahei River in Hohhot, Zhaojun's Tomb is the burial place of Wang Zhaojun, a Han Dynasty woman who married a Mongolian Khan and brought peace between the Han and Mongolian peoples. The tomb is 108 feet tall in the shape of an Aobao or stone mound.

Zhaojun's tomb is regarded as a symbol of Chinese unity.

Ten-Thousand Huayanjing Pagoda

The Ten-Thousand Huayanjing pagoda is also called the White Pagoda. Located in the east suburb of Hohhot, it was built during the late Liao Dynasty and holds a vast amount of Huayan scripture and other works in Chinese, Kitan, Manchu, Mongolian, and Tibetan.

The only well preserved Liao structure in Fengzhou. (From Colphoto)

Hilamuren Grassland

The Hilamuren grassland is about 56 miles north of

The statue in front of Zhaojun's Tomb is a symbol of the friendship between the Han and Mongolian tribes. (From CFP)

Staying in a Mongolian tent is an indispensable feature of tourism here. (From Quanjing)

Hohhot. The nearest grassland to Hohhot, the scenery is spectacular with large expanses of rolling grassland, grazing flocks and herds, and the famous mushroom-shaped yurts. There are more than 62 "tents" for visitors to get a feeling of the ethnic Mongolian yurts but with modern conveniences. The Nadamu meeting is held here every summer.

The temperature in July and August hovers between 64 and 68°F. Remember to take warm sweaters and a coat because the temperature falls dramatically during the afternoon and evening.

Gegentala Grassland

The Gegentala grassland is near Sumu Township, which is 93 miles north of Hohhot.The fertile grassland plain makes a perfect meadow. In addition to watching Mongolian horse riding and song-and-dance performances, you can also participate in horse and camel riding, archery, and other ethnic sports.

Alongside traditional Mongolian tents, modern luxurious Mongolian yurts, night clubs, saunas, and the like cater to tourists.

Nadamu Meeting

Nadamu is a traditional Mongolian festival drawing participants from all over the country. In July and August, when grassland is fertile and livestock grow fat, the Nadamu Meeting takes place with traditional events such as wrestling, horse riding, archery, rodeos, and Mongolian chess. Many tourists are thrilled to watch and join in ethnic singing, dancing, and sports contests.

Baotou Region

Best Time to Travel

Baotou is situated on the south Mongolian plateau, where spring and summer are the best seasons for tourists.

Wu Dang Zhao

Wu Dang Zhao (monastery built near willow trees) is in Wudanggou Valley, less than 50 miles northeast of Baotou. It was built in 1749 and originally called Badagaer, according to the blueprint brought back from Tibet by the first Living Buddha Lobusanga.

There are 2,538 building units in Wu Dang Zhao, most of which are in Tibetan style. (From CFP)

The solid silver Buddha is called Mei Dai Buddha, the Mongolian name for Buddha Sakyamuni. (From ImagineChina)

The temple is built against the side of the mountain; the monastery itself has no outer walls, more than 2,500 rooms, and many Buddhist artifacts and scriptures. It is the largest Tibetan Lama temple in the Inner Mongolia region.

Kun Du Lun Zhao

Kun Du Lun Zhao was first built in 1729 at the foot of Ura Hill, northwest of Baotou. Originally named Faxi Temple by Qianlong, a Qing emperor, it is commonly known as Kun Du Lun Zhao because of its location on the banks of the Kundu River. The Zhao Great Wall (Summer and Winter period) is behind the temple grounds.

Mei Dai Zhao

Mei Dai Zhao temple, built on Daqing mountain, is a Lama temple built by Alatan Khan, a Ming Dynasty Mongolian chieftain, and is the only multifunctional building in Inner Mongolia comprising temple, fortress, and residence.

Tomb of Genghis Khan

The tomb of Genghis Khan is located in the Gandeli grassland in Yijinhuoluo County, about 115 miles from Baotou. The complex comprises four magnificent areas, or palaces, all in the shape of Mongolian yurts. The main palace has a 16-foot-tall statue of Genghis Khan; the other halls contain artifacts and the coffins of Genghis Khan's wife and fourth son. Originally built in 1946 by the Inner Mongolian government, the treasures and original structures were destroyed in the Cultural Revolution. The complex has been completely reconstructed and renovated, and there are replicas of many of the lost treasures.

The Genghis Khan palace, a short distance from the tomb, hosts four commemorative ceremonies each year: March 21, May 15, September 21, and October 3.

The roofs of the halls are covered with blue and gold glazed tiles. (From CFP)

When people slide down the slope, it makes a roaring sound. (From Colphoto)

Chifeng Region

Best Time to Travel

June to September is the optimal time to visit Chifeng. The winters are cold and arid, summers warm and wet. Temperature change greatly from daylight hours to nighttime, so remember to take extra sweaters.

Ruins of Liao's Central Capital

The ruins of the ancient Liao capital on the north bank of the Laoha River between the Tiejiangyingzi Township and Daming, is 9 miles west of Tianyi.The largest provisional capital, it was built in 1007 and had great influence on Liao's economic and military strength.

Ruins of Liao's Upper Capital

The ruins of Liao's upper capital are located in the southern suburb of Lindong in Balin. It was built in 918 and was the first and largest capital of the Liao Dynasty.

Take a bus at Chifeng to Lindong, then a taxi to the site.

Sounding Sand Slope

The Sounding Sand Slope, so called because of the roaring sound made by stepping on the sand, is in the Kubuki Desert. The slope is about 361 feet high, with a rising angle of 45 degrees. The slope itself forms a half circle and becomes a huge echo chamber. When you slide down the slope, the slope makes a loud rattling sound somewhat like a jet plane. You can also see and participate in desert adventures, horse riding, camel riding, parachuting, shooting, archery, boating, and swimming.

There is no direct bus to the slope, but you can rent a car or minivan.

Liao Grottoes

These grottoes, about 15.5 miles southwest of Lindong, were built around 1109. Divided into three sections (central grottoes, south grottoes, north grottoes) you will find Devanagari (Sanskrit) scriptures on stones and walls.

Take a bus at Chifeng to Lindong, then a taxi to the grottoes.

The Buddhist sculptures are in Kitan style. (From Colphoto)

Dalainoer

Dalainoer lies in the southwest of Gongaer grassland, which is 56 miles from Pengzhen. Known as "Birds' Heaven," it is one of the four largest lakes in Inner Mongolia; hundreds of migrant birds, including swans and cranes, make this lake a bird-watcher's paradise.

Balin Stone Museum

The museum, built in 1995 on Mulun Street in Daban, boasts three exhibition halls and a souvenir hall, in which over 5,000 precious stones are displayed and sold.

> You can buy different kinds of stones and perhaps a precious gem from street vendors in front of the Balin Stone Museum.

Residence of Duke of Kharachin Territory

The ducal residence in Dachengzi, Chifeng, was built in 1679 and housed 12 Kharachin territory dukes in its long history. Now a mini theme park, you can enjoy the fun of being a Chinese duke for one day and attend a royal Mongolian banquet.

> Many interesting tourist programs, such as "living as a duke for one day" and "enjoying royal dinners," are offered here.

Longquan Temple

The Longquan Temple, about 2 miles northwest of Gongyefu in Kharachin, was named after an ancient well, the Longquan spring. Located about 50 feet west of the temple, it never dries up. The temple was first built in 1287 and rebuilt in the Qing Dynasty.

Ashatu Stone Forest

Ashatu means "rugged stones" in Mongolian. This granite forest is on Bedashan Mountain, which is 25 miles north of the Huanglianggang Peak of the Daxing'anling Mountains in Hexigten, Chifeng. The stone forest often changes its appearance and color with the seasons.

> Cell-phone service is restricted in the area, but there is a landline phone at the local government building. There is also no gas station in the area, so we recommend filling the gas tank before setting off for this site.

Eroded by ancient glacial movements, the stones in Ashatu Stone Forest look like pages of a book. (From Colphoto)

Reshuitang Hot Spring

The thousand-year-old Reshuitang Hot Spring is about 18 miles from Hexigten, Ningcheng County, and 143 miles from Chifeng. With an average temperature of 116–181°F, this ancient spa is said to cure many diseases in addition to being a relaxing place to bathe because the water contains trace elements that soothe and purify the skin. The waters at Reshuitang are good for joint and skin diseases.

Alashan League Region

Best Time to Travel

From mid-August to September the climate is mild in Alashan League, and it is the best time to visit the deserts. Summers are the optimal time to travel to the Helan Mountains.

Tengri Deserts

The Tengri Deserts (Badain Jaran, Tengger, and Kubuqi are the three most famous) are located at the border between Alashan League and Gansu Province. Surrounded by Helan Mountains in the east, the Great Wall in the south, Abrai Mountains in the west, the deserts cover 14,170 square miles and are about 2,000 feet above sea level, making them among the coldest deserts on the planet. The area is an archeologist's mecca: Dinosaur eggs and fossils, stone tools and other utensils, and a recently discovered 7,000-year-old stonemason's workshop have been found here. It is believed that more than 4,000 years ago this area was once fertile farmland.

There is a desert adventure camp at moon Lake. The water and mud in the lake is said to have medicinal effects. Travel in the Gobi is safe and fascinating.

In the early twentieth century, these ruins were unearthed by archeologists. (From ImagineChina)

Heicheng Ruins

The Heicheng Ruins, located at the edge of the Badan Jaran Desert and close to Dalai (Ejin Nue League), is the only ancient city still intact on the Silk Road. There are abundant cultural artifacts from the Han Dynasty, including houses and a church with vaulted roofing. The "magic black dune" surrounds the city ruins, and is of great interest to tourists and archeologists alike.

Camels in Tengri Desert. (From Colphoto)

In the milking dance and rainbow dance, the girls shake shoulders and turn wrists to the accompaniment of brisk music. The dances display the softness and grace of females. (From ImagineChina)

Inner Mongolia Style

Charming and Colorful Mongolian Customs

Dance

Mongolian dances enjoy a very long history. It's said that early in the twelfth century, there existed a kind of dance called "Tage" in the Mongolian grassland. The Mongolian dances are mostly the representations of daily grassland and livestock farming life and culture. The males' dancing shows the beauty of manliness, labor, and strength. In the milking dance and rainbow dance, the girls shake shoulders and turn wrists to the accompaniment of brisk music. The dances display the softness and grace of females as well as their characteristics of diligence, candor, and warmth. With rich themes and strong expressive force, the Mongolian dances are the artistic portrayal of grassland life and nomadic culture.

Wedding in Erdos Grassland

The Mongolian weddings are always grand and unique, especially the traditional Mongolian weddings in Erdos grassland which enjoy a history of more than 700 years. The weddings are often held in the last or the first month of the lunar year. The young couples are supposed to enter into betrothal first. And then the girl should comb her hair into one major braid, and six minor ones by each side of her forehead, which means that she

(From Colphoto)

An older man playing the matouqin (From Imagine-China)

is engaged. Then they will select a lucky day for the wedding and invite their relatives and friends to participate. Dressed in beautiful clothes and riding on horses, the guests go to celebrate the wedding with gifts. At the wedding, everybody drinks and sings to their content. With the passing of time, the traditional wedding customs in Erdos grassland are changing. The scale and procedures are not as great and complicated as before.

Matouqin

The matouqin (horse-head fiddle) is the most representative musical instrument of the Mongolians. The instrument is named after the horse head decorated on the top end of the fiddle body. With a simple structure, the maotouqin consists of two parts: fiddle body and fiddle stick. It can be played for solo as well as for ensemble and concerto. It provides a strong expressive force with its low and deep, broad and melodious sounds. A legend has it that long, long ago, there lived in the grassland a little shepherd boy named Suhe. He took good care of a little white horse that had lost its way. Suhe and his horse won the race at the Nadam Fair that year. Unexpectedly, the outraged Duke wanted to snatch the horse forcibly. But the horse ran away and was determined to go back to Suhe. The angry Duke ordered his man to shoot the horse. Grief-stricken by the death of his horse, Suhe made a fiddle with the bone of the white horse and carved a horse head resembling the head of the white horse on the pole. From then on, Suhe and the fiddle were never apart.

Koumiss and Shouba Lamb

The Mongolian women store horse milk in a leather bag and stir it. After several days, the horse milk ferments into koumiss. As one of "eight treasures of Mongolians," koumiss is warm and has many health functions including dispelling cold, promoting blood circulation, relaxing muscles and tendons, and promoting digestion. In summer days, koumiss is also a good drink for guests. Traditional Mongolian doctors use koumiss in

(From Jin Yongji)

Roasted whole sheep (From Colphoto)

the treatment of hypertension, diabetes and intestinal tract disease. The curative effect is remarkable. Shouba lamb is a popular traditional dish of the Mongolians. The lamb is first cut into big slices and then put into water to cook. When the water is boiled and the meat is done, take out the meat and put it on a large plate. You can cut it into smaller pieces with the Mongolian knife and eat it. It is impressive that the Mongolians treat their guests with koumiss and shouba lamb not only because of the delicious food but also as an expression of the generosity of the host.

Milk Tea

Milk tea is not only a daily drink for the Mongolians, but also a necessary drink the Mongolians prepare for guests. Milk tea is made by boiling tea together with fresh milk in a proportion of 6 to1. Milk tea is nutritious and helps to refresh oneself, stimulate the appetite, and improve digestion.

Millet Stir-fried in Butter

Millet stir-fried in butter is one of the staple foods of the Mongolians. It tastes delicious and can satisfy hunger.

Roasted Whole Sheep

The roasted whole sheep is a famous traditional dish of the Mongolians. Butcher a sheep and get rid of its entrails. Then roast the whole sheep with a mixture of ginger, scallions, pepper and salt on the inside. The roasted whole sheep has a savory taste.

During the Nadamu Meeting, nomadic Mongolian tribes from all over China travel here to join the festivities in native dress. (From Quanjing)

Heilongjiang

Geography at a Glance

Heilongjiang Province, or Hei, located in Northeast China, is the northernmost province of the entire country. It covers an area of 177,607 square miles, with a population of 37,670,000 (2000 census). Its name derives from the province's major river, the Heilongjiang River. Standing in the northwest is the Daxing'anling Range, extending into the northeast; in the north is the Xiaoxing'anling Range; in the southeast there are two parallel ranges, the Zhangguangcai and Laoye ranges, which stretch from the northeast to the southwest. The western part of the province is the Songnen Plain. The whole area falls in the temperate zone and is influenced by the continental monsoon climate. The winters here are long, dry, and bitterly cold, with the lowest temperature reaching down to almost –62°F. Summers are short and rainy, and the highest temperature can reach as high as 100°F. The average annual precipitation here measures about 16 to 26 inches.

(From ImagineChina)

Featured Cuisine

Big meat pies, cool noodles, local dumplings, hemp flowers, dough twists, sliced yellow rice cake, meat bread, Dingfeng cakes, soy cheese, peanut candy, Hongmei candy, smoked chicken, oil sausage, smoked pork elbow, dried sheep intestines, crystallized pork belly, pine nut and pork belly, dried pork tongue, cooked lobster, beef jerky, boiled ferns, sliced dried fish, and monkey-head mushroom.

Red-crowned crane in Zhalong Nature Reserve Area (From CFP)

Featured Commodities

Herbal Medicines

Ginseng, hairy deer horn, tiger bone, musk, red pine seed, Siberian ginseng (devil's root), parsnip bear palm, forest frog oil.

Special Local Products

Ginseng, mink fur, deer horn, soybeans, salmon, Beidacang wine, white fish from Lake Xingkai, Heilongjiang yellow chicken, Boli black pottery, Harbin smoked chicken, Qiulin bread, monkey head, iron-plate squid, red sausage, Habulong vegetable, ginseng and royal jelly liquid, small day lily.

Local Handicrafts

Helen cut paper, Longjiang agate engraving, Baomazi tea caddies, brush pen, Songjiang knotted embroidery, willow weaving, pictures made from oxhorn, feather-pasted pictures, wheat-stock pasted pictures.

Fruits and Delicacies

Hazelnuts, hickory nuts, acorns, Mohedadu kaki, Yue oranges.

Transportation Tips

By Bus

Heilongjiang is dotted with expressways and national and provincial highways. More than 20 main expressways radiate from Harbin to Manzhouli, the Suifen River, Qiqihar, and other locations.

By Train

Trains are the most convenient way for visitors to tour Heilongjiang Province, which has the longest railroad line in China. The main railroads that run trips to this province are the Beijing-Harbin, the Siping-Qiqihar, the Lasa-Harbin,

Notes 

❶ Visitors to Heilongjiang are advised to take their warmest clothing to protect them against the bitterly cold weather. Sunglasses are a necessity to protect the eyes from the glare of the snow.

❷ Cameras need to be wrapped to prevent any movable parts from freezing and the batteries from running down. Once indoors, place the camera in a refrigerator or cooler to keep the camera lens from frosting up.

the Tumen-Mudanjiang, and the Tongliao-Ranghu lines.

By Plane

There are five airports serving more than 70 national airlines in Heilongjiang Province, located in Harbin, Qiqihar, Mudanjiang, Jiamusi, and Heihe. The Harbin (Pacific) International Airport runs regular flights to cities such as Beijing, Tianjin, Shanghai, Nanjing, Qingdao, Xiamen, Guangzhou, Shenzhen, Shenyang, Dalian, and Xi'an. Shorter flights to smaller cities are also available.

Recommended Routes

Classical Routes

Two-day tour of Jinyuan culture

Day 1 Harbin→Mount Songfeng→Pingshan County→Xiquanyan (West Spring Well) Reservoir→Mount Suping Holiday Village.

Day 2 Pingshan County→Acheng City→Jinshangjing Museum→Mausoleum of Wanyan'aguda→Jinshangjing Historic Site at Huining Residence.

Yinchun Natural-Ecological five-day tour

Day 1 Arrival in Harbin. Lodging: Wanda Holiday Inn of Harbin.

Day 2 Harbin-Yinchun-Resource House of Xiaoxing'anling-Botanic Park of Xiaoxing'anling→Dinosaur Museum of Xiaoxing'anling. Lodging: Yinchun Hotel.

POPULAR FESTIVALS

Harbin International Ice and Snow Festival

Ice lantern fair and sports competition on ice are held on from January 5 to February 5 in Harbin.

Five Great Linked Pool Lake Water Festival

Visitors can enjoy open-air movies, fairs, and fireworks, water sports, hiking, and a visit to Mount Yaoquan. The festivities are held yearly on May 4, 5, and 6 of the lunar year.

Mohe Solstice Festival

Held during the nine days around the summer solstice from June 15 to June 25. Visitors can enjoy the mild sunny weather, the spectacular northern lights, and the white night phenomenon.

Tongjiang Hezhe Ethnic Minority Cheer Festival

On June 28 every three years, the Hezhe ethnic group holds a Wurigong (meaning "happy and festive") festival, with folk songs, dancing and instrument performances, sports competitions, and special local foods.

Qiqihar Crane Watching Festival

From August 12 to 16, this festival celebrates the protected red-crowned crane and it's habitat in the Zhalong Nature Reserve. You can watch plays, dances, and acrobatics; local food and souvenirs are for sale, and there are also many ethnic products.

Golden Autumn Festival of Lake Jingbo

Various activities, sports, and fireworks take place in downtown Mudanjiang, Lake Jingbo park, and other locations to celebrate the golden autumn every year on August 15.

Day 3 Wuying National Forest Park→Songxiang Bridge→Wave Tower. Lodging: Yinchun Hotel.

Day 4 Fenglin National Reservation Park. Lodging: Yinchun Hotel.

Day 5 End of tour.

Heilongjiang typical six-day tour

Day 1 Arrival in Qiqihar. Lodging: Qiqihar White Crane Hotel.

Day 2 Qiqihar-Zhalong Nature Reserve. Lodging: Qiqihar White Crane Hotel.

Day 3 Qiqihar-Bei'an City–Five Linked Lakes. Lodging in Bei'an City.

Day 4 Bei'an City-Harbin. Lodging: Wanda Holiday Inn of Harbin

Day 5 Harbin→Mudanjiang→Lake Jingbo. Lodging: Mudanjiang Hotel.

Day 6 End of tour.

Traditional Routes

Two-day tour of Harbin

Day 1 Songhuajiang→Ice Lantern Park Fair→Wen Temple→St. Sophia Church→Pedestrian Mall of the Central Street.

Day 2 Sun Island→Pedestrian Mall of China→Russian local products→Tiger Park. End of tour.

Five-day tour of famous sites of Harbin

Day 1 Arrival in Harbin.

Day 2 Banks of the Songhuajiang River→Memorial Tower→Sun Island.

Day 3 Wen Temple→St. Sophia Church→Main Street.

Day 4 Harbin→Hulan→Former residence of Xiaohong.

Day 5 End of tour.

Two-day skiing tour

Day 1 Yabuli Ski Complex→Skiing→Other ice and snow sports.

Day 2 Skiing→Windmill network. End of tour.

Five-day tour of Five Linked Pool

Day 1 Arrival in Harbin.

Day 2 Harbin-Bei'an City→Scenery park of Five Linked Lakes→Longevity Park, Health Park.

Day 3 Volcano area of Mount Heilong (crater, Fairy Cave, Stone Sea) →Mount Flame→Second and third of the Five Linked Lakes→Mount Yaoquan→Zhongling Temple→Dual Dragon Spring Mouth.

Day 4 Mount Geqiu→Bath Pool of Fairies →Bird Singing Forest→Hunting Ground.

Day 5 End of tour.

Self-Guided Tours

Heilongjiang landscape and Russian town

Depart from Qiqihar and visit Zhalong Nature Reserve; travel to Bei'an to view Five Linked Lakes and Mount Yaoquan. Trains are available to Heihe, and you can stop at a small Russian town for local and ethnic souvenirs. The tour ends in Harbin. Return to Qiqihar.

Heilongjiang ecological tour

Depart from Harbin for Bei'an on National Highway 202,which leads to the Five Linked Pools Scenery Park and Heihe City. The next stopping place is Yinchun, where you can join an educational ecological tour. Return to Harbin.

Addresses and Phone Numbers

Haiyan Grand Hotel	19 Xizhi (West Direct) Street, Nangang District, Harbin	0451-82832698
Wanda Holiday Hotel	90 Jingwei Street, Daoli District, Harbin	0451-84226666
Normandy Hotel	178 Shangzhi Street, Daoli District, Harbin	0451-86775555
Huayi Hotel	15 Songhuajiang Street, Nangang District, Harbin	0451-53679898
Bost Hotel	147 Post Street, Nangang District, Harbin	0451-53626888
Triumph Business Hotel of Songhuajiang	257 Central Street of the Daoli District, Harbin	0451-84638855
Lakeside Hotel of Qiqihar	2 Culture Street, Qiqihar	0452-2742399
White Crane Hotel of Qiqihar	85 Zhanqian Street, Qiqihar	0452-2125258
Mudanjiang Hotel	8 Guanghua Street, Mudanjing	0453-6925833
Yinchun Hotel	8 Yinchun District, Yinchun	0458-3081111

Harbin Region

Best Time to Travel

The Harbin Ice and Snow Festival takes place every year around the first day of the lunar year. Travel plans need to be made well in advance.

Shopping Tips

Central Street between the Flood-Resistance Monument and Jingwei Street is the most upscale area of Harbin. Don't miss shopping at the Central Business City Mall at 100 Central Street; all kinds of stores, food courts, and movie theaters are here, and the mall is also a good place to relax and people-watch.

Heart Shopping Square, located at 118 Xizhi Street in Nangang District, is another large mall with every service imaginable. Take Bus No. 10, 11, 63, 64, 104, or 107 and get off at West Bridge.

Sun Island

Sun Island is in the middle of the Songhuajiang River. It is a wonderful place to sunbathe and swim when the weather permits. There are plenty of sandy beaches, and two amusement parks

Sun Island Park is filled with lush woodland and beautiful beaches. Summer is the best time to visit. (From CFP)

(Paradise on Water and Ice World), which offer entertainment and recreational activities.The total size of the island is 14.5 square miles and includes Sun Mountain, Sun Bridge, Sun Lake, and Lilac Park.

Take any bus from downtown to the river, then board the ferry for Sun Island.

Ecstasy Temple

Ecstasy Temple is at the end of Dongzhi (East Direct) Street, in the Nangang District, in Harbin. It was built in the 1920s and, with an area of 57,000 square meters, is ranked as the largest temple complex in Heilongjiang Province. The temple faces south and is divided into the Main Yard, the East Yard, and West Yard. The design, construction, and layout maintain the traditional Chinese temple style.

Temple fairs are held on April 4, 18, and 28 of the lunar calendar.

Northeast Tiger Park

This zoological park is located in the Songbei Development Zone of Harbin, on Sun Island and is the largest tiger reserve in the world. The total area of the park is about half a square mile. More than 200 Siberian tigers live here; the aim of the park is to breed and release tigers. Be sure to visit the Science Exhibit, which is informative and fascinating. Visitors can watch the tigers in the reserve's naturalized habitat in specially designed cages, and there are future plans for a safari-like tour.

St. Sophia Church

The St. Sophia Church, located on the south bank of the Songhuajiang River, is the largest Eastern Orthodox church in the Far East. Built in the form of a Latin cross, it is 175 feet tall and covers an area of about 7,761 square feet. Russian soldiers initially built the church of wood in 1907; later reconstructions rebuilt the walls with red brick, and a traditional gold onion dome tops the body of the church. The completely refurbished building (1997) is now the Harbin Art Gallery; murals, dome, and bell tower are well worth seeing now in their original splendor.

The bronze sculpture of Siddhatra the Buddha in Daxiong Hall, along with a four-eyed and four-handed bronze statue of Kwan-yin seated on a lotus blossom (From CFP)

Take Bus No. 1, 2, or 13 and get off at the First Department Store stop. The church is immediately in front of you.

Dual Dragon Scenery Park

The Dual Dragon Scenery Park, located in southwestern Bin County, 31 miles east of Harbin, attracts

As the largest ski area in China, Dual Dragon Mountain is high on the winter sports list. (From CFP)

many tourists each year. The Dragon Pearl Ski Area on the mountain is the largest tourist ski complex in the area. The eight ski lifts and two immense ski slopes allow more than 2,000 skiers at a time. You can also take part in various other activities, such as zip lines, summer sledding, paragliding, and fishing.

Five Linked Lakes

The volcanic Five Linked Lakes, situated on the west side of the Xiaoxing'anling Range, are famous throughout China. Between 1719 and 1721, lava from the volcano flowed down the mountains, blocked the rivers, and thus formed five connected lakes. Together with the strange volcanic landforms, the five lakes make a harmonious and elegant landscape.

Five Linked Lakes is the largest nature reserve of volcanic lakes. The mineral water here is sparkling clear, cool, and refreshing. (From ImagineChina)

Mudanjiang Scenic Park

Best Time to Travel

June and September are the best months to visit Mudanjiang, when the lakes are full of water, and the waterfalls are at their best. Summer and autumn are cool and serene.

Yabuli Ski Area

Yabuli Ski Area is located in Shangzhi, 120 miles from Harbin. The highest point is 4,500 feet. The entire ground is covered by thick forest and gorgeous landscape. There are altogether 11 trails of varying difficulty, and all are equipped with the latest technology. The high ski trails rank as the longest in Asia. The area is well-lit for night skiing and winter sports competitions.

Jingbo Villas, on the north shore of Lake Jingbo, are the only hotels in the area. The lake and waterfalls are spectacular at any season. (From Quanjing)

Lake Jingbo

Located in Anning, southwest of Mudanjiang, and with a total area of 36 square miles, Lake Jingbo is famous as the "West Lake of the East" and is beautifully graced with islands, waterfalls, underground lava tunnels, and underground forests. The waterfall at the Water-Elevating Pavilion rushes down like a billion stars falling, making for an awesome sight.

The stone lamp in front of the Daxiong Great Hall is a relic of the Bohai State. (From Colphoto)

Prosperity Temple

Prosperity Temple in the city of Ning'an in Bohai County was built in the first year of Emperor Kangxi's reign. The temple complex was constructed originally in the Qing architectural style. Part of it was ruined by fire but was rebuilt in subsequent dynasties. Today the temple consists of five halls: Ma King Hall, Guan General Hall, Heaven King Hall, Daxiong Hall, and Three-Saint Hall. All are made of wooden arch-like structures, with aisles decorated with red grids, carved beams, and painted pillars. Buddha statues abound.

Historic Ruins of Longquan Residence of Shangjing, Bohai State

The ruins of the Longquan Residence of the Bohai State are located northeast of Mudanjiang River. Once the capital and one of the five major cities of the Bohai State, Shangjing was built according to the model of Chang'an, capital of the Tang Dynasty. The residence was rectangular in layout, with cities inside cities, and halls inside halls. The ruins consist of three parts: the outer city, inner city, and palace city.

Qiqihar Region

Best Time to Travel

Qiqihar, with its dry and cold climate, is located at the northernmost point of the northeast Manchurian Plain. The average annual temperature is about 37°F. Winters are bitterly cold and windy, but late spring and early summer are cool and refreshing, making these the best times to visit.

The Siberian or Northeast tiger (an ancestor of the South China tiger and Bengal tiger) is native to Heilongjiang. More than 200 of these endangered tigers live in the Northeast Tiger Zoological Park in Harbin. (From CFP)

Bright Moon Island is a sister of Sun Island. It is a good place to picnic and engage in water sports in summer, and the best location to enjoy the striking northern landscape and snow and ice activities in winter. (From CFP)

Bright Moon Island

Bright Moon Island, 4,350 miles northwest of Qiqihar, is about 1,893 acres in area and is located in the middle of the Nanjiang River. It is named for its moonlike overlook and is surrounded by blue clear waters. In midsummer, the waters and trees combine to make a heavenly view, bright and serene. At the center of the island stands Wanshan Temple and a number of ancient pavilions—Yuquan Pavilion, Sanqing Pavilion, Baiyang Pavilion, and Sanxing Pavilion—all of which are built in the ancient and elegant Chinese architectural style. There is a mini-train to take visitors around the island for some spectacular scenic views.

Longsha Park

Longsha Park, located in the Longsha district of central Qiqihar, has the most extensive facilities and is the largest and oldest city park in northeast China. Built in the late Qing Dynasty, it has been renovated and improved many times and now consists mainly of five separate parts. The best place to see the entire park is at the Far-Sky Pavilion on Shenglong Mountain. There you can see three of the most beautiful structures: the Wangjiang Pavilion, General Guan Temple, and the Book Depository Pavilion.

Zhalong Nature Reserve Area

The Zhalong Nature Reserve Area, almost 17 miles southeast of Qiqihar, was listed as one of the "most important marshes of the

Daxing'anling is covered with thick and thriving primitive forests. The photograph shows the vast amount of timber cut by the local forest bureau. (From Quanjing)

There are 35 rare bird species protected by China's bird protection laws. The Zhalong State Nature Reserve is the largest artificial breeding center for the endangered red-crowned crane. (From CFP)

world" in 1992. It covers 386 square miles and protects over 260 kinds of birds, more than 120 breeds of waterfowl, as well as other animals, with endangered birds like the red-crowned crane as its most protected species. This nature reserve is a major tourist destination for bird-watching, and its science and research center is world-famous. The reserve is the natural habitat for 6 of the world's 15 breeds of crane.There are about 500 red-crowned cranes in this area, amounting to one-fourth of the total number of this species in the world.

Zigong Region

Best Time to Travel

The Daxing'anling Range lies at the northernmost reach of the Chinese mainland. Because of its latitude, winters here last more than seven months and the two-month summers are cool but pleasant. Winter days are very short, while in summer the daytime lasts about 17 hours.

North Pole Village

Located at the northernmost point of Mohe County, the tiny (only 6 square miles) North Pole Village is the coldest area of China, with an average temperature of 23°F and the lowest temperature sinking to about –60°F. Around the summer solstice, daylight lasts almost 24 hours, and the village is often referred to as "the nightless city." Summer is also the best time to see the northern lights and the white night phenomenon.

An Orqen hunter in Daxing'anling (From CFP)

Heilongjing Style

Fishing and Hunting Ethnic Group in North China

Hezhen Ethnic Group

The Hezhens mainly inhabit Raohe County and Fuyuan County in Heilongjiang Province. They all fish and hunt for a living because there are many mountains and rivers nearby, which makes it convenient for these activities. Every Hezhen person, old or young, male or female, is good at fishing. They also give full expression to their own history, heroes, social life, customs, and beliefs through *Yimakan,* their unique art form, which is a rich oral literature equivalent to a "cultural encyclopedia." Their works of art include *Hero An Cu* and *Hero Xiang Sou* as well as other short works that involve songs about life and love stories.

Orqen Ethnic Group

Most of the Orqens inhabit Heilongjiang Province while the rest live in Inner Mongolia. The Orqens have been living on Daxing'an Mountain and Xiaoxing'an Mountain for generations. They make their living mainly by means of hunting, but

The Hezhen woman is making clothes with fish scales. (From ImagineChina)

sometimes also by fishing. The Orqens are experienced in hunting, gathering, and fishing and have a system of hunting methods for different seasons. They are simple and warmhearted, and excel at horsemanship and archery. The females are good at embroidery and making leather.

Harbin Zhaolin Park Ice Lantern Exhibitions

Creating ice lanterns is a unique artistic form in the north of China. Harbin ice lanterns are considered the best of all. Harbin ice lantern exhibitions have been held annually in Zhaolin Park since 1963. From January 5 to the end of February every year, there are thousands of scenic sites in Zhaolin Park, which becomes a world of ice lanterns. In recent years, people precolor the ice used for the ice sculptures, which allows the artistic work to blossom in multicolored splendor. The ice lantern exhibitions have become a popular cultural attraction.

(From Quanjing)

Jilin

Geography at a Glance

Jinlin Province, known as Ji, is at the center of the three northeastern provinces of China. It borders Russia on the east and faces Korea southeast across the Tumen and Yalu rivers; Liaoning Province is to the south, Inner Mongolia to the west, and Heilongjiang province lies to the north. The capital city is Changchun. The total area of the province is more than 70,000 square miles, occupying 2 percent of the total Chinese territory. It is 403 miles wide from the west to the east and 186 miles from south to north. The population, consisting of different ethnic groups such as Han, Korean, Man, Hui, Mongolian, and Xibo, is 27.28 million (2000 census).

The province is rich in resources and is one of the three world-famous "black lands," boasting fertile soil, rich products, dense forests, and minerals. The forest covers about 30,000 square miles, approximately 42 percent of the whole province. The region's wood production ranks sixth in China. There are also many rivers and lakes, including Mudanjiang River, Tumenjiang River, and the Heaven Pool (Tianchi). The province is home to the "three treasures of the northeast": ginseng, marten fur, and hairy deer horn. The expanding economic climate relies on light industry (e.g., watches, toys, food), paper mills, car manufacturing, hydroelectric power plants, metallurgy, and household appliances.

There are tall mountains in the east of the province, plains in the middle, and prairies in the west. Summers are very short, winters, long and snowy; and spring and autumn are usually windy but mild. The entire province is influenced by the continental monsoon

(From Quanjing)

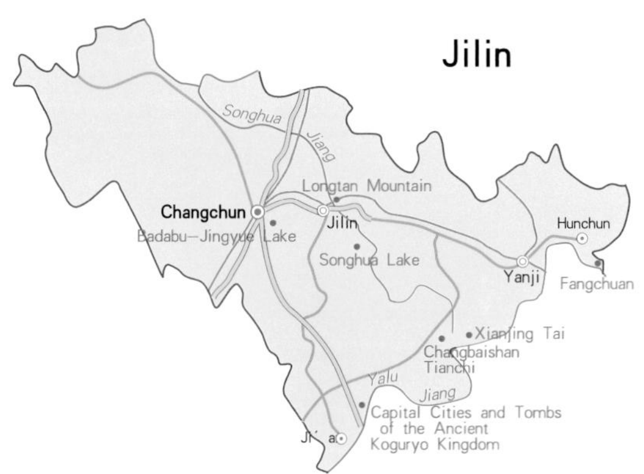

Frost viewing (From ImagineChina)

climate of the temperate zone, with plentiful rain and four distinct seasons. Mount Changbai (Ever White Mountain), the most famous range in the province, is covered with bright white snow in winter and, in combination with stands of pine trees and the snowmelt of Heaven Pool (Tianchi), the mountain is extremely beautiful, earning it the name " A World of White Mountains, Pines and Waters."

Featured Cuisine

Tomato and eggplant casserole, whitefish, hot pot, ginseng, medlar, chicken, cool noodles, hotcakes, Sanzhangdan pies, Qianguo sandwich pies, pork and vermicelli, pickle and pork hot pot, Korean cool noodles.

Featured Commodities

Changchun

Wood carving, Dehui straw weaving, Laomaosheng sweets, Huidingzhen pastry, Zhenbutong pickles, painted plates.

Jilin

Baishan wood pictures, pheasant, hawthorn, strawberries, bracken ferns, paper cuttings, stone carving.

Mount Changbai

Ginseng, hairy deer horn, Songhua inkstone, Changbai hawk, lucid ganoderma lucidum (the "wonder herb," or reishi mushroom), ear-shaped jelly fungus, Songkou mushroom, Yuhuang mushroom.

Notes 

❶ Visitors are advised to travel with a competent guide in this area. Hiking boots or heavy shoes are indispensable, as is warm clothing.

❷ The mountain is steep and high, the peak windy and rainy; tourists need to wear warm clothes and bring rain gear.

❸ A high-resolution telescope and a good camera are necessities, not just for the exceptional mountain scenery but perhaps for a glimpse of the "monster of Tianchi." Tianchi Lake is on the border between China and North Korea and is the world's highest crater lake.

Transportation Tips

By Bus

Highways radiate from Changchun in all directions, reaching Siping, Jilin, and Tumen, and other places. Some roads cross the border into Korea through Tumen and Sanhe. The Jilin highway system ranks seventh in China.

By Train

Jilin province has a dense network of railways, including the Beijing-Harbin line, the Changchun-Dalian line, the Changchun-Baicheng line, the Changchun-Tumen line, and the Baicheng-Yinghua line. With Changchun as the hub, these lines connect the whole province. Besides the 28 main and branch lines inside the province, there is also the Huichun Railway, which is tied into the Russian network.

By Plane

There are three airports in Jilin: Changchun and Yanji (both international airports), and Jilin. More than 44 airlines connect the province with Bejing, Shanghai, Shenzhen, Hong Kong, and other major cities, including many locations in Korea, Japan, and Russia.

POPULAR FESTIVALS

Frost, Ice, and Snow Festival

One of the four natural wonders of China, the frost along the Songhua River gives rise to this well-known fair. Held every January in Jilin, this festival offers ice and snow sculptures, food, souvenirs, and winter sports opportunities.

North Mountain Temple Fair

This fair is held on April 8 in Jilin. There are various programs of entertainment, goods, special foods, and temple tours.

Mongolian Local Custom Festival of the Chagan Lake Area

This lengthy fair (held between the end of July and the beginning of October in the Chagan lake area of Jilin) consists of folk music performances, folk exhibits, Aobao worship ritual, and tours.

Yanbian Local Custom Festival

Organized by the Yanbian Korean autonomous prefecture, this festival takes place between the end of August and the first week in September. Wrestling, tugs-of-war, and soccer are the main activities of the festival, in addition to local performances and exhibits, and a business and trade fair.

Mountain Produce Festival of Changbai Mountain

Held in the first full week in September, this fair reminds the visitor of a state fair with exhibits and judged contests of mountain produce and goods. There are organized sightseeing tours to the splendid landscape of the west slope of Changbai Mountain.

Movie Festival of Changchun

Established in 1992, this international movie festival is sponsored by the Ministry of Radio, Cinema, and Television. It is held every other year and maintains friendship, communication, and progress as its objective. The Changchun Film Group has invested in a 3-million-square-foot movie park, which will offer the latest in motion picture technology.

Recommended Routes

Recommended Tours

Ten-day border tour of Jilin–Korea–Russia

Day 1 Arrival in Changchun. Lodging: Province Hotel.

Day 2 Changchun→Changbai Mountain →Tianchi→Thermal Spring→Yue Birch Forest→Waterfall→Vertical Vista→Minor Tianchi→Thermal Springs. Lodging: Changbai International Tourist Hotel.

Day 3 Underground forest→Spotted deer ranch→Bear's House→Huichun. Lodging: Huichun Hotel.

Day 4 Huichun→Quanhe Ferry→Luojin →Revolutionary memorial sites→Artistic performance by children→Liberty Ferry at Huichun→British Royal Entertainment City. Lodging: Luojin.

Day 5 Beach activities→Free market→ Scenery Park of Pipa Island→Huichun. Lodging: Huichun Hotel.

Day 6 Huichun→Huichun Port-Slavyangka→Haishenwei.

Day 7 Haishenwei→Old train station→ Peak Point→Aquarium→Sumarine Exploit →fortress. Lodging: Haishenwei.

Day 8 Haishenwei→Military port→Russian market→Department store→Shopping. Lodging: In Haishenwie.

Day 9 Haishenwei→Slavyangka→Huichun. Lodging: Huichun Hotel.

Day 10 Huichun→Changchun. End of tour.

Four-day tour of Man ethnic group

Day 1 Arrival in Siping. Lodging: Jiping Hotel.

Day 2 Shanmen scenery park→Man scenic park→Dual Dragon Lake scenic park. Lodging: Jiping hotel.

Day 3 Siping→Man tourist zone (Man ethnic museum, Green Height, volcano landscape). Lodging: Yintong.

Day 4 End of tour.

Traditional Routes

Two-day tour of Changchun

Day 1 Arrival in Changchun.

Day 2 Royal palace of Manchurian (Man ethnic group) puppet government→Military headquarters→Geography Exhibition of Changchun→Culture Square→State Council Exhibition of Man puppet government→Eight military divisions, Manchurian puppet government.

Six-day tour of Jilin

Day 1 Arrival in Changchun.

Day 2 Royal palace of Manchurian puppet government→Eight military divisions→ Changchun movie park→Jilin →Middle Songhuagjing Road→Century Square.

Day 3 Songhua Lake→Dunhua.

Day 4 Dunhua→White River County→ Changbai Mountain Museum.

A Korean man turns 60 years old. (From Jin Yongji)

Addresses and Phone Numbers

Jilin Hotel	2598 Changchun People's Street	0431-88488999
Changbai Mountain Hotel	1448 Changchun New People's Street	0431-85588888
Changchun Hotel	458 Changchun New China Road	0431-88791888
Changchun National Trades Hotel	2059 Changchun People's Street	0431-88487888
Changchun Restaurant	57 Changchun Chongqing Road	0431-88939431
Jilin Rime Hotel	29 Jilin Longtan Street, Longtan County	0432-3986200
Divine Land Restaurant	21 Jilin East Songhuajing Road	0432-2161000
Changbai International Tourist Hotel	Inside the scenic site of Changbai mountain	0433-5746001
Jiping Hotel	1101 South New China Street, Siping	0434-3249166
Baicheng City Hotel	102 Baicheng Patriotic Street	0436-3268666
Huichun Hotel	235 Huichun Street, Huichun	0433-7558888

Day 5 Changbai waterfall→Tianchi→White River County.

Day 6 White River County→Dunhua. End of tour.

Four-day tour of Jilin–Beida Lake

Day 1 Arrival in Jilin.

Day 2 Jilin→Ice-free Songhuajiang River and the odd-shaped frost formations→Beida Lake ski slope.

Day 3 Catholic church→PRC Square →Riverside Gate Bridge→Century Square.

Day 4 End of tour.

View of Jinlin (From Jin Yongji)

Self-Guided Tours

Ecological tour of Jinlin

Begin in Changchun and end in Jilin. Visit cities including Yintong, Huinan, Fusong, Antu, Dunhua, and Wenhe. The major scenic sites include Man Ethnic Museum, Green Height, volcano landscape, Big Dragon Bay, Small Dragon Bay, Triangle Dragon Bay, Diaoshuihu waterfalls, thermal spring of God Bridge in Wusong, Changbai Mountain scenic park, forest hunting ground of Dew River, Ecological Bay of Wusong, Cultural Exhibition Hall, Awakening Temple, Lafa Mountain, Qingling scenic park, Songhua Lake, North Mountain Park.

Jilin–Harbin winter ice tour

Begin in Jilin City and end in Harbin. Visit north mountain of Jilin City for skiing. Tour of the river ice formations and visit Gaojuli City on Longtan Mountain and Songhua Lake. Tour Harbin, Sun Island, and take part in the Ice Festival activities on Songhuajiang River, and afterward ski at Yabuli Ski Area, the largest ski spot in Heilongjiang Province.

Changchun Region

Best Time to Travel

Each season in Changchun is distinctive: Winter is long and cold; summer, short and warm; spring is dry and windy; while autumn is sunny and has highly variable day and night temperatures. The high tourist seasons are spring and autumn.

The Clear Moon ski area attracts skiers and other winter sports enthusiasts with its beautiful landscape and good facilities. (From Colphoto)

Shopping Tips

For fashionable citizens of Changchun, Guilin Road is the place to shop. Guilin Pedestrian Street is an upscale place that incorporates shopping, relaxation, tourism, food, and entertainment.

Royal Palace of the Former Man Puppet Government

The palace is situated at 3rd, Recovery Road, northeast of Changchun. Covering an area of 106 acres and built under the reign of Emperor Puyi of the Qing Dynasty, it survived the invasion of the Japanese army in the early twentieth century. It was renovated and expanded in 1934.

Clear Moon Pool

Clear Moon Pool, located about 13 miles southeast of Changchun, is an extraordinary scenic spot surrounded by hills and covered by thick forests. The name corresponds to the Sun and Moon Pool in Taiwan Province and is thus called Sister of the Sun and Moon Pool. The clear mirror-like surface of the pool covers about 1.5 square miles.

Ski Area at Clear Moon Pool

Situated inside Clear Moon Pool park, this area has snow almost 150 days of the year. The best time to ski is between mid-November and

Changchun Movie City is a well-equipped and multifunctional theme park with entertainment centers, food courts, motion picture technique and equipment exhibitions, movie theaters, and scenic areas. (From CFP)

mid-March. The ski run is 3 miles long and is often used by professional skiing teams from Russia, Japan, North Korea, South Korea, and China. The area has every kind of high-tech facility for expert and amateur skiing, ski equipment, cables, and all grades of ski runs, providing entertainment for the whole family.

Songhua Lake is picturesque and attractive, surrounded by high peaks and thriving forests, and dotted with pavilions. (From CFP)

Jilin Region

Best Time to Travel

There is frost for about three months every year in the city of Jilin. The best time to visit Jilin is from October to April. Jilin is also a good place for skiing and winter sports with its seven-month snow season.

Shopping Tips

The Oriental Mall and Jilin Department Store are the most frequently visited shopping places. Clothing, furniture, exotic foods, and souvenirs are among many of the goods available.

North Mountain

North Mountain sits in the northwestern part of Jilin city. It covers an area of 0.5 square miles and is 885 feet above sea level. The ancient buildings in some of the special temple complexes include Jade Emperor Pavilion, Medicine King Temple, Kanli Palace, and General Guan's Temple, all of which are situated on the east peak of the mountain.

Songhua Lake

Songhua Lake, the biggest man-made lake in Jilin Province, lies on the Songhua River, about 15 miles southeast of Jilin city. The Songhua Lake is narrow and long, surrounded by steep hills and hazardous peaks. The major scenic spots include Golden Turtle Island, Camel Peak, North Tian Mountain, Five-Tiger Island, Crouching Dragon Pool, Phoenix Dancing Pool, Stone Dragon Wall, and Intoxicated Stone Slope. From December through March is the prime time for sking in the Songhua Lake ski area. The area encompasses two high mountain ski runs, a cable lift, a 16,400-foot-long natural ski slope, a 164-foot ski jump, and two hunting areas.

The ancient temple fair at North Mountain (From ImagineChina)

The Jilin frost and the winter festivals are world-famous. (From CFP)

Frost Viewing

The two banks of the Songhuajiang River are covered by dense forests. In winter, fog from the ice-free water of the river hovers in the air and freezes on the trees to form beautiful frost patterns, which is called "rime" or "tree hangs" in the local dialect. Together with the landscape of Guilin, the stone forest in Yunnan, and the Three Gorges of the Yangtze River, the river rime is listed as one of the four wonders of China. In the depths of winter, the whole province is covered with ice and snow; Songhuajiang City dresses itself in jade and silvery white, resembling clouds and snow banks viewed from a distance. Since 1991, Jilin has held its Rime Ice and Snow Festival every January, with large-scale ice lantern fairs, ice skating, sledding, and fireworks.

Gaogouli Mountain City on Dragon Pool Mountain

On Dragon Pool Mountain, about 4 miles southeast of Jilin Province, sits a city that is more than a thousand years old. In the second century, the Gaogouli Dynasty built its capital here. The city itself was a typical military fortress, with gates, moats, high walls, and interior dungeons.

Ji'an Region

Ji'an Museum

The Ji'an Museum is located at 88 Yingbin Road, north of the city of Ji'an. Built in 1958, it contains 11,000 cultural artifacts, many of which are priceless. The museum is divided into three separate halls. The central hall exhibits various rubbings from the Super King Monument, on which the inscriptions and characters are legible and complete. The west hall exhibits different tools and agricultural implements, weapons, and everyday utensils from the Gaogouli Kingdom. In the east hall are various tombs, frescoes, and murals. These paintings demonstrate the extraodinary artistic talents and are gems of East Asia.

Meteorite Museum

This is the only museum in China dedicated solely to meteorites. This souvenir from outer space fell on the suburbs of Jilin in March 1976, leaving behind the world's largest meteorite. Called Jilin No. 1 Meteorite, it weighs 3,902 pounds. More than 3,000 meteorite fragments and a host of information on outer space make up the interesting exhibits in this museum.

Known as the oriental pyramid, the famous fifth-century general's grave is built in the shape of an Egyptian pyramid. (From Colphoto)

Tumulus Group of Donggou

This large collection of mounds, the Gaogouli tumuli, is located beside the Donggou River in Ji'an. There are more than 10,000 ancient tombs, which, according to their structure and appearance, fall into three main groups: stone, soil, and the royal clothing tumulus. The stone tumuli were built from gravel and pebbles, while the soil tumuli were built with stones inside and covered by soil on top. The big stone tumuli include the Tai Emperor Mausoleum, generals' graves, and the Tumulus of the Endless Vista of Time. Most of the tombs have wall frescoes that depict the life and social customs of the Gaogouli kingdom.

Changbai Mountain Scenic Park

Changbai Mountain Scenic Park, located at the juncture of Antu, Fusong, and Changbai, is China's largest nature reserve. Baiyun Peak, known as the "first peak of Guandong," is about 8,900 feet high. The saying "Snow of centuries and pines of millennium, see them on the first peak of the world" typifies the spectacular views. Tianchi Lake and the four vertical landscapes are the most extraordinary.

Changbai Mountain is rich in natural resources such as ginseng, marten fur, and hairy deer horns. (From Jin Yongji)

Rare vertical forests can be seen on the western slope of Changbai Mountain. (From Colphoto)

Drum Dance (From Colphoto)

Jilin Style

Korean Ethnic Group

The Korean ethnic group in China has its origin in Korean migrations into the Northeast of China from the Korean Peninsula. The current Korean population in China is mainly descended from migrants who came to China since the end of the Ming Dynasty and early Qing Dynasty. The Koreans have overcome great difficulties to cultivate rice in the northeast of China. They have their own language. A common saying among the Koreans goes like this: "No matter how poor life is, the children are supposed to get an education." The Koreans have a unique custom of "beating clothes." They are good at singing and dancing. Typical recreational activities include playing on springboards and swings, and wrestling.

Korean Cuisine

Among Korean foods, cold noodles and kimchi are the most well-known. Cold noodles are often eaten in summer. The noodles are made from wheat flour and sweet potato flour. The ice, pepper, beef seasoned with soy sauce, apple slices, and other flavorings are added to the noodles after they are cooked in the cattle bone broth. The cold noodles are chewy and spicy. Kimchi refers to the pickled vegetables made by the Koreans, including sour and spicy cabbage, green pepper, radish pieces, and dried fish. There are also a variety of cold dishes and soups.

Korean Song and Dance

The Koreans are very fond of singing and dancing. The art of song and dance among Koreans has a long history and is very popular with the people. Well-known Korean dances include the Happiness Dance, the Drum Dance, the Fan Dance, and water-carrying. In the Yanji and Longjing areas in Yanbian Korean Autonomous Prefecture, the people like to heartily celebrate happy occasions and hold festivals, which often seem like big family parties.

Liaoning

Geography at a Glance

Liaoning Province (Liao), known as the "Golden Triangle," is located in the southern part of northeast China. Bordering on the Yellow Sea, the Bohai Gulf, and the Yalu River, it covers an area of nearly 58,000 square miles and has a population of about 40 million (2000 census). The northeast and west are mountainous and forested, while the middle is the vast Liaohe Plain. Because of its proximity to the sea, this southernmost province of the three large provinces in northeast China has had both commercial and strategic advantages. Because of the high latitude, the offshore area of Liao also has the lowest water temperature in China. The province belongs to the temperate zone and is influenced by the warm monsoon climate, yet the climate differs between areas because of the relative positions of sea and land. The annual average temperature is 43 to 52°F and annual precipitation averages 15 to 40 inches. There are beautiful beachfront towns with picturesque landscapes, including the cities of Dalian, Dandong, and Cucurbit Island.

Featured Cuisine

Red-baked lobster, complete Man-Han feast, Jiaji fish, snow scallops, Korean hotcakes, baked beef, stuffed buns, dumplings, Hai-

(From CFP)

cheng pie, smoked meat pies, steamed dumplings, oven-baked pies, yellow cake, mutton feast, Mongolian pie.

Transportation Tips

By Bus

The roads in Liaoning Province are excellent. There are close to 25,000 miles of paved expressways and secondary highways. The complete Shenyang-Changda loop is a prime example of highway construction on the mainland and has since opened up the East Liao Peninsula to the outside world.

By Train

Liaoning has the densest rail network in China. The six national trunk lines and five local lines reach almost every corner of the province and connect small towns and villages.

By Plane

There are now four airports in Liaoning: Shenyang, Dalian, Dandong, and Chaoyang. More than 90 airlines serve the province, connecting it to the rest of China and to Japan, Hong Kong, Korea, and Russia as well.

By Ship

Liaoning has five major ports: Dalian, Yingkou, Dandong, Jinzhou, and Cucurbit. Shipping from here reaches more than 50 countries and regions—more than 300 foreign and national ports altogether.

The Manchus are distributed mainly throughout Liaoning Province and Hebei Province; Liaoning Province is the birthplace of the ethnic group. The Manchus have their own alphabet and language, and nowadays adopt Mandarin Chinese as their language, too. (From Jin Yongji)

Notes 

❶ Xingcheng is a well-known seaside town. Swimming, sunbathing, and other beach activities are a great way to spend your vacation.

❷ Xingcheng is the largest seafood supplier in West Liao. The middle of July is prime time for fresh seafood. The Mid-Autumn Festival is the best time of year for crabs.

❸ Fresh fish and crabs are widely available in stores and restaurants.

Recommended Routes

Featured Routes

Six-day tour of Huludao

Day 1 Arrival in Dandong. Lodging: Dandong Hotel.

Day 2 Great wall of Tiger Mountain→Jinjiang Mountain Park→Korean War Memorial→Yalujiang Bridge→Departure for Dalian.

Day 3 Zhongshan Square→Hutan Ocean Park→Bangchui Island→Fu Village→Xinghai Beach→Xinghai Park→Black Stone →People's Square. Lodging: Dalian Hotel.

Day 4 Lushun→Historic Relic of the

POPULAR FESTIVALS

Ice Lantern Festival of Dalian Ice Valley

Held in the Ice Valley of Zhuanghe County in Dalian for two months (January and February).

Shenyang Lantern Festival

Held every January 15 in Zhongshan Park in Shenyang, this festival shows off every variety of flowered lantern, colored lantern, and specially designed lantern.

Phoenix Mountain Fair

The Medicine King Meeting is held here every year on April 28 in Fengcheng city in Dandong. Traditional herbal medicines, local specialties, and tours of the temples draw many locals and visitors alike.

Dalian Sophora Viewing Festival

A flower show held in Dalian every May. Competitions for flower arranging, new species, and fantastic flower displays take pride of place at this time.

Spring Fireworks Festival

Celebrating the return of spring, a great fireworks celebration is held here each May.

Oriental Silk Road Festival

Held in May in Dandong, this festival celebrates the famous and ancient Silk Road with songs and dance performances, concerts by renowned orchestras, fireworks, and other sorts of entertainment.

Myriad Mountain Festival

This festival is held every June in Anshan.

Lotus Festival

Held every year from late July to mid-September in Xinmin County at Shenyang West Lake, a well-known vacation resort. Lotus flowers, symbols of beauty and fertility, are the stars of this summer fair.

Dalian International Fashion Festival

Trade, culture, and tourism are featured at this annual festival, held from late August to early September. Top models from all over the world parade the newest fashions.

The Qing Culture Festival

Held in Shenyang in late September. Folk dancing contests, parades, and band competitions are the main attractions. Don't miss the local folk and ethnic group exhibits.

Japan-Russia War and Jiawu War→Dalian. Lodging: Dalian Hotel.

Day 5 Dalian→Cucurbit Island→Bijia Mountain. Lodging: Golden State Hotel.

Day 6 Chrysanthemum Island→Xingcheng →Ningyuan Ancient City→Street of Ming and Qing. Lodging: Xingcheng Environmental Protection Center. End of tour.

Eight-day tour of Liaoning-Korea

Day 1 Arrival in Shenyang. Lodging: Liaoning Hotel.

Day 2 Royal Palace of Shenyang→Former Residence of Zhang Xueliang→Zhao Mausoleum. Lodging: Liaoning Hotel.

Day 3 Shenyang→Dandong→Yalujiang Park. Lodging: Dandong Hotel.

Day 4 Dandong→Pyogyang. Lodging: In Pyongyang.

Day 5 Wanjing Platform→Mind Tower→ Triumph Arch→Longevity Monument→ Jinricheng Square→Winged Steed Bronze Sulpture. Lodging: In Pyongyang.

Day 6 Pyongyang→Kaicheng→ Banmendian border between South Korea and North Korea→Gaoli Museum. Lodging: In Pyongyang.

Day 7 Kaicheng→Pyongyang→Dandong. Lodging: Dandong Hotel.

Day 8 End of tour.

Seven-day business tour of Liaoning

Day 1 Arrival in Dalian Lodging: Dalian Hotel.

Day 2 Binhai Road→Economic Development Zone→Colorful City. Lodging: Dalian Hotel.

Day 3 Dalian→Yingko→Economic Development Zone. Lodging: Dalian Hotel.

Day 4 Jade Buddha Yard→Tanggangzi Thermal Spring. Lodging: Anshan Restaurant.

Day 5 Anshan→Shenyang Economic Development Zone→Royal palace→Zhao Mausoleum. Lodging: Liaoning Hotel.

Day 6 Shenyang→Dandong→Border Economic Cooperation Zone→Yalujiang. Lodging: Dandong Hotel.

Day 7 Dandong→Dalian→Jinshitan Holiday Villa. End of tour.

Traditional Routes

Qing Culture three-day tour

Day 1 Shenyang Royal Palace→Fu Mausoleum→Zhao Mausoleum.

Day 2 Xinbinhetuala Ancient City→Yong Mausoleum.

The main building of the September 18 History Museum. Seen from a distance, the complex looks like the map of the northeast's three provinces. The Monument of Remembered History is nearly 60 feet tall and shaped like a three-dimensional desk calendar, on the right side of which is carved "Sept. 18, 1931, the 7th day of the 8th lunar month in the Sheep Year of the 8th Heavenly Items (Friday)"; the left side lists the historical facts of the Japanese invasion. (From CFP)

Addresses and Phone Numbers

Liaoning Hotel	97 Zhongshan Road, Heping District, Shenyang	024-23839166
Kailai Grand Restaurant of Shenyang	32 Yingbin Street, Shenhe District, Shenyang	024-22528855
Shenyang Holiday Inn	204 North Nanjing Street, Heping District, Shenyang	024-23341888
Dalian Restaurant	6 Shanghai Road, Zhongshan District, Dalian	0411-82633171
Dalian Hotel	4 Zhongshan Square, Dalian	0411-82633111
Jinzhou Hotel	412 Stalin Road, Jinzhou District, Dalian	0411-87692172
International Grand Restaurant	219 Yuanlin Rood, Anshan	0412-5555888
Dandong Hotel	69 Shanshang Street, Dandong	0415-2101618
Jinzhou Building Hotel	58 Central Street, Guta District, Jinzhou	0416-2160000

Day 3 Yiwulu Mountain→Beizhen Temple. End of tour.

Four-day tour of Dalian-Lushun

Day 1 Arrival in Dalian.

Day 2 Hutan Amusement Park→Binhai Road→Beida Bridge→Bay Square→People's Square→Zhongshan Music Square→Russian-style street.

Day 3 Xinghai Park→Xinghai Square→International Conference and Exhibition Outlook→Aolianna Ocean Liner.

Day 4 Dalian→Lushun→Victory Tower→Friendship Tower→Military port→Loyalty Mausoleum→Pearls Park. End of tour.

Self-Guided Tours

Five-city landscape tour of Liaoning

Start in Shenyang and end in Dalian. Along the way visit Anshan, Benxi, and Dandong. The major sites of this tour include the Royal Palace of Shenyang, Former Residence of Zhang Xueliang, Qian Mountain, Jade Buddha Yard, Water Cave of Benxi, thermal spring of Wubei Mountain, Great Wall of Hushan, Jinjiangshan Park, Korean War Memorial, Yalujiang Bridge, Yalujiang Park, Yalujiang Duan Bridge, Zhongshan Square, Hutan Ocean Park, Bangchui Island, Polar Aquarium, Xinghai Square, Ecology Museum, and Jinshi Bay.

Liaoning Holiday Tour

Start in Dalian and end in Benxi. Visit Yingkou, Anshan, and Shenyang. Major sightseeing stops include Jinshi Bay, West Lake Holiday Village, Ice Valley Holiday Village, Xianren Island Holiday Village, Baisha Bay, Xianren Island, Yueya Bay, Son-Expecting Mountain, Shuangtaizi Thermal Spring, Tanggangzi, Qianshan Thermal Spring, Huishan, Benxi Water Cave, and Tanggou Thermal Spring.

Shenyang and Anshan Region

Best Time to Travel

April through October is the best time to visit. Like other places in northeastern China, the climate is characterized by long, cold winters, warm but rainy summers, and short springs and autumns. January is the coldest month, July the warmest. Remember to take warm sweaters when traveling through mountainous areas.

Shopping Tips

Taiyuan Street, located in the central area of Shenyang, has everything a tourist might want. Dominated mainly by department stores, exclusive shops, and outdoor stands, it is a great place to sightsee and shop.

Zhong Street is one of the old shopping meccas, with businesses, restaurants, movie theaters, and plenty of places for people to watch. Recently renovated, this is Shenyang's "greenest" location.

Zhao Mausoleum of the Qing Dynasty

Also called North Mausoleum because of its location, Zhao Mausoleum is the grave of Emperor Huangtaiji of the Qing Dynasty and his wife. The surrounding area is now a park, located at 12 Taishan Road, Huanggu District. Bejing Park is the largest park in Shenyang. There are two lakes, East Lake and Youth Lake, Fangxiu Garden, and hundreds of trees and flowers.

Dragon: the external major motif of every palace gate design. (From CFP)

The Royal Couch and splendid screen walls in Chongzheng Hall of the Royal Palace are well worth a visit. (From Quanjing)

Shenyang Royal Palace

Shenyang Royal Palace was once the center of the ancient city; now it is in the neighborhood of Zhong Street. Built and used by Emperor Nuerhachi and Emperor Huangtaiji, it is the earliest palace group still intact today.The complex's construction began in 1625 and took more than ten years to complete. Covering an area of more than 0.13 square miles, its three main structures contain 90 buildings swith 300 rooms. The majestic palace combines the traditional style of Qing Dynasty architecture with characteristics of the Manchurian ethnic style.

Fu Mausoleum of the Qing Dynasty

Located inside Dongling Park (East Mausoleum Park) in the eastern suburbs of

In 1626, Nuerhachi was injured during his war on Ningyuan and died on his way back home. His mausoleum was begun three years later. (From Quanjing)

Shenyang, this is the tomb of Nuerharchi, the first emperor of the Qing Dynasty, and his wife. Construction began in 1629 and was completed in 1651; it is similar to that of the Zhao Mausoleum. The famous 108 steps symbolize 36 constellations and 72 Earth Devils. It faces the Hun River and has Tianzhu Mountain as a backdrop.

September 18 History Museum

The museum was built in May 1991 and opened to the public on September 18, 1991, to commemorate the invasion of Shenyang by the Japanese Army in 1931. Located at 46 Wanghua South Street, Dadong District, where the incident happened, the museum holds more than 600 photographs, 448 documents, 54 reference books, and various guns, Japanese swords, sabers, and telescopes. On the memorial day, sirens and tolling bells mark the hour of the invasion. The exhibition's main focus is on the historical facts before and after the September 18th incident.

The buildings of the museum combine the Monument of Remembered History and the Exhibition Hall.

Liaoyang White Tower (Baita)

Liaoyang White Tower, also called Chuiqing Convent Tower, is in White Tower Park, Liaoyang. Built of bricks in the Jin Dynasty (1161–1189), the octagonal tower is 231 feet tall and has 13 levels. The Sumeru pedestal with bucket arches was built to support the tower body; each of the eight sides has a niche for Buddha, majestic and peaceful, seated on a lotus flower. The Buddhas on either side appear solemn. It is a representative work of the Qidan ethnic group, successfully combined with the Han and Buddhist culture.

Strange Slope (Guaipo)

Strange Slope was discovered in April 1994, on the west side of Mount Hat (Maoshan),

The base of White Tower is carved with lotus flowers, bucket arches, and winged figures. (From Colphoto)

Qingshuitai, Xinchengzi District. If you stop your car at the foot of the slope, the car will roll to the top of the slope by itself. About 300 feet from Strange Slope, there is a 1.5-mile hill; if you stomp hard on the ground, you will hear a loud roaring, thus the hill is called Loudness Mountain (Xiangshan).

The unusual phenomenon on Strange Slope is due mostly to a visual aberration. Because the grade here is so slight, it is hard for human eyes to distinguish which end is higher.

Anshan Jade Buddha Park (Yufoyuan)

This enormous park is in the eastern Thousand Mountain (Qianshan) Park and comprises Jade Buddha Pavilion (Yufoge), Jade Belt Bridge (Yudaiqiao), Gate to the Park (Shanmen), Lotus Pond (Lianhuachi), Flowers and Fruits Island (Huaguodao), and other interesting sites. Built relatively recently as a tourist attraction, the buildings reflect the ancient architectural style, with palaces, temples, and Chinese gardens. Inside Jade Buddha Pavilion, the world's biggest jade Buddha, carved from a single piece of jade weighing 287 tons, rises nearly 23 feet into the air. Crafted with a majestic and solemn Sakyamuni on the front side and Avalokitesvara sailing over the sea on the reverse, this figure was made expressly to earn a Guinness world record. The buildings and jade figures are worth a visit.

The central Chinese garden in Tanggangzi Thermal Spring Park (From Colphoto)

Take the 308 bus from Anshan Railway Station to Thousand Mountain; the trip takes about 30 minutes.

Tanggangzi Thermal Spring (Wenquan)

This ancient and still popular spa dates from the twelfth century and is 9 miles south of Anshan city. There are eighteen mineral springs with water temperatures ranging from 130 to 158°F. Visited mainly for spa vacations and the treatment of rheumatism, these thermal springs are part of one of the four most famous convalescent hospitals in China.

The well-known Tanggangzi Convalescent and Physical Therapy Center (Tanggangzi Hospital) was built here in the 1930s.

Dalian Region

Best Time to Travel

With favorable weather anytime of year, Dalian has the most temperate and pleasant climate of the northeast provinces. Beaches and fairs provide the spring, summer, and fall attractions, while winter sports rule from December through March.

Dalian Seashore

Dalian Seashore sits at the southern tip of the Liaodong Peninsula. It is bordered by the Bohai Sea and the Yellow Sea and has a 19-mile-long coastline. The beach is a popular place for summer vacationers: The weather is perfect, and there are many opportunities for sightseeing, nightlife, fine seafood dining, and local fairs.

Beaches, water sports, and cycling are great summer attractions in Dalian.

Star Sea Square (Xinghai Square)

Star Sea Square, named after the beautiful Star Sea Bay (Xinghai), was built in 1997 to celebrate and commemorate Hong Kong's return to China. Cliffs tower above the sea at the eastern and western ends of the park, and from the top of the cliffs you can see the sky and sea blend together on the distant horizon. The square itself has streets radiating from the center, where one of China's tallest carved marble pillars takes pride of place. The pillar is 62 feet high and about 6.5 feet in diameter. The base is carved with eight dragons on the body of a larger dragon, symbolizing China's nine ancient states. There are also large musical fountains around the square.

Tiger Beach Ocean Park

This is Coney Island in China. Almost 2.5 miles of beachfront is the main attraction here, and there is a first-rate Polar Aquarium and a wild bird park. Tiny seafood restaurants and boardwalk entertainment abound, and the scenery from the beach, with the sea bordering the south and mountains on the other sides, is spectacular.

Golden Stone Beach (Jinshitan) Scenic Area

About 63 miles northeast of Dalian, Golden Stone Beach faces the Yellow Sea. Famous for its marine abrasion landforms, including banks, caves, and pillars, this beach is a safe and interesting place to beachcomb. Often called the "Stone Forest,"

Dalian, a beautiful beachfront city, is known for its spectacular scenery, pristine beaches, and garden-like streets. (From Quanjing)

Golf course in Golden Stone Beach Scenic Area (From ImagineChina)

this beach is a natural museum of geology. There is also a first-rate golf course, an amusement park, a motocross area, and a hunting preserve.

You can take the light rail from Dalian or any one of several buses from Dalian Railway Station or Dalian Port.

Shengya Ocean World

Shengya (Sun Asia) Ocean World is in Star Sea Park. Not as large or as imposing as Tiger Beach's aquarium, this one is just as fascinating. A 387-foot-walk through an underwater tunnel gives you a fish-eye's view of fascinating sea creatures. English-speaking guides are available if you call beforehand.

Lushunkou

Lushunkou is in the west of Dalian, on the southernmost tip of Liaodong Peninsula. It is by the Yellow Sea and the Bohai Sea, with Shandong Peninsula across the bay. The world-famous ice-free Lushun Harbor is the gateway to Beijing and Tianjin, and a brand-new port links Liadong Peninsula to Shandong. Be sure to visit the Snake Museum on Snake Island, Bird Island, Old Iron Mountain, Bird Migration Resting Spot, excellent beaches, and the natural boundary line between the Yellow Sea and the Bohai Sea.

Lushun Japan-Russia Prison was once the largest prison in northeast China. The building is now a memorial museum and well worth a visit to learn about its infamous history. (From Colphoto)

Lushun Japan-Russia Prison

Built in 1902 by Russian invaders, this prison served as the barracks for cavalry and as a field hospital. After the Japan-Russia War, the Japanese expanded the prison in 1907. The building is now a museum with exhibits on the war. Tours are available, and there are some fascinating secret rooms to view.

The site of the prison now allows public accessibility, and receives hundreds of thousands of visitors each year.

Dandong Region

Best Time to Travel

Travel here at any time of the year; Dandong's weather is controlled by the continental monsoon and falls into the warm temperate zone. Winters and summers are relatively short, and tourists find that the long spring and fall are the best times to travel throughout the area.

The Yalu River

The Yalu River is the boundary line between China and North Korea. With its source on the south side of Changbai Mountain, the 494-mile-long river runs through Dandong and then into the Yellow Sea. Yalu River Park has more than 100 scenic spots—mainly beautiful river views with mountains as a foil. Although most visitors cannot travel into North Korea, they can see the mountains and riverside activities from the Yalu riverbank.

It takes only 10 minutes to walk from downtown Dandong to the banks of the Yalu.

Korean War Memorial

Known in China as the Memorial Hall of the Korean War, this memorial is located at 68 Jinjiangshan Street, Dandong. Construction began in 1958 and it opened to the public in July 1993. This museum comprises a large exhibition hall, a picture and photo gallery, and a memorial tower. The actual war exhibit has 12 sections, and there are more than 500 photos and 1,000 objects on display.

In 1950, the China People's Volunteer Army marched across the Yalu River to resist the U.S. forces and aid Korea. Thus, the Great Yalu River Bridge became a route of major military importance. (From ImagineChina)

Some of the temples on Phoenix Mountain were built in the Ming and Qing dynasties. There are also many stone tablets and inscriptions on the cliff wall. (From CFP)

Phoenix Mountain (Fenghuangshan)

Phoenix Mountain is 31 miles from the northwestern part of Dandong. Shaped like a flying phoenix and just one of Changbai's ranges, it covers an area of about 83 square miles. It is famous for its steep cliffs, peaceful spring caves, beautiful trees, and lush flowers. Phoenix Mountain, Yiwulu Mountain, Thousand Mountain (Qianshan), and Herb Mountain (Yaoshan), have been called the "Four Big

Mountains of Fengtian" since the Qing Dynasty. The main peak, Cloud Gathering Mountain (Cuanyunfeng), is 2,743 feet above sea level.

To visit Phoenix Mountain, take the bus from Dandong to Fengcheng, and then change to a shuttle bus, which will take you to the site.

Qingshan Valley

Qingshan Valley lies in the northern mountainous area of Kuandian, Dandong, between Thousand Levels Mountain (Qiancengshan) and the north side of Almighty Mountain (Bamianweishan). Covering an area of 49 square miles, this scenic valley has three famous spots: Lake Qingshan (Qingshanhu), Cascading Waterfalls Valley (Feipujian), and Tiger Pond Valley (Hutanggou), all of which present spectacular views, waterfalls, and clear lakes.

The tourist season in Qingshan Valley is from March to October. Remember to carry a warm sweater or coat, as the temperature varies greatly from that of the surrounding area.

Jinzhou, Huludao, Fuxin, and Panjin Region

Best Time to Travel

Summer is the prime tourist season. The cities in this area are in the North Temperate Zone (NTZ), with a continental monsoon climate.

Guangji Temple

Guangji Temple, also known as Great Buddha Temple, is in the downtown section of Jinzhou. It was originally built during the Liao Dynasty and has gone through centuries of devastation and reconstruction. Now the site of the Jinzhou Museum, the buildings are in a quadrangle, around which are the Guangji Temple and the celebrated Liao Tower, with its 940-year history, which was constructed to preserve the Buddha's relics.

Brush-Holder Mountain (Bijiashan)

Brush-Holder Mountain lies in the village of Zhujiakou, Tianqiao, and is about 22 miles from the southeastern part of

Heaven Bridge is one of the Eight Great Scenery Sites of Jinzhou. At high tide, this pebbled path sometimes disappears. (From ImagineChina)

Jinzhou. Rising from the sea, it is 656 feet above sea level and covers an area of less than 1 square mile. Heaven Bridge (Tianqiao) is a mile-long, 98-foot-wide natural path paved with pebbles, which connects the mountain and the north bank.

Xingcheng Seashore

Xingcheng Seashore is about 5 miles from downtown Xingcheng, located at the foot of a mountain and beside the sea. With a coastline of nearly 8.5 miles, this large area is divided into five sections. Head Mountain (Shoushan) is shaped like a human head and is a mile and a half from southeast Xingcheng. On the rocks at the southern tip, there are three pavilions where you can relax and observe the stunning ocean and mountain views.

The large Buddhas of the Liao Dynasty in the hall of ceremony (From ImagineChina)

> The best time to visit Xingcheng Seashore is from May to October, when the water temperature is warm enough for swimming and other water sports, and the seafood is fresh, abundant, and inexpensive.

The Graveyard of Zhu Mei

The Graveyard of Zhu Mei is in Shipaifang Village, Lijia, Suizhong County, Huludao. The central government at that time built the graveyard for Zhu Mei, a famous Ming Dynasty general, to commemorate his brilliant achievements in battle. With mountains on the north and the Jin River on the south, the site stretches 1,148 feet from north to south and 361 feet from east to west. Many stone carvings are preserved here, along with ancient pillars, stone lions, tablets, and arched gates.

Fengguo Temple

Fengguo Temple, built in the Ninth Kaitai Year of the Liao Dynasty (1020), is in Yi County. The temple complex consists of the ceremonial hall, bell tower, Wuliang Palace, stone arches, the living area of the monks, and an extraordinary stone gate. Fengguo is a majestic and well-preserved ancient temple as well as the largest wood-frame building from the Liao Dynasty.

Ten Thousand Buddha (Wanfotang) Grottoes

In Jinzhou, the Ten Thousand Buddha Grottoes is an ancient grotto complex in the far northern part of China. Most of the grottoes were carved on the cliffs on the north bank of Daling River, near the Three Gorges. More than 328 feet in length, all 16 original grottoes have survived the centuries. The largest and most interesting Buddha is in Grotto 6.

Buddhist Sculpture on Cherry-Apple Tree Mountain

The Buddhist Sculpture on Cherry-apple Tree Mountain can be seen in the Pu'an Temple, Fuxin, the only well-preserved cliff sculpture complex in China. These 260 Buddhist figures are an important part of the religious activities in Pu'an. On the cliff are also the sutras and inscriptions stating the completion dates and the names of donors and craftsmen in Zang, Mongolian, Man, and Han characters.

Yiwulu Mountain (Yiwulushan)

Yiwulu Mountain is 3 miles northwest of downtown Beining, stretching 28 miles from north to south. It has been one of the sacred mountains of Youzhou since the Sui Dynasty. Most of the other temples and other buildings on the mountain have been destroyed throughout the centuries as a result of warfare, weather, and age. The Mountain God Temple is worth a visit.

Pu'an Temple, built in 1683, has hundreds of Buddhist carvings. (From Colphoto)

Red Beach presents an extraordinary sight. (From Colphoto)

> It is said that the famous Emperor Qianlong of the Qing Dynasty once played I-go near the Mountain God Temple.

Red Beach

This ecological wonder is in the southwestern part of Panjin. Known as Red Beach, it is covered with a special variety of beach grass. The grass changes from green to red, and then to violet, because of the angle of the sun and the action of the tides. When this occurs, the whole beach looks like a red carpet, stretching more than 30 miles.

> Red Beach is in Zhaoquanhe, Dawa County, Panjin. Take the bus from Panjin to Dawa, then rent a car to drive to Red Beach.

Shandong

Geography at a Glance

Located in the east of China, where the Yellow River joins the Bohai Sea, Shandong Province, "Lu" for short, covers a total area of over 57,915 square miles, with a population of 90.79 million (2000 census). Jinan is its capital city. The province is one of the cradles of Chinese civilization. Important discoveries here include Dawenkou Pottery inscriptions and Longshan Pottery inscriptions, which are the earliest Chinese characters ever found; Chengziya Longshan Ancient City, the earliest city-state in China; and the Qi Great Wall, the oldest preserved section of the Great Wall in China. Shandong Province is also one of the birthplaces for pottery and silk cloth. Situated in the temperate zone, it has a humid or semihumid monsoon climate, with an average annual temperature range of 51 to 56°F. The average monthly temperature is 25 to 33°F in January and 75 to 81°F in July. The average annual precipitation here is 22 to 37 inches.

Featured Cuisine

Shepherd's-purse spring rolls, Chinese onion with brown sauce, Shandong spiced pickles, Jinmeng braised rabbit head with brown sauce, pan-fried stuffed buns, melon pickles, Kong Family banquet, apples in hot toffee, Qufu smoked bean curd, dough thread coils fried in peanut oil, Qilin salmon, fried rice cakes, Yellow River carp, salted donkey meat with sauce, diced chicken with pepper, stewed large intestines, grilled mandarin fish.

(From ImagineChina)

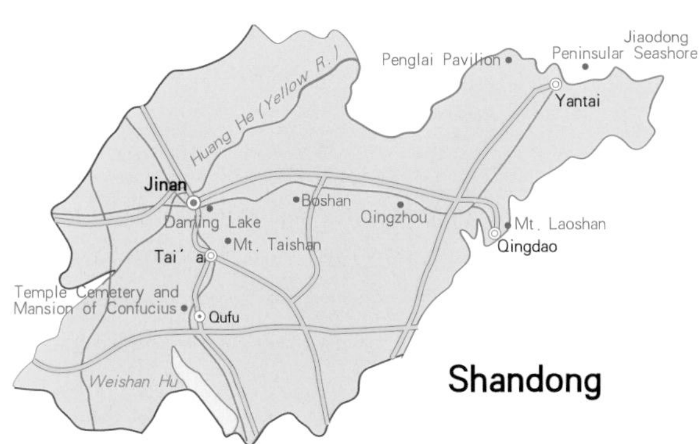

Weifang is the World Kite Capital, selected by world kite organizations, and is well known for its kite art and annual International Kite Festival. (From Imagine-China)

Featured Commodities

Herbal Medicine

Ejiao (donkeyhide giue).

Special Local Products

Kong Family wine, abalone, scallops, prawn, Muping silk, Longkou mung bean noodles.

Local Handicrafts

Shandong embroidery, pictures made with feathers, Kai-wood (Chinese pistachio tree) carving, inkstone, carpet, lace, rush mats, shell carvings, wooden molds, clay toys, Laizhou embroidery, Laizhou straw handiwork, pottery tea sets.

Fruits and Delicacies

Red jade apricots, Mount Tai small white pears, persimmons, Pingyin County rose oil, Yantai apples, Laiyang pears.

Transportation Tips

By Bus

Shandong highway reaches all the major scenic sites in the province.

By Train

The two major railways in Shandong are the Jinghu (Beijing-Shanghai) line and the Jiaoji (Jinan-Qingdao) line, which serve all major cities in China.

By Plane

Shandong has a well-developed airline system, with airports in each of the larger cities, including Jinan, Qingdao, Yantai, Weihai, Weifang, and Jining. Fourteen international airlines serve the airports in Jinan, Qingdao, and Yantai.

Notes 

Yantai and Weihai are port cities. Their fishing villages have unique customs. Tourists are asked to respect their customs when visiting these villages. For example, for those who speak Chinese, it is taboo among fishermen here to say words with the same pronunciation as "fun" or "cow" (which are similar to the pronunciation of Chinese words indicating a shipwreck). When aboard a sailing boat, visitors are advised not to whistle, run, jump, or sit at the bow. Always follow the instructions of your tour guide on such topics as local customs and taboos.

By Water

Shandong is the "gold coast" in this part of the world, with ships arriving and departing from Yantai, Weihai, Penglai, and Longkou to Dalian every day. Every summer ships, ply the waters between Yantai and Tianjin New Port and between Qingdao and Shanghai. There are also regular liners from Qingdao and Yantai to South Korea and Japan.

Recommended Routes

Classical Routes

Ten-day tour of Shandong

Day 1 Arrival in Qingdao.

Day 2 Zhanqiao Pier→Small Qingdao Island (Xiao Qingdao Gongyuan)→Xiaoyu Mountain (Xiaoyu Shan)→Aquatic Product Museum.

Day 3 Laoshan Mountain Scenic Area→Longtan Waterfall (Dragon Pool Waterfall)→Taiqing Temple (Taiqing Gong)→The Stone Old Man→May 4th Square→Badaguan (the Eight Great Passes) Scenic Park→Public Swimming Beach.

Day 4 Weihai→Liugong Island (Liugong Dao)→Governor's Mansion→Museum of Sino-Japanese War of 1894–1895—Huan-

POPULAR FESTIVALS

Sugar-Coated Hawthorn Fair at Haiyun Buddhist Convent (Haiyun An)

Held from lunar January 10 to 18 including a temple fair. Tasting various sugared fruits is high on the agenda.

Yuhuangding Temple Fair

Held annually on lunar January 19, including performances of Beijing opera, Chinese Yangge dances, and folk handicrafts.

March 3 Fair

Held on lunar March 3, highlighting such activities as the Dragon Lantern Dance and cock-fighting.

Weifang International Kite Festival

Held from April 20 to May 7 in Weifang, with various kinds of traditional folk art and kite–flying contests.

International Fisher's Festival in Rongcheng, Weihai

Held from May 20 to 22, with folk kung fu shows, an exploration of the origin of the Quanzhen School of Taoism, research on calligraphy and stone inscriptions, and more.

Qianfo Mountain Climbing

On lunar September 9, people in Jinan climb Qianfo Mountain and buy special products offered along the way. There are also exhibitions and fairs of various folk handicrafts.

Confucius International Cultural Festival

September 28 in Qufu, the birthplace of Confucius, with large-scale sacrificial dances accompanied by music, an exhibition of cultural artifacts of the Kong Family, an exhibit of the folk customs of Confucius's birthplace, and other activities.

cuilou (Building Surrounded by Green Jade) Park→Korean Clothing City.

Day 5 Penglai→Penglai Pavilion (Penglai Ge)→Penglai Water City (Penglai Shuicheng)→Antique Boat Exhibition Hall →Weifang.

Day 6 Ten-Scepter Garden (Shihu Yuan)→Weifang World Kite Museum→Qingzhou →Yunmen (Cloud Gate) Mountain (Yunmen Shan)→Fangong Pavilion (Fangong Ting).

Day 7 Chinese Ancient Chariot Museum in Zibo→Buried Horse Pit.

Day 8 Daming Lake (Daming Hu)→Baotu Spring (Baotu Quan)→Qufu→Cemetery of Confucius→Kong Family Mansion→Temple of Confucius.

Day 9 Tai'an→Mount Tai→Dai Temple (Dai Miao)→Gate to Mid-Heaven (Zhongtian Men)→Zhanyundeng→Southern Heavenly Gate (Nantian Men)→Eighteen Bends (Shiba Pan)→Street in Heaven (Tian Jie)→Jade Emperor Summit (Yuhuang Ding).

Day 10 End of tour.

Three-Day tour of Mount Tai and Qufu

Day 1 Arrival in Tai'an.

Day 2 Mount Tai→Dai Temple→Gate to Mid-Heaven→Zhanyundeng→Southern Heavenly Gate→Eighteen Bends→Street in Heaven→Jade Emperor Summit. Lodging: Taishan Hotel.

Day 3 Temple of Confucius→Cemetery of Confucius→Kong Family Mansion. End of tour.

Three-day tour of Penglai and Weihai

Day 1 Arrival in Penglai.

Day 2 Penglai Pavilion→Penglai Water City→Antique Boat Exhibition Hall→Dengzhou Ancient Bazaar. Lodging: Penglai.

Day 3 Weihai→Liugong Island→Museum of the Sino-Japanese War of 1894–1895→Korean Clothing City. End of tour.

One-day tour of Qingdao Beach

Zhanqiao Pier→Mid-Air Garden→Qingdao Olympic Hall→Little Qingdao→Badaguan →Beach→May 4th Square→Sculpture Street in Donghai (East Sea) Road→Shell Carving Factory.

One-day tour of Laoshan Mountain

Laoshan Mountain→Golden Beach→The Stone Old Man→the Frog Stone→Bashui River→Longtan Waterfall→Taiqing Temple.

Self-Guided Tours

Cultural tour of one mountain, two rivers, and three Confucius sites

Start from Jinan and end in Xuzhou by way of Tai'an and Qufu. From Jinan, the major scenic spots are Daming Lake, Baotu Spring, Qianfo Mountain, Xingguo Temple, Lingyan Temple, Qingzhou Museum, Dai Temple, Mount Tai, Jining Iron Pagoda, Jining Taibai Building, Shaohao Tomb, Temple of Yan Hui, Zhougong Temple, Liangshan Shuipo relics, Caozhou Peony Garden, Temple of Confucius, Kong Family Mansion, Cemetery of Confucius,

Daming Lake scenic area (From ImagineChina)

and the beautiful scenery along the Yellow and Huai rivers.

Tour of Laoshan Mountain, Weifang, and Zibo

Start from Laoshan Mountain and end in Zibo. Major scenic spots are Longtan Waterfall, Taiqing Temple, Badaguan Scenic Area, public beach, Ten-Scepter Garden, Weifang World Kite Museum, Yunmen Mountain, Fangong Pavilion, Qingzhou Museum, Chinese Ancient Chariot Museum in Zibo, and Buried Horse Pit. This tour features a combination of culture, folk customs, and leisure time.

Jinan Region

Best Time to Travel

Autumn is the best tourist season. Jinan is cold in winter and hot in summer; spring is windy and dusty. However, Daming Lake in winter and Baotu Spring in springtime are spectacular.

Daming Lake

Daming Lake, a spring-formed natural lake, is situated at the center of the city proper of Jinan. The area of the whole park is 330,000 square miles, while the lake surface is more than 177,000 square miles. Lixia Pavilion, Huiquan (Place Where Springs Gather) Hall, Huxin (Center of the Lake) Island, and other big and small islets are scattered around this huge lake. The natural scenery of the park is magnificent.

Be sure not to miss a visit to Jiaxuan Temple on the southern bank of the lake.

Addresses and Phone Numbers

Wanghai (Ocean-View) Hotel	8 Huanshan Road, Yantai	0535-6888405
Yantai Pacific Hotel	74 Shifu Street, Yantai	0535-6588866
Golden Beach Hotel	Stone Old Man National Tourism Resort, Qingdao	0532-88897888
Debao Garden Hotel	122 Hong Kong Road, Qingdao	0532-85899898
Dongfang Hotel	4 College Road, Qingdao	0532-82865888
Zhanqiao Hotel	31 Taiping Road, Qingdao	0532-82888666
Jinan Hotel	Intersection of Jinan's Jinsi and Weiliu Roads	0531-87938981
Qilu Hotel	8 Qianfoshan Road	0531-82966888
Taishan Hotel	26 Hongmen Road, Tai'an	0538-8224678
Tai'an Dongfang Hotel	65 Longtan Road, Tai'an	0538-6216208

It is rare to have such beautiful scenery in the middle of a town. (From ImagineChina)

Seventy-two Springs

Jinan is described as having "springs and weeping willows in every household" because of its numerous springs. The expression "seventy-two springs" originated in the "pillar of Famous Springs," written during the Jin Dynasty and recorded in the book *Qisheng* by Yu Qin of the Yuan Dynasty (1206–1368). Each of the 72 springs is listed by name on the pillar, but the actual number of springs in Jinan is much greater, for there are more than a hundred in the city area alone. Here, the number 72 indicates "plenty."

Qianfo Mountain

Qianfo Mountain, one of the three most famous scenic spots in Jinan, is in the southern part of the city, with an altitude of only 946 feet and an area of about 641,000 square miles. Originally called Lishan Mountain, the name Qianfo Mountain came from the numerous Buddha figures carved on the mountain and the construction of Qianfo Temple during the Kaihuang period (581–600) during the Sui Dynasty.

On the northern side of Qianfo Mountain is Wanfo (Ten-Thousand Buddha) Cave containing the four great Chinese grottoes, where tourists can get a look at the magnificent figure-carving skills of the Northern Wei, Tang, and Song dynasties.

Liubu

Situated in the southern part of Jinan on the ancient border between the states of Qi and Lu, Liubu has been a crucial trading place in Shandong since the Sui (581–618) and Tang (618–907) dynasties. Here you will find natural beauty, cultural artifacts, and scenic sites, among which are the famous Simen (Four Gates) Pagoda, Longhu (Dragon and Tiger) Pagoda, Jiuding (Nine Roofs) Pagoda, and Qianfo Cliff, collectively referred to as "three pagodas and a cliff."

The old water supply in Shui Lianxia Scenic Area, Liubu. (From ImagineChina)

Lingyan (Magic Rock) Temple

Lingyan Temple is at the foot of a mountain in southeastern Changqing County, with Mount Tai to the southeast. Built during the Northern Wei Dynasty and at its most splendid during the Tang and Song dynasties, the temple once held more than 40 halls, 500 meditation rooms, and around 500 monks. It ranks as one of the most famous temples in China, the other three being Guoqing Temple in Tiantai (Zhejiang Province), Yuquan Temple in Jiangling (Hubei Province), and Qixia Temple in Nanjing (Jiangsu Province).

The residence of Pu Songling that tourists see today was restored in 1954 to its original appearance. (From ImagineChina)

To get to Lingyan Temple, take the bus for Tai'an and get off in Wande, then proceed to Lingyan Temple by taxi. In Jinan there are also special tourist buses to Lingyan Temple.

In Lingyan Temple there are precious cultural relics such as the rock grotto sculptures dating back to the Northern Wei Dynasty, Pizhi Pagoda built during the Tang Dynasty, and clay luohan (arhat) figures from the Song Dynasty. (From Quanjing)

Tombstone Temple of the Guo Family in Xiaotang (Hall of Brotherhood) Mountain

This temple is located on Xiaotang Mountain, south of the village of Xiaoli, in Changqing County in Jinan. Built at the beginning of the East Han Dynasty, it is a sacrificial hall in front of a tomb and is the earliest existing building above ground level in China. The temple faces south and forms a 12-foot-long, 7-foot-wide rectangle. It is 8.5 feet high, built entirely of black stone. Each of the structural elements in the temple has been decorated with Tibetan-style engravings, such as figures, hanging curtains, and diamonds. The figures are cut directly into the raw material, with no background decoration, which is unique among the engraved stones of the Han Dynasty.

Former Residence of Pu Songling

This is a quiet and simply designed house located in the village of Pujia, in Hongshan, Zichuan District in Zibo. The house has four courtyards, with a west-wing yard and a gate facing south. In the northern courtyard there are three sitting rooms, including Pu Songling's birthplace and his study, Liaozhai Room. Behind Liaozhai Room are six exhibition rooms, displaying a variety of works by domestic and foreign researchers into the history of Pu Songling as well as more than 100 pieces of calligraphy, paintings, and dedications from prominent cultural personalities, calligraphers, and artists.

Liuquan (Willow Spring)

Liuquan, also called Manjing, is situated in the valley about 328 feet from Pujia, in the Zichuan District. It is said that Pu Songling often stayed here, offering tea to passerbys and collecting materials for his masterpiece, *Liaozhai Zhiyi.* Pu Songling loved this place and referred to himself as the "Liuquan Hermit," after its name. Longwang (Dragon King) Temple, also called Manjing Temple, once stood in the north of Liuquan. Its west-wing hall originally held the Pillar of the Newly Built Longwang Temple, said to have been written by Pu Songling. Now the temple is gone (date unknown), and the pillar has been moved to the former residence of Pu Songling.

Grottoes on Yunmen Mountain

These grottoes are located to the northeast of Wangjia village (Wangjia Zhuang), about 2.5 miles southeast of Qingzhou. The 272 stone figures are carved in five grottoes of different sizes on the southern cliff of Yunmen Mountain. The first and second shrines from the west are quite large, and the bodhisattva figures there are masterpieces of Sui Dynasty sculpture. The third, fourth, and fifth caves are small, with similar subject matter and style; carved in each grotto are Buddha, two bodhisattvas, two Buddhist warrior attendants, and two Heavenly Kings.

Grottoes on Camel Mountain (Tuo Shan)

These grottoes are situated on Camel Mountain, 3.7 miles southwest of Qingzhou. Six hundred thirty-eight stone Buddhas, big and small, are located in five grottoes and one shrine, which extend from north to south on the southeastern cliff of the main peak of Camel Mountain. Being the largest stone figure group in eastern China, the cliff grottoes of Camel Mountain contain a collection of works from three dynasties: the Northern Zhou, the Sui, and the Tang.

Dai Temple (Dai Miao)

Also called Tai Temple (Tai Miao), Dai is located in the northern part of the city of Tai'an with Mount Tai to its north. It is dedicated to the god of Mount Tai, where ancient emperors lived and carried out ceremonies when they came to hold the Fengshan Sacrifices. It stretches 1,331 feet from north to south and 777 feet from east to west. Its design is a replica of the traditional imperial palace and is divided into eastern, middle, and western parts. The centerpiece, Palace of Heavenly Blessings (Tiankuang Dian), is located at the back of Dai Temple; it was built during the Song Dynasty and renamed Junji Palace later in the Ming Dynasty.

Dai Temple Arch (Dai Miao Fang), located in front of Zhengyang Gate (Zhengyang Men) at the Dai Temple, was built in 1672 in the Qing Dynasty, with a multiple-beam-and-four-column design and relief carvings. On the Drum Changing Stones (Huan Gu Shi) at its front and back are eight lifelike crouching stone lions. (From ImagineChina)

Southern Heavenly Gate, Mount Tai. (From Quanjing)

Mount Tai

Mount Tai, the first of China's five great mountains, is located at the center of Shandong Province, surrounded by Jinan, Changqing, Feicheng, and Tai'an, with an area of 164 square miles. Its main peak is located in Tai'an, at an altitude of a little more than 5,000 feet. Mount Tai is famous not only for its beautiful natural scenery but also for its reputation as the only mountain on which ancient emperors carried out the Fengshan ceremony. Dating back from the Xia and Shang dynasties, there are a total of 72 kings and emperors who came to Mount Tai to meet their subjects, consolidate their rule over the country, and leave stone inscriptions. UNESCO listed it as a World Natural and Cultural Heritage Site in 1987.

The best times to watch the sunrise on the peak of Mount Tai are around the summer and winter solstices.

Qingdao Region

Best Time to Travel

Qingdao has mountains at its back, and the sea to its front, and it abounds in trees, with a short summer of only 65 days. The best months for visiting are from April to October, and the peak tourist season is from July to September.

Shopping Tips

Zhongshan Road is the major shopping street in Qingdao. It is a good idea for tourists to buy seafood in state-run seafood shops beside Guohuo Plaza, where both the price and the quality of the seafood can be guaranteed.

Zhanqiao Pier (Qianhai Zhanqiao)

Zhanqiao Pier, the symbol of Qingdao, lies at the tip of Qingdao Bay off Zhongshan Road, the most prosperous street in Qingdao. It enjoys a reputation as being "the rainbow that reaches far away" because it extends quite a long distance from the beach to the water. It was originally built as a wooden

The decorated Zhanqiao Pier has recently been renovated and developed and is now an amazing place where people can enjoy themselves and watch the sea. (From ImagineChina)

bridge in 1890 and was later rebuilt as a reinforced concrete structure. Zhanqiao Pier is now 26 feet wide, 1,444 feet long, and holds a two-story octagonal pavilion called Billow Returning Pavilion (Hui Lan Ge). It is in typical Chinese style with golden tiles and vermeil walls, a helmet-shaped top, and upturned eaves.

Eight-Great-Pass (Badaguan) Villas Area

Located to the east of Huiquan Corner of Qingdao, Eight-Great-Pass Villas Area is a resort combining the high-class art of world architecture and the unique art of courtyard gardening. It gets its name from the eight roads (now ten) named after famous passes in China: Shanhai, Jiayu, Wusheng, Ningwu, Juyong, Shao, Zijing, Zhengyang, Hangu, and Linhuai.

> To the south of Eight Great Passes is Small Fish Mountain (Xiaoyu Shan). It faces Huiquan Bay, opposite the Billow Returning Pavilion on Zhanqiao Pier in the distance. The works of architecture on the mountain are built according to the shape of the mountain, highlighting the theme of the sea and the pattern of fish. Thus all the architectural works combine into an organic whole that reveals the beauty of nature, of the architecture, and of art.

Bathing Beach

The seashore at Qingdao has 12 beaches. Located in Huiquan Bay is Beach No.1, which is reputed to be the best in East Asia because of its fine sand and clear, calm water. The Stone Old Man Bathing Beach, located in Stone Old Man National Tourism Resort, is the largest beach in Qingdao, stretching 3,609 feet from east to west with a width of more than 600 feet.

> The bathing beach is admission free, but tourists are expected to pay for freshwater baths, lockers, and rented swimming articles.

Laoshan Mountain (Lao Shan) Scenery Park

Laoshan Mountain, known as China's premier mountain by the sea, is located in Laoshan District, Qingdao, and faces the Huanghai Sea. Its main peak is Gigantic Peak (Ju Feng) at 3,717 feet above sea level. The scenic park is made up of nine

The coastline at Laoshan Mountain is 11 miles long, with 18 islands just off the beach. When tourists walk on the beach, to their left is the roaring sea extending to the horizon, and on the right are peaks and rocks of amazing shapes. By just turning your head, you can enjoy the beautiful scenery of both the mountain and the sea. (From ImagineChina)

sections: Jufeng, Liuqing, Shangqing, Taiqing, Chessboard Stone (Qipanshi), Yangkou, Northern Nine Waters (Beijiushui), Hualou, and Dengying.

Entrance to Huayan Si Temple in Laoshan (From ImagineChina)

Stone Forest (Shi Lin) on Horse Mountain (Ma Shan)

Horse Mountain, located about 4 miles west of Jimo, abounds in Anshan porphyrite, unusually grayish green or grayish brown in color, which is the magma that solidified after it erupted from the earth about 100 million years ago. Anshan porphyrite makes excellent raw material for stone architectural ornaments. The geological junction at the southwestern part of the mountain consists of column-shaped cuboids, which stand straight as a thick forest, hence the name Horse Mountain Stone Forest after this amazing scene.

Yantai Region

Best Time to Travel

Neighboring mountains and the sea, this area is pleasant in summer and cool in winter, which makes Yantai an ideal summer resort. The best months to visit are from April to October.

Shopping Tips

Keeping up with the thriving Korean trends, the Korean Clothing City in Yantai is worth a visit. It offers a wide selection of clothes, shoes, and hats that enjoy worldwide popularity. These clothes are well made and very inexpensive.

Yuhuangding Park

Yuhuangding Park, also called "small Penglai (Xiao Penglai)," is located on a 236-foot-high hill at the center of the Zhifu district, in Yantai, where you can find several magnificent architectural works. Originally called the Jade Emperor Summit, Yuhuangding Temple was originally built in the Yuan Dynasty. In 1876, the Jade Emperor Temple (Yuhuang Miao) was rebuilt into an independent courtyard surrounded by low walls. The temple has three yards, which contain the gate to the monastery, the middle palace, the back hall, and the east and west wings. On each side of the gate is a bell tower and a drum

Scenery in Yuhuangding Park (From Colphoto)

tower with upturned eaves and a bucket arch. There is a statue of the Jade Emperor in the middle hall.

> At No. 3 Park Road (Gongyuan Lu), east of Xianhe Park in the eastern part of Yantai suburb, is a shop selling red porcelain teapots and other ancient-style utensils for daily use, appreciation, and collection. This shop is worth a visit for souvenirs and antiques.

Fujian Guild Hall (Fujian Huiguan)

Fujian Guild Hall, also called Heavenly Queen's Palace for Short Stays (Tianhou Xinggong), is in Yugang Street in Yantai. Built in 1884 with funds raised by maritime merchants and boatmen, the guild hall covers 1,351 square miles. It is composed of a gate to the monastery, a large palace, a back palace, a theater, and east and west wings. The whole building is of the southern Fujian construction style, with wonderful wood and stone carvings, which make the building a must-see.

Penglai Pavilion (Penglai Ge)

Penglai Pavilion sits on the cliff of Danya Mountain (Danya Shan), close to the sea north of the city of Penglai and was built in the Song Dynasty (1056–1063) with a total area of 12,664 square miles. Many towers and pavilions stand high on the cliff as if hanging in midair with the sea below, which earns this place the reputation as paradise on earth. Together with the Yellow Crane Tower (Huanghe Lou), Yueyang Tower (Yueyang Lou), and Prince Teng Pavilion (Tengwang Ge), Penglai Pavilion is one of the four famous pavilions in China. Constructed with double-deck wood, it faces the south. In the east is Sugong Temple (Sugong Ci), in the south Billow Viewing Pavilion (Guanlan Ting), and in the east Wind Shelter Pavilion (Bifeng Ting), also called Mirage Pavilion (Haishi Ting). The walls of these halls and pavilions bear couplets, calligraphy, and paintings of well-known personages from dynasties, in addition to more than 200 stone inscriptions about the view.

Penglai Pavilion is surrounded by architectural works of many different styles. Below the pavilion is the Fairy Bridge (Xianren Qiao) from which, according to legend, eight immortals crossed the sea. (From ImagineChina)

> To the east of Penglai Pavilion is the famous Penglai Water City (Penglai Shui Cheng), or Dengzhou Ancient Port (Dengzhou Gu Gang), which is the oldest intact naval base in China.

Mu Family Manor

Situated in the village of Du, in the town of Guzhen, Qixia city, Mu Family Manor is often called Manor of Mu's Second Dark Son (Mu'erheizi Zhuangyuan). Construction on it began in 1723 and was gradually completed during 200 consecutive years of building by the Mu family. The manor is known as the "small Imperial Palace among the people." Facing south, the manor covers an area of about 215,278 square feet and contains more than 480 rooms, which is the largest intact and most typical feudal landlord manor in northern China.

Long Island National Nature Reserve

Located in Long Island County (Changdao Xian), Long Island National Nature Reserve is made up of 32 islands, with a coastline of about 91 miles. This place is called Fairy Mountain (Xian Shan) because of its beautiful scenery and pleasing year-round climate. Also called the Hotel of Migrants, the pristine natural environment makes this reserve a stopping place for migratory birds.

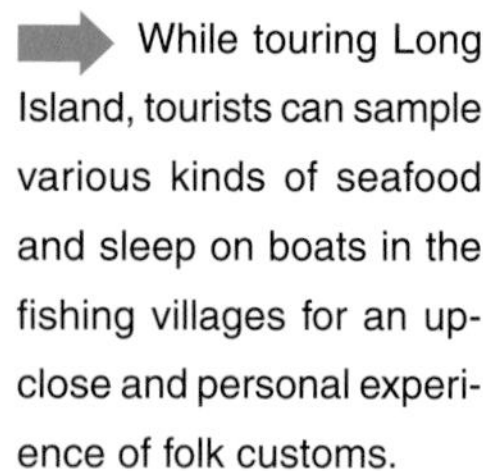

While touring Long Island, tourists can sample various kinds of seafood and sleep on boats in the fishing villages for an up-close and personal experience of folk customs.

Chengshan Cape (Chengshan Tou)

Chengshan Cape, also called "the end of the sky," is at the very eastern tip of Chengshan Mountain in the town of Longxu Island (Longxu Dao), in Rongcheng city. Chengshan Cape is surrounded by water in three directions. It faces South Korea across the sea and has been known as "the place where the sun rises" since ancient times in addition to "China's Cape of Good Hope" because it is located at the easternmost place where the land and sea meet. The highest point of Chengshan Cape is 656 feet above sea level. The magnificent blue sea, the majestic steep cliffs, and the snowy surf crashing against the cliff make this place an ideal tourist resort.

Chengshan Cape has long been believed by ancient Chinese to be where the god of the sun lives; many of the ancient emperors came here to worship the sun god and watch the sunrise. (From Colphoto)

Long Island is a major area for avian research. (From CFP)

It is extremely dangerous to swim in the sea below Chengshan Cape because of the undercurrents.

Office of Commander in Chief of the Beiyang Fleet

This is the command center of the first modern navy of China and the only senior military yamen of the Qing Dynasty still intact. Located on Liugong Island (Liugong Dao), Weihai city, the office occupies 6,564 square miles. Twelve years into Emperor Guangxu's reign in the Qing Dynasty, the government set up the Beiyang Fleet and located the office on Liugong Island, which was the headquarters of the fleet, habitually called the Beiyang Fleet Commander's Yamen. Backing against the mountain in the north and facing the sea in the south, the yamen is a brick-and-wood structure surrounded by a long wall. Along its ordinate axis there are three courtyards in the front, the middle, and the back. The whole building group is decorated with upturned eaves and painted beams.

Commander in Chief Ding Ruchang's residence is about 700 feet southwest of the yamen.

Jining Tourist Area

Best Time to Travel

April to June are the optimal months to visit.

Shopping Tips

Qufu Queli pedestrian–only street, east of the Temple of Confucius, is a shopping mall with all kinds of shops and department stores, and several food courts. The fun here is in people-watching and strolling among the different shops.

Jining Iron Pagoda

Jining Iron Pagoda is situated in the former Temple of Iron Pagoda (Tieta Si) on the north side of Tietasi Street in Jining. Originally called Chongjue Temple or Shijia Temple, it was built in 1105 as a votive temple by Xu Yong'an's wife, whose maiden name was Chang. Made of pig iron, the pagoda originally had seven stories, with two more added in 1581. It is perfectly structured, displaying a high level of ancient Chinese smelting skills and architectural art.

Jining Taibai Tower

Jining Taibai Tower is on the northern bank of the ancient canal in Jining, which is the former residence of the famous poet Li Bai of the Tang Dynasty. Between 740 and 755, Li Bai moved from Anlu, Hubei, to Jining and lived there for 16 years with his wife and his daughter, Pingyang. The original tower was destroyed in wartime; the one tourists see today was rebuilt much later. It is a majestic and magnificent two-story tower over 65 feet high, with upturned eaves and xieshan-style roof.

In the Cemetery of Confucius there are more than 100,000 graves, 85 pairs of pillars, 400 tombstones, and about 42,000 trees, which have lasted for 2,400 years. (From ImagineChina)

Kong Family Mansion, the Temple, and the Cemetery of Confucius (Kong Fu, Kong Miao, and Kong Lin)

Called collectively the Three Kongs (San Kong), these three complexes are a symbol of China's long-standing tradition of holding Confucius and Confucianism in esteem. The Temple of Confucius, also called Temple of the Sage (Zhisheng Miao), recalls the time

The Kong Family Mansion is the office and residence of the eldest son borne by the legal wife of the Kong Family. It is the third-largest mansion after the palaces of the emperors of the Ming and Qing dynasties. (From Quanjing)

when sacrifices were offered to Confucius in the feudal dynasties of ancient China. At the center of the city of Qufu is a large group of majestic historic buildings in typical oriental architectural style. The Three Kongs have been listed as UNESCO World Heritage sites since 1994.

Temple of Yan Hui (Yan Miao)

Dedicated to Yan Hui, the Temple of Yan Hui, also called Fusheng Temple, is located at the northern end of Louxiang Street, in the town of Gucheng, in Qufu. During the Jin Dynasty, the temple was located in the northeast of the ancient city of the state of Lu. At the end of the Dade period of the Yuan Dynasty, the original temple was destroyed and a new one was built in Louxiang Street. In 1594 the temple was completely renovated, laying the foundation for the scale of the temple today. There are 25 buildings of the Yuan, Ming, and Qing dynasties, with 159 rooms and more than 60 stone tablets.

Tourists can take Bus No.1 to the temple or walk there from the Kong Family Mansion along Drum Tower Street (Gulou Dajie).

Liangshan Po Ruins

Liangshan Po Ruins, in Liangshan County, enjoys worldwide fame because of the Chinese classic novel *Water Margin*. Liangshan Mountain (Liang Shan) neighbors the Yellow River in the west, the Beijing-Hangzhou Grand Canal in the east, and Dongping Lake and the ruins of Liangshan Po in the north. In the last years of the Northern Song Dynasty, Song Jiang made friends with heroes across the country, and they gathered here to fight the injustice of the rulers at the time. Backed by the natural barrier of Liangshan Po, they became famous for their rebellious efforts.

Zhougong Temple

Zhougong Temple, located on Gaofu Street in the eastern part of Qufu city, was first built in 1008 and then enlarged and renovated during the Song, Yuan, Ming, and Qing dynasties. There are three courtyards and 57 halls, pavilions, and other rooms. The yards are covered with ancient junipers, cypresses, Chinese toons, and Chinese scholar trees, which create a magnificent sight.

One-Hundred-Lion Arch (Baishi Fang) and One-Hundred-Year Longevity Arch (Baishou Fang)

Located on Paifang Street (Paifang Jie), these structures display the typical stone-carving architecture of the Qing Dynasty. The arch is 46 feet high and 30 feet wide, with four columns, three parts, and five decks completely made of stone. In front and at the back of the arch are eight columns, on which are carved 100 lions. The other arch, also called the Arch of the Zhu Family (Zhujia Paifang), is located 328 feet southwest of the lion arch, and gets its name from the 100 different versions of the Chinese character for "longevity" carved in relief on the center and margins of the square column of the arch.

Making Chinese pancakes (From CFP)

Shandong Style

Local Delicacies

Rolled Pancakes with Chinese Onion

Rolled pancake with chinese onion is a dish that best represents the local flavor of Shandong delicacies. The pancake is made from millet flour or cornmeal. The pancakes from Tai'an and the Chinese onions from Zhangqiu of Jinan are the best.

Crisp Jujube of Liaocheng

Crisp jujube is the traditional snack of Liaocheng. It is made by soaking, washing, sunning, and drying the large jujube fruit of Liaocheng. Crisp jujube is characterized by its aromatic and sweet taste and has been a familiar snack for more than 100 years.

Huoshao Made by Stick

Huoshao made by stick is a popular snack from Weifang. Huoshao is actually a kind of baked wheat cake that is very hard. The dough used to make the snack is so tough that a stick is necessary to knead it—hence the name of this snack.

San

San is a special snack from the Linyi area. It is popular because it is aromatic and spicy, rich but not greasy. It also has the function of warding off the wind and cold, stimulating the appetite and improving the digestion.

Huoshao Made by Stick (From Colphoto)

San literally means a "thick meat soup." It is said that san was originally a breakfast food of the ancient Huis living in the western area. In the Yuan Dynasty, a Hui couple came to Linyi to sell san, which was called meat paste at that time. It was named san later in the Ming Dynasty. But according to the county annals of Linyi, san was created by the Linyi people during the last years of the Ming Dynasty and developed into a unique delicacy of Linyi later. There were only 8 san shops in Linyi before 1949, but now there are more than 100. San should be hot, spicy, aromatic, and rich if you want to drink it. A bowl of hot san, together with some deep-fried twisted dough sticks and baked wheat cakes, is an indisputably delicious breakfast. There are three kinds of san: Chicken san, mutton san, and beef san, of which mutton san is the most common and chicken san is the most unusual.

Sesame Seed Cake of Zhoucun

The sesame seed cake of Zhoucun has a long history and is famous for its thinness, aroma, flakiness, and crispness. The ingredients used to make this sesame seed cake are very simple: flour, sesame seeds, sugar, and salt. There are special requirements for the process. The recipe, how you form the cake, and the baking are critical factors, the most important of which is baking. The baking temperature determines the quality of the cake. In the last years of the Qing Dynasty, the royals frequently ordered tributes consisting of the sesame seed cake of Zhoucun. At that time, Badayang, a famous shop in Shandong, ordered boxes of this cake and delivered them to other areas as very desirable gifts. In 1951, the Zhoucun people conveyed their solicitude for the

(From Colphoto)

Chinese People's Voluntary Army during the war to resist U.S. aggression in Korea with the sesame seed cake of Zhoucun as their gift.

Braised Rabbit Head

Braised rabbit head is a popular local snack in the Mengyin area. Rabbit heads (of 3- to 4-month-old rabbits), along with dozens of Chinese traditional medicines from Mengshan and a like number of procedures are required to cook the dish. Braised rabbit head, with its unique flavor and attractive color and luster, tastes hot, spicy, salty, and delicious. It is also nourishing and improves your complexion.

Deep-Fried Luosi Cake

Deep-fried Luosi cake is a traditional delicacy of Jinan. It is crisp, tender, and aromatic. Legend has it that three brothers from the Xu family brought this snack from Nanjing 100 years ago. In order to meet the taste of the local Jinan people, the brothers improved the ingredients in the cake, and it soon became so popular in the north of China that it was even called the "Luosi Cake of Xu." Later, many restaurants began to imitate it and deep-fried Luosi cake became a traditional delicacy of Jinan.

Kai sculpture (From CFP)

Local Specialties of Shandong

Shandong Embroidery

Shandong embroidery was renowned even during the Spring and Autumn Period, called *Qiwan* and *Lugao* at that time. Hair and silk embroidery is the representative form of Shandong embroidery, which is produced by combining hair and silk threads by hand. The subjects used for Shandong embroidery consist of figures, birds, and beasts as well as Chinese wash paintings. Shandong embroidery is famous for its exquisite style, fine materials, and excellent handiwork.

Feather Painting

This art had once been lost for a long period. In 1960s, the craft of feather painting was revived by the Jinan Arts and Crafts Research Institute. It characteristically employs vivid images drawn from various subjects.

Kai Sculpture

Kai sculpture is made of Kai (a kind of tree) wood. It is said that after the death of Confucius, one of his disciples, Zigong, transplanted Kai beside the tomb and carved the wood into the figure of Confucius to express his sorrow and grief. Kai wood is hard yet pliable, close-grained, and golden in color. The sculptures made of Kai wood are pliable and exquisite. Kai sculpture products include traditional walking sticks and Ruyi as well as statues of Confucius, brush pots, and screens.

Zhangyu Wine

Yantai Zhangyu Wine Company was founded in 1892 by Zhang Bishi, a famous overseas Chinese merchant. Zhangyu Wine Company is the first industrial production company for wine in China. Its products include brandy, wine, champagne, medicinal wine, and white liquor.

Tsingtao Beer

Tsingtao Beer is the most famous brand of beer in China. It is produced using high-quality materials and special yeast by applying classic brewing technologies. It is famous for its pleasant aroma and well-balanced taste. It is now being sold in the domestic market as well as abroad.

Feather painting (From ImagineChina)

Jiangxi

Geography at a Glance

Jiangxi is called "Gan" for short. It is located to the south of the middle-lower reaches of the Changjiang River, neighboring Zhejiang and Fujian in the east, Hubei and Anhui in the north, and Hunan in the west, with a total area of 62,000 square miles and a population of 41.4 million (2000 census). Jiangxi features mountainous and hilly areas, surrounded by Wuyi Mountain (Wuyi Shan), Luoxiao Mountain (Luoxiao Shan), and Nanling Mountain (Nanling Shan). In the northern part is Poyang Lake (Poyang Hu) Plain and in the middle is a hilly area. The largest river system is the Ganjiang River (Gan Jiang), with the rivers of Wujiang, Xinjiang, Raojiang, and Xiujiang following it, all of which enter Poyang Lake and then the Changjiang River.

Jiangxi is located near the Tropic of Cancer and has a subtropical monsoon climate. There are four distinct seasons, with a climate that is changeable in spring; moist and rainy at the end of spring and the beginning of summer; sunny, hot, and dry in summer; and cold and dry in winter. The yearly average temperature here is 65°F, with an average annual precipitation of 39 to 71 inches.

(From Quanjing)

Featured Cuisine

Ganzhou stir-fried pork, vagabond chicken, rice cakes boiled with shrimp, stewed Chinese yam and pork, coin-shaped Chinese yam pancakes, crisp fried chukar leg, cuttlefish, rice-dough noodles, Nanchang raisin-like fermented soybeans, Nanchang dried meat, stewed white duck, Nankang roasted lamb ribs, dog meat stewed in an earthen bowl, Xingguo steamed fish slices with rice flour, Dahui pancakes, pancake-shaped candy made of rice and sesame.

A delicate porcelain bottle produced in Jingde Town. (From Colphoto)

Featured Commodities

Special Local Products

Silver fish of Poyang Lake, Donggu Mountain (Donggu Shan) pickled fish, Dongshan Mountain life-prolonging (Yanshou) wine, Shangrao Daqu wine, Lushan Mountain cloud-and-mist (Yunwu) tea, Wuyuan green tea, Dog-Head Mountain (Gougunao Shan) tea, Jinggang Mountain (Jinggang Shan) green tea.

Local handicrafts

Lidu writing brushes, Wuyuan Dragon-tail inkstones, Jingde Town porcelain, Jinggang Mountain bambooware, Yichun bodiless lacquerware, Wuyuan Chinese ink, golden-star inkstones, Jade Mountain (Yu Shan) inkstones with silk-like grain, Lianshi paper, Jiangxi handmade paper, Nanchang porcelain painting, Ruijing Jade-button (Yukou) paper, Maobian paper, Wanzai Summer (Xia) cloth, Yinchuan tan-sheep brand jacquard blankets, snuff pots, folding screens.

Transportation Tips

By Bus

There are 10 national highways and 91 provincial highways, which form a network that covers the whole province and connects its neighboring six provinces, with Nanchang, the capital city of Jiangxi, as its center. Within this network there is the Beijing-Nanchang-Fuzhou National Highway and the Shanghai-Ruili National Highway, in addition to many other high-quality highways and roads that connect the entire province with most major cities. The total length of Jiangxi highways is over 621 miles, and six other interprovincial highways are under construction.

Notes 

❶ The folk customs in Jiangxi display primitive simplicity. There are ancient-style houses in fishing villages and old towns in southern and northeastern Jiangxi and beside Poyang Lake.

❷ Jiangxi is one of the regions south of the Changjiang River and in ancient times it was known for its favorable geographical position, called "head of the Wu State, tail of the Chu state, Gate of Guangdong, and yard of Fujian". Its unique geographical environment, together with its numerous rivers and plentiful rainfall, earns it the appellation of "a fertile land of fish and rice south of the Changjiang River."

POPULAR FESTIVALS

Bean Curd Festival

Lunar December 28 is the festival for the porcelain workers of Duchang origin, whose surnames are Yu and Zou. On this day all the feast dishes are made of bean curd.

Asking-for-Candles

This is one of the traditional spring festivities unique to the town of Jingde. From lunar December 30 to January 15, children go in twos and threes to every household or store to ask for candles with a dragon-head lantern while striking a little gong.

The International Dragon Boat Festival

This is held in Jiujiang annually on lunar May 5 with water festivities such as a dragon boat race, water skiing performances, and more.

Making-Peace-Kiln

This folk festival is unique to Jingde Town, with a history of more than 100 years. On the night of Mid-Autumn Day, every household in the town makes a "peace kiln" (*Taiping Yao*) and lights a fire.

International Pottery and Porcelain Festival

Held in Jingde Town annually from October 11 to 14, this festival features activities such as porcelain shows with judging and exhibitions of porcelain-making skills.

By Train

Jiangxi has within its borders nine arterial railways including Beijing-Kowloon, Zhejiang-Jiangxi, Yingtan-Xiamen, Ningxia-Jiangxi, Xiangtang-Jiujiang, Xiangtang-Ji'an, and Wuchang-Jiujiang lines, as well as more than ten branch railways.

By Plane

Jiangxi has five airports: Xiangtang Airport in Nanchang, Huangjin Airport in Ganzhou, Lukou Airport in Ji'an, Luojia Airport in Jingde Town, and Mahuiling Airport in Jiujiang. There are flights to Beijing, Shanghai, Guangzhou, Wuhan, Xi'an, Chengdu, Fuzhou, Xiamen, Shenzhen, and Haikou, in addition to chartered airliners to Hong Kong.

By Water

Jiangxi is famous for being a world of water, dotted with lakes and crisscrossed by rivers. The Ganjiang River and Poyang Lake are its major waterways, connecting 62 other rivers (such as the Wujiang, the Xinjiang, the Raojiang, and the Xiujiang rivers and forming a useful and convenient network. The six major ports in Jiangxi are Jiujiang, Nanchang, Zhangshu, Ji'an, Ganzhou, and Boyang, with Nanchang as the largest and busiest.

Recommended Routes

Classical Routes

Five-day tour of Nanchang, Wuyuan, and Jingde Town

Day 1 Arrival in Nanchang. Lodging: Jiangxi Hotel.

Day 2 Nanchang→Jiujiang. Lodging: Jiujiang Hotel.

Day 3 Jiujiang→Wuyuan→Jiangwan→Yan Village (Yan Cun)→Rainbow Bridge

→Jingde Town (Jingde Zhen) Porcelain Museum→Porcelain Street of Jingde Town. Lodging: Joint Venture Hotel of Jingde Town.

Day 4 Jingde Town→Memorial Hall to the Nanchang August 1 Uprising. Lodging: Jiangxi Hotel.

Day 5 End of tour.

Four-day holiday tour of Fuzhou

Day 1 Fuzhou→Earthly Paradise (Dongtianfudi)→Magu Mountain (Magu Shan)→ Spoonful Fountain (Yishaozhiduo) →Two-Flying-Jade-Ribbon Waterfall (Yulian Shuangfei)→Zixiao Taoist Temple (Zixiao Guan)→Orange orchards. Lodging: Nanfeng County Inn.

Day 2 Nanfeng→Dingxin Temple (Dingxin Si)→Temple of the Crown Prince (Taizi Miao)→Wild Goose Pagoda (Yan Ta)→ Penholder Mountain (Bijia Shan)→Toad Peak (Hama Feng)→Dinosaur Exhibition Hall→Tai Ji Rock (Taiji Yan) Scenery Park. Lodging: Yihuang County Inn.

Day 3 Yihuang→Le'an Five Jinshi Arch (Le'an Wugui Fang)→No. 1 Scholar Tower (Zhuangyuan Lou)→Village within a Village (Cun Zhong Cun) →Tang Xianzu Memorial Hall. Lodging: Yuming Hotel.

Day 4 Wang Anshi Memorial Hall→Third-Largest Cathedral in China. End of tour.

Traditional Routes

Four-day tour of Lushan Mountain

Day 1 Arrival in Jiujiang.

Day 2 Jiujiang→Lushan Mountain→ Flower Pathway (Hua Jing) Park→Brocade Valley (Jinxiu Gu)→Broken Bridge (Duan Qiao)→Perilous Peak (Xian Feng) →Immortals Cavern (Xianren Dong)→ Lulin Lake (Lulin Hu)→ Yellow Dragon Temple (Huanglong Si)→Yellow Dragon Pool (Huanglong Tan)→Black Dragon Pool (Wulong Tan).

Day 3 Hanpo Pass (Hanpo Kou)→Five Elderly Men Peak (Wulao Feng)→Three-Stage Spring (Sandie Quan).

Day 4 End of tour.

Six-day tour of Nanchang and Lushan Mountain

Day 1 Arrival in Nanchang.

Day 2 Prince Teng Pavilion (Tengwang Ge)→August 1st Square→Memorial Tower to Nanchang August 1st Uprising→Lushan Mountain.

Day 3 Yellow Dragon Pool→Black Dragon Pool→Three Precious Trees (San Bao Shu)→Lulin Bridge (Lulin Qiao)→ Lulin Lake (Lulin Hu)→Museum.

Day 4 Hanpo Pass (Hanpo Kou)→ Five Elderly Men Peak (Wulao Feng)→Three-Stage Spring (Sandie Quan)→Botanical garden.

Day 5 Flower Pathway (Hua Jing) Park→ Brocade Valley (Jinxiu Gu)→ Immortal's Cavern (Xianren Dong)→ Perilous Peak (Xian Feng)→ Heavenly Pool (Tian Chi)→ Imperial Tablet Pavilion (Yubei Ting)→ Dragon Head Cliff (Longshou Ya)→ Heavenly Bridge (Tian Qiao).

Day 6 End of tour.

Three-day tour of Wuyuan

Day 1 Lake of Mandarin Duck (Yuanyang Hu)→Ancient buildings of Xucun Village (Xu Cun)→Ancient firs of Wengong Mountain (Wengong Shan)→ Gaosha Pendant-shaped red carp fishery→ Wuyuan Museum.

Day 2 Likeng→ Temple of the Yu Family in Wangkou→ Jiangwan→ ancient buildings of Up and Down Xiaoqi (Shangxia Xiaoqi)→ scenery of Jiangling→ ancient village of Qingyuan.

Day 3 Ancient buildings of Yancun Village (Yan Cun)→ Qinghua Rainbow Bridge→Tuochuan Likeng official residence→Zheyuan Longtian Pagoda (Longtian Ta)→Former residence of Zhan Tianyou in Lukeng→No.1 camphor tree of regions south of the Changjiang River (located in Hongguan)→ Ancient villages of the Ming and Qing dynasties. End of tour.

Two-day tour of Jinggang Mountain

Day 1 Ciping→ Big Well Village (Da Jing) → Small Well Village (Xiao Jing)→ Dragon Pool (Long Tan)→ Five Major Sentry Posts (Wudashaokou)→ Maoping→ Ciping.

Day 2 Ciping→Stone Swallow Cave (Shiyan Dong)→ Five Horses Peaks (Wuma Chaotian)→ Five Fingers Peak (Wuzhi Feng) → Penholder Mountain (Bijia Shan). End of tour.

One-day tour of Nanchang

Prince Teng Pavilion (Tengwang Ge)→ Memorial Hall to Badashanren→ August 1st Square→ Memorial Hall to Nanchang August 1st Uprising→Nanchang Port→Ancient town of Wuqi.

Self-Guided Tours

The "Red Tour"

Start from Jinggang Mountain and end in Ruijin by way of Suichuan, Ganzhou, and Yudu. Major scenic spots: Huangyangjie, Big Well Village, Small Well Village, Dragon Pool Waterfall, Yugu Terrace (Yugu Tai), ancient city wall, Bajing Terrace (Bajing Tai), Tongtian Rock (Tongtian Yan), Ruijin, former site of the Soviet government of China in Yeping, former site of the first national congress of the Soviet Republic of China, former site of Xinhua Press, Memorial Tower to the Martyrs, reviewing stand, Shazhouba Village, grand hall of the interim Soviet government, former residence of Mao Zedong.

A tour of the Jiangxi scenery

Start from the city of Jiujiang and end in Nanchang by way of Lushan Mountain, Jingde Town, city of Dexing, Yushan, Shangrao, Hengfeng, Yiyang, Guixi, Yingtan, Yujiang, Dongxiang, Jinxian, and so on. Major scenic spots include Lushan Mountain Scenic Park, Hanpo Pass, Five Elderly Men Peak, Three-Stage Spring, Mist and Water Pavilion (Yanshui Ting), Xunyang Tower (Xunyang Lou), Jiujiang Changjiang River Bridge, ancient-style porcelain factory, Museum of Ceramic History, Sanqing Mountain (Sanqing Shan), Dragon and Tiger Mountain (Long Hu Shan), residence of the Taoist master (Tianshi Fu), ancient town of Shangqing, Fairy Rock and Water Rock (Xianshui Yan), Prince Teng Pavilion, and the August 1st Square.

Folk-custom show in Jiangxi (From CFP)

Addresses and Phone Numbers 

Jiangxi Hotel	368 Bayi Avenue, Nanchang	0791-6206666
Jiujiang Hotel	118 Nanhu Road, Jiujiang	0792-8981888
Lushan Hotel	70 Hexi Road, Lushan	0792-8282060
Shangrao Hotel	66 Zhongshan Road, Shangrao	0793-8323888
Yuming Hotel	501 Gandong Avenue, Fuzhou	0794-8252888
Jinggangshan Hotel	10 North Hongjun Road, Ciping, Jinggangshan	0796-6552272
Ruijing Hotel	100 Dongsheng Street, Xianghu, Ruijin	0797-2522001
Gannan Hotel	86 Houde Road, Ganzhou	0797-8265166
New Changjiang Hotel	1056 Cidu Avenue, Jingde Town	0798-8576666

Nanchang and Yingtan Region

Best Time to Travel

Nanchang, one of China's so-called four stoves, has a typical climate of cold winters and hot summers, which makes spring and autumn the best seasons for tourists.

Shopping Tips

The well-known Women's Street (Nuren Jie) in Nanchang features shops with small items, clothes, shoes, and hats. Bargaining is allowed and expected.

Zhongshan Road shopping street is the traditional prosperous shopping area in Nanchang. The goods here are inexpensive but of high quality.

Shengli Road pedestrian-only street features leisure activities, shopping, and entertainment. This 3,150-foot-long street is a good place for tourists to shop and people-watch.

Memorial Tower to the August 1st Nanchang Uprising (From CFP)

Former site of the General Headquarters of the August 1st Nanchang Uprising

Originally built in 1924 as Jiangxi Grand Hotel (Jiangxi Dalushe), the former site of the general headquarters of the August 1st Nanchang Uprising is located at Horse-washing Pond (Xima Chi), Zhongshan Road, Nanchang. It is a five-story gray building with 96 rooms. The first floor has been rebuilt

This is the huge copper Buddha statue, which weighs 39,000 pounds, in the back hall of Youmin Temple. Before 1949 there was a saying: "However poor Nanchang is, it still gets 39,999 kilos of copper." (From Colphoto)

as the original 1927 conference hall. On the second and the third floors are four exhibition halls and a room for dedications, in which many historical documents, pictures, photos, and artifacts tell the story of the Nanchang uprising. Outside the site is August 1st Square, with the 149-foot-tall Memorial Tower to the August 1st Nanchang Uprising.

Youmin Temple (Youmin Si)

Originally called Shanglan Temple (Shanglan Si), Youmin Temple is located midway along Minde Road, Nanchang. It is the only intact ancient temple in the city of Nanchang. Built during the Tianjian Period (502–519) of the Southern Liang Dynasty, the copper Buddha figure and the copper bell of this temple, together with the iron elephant in Puxian Temple, are called the "three treasures of Nanchang." Inside is the Hall of the Heavenly King, the Great Buddha's Hall, and the Hall of the Medicine Buddha, all of which attract many worshippers.

Qingyunpu Qingyunpu

Located 3 miles south of Nanchang, Qingyunpu is the former residence of the artist Badashanren, originally built during the Western Han Dynasty as the Temple of the Plum Fairy (Meixian Ci). It was renamed Qingyunpu ("as clean and high as a cloud") in 1661. The garden features ancient trees, zigzagging paths, and beautiful pavilions and other buildings. Some of Badashanren's paintings are stored in this garden.

Prince Teng Pavilion

Prince Teng Pavilion is located south of the junction of North Yanjiang Road and

The current Prince Teng Pavilion was built in 1983—the twenty-ninth reconstruction of the pavilion. (From CFP)

Dieshan Road, at the confluence of the Gan and the Fu rivers. With Nanchang city at its back and the rivers at its front, the pavilion is a favorite and lovely place to visit. The existing major part of the pavilion is of the Song Dynasty style, with nine stories and a 140-foot-high base. The whole pavilion is 189 feet tall. The main structure has seven stories, three of which are above the ground; the other four are hidden inside. The two wings of the building are two symmetrical terraces. In the south is the Yajiang Pavilion and in the north the Yicui Pavilion, with double eaves, green tiles, and carved and painted beams. Here tourists and locals alike can get a bird's-eye view of Nanchang.

Gold Rope Pagoda

Built during the Tianyou Period, in the Tang Dynasty (904–907), Gold Rope Pagoda is on the east side of Shengjinta Street (originally outside the Jinxian Gate of the ancient city), Xihu District, Nanchang. Legend has it that when the pagoda was under construction, workers dug into the ground and found four bundles of gold ropes, three ancient swords, and 300 sariras (crystalized remains after cremation). It has been rebuilt and repaired many times; the existing pagoda is made of brick and wood, simple and elegant, which is typical of the architectural style in regions south of the Changjiang River.

The octagonal Gold Rope Pagoda is 194 feet high. On its upturned eaves hang copper bells, which produce different sounds on the different levels. The bells on all seven stories make up a complete musical scale. (From ImagineChina)

Dragon and Tiger Scenic Park

Located in the city of Yingtan, Jiangxi Province, with a total area of 77 square miles, the park was originally named Brocade Mountain (Yunjin Shan) because of a huge colorful rock on the mountain. The rock itself is about 328 feet high and several hundred feet wide and resembles a gigantic piece of brocade. It was renamed Dragon and Tiger Mountain because the Taoist master once made pills of immortality here; when he succeeded, dragons and tigers appeared on the mountain. With the Xi River as its center, the scenic park features one major tour line (the tour line on the Luxi River) and five major scenic spots: Shangqing, Dragon and Tiger Mountain, Fairy Rock and Water Rock, Paiya Peak (Paiya Feng), and Mazu Rock (Mazu Yan).

The Taoist Culture Festival of Dragon and Tiger Mountain is held from October 3 to 9 when Taoists from home and abroad gather here to participate in traditional rituals.

Scene from Dragon and Tiger Scenic Park (From ImagineChina)

Jingde Town and Shangrao Region

Delicate porcelain bottles produced in Jingde Town. (From ImagineChina)

Best Time to Travel

Spring and summer are the optimal months in which to visit Jingde Town.

Sanqing Mountain Scenic Park

Exquisitely beautiful Sanqing Mountain is located 31 miles north of Yushan County, Shangrao. It gets its name because it looks like the three founders of Taoism—Yuqing, Shangqing, and Taiqing—are sitting on its three biggest peaks, Yujing Peak, Yuxu Peak, and Yuhua Peak. The main peak, Yujing Peak, is 5,961 feet above sea level. Sanqing Mountain is famous for its Taoist traditions and culture. It is said that the immortal Ge (Ge Xian) once practiced Taoism here during the Eastern Jin Dynasty.

Unfortunately, there are great numbers of mosquitoes on the mountain; tourists should bring insect repellant. The way upward is narrow and sometimes steep, and all visitors need to be careful.

Sanqing Mountain is perilous, marvelous, and beautiful, with the magnificence of Mount Tai, the wonder of Yellow Mountain, and the beauty of Lushan Mountain. (From ImagineChina)

Jingde Town (Jingde Zhen) Porcelain Museum

Built in 1954, the museum is located on Lianshe Road, Jingde Town. There are over 2,400 pieces of porcelain ware, the history of which can be dated back to the Five Dynasties. Here the four famous kinds of Jingde Town porcelain are on display: Blue Flower Porcelain (Qinghua), Linglong Porcelain (Linglong), Pink Color Porcelain (Fencai), and Colored Glaze Porcelain (Yanse You). The entire museum, dedicated as it is to porcelain, is divided by floor into the history exhibit and the current role of porcelain in China.

There is also an ancient porcelain exhibition at Panlonggang, west of Jingde Town. The old porcelain factory is an in-depth exhibition vividly representing the entire process of ancient-style porcelain production in Jingde Town.

The Xiangji Lane Civilian Houses

Situated in Xiangji Up Lane (Xiangji Shangnong), Jingde Town, the housing complex is a relatively intact lane of Ming Dynasty style. Take a close look at buildings 3 and 11, both of which represent the traditional and typical Ming architectural style.

Ancient Sanlu Temple Street

This site is located near a Ming-style street and a Qing-style street, on the west bank of the Changjiang River, in Jingde Town. The only road to Jingde Town from places in Anhui and Jiangxi, this street was once very prosperous in the Ming and Qing dynasties. The old street area has 136 ancient buildings, including houses, stores, temples, and arches. The Qing-style street to the north consists entirely of Qing Dynasty buildings. On the stone-paved road visitors can still see the prints of single-wheeled carts several inches deep.

Lingyan Cave Group (Lingyan Dongqun)

Lingyan Cave Group is located in Lingyan Cave National Forest Park in Tongyuanguan Village (Tongyuanguan Cun), Gutan Township, about 37 miles from Wuyuan County. The group is made up of 37 limestone caves with more than 2,000 dedication poems from well-known personages such as Yue Fei, Zong Ze, and Zhu Xi.

Ancient buiding in Wuyuan (From ImagineChina)

Wuyuan Ancient Building Group

Located in Wuyuan County, Shangrao, these ancient buildings are still relatively intact. Known far and wide as the "museum of ancient architecture," the houses are typical of Anhui style.

The house groups here are typical of the Anhui style, among which are Ming and Qing ancient building groups. (From ImagineChina)

Jiujiang Changjiang River Bridge connects the two banks of the Changjiang River and gives impetus to the economic development both north and south of the Changjiang River. (From CFP)

Jiujiang Region

Best Time to Travel

Jiujiang has a mild climate with short winters and long summers, which makes it a good year-round vacation spot.

Lushan Mountain Scenic Park

Lushan Mountain Park, south of Jiujiang city, neighboring the Changjiang River in the north and Poyang Lake in the east, is a spectacular scenic park that combines the beauty of a great river, an immense lake, and a magnificant mountain. Lushan Mountain itself is a sacred place in Buddhism with more than 300 temples, among which West Lin Temple (Xilin Si), East Lin Temple (Donglin Si), and Grand Lin Temple (Dalin Si), are the most famous. In 1996 Lushan Mountain was listed as a World Heritage site by UNESCO. At the foot of

Small Heavenly Pool situated on the top of northern Lushan Mountain. It never runs dry, even in drought, and its water never overflows the pool in rainy weather. (From CFP)

Lushan Mountain Villa Group (From CFP)

Located at the northwestern foot of Lushan Mountain is the Lushan Iron Buddha Temple (Lushan Tiefo Si), where there are more than 600 Buddha statues. One figure is almost 7 feet tall. The most prosperous street is the winding Guling Street (Guling Jie). Stores, dining areas, and restaurants selling local specialties are hidden by green trees, which form a picture of a secluded yet accessible street.

Zhibi Peak (Zhibi Feng), the former location of the 1959 Lushan Conference has been transformed into the Lushan Conference Memorial Hall, where historical records, photos, and documents are kept.

Lushan Mountain Villa Group

Lushan Mountain Villa Group is located in East Valley (Dong Gu), Lushan Mountain. It represents the Western architectural style and a perfect combination of fine architecture and pleasing environment.

Jiujiang Changjiang River Bridge

With the Jiujiang city of Jiangxi on its southern bank, the Jiujiang Changjiang River Bridge is situated on the border of Hubei Province and Jiangxi Province, and is the longest highway/railroad combination bridge in China that was built after the Wuhan Changjiang River Bridge and the Nanjing Changjiang River Bridge. Completed toward the end of 1991, the highway part is 14,600 feet long, and the railway part is 25,180 feet long. The section above the Changjiang River is 5,925 feet long. Both the Beijing-Kowloon railroad line and the Hefei–Jiujiang line use this bridge.

Ganzhou Region

Best Time to Travel

Spring and autumn are the best seasons in which to tour Ganzhou.

Northern Song Ancient City Wall

Now called the Ganzhou ancient city wall, it runs from the Xijin Gate (Xijin Men) to Bajing Terrace (along the Zhang River) and ends at the bridgehead of the East River by way of the Yongjin Gate (Yongjin Men) and the Jianchun Gate (Jianchun Men). It was first built as an earthen wall in the Later Liang Dynasty. After repair and consolidation during the dynasties that followed, it was turned into a 4-mile-long brick wall. At present 12,139 feet of the ancient city wall still exists and is about 23 feet high and 13 feet wide. There are 10 watchtowers and 1 attached tower (Ma Mian) left on the city wall. Bajing Terrace on the northeastern wall is the only restored gate tower; the cannon tower of the West Gate (Ximen Paocheng) is also extant. There is a treasure trove of 521 different kinds of bricks in the wall, on which there are many inscriptions.

Buses and taxis play a major role in the urban transportation of the Ganzhou city area.

Northern Song Ancient City Wall (From Colphoto)

The West Gate on Northern Song Ancient City Wall (From CFP)

Tongtian Rock Grotto (Tongtian Yan Shiku)

Tongtian Rock Grotto is situated about 6 miles northwest of Ganzhou City. Constructed during the Tang Dynasty, it reached its peak in the Song Dynasty.There are 359 figurines carved in the grotto from both the Tang and the Song dynasties, along with 128 inscriptions dating from the Song Dynasty to the Republic of China. At present the grotto consists of Wanggui Rock (Wanggui Yan), Tongxin Rock (Tongxin Yan), Tongtian Rock (Tongtian Yan), and Cuiwei Rock (Cuiwei Yan). On the cliffside of the grotto there are figurines and inscriptions, which make the spot look like an open-air museum. Tongtian Rock has been a famous mountain for Buddhists ever since the Tang and Song dynasties.

Yugu Terrace (Yugu Tai)

Located on Helan Mountain (Helan Shan) and locally known as Escargot Mountain (Tianluo Ling), northwest of Ganzhou city, Yugu Terrace was built during the Guangde and Dali periods of the Tang Dynasty (763–779).The three-story terrace is 56 feet high, with a total area of about 116 square miles. The terrace is magnificent with its carved and painted beams; it also attracted men of letters from different dynasties to leave their dedications here. In 1094, Su Shi, a famous eleventh-century poet and calligrapher, was exiled to Lingnan. When he passed by Ganzhou, he went to Yugu Terrace and wrote the poem "Composed on the Yugu Terrace, Qianzhou."

Tongtian Rock's carvings (From ImagineChina)

Former Site of the Revolution in Ruijin

Located in Ruijin at the western foot of Wuyi Mountain (Wuyi Shan), this group of historical buildings includes Yeping and Shazhou Ba and several memorial buildings. Yeping is 3 miles northeast of Ruijin City, which was the headquarters of the Chinese Communist Party (CCP) from 1931 to 1933. Shazhou Ba is 3 miles southwest of the city. In April 1933, the interim central government moved here from Yeping. The former site of the Executive Committee of the interim central government is located in Yuantai House (Yuantai Wu), where leaders such as Mao Zedong, Xu Teli, and Xie Juezai lived.

Ji'an Region

The Bajing Terrace tourists see today is an ancient-style building made of reinforced concrete. (From Colphoto)

Bajing Terrace (Bajing Tai)

At the confluence of the Zhang River (Zhang Shui) and the Gong River (Gong Shui), north of Ganzhou city, Bajing Terrace is the symbol of the ancient Ganzhou city.Visitors have a panoramic view of the eight scenic spots of Ganzhou from the terrace. It is a three-story ancient-style building, with a height of 93.5 feet. According to historical records, this terrace was originally made of stone, built by Kong Zonghan in the Northern Song Dynasty (1056–1063).

Heavenly Queen Temple (Tianhou Gong)

Located on Zhonghua Road, Heavenly Queen Temple was built during the Kangxi Period of the Qing Dynasty (1662–1722) for merchants of Fujian origin to offer their sacrifices. This temple was built by d'Entrecolles, a French missionary. It is said that a wealthy Frenchman survived a shipwreck when he was crossing the Atlantic because of the blessing by the Heavenly Queen, so he promised to build a temple for her with all his property. He chose this site to build the temple. Inside there is an arch, a stage, the Heavenly Queen Palace, the Sanzun Palace, and other fascinating and lovely structures. The subject of the relief sculptures inside the palace is mostly sea transportation.

Qingyuan Mountain (Qingyuan Shan)

Situated 9 miles southeast of Ji'an city, this mountain is more than 6 miles long and 1,050 feet above sea level. There are more than 30 pools, springs, rivers, and gorges, earning the mountain the reputation as the "No. 1 best view of mountain and water in Jiangxi." Ever since the Tang Dynasty, the mountain has been a sacred place in Buddhism, where rites of the Qingyuan School of the Zen Sect take place. It plays an important role in the history of Buddhism.

Drum tower in Qingyuan mountain (From Colphoto)

Making straw sandals (From CFP)

Ancient Building Group in Liukeng Village (Liukeng Cun)

Located in Liukeng Village along the Wu River, southeast of the township of Niutian, Le'an County, in Fuzhou city, Liukeng Village was built during the Kaiyuan period of the Southern Tang Dynasty (937–942) in the Five Dynasties Period. Most of the villagers here had Dong as their family name and regarded Dong Zhongshu, a knowledgeable scholar in the Han Dynasty, as their ancestor and Dong He as the creator of the Liukeng Village. There are more than 500 ancient buildings, among which are 309 buildings of the Ming or Qing dynasties, nearly 100 temples, and dozens of schools. The stage, the Jade Emperor Pavilion (Yuhuang Ge), the Tower of the God of Literature (Kuixing Lou), the arch, and the screen wall facing the gate in this village are still intact. In the village there are now about 170 wooden horizontal inscribed boards, over 250 inscribed boards for wall decoration, and at least 100 couplets written on scrolls from the Ming and Qing dynasties.

Liukeng Cun is a miniature of feudal Chinese patriarchal society. The remains of the patriarchal rituals performed here before can be seen everywhere in the village.

Jinggang Mountain Scenic Park

Located in the middle of the Luoxiao Mountains in the south of Jiangxi Province, with a total area of about 259 square miles and situated on the border of Jiangxi and Hunan, Jinggang Mountain has an important place in the history of the Chinese revolution. The mountain is a collection of

Since the middle of the Ming Dynasty, Liukeng Village has been making bamboo and wooden utensils and furniture. (From CFP)

over 500 peaks of different heights. It is higher in the west and lower in the east. The peaks in the middle are usually above 3,281 feet high; the main peak, Five Fingers Peak, has an altitude of 4,717 feet. The scenic park features perilous cliffs and deep valleys, and is dotted with brooks. It looks even more beautiful with its landscape filled with green bamboo and azalea. Jinggang Mountain Scenic Park is an ideal summer resort for both tourism and recuperation.

There are beautiful landscapes inside the thick forest of the Jinggang Mountain. (From Quanjing)

The optimal time to tour Jinggang Mountain is from April to October, especially in April and May when the azaleas are in full bloom.

The green Jinggang bamboo all over the mountain creates a serene and beautiful view. (From CFP)

Diaoyuan Village (Diaoyuan Cun)

Located 11 miles from Ji'an city, Diaoyuan Village is a place where the descendants of Ouyang Xiu, a famous man of letters in the Northern Song Dynasty, lived. The village itself is more than 1,100 years old and consists of two naturally formed villages, Weixi and Zhuangshan, separated from each other by an S-shaped mountain, Chang'an Mountain (Chang'an Ling). In the village of Zhuangshan there is a chain of ponds, and in the north is Duimen Mountain (Duimen Shan), both of which run east to west, as does Chang'an Mountain. The two mountains, with the chain of ponds in between, resemble the Li Diagram of the traditional Eight Diagrams. The Temple to Wenzhong Gong (Wenzhong Gong Ci) in the village is a modestly ornate temple in memory of Ouyang Xiu.

Jiangsu

Geography at a Glance

Jiangsu is a coastal province in East China, situated beside the Changjiang River and the Huai River. It gets its name from the first character of the Jiangning Fu (Nanjing) (Jiang) and the Suzhou Fu (Su), and is called "Su" for short. With a total area of over 38,600 square miles, Jiangsu Province has a population of 74.38 million (2000 census), about 743 persons per square mile, making it the most densely populated place in China. Jiangsu Province has the lowest altitude among all the provinces of China, half of which is below an altitude of about 164 feet. Located in the northeast of the province, Yuntai Mountain (Yuntai Shan) is the highest mountain in Jiangsu. The province is divided into two parts: the Changjiang River basin, and the Huai River basin. Here, the Changjiang river system, the Taihu Lake system, the Huai river system, and the Yishu river system flow into the two basins. Most of the rivers and lakes of the province are connected to each other, among which the Beijing-Hangzhou Grand Canal winds through the entire province from north to south, connecting Weishan Lake (Weishan Hu), Luoma Lake (Luoma Hu), Hongze Lake (Hongze Hu), Gaobao Lake (Gaobao Hu), Shanbo Lake (Shanbo Hu), and Tai Lake (Tai Hu), which makes it the arterial channel for Jiangsu Province to carry out cross-basin water transfer. The average temperature of the province is above 32˚F in January (except in places north of Xuzhou city) and around 82˚F in July. The average annual precipitation here is around 40 inches, with "plum rain" in June and July and typhoons in summer and autumn.

Nanjing, the capital city of Jiangsu, is located along the Qinhuai River (Qinhuai He). Since ancient times it has been a city of stunning

(From CFP)

Su embroidery for daily use, with even stitches as well as harmonious and bright colors, is highly decorative. (From ImagineChina)

women and scenery. This, in addition to the beauty of a region of rivers and lakes, forms the unique charm of Jiangsu Province.

Featured Cuisine

Jinling saltwater duck, stewed meatball with crab meat, deeply boiled shreds of dried bean curd, crystal pig trotters, Liangxi crisp eel, squirrel salmon, Ping Bridge bean curd, Xuyi lobster, Yangzhou Yechun steamed buns, Wuxi small wontons, Suzhou Huangtianyuan rice cakes, Taizhou Yellow Bridge pancakes, Nanjing Yuhua dough and soup, Pei County dog meat, stir-fried spiral shells and Chinese chives, Nanjing potherb, honey ham slices, Changshu beggar's chicken, Huai'an stir-fried eel, steamed buns filled with gravy and crab roe, Yangzhou stir-fried rice, braised silver carp head.

Featured Commodities

Local Special Products

Velvet, pressed salted duck, pearls, silk cream, Hui Spring (Huiquan) wine, Yuhua colorful pebbles.

Local Handicrafts

Cloud brocade, ancient-style ivory carving, wood carving, Jiangsu embroidery, Song brocade, tapestry with fine silk and gold thread, Taohuawu woodcut New Year's pictures, Huishan clay figures, Wuxi embroidery, Yixing violet pottery tea sets.

Notes 

❶ In Jiangsu, it is most convenient to travel by bus. There are numerous bus stations throughout the cities.

❷ In the past, Nanjing in summer was referred to as "a stove." However, in recent years the green areas in Nanjing have begun to change the overall climate of the city.

Transportation Tips

By Bus

Jiangsu has a well-developed highway system. The Beijin-Shanghai Highway, the Nanjing-Lianyungang Highway, and the Nanjing-Hefei Highway help ensure a smooth flow of traffic.

By Train

The train transportation in Jiangsu is also very convenient. Railroads like the Beijing-Shanghai line, the Longhai line, and the Ningbo-Wuhu line connect major cities in and out of the province, which make Nanjing and Xuzhou transportation hubs that connect the north and the south. The Beijing-Shanghai line joins the Nanjing-Tongling line in Nanjing and joins the Longhai line in Xuzhou.

By Plane

Jiangsu Province has nine airports, including the newly built Nanjing Lukou International

POPULAR FESTIVALS

Listening to the bell in Hanshan Temple (Hanshan Si) on New Year's Eve

"Inside the boat at midnight, I heard the bell in Hanshan Temple outside the Gusu City" (from a famous poem by Zhang Ji of the Tang Dynasty). On New Year's Eve, the abbot of Hanshan Temple strikes the temple bell 108 times to welcome the new year and invite good luck and happiness.

Jinling Lantern Festival

This festival is held lunar January 1–31, on Fuzi Temple (Fuzi Miao) Square and around Dacheng Hall (Dacheng Dian). There are great displays of thousands of unique lanterns of all different shapes.

Nanjing International Plum-Blossom Festival

This festival is held from the last Saturday of February to March 18.

Cloud and Dragon Mountain (Yunlong Shan) Temple Fair

This festival is held from March 28 to April 3. Lion dances, stilt walking, singing, and all kinds of delicate folk handicraft works.

Enjoying the Full Moon around Mid-Autumn Day on Taihu Lake (Tai Hu)

This celebration involves boating on Taihu Lake in Wuxi and enjoying the beautiful view of the full moon and the natural scenery.

Qintong Boat Festival

On the day following the Qingming Festival (April 5, Tomb-Sweeping Day in China), people in Qintong, Yangzhou, perform dragon and lion dances and have boat races to celebrate the Boat Festival.

Xuyi Lobster Festival

This festival is held in late June. The thirteen-flavor lobster (Shisanxiang Lobster) is famous for its bright color and tasty flavor.

Tiger Hill (Hu Qiu) Temple Fair

Beginning in October, a 62-day temple fair is held on Tiger Hill featuring folk art, performances, handicraft shows, local delicacies, exhibitions, and buying and selling goods.

Airport, with a number of airlines. It is easy and convenient for tourists to fly to Jiangsu from any major city.

By Water

Jiangsu is a province of water transportation. Tourists can enter Jiangsu by boat from Wuhan or places west of the Changjiang River. Along the shipping lanes of the Changjiang River there are major passenger-transportation ports such as Nanjing, Zhenjiang, Taizhou, Jiangyin, and Nantong. On the shipping lanes of the Grand Canal there are ships that start from Suzhou and Wuxi in the morning and reach Hangzhou in the evening.

Recommended Routes

Classical Routes

Four-day tour of the ancient towns of rivers and lakes

Day 1 Arrival in Suzhou. Lodging: Zhonghuayuan Hotel.

Day 2 Tiger Hill (Hu Qiu)→Lion Grove Garden (Shizi Lin)→Humble Administrator's Garden (Zhuozheng Yuan)→Hanshan Temple (Hanshan Si)→ Guanqian Street (Guanqian Jie). Lodging: Zhonghuayuan Hotel.

Day 3 Town of Tongli→ Tuisi Garden (Tuisi Yuan)→ Chongbentang Hall (Chongbentang)→Three Bridges (San Qiao) (Bridges of Peace, Auspiciousness, and Celebration)→Ming- and Qing-style Street (Ming Qing Jie)→Shidetang Hall (Shidetang)→Luoxing Island (Luoxing Zhou)→Zhouzhuang Town (Zhou Zhuang). Lodging: Jinfeng Folk House Restaurant.

Day 4 Zhouzhuang →Zhang Hall (Zhang Ting)→ Twin Bridge (Shuang Qiao)→Richness and Peace Bridge (Fu'an Qiao)→Shen Hall (Shen Ting)→Folk Custom Museum→Baosheng Temple (Baosheng Si). End of tour.

Six-day tour in "flowery March"

Day 1 Arrival in Zhenjiang. Lodging: Zhenjiang Hotel

Day 2 Gold Hill Temple (Jinshan Si)→No. 1 Spring under Heaven→Song- and Yuan-style Street→Former residence of Pearl S. Buck→Jiaoshan Mountain (Jiao Shan). Lodging: Zhenjiang Hotel.

Day 3 Yangzhou→the Narrow West Lake (Shou Xihu)→Twenty-four Bridges →Daming Temple (Daming Si). Lodging: New Century Hotel.

Day 4 Fuchun Tea House→Ge Garden (Ge Yuan)→Yechun Garden (Yechun Yuan)→ Wang Residence (Wangshi Xiaoyuan)→ Zhenhuai Tower. Lodging: Huai'an Yingbin Hotel.

Day 5 Xihua Hall (Xihua Ting)→Memorial Hall to Zhou Enlai→Former residence of Zhou Enlai→Temple of Han Xin (Hanxin Ci)→Former residence of Wu Cheng'en→Temple of Piao Mu (Piaomu Ci). Lodging: Huai'an Yingbin Hotel.

Day 6 Mausoleum of Dr. Sun Yat-sen (Zhongshan Ling)→Mausoleum of Zhu Yuanzhang (Ming Xiao Ling)→Presidential Palace→Qinhuai River→Fuzi Temple (Fuzi Miao). End of tour.

Traditional Routes

Five-day tour of the ancient capital Jinling (Nanjing)

Day 1 Arrival in Nanjing.

Day 2 Egret Island Park (Bailuzhou Park)→ Fuzi Temple→Zhan Garden (Zhan Yuan)→Mochou Lake (Mochou Hu)→ Mausoleum of Dr. Sun Yat-sen→Linggu Temple (Linggu Si).

Day 3 Xuanwu Lake (Xuanwu Hu)→ Qixia Temple (Qixia Si)→Nanjing Changjiang River Bridge→Swallow Stone (Yanzi Ji).

Day 4 Toutai Cave (Toutai Dong)→ Ertai Cave (Ertai Dong)→Santai Cave (Santai Dong)→Mausoleum of Zhu Yuanzhang→Former site of the Palace of Heavenly King of Taiping Celestial Kingdom (Taiping Tianguo Tianwang Fu)→New Village of Plum Garden (Meiyuan Xincun)→Yuhua Terrace (Yuhua Tai).

Day 5 End of tour.

Five-day tour of gardens in Suzhou

Day 1 Arrival in Suzhou.

Day 2 North Temple Pagoda (Bei Si Ta)→ Humble Administrator's Garden (Zhuozheng Yuan)→ Lion Grove Garden (Shizi Lin)→ Yi Garden (Yi Yuan)→ Ou Garden (Ou Yuan) →Wangshi Garden (Wangshi Yuan)→ Canglang Pavilion Garden (Canglang Ting).

Day 3 Mountain Villa of Secluded Beauty (Huanxiu Shanzhuang)→Tiger Hill→Lingering Garden (Liu Yuan)→ West Garden (Xi Yuan)→ Hanshan Temple→Maple Bridge (Feng Qiao).

Day 4 Tianping Mountain (Tianping Shan)→Lingyan Mountain (Lingyan Shan)→ Purple Gold Nunnery (Zijin An)→East and West Dongting Hill (Dongxi Dongting Shan).

Day 5 End of tour.

Seven-day tour of the region of rivers and lakes

Day 1 Arrival in Suzhou.

Day 2 Panshan Mountain Scenery Park →Humble Administrator's Garden→Tiger Hill→Hanshan Temple→Guanqian Street.

Day 3 Wuxi→Taihu Lake→Yuantouzhu Park→Plum Garden (Mei Yuan).

Day 4 Changzhou→Tianning Temple (Tianning Si)→Museum of Combs→Dinosaur Park→Zhenjiang→Gold Hill Temple→Beigu Mountain (Beigu Shan)→ Jiaoshan Mountain (Jiao Shan).

Day 5 Yangzhou→Narrow West Lake→Daming Temple→He Garden (He Yuan)→Ge Garden (Ge Yuan) →Gaoyou→Mengcheng Post (Mengcheng Yi)→Wenyou Terrace (Wenyou Tai).

Day 6 Huai'an→Zhenhuai Tower (Zhenhuai Lou)→Memorial Hall to Zhou Enlai→Former residence of Wu Cheng'en.

Day 7 Suqian→Hometown of Xiangyu→Park of King Xiang (Xiangwang Park)→ Street of Chu Culture→Sanzhuang Han Tomb. End of tour.

Self-Guided Tours

Boating on Taihu Lake

Board at Xiaoqishan Port, tour Taihu Lake, Yuantouzhu, Immortal Island (Shenxian Dao), and places neighboring the Lake, in addition to beautiful sites such as Taiping Lake (Taiping Hu) and Water Base of the Three Kindoms.

A tour of the ancient canal

Jiangsu is famous for its rivers and lakes. Just as the old saying "Suzhou and Hangzhou are the paradise on earth" states, tourists will savor more of the beauty of this region of rivers and lakes by way of the ancient canal. Boarding a tour boat at the Xishan port, sightseers can have a good view of the beauty of the old and the new canal, experiencing the loveliness of this region and its simple and unsophisticated folk customs.

Addresses and Phone Numbers

Jinling Hotel	2 Hanzhong Road, Xinjiekou, Nanjing	025-84711888
Liuyuan Hotel	38 Jinxianghe Road, Nanjing	025-83600111
Wuxi Grand Hotel	1 Liangqing Road, Wuxi	0510-85806789
Zhenjiang Hotel	92 West Zhongshan Road, Zhenjiang	0511-85233888
Yunhai Resort	32 Yunhai Road, Zhouzhuang, Kunshan	0512-57211977
Jinfeng Folk House Restaurant	145 Zhuhang Street, Tongli	0512-63338220
Zhonghuayuan Hotel	198 Jinshan Road, Mudu, Suzhou	0512-66256666
Qidong Hotel	490 Middle Minle Road, Qidong	0513-83316621
New Century Hotel	101 Weiyang Road, Yangzhou	0514-7878888
Hanyuan Hotel	246 South Jiefang Road, Xuzhou	0516-87889999
Huai'an Yingbin Hotel	121 North Huaihai Road, Huai'an	0517-83180888
Lianyungang Shenzhou Hotel	215 North Haitang Road, Xugou, Lianyungang	0518-2310088
Taizhou Hotel	88 Yingbin Road, Taizhou	0523-86669898

Nanjing Region

Best Time to Travel

From mid-June to the beginning of July, Nanjing is extremely hot. Spring and autumn are the optimal times to tour Nanjing. The city is famous for the clouds and mist on Bull Head Mountain (Niushou Shan) in spring, the clouds on Purple Mountain in summer, and the snow in Stone City in winter.

Shopping Tips

On Jinling Road near the Fuzi Temple in Nanjing is the biggest flower and bird market of the whole city, where flowers, plants, birds, scrolls of painting or calligraphy, and Yuhua colorful pebbles are sold. Tourists can savor the aesthetic taste of the ancient capital even if they buy nothing here.

In China Silk Fabrics Village in Nanjing, visitors can view the different weaving skills and fabric collections, and buy handcrafted silk fabrics and clothings.

Hunan Road is a new shopping street in Nanjing. (From ImagineChina)

Mausoleum of Dr. Sun Yat-sen

Neighboring the Mausoleum of Zhu Yuanzhang in the west and Linggu Temple in the east, the mausoleum of Dr. Sun Yat-sen is located at the southern foot of Xiaomao Mountain, which is the eastern peak of Zhongshan Mountain (Zhong Shan) in the eastern suburb of Nanjing. The mausoleum is designed by Lu Yan, a famous architect. The entire complex is built upward following the slope of the mountain; the crypt itself is situated 518 feet above sea level. Around the mausoleum are memorial buildings, built from donations raised by people from all countries and all walks of life.

At the gate of the mausoleum, old-style motorbikes are available.

Inside the mausoleum from the arch to the memorial hall there are 392 steps and eight terraces built from Suzhou granite. (From Quanjing)

Nanjing Museum

Located inside Chaotian Palace (Chaotian Gong) on Wangfu Street, Nanjing Museum was built in 1962 as a comprehensive historical museum, with an area of over 27,000 square miles and a collection of more than 60,000 cultural artifacts, both ancient and contemporary. The majority of these artifacts were unearthed from tombs of the Six Dynasties and the Ming Dynasty.

Zhonghua Gate (Zhonghua Men)

Called Treasure Gate (Jubao Men) in ancient times, the castle-like Zhonghua Gate was the largest gate in the city wall of Nanjing and the biggest castle in China. It is also called Jar Gate (Wong Men) for its jar-shaped appearance, designed to resist attacks from enemies. Inside the castle there are 24 caves that can hold 3,000 soldiers. The gate occupies an important position in the history of the architecture of Chinese city walls because of its magnificent scale, complex structure, and intelligent design.

There were once four gates in the castle of Zhonghua Gate; now only ruins of the base are left. (From CFP)

Yuhua Terrace Cemetery of Revolutionary Martyrs

This cemetery is located about a half-mile south of Zhonghua Gate in Nanjing, on a hill 199 feet above sea level. From 1927 to 1949 this area was the execution site where the Kuomintang massacred tens of thousands of Communist Party members and revolutionaries. In the memorial hall are the stories of these revolutionary martyrs. Many historical letters, photographs, and mementos of the martyrs are also exhibited here.

Take Bus No. 2 or No.16 to the cemetery, or walk about 15 minutes from Zhonghua Gate.

On the cemetery square is a group sculpture of martyrs built from 179 pieces of granite. (From ImagineChina)

The Mausoleum of Zhu Yuanzhang (Ming Xiao Ling)

Located at the foot of Playing Pearl Peak (Wanzhu Feng) at the southern side of Zhongshan Mountain, the Mausoleum of Zhu Yuanzhang is where Zhu Yuanzhang, the first emperor of the Ming Dynasty, and Empress Ma, his wife, were buried. The mausoleum was built in 1381. Inside it is a huge stone turtle, head turned skyward, with a stone pillar on its back. On the pillar is a 2,746-word inscription composed by Zhu Di, one of the emperors of the Ming Dynasty, which tells of Zhu Yuanzhang's wise decisions and good deeds. The pillar is some 29 feet tall, making it the tallest among all the existing ground pillars in Nanjing.

Nanjing Changjiang River Bridge

Located between Xiaguan and Pukou, northwest of Nanjing, the Nanjing Changjiang River Bridge is a double-deck, double-line bridge for highway and railway. Completed on December 29, 1968, the highway part on the upper deck is 15,056 feet long and the railway part on the lower deck 22,218 feet long, with two sets of rails, enabling two trains to run at the same time.

Purple Mountain Observatory

Located on the third peak of Purple Mountain in the eastern suburb of Nanjing, Purple Mountain Observatory was completed in September 1934 as the first modern astronomical research institution built by China independently. During its long-term work of astronomical observation, the observatory has discovered a large number of planetoids, of which 100 have received their official serial number and the right to be named from the Minor Planet Center.

The observatory is the best place to get a bird's-eye view of the city of Nanjing.

Stone tortoise at the Mausoleum of Zhu Yuanzhang. (From ImagineChina)

New Village of Plum Garden Museum

This museum is located at the east end of Changjiang Road, in the northern part of Hanfu Street. Numbers 30, 17, and 35 on this block were the workplaces of the CCP Delegation. House No. 30 in the New Village of Plum Garden is where Zhou Enlai and Deng Yingchao lived and worked. There is an exhibit of various items from Zhou's desk.

Memorial Hall for Compatriots Killed in the Nanjing Massacre in the Sino-Japanese War

This memorial hall, located at 195 East Chating Street in Nanjing, was built in 1985 in honor of the hundreds of Chinese who were massacred and buried during the Sino-Japanese War.

Fuzi Temple (Fuzi Miao)

Built in the Song Dynasty, the Fuzi Temple (Temple of Confucius) is located south of Jiankang Road, beside Gongyuan Street north of the Qinhuai River in Nanjing. The temple neighbors the Qinhuai River, the stone wall along the southern bank of which is the screen wall of the temple. This 361-foot screen wall is the longest in China. The name "Fuzi Temple" refers to the three major architecture groups of the Temple of Confucius, the Palace of Study (Xue Gong), and Gong Yuan (where examinations were carried out), as well as their surroundings.

> Surrounding Fuzi Temple are famous places of interest such as the Beauty and Fragrance Tower (Meixiang Lou), Black Clothes Alley (Wuyi Xiang), and the former residence of Wang Dao and Xie An.

Zhan Garden (Zhan Yuan)

Situated at 208 Zhanyuan Road in Nanjing, Zhan Garden is the oldest existing garden in Nanjing. It was once the residence of Prince Wu, where Zhu Yuanzhang, the first emperor of the Ming Dynasty, lived before he claimed the crown. In the Qing Dynasty, when Emperor Qianlong made his inspection tour of southern China, he wrote a dedication to this garden. The western section of the garden exemplifies the classical gardening art of Suzhou with its delicate layout.

Snow covers the roofs of houses and boats but never the crystal water of the Qinhuai River. The beauty of the river stands out against the background of the white snow. (From Quanjing)

Zhenjiang Region

Best Time to Travel

The mild climate of spring and autumn are the optimal months to tour Zhenjiang.

Gold Hill Temple has a long-standing history. The temple holds many ancient relics. The photo shows Guanyin Pavilion near the top of the hill. (From ImagineChina)

The Gold Hill Temple (Jinshan Si)

Located on Gold Hill (Jin Shan), this temple got its name during the Tang Dynasty after people discovered gold here. This is the place of origin of the Water and Land Dharma Functions and one of the four greatest temples of the zen sect.

> Four Treasures of the Gold Hill Temple are the Zhou Dynasty copper tripod, the drum of Zhuge Liang, the jade belt of Su Dongpo, and *The Picture of the Gold Hill* by Wen Zhengming.

Zhongling Spring

Zhongling Spring, with its crystal clear, sweet water, beside the Lake of Pagoda's Reflection (Taying Hu) and west of Gold Hill in Zhenjiang, was regarded as the number one spring in the world by Lu Yu, Sage of Tea, in the Tang Dynasty. Originally located in the whirlpools of the Changjiang River, the spring changed its location from the middle of the river to the land because the sediment in the Changjiang River merged into Gold Hill and the southern bank of the river.

Jiaoshan Mountain (Jiao Shan)

Also called Qiaoshan Mountain (Qiao Shan), Jiaoshan Mountain is located in the Yangtze River about 3 miles northeast of Zhenjiang proper. It was named after Jiao Guang, a hermit from the East Han Dynasty who lived here. The major structure on the mountain is Dinghui Temple (Dinghui Si), built toward the end of the East Han Dynasty (25–220 CE). The magnificent Great Buddha's Hall (Daxiong Baodian) in the temple is in the Ming style. Starting northward from Guanlan

Jiaoshan Mountain has long been famous for its ancient trees and well-known pillars. The buildings of its temples are all hidden behind ancient yet still flourishing trees. (From ImagineChina)

Pavilion (Guanlan Ge) east of Dinghui Temple is the Jiaoshan Forest of Pillars, also called Baomo Veranda (Baomo Xuan). Over 460 pillar inscriptions are located here, which makes the Jiaoshan Forest of Pillars the largest one in the regions south of the Changjiang River.

Sweet Dew Temple (Ganlu Si)

On the back peak of Beigu Mountain in Zhenjiang, Sweet Dew Temple was originally built in the time of the Three Kingdoms (265). Since then, the temple has been destroyed and reconstructed many times. Now the existing buildings include the Grand Hall (Da Dian), Laojun Hall (Laojun Dian), Guanyin Hall (Guanyin Dian), Jiangsheng Pavilion (Jiangsheng Ge), and a few others. In the small garden beside the temple there was once a nine-story iron pagoda, which was later destroyed by lightning. In 1960, many cultural artifacts were unearthed from the base of the pagoda, including stone boxes, gold and silver coffins, Buddhist relics, and stone inscriptions.

Zhao Pass Stone Pagoda (Zhaoguan Shita) on Song Street

In northwestern Zhenjiang there is an ancient street constructed during the Song Dynasty and thus named Song Street, which once was an important ancient ferry on the Changjiang River. Zhao Pass Stone Pagoda is located right in the middle of the street. It is 16 feet high and was built of stones during the Yuan Dynasty. The pagoda sits on two stone bases, one on top of the other, with an I-shaped cross section. Atop the base is a round platform with lotus carvings and the drum-shaped pagoda. Farther up on the pagoda walls are 13 belts of relief sculptures, symbolizing the 13 layers of heaven.

Wuxi Region

Best Time to Travel

Wuxi has a temperate climate all the year round, which makes the whole year perfect for a tour here. The high tourist season is from April to October.

Li Garden (Li Yuan)

Li Garden is located on the northern bank of the Lihu Lake (Li Hu), 1.5 miles southwest of Wuxi. It is said that Fan Li, an official of the state of Yue, used to go boating here with the famous beauty Xi Shi. Later, people renamed the lake (originally called Qihu Lake) in memory of him. The current garden area is a combination of the original Li Garden built in 1927 and the Fishing Village (Yu Zhuang) built in 1930.

Li Garden is surrounded by the lake on three sides. Beside the lake are stones of amazing shapes, twisting verandas, and fragrant grass and trees, the rich colors of which make this area stand out among all gardens in the region south of the Changjiang River. (From ImagineChina)

Plum trees and the mountain enhance each other's beauty. Inside Plum Garden, the beauty and fragrance of the plum trees are stunning and well worth a visit. (From ImagineChina)

Plum Garden

Located on the southern side of East Mountain (Dong Shan) and Hushan Mountain (Hu Shan) in the western suburb of Wuxi, Plum Garden is filled with plum trees, which make it one of the best places south of the Changjiang River to appreciate their delicate beauty. Now with a total area of 208,495 square miles, Plum Garden was built in 1912 by the Rong Brothers (Rong Zongjing and Rong Desheng), two famous national capitalists. In the scenic park of Plum Garden there are three major sections: the plum blossom area, the architecture area including the Plum Culture Museum, and Suihan Grass Hall. The garden expo features an interesting combination of natural scenery and horticultural art of many different styles.

➡ Take Bus No. 2, the special tourist bus from the Wuxi train station.

Xihui Park

Located in suburban Wuxi, Xihui Park neighbors the ancient canal in the south and Huishan Mountain in the north. Inside the park, hills and peaks are green and beautiful. Xishan Mountain (Xi Shan) and Huishan Mountain (Hui Shan) face each other, with Mountain Reflection Lake (Yingshan Hu) in between. North of Huishan Temple (Huishan Si) in Xihui Park is Jichang Garden (Jichang Yuan), also named Qin Garden (Qin Yuan), which used to be monks' living quarters during the Yuan Dynasty. In the Ming Dynasty (1368–1644), Qin Jin, an important minister, rebuilt this place into a garden and named it Feng Gu Xing Wo, which was later changed to Jichang Garden by Qin Yao. Tourists can enter Xihui Park by way of Guhua Gate and go directly to Huishan Temple and Jichang Garden.

Inside Jichang Garden in Xihui Park, bamboo, bridges, and pools highlight the simplicity and tranquility of the garden. (From CFP)

Wuxi Movie and TV Studio Town

The studio town for CCTV includes movie and TV bases such as the City of Three Kingdoms (Sanguo Cheng), the City of the Water Margin (Shuihu Cheng), the City of the Tang Dynasty, and the City of Europe. The City of Three Kingdoms is located in the southwestern suburbs of Wuxi. Inside the city are large-scale sites in the Han Dynasty style, such as the Palace of the King of Wu, Sweet Dew Temple, Water Base of the Cao Army, a sentry tower, barracks, warships, and the port. Neighboring it is the City of the Water Margin, east of Taihu Lake. Buildings in this city are of the same style but in different forms. Ranging from palaces and official residences to folk houses and grass cabins, buildings in this city represent the unique historical background and folk customs of the Song Dynasty.

Taihu Lake

Called Zhenze Lake in ancient times, Taihu Lake is the third-largest freshwater lake in China, with an area of about 869 square miles, crossing Jiangsu and Zhejiang provinces. Wuxi occupies the most beautiful part of the lake's northern bank. The lake is dotted with 48 islands, which are collectively called Seventy-two Peaks, and surrounded by mountains and peninsulas. The islands are extensions of Heaven's Eye Mountain (Tianmu Shan) in Zhejiang Province, which, embraced by the lake, form a beautiful natural picture of mountains and lakes.

October 10 is the Taihu International Fishing Festival. Fishing aficionados from all over the world gather here and compete with each other.

Scene of Taihu Lake (From ImagineChina)

Suzhou Region

Best Time to Travel

Suzhou has a warm and damp climate, which extends the tour season here to the whole year. The period from April to October is best, with April being the most beautiful.

Shopping Tips

Guanqian Street in Suzhou is the equal of Heaven Bridge (Tian Qiao) in Beijing and Town God's Temple (Chenghuang Miao) in Shanghai. This is a worldclass market for all kinds of entertainment and food. Here tourists can buy special local products like Jiangsu embroidery, Biluochun tea (one of the ten famous kinds of tea), and Taohuawu woodcuts.

Tiger Hill (Hu Qiu)

Also called Haiyong Mountain (Haiyong Shan), Haiyong Peak (Haiyong Feng), or Hufu Mountain (Hu Fu), Tiger Hill is located in the Suzhou suburbs, about 2 miles from Chang Gate (Chang Men) northwest of the ancient city of Suzhou. It is only 142 feet above sea level. Historical records say that toward the end of the Spring and Autumn Period, Fu Chai, king of the state of Wu, buried his father, He Lu, on this hill. Three days after the burial, a white tiger was seen here, hence the name Tiger Hill. Though small, this hill has many scenic spots. Along the path up are the famous 18 sites of Tiger Hill, including Broken Beam Hall (Duanliang Dian), Hanhan Spring (Hanhan Quan), the Sword-Testing Stone (Shijian Shi), the Tomb of Zhenniang (Zhenniang Mu), One Thousand People Stone (Qianren Shi), Er Pavilion (Er Ting), Fifty-three Steps (Fifty-three Can), and Quyan Pagoda (Quyan Ta). The most interesting site is Yunyan Temple Pagoda (Yunyan Si Ta), also called Tiger Hill Pagoda (Huqiu Ta). In 1956 numerous cultural artifacts were discovered inside the pagoda, including rare art treasures such as the lotus porcelain bowl of Yue Yao.

Take Tourist Bus No. 1 and 2 or Public Bus 8 and 48. The high season is from March to May and from September to November, when flower fairs and temple fairs take place.

Garden of the Humble Administrator

Located on Northeast Street (Dongbei Jie) in Suzhou, this is one of the four famous gardens in the city. Originally built during the Jiajing period in the Ming Dynasty (1522–1566), the garden received its name from a remark made by

Every corner of the Garden of the Humble Administrator is beautiful. (From ImagineChina)

Pan Yue, a man of letters in the Jin Dynasty: "Those who are humble can make good administrators." The garden is divided into eastern, middle, and western sections. The garden now is much different from what it was originally, but its layout is basically of the Ming Dynasty style, featuring a pond at its center, around which the temples, pavilions, and verandas have been built.

Lingering Garden

Located on Liuyuan Road outside the Chang Gate in Suzhou, Lingering Garden is one of the four famous gardens in Suzhou. Built in 1460, the garden was originally the eastern part of Xu Shitai's garden. During the Qing Dynasty, Liu Rongfeng was the owner of the garden and named it after his own surname—Liu Yuan. Later, the garden was owned by Sheng Xuren and renamed Lingering Garden (Liu Yuan). It comprises four parts; the central part, the Cold and Green Mountain Villa (Hanbi Shanzhuang), captures the essence of the whole garden. There is a pond at the center of the garden, surrounded by stones, towers, and pavilions, which are connected by verandas and bridges.

Wangshi Garden

Situated in Kuojiatou Alley, southeast of the ancient the city of Suzhou, Wangshi Garden represents the typical style of smaller gardens. The main part features various works of architecture and the beauty of the hills and lakes, and the auxiliary part adds to the beauty. The garden is a masterpiece of middle-scale gardens in Suzhou.

Wangshi Garden is open in the evening, which is rare among gardens in Suzhou.

Lion Grove Garden

Situated at 23 Yuanlin Road in the northeastern corner of Suzhou city proper, Lion Grove Garden is another of the four famous gardens in Suzhou. Built during the Yuan Dynasty (1341–1368),

Lingering Garden (Liu Yuan) is famous for its stones of amazing shapes. (From Quanjing)

Outside Canglang Pavilion is a crystal brook, along which are verandas, rock gardens, and trees. (From ImagineChina)

it is a great representative of Suzhou classic gardens. It is well known for its ancient rock gardens, which are the largest existing ones in China.

Canglang Pavilion

Located at Sanyuanfang in the southern part of Suzhou, the Canglang Pavilion was originally the garden of the Guangling King of the state of Wuyue during the Five Dynasties. In 1044 Su Shunqin, a poet, built a pavilion beside the brook and named it Canglang Pavilion. In the Southern Song Dynasty it was the residence of Han Shizhong, a famous general in wars against the state of Jin. The garden features a natural design of simplicity, without any touch of pretention.

Hanshan Temple

Also called Maple Bridge Temple (Fengqiao Si), Hanshan Temple is located in the Maple Bridge neighborhood in the western part of Suzhou. It gets its fame from a well-known poem written by Zhang Ji, a poet of the Tang Dynasty. The temple was built during the Tianjian period in the Southern Dynasty (502–159) and named after an abbot.

Pan Gate

Built in the Spring and Autumn Period (514 BCE) and rebuilt toward the end of the Yuan Dynasty, this is the only intact water-and-land city gate. It is made up of two water passes, three gates, and a jar-shaped building. The gates are further divided into outer and inner sections, between which is the jar-shaped building that can hold hundreds of soldiers. The water gates are close to the land gates, which are also divided into two sections and are constructed of bricks.

Tourists can climb the city wall through the stone slope in the northern part of Suzhou.

There used to be a fortress at Pan Gate, but it was burned during the Sino-Japanese War. The newly built fortress is of pavilion style, with two decks and upturned eaves. (From CFP)

Treasure Belt Bridge

Located 4.6 miles southeast of Suzhou, Treasure Belt Bridge crosses the Daihe River between the Grand Canal and Dantai Lake. Built during the Yuanhe period in the Tang Dynasty, the bridge is more than 1,300 feet long and about 13 feet wide. The piers of the bridge are unique and fall into two categories, flexible ones and rigid ones, making them not only strong but attractive.

Luzhi

Located in the eastern suburbs of Suzhou and neighboring Shanghai, Luzhi was built in 503 and ranks as one of the six famous ancient towns in the region south of the Changjiang River. There are 41 ancient bridges, Tang-style arhat figures, folk houses, and very old streets.

> Luzhi is 15.5 miles from Suzhou, 30 miles from Zhou village, and 40 miles from Tongli, with convenient highway transportation between the three places.

Dongting West Hill

Located on the largest and prettiest island on Taihu Lake, about 50 miles west of Suzhou, it faces Dongting East Hill (Dongting Dongshan) on another island on the Taihu Lake. West Hill has 41 of the Taihu Seventy-two Peaks. Besides temples and resort buildings, its unique scenes include the moon in autumn, the mist at night, and snow.

> West Hill has the most white plum trees in Jiangsu. There are about 100,000 plum trees near Linwu Mountain (Linwu Shan), which are most beautiful in early spring.

Tongli

Located east of the ancient canal in northeastern Wujiang, the town of Tongli ranks as one of the six famous regions of rivers south of the Changjiang River. The town has a total area of about 24 square miles and is the most intact ancient water town in Jiangsu. Surrounded by water and including five lakes (Tongli Lake, Jiuli Lake, Yeze Lake, Nanxing Lake, and Pangshan Lake), the town is divided into seven small islands by its 15 rivers, all of which are connected by 49 ancient bridges.

> Tourists can take a 30-minute ride to Tongli in minibuses from the westernmost bridge in Zhou village.

Tuisi Garden

Located on Dongxi Street in the town of Tongli in Wujiang, this garden was built during the period between the eleventh and thirteenth years of Emperor Guangxu in the Qing Dynasty (1885–1887). The Chinese phrase *tui si* means "to step back and reflect."

A beautiful scene of a garden in Tongli. (From CFP)

The owner, Ren Lansheng, was impeached and removed from his post, so he named his garden in expectation that it would remedy his situation. The western part of the garden is the residence, the middle part the courtyard, and the eastern part the garden. The residence is further divided into outer and inner sections, the outer one made up of Sedan Chair Hall (Jiao Ting), Flower Hall (Hua Ting), and Central Hall (Zheng Ting). Buildings in the courtyard are connected by verandas with French windows on two sides. The two gates on either side of the garden are designed to resist fire and thieves. Tuisi Garden is a masterpiece of classic Chinese gardens.

Zhou Village

Originally called Zhenfengli, Zhou village is located at the southern part of Kunshan Mountain in the city of Kunshan. It was renamed after Zhou, a Buddhist landlord who donated the land to Quanfu Temple. Rivers crisscross the town, where there are over 100 structures and folk houses of the Ming and Qing dynasties, 24 stone bridges, and over 60 gate towers of carved bricks. South of Zhou village is South Lake (Nan Hu), about

Scene of Zhou village (From ImagineChina)

a third of which lies within the village. The most famous sites in this village are Fu'an Bridge (Fu'an Qiao), Twin Bridge (Shuang Qiao), and Shen Hall (Shen Ting).

Yangzhou Region

Best Time to Travel

Yangzhou has a cold winter and a hot summer, making spring and autumn the optimal time to travel, especially in April and May.

Narrow West Lake

Located in the western suburbs of Yangzhou, this lake was originally named Baozhang Lake (Baozhang Hu). It's now

Narrow West Lake has long been a scenic site. Five-Pavilion Bridge (Wuting Qiao), one of its scenic spots, was built in 1757. (From Quanjing)

called Narrow West Lake because it is narrower than the West Lake in Hangzhou. The most famous vistas are the willows on the long banks in the spring, Xu Garden (Xu Yuan), Small Gold Hill (Xiao Jinshan), the mist and rain over the four bridges, Blowing Terrace (Chui Tai), Five-Pavilion Bridge, and the White Pagoda (Bai Ta).

In the western part of He Garden, there is a pond in the middle, to the east of which is a square pavilion surrounded by stone railings. Two stone bridges are situated north and south of the pavilion. (From CFP)

Daming Temple

Located on Shugangzhong Peak (Shugangzhong Feng) outside the North Gate of Yangzhou, Daming Temple was built in the fifth century. Inside the gate of the temple, statues of the Four Davarajas stand on both sides. In Great Buddha's Hall there is a statue of Sakyamuni. On either side of the hall sit the Eight Arhats. The Memorial Hall to Jianzhen in the temple is in the Tang Dynasty style; the foundation was laid in 1963, the twelve-hundredth anniversary of Jianzhen's death, and it was completed in 1973.

He Garden

Located at 7 Xuningmen Street in Yangzhou, He Garden was owned by He Zhi. Built in 1883, it is also known as Jixiao Mountain Villa. The eastern garden features a boat-shaped hall made of nanmu (an evergreen laurel). In the center of the western garden is a pond and a veranda. A two-story tower stands south of this veranda in a tranquil environment.

> Tourists can reach He Garden by taking Bus 1 at the Heyuan Bus Station or Bus 19 at the West Bus Station.

Ge Garden

Ge Garden is located in Dongguan Street in Yangzhou. The Four Seasons Rock Garden is a masterpiece, which, according to legends, is the work of Shi Tao, a famous painter from the Qing Dynasty. The Spring Rock Garden is at the south of the garden proper, where the gate is located. The Chinese character ge is written on the stone horizontal tablet of the gate and takes the shape of three bamboo leaves. The Summer Rock Garden faces south and bathes in the sun, looking delicate and crystal-like. Located in the eastern part of the garden, the Autumn section is made of yellow stones, reflecting the color of autumn. The Winter part is in front of the Veranda of A-Touch-of-Wind-and-Moon (Toufeng-louyue Xuan). Quartz in the rocks makes this section appear white like snow in the shadows.

Huai'an Region

Best Time to Travel

Situated in the temperate zone, Huai'an has a monsoon climate with distinct seasons. The whole year is good for travel except the rainy season from mid-June to early July.

Wintong Pagoda (Wentong Ta)

Originally named Zunsheng Pagoda (Zybsgebg Ta), Wintong Pagoda is situated beside the canal and Shaohu Lake in the northwestern corner of the ancient city in Huai'an. This example of classical Buddhist architecture was built in the second year of Emperor Zhangzong in the Tang Dynasty (708). It was originally an all-wood pagoda but was rebuilt as a brick pagoda in 984. The pagoda is a seven-story octagon, exactly 100 feet tall. The shape of the pagoda itself actually resembles two parabolas. The pagoda holds a statue of the Goddess of Mercy (Guanyin) and four statues of Sakyamuni.

Wintong Pagoda is empty inside. The inner stairs and the first three floors have been restored. In the southeast a new ancient-style tracery wall has been built to guard the pagoda. On the horizontal tablet of the gate is written "the garden of the Wintong Pagoda (Wen Tong Ta Yuan)." (From ImagineChina)

Former Residence of Zhou Enlai

The former residence of Zhou Enlai is situated in Fuma Alley (Fuma Xiang), less than 1,000 feet from the northwest corner of Zhenhuai Tower in Huai'an. The residence is made up of two old-style courtyards, the east one neighboring Fuma Pier (Fuma Bu), and the west one near Linju Alley (Linju Xiang). The living quarters are of typical northern Jiangsu style, and it is very close to the Memorial Hall to Zhou Enlai.

Former Residence of Wu Cheng'en

The former residence of Wu Cheng'en is located in Datong Alley (Datong Xiang), in the town of Xiahe, northwest of Huai'an. The original building was destroyed, and the existing one, built on the four-hundredth anniversary of Wu's death in 1980, was constructed on the same site and followed its original design. The residence is a courtyard in the Ming Dynasty style, made up of verandas, a study, a back garden, and other structures. The dedication on the horizontal tablet of the house is from Shu Tong, a famous calligrapher.

Mingzu Mausoleum

Situated at the spot where the Huaihe River empties into Hongze Lake, 5 miles northwest of Xuyi, Mingzu Mausoleum is the number one mausoleum of Ming Dynasty tombs. Built by Zhu Yuanzhang as a cenotaph honoring three generations from his grandfather and the place where his grandfather is actually buried, its construction began in 1385. The stone carvings in front of the tomb are masterpieces of Ming stone sculpture.

 Lodging in Xuyi is very inexpensive.

The owner of the Han terra-cotta pit on Lion Mountain is Liu Wu, the third Chu king who was assigned to Xuzhou in the early Western Han Dynasty. (From ImagineChina)

Xuzhou Region

Best Time to Travel

Xuzhou has a mild climate, but the optimal time to visit is in the spring and autumn.

Tomb of the Chu King on Lion Mountain

Located near Lion Mountain in the eastern suburbs of Xuzhou, this tomb was once owned by the second Chu King, Liu Ying. It has an amazing structure and is indeed magnificent. More than 2,000 cultural artifacts of gold, silver, copper, iron, jade, stone, and clay have been excavated from this site. The discovery of this tomb bridges the gap in the research of the oriental Han culture of the early Western Han Dynasty.

Han Stone Sculpture Museum in Xuzhou

Situated in the west on Yunlong Mountain, this museum was built to follow the slope of the mountain. It houses over 800 pieces of Han stone sculpture, 177 of which are currently on display.

Lianyungang Region

Best Time to Travel

Lianyungang is an ideal tourist destination all year round, but the period from April to October is the best time to visit.

"General" Cliff Rock Paintings

These rock paintings are on the southern side of Jinping Mountain in the town of Jinping, in Lianyungang. Painted on the eastern cliff of the peak is a general on a horse, hence the name of the cliff. The paintings were made around the middle or late Neolithic Age and extend 72 feet from north to south and 50 feet from east to west. Experts estimate that these paintings date back at least 4,000 years. These rock paintings are the only ones in China that reflect the production and life of an agricultural tribe.

Other petroglyphs at the General Cliff rock paintings are human faces, birds, beasts, astronomical phenomena, and some symbols. (From Colphoto)

Flower and Fruit Mountain

Flower and Fruit Mountain (Huaguo Shan) is located within Yuntai Mountain Scenic Park, about 4 miles from the city proper. Yuntai Mountain has 136 peaks, among which Flower and Fruit Mountain is the highest, at 2,051 feet. Also the highest in Jiangsu Province, Flower and Fruit Mountain is the model for Monkey King's Mountain in the famous Chinese novel *A Journey to the West*.

Kunqu Qinlan Hall

Address: North of Guanqian Garden, Furenfang Lane

Suzhou Kunqu troupe of Jiangsu Province

Address: No.9 Jiaochang Road, Suzhou TEL:0512-67532349

(From ImagineChina)

Jiangsu Style

Pingtan Performances

Pingtan, a form of storytelling and ballad singing in the Suzhou dialect, is often performed in the many gardens of Suzhou. The performances are usually enjoyed in the teahouses at a low price. You can order a cup of Biluochun tea and ask for a Pingtan performance such as *Lin Chong Ye Ben* or *Dian Qiu Xiang,* for your amusement.

Yuanxiang Hall in the Garden of the Humble Administrator features Pingtan. A cup of tea there costs 10 yuan and a Pingtan performance costs 30 yuan.

Kunqu Performances

Suzhou is the cradle of Kunqu. In the past, the audience for Kunqu was dwindling. However, Kunqu has been revived in Suzhou since it was selected as representative work of Human Verbal and Nonmaterial Cultural Heritage. Fans of Kunqu can now enjoy the performances in many of the gardens of Suzhou.

Wuzhong District Pingtan Troupe Place: Meizhu Reading Hall (Stone Road) Guangyu Reading Hall (NO. 5 of Pearl Lane) Time:13:30~15:30 TEL:0512-65251108 (From ImagineChina)

Su Embroidery

Su embroidery is a traditional craft of Suzhou, dating back to the Spring and Autumn Period. The embroidery technique was improved greatly during the Song Dynasty and developed its own characteristics in terms of material, stitches and colors in the Ming Dynasty. Su embroidery is well known for its fine, exquisite, and neat design. Pieces of Su embroidery are characterized by their distinct themes, vivid images, and profound artistic conception.

Shanghai

Geography at a Glance

Shanghai—"Hu" or "Shen" for short—is situated on the estuary of the Yangtze River and is the largest city in China. Shanghai lies in the south of the Yangtze River valley with Jiangsu and Zhejiang provinces to its west, the East Sea to its east, and Hangzhou Bay to its south. Covering an area of 2,316 square miles, Shanghai has a population of 16.73 million (2000 census).

Shanghai has excellent, modern, and convenient transportation facilities and a vast, favorable terrain. It's a natural harbor, having Huangpu River and Ding Mountain Lake. There are no high mountains or highland in Shanghai, but there are lower mountain chains such as the Tianma and She. Shanghai's weather is moderate with an annual average temperature of 60°F. It has the north subtropical monsoon climate, so the four seasons are not as distinct as in the north. The "plum rain" season (frequent light rain) occurs from mid-June to early July. July and August are Shanghai's hottest months when the temperature reaches 82°F. It seldom snows in Shanghai. January, with an average temperature of 37°F, is its coldest month. The frost-free period lasts for 241 days, and the annual precipitation is 47 inches.

Featured Cuisine

Duck stuffed with the eight treasures, zaobotou, three shreds, beche-de-mer with shrimp roe, chicken bone purée, bamboo soup, stewed fish lips with shrimp, sautéed shredded eel with spicy sauce, steamed turtle in

(From Quanjing)

The world-famous Shanghai maglev train line starts from south of Longyang Road Subway station Line 2 in the west and ends east of the first phase airport terminal building of Pudong International Airport. The total length is 19.37 miles, and the designed speed and running speed are respectively 314 miles and 267 miles per hour. After the full line is open for business, passengers need only seven minutes to arrive at the urban area of Shanghai from Pudong International Airport. (From CFP)

crystal sugar broth, stir-fried spring sprouts, chicken congee, chicken and duck's blood soup, Nanxiang's steamed stuffed bun, spareribs New Year cake, pan-fried turnip cake, crisp cake in shape of eyebrow, fried king prawn shaomai, sliced lotus root with sweet sauce, pan-fried noodle with chicken, condensed bean curd jelly, mixed noodles with spring scallion, oil and soy sauce, shrimp wonton.

Featured Commodities

Special Local Products

Jiading garlic, scented rice, taro, anchovy, Pudong chicken, whitebait, Chong Ming narcissus.

Local Handicrafts

Shanghai inkstone, Ji Yunge engraved characters, Cao Sugong ink, Jiading bamboo carving, Jiading yellow straw knitting, tooth carving, embroidery, woolen embroidery, silk, lacquerware, jade carving, wood carving.

Transportation Tips

By Bus

Shanghai has an excellent public transportation system. Except for the most congested roads, Shanghai's highway network is well developed. There are expressways from Shanghai to Hangzhou, Nanjing, and other surrounding cities.

Notes 

❶ Because of ongoing highway and road construction, tourists should write down the name and phone number of the hotel in case they get lost.

❷ Shanghai has many scenic spots and places of historical and cultural interest.

By Train

The three train stations in Shanghai are Shanghai (Main) Railway Station, Shanghai South, and Shanghai West. The main station has 70 trains departing to large cities in the middle of China. Shanghai South Station runs from Shanghai to Hangzhou, Jiashan and Jinshan. Shanghai West Station has through trains to Zhang Jiajie and runs from Shanghai to Baotou, Qi Qihaer, Yantai, Changchun, Zaozhuang, Hengyang, Ganzhou, and Chengdu.

By Plane

Shanghai has two airports: Pudong and Hongqiao. International flights depart from and arrive at Pudong. Hongqiao, located in the west part of the city, controls the departure and arrival of all domestic flights and some international flights. There are hundreds of taxis and rental cars available at the airport.

By Water

Shanghai is the largest harbor in China; there are many options available, such as cruise lines, ferries, and local boat trips.

Recommended Routes

Classical Routes

Tour of New Shanghai at night

Jiading→Shanghai-Jiading Expressway→Second West Ring Road→Yan'an Road Viaduct→Bund→People's Square→Pudong New Area→Jinmao Building→Oriental Pearl TV Tower→Shanghai Ocean Aquarium.

Tour of Lupu Bridge at night (Lupu da qiao)

The Bund→People's Square→Shanghai Urban Planning Exhibition Hall→Shanghai Museum→Shanghai Grand Theater→Lupu Bridge.

Tour of Pudong New Area

People's Square→Shanghai Grand Theatre→Shanghai Museum→the Oriental Pearl TV Tower→Binjiang Road→the Jinmao

POPULAR FESTIVALS

Striking the Longhua Bell to Welcome the New Year's Arrival

It is held from December 31 to January 1. Striking the famous bell to bring good luck and happiness is the main event of this New Year's festival.

Nanhui Peach Blossom Festival

It is held from April 1 to April 20 when the blooming peach trees are at their height of splendor.

Longhua Temple Fair

Longhua Temple holds a temple fair in the first two weeks of April with folk dances, singing, plays, and stands with local food.

Shanghai International Tea Cultural Festival

Zhabei District hosts cultural learning activities centered around the selection and preparation of tea from April 26 to May 21.

Shanghai Osmanthus Flower Festival

Cao River area holds this festival is appreciation of the osmanthus (royal palm) flowers from September 28 to October 15.

Building → "Olianna" Tourist Ship→Lu Jiazui Financial Trade Zone→Huaxia Tourist City.

Tour in the Peripheral Area of Shanghai

Jiading Wistaria Park→Kong Temple (Kong Miao)→Qiuxia Gargen (Qiuxia Pu)→Millennium Tree Garden→Xin Ze Yuan →Hundred Buddha Garden.

Tour of Chongming Island

Village of Qianwei→Gymnasium→Fishing House→Square for Fun and Leisure →Yingzhou Ancient Village→Ecological Marsh Park→Chongming Forest Park.

Traditional Routes

One-day tour of Old Shanghai

Shanghai Square Tower Garden→White Pool Park→Zhongshan Mid-Road→Huating Old Street College Town.

Two-day tour of Changing Shanghai Lin Chan

Day 1 Shanghai Film and TV Amusement Park→Songjiang Industrial Estate→Square Tower Garden→White Pool Park →Xi Lin Chan→Songjiang New City→Songjiang New City Center Park (tour of Miaoqian Street at night, Changqiao Street, Huating Old Street, Zhongshan Mid-Road).

Day 2 Oriental Pearl TV Tower→Bund→Nanjing Road→Old City God's Temple.

Two-day ecological leisure tour of Songjiang

Day 1 Tomato Farm.

Day 2 Qingqing Tourist World→Jiaotong University Agricultural Technology New Bridge Flower District.

Two-day tour of natural scenery

Day 1 Sheshan Catholic Church→Sheshan Astronomical Observatory→Hundred Birds Garden→Butterfly Garden→Tianma Mountain Park→Songjiang College Town→Shanghai Square Tower Garden.

Day 2 Tour of Songjiang Industrial Estate by car→Shanghai Film and TV Amusement Park→Shanghai Qingqing Tourist World→Jiaotong University Agricultural Technology New Bridge Flower District.

Self-Guided Tours

Information for Shanghai's tours

Tourists might find it more convenient to stay at hotels in the Xu Jiahui District and start the tour at the Longhua Temple in the morning, then stroll around the Old City God's Temple, Yu Garden Bazaar, and Yu Garden. Take time to eat at local restaurants or from street carts. In the afternoon, visit People's Square, Shanghai Museum, and Nanjing Road, a pedestrian-only street. Explore the Bund at dusk to see the Lu Jiazui Financial Trade Zone, then cross the river by subway through the tunnel and climb the Oriental Pearl TV Tower to appreciate Shanghai's beautiful night skyline.

Decorations adorn the Chenghuang Temple during the Chinese New Year. (From CFP)

Addresses and Phone Numbers

Pujiang Hotel	15 Huangpu Road	021-63068888
East Lake Hotel	70 East Lake Road	021-64158158
Linglong Hotel	939 West Yan'an Road	021-62250360
Fudan University Medical College East Garden Rest House	139 Medical College Road, Xuhui district (outside the east door of the college)	021-54237901
City Hotel	661 Zhejiang Mid-Road	021-63514685

Shanghai Tourist Area

Best Time to Travel

Shanghai's seasons are typically warm in spring, hot in summer, cool in autumn, and cold in winter. It rains almost one-third of the year. January and February are Shanghai's coldest months. The "plum rain" season (frequent light rain) is from mid-June to early July. Always prepare for rain by keeping an umbrella and raincoat handy.

Shopping Tips

Nanjing Road, known as "China's finest commercial street," has become a symbol of Shanghai. It goes without saying that tourists new to Shanghai must stroll around the Nanjing Road, whether they shop or not.

Shanghai's largest bookstore, Shanghai Book City on Fuzhou Road. is an essential place for readers and browsers. Books and magazines in all languages are for sale here. Huaihai Road, the former Xiafei Road, is full of fashionable shops reflecting the newest trends.

Shanghai Sanlian Bookstore Press, Shanghai Culture Press, Shanghai Wenhui Press, Shanghai People's Press, and other famous publishers are all on Shaoxing Press Street. There are also art galleries and small bookstores for special interests. Be sure to visit the Angle Gallery, Hanyuan Bookstore, Reading Club, and Haichen Tea Ceremony House.

North Sichuan Road Business Street has department stores, as well as hardware and grocery stores.

In China Silk Fabrics Village of Nanjing, visitors can view the different weaving skills and fabrics collections, and also buy some silk handcrafted fabrics and clothing.

Huangpu River

With its source in Taihu Lake, the 70-mile-long Huangpu River is located in the southeast part of the Taihu drainage area and

A gold store in the Cheng Huang Temple, Shanghai (From CFP)

The Huangpu River is the major river as well as a distinguishing feature of Shanghai. The essence of life and culture in Shanghai can be viewed along the river. (From ImagineChina)

flows into the Yangtze River in northeast Shanghai. The river is named for the yellow sand in the water.

> Thanks to the Cross-River Tunnel, which connects the Bund in East Nanjing Road with the Oriental Pearl TV Tower under Huanghu River, it's quick and easy to get from one side to the other in a matter of minutes.

The Bund

The Bund (also named East First Zhongshan Road) lies along the west bank of the Huangpu River. In 1845, the Bund was leased to the United States. Along this 2.5-mile-long thoroughfare, there are buildings of different Chinese and Western architectural styles. It is locally called "the contemporary world expo of architecture." In the past few decades, as China has opened up to the outside world, many modern skyscrapers have been built here. The combination of these old and new buildings is an architectural symbol of Shanghai.

Shanghai Great World

Shanghai Great World, a hexagonal, yellow, pinnacled building, stands at the junction of Yan'an Road and Xizang Road. Opened in 1917, the Great World is Shanghai's largest amuse-

Buildings in the Bund are all decorated with advanced lighting, making the night skyline brilliant and fantastic. (From Quanjing)

The Shanghai Museum (From CFP)

ment park as well as the main spot for the recreational activities, vaudevilles, plays and operas, and folk arts. Having distinctive architectural characteristics, Shanghai Great World is supported by twelve columns. Three four-story architectural complexes constitute its main buildings, two facing west and one facing north.

Near Dingshan Lake, the Shanghai Water Park is a brand-new area for camping, vacationing, entertainment, and business.

Shanghai Museum

Shanghai Museum, covering about 237,000 square feet, was originally housed within the Shanghai Library in 1975. Now situated to the south of the People's Square, this spectacular building is the centerpiece of People's Square. The museum is a harmonious combination of squares and circles, epitomizing the Chinese traditional concept that imagines Heaven as round and Earth as square. The museum has 12 exhibition halls and boasts over 120,000 of historical and cultural artifacts.

People's Square

People's Square, Shanghai's largest public square, is located in the center of Shanghai, south of the People's Road. In the center of the square is a round three-story-high fountain. Its colorful rings are formed by glass steps of red, yellow, and blue. The Building of Shanghai Municipal Government, Shanghai Museum, and Shanghai Great Theater are also important tourist sights of the People's Square.

In the "1930 Life-Style Street of Shanghai," located beside the square, tourists can see the architectural features and folk customs of the old Shanghai.

The People's Square, previously a racecourse built by Westerners, is now the political, financial, and cultural center of Shanghai. Activities and performances that attract large audiences are also held here. (From ImagineChina)

Night scene at the Yuyuan Garden (From CFP)

The Yuyuan Garden

Construction of Yuyuan Garden began in 1559. Located not far from the Bund in the southwestern side of the city, it is a classical landscape in the southern Chinese style with a history of more than 400 years. Pavilions, halls, rock gardens, and ponds display the finest in landscaping as typified in the Ming and Qing dynasties. Five scenic spots and more than 30 landscapes have been ingeniously separated by latticed walls, winding corridors, and latticed windows. The large rock garden is the oldest and most elegant of its kind in the Jiangnan area.

Yu Garden Bazaar, the former Old City God's Temple market, grew out of the Old City God's Temple Fair and is now Shanghai's famous small commodities market.

Site of the First National Congress of the Communist Party of China

Located at No. 76 Xingye Road (previously 106 Wangzhi Road), the building was originally the residence of Li Shucheng, the brother of one of the delegates at the First National Congress of the Communist Party. On July 23, 1921, that Congress was held in this building. In the last 50 years, more than 38,000 items of historical value have been collected here.

Open from 8:30 am. to 4:00 p.m. except Monday and Thursday. Take subway line 1 and get off at South Huangpi Road station; then take No.10, 17, 24, 146, or 581; the free sightseeing bus of Huaihai Road is also an option. The Huiahai Road business street, Sun Yatsen's Residence, the Residence of Zhou and Xin Tiandi, and other scenic spots are all nearby.

Sun Yat-sen's Residence

Located at No. 7 Xiangshan Road, the house was bought for Dr. Sun by Chinese people living in Canada in support of his revolutionary activities. He and his wife, Song Qingling, stayed in this Western-style villa from 1920 to the end of 1924.

Song Qingling's Residence

Song Qingling's Residence, located at 1843 Middle Huaihai Road, is a quadrate courtyard covering 14,225 square feet. From 1948 to 1963, Song Qingling lived and worked here. In January 1994, it was renamed as Shanghai Song Qingling's Residence Memorial. The main building was built in 1920 and is a Western-style three-story villa. Upstairs are Song Qingling's bedroom and office, which display things that she used during her lifetime.

Longhua Temple

Longhua Temple, located in Longhua Town, Xu Jiahui area, is the oldest and largest temple in Shanghai. The main building includes the Maitreya Hall, the Hall of Heavenly Kings, the Hall of Sakyamuni, and the Abbot House. In the front of the temple is Longhua Pagoda with its famous bell. It is said that the pagoda was built in 249 as a seven-tier octagonal brick tower with a total height of 132.5 feet. This magnificent and graceful pagoda is one of the best-preserved pagodas in Shanghai.

The picture shows Song Qingling's simple and elegant lobby. There are also many works of art hung on the walls, which Song Qingling collected during her lifetime. (From ImagineChina)

Museum of the Chinese League of Left-Wing Writers (1930–1936) on the Duolun Road. (From ImagineChina)

Cultural Street on the Duolun Road

Duolun Road is a narrow, short street, north of the North Sichuan Road trade area. Along the red-colored road, a decorated silver-gray archway, with characteristics of the Shikumen style, can be seen at the north entrance of Duolun Road. Not far away is the Kong Residence, home of one of the four most important Chinese families before the People's Republic of China. The adjacent Spanish garden villa holds China's Jinquan Coin Museum.

Along the Duolun Road, there are many other buildings, such as the Unique Stone Museum, the Chopsticks Collection House, the Jade Collection House, and the Suzhou Embroidery Hall.

Shanghai Old Street (Laojie)

Previously known as Fangbang Road, Shanghai Old Street is 2,707 feet long. It runs adjacent to the Sixteen Store (Little East Door), the City God's Temple, and the Yuyuan Garden. A number of Shanghai's earliest banking houses, gold stores, silverware shops, wineshops, teahouses, theaters, and trading companies are built along this street.

The old teahouse on Shanghai Old Street is well worth a visit. There is a performance of Pingtan (storytelling combined with ballad singing in Suzhou dialect) in the afternoon on Saturdays and Sundays. More than 50 cheongsams of the 1930s are exhibited in the "Old Shanghai" teahouse.

Jade Buddha Temple (Yufo Si)

The Jade Buddha Temple was built during the Guangxu period of the Qing Dynasty (1875–1909) and burned down in the early twentieth century. In 1918 the temple was rebuilt on Anyuan Road, north of Shanghai. The construction is in the impressive architectural style of the Song Dynasty. Jade Buddha Temple is dedicated to a jade Sitting Buddha statue 6 feet high and weighing about 2,200 pounds.

Hongkou Park (Luxun Park)

The former residence of Luxun is located at No. 9 and 10 New Continental Village, Shanyin Road. In October 1956, the New Shanghai Luxun Memorial was built in Luxun Park, and Luxun Tomb was moved there. The new memorial reconstructed the living environment at that time, including the study and bedroom combination and the Zhongshan University school administration meeting room.

The Oriental Pearl TV Tower

The Oriental Pearl TV Tower stands in Pudong Park in the newly developed Lu Jiazui District on the banks of the Huangpu River. With typical oriental architectural style, the tower is 1,535 feet high and is the tallest in Asia and the third tallest in the world.

The Scientific Fantasy City under the Oriental Pearl Tower is really a small amusement and theme park. Such venues as the Forest Tour, Tour to South Pole, Magic Tour, Treasure Cave, and Dynamic Movie Theatre are highlights of this area.

The upper sphere of the oriental Pearl TV Tower, 876 feet high, is the largest revolving restaurant in Asia. It can accommodate 350 people for dining, drinking, and enjoying the panoramic view of the city. (From Colphoto)

The Jinmao Building (From Colphoto)

The Jinmao Building

Along with the Oriental Pearl TV Tower, the Jinmao Building is an 88-story skyscraper in the center of the Lu Jiazui Finance and Trade Zone. The building is a superb design, combining elements of traditional Chinese architecture and current high-tech features. It adds yet another spectacular high-rise to the skyline of Shanghai.

Elevators in the Jinmao Building can reach the top floor from the basement in 45 seconds.

Century Park

Century Park, located in the administrative and cultural center of Pudong New Area, is an enormous ecological city park, rich in natural features even though it is in the middle of this modern city.

Take Bus No. 640, 788, 794, or 983; Shenbao Line B Line; subway line 2, or Jiangyuan sightseeing minibus.

Former Residence of Zhang Wentian

In Dengsan Village, Shiwan Township, New Pudong Area, there is a rural residence characteristic of local houses. With one central room and two rooms on the wings, it is the former residence of Zhang Wentian. Zhang Wentian was born here on August 30, 1900. Inside is the "Exhibition Room of Zhang Wentian's Revolutionary Activities." More than 400 artifacts, including the Address at Lushan Conference, books, other scripts and documents, and the jade ink stone are all on display here.

Pudong International Airport, Wu Changshuo Memorial, and the Former Residence of Huang Yanpei are all close by.

Zhu Jiajiao Town

Zhu Jiajiao Town is located in the western suburb of Shanghai, beside Dingshan Lake. Endowed with another elegant name, "Pearl of South China," the little town has been a business quarter since ancient times. Situated along the stream, North Street is only 10 to 13 feet wide and goes through the town's business center. Only a tiny piece of sky can be seen at its narrowest part. The private residences, built in the Ming and Qing periods, are well-preserved and worth a visit.

Scenery of a water village in Zhu Jiajiao Town. (From ImagineChina)

Shanghai local cuisine (From ImagineChina)

Shanghai Style

Shanghai Local Cuisine

Shanghai cuisine, which is one of the major Chinese cuisines, is also called "overseas style cuisine." Its development is mainly due to the geographic advantages of the natural environment. Located in a fertile land south of the lower reaches of the Changjiang River, the states of Chu and Yue were said to "take rice as food and fish as soup." Shanghai is located in the central point of the continental coast of China. Its climate is mild, its transportation is convenient, and there are abundant vegetables, seafood, and food imported from across the country and overseas. Such abundant resources provide broad flexibility for Shanghai cuisine, which forms the possibilities of selecting different foods for different seasons. Since Shanghai is a commercial port that is connected with the entire country internally and linked to the whole world externally, its cuisine is adapted to the needs of people from various places, Shanghai cuisine represents the overseas style of compatibility, variety, simplicity, elegance, freshness, and purity as well as openness to change. It sets the trends for cuisines throughout the country.

Shanghai Alleys

Alleys, the most important component of Shanghai local culture in modern times,

(From ImagineChina)

compose the most important architectural features of modern Shanghai. To know alleys is to know Shanghai and Shanghai people. Alleys contain the the typical houses in Shanghai, which integrate the traditional Chinese lifestyle and modern commercial culture. Alleys are connected clusters of houses that have uniform style and spread in the form of a fishbone. The only gate connected with the street is the alley porch, which is usually an arcaded building. There is a small atrium in every house in the alley and there is a small "pavilion booth" and terrace in the rear end of each house. Typical examples include Bugao Alley and Jianye Alley on West Jianguo Road, and Nianwuxincun and Simingcun on Middle Yan'an Road.

In the 1930s, Shanghai developed into a world famous metropolis with plenty of exotic new alleys emerging. Although new alleys retained the basic pattern, they were obviously westernized and modernized. Typical examples include Verdun Garden on South Shanxi Road, Huaihaifang on Middel Huaihai Road, Jing'an Villa on West Nanjing Road, and Yongquanfang on Yuyuan Road.

Xintiandi Plaza's bars in Shanghai (From Imagine-China)

Elegance of Bars

There are plenty of bars throughout Shanghai, which have become a unique part of Shanghai's night life. Bars are mostly concentrated in the area of Hengshan Road, Maoming Road, Huashan Road, Huaihai Road, and Changle Road. Their style is often European and the appearances are largely identical but with minor differences. Foreigners and young and trendy Chinese people are familiar with the drinks and entertainment of the West.

Bars on Hengshan Road

Hengshan Road has the largest concentration of bars in Shanghai. It is also called the "Avenue des Champs Elysées in Shanghai." As it is located near the consulates, it is international and diverse. Nowadays, in people's perception, it also includes the restaurants on Dongping Road and Wuxin Road. On Hengshan Road and the crossing roads there are over 100 bars, teahouses, hotels, recreation centers, beauty parlors, and galleries which attract the young and affluent.

Cuisine on Hengshan Road is more cosmopolitan. There are restaurants such as Mr. Stone from Australia, chain stores such as Friday's from the United States, Bourbon Street from New Orleans, French food at Sasha's, Mediterranean cuisine at 1001 Nights Restaurant, Hong Fan Indian Pub Restaurant, Sumo Sushi with Japanese food, Landhaus Restaurant & Bar with German cuisine, Simply Thai, Pasta Fresca Da Salvatore with classic Italian cuisine, and many Chinese-style restaurants with elegant environments such as Xiangzhang Garden,

Xijia Garden, Yangjia Kitchen, and Jingting Restaurant.

For recreational activities, in addition to the Orden Bowling Center, there are tennis courts, indoor golf, and a swimming pool at the Shanghai International Tennis Center in the Regal International East Asia Hotel, not to mention Shanghai's Real Love Disco. Even if bars in other places in Shanghai were as numerous as stars, people would still come here for its reputation. It is the first choice for witnessing Shanghai's fascinating charm.

Xintiandi has borrowed its old-Shanghai style from Shikumen architecture. (From ImagineChina company)

Xintiandi Plaza

Located on Lane 181 Taicang Road, Xintiandi Plaza is a fashionable pedestrian-only street composed of older architectural styles, such as the residential quadrangle with stone-ringed doors, and modern architecture. It contains the historic and cultural features of the past as well as the fashionable recreation and entertainment of the present.

The current Xintiandi Plaza is divided into North Lane and South Lane with Xinye Road as the dividing line. North Lane has retained most of its residential quadrangles with stone-ringed doors, which are now mostly bars, chambers, art galleries, thematic restaurants and entertainment centers, and museums.

Xintiandi Plaza is now called "Lan Kwai Fong in Shanghai," a place in the forefront of vogue and fashion. Therefore, Xintiandi Plaza is the first choice for recreation and sightseeing. Fashionable men and women, tourists from far and wide, and the constant fashion promotion shows make Xintiandi Plaza an elegant hot spot in Shanghai.

Xintiandi Plaza is composed of Taicang Road, South Huangpo Road, Madang Road, and Zizhong Road. It is located in the central zone of the city and near the business area on Middle Huaihai Road.

Anhui

Geography at a Glance

Anhui Province, or "Wan" for short, is located in the southeastern part of China, near the lower reaches of the Yangtze River. Anhui covers a total area of more than 50,000 square miles and has a general population of 63,690,000 (2000 census). Anhui has complex landforms, with alternating plains, hills, and mountains. The land area slopes downward from the southwest to the northeast. The plains north of the Huaihe River are in the northern part of the province, the hilly land between the Huaihe River and Yangtze River is in the east, Dabieshan Mountain range is in the west, and there are more hilly areas in the south. Well-known bodies of water in Anhui include the Huaihe River, Chuhe River, Chaohu Lake, and Yangtze River. Mountain ranges include the Yellow Mountains, Jiuhua Mountains, and Zhangbaling Mountains.

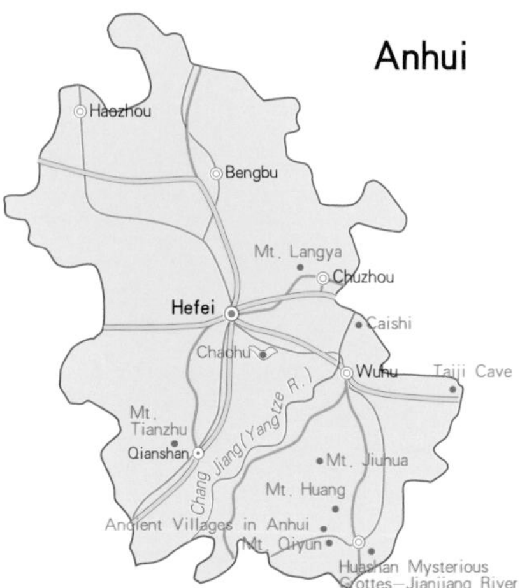

(From Quanjing)

Featured Cuisine

Smoked duck, gold and silver chicken, fish stroganoff, Li Hongzhang hotchpotch, Wenzheng wild bamboo shoots, mountain Bagong bean curd, Jiang Wanchun boiled dumplings, Luyang dumplings, crab shell yellow fried cakes, Huizhou double winter meat, duck's oil shaomai, crab fried dumplings, mung bean hum zongzi, dried shrimp roe noodles, steamed turtle, Baohe crucian, Maofeng follet, stewed hen with stone mushrooms, Tunxi drunken shrimp, Fenghuang roast chicken, braised head and tail, fish tails in brown sauce.

Anhui cuisine consists of cooking styles from three localities: southern Anhui, the region along the Yangtze River, and the region along the Huaihe River. The cuisine in southern Anhui is most typical. With top-quality ingredients, Anhui cuisine offers fresh river catches and domestic fowl deliciously prepared. Cooking methods here include more boiling, stewing, or steaming and less quick-frying or stir-frying. Great importance is attached to oil, color and temperature control. (From CFP)

Featured Commodities

Herbal Medicines

Root of herbaceous peony, Bozhou chrysanthemum, Chuzhou chrysanthemum, Bo flower powder, Bo Clary, Tianzhu glossy ferns, Tianzhu wild mushrooms, and other specifically Chinese herbs and spices. Always consult with your tour guide about buying these products. Note that tourists from the West cannot take herbs or plants home with them.

Special Local Products

Mountain Bagong bean curd, Tongling ginger, Wuhu melon seeds, Anqing horsebean chili paste, Gujing wine, Qianshan Snow Lake lotus root, Shuzhou bamboo-strip mats, Tianzhu Qingxue tea, Huangshan unprocessed tea, Liu'an Guapian (a green tea produced in Anhui Province), Taiping Houkui (green tea), Qimen black tea, Tunxi green tea, Huangshan green peony, Jiu Huashan fog tea.

Local Handicrafts

Huizhou bamboo basketwork, Jiuhua bambooware, Jiuhua stone carving, exquisite writing brushes made in Xuancheng, Hui inksticks produced in Huizhou, Xuan paper, Shexian inkstones, Wuhu iron pictures.

Transportation Tips

By Bus

The major long-distance transportation routes in Anhui are nine national highways, which constitute the main arteries

Notes 

❶ Besides the Yellow Mountains, there are several other famous ranges in Anhui Province, such as the Jiuhua Mountains and Qiyun Mountains.

❷ The traditional "four treasures of the study" in Anhui have acquired a great reputation at home and abroad. It's worth taking back an ink slab from She, Hui ink stick, Xuan paper, and Xuan writing brush as souvenirs.

from inside the province to the outside. You can get to all the major cities in Anhui from almost every other location in China.

By Train

There are almost 1,600 miles of railroad in Anhui Province. Among the 15 main lines, Beijing-Jiujiang, Beijing-Shanghai, and Lianyungang-Lanzhou railroads are the dominant ones; Hefei, Fuyang, and Bengbu are the three main railroad stations.

By Plane

Luogang Airport in the capital city of Hefei and Tunxi Airport in Huangshan offer flights to many cities in the province and throughout China. Anqing and Fuyang airports offer flights to only a few other cities. Bengbu airport has only nonstop flights to Beijing.

By Water

The Yangtze River is the main waterway in Anhui. From Hubei Province and Jiangxi Province in the upper reaches, people can travel through Anqing, Chizhou, Tongling, Wuhu, and Ma'anshan Port to Shanghai.

Recommended Routes

Classical Routes

Three-day scientific and educational tour of Hefei

Day 1 Arrival in Hefei. Lodging: Anhui Hotel.

Day 2 University of Science and Technology of China→Anhui Museum→Hefei Science and Technology Museum→Anhui Weather Science and Technology Museum→Anhui Science and Technology Museum→Anhui Museum of Famous Persons→PLA Artillery College→Hefei Wild Animal Zoo→Hui Garden. Lodging: Anhui Hotel.

Day 3 End of tour.

POPULAR FESTIVALS

Lantern Festival in Zhangou

Large-scale lantern exhibitions are held on the 15th day of the first lunar month in Zhangou southeast of Lixin County.

Temple Fair on Langye Mountain

The temple fair is held on the 16th day of the first lunar month on Langye Mountain in Chuzhou. Many activities take place, attracting a great many tourists.

Temple Fair in Shouzhou

Traditional trade fairs take place on the 15th day of the third lunar month on Siding Mountain in Shouzhou.

Mulan Festival in Bozhou

Activities such as dragon lanterns, lion dances, and martial arts performances are held on the 8th day of the fourth lunar month in Bozhou.

International Tourism Festival in Huangshan

This festival is held October 25–27 in Huangshan. The main thrust is the convention of travel guides and tour companies, in addition to sightseeing in the Yellow Mountains and other scenic spots.

Five-day tour of Guniujiang-Hongcun

Day 1 Arrival at Yellow Mountains. Lodging: Huangshan Hotel.

Day 2 Tunxi→Guniujiang Natural Reserve (visit the relics of the Guniujiang Guanyin Hall, Huanglong Pond, Heilong Pond, Guniu Lake, etc.). Lodging: Guniu Hotel.

Day 3 Xianrenjuhui→Luohan Pine→Heilong Pond→Xiannu Pond→Carp Salutes Guanyin→Nine-Dragon Pond (Qiyu Platform, Xue-tangji, China Stone, Zuochan Guanyin, Crouching Lion, Sword Testing Stone, Three-Layer Waterfall, Fairy Maidens' Foot Basin)→Yi County (visit Hongcun). Lodging: Local residence in Hongcun.

Day 4 Yi County→Tunxi (visit modern Song Street→Tunxi Ancient-style Street). Lodging: Huangshan Hotel.

Day 5 End of tour.

Traditional Routes

Seven-day tour of the former residence of Huizhou

Day 1 Arrival in Huizhou.

Day 2 Tangyue Archway Group→Tangmotangan Garden→Qiankou Civilian Residence→Chengkanluodongshu Temple.

Day 3 Ancestral Temple of Hu Family →Ancestral Temple of Zhang Family →Shangzhuang.

Day 4 Former Residence of Hushi→Frescoes of the Taiping Heavenly Kingdom period→Kuixing Pavilion→Tianzi Tomb.

Day 5 Xidi Village→Hongcun→Nanping.

Day 6 Three River Town→Chencun→Chaji.

Day 7 End of tour.

Four-day tour of the Yellow Mountains

Day 1 Arrival in Huangshan City (visit the old city).

Day 2 Huangshan City→Yellow Mountain Tour Section (You Shixin Peak, Lion Peak, Paiyun Pavilion, Feilai Stone).

Day 3 View sunrise→Mountain Qian→Guangming Peak→Aoyu Peak→A Line of Sky→Lianhua Peak→Yuping Building→Banshan Temple→Ciguang Temple.

Day 4 End of tour.

Three-day tour of Mount Tianzhu

Day 1 Arrival at Mount Tianzhu.

Day 2 Sanzu Temple→Shiniugu Cave→Mystery Vale→Tianzhu Peak→June Snow→Liandan Lake.

Day 3 End of tour.

Four-day tour of the Jiuhua Mountains

Day 1 Scenery of Wuxi→Two Sages Hall→Taoya Waterfall→Ganlu Temple.

Day 2 Diyuan Temple→Taibai Ancient School→Tonghui Convent→Li

Huangmei Opera (From ImagineChina)

Temple→Huacheng Temple→Jiuhua Mountain Museum→Shangchan Hall→Zhantanlin→Roushen Hall→Cloud Sea→Dongyayunfang→Baisui Palace.

Day 3 Huixiang Temple→Phoenix Old Pine→Huiju Temple→Huayan Temple.

Day 4 Banshan Temple→Guanyin Peak→Ancient Baijing Platform→Tiantai Peak→Tiantai Temple→Tiantai sunrise→Cloud Gorge.

Self-Guided Tours

Tour of Famous Mountains and Folk Customs

Start from Hefei to Chuzhou via Chaohu, Yangtse River, Wuhu, City Xuan, Jixi, She County, Yi County, Xiuning, Tongling, Chuzhou. Main scenic spots include Ancestral Temple of Hu Family, Minister MemoLuan's memorial Arch, Tangyue Archway Group, Xuguo Stone Store, Xidi Ancient Village, Hongcun Ancient Village, ShuQingyu Hall, Mountain Qiyun, Yellow Mountains, Jiuhau Mountains, Langye Mountains.

Tour of northern Anhui

Start from Hefei to Shou County via Chuzhou, Fengyang, Meng City, Bozhou, Shou County. Main scenic spots include Xiaoyao Ford Park, Temple of Bao, Li Hongzhang's Former Residence, Tomb of Bao, Mountain Langye, Zuiweng Pavilion, Fengyang Royal Mausoleum of the Ming Dynasty, Zhuangzhou's Former Residence, Ancient City Wall of Shou County, Liu'an Tomb.

Addresses and Phone Numbers

Anhui Hotel	18 Meishan Road, Hefei	0551-2218888
Nanshan Hotel	168 Zhongshan Road, Bengbu	0552-2049999
Tieshan Hotel	3 Gengxing Road, Wuhu	0553-3718888
Dongshan Hotel	1 Yingbin Road, Tian Jia'an District, Huainan	0554-6644923
ZhuangyuanFu Hotel	77 Xiaosu Road, Anqing	0556-5542871
Gujing Hotel	105 South Qiaoling Road, Bozhou	0558-5534270
Huangshan Hotel	Hot spring tourist area in Huangshan	0559-5585808
Huaxi Hotel	1 Xizhen Street, Tunxi District, Huangshan	0559-2328000
Xiang WangFu Hotel	1 Meicheng Road, Huaibei	0561-3030081
Chengzhong Hotel	90 Zhong Road, Lujiang County, Chaohu	0565-7336328
Jinyi Holiday Inn	Luchao Road, Lujiang County, Chaohu	0565-7312888
Jiuhua Mountain Julong Hotel	Jiuhua Mountain tourist area, Guichi District, Chizhou	0566-2831368

Hefei, Chaohu, and Chuzhou Region

Best Time to Travel

April to October is the best time for visiting Hefei.

Shopping Tips

Huaihe Road, is a historically well-known business street in Hefei. It is now a financial and cultural center.

The statue of Zhangliao on an island at the center of Xiaoyaojin Lake. (From Colphoto)

As the busiest downtown area in Anhui Province, Middle Changjiang Road has hundreds of stores as well as party and government headquarters.

In the main hall, there is a bronze statue of Lord Bao sitting upright. One of his hands is placed on the arm of the chair with the other clenched, which shows his integrity and incorruptibility. (From CFP)

Hefei Department Store, located at No. 124 Changjiang Road, is the largest retail store in Anhui Province. Every imaginable commodity is available here.

Temple of Bao (Baogong Ci)

The Temple of Bao, in the southeastern part of Hefei, and at the western end of Baohe Park, was built in 1882 on the foundations of a fourteenth-century temple and restored in 1946. It stands at the place where Baozheng, a famous official during the Northern Song Dynasty (960–1127), pursued his studies. He was very popular with the people because of his moral integrity and incorruptibility.

Baogong Tomb, east of the Temple of Bao and on the south bank of Baohe, is located here and is well worth a visit.

Xiaoyao Ferry (Xiaoyaojin)

The Xiaoyao Ferry, located at the northeastern corner of Hefei's old city area, is both a ferry across the Fei waters as well as a famous ancient battlefield from the Three Kingdoms Period (222–265 CE). It is now a comprehensive park, covering 12 square miles.

> The crossbow platform, commonly known as the Caocao Appointment Platform, is located beside the park.

Chaohu Lake Scenic Area

As one of the five largest freshwater lakes in China, Chaohu Lake occupies an area of more than 300 square miles, one-third of which is within the boundaries of Hefei. With three famous hot springs, four national forest parks, and five caves, Chaohu Lake Scenic Area has numerous tourist attractions. It is widely known as the Land of Fish and Rice for its plentiful biological resources.

> Whitebait, shelled shrimp, and crabs are called "the three delicacies of Chaohu Lake."

Mount Langye Scenic Zone (Langye Shan)

Mount Langye, on the southwestern outskirts of Chuzhou, is well known for its scenic charm. It was called Muotuo Ridge (Muotuo Ling) in ancient times. It is densely wooded, with many secluded ravines and sparkling mountain streams. Mount Langye includes three major scenic areas: Chengxi Lake, Gushan Lake, and Sangu. It is the most famous tourist attraction in the East Wan area. Here on the mountain are found the Tang Dynasty Langye Si (Temple of Langye), the Song Dynasty Pavilion of the old Drunkard (Zuiweng Ting), and many cliff-face carvings and inscribed tablets, some of which date back to the Tang and Song dynasties.

A great number of scenic spots and pseudo-classic structures on Mount Langye were rebuilt or repaired and now blend well with the old roads and architectural styles on the mountain. (From CFP)

The Central Capital Town of the Ming Dynasty

Located in Fengyang County, in the city of Chuzhou, this town was built by Zhu Yuanzhang in 1369. All the palaces have

Chaohu (Nest) Lake is so named because it looks like a bird's nest. The people fish for a living. (From CFP)

been destroyed, and only the ruins of the foundations can be seen at this time. The architectural style of the whole city drew from the tradition of the Song and Yuan dynasties and initiated a new style for Ming and Qing dynasties.

Fengyang Royal Mausoleum of the Ming Dynasty

Located 4 miles south of Fengyang County, the mausoleum is the tomb of the parents of Zhu Yuanzhang. Construction of the tomb began in 1366. In 1635, Zhang Xianzhong captured Fengyang, and all the buildings were burned by the insurrection army; only 36 pairs of stone statues of human figures and animals were left.

Longxing Temple

Longxing Temple, also called Huangjue Temple, at the foot of Phoenix Mountain (Fenghuang Shan), Fengyang County, has been relocated to Xiaoli village, in the Ershiying area in Fengyang County. Construction of the temple began in the Song Dynasty, and it was rebuilt in 1383. There are two main architectural complexes in Longxing Temple, one of which is a simple and intact small temple called Old Longxing Temple.

Bozhou Region

Best Time to Travel

Spring and autumn are the best seasons for travel in Bozhou.

Flower Theater

Located in Grand Guandi Temple at God Fire Temple Street in the northern part of the city of Bozhou, the Flower Theater, also known as Playing Platform, is a large stage for theatrical performances. This three-story building was constructed in the shape of an archway and covers 10,700 square feet. The facades look like wood but are really textured brick. They are decorated with three-dimensional carvings of figures, vehicles and horses, mountains and woods, flowers, and various animals. There are six integrated theatrical narratives and more than 70 other stories, designs, and decorative patterns sculpted on the building. The colorful paintings and skillful carvings are representative of the prosperous period of the Qing Dynasty.

The name "Flower Theater" comes from the hundreds, maybe thousands, of carved ornamental flowers, animals, and narratives on the walls.

A pair of iron flagpoles, about 52 feet tall and weighing about 26,500 pounds, stand in front of the Flower Theater Building. (From ImagineChina)

Tombs of the Cao Family

Located in the southern suburbs of Bozhou, these tombs include that of Caocao's father, Caosong; his grandfather, Caoteng; and other ancestors.

Stone animals beside the walkway of the tombs of the Cao Family

Huazu Temple

In Bozhou city proper, Huazu Temple was built in honor of Hua Tuo, a famous medicial doctor in the Eastern Han Dynasty. The construction of the temple took place in the Tang (618–907) and Song (960–1279) dynasties.

Underground Troop Course

This underground tunnel was built by Caocao for transporting troops secretly. The entire area is exquisitely laid out, with a complicated structure; this troop course is the earliest and largest military underground passage ever found.

Yellow Mountain, Xuan City, and Chizhou Region

>>>

Best Time to Travel

The scenery of the Yellow Mountains is beautiful, and tourists can visit here at any time of the year. Although winter is the best season for viewing the cloud sea, the tourist areas of Mount Tiandu and White Cloud Stream are closed at that time. July and August attract the most tourists to the Yellow Mountains.

Ancient Street in Tunxi

The 4,920-foot-long Ancient Street in Tunxi was built in the Southern Song Dynasty. Lined on both sides with Ming- and Qing-style buildings, it has become a commercial center. The buildings here are mainly brick and wooden structures topped by gray tiles and decorated with wood carvings. At the back of most stores and shops are workshops or residences. The towers are exquisite and elegant, with small doors, big halls, small yards, and narrow lanes.

Former Residence of Cheng Dawei

The former residence of Cheng Dawei is located in Tunxi, in the city of Huangshan. It was built by Cheng's descendants during the Qing Dynasty to commemorate Master Cheng's great achievements with the abacus and in mathematics.

Yellow Mountain (Huang Shan)

The Yellow Mountains, in the eastern part of China, are famous for their marvelous and beautiful scenery. This is one of the most popular tourist areas in China. The landform of the Yellow Mountains is typical of granite mountains and forests, but the Yellow Mountains are justly famous for their four natural wonders: pine trees growing in strange shapes, grotesquely formed stone masses, the sea of cloud through which the peaks protrude, and hot springs. This area brings together all the strong points of other mountains—being grand, strange, baffling, arduous, steep, flourishing, quiet, and expansive. In December 1990, UNESCO listed the Yellow Mountains as a World Natural and Cultural Heritage site.

Mount Qiyun Scenic Spot

Mount Qiyun, known as the White Mountain in ancient times, is located near Yanqian, 9 miles west of Xiuning County, in Anhui Province. It is a national scenic spot, with rolling hills and beautiful landscapes. Mount Qiyun is famous for its Danxia geomorphology (red sandstone, large rock forms, etc.) with hundreds of fantastic rock gardens and secluded caves. It is one of the four famous mountains held sacred by Taoism in China.

 Take a bus from Tunxi bus station.

Tangyue Memorial Archway Group

Tangyue Memorial Archways are located in the village of Tangyue, west of She County. At the entrance to the village are seven magnificent stone memorial archways—three built in the Ming Dynasty and four in the Qing Dynasty—in successive order of loyalty, filial piety, women's chastity, and charity. Alongside the archways are two ancient ancestral halls of the Bao family: one for men (Dun Ben Tang, which means "hall of honesty"); the other for women (Qing Yi Tang, which means "hall of good examples"). Both halls provide vivid examples for studying and

The scenery of the Yellow Mountains is changeable and magnificent in any season. (From ImagineChina)

Dwellings in Hongcun are connected by water. (From Quanjing)

understanding the life and work of the local merchant families in the patriarchal-feudal system, which evolved in the Huizhou area. The construction of a women's hall in the mid-nineteenth century was a rare symbol of women's victory over the feudal admonition that women were not allowed to enter the ancestral hall.

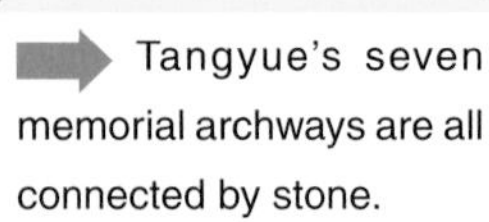

Ancient Village of Xidi

The traditional village of Xidi, located in Yi County at the foot of the Yellow Mountains, preserves to a remarkable extent the appearance of rural settlements of a type that has largely disappeared or has been transformed in the past century. Nearly 1,000 Ming (1368–1644) and Qing (1644–1911) residential buildings have been preserved, re-creating the village life in southern Anhui Province of a few centuries ago. The street patterns, the architecture and decoration, and the integration of houses with comprehensive water systems are unique remnants. The village was listed as a UNESCO World Heritage site in 2000.

Hongcun

The ancient village of Hongcun, located 7 miles from Yi County, was listed as a UNESCO World Heritage site in 2001. From a bird's-eye view, the village takes the shape of a resting water buffalo. The village, covering more than 12 acres, is renowned for its water-supply system. The running water flows through the winding ditches to every household and collects in

Mount Qiyun scenic spot (From ImagineChina)

a little lake at the entrance to the village. The peaceful environment and beautiful surroundings present a pleasing and tranquil picture of typical country life in ancient southern China.

After about a 30-minute ride by three-wheeler, tourists can reach the ancient village of Hongcun from Yi County.

Chaji Ancient Architectures

Located 37 miles west of Wannan, in Jing County, Chaji village has 80 well-preserved structures from the Ming Dynasty and 109 from the Qing Dynasty. These ancient examples of residential architecture stretch for 3 miles along the Chaji River.

Peach Blossom Pond

Located on the shores of Taiping Lake in Jing County, Peach Blossom Pond is part of the Qingyi River system from Zhaicun to Wancun. The terrain here is level and expansive. It is by this pond that the great ancient Chinese poet Li Bai, in the Tang Dynasty, was seen off by his friend Wang Lun, who wrote him the famous poem "To Wang Lun": "I'm on board, about to sail.

The beautiful scenery as well as human activity imbue Peach Blossom Pond with poetic sentiment. (From CFP)

There are ten of these 13-foot-high windows on each side of the main hall of the Ancestral Temple of the Hu Family. (From CFP)

When there's stamping and singing on shore; the Peach Blossom Pond is a thousand feet deep, Yet not so deep, Wang Lun, as your love for me."

The Ruins of the New Fourth Army Headquarters

The ruins of the New Fourth Army Headquarters are located in Yunling, in Jing County. They include the headquarters, government offices, and the hall.

Ancestral Temple of the Hu Family

Located in Yingzhou, in Jixi County, this is the ancestral temple of Hu Fu, minister of revenue, and Hu Zongxian, minister of war, from the Ming Dynasty. The temple covers an area of 12,330 square feet and has elegant carvings on the pillars and beams. These carvings are the best examples of the wood carvings of the Hui School.

Fengcun Ancient Villages

Located 24 miles north of Jixi County, these ancient villages were built by Feng Jianpu in 865, in the Tang Dynasty. Even after thousands of years, most of the ancient residences, bridges, and workshops are still well preserved.

Shijia Village Chessboard Street

Located 17 miles northwest of Jixi County, Shijia Village Chessboard Street has a long history. It is located at the eastern foot of the Yellow Mountains, near Mount Wang to the south and facing Peach Blossom Stream to the north. The layout of the street looks very much like a chessboard, thus its name.

Mount Jiuhua (Jiuhua Shan)

Mount Jiuhua, southeast of Wuhu, is one of the Four Holy Mountains revered by Chinese Buddhists. Its highest point is the summit of the Ten Kings (Shiwang Feng), which is 4,400 feet high. All its major scenic spots and temples are found within an area of 39 square miles. These include 86 temples enshrined with 6,800 Buddhist statues and inhabited by 700 or so monks and nuns. Large numbers of monasteries were built here in the Eastern Jin period; there were some 300 in existence in the seventeenth century, providing accommodation for more than 5,000 monks. Fifty-six of these sacred buildings remain intact and house over 1,300 old documents.

A worker making Hui Mo (ink made in Anhui Province) at a plant in Jixi County. (From ImagineChina)

Tiantai is the best place for viewing the cloud sea. Spring and summer are the best seasons for visiting Mount Jiuhua.

The Baijing platform on Mount Jiuhua is located under Tiantai peak. The main structures here are the Hall of Sakyamuni and the Sea Island. (From ImagineChina)

With the flavor of the local yangge dancing and a brisk tempo, Fengyang flower drum is widely enjoyed by the people. (From CFP)

Anhui Style

Fengyang Flower Drum

The double-stick drum, the flower drum song, and the flower-drum-lantern dance are collectively called "Fengyang flower drum." Double-stick drum is also called "flower drum with small gong," and it is derived from a type of yangge dance from the Ming Dynasty. It is popular in areas around Lantern Temple, in Fengyang. As the hometown of Zhu Yuanzhang, the founder of the Ming Dynasty, Fengyang was said to be devastated after Zhu Yuanzhang ascended to the throne. Unable to make a living by ordinary means, many women were forced to perform street singing with a flower drum and a small gong. Fengyang flower drum has been popular in the Jiangsu and Zhejiang provinces as well as in Beijing for a long time.

Huangmei Opera

Huangmei opera is popular in Anhui and parts of the Hubei and Jiangxi provinces. It developed from tea-picking songs in Huangmei County, Hubei Province, which were brought into Anqing, Anhui Province, in the late reign of the Qianlong Emperor in the Qing Dynasty. Three types of music are used: coloratura, character songs, and basic tunes. Traditional plays include *Collecting Green Feed for Pigs, Marrying a Fairy,* and *Emperor's Female Son-in-law.* Huangmei opera is characterized by mild and pleasant melodies, lively and graceful movements, simple language, and closeness to real life. Its fans can be found both in China and in other countries.

(From Colphoto)

Zhejiang

Geography at a Glance

Zhejiang Province, or "Zhe," is situated on China's southeastern coast and faces the East China Sea. The province covers a total area of more than 38,620 square miles and has a permanent population of 46,770,000 (2000 census). The southwestern part of the territory is mountainous, with an average altitude of 2,625 feet above sea level. The middle part of Zhejiang is hilly, scattered with many large and small valleys. The northeastern part is a low and flat alluvial plain. The mountain ranges stretch toward the East China Sea, forming peninsulas and islands. Zhejiang has a coastline (including islands) of 4,030 miles. This province also has the largest number of islands in China, with more than 2,000 off the coast. Situated in the subtropical region, the province has a warm and rainy climate. A 20-day rainy season comes between spring and summer, and large typhoons hit the area between summer and autumn.

Zhejiang

(From ImagineChina)

Featured Cuisine

Huixiangdou in Shaoxing, stewed fish head with bean curd in clay pot, steamed pork wrapped in lotus leaf, Ningbo clam, steamed pork with preserved vegetables, West Lake sour fish, stir-fried prawn with Longjing tea, braised bamboo shoots, braised pork, soup with West Lake water shield, the Song fish soup, beggar's spring chicken, fish balls in clear soup, turtle stewed with crystal sugar, baked algae, goose liver wrapped in lard, steamed river eel, whole chicken stewed with ham.

The tea master is cooking Longjing tea leaves. (From ImagineChina)

Featured Commodities

Special Local Products

Shaoxing silk, pearl tea in Pingshui, preserved bean curd of Shaoxing, preserved vegetables, Shaoxing laojiu, beef jerky of Wenzhou, bone and wood mosaic, straw mat of Ningbo, Longjing tea, zhen mei tea of Wenzhou, jasmine tea of Jinhua, Ou embroidery of Wenzhou, Xiaoshan lace, canned fish of Zhoushan, chamomile of Hangzhou, embroidery of Hangzhou, silk of Hangzhou, sindhu chopsticks, lotus root starch from West Lake.

Local Handicrafts

Longquan celadon, boxwood carving, Dongyang wood carving, Qingtian stone carving, Wenzhou Qu sculpture, Shaoxing gold and silver jewelery, Zhang Xiaoquan scissors, West Lake silk parasol, silk fan, gold stone stamp, Longquan sword, Hu writing brushes.

Transportation Tips

By Bus

Hangzhou is the center of the expressway network in Zhejiang. At present, the province has completed several other expressways such as Shanghai-Hangzhou, Hangzhou-Ningbo, Shangpu-Sanmen, and 104, 320, 329, and 330 national roads. Highways are convenient ways to travel in Zhejiang.

By Train

There are two main railroad lines inside the province: the Shanghai-Hangzhou railway and the Zhejiang-Jiangxi railway, and several sublines such as Xiaoshan-Ningbo,

Notes 

❶ Because of the southeastern monsoons, Zhejiang is perennially wet. The mountainous area is even rainier than the coastal area. Be prepared with raincoats or umbrellas when traveling in Zhejiang.

❷ Wenzhou and Ningbo have convenient air and sea connections from Zhejiang.

❸ Longjing (dragon well) tea is a local product and is produced in very small amounts, most of which is for export.

Xuan Cheng-Hangzhou, Jinhua-Thousand-Islet Lake, and Jinhua-Wenzhou. Hangzhou, Ningbo, and Wenzhou are major departure cities. Hangzhou East Railway Station and Jinhua West Railway Station are the two most important transfer stations in Zhejiang Province.

By Plane

There are seven regional airports in Zhejiang Province: Wenzhou, Ningbo, Wenzhou, Yiwu, Huangyan, Quzhou, and Zhoushan. International flights leave from Hangzhou-Xiaoshan and Ningbo-Yueshe airports.

By Water

Zhejiang, with its hundreds of lakes, has a well-developed water transportation system. Several passenger liners travel to and from Ningbo, Shanghai, and Zhoushan Archipelago every day, the so-called Golden Triangle, forming the busiest sea passenger

POPULAR FESTIVALS

Auspicious Bell-Ringing in Jingci Temple on New Year's Day

Held on January 1 at Jingci Temple in Hangzhou, there are performances of classical musical instruments of South China, Sizhu shows, and night bell ringing in Nanping.

Lanting Calligraphy Festival

The National Lanting Calligraphy Festival is held annually on the 3rd day of the third lunar month in Shaoxing. Activities include offerings to the great calligraphy master Wang Xizhi, a purification worship ceremony, and calligraphy exhibitions.

Loquat Festival in Tangxi

Held in June in the town of Tangxi, Yuhang District of Hangzhou, the festival features loquat dishes, recipes, and feasts.

Summer of Xin'an River Tourism Festival in Hangzhou

Held from July 15 to July 18 in the town of Xin'an River in Jiande, it features exhibitions, conferences, and tours.

The Grand Canal Cultural Tourism Festival in Hangzhou

Held between July and August by the banks of the Grand Canal in Hanghzou. The festival features parades, conferences, feasts, and tours.

Festival of Clear Water in Thousand-Islet Lake in Chun'an County

It is held in September in the town of Thousand-Islet Lake in Chun'an County.

Traditional Folk Drama Shexi in the Water Village

Held between September and December in Shaoxing City, it features drama and music performances, ethnic foods, and local goods.

Festival of Watching the Tide of Qiantang River

People observe the tidal movement of Qiantang River on the bank from the 16th to the 19th day of the eighth lunar month.

International Yacht Festival in West Lake of Hangzhou

Held from October 5 to 7 in West Lake in Hangzhou City, the festival features boat races, regattas, local food and goods, and yacht competitions.

transportation area in China. There is also a cruise ship, which leaves at sunset and arrives at sunrise, and travels along the Beijing-Hangzhou Grand Canal.

Recommended Routes

Classical Routes

Seven-day tour of "Water Village and Buddhist Country" in East Zhejiang

Day 1 Arrival in Hangzhou. Lodging: Wuzhou Hotel (Five Continents Hotel).

Day 2 Hangzhou-Keqiao (ancient track road and foot-propelled boat)→Sanweishuwu (Three Tastes Private School)→Bazi Bridge (Eight Words Bridge). Lodging: Xianheng Hotel.

Day 3 East Lake→Lanting→Cao'e Temple →Hemudu→Ningbo. Lodging: Ningbo Hotel.

Day 4 Xikou of Ningbo→Tianyige. Lodging: Ningbo Hotel.

Day 5 Tiantong Temple→Gate of Shens→ Putuo Mountain. Lodging: Mount Putuo Hotel.

Day 6 Puji Temple→Fayu Temple→Huiji Temple→Giant Buddha in open air. Lodging: Mount Putuo Hotel.

Day 7 End of tour.

Six-day tour of mountains and rivers in West Zhejiang

Day 1 Arrival in Hangzhou. Lodging: Wuzhou Hotel (Five Continents Hotel).

Day 2 One day tour of West Lake. Lodging: Wuzhou Hotel (Five Continents Hotel).

Day 3 Hangzhou→Fuyang→Tonglu Fishing Platform→Drifting in Tianmu Creek→Fuchun River→Meicheng→Jiande River. Lodging: Jiande Hotel.

Day 4 Jiande River→Zhuge Liang Bagua (Eight Diagram) Village in Lanxi→Chun'an. Lodging: Thousand-Islet Lake Holiday Inn.

Day 5 One day tour of Thousand-Islet Lake. Lodging: Thousand-Islet Lake Holiday Inn.

Day 6 End of tour.

Traditional Routes

Two-day tour of Hangzhou

Day 1 Lingyin Temple→Carved stone statues on peak flown from afar→Longjing (Dragon Well) Tea Field→Snowfall Over Broken Bridge→Bai Causeway→Gu Mountain→Xiling Seal Club→Santan Yinyue Yingzhou Isle (Three Pools Mirroring the Moon)→Quyuan Garden→Yuefei Temple.

Day 2 Song City→Six Harmonies (Liuhe) Pagoda→Qiantang Bridge→Dreaming of the Tiger Spring→Manlongguiyu→Prince Bay Park→Fish Wonder at Huagang Crook→Spring Dawn at Su Causeway→ Night Bell in Nanping→Chinese Silk Museum→Orioles Singing in the Willows. End of tour.

Silk products in Hangzhou (From ImagineChina)

Five-day tour of Jiaxing

Day 1 Arrival at Haiyan.

Day 2 Watching the tide in Haining→Former Residence of Chen Gelao→Sea God Temple→Former Residence of Wang Guowei.

Day 3 South Lake→South Lake Memorial Hall→Yanyu Building→Red Boat→Jiashan.

Day 4 Ancient Town of Xitang→Memorial Hall in the Town of Wu.

Day 5 End of tour.

Three-day tour from Ningbo, Fenghua, and Xikou to Putuo Mountain

Day 1 Hangzhou→Fenghua→Former Residence of Jiang in Xikou→Rock of Tens of Thousands Feet High→Xuedou Temple.

Day 2 Fenghua→County of Yin→Tiantong Temple→Temple of Asoka→Putuo Mountain.

Day 3 Mountain of the Top of the Buddha→Huiji Temple→Fayu Temple→Beach of Thousand Steps→Zizhu Forest→Cave of Sound of Tide→Puji Temple. End of tour.

Self-Guided Tours

Tracing spots cited in poems of Tang Dynasty

Starts from Hangzhou and ends in Ningbo by way of Keqiao, Shaoxing, Shangyu, Shengxian, Xinchang, Tiantai, and Linhai. The main scenic spots include Memorial Temple of He Zhizhang, Lanting, Ruoye Crook, Mausoleum and Temple of King Yu, Wanwei Mountain, Yumen Temple, Cao'e Temple, Tomb of Wang Xizhi, Tens of Thousand-Feet Deep

Addresses and Phone Numbers 

Wuzhou (Five Continents) Hotel in Hangzhou	2 Pinghai Road, Hangzhou	0571-87088088
Thousand-Islet Lake Holiday Inn	9 South Huanghu Road, Town of Thousand-Islet Lake, Chun'an	0571-64880088
Economy and Trade Hotel	37 Xindian Road, Jiande	0571-64791385
Huzhou Hotel	43 Red Flag Road, Huzhou	0572-2020162
Jiaxing Hotel	699 Zhongshan Road, Jiaxing	0573-82067788
Xianheng Hotel	680 South Jiefang Road, Shaoxing	0575-88068688
Wenzhou Hotel	111 Park Road, Wenzhou	0577-88822222
Ningbo Hotel	251 Mayuan Road, Ningbo	0574-87097888
Tiantai Hotel	Guoqing Road, Tiantai, by side of Guoqing Temple	0576-83988999
Linhai Hotel	Great Oriental Road, Linhai	0576-85389288
Yandang Hotel	12 Xiangling Street, Yandang Town, Leqing	0577-62243630
Hotel of Putuo Mountain	Putuo Mountain Scenery Park in Zhoushan	0580-6092828

Cave, South Rock, Wozhou Lake, Banzhu Village, Guoqing Temple, Ancient City of Linhai, Longxing Temple, and Tianyige.

Tour of Taoism in Zhejiang and Jiangxi

Starts from Hangzhou and ends in Nanchang by way of Tonglu, Lanxi, Jinhua, Quzhou, Yushan, Dexing, Shangrao, and Yingtan. The main scenic spots include Geling, Yuhuang Mountain, West Lake, Fishing Platform of Yan Ziling, Zhuge Liang Bagua (Eight Diagrams) Village, Chisong Palace, Double Dragon Cave, Taichi Star Image Village in Yuyuan, Lanke Mountain, Jianglang Mountain, Sanqing Mountain, and the Dragon and Tiger Mountain.

Sightseeing tour of ancient folk houses in Zhejiang, Jiangxi, and Anhui

Starts from Hangzhou, and ends in Huangshan City by way of Fuyang, Tonglu, Lanxi, Jinhua, Dongyang, Hengdian, Quzhou, Jiangshan, Wuyuan, Yixian, and Shexian. The main scenic spots include Town of Longmen, Fishing Platform of Yan Ziling, Zhuge Liang Bagua (Eight Diagrams) Village, Changle Village, Former Residence of Lu, Palace of the First Qin Emperor, Jianglang Mountain, Ershibadu, Ancient Folk House in Wuyuan, Xidi Village, Hong Village, Ancient Stone Memorial Archway in Shexian.

Scenery of West Lake (From CFP)

Hangzhou Region

Best Time to Travel

With its subtropical climate, Hangzhou is warm and humid with lots of rain. The optimal seasons to visit are spring, summer, and autumn.

Shopping Tips

Jiefang Road is the busiest commercial street in Hangzhou, extending from Jinyazhuang on the East Ring Road to the intersection between Nanshan Road and Hubin Road on the west side. Here, restaurants and department stores are clustered side by side. Guanxiangkou, at the intersection between the Jiefang Road and the Zhongshan Road, is one of the busiest commercial centers in downtown Hangzhou.

Yan'an Road, also one of the busiest commercial streets in Hangzhou, is almost 2 miles long. The road is flanked by the Provincial Great Hall of the People and many commercial, cultural, and recreational centers. Don't miss a chance to eat at the Hangzhou Restaurant and visit the Hangzhou Department Store.

West Lake

Located in Hangzhou, provincial capital of Zhejiang Province, West Lake is one of great tourist attractions in China. For centuries, West Lake has been known for its picturesque landscape. The landscape area of West Lake includes the surrounding hills and nearby historical sites as well as the lake itself. The lake area is approximately 23 square miles.

Tourists can rent motorboats or rowboats on West Lake to visit the three islands in the middle of the lake.

Yue Fei's Tomb

Yue Fei's Tomb is situated at the southern foot of Qixia Hill. This tomb was built to commemorate Yue Fei, a famous general in the Southern Song Dynasty and an outstanding national hero of China. Yue Fei's statue in martial attire stands in the middle of Loyalty Hall along with a plaque inscribed "Retrieve Our Lost Territories."

Yue Fei's Tomb is on one side of Loyalty Hall. There are 127 carved pillars in the south and north corridors of the courtyard.

Pillars and brackets of the Six Harmonies Pagoda (From Imagine-China)

Six Harmonies Pagoda (Liuhe Ta)

The Six Harmonies Pagoda is on Yuelun Hill on the north bank of the Qiantang River in Hangzhou, Zhejiang Province. The name comes from the six Buddhist harmonies of the heaven, earth, north, south, east, and west. The pagoda was first built in 971 by the King of Wuyue State, who intended to demonstrate his authority by conquering the floods of the Qiantang River. In 1153 the pagoda got a full restoration. Seen from the outside, the pagoda looks like a 13-story building; in actuality, there are only seven stories.

Lingyin Temple (Lingyin Si)

Situated at the foot of Lingyin Mountain, Lingyin

Temple (Temple of Inspired Seclusion) is one of the ten most famous ancient Buddhist temples in China. First built by the Indian monk Huili in 326 during the Eastern Jin Dynasty (317–420), the temple was named Lingyin due to its beautiful and serene locale, suitable for "gods resting in seclusion." On the compound's central axis stands the Hall of Heavenly Kings and Daxiongbaodian Hall (Grand Hall of Buddha), the main hall of the temple. It is seven rooms wide and five rooms deep, with one story, double-layer eaves, and a pinnacle roof 110 feet tall, famed as one of China's tallest one-story buildings.

Tourists are welcomed to a delicious vegetarian meal in the Lingyin dining room beside the temple.

Hu Qingyu Traditional Chinese Medicine Museum

Located in Dajing Lane at the foot of Wu Hill, the museum was founded by a famous Qing Dynasty businessman, Hu Xueyan. It used to be a shop for selling herbal medications. The building is a traditional court-style structure of the Qing Dynasty, elegant and magnificent. The museum, covering an area of 29,000 square feet, is the only one specifically exhibiting traditional Chinese herbal medicines in the country.

Mountain Ling's Fairyland

Located on Mountain Ling southwest of the suburb of Hangzhou, Mountain Ling's Fairyland is the general term for Lingshan Cave, Qingxudongtian, and Xianqiao Cave. It is famous for its wonderful scenery.

Boards hanging in the Hu Qingyu Medicine Museum, each with the name of a kind of herbal medicine in the upper part and its functions stated below. (From ImagineChina)

Tianmu Mountain

In northwest Zhejiang and originally named Fuyu Mountain, Tianmu Mountain is about 19 miles from Hangzhou. The Tianmu Mountain comprises two peaks: East Tianmu at 4,850 feet, and West Tianmu with a height of 4,940 feet.

Fuchun River-Xin'an River Scenic Area

Straddling Fuyang, Tonglu, Jiande, and Chun'an, the Fuchun River-Xin'an River area includes those two rivers and Qiandao Lake. It has been called the "Golden Tour Area" for its beautiful scenery and long-standing history.

➡ About a two-hour ride from Hangzhou West Bus Station to Meicheng, tourists can get to the Xin'an River either by another bus or by tour boat.

Daci Rock

About 15 miles from Jiande, Daci Rock perfectly merges Buddhist serenity and a pleasant landscape. In a cliff-side cave 10 feet high, 200 feet long, and 65 feet wide, the main temple was built half in the air and half in the stone.

Yaolin Fairyland is well known for its winding cave trails and brilliant stalactites. (From Colphoto)

Yaolin Cavern

Located at the foot of the Camel Mountain, Hangzhou City, Yaolin Cavern is also called Yaolin Fairyland. It is famous for its elegant and delicate stalactites.

Qiandao Lake

Qiandao Lake in Chun'an County, west of Hangzhou, is one of the most stunning scenic spots and is the largest national forest park in China. The lake covers 220 square miles including more than 1,000 islands.

Islands in the Qiandao Lake are of different sizes and shapes. (From ImagineChina)

Jiaxing Tour Area

Best Time to Travel

With its pleasant year-round weather, any season is a good time to visit Jiaxing. Spring and summer are the top tourist months because of the many festivals and celebrations.

Inside Xitang Ancient Town, streams, old residences, and red lanterns compose a lovely picture of the old days. (From ImagineChina)

South Lake

South Lake in Jiaxing, West Lake in Hangzhou, and East Lake in Shaoxing constitute the three major lakes in Zhejiang Province. Located in the southern part of Jiaxing, South Lake's two parts look like a pair of mandarin ducks. The lake was first formed in the Five Dynasties and Ten Kingdoms era (907–960). At the lakeside, there used to be an ancient and elegant building with a double-eaved roof, which took its name "Yanyulou" (Tower of Mist and Rain) from a poem by Du Mu, a well-known Tang Dynasty poet. In July 1921, the first congress of the Chinese Communist Party was held on a cruise boat on the South Lake. Visitors can see the pavilion-like boat, a replica of the original, moored in the lake.

Qiantang River Tide

The Qiantang River tidal bore was formed by the combined action of the tides and the special topography of Hangzhou Bay. Known for its high tides, numerous twists, turbulent waves, and astounding views, the tidal bore is world famous.

From the 16th to 20th of the eighth month of the Chinese lunar calendar, thousands of tourists gather in Haining to view the spectacular sight of the tidal bore. Be sure to check with local authorities for the exact times of the tides.

Xitang Town

Xitang Town is under the municipality of Jiashan County, Jiaxing. Located at the juncture of three provinces (Jiangsu, Zhejiang, and Shanghai), the town comprises 9 rivers, 27 bridges, and 122 lanes, all of which are connected with residences.

Former Residence of Maodun

The well-known novelist and journalist Mao Dun (pen name of Shen Yanbing) was born in July 4, 1896, in Wuzhen and spent his boyhood there. The residence was purchased by his grandfather Shenhuan in 1885. From

1934 to 1937, Mao Dun returned to Wuzhen several times to write his novels.

Wuzhen Water Town

Wuzhen (Wu Town) lies in the north of Zhejiang Province at the west side of the Jinghang Grand Canal. A place of strategic importance for both land and water transportation, it is a famous ancient town south of the Yangtse River. With its long history, Wuzhen boasts of many famous historical cultural sites, especially the houses built in the later years of the Qing Dynasty.

The layout of Jiaye Library is exceptionally comfortable for reading. (From CFP)

Wuzhen Water Town (From Quanjing)

Huzhou Tour Area

Best Time to Travel

Huzhou's weather is moderate, belonging to the north subtropical monsoon zone, so the four seasons are not as distinct as in the north. Although tourists can visit Huzhou at any time, spring and autumn are the best seasons.

Feiying Tower

Located in downtown Huzhou, Feiying Tower is a tower within a tower. Built in 884 during the Tang Dynasty next to the Feiying Temple, the stone tower has been rebuilt and renovated many times over the centuries. Octagonal in shape, the tower is five stories tall at 48 feet.

Jiaye Library

Located on the banks of the Zhegu Stream, Nanxun, Huzhou, Jiaye Library is the private collection of Liu Chenggan, an aristocrat and collector of fine books and art prints.

The construction of Nanxun can date back to 745 years ago. In China's modern history, Nanxun was one of the few wealthy towns. The valuable collection in Liu Chenggan's library owes its existence to the grand fortune he had inherited.

The Buildings of Zhang's Former Residence in Nanxun

The private mansion of Zhang Shiming (cousin of an old member of Kuomintang named Zhang Jingjiang) is located in Nanxi Street, Nanxun, in Huzhou. Built in the later years of the

Qing Dynasty, the house has 224 rooms, a blend of Western European baroque and traditional Chinese-style architecture. Combining both oriental and occidental architecture, culture and artistry, the large mansion is of great historical and artistic value.

Nanxun has many old mansions. (From CFP)

Mogan Mountain

Located in Deqing County, Huzhou, Mogan Mountain is known as one of the four best summer resorts in China, along with Beidaihe Scenic Spot, Mount Lushan, and Jigong Mountain. With an altitude of 2,360 feet and a location in the center of the "golden triangle" (Shanghai, Ningbo, and Hangzhou), Mogan Mountain is famous for its bamboo, springs, clouds, and tranquil atmosphere and is one of the best places to escape the summer heat. With the lush bamboo stands, hundreds of springs and waterfalls , and many villas of various styles dotted here and there, Mogan Mountain abounds with natural beauty. Visitors should not miss the legendary Sword Pond and Sword-Milling Stone where Gan Jiang and Mo Ye cast two swords in the Spring and Autumn Period.

You can take a direct bus to Mogan Mountain from the North Hangzhou Station every day. The trip takes about one hour.

Shaoxing and Taizhou Region

Best Time to Travel

Shaoxing has a subtropical monsoon climate with four distinct seasons and plenty of rainfall. Any month of the year is suitable for a visit to Shaoxing.

Luxun Memorial

Lunxun Memorial, built to honor the founder of modern Chinese literature, is located at the end of Dongchang

In the center of the Three Flavor Study is a square table and a wooden chair for the teacher, while the students of those years sat under the windows. Luxun's desk with two drawers is in the northeast of the study. (From CFP)

Road in Shaoxing. The complex comprises Luxun's former residence, Baicao Park (Baicao Yuan), Three Flavor Study (Sanwei Shu Wu), and an exhibition hall for his life story. Luxun's residence at Xintaimen in Dongchang Road, with its 100 rooms, served as a gathering place for the large Zhou family. On the east of the residence is the Three Flavor Study, where Luxun studied for five years.

The indoor scene of Zhou Enlai's former residence (From Imagine-China)

Tomb of Yu the Great (Dayu Ling)

Tomb of Yu the Great is the burial ground of Yu, the hero of flood control in ancient China and first emperor to found a state. It is located at the rear of Huiji Mountain in the southeast suburb of Shaoxing. According to the literature, Yu was buried there. His son, Qi, had a memorial ceremony held for his father every year, and he also built an ancestral temple abutting the Tomb of Yu the Great on Nan Mountain (Nan Shan).

Many residents near the tomb with the family name of Si are the offspring of Yu: 144 generations up to now.

Ancestral Residence of Zhou Enlai

The Ancestral Residence of Zhou Enlai is located on the banks of the Blessing River (Baoyou He) in Shaoxing. According to local records, the Zhou family moved to the city during the Ming Dynasty (1368–1644). Formerly called "Xiyang Tang," the home is a tile bungalow of Ming Dynasty style. The west wing room is where the late premier Zhou Enlai slept. Covering less than 100 square feet, this tiny room has simple furnishings—a bed, a table, and a chair.

Qiu Jin's Former Residence

Also known as Hechangtang, this dwelling is located in Shaoxing. Its wooden construction is representative of the traditional style of dwellings in southeast China. Qiu Jin died a heroic death at the age of 28 at Xuantingkou in Shaoxing in 1907. Once a part of the villa of Zhu Geng, a scholar in the Ming Dynasty, Qiu Jin's house was built at the foot of a hill.

Shaoxing Bazi Bridge (Bazi Qiao)

Bazi Bridge lies between Guangning Bridge (Guangning Qiao) and Dongshuang Bridge (Dongshuang Qiao) to the east of Baziqiao Straight Street in Shaoxing. It was built during the Jiatai Period of the South Song Dynasty (1201–1204). The book *Jia Tai Kuaiji Records* says that the bridge was so named because it looked like the number eight written in Chinese. The bridge is a junction of three streets, three rivers, and four roads.

Orchid Pavilion (Lan Ting)

Located at the foot of Lanzhu Mountain eight miles to the southwest of Shaoxing, the Orchid Pavilion is renowned as the "calligraphic mecca." The famous calligrapher Wang Xizhi wrote the famous *Preface to the Orchid Pavilion* here. These ancient constructions, viewed as his memorial, include Yubei Pavilion (Yubei Ting), Liushang Pavilion (Liushang Ting), and Wang Xizhi Memorial Temple.

Tourists can get copies of Wang Xizhi's famous third-century *Preface to the Orchid Pavilion* here.

A delicate bridge over the East Lake in the Shen Garden (From ImagineChina)

Shen Garden (Shenshi Yuan)

Shen Garden, also called Shenshi Yuan, is located between Yan'an Road and Luxun Road in Shaoxing and was a private garden of the Shen family that was built in 1156. Here in the garden Luyou, known as "the patriotic poet of the Southern Song Dynasty" for his lyric poems, wrote a poem named "Chaitoufeng" on a wall of the garden. After the Song Dynasty, the garden fell into ruin except for one small part. In 1984 the entire garden was reconstructed according to the original Shen Garden map.

Fu Mountain (Fu Shan)

Fu Mountain, also called Wolong Mountain, is located to the west of Shaoxing, with an altitude of 243 feet. In the Spring and Autumn Period, Fu Mountain was the palace of the Yue State. A senior official named Wen Zhong was buried there and the mountain was also called "Zhong Shan." Later, the Shaoxing government headquarters was established at the eastern foot of the mountain, and the name changed again into "Fu Shan." There are numerous historical sites in the mountain, including more than 10 locations of cultural artifacts. At the southeast foot of the Fu Mountain is the Terrace of King Yue (Yuewang Tai). The high terrace is a structure with a single-eaved Chinese hip-and-gable roof, in memory of Gou Jian, the King of Yue.

In East Lake, the Taogong Cave and the Xiantao Cave are the most interesting. Along the bank, there are the Tingqiu, Yinlu, and Xiangji Pavilions as well as other beautiful and scenic spots. (From ImagineChina)

East Lake

East Lake is situated at the foot of Ruokui Mountain (Ruokui Shan) to the east of the Shaoxing. When the first emperor of Qin Dynasty made his eastward tour to Kuaiji (today's Shaoxing), the troops stopped here to feed the horses, after which the Ruokui Mountain was named. East Lake was once a bluestone mountain full of hard rocks and lush bamboo and other trees. Since the Sui and Tang dynasties, stoneworkers quarried materials from the mountain, creating a hollowed-out spot, leaving only steep cliffs and a deep pool.

Visitors can explore the lake on a tour boat or in rental boats.

Ancient Track Road in Ruanshe

Located over the Zhedong Canal in Shaoxing County, the Ruanshe Ancient Track Road (Track Road Bridge) was built in 815 in the Tang Dynasty. Meng Jian, envoy of Zhedong, built the bridge when he was trying to control the canal. This ancient road stretches for more than 31 miles, flanked by water on one side and bank on the other or water on both sides. Here, the road, the bridge, the water, and the boats together form a harmonious picture.

Keyan Scenic Area

Located 7.5 miles west of Shaoxing, covering 43 square miles, the Keyan Scenic Area has been a famous tourist location since the Sui Dynasty. During the Qing Dynasty, the well-known "eight scenic spots of Keyan" came into being and have been places of great interest at the core of the ancient Yue State. Now this area has been developed into a four-star tourist resort and includes other such interesting and spectacular sites such as Yuanshan Park (Yuanshan Yuan), Stone Figures of Buddha Scenic Area, Jingshui Bay Scenic Area, and Yuezhong Celebrities Garden. This entire area is now a national tourist area, integrating nature, beauty, gardens, religion, and entertainment.

The Keyan Stone in the Keyan Scenic Area is more than 98 feet high. Its broad top and narrow base make it look like an upside-down pagoda. (From Quanjing)

Wuxie Scenic Area

Located 14 miles northwest of Zhuji, this magnificent area has 72 peaks, 36 lawns, 25 cliffs, 10 rocks, 5 waterfalls, 5 valleys, 2 brooks, and 1 lake, comprising the beautiful natural scenery of Wuxie. Wuxie waterfall is 735 feet high and drops 265 feet, cascading down five giant levels. The grotesque rocks and stunning views have drawn visitors since the North Wei Dynasty, some 1,400 years ago.

Tiantai Mountain (Tiantai Shan)

Tiantai Mountain is located in the Tiantai County in Taizhou. Its highest peak, Huading, is 3,730 feet tall and is divided into 13 scenic sections, including more than 100 scenic spots. Tiantai Mountain boasts unique natural scenery and splendid ancient artifacts. It is known as the "mystical and beautiful hills and waters."

> It takes about 2 hours to drive from Hangzhou or Ningbo to Tiantai Mountain, and four hours from Shanghai to the mountain.

Xinchang Great Buddha

The Xinchang Great Buddha is located in the Great Buddha Temple in southwest Xinchang County of Shaoxing. The stone statuary of the Mi-le Buddha, carved between the year 486 and the year 516, is the earliest known example of grotto art in south China.

Ningbo and Zhoushan Region

Best Time to Travel

You can visit Ningbo in any of the four seasons due to its pleasant climate. However, it's better to avoid June's massive rainfall and September's typhoon.

Tianyi Pavilion (Tianyi Ge)

Located west of Moon Lake (Yue Hu) in Ningbo, the Tianyi Pavilion is the oldest private library in China. It was built in 1561 in the Ming Dynasty, and its founder, Fan Qin, was an important official in the War Cabinet. For centuries it has been known as the "Book City of South China" for its giant collection of highly valued ancient books and documents. Borrowing an idea from *The Book of Changes* ("Heaven embodied in One gives birth to water, while Earth represented in Six makes it grow"), Fan Qin named the new house "Tianyi Pavilion" or Pavilion of Heaven and One. Books are most vulnerable to fire, but water can extinguish fire. Thus the name hints that the books might forever be clear of the destructive might of flames. The library has a large room on the upper floor, and six chambers downstairs. The galleries in front of and behind the library are connected. Just in case of fire, there is a large pond in front of the house for emergencies.

> The Garden Entertainment Section in the East Garden of Tianyi Pavilion includes many scenic spots such as Ming Pond, Long Gallery, Forest of Pillars, Bai'e Pavilion (Bai'e Ting), and Ninghui Hall (Ninghui Tang).

Baoguo Temple

Seated at the foot of the Ling Mountain in the suburb of Ningbo, Baoguo Temple is the oldest (more than 970 years of history) and most completely preserved wooden structure in south China. It was initially es-

The Four Branches of Literature in the Tianyi Pavilion. It currently has a collection of more than 300,000 volumes of books, among which are 80,000 precious ones. The most valuable ones are Ming Dynasty local and imperial records. (From Imagine-China)

tablished in the Eastern Han Dynasty and fomerly called Lingshan Temple. In 845, Buddhism was in danger of being extinguished, and the temple was destroyed. In 880 it was rebuilt and renamed as Baoguo Temple. The Grand Prayer Hall (Daxiong Baodian) in the Grand Hall (Da Dian) are the most interesting buildings in the Baoguo Temple complex. The Grand Hall's depth is larger than its width, hence it forms a vertical rectangle. The roof is made of overlapping and interlocking wooden beams, and no nails were used in its construction. Legend says that no birds, spiders, or dust have ever found their way into the hall.

Hemudu Historical Sites Museum

The Hemudu Historical Sites Museum is near the village of Hemudu in Luojiang, Yuyao. More than 7,000 cultural relics were unealthed from the sites in 1973 and 1977. It is one of the oldest cultural historical sites that have been discovered in China up to this point. The museum is composed of the Cultural Relics Exhibition and the excavation site. In the west side of the site, there are six buildings that connect with each other through porches. The exhibition displays over 400 cultural relics, photos, diagrams, and models, which are used to introduce the everyday life and work of the Hemudu people.

Baoben Hall in Jiang Jieshi's former residence, Fenggao House, is the central place for ancestor and general worship. (From CFP)

Long Mountain Yu's Former Residence

Located in the village of Shanxia, Longshan, Cixi, this site is the private residence of Yu Qiaqing, a noted figure in the business circles before the founding of the People's Republic of China. The house includes two independent parts comprising five separate building rows, altogether 194 feet wide and 308 feet deep, each row with nine rooms and two alleys. The construction represents the neoclassical architectural style and borrows widely from other styles. Yu's former residence typifies the Chinese approach to architectural style.

Fenggao House (Fenggao Fang)

Located on West Wuling Road in the town of Xikou of Fenghua, the Fenggao House is the former residence of Jiang Jieshi and his son Jiang Jingguo. The house covers 51,666 square feet, including halls both in the front and at the back, two wing rooms, porches, and connecting eaves. The Baoben Hall (Baoben Tang) in the middle of the back line of halls is used for worshipping ancestors and the gods. The pillar inscription of "Baoben Hall" is written by Wu Jingheng, while the couplet hung on the columns of the hall is the handwriting of Jiang Jieshi.

Xuedou Mountain Scenic Area

Located at the eastern edge of the Siming Mountain (Siming Shan), Xuedou Mountain scenic area is composed of three separate sections: the town of Xikou, Xuedou Mountain, and Tingxia Lake. The mountain is also famous for the Shanshui Buddhist Temple, the hometown of Jiang Jieshi, and the valley with waterfalls.

Tiantong Temple

Located at the foot of Taibai Mountain in the town of Tiantong, Yin County, in Ningbo, this temple is recognized as the Buddhist territory in southeastern China and is one of the five renowned Buddhist temples in China. It is built on a mountain range with a ladder layout, including more than 720 buildings, such as Outer Wangong Pond (Wai Wangong Chi), Seven Towers (Qi Ta), Inner Wangong Pond (Nei Wangong Chi), Tianwang Hall (Tianwang Dian), Grand Prayer Hall (Daxiong Baodian), Fatang (House of Buddhist Texts), Luohan Hall (Luohan Tang, or Arhat House), and House of Imperial Inscriptions (Yushu Lou).

King Ayu Temple

King Ayu Temple, a famous Zen temple in China, is located below the Huading Peak of the Taibai Mountain in Ningbo. It was built in 282, during the Western Jin Dynasty. The temple is said to house a piece of Sakyamuni's parietal bone in the Buddhist Shrine Tower (Sheli Ta), which makes the temple well known and revered in worldwide Buddhist circles. The 1,000-year-old King Ayu Temple is the only preserved temple named after the Indian, King Ayu.

Xuedou Mountain has small peaks and spectacular milky-white waterfalls. (From ImagineChina)

Close to cliffs and the sea, Chaoyang Pavilion (Chaoyang Ge) is the optimal place to watch the sunrise. (From ImagineChina)

Putuo Mountain (Putuo Shan)

Putuo Mountain is located in Zhoushan. Standing in great numbers on the mountain, resplendent and magnificent Buddhist temples form a large scenic area, making Putuo Mountain uniquely attractive among the Chinese religious spots. As one of the four greatest Buddhist mountains, the Putuo Mountain is known for its splendid view of the sea and sky as well as its deep mountain forest.

> Be especially careful on the reefs near the sea. Smoking or fires of any form are forbidden in the forest.

Zhoushan Archipelago (Zhoushan Qundao)

Located at the southern flank of the Yangtse River estuary and outer edge of Hangzhou Bay in Zhejiang Province, the Zhoushan Archipelago is composed of 1,339 islands of different sizes. It is viewed as the largest archipelago of the China coast and is called "the bright pearl of the East Sea." In the section where the Tiantai Mountain extends into the sea, rugged rocks and odd-shaped stones abound. The beautiful natural scenery and pleasant climate make the archipelago an enjoyable tourist destination.

> Zhujiajian Island, located on the Lotus Flower Ocean in the southeast Zhoushan Archipelago, is a scenic site known throughout China as "Yandang on the Sea" or "Hawaii in the East."

Shengsi Isles

North of Zhoushan Archipelago at the junction of the Yangtse River estuary and Hangzhou Bay, Shengsi Isles are famous for their stunning scenery, the vast blue sea, golden sand beach, beautiful reefs, and deep fishing area. Its comfortable and temperate climate gain the Isles a reputation as the "celestial mountain on the sea." The Shengsi Isles, 66 miles long from east to west and 16 miles south to north, include four scenic spots: Sijiao, Hualu, Shengshan-Gouqi, and Yangshan. Sijiao is famous for its golden sand, and its Jihu Sand Beach is well worth a visit. Hualu boasts an important lighthouse, the

The Shengsi Isles in the Zhoushan Archipelago have many odd reefs and beautiful islands. (From Imagine-China)

Puji Temple on Daishan Island is the main Kwan-yin temple. (From Imagine-China)

Huaniao Lighthouse, which is an important marker for the entrance to the Shanghai Port and the south-north sea route of the China coast.

Daishan Island

Daishan Island is to the east of Changtu Mountain (Changtu Shan). Neolithic cultural sites have been discovered in the rear area of the Dashun Temple in the eastern part of the island as well as in Bendou in western Dongsha. The island includes the Gaoting, Xiushan, Jushan, and Changtu scenic spots and is famous for the "ten featured spots in Penglai (a fabled abode of immortals) Fairyland." Here, the visitor can see ten representative landscapes, including the dawn sunlight, dusk sunshine on stonewall, Kwan-yin Riding-on-Fog (Guanyin Jiawu), Jiuzi Sandbeach (Jiuzi Shatan), and others. Kwan-yin Mountain (Guanyin Shan), viewed as "the Second Buddhist State on the East Sea" and the sister of the Putuo Mountain, is an important and holy Buddhist destination.

On the pillars in the Imperial Pillar Pavilion (Yubei Ting) of Puji Temple (Puji Si), Emperor Yongzheng inscribed the establishment and development of Puji Temple and the history of Putuo Mountain.

Wenzhou Region

Best Time to Travel

Wenzhou's comfortable climate, fertile land, long rivers, and broad sea make it an ideal place for a vacation.The overall mild yet humid weather contributes to lush flora and abundant fauna. On average, the annual rainfall is about 71 inches, the annual temperature is 65°F, and annually there are 280 frost-free days.

Jiangxinyu Island

Located in the center of Oujiang River to the north of Wenzhou, Jiangxinyu Island is longer from east to west than from south to north. In ancient times there were just two small islands. Nowadays grand halls and pavilions, as well as cultural and historical attractions, are everywhere on the island. The island features various kinds of ancient trees, and it is known as the "Penglai of the Oujiang River" due to its beautiful natural scenery. Scattered throughout the island there are more than 500 odes by poets from all dynasties praising its beauty.

Yaoxi Scenic Area

Yaoxi Scenic Area is located northeast of Daluoshan Mountain and southwest of the new industry zone of Long Bay in Wenzhou. Here, you can look into the distant East Sea and watch the sunrise.

Yongchang Blockhouse (Yongchang Bao)

Located in Wenzhou, between the East Sea shore and the foot of the Daluo Mountain, the Yongchang Blockhouse, in the village of Xincheng, Yongchang, Ouhai District, is the most completely preserved historic site of the Sino-Japanese War in the southern Zhejiang Province. This blockhouse is in a coastal defense outpost. The spectacular Yongchang Fort is 2,552 feet long from south to north and 1,460 feet long from east to west. Its wall is 26 feet high and almost 10,000 feet around. Both the inner and the outer sides of the wall are built with beveled stones.

North Yandang Mountain

North Yandang Mountain, northeast of Leqing City, is 43 miles from Wenzhou. Recognized for its unique scenery, the area stretches from the Fang Mountain (Fang Shan) in the east to Juban Mountain (Juban Ling) in the west, to the entrance of Jinzhu Cave in the south, and to Liuping Mountain in the north. The mountain is divided into eight sections: Lingfeng, Lingyan, Dalongqiu, Yan Lake (Yan Hu), Sanzhe Waterfalls (Sanzhe Pu), Xiansheng Door (Xiansheng Men), Xianqiao, and Yangjiaodong.

Shen Kuo, a famous scientist in the Northern Song Dynasty, explored North Yandang Mountain four times and praised it as "a rare beauty in the world." (From Quanjing)

In the dim light of night, Lingfeng has a distinctive view, with the rocks and peaks looking like various shapes of animals emerging from the dusk.

Much of the countryside near the Nanxi River has preserved ancient buildings of the Song, Ming, and Qing Dynasties. (From ImagineChina)

Nanxi River

Located in the Yongjia County in Wenzhou, 14 miles from Wenzhou and abutting the Yandang Mountain Scenic Area, the Nanxi River Scenic Area boasts more than 800 picturesque landscapes.

Taishun Ancient Bridge

Taishun lies in Wenzhou in southern Zhejiang Province, bordering on Wencheng County in the northeast and Jingning County in the northwest, and abutting Fujian Province in the south. With numerous ancient bridges of various designs, Taishun is known as the "ancient bridge museum of China." More than 200 wooden-corridor arch bridges are preserved in Taishun, and of these, 30 were built in the Ming or Qing Dynasties. The Sister Bridge near Sixi, Xuezhai Bridge near Sankui, Xianju Bridge, Wenxing Bridge near Xiaocun, and the Santiao Bridge are significant in the history of bridges in the

The Wenxing Bridge is 151 feet long and 16 feet wide. It was built solely by the villagers of Xiaochun and is now more than 100 years old. (From ImagineChina)

world and have been called "the most beautiful corridor bridges in the world."

June to October are the best months to visit Taishun. About every half an hour, a coach goes to Taishun from the Passenger Transport Center, located at No. 50 North Niushan Road in Wenzhou.

Chengtian Hot Spring (Chengtian Wenquan)

Called "Divine Water and Precious Land," this hot spring is in the Huija Canyon, near Chengtian at the foot of Yulong Mountain. The average temperature of the water is 62°F. Rich in minerals, the water is especially beneficial for treating psoriasis, rheumatism, arthritis, dermatitis, and the like. The Chengtian Hot Spring is a wonderful spa for relaxing.

Jinhua Region

Tianning Temple (Tianning Si)

On the northern side of the Piaoping Road in the Jinhua urban district and facing the south, Tianning Temple, formerly named "Dazang Yard" (Dazang Yuan), was built in the Northern Song Dynasty between 1008 and 1016. The roof beam structure between the palace and the hall is rare in the preserved ancient structures in China.

Site of King Shiwang's Residence of the Taiping Heavenly Kingdom (Taiping Tianguo Shiwang Fu)

Located in Jiufang Lane in Jinhua, this site was once the military command post of King Shiwang (Li Shixian) of Taiping

Heavenly Kingdom. The residence is immense and divided into east and west courtyards. The main hall in the east yard was where Li Shixian held important military conferences. The west yard comprised the living quarters. The open ground to the southwest of the hall of the west yard was a drill ground.

In Zhuge Village, 209 private residence constructions of the Ming and Qing dynasties have been preserved. The architecture styles of the upstairs halls and the back-hall buildings are quite rare in China. (From Colphoto)

Shuanglong Scenic Area

About 9 miles from Jinhua, this scenic area is famous for its immense forest, boundless grassland, unique landscapes, odd caves, and Taoist mountains. Here visitors can relax in a boat, watch waterfalls, view stones, and explore.

Zhuge Village

Situated inside Lanxi, Zhuge Village is the largest settlement of Zhuge Liang's descendants. In the late years of the Southern Song Dynasty, the twenty-eighth grandson of Zhuge Liang (Zhuge Dashi) moved to the village. He redesigned the whole structure and constructed it based on the "nine zodial spaces and eight diagrams" pattern, in order to commemorate his ancestors. In the center of this village is the Zhong Pond. It is half pool and half land, with a well on both sides, looking like a fish-shaped Taiji figure.

The carved stone dragon on a screen wall in King Shiwang's Residence. (From Colphoto)

Lu's Residence

Located in the east of the Dongyang urban district, facing the Bijia Mountain to the south, and adjacent to the Dongyang River to the north, the Lu's Residence is a well-known group of ancient structures of the Ming and Qing Dynasties in south China. There are more than 60 large-sized dwellings and over 20 memorial archways. Surrounded by the Yaxi River, with Suyong

Hall as its principal part, the Lu's Residence has over ten alleys, dividing several sections according to family clans.

Yuyuan Ancient Village

The layout of Yuyuan Ancient Village in the town of Yuyuan of Wuyi County in Jinhua is based on the "configurations of celestial body" pattern. Almost all of the architectural styles of the Ming and Qing Dynasties can be found here.

Zheng's Former Residence

Located in the center of Zhengzhai, over 6 miles east of Pujiang County, 15 generations of the Zheng family lived here, spanning 360 years from their primogenitor Zheng Qi. *The Zheng Family Code of Conduct* is a rare and ancient family code, and is known as "the Greatest Family Rules."

Longyou Grotto

The Longyou Grotto is in the village of Shiyanbei in southeastern Xiaonanhai, on the north bank of the Qujiang River, and to the north of Longyou County in Quzhou. Within a circumference of about 100 feet on a mountain, there are 24 caves of various sizes and shapes. Decorative patterns of half leaves are carved on the walls, ceilings, and pillars. Even after 1,000 years, no one knows when it was built, who built it, what its layout was like, and what its function was.

Xiandu Scenic Area

Xiandu Scenic Area, 4 miles east of Jinyun County in Lishui, was well-known since the Sui Dynasty. In the ancient times it was called Jinyun Mountain. According to legend, this is where the Emperor Huang was ascended to Heaven and where immortals gathered. The scenic area features an enchanting landscape of odd-shaped peaks and serene waters in harmony with the rural scenery and historical setting.

The image of Kwan-yin in the Zhulin zen Temple (Zhulinchan Si) in the Longyou Grotto. (From Colphoto)

People are collecting Longjing Tea in a tea garden. (From ImagineChina)

Zhejiang Style

Longjing Tea

Longjing tea is mainly produced in the village of Longjing in the mountains southwest of the West Lake in Hangzhou. According to *Tea Classic* of Lu Yu, Father of Tea in the Tang Dynasty, Tianzhu and Lingyin temples produced very good tea. The tea was named "Longjing" in the Song Dynasty and became well known in the Qing Dynasty. Today it remains a famous tea and an ideal gift choice. Longjing tea is famous both at home and abroad for its green color, strong aroma, and sweet taste. The tea leaf is straight, flat, smooth, and even with green and slightly yellow colors. Steeped tea is clear and bright and is acclaimed as "golden bud." Steeping the tea in the water of Hupao Fountain will make it taste even better. Longjing tea falls into three types: Shifeng Longjing tea, Wengjiashan Longjing tea and Meijiawu Longjing tea, among which Shifeng Longjing tea is the best. Literary figures and scholars of all dynasties spoke highly of Longjing tea. Emperor Qianlong of the Qing Dynasty toured the region south of the Yangtse River six times, four of which included a visit to the Longjing tea production area. He also designated the tea as "royal tea." After the founding of the People's Republic of China, the *Tea Plucking Song* was composed and enjoyed great popularity.

Louwailou Restaurant

"With gentle breeze and bright moonlight, why not drink our fill; even if we are all drunk, the beautiful scene of lake and mountain will feast our eyes." The scene depicted in the couplet is from Louwailou, a famous restaurant beside the West Lake in Hangzhou.

It is said that Louwailou started business furing the Daoguang period of the Qing Dynasty (1848). The owner of the restaurant was an intellectual who failed the imperial examinations. He and his wife Tao Xiuying moved from Shaoxing East Lake to Qiantang after their parents passed away and settled in the neighborhood of Xiling Bridge at the foot of Gushan Mountain, where they made a living as fishermen. Coming from Shaoxing, a land teeming with fish and rice, the couple had peculiar talent in cooking fresh fish and shrimp. In the very beginning, they just cooked selected fishes and shrimps and put them on sale. Later on, considering that there was no restaurant in the vicinity of Xiling Bridge, they started a small restaurant with their savings, which came to attract more and more patrons. In 1968, the restaurant moved from the outer flank of Yulou Tower to Gushan. Taking its name from a line written by poet Lin Sheng during the South Song Dynasty, the restaurant serves many famous dishes, including Sister Song's Fish Sound, Vinegar-flavored West Lake Carp, Braised Ham with Honey Sauce and Longjing Peeled Shrimp. Domestic celebrities Sun Zhongshan, Lu Xun, Zhou Enlai, Chen Yi, and foreign distinguished guests such as Norodom Sihanouk have savored these famous dishes in this most renowned traditional restaurant in Hangzhou. Among all dishes the restaurant serves, Dongpo Meat in particular is of great appeal for one's appetite and senses. Vinegar-flavored West Lake Carp is another delicious dish of the restaurant. The carp is fished in the West Lake only when guests order the dish. This special service is only available in this restaurant.

China National Silk Museum

Located at the foot of Lianhua Peak of Yuhuang Mountain in Hangzhou, the China National Silk Museum boasts a total of eight permanent exhibition halls: Introduction Hall, Historical Relic Hall, Folk Custom Hall, Silk Hall, Silk Reeling Hall, Silk Product Hall, Silk Dying and Weaving Hall, and Modern Achievement Hall to introduce the history of Chinese silk and the technical process of silk production from the perspective of social and natural science.

Tourists interested in silk products can take Bus No.11 and 28 to the museum, which is located near the beautiful West Lake.

White Chrysanthemum Tea

As famous as Longjing tea, white chrysanthemum tea used to be an object of tribute in ancient times. It is made of fresh white chrysanthemum, a kind of perennial herb that is braised, cooked, and dried. The tea liquor is light green and aromatic when steeped in boiled water. White chrysanthemum tea can disperse pathogenic wind, discharge inner heat, improve eyesight, and remove the effects of poison. White chrysanthemum tea can be divided into Huju tea, Xiaoyangju tea, Dayangju tea, Xiaobaiju tea, and Xiaohuhuang tea. Indigenous to Tongxiang, white chrysanthemum tea boasts a long history of vast harvest yielding high production and high quality. Ancient tea traders of Tongxiang named the Xiaobaiju tea "Hangzhou," a name that remains today.

The women are collecting white chrysanthemum. (From CFP)

Fujian

Geography at a Glance

Fujian Province or "Min" for short, is located on China's southeastern coast. It borders on the three provinces of Zhejiang, Jiangxi, and Guangdong, and faces the island province of Taiwan with Taiwan Strait to the east. Fujian occupies an area of around 46,332 square miles. Its population of permanent residents is slightly above 34,700,000 (2000 census). Besides the Han nationality, other ethnic groups living in Fujian Province are Hui, Miao, Manchu, and Gaoshan.

Fujian Province has a coastline more than 2,050 miles long. It has a winding coast, harbors, and 1,401 scattered islands, the most famous of which are Xiamen, Dongshan, Pingtan, and Jinmen. There are four major rivers in the province: the Minjiang, Jiulongjiang, Jinjiang, and Tingjiang. Minjiang River, the largest river in Fujian, is 358 miles long. Fujian's weather is typical of a subtropical humid monsoon climate. The Xiamen, Zhangzhou, and Quanzhou regions have gained the reputation of "natural greenhouse." May and June are rainy seasons, and there is always the possibility of a typhoon in late summer and autumn.

Featured Cuisine

Mashed taro, oyster cake, rice with seafood soup, Qi Jiguang cake, spring roll, steamed meat and rice dumpling, noodles in peanut

(From Quanjing)

Indoor scene of earthen building (From ImagineChina)

sauce, sesame and potato, radish cake, fried Chinese dates, pan-fried oyster, pork soup, Ximen jellied sandworm, glutinous rice congee with sea crab.

Featured Commodities

Fuzhou

Horn comb, olives, tangerines, longan, litchi, Furong plums, shell carving, chinaware.

Quanzhou

Dehua china, Hui'an stone carving, Anxi oolong, Yongchun aged vinegar, Yuanhetang confiture, Quanzhou puppet head, Yongchun lacquer basket.

Zhangzhou

Flowers, litchi, banana, longan, grapefruit, pineapple, dried seafood, eight-treasure inkpad, pearl cream.

Xiamen

Peanut, Xiamen beaded-embroidery, lacquer thread sculpture, Xiamen painted sculpture, Xiamen porcelain sculpture, Xianggu mushroom meat paste, dried seafood.

Notes 

❶ Don't miss a chance to try the local snacks of Fuzhou. Go to the restaurant street in the Taijiang District. If seafood is your favorite, go to another street named "Chixian Yitiao Jie" in Jin'an District, which is also full of restaurants. The food there is inexpensive and of excellent quality.

❷ Although the Xiamen speech belongs to the Minnan dialect, there is no problem communicating with the local people in Mandarin.

❸ June through September is the typhoon season. Always check the weather forecast before setting out.

- **Wuyi Mountain**

Wuyi rock tea, Xianggu mushroom, bamboo shoot, Fujian lotus.

Transportation Tips

- **By Bus**

In Fujian there are 5 national highways and 29 main expressways, totalling almost 25,000 miles. Fujian is tenth among provinces in China in highway distributation density. It has a road network connecting all the cities in the province and most counties and towns. Fuzhou, Pingnan, Quanzhou, Zhangzhou, and Longyan are the centers.

- **By Train**

Since Fujian is a hilly province, the train slows down when passing through it, but it remains an important means of transportation. Yingxia Railway (Yingtan-Xiamen) has joined the National Railway Network. Hengnan Route (Hengfeng-Nanping) and Fuzhou-Longyan-Shenzhen Route are two main rail lines that connect Fujiang to other provinces.

- **By Plane**

Plane is the most convenient way to get from place to place in this area. At this point there are four airports in Fujian: Gaoqi International Airport in Xiamen, Changle International Airport in Fuzhou, Jinjiang Airport in Quanzhou, and Wuyishan Airport in Nanping.

POPULAR FESTIVALS

Relatives Reunion Festival (Huiqin Jie)

Held on February 2 of the lunar calendar, it is when the men and women of the She ethnic group in Shuanghua of Fuding County visit relatives and friends.

Panwang Festival

Held on February 15, July 15, and August 15 of the lunar calendar, the purpose of the festival is to worship ancestors as well as the foremost She ancestor, King Pan Hu.

Black Rice Festival (Wufan Jie)

Held on March 3 of the lunar calendar; it commemorates the heroes of She ethnic group, Lei Wanxing and Lan Fenggao.

Fenlong Festival (Fenlong Jie)

It is said that, in April, the Jade Emperor distributes rain to the She Mountain. During the festival it is taboo to go into the fields with anything made of iron.

Mazu Festival

It is held on April 25 in Meizhou, Fujian Province, to worship Mazu, the goddess of the sea.

Baiyun Mountain Singing Festival (Baiyunshan Gehui)

It is held on June 1 of the lunar calendar on Baiyun Mountain in Fu'an County. The traditional songs from Fu'an and Ningde counties are the highlights of this festival.

Mulian Mountain Singing Festival (Mulian Shan Gehui)

It is held on September 9 of the lunar calendar by people of the She nationality in Mayang and Xinan of Xiapu County to show their respect to a local monk.

Recommended Routes

Classical Routes

Two-day tour of history and culture

Day 1 Fuzhou Museum→Lin Zexu Memorial Hall. Lodging: Fuzhou Grand Hotel.

Day 2 Fujian Revolutionary History Memorial Hall→Hot Spring Park. End of tour.

Three-day tour of Xiamen, Quanzhou, and Shishi

Day 1 Gulangyu Island→Wanguo Architecture Extensive Sightseeing Line→Sunlight Rock (Riguang Yan)→Funicular Railway→Bainiao Park→Zheng Chenggong Memorial Hall→Jizhuang Garden→Piano Museum. Lodging: Yuehua Hotel.

Day 2 Jimei School Village→Ao Park→Former Residence of Chen Jiageng→Quanzhou Kaiyuan Temple→Laojun Rock→Shopping in Shishi→Xiamen. Lodging: Yuehua Hotel.

Day 3 Wanshi Arboretum→South Putuo Temple→Hulishan Cannon Fort. End of tour.

Five-day tour of Xiamen, Wuyi Mountain, and Fuzhou

Day 1 Gulangyu Island→Wanguo Architecture Extensive Sightseeing Line→Sunlight Rock (Riguang Yan)→Funicular Railway→Bainiao Park→Zheng Chenggong Memorial Hall→Jizhuang Garden→Piano Museum. Lodging: Yuehua Hotel.

Day 2 Jimei School Village→Ao Park→Former Residence of Chen Jiageng→Wanshi Arboretum→South Putuo Temple→Hulishan Cannon Fort→Wuyi Mountain. Lodging: Wuyishan Villa.

Day 3 Tianyou Peak Scenic Spot→Cloud Nest (Yun Wo)→Tea Cave→Shaibu Rock→Rafting on Jiuqu Brook→Wuyi Palace→Song-Dynasty-Style Ancient Street. Lodging: Wuyishan Villa.

Day 4 Huxiao Rock→Wind Cave (Feng Dong)→Ling Cave→One Line Sky→Fuzhou. Lodging: Fuzhou Grand Hotel.

Day 5 Gu Mountain→Yongquan Temple→Lin Zexu Memorial Hall→West Lake Park. End of tour.

Traditional Routes

Three-day tour of sea-eroded landforms

Day 1 Fuzhou→Pingtan County→Panyang Stone Sails→Changjiang Wind Power Plant→Red Rock Villa→Longfengtou Shore Beach.

Day 2 East Sea Fairyland (Xianren Well)→Thirty-Six Feet Lake→Dong'ao Steamship Berth Spot→Jinkun Kangle Holiday Entertainment Center.

Day 3 General Mountain→South Village Stone Forest. End of tour.

Five-day tour of historic cities

Day 1 Arrival in Longhai City.

Day 2 Yundong Rock→Ciji Palace→Jiangdong Bridge→Hua'an.

Day 3 Hua'an→Zhangzhou→Eryi Building→Xianzi Deep Pool→Zhangzhou Ming-and-Qing-Dynasty Stele Lane.

Day 4 Zhangzhou→East Mountain (Dong Shan)→Guandi Temple→Tongling Ancient City→Fengdong Stone→East Gate Island→Maluan Bay.

Day 5 East Mountain→Zhangzhou. End of tour.

■ **Self-Guided Tours**

Tour of famous mountains and folk customs

Start from Fuzhou and end in Hui'an. Through Shaowu to Wuyi Mountain, major sights include Jiuqu Brook, Huxiao's eight scenic spots, One Line Sky, and Wuyishan Nature Reserve. Then travel to Xiamen and visit South Putuo Mountain, Hulishan Cannon Fort, Jimei School Village, and Gulangyu Island. Then head for Quanzhou and tour Kaiyuan Templea and Qingyuan Mountain. From Shishi to Putian, tour Meizhou Mazu Temple and Guanghua Temple. Last stop should be a visit to the legendary Hui'an women.

Famous temple self-guided tour

Start from Zhangzhou through Xiamen, Quanzhou, Putian, Fuzhou, and Ningde, and end in Nanping. Famous temples include South Mountain Temple and Sanping Temple in Zhangzhou; Ciji Palace and South Putuo Temple in Xiamen; Kaiyuan Temple in Quanzhou; Qingshui Rock in Anxi; Guanghua Temple and Cishou Temple in Putian; Gushan Yongquan Temple, Xichan Temple, Linyang Temple and Dizang Temple in Fuzhou; Xuefeng Temple in Minhou County; Wanfu Temple in Fuqing; Zhiti Temple in Ningde; Tianxin Yongle Temple in Wuyi Mountain in Nanping; and Guangxiao Temple in Jian'ou City.

Addresses and Phone Numbers

Fuzhou Grand Hotel	1 Doudong Road, Fuzhou	0591-83333333
Apollo Grand Hotel	132 Middle Wuyi Road, Fuzhou	0591-83055555
Fujian Zuohai Mansion	36 Tongpan Road, Fuzhou	0591-87098888
Fujian West Lake Hotel	158 Hubin Road, Fuzhou	0591-87839888
Jinyuan International Grand Hotel	59 Hot Spring Road, Fuzhou	0591-87088888
Jinhai'an Grand Hotel	40 North Hubin Road, Xiamen District	0592-5303333
Yuehua Grand Hotel	101 Yuehua Road, Xiamen	0592-6023333
Jingmin Center Hotel	158 Yuhou Nanli, Xiamen District	0592-5123333
Jindi Hotel	189 Western Xianyue Road, Xiamen	0592-5111888
Xiamen Airlines Jinyan Hotel	99 South Hubin Road, Xiamen	0592-2218888
Huaqiao Mansion	Baiyuan Road, Quanzhou	0595-22282192
Quanzhou Grand Hotel	22 Zhuangfu Lane, Quanzhou	0595-22289958
Wuyi Mountain Villa	Near Wuyi Palace in Wuyimountain	0599-5251888
Wuyi Mountain International Hotel	Inside the Wuyi Mountain National Tourist Vacation Area	0599-5252521

Fuzhou and Putian Region

Best Time to Travel

March and April in Fuzhou is cool and rainy. From May to September, it is hot and often stormy. October and November, when the weather is cool and pleasant, are the best months to visit.

Yu Mountain

Located in the center of the Fuzhou urban district, Yu Mountain's highest peak is 192 feet in altitude. On the mountain there are 24 historic and scenic sites, including the Qigong Temple, Qijiguang Pingyuan Platform, Drunk Stone (Zui Shi), Penglai Pavilion, Fayu Hall, Wansui Temple, and Dingguang Pagoda. The largest temple here is the Nine Immortals Taoist Temple (Jiuxian Guan), which exhibits 19 pillars from ancient dynasties. On the south side of the mountain stands the largest pillar in Fuzhou, which is 11 feet high and 15 feet wide. It holds 319 inscribed words. Each word is about 8 inches tall.

The top of the White Pagoda (Baita) commands a view of the whole city. Tourists may also pay a visit to the Dashi Hall at the top of the Yu Mountain, where the Fuzhou Museum is located.

Yu Mountain has many small and exquisite pavilions such as Wanxiang Pavilion, Xicui Pavilion, and Bushanjing, all standing among trees and flowers. (From CFP)

A pelican in the Birds' Words Woods (Niaoyu Lin) in Fuzhou National Forest Park. (From Colphoto)

Ruiyan Mountain

Located north of Haikou and 6 miles to the east of Fuquing, Ruiyan Mountain boasts the most distinctive scenery area in Fujian Province. Here you can visit Ruiyan Temple, which include Tianwang Hall (Tianwang Dian), Bell and Drum Towen (Zhonggu Lou), Grand Prayer Hall (Daxiong Baodian), and Xianju Tower. The temple was built against the Rriyan Mountain facing Haikou. Outside of the southwestern wall of Ruiyan Temple is a tall stone Buddha.

Fuzhou National Forest Park

Located in Chiqiao of Xindian in the north suburb of the city, Fuzhou National Forest Park is one of the nine largest forest parks of China. Its former name was Fuzhou Tree Garden (Fuzhou Shumu Yuan). It is dedicated to both scientific research and sightseeing.

Mawei Scenic Area

The little port town of Mawei is located at the entrance of the Minjiang River, about 20 minutes drive from Fuzhou. Due to its strategic location, Mawei is the gateway to the sea of Fujian Province.It is hard to access and guards the lower reaches of the Minjiang River. Most featured terrain of Mawei is low mountains and hills, and the local scenery features beautiful mountains, odd-shaped stones, clear streams, and tranquil forests. Typical of the South Asian tropical ocean monsoon climate, Mawei is mild and rainy year-round and is a good place for a summer vacation. The famous scenery and historic sites in Mawei include Luoxing Pagoda, Zhaozhong Temple in Majiang, and the Modern Chinese Navy Museum, which features the historical exhibit of the 1880 French attack on the Mawei dockyard.

Meizhou Mazu Temple

This temple is located on Meizhou Island, Putian City. As the oldest Mazu Temple, it has been destroyed and rebuilt several times oer the centuries.

Fuzhou lies at the foot of a mountain and beside the sea, and has a comfortable climate. Since banyan trees started to be planted here over 900 years ago, Fuzhou is also called "Banyan City" (Rong Cheng). In the Five Dynasties, Fuzhou was expanded to include the beautiful Wu Mountain, Yu Mountain, and Ping Mountain. Since then, Fuzhou has become a unique city characterized as "a city that lies in a mountain." (From Quanjing)

The 13-foot-high stone statue of Mazu stands facing the sea. (From CFP)

March 23 of the lunar calendar each year is the birthday of Mazu. On that day pilgrims from all around China and abroad pour into the temple to worship the sea goddess.

Haitan Island

Located in Pingtan County in Fujian Province, with an area of 139 square miles, Haitan Island, or Pingtan Island, is the largest island in the province. On the island is the Thirty-Six-Feet Lake (Sanshiliu Jiao Hu), which is 52 feet deep and 49 feet above sea level. It is the largest natural freshwater lake in Fujian.

Fangguang Rock (Fangguang Yan)

Located in the middle of Ge Mountain (Ge Ling) in Yongtai County, Fuzhou, Fangguang Rock is a natural grotto 66 feet high and 131 feet wide. At the top of the grotto stretches a huge stone, which hangs over more than 11,000 square feet above the ground. Buddhist pavilions were built in the Qingli period of the Northern Song Dynasty (1041-1048). The waterfalls from the rock are a magnificent sight.

Nanshan Guanghua Temple (Nanshan Guanghua Si)

Located at the foot of the Phoenix Mountain (Fenghuang Shan, or Nanshan) in the south of Putian, this temple was established in 558. It is one of the four largest Buddhist temples in Fujian. After it was renamed as Guanghua Temple in 976 (in the Song Dynasty), it has been destroyed and rebuilt several times. The current buildings were constructed in 1890.

Xiamen Region

Best Time to Travel

Xiamen can be very hot in July and August. The optimal time to visit Xiamen is from November to April.

Shopping Tips

Zhongshan Road as well as North and South Siming Roads are prosperous commercial areas in Xiamen. The large shopping centers, together with a variety of small retail stores, have many items which are reasonably priced.

Longtou Road is the main commercial street on Gulangyu Island. There are quite a few small shops and street vendors selling handicrafts, calligraphy, and paintings.

Gulangyu Island

Gulangyu Island is located in the southwest corner of Xiamen Island, facing Xiamen. It was formerly named as "Yuanshazhou Island." The island got its present name from the huge reef surrounding it. When the tide comes in, the waves pound the reef, and it sounds like the beating of

Gulangyu Island preserves many buildings of various foreign or Chinese architectural styles and is known as the "International Architectural Museum." (From Jin Yongji)

a drum. The island came to be named "Gulang" (which means "drum waves") during the Ming Dynasty. The island is known for its comfortable climate, delicate natural beauty, ancient artifacts, and varied architecture.

Jimei Ao Park

Jimei Ao Park, lying on the southeast seashore of Jimei in Xiamen, covers an area of nearly 97,000 square feet. Jimei Ao Park is composed of three parts: the tomb of Mr. Chen Jiageng, the Jimei Liberation Monument, and a corridor. The side walls of the corridor are inscribed with about 40 reliefs telling the stories of Chinese historical characters.

Qingjiao Ciji Palace

Qingjiao Ciji Palace is located in the Dongming Mountain in Haicang, Xinglin District. It was originally built in the Southern Song Dynasty in 1151 to honor Wu Zhenren, a "medical saint" of the Northern Song Dynasty. It has been renovated several times over the centuries. Qingjiao Ciji Palace has 12 dragon pillars inside, two of which are uniquely vase-shaped. The left ceiling of the front palace is painted with designs of phoenix heads, tortoise backs, dragon claws, and lion's feet. The palace is historically important for studying ancient Chinese architecture, sculpture, and painting as well as the expression of folk beliefs.

Wanshi Mountain Scenic Area

Located at the north foot of the Shi Mountain east of Xiamen, the area is named "Wanshi" for the diverse and odd-shaped rocks there. The Wanshiyan Reservoir is filled with clear water. The fields around it are decorated with flowers and trees surrounding exquisite temples and pavilions. Other sights include the Martyr Memorial, Garden Arboretum, and the Zhongshan Park.

Hulishan Cannon Fort

Hulishan Cannon Fort lies on Huli Mountain to the east of Xiamen Island. Built in 1891, it took five years to complete. Along with the castle, the cannon fort covers about 140,000 square feet. It was constructed as a mixture of the European demi-blockhouse style with the Ming and Qing bastion style and formed a sound defensive system. The city gates and walls, gate towers, moats, barracks of the Qing Army, and the drill ground are all very well preserved.

Nanputuo Temple

Situated at the foot of Wulaofeng (Mountain of Five

Springtime view of the Ao Park. (From ImagineChina)

Old Men) in the south of Xiamen, Nanputuo Temple was first established in the Tang Dynasty. Built to worship Kwan-yin (like the Puji Temple in the Putuo Mountain of Zhejiang), and located to the south of Putuo Mountain, the temple was named "Nanputuo." The Sutra-Keeping Pavilion in the temple houses thousands of Buddhist scriptures, Buddhist images, sculptures, bronze bells of the Song Dynasty, ancient books, and other artifacts. The back wall of the temple is inscribed with a stone-carved Chinese character "Buddha," which is 13 feet tall and 10 feet wide.

Hakka Earthen Buildings

The Hakka Earthen buildings represent the unique and traditional residential style in which large Hakka families live together in harmony. The buildings can be found in several cities and counties in the southwest of Fujian and the northeast of Guangdong. Most of these buildings are in round and square shapes. The square ones represent stronger hierarchical clan structures than the round ones. The round earthen buildings are the common private residences with more defensive functions.

In addition to the defensive functions, earthen buildings are also quakeproof, fireproof, and extremely secure. The rooms are often ventilated and bright. (From ImagineChina)

Ancient City of Tongshan

Located in Tongling 6 miles northeast of Dongshan County of Zhangzhou, the Ancient City of Tongshan is renowned as the "Oriental Hawaii" for its broad bay, smooth beach, and green trees. In order to protect the city from Japanese pirates, the first emperor of the Ming Dynasty had his officials build towers and other defensive structures along the Zhangzhou coastline. City walls were built by laying stones at different heights in accordance with the topography of the land, with a total length of 6,234 feet and a height of 23 feet.

Fengdong Stone

Fengdong Stone, which means "stone shaking in the wind," is situated on a stone cliff to the north of the east gate of Tongshan Ancient City. With a cuspate top and a round bottom, the stone is shaped like a peach. It is 14 feet high, 14.5 feet wide, and 15 feet long. The interface of the two stones only covers an area of some 1.5 square inches. It is balanced so precariously that it seems the upper stone is shaking when the sea wind blows.

The Fengdong Stone in Dongshan is the most astonishing and wondrous of the more than 60 Fengdong Stones in China. It is an icon of Dongshan Island. (From CFP)

Quanzhou Region

Best Time to Travel

Quanzhou's weather is good for tourists year-round. Flowers bloom in each season, and there is no snow in winter.

Shopping Tips

Houcheng Street is located between Tumen and Jiuyi streets. Abutting the Qiaoxiang Street to the east, connecting the Baiyuan Road to the west, and linking the Qingjing mosque and Guandi Temple to the south, this street is a shopping mecca as well as a great location for eating, drinking, and entertainment.

Grand Prayer Hall in Kaiyuan Temple was first built in the Tang Dynasty. The current building is a Ming restoration,which preserves the grandiose architectural style of the Tang Dynasty. (From Quanjing)

The builders of Luoyang Bridge creatively used the "raft-shaped foundation" to build the pier. Stones were laid along the middle axis of the bridge, forming a low stone mound that connected to the bottom of Luoyang River. (From ImagineChina)

Kaiyuan Temple

Located on West Street in the Licheng District of Quanzhou City, the Kaiyuan Temple was built in 686 and is listed as the largest temple in Fujian Province. Because of its 86 stone pillars, the Grand Prayer Hall (Daxiong Baodian) is also called "Hundred Pillar Palace" (Baizhu Dian). The west and the east pagodas are symbols of the Quanzhou Old City.

Luoyang Bridge

Located on the Luoyang River in the east of Quanzhou, the Luoyang Bridge is the oldest stone-beam sea bridge in China, and also represents the earliest use of the "raft-shaped foundation" in the world. The Luoyang Bridge is one of the four most famous ancient bridges in China, which also include the Lugou Bridge in Beijing, the Zhaozhou Bridge in Hebei, and the Guangji Bridge in Guangdong.

Qingjing Mosque

Located on the Nantumen Street in Quanzhou, the Qingjing Mosque was first built in 400 of the Islamic calendar (1009 of the Gregorian calendar) and is similar to the Grand Mosque in Damascus, Syria. The temple is believed to be the oldest preserved Islamic mosque in China.

The tomb of a Muslim saint at the south foot of the Ling Mountain outside the East Gate of Quanzhou is well worth a visit.

Anping Qiao

Located in the town of Anhai in Jinjiang, Anping Bridge is the longest ancient stone bridge in China. The bridge, 6,791 feet long and 10 feet wide, spans a little more than 1 mile of ocean between Anhai in Jinjang and the town of Shuitou in Nan'an. First constructed in 1138, the deck is made of huge flagstones, and on both sides are balusters. In addition, there are several pavilions and a small temple on the bridge itself. It is a great place to walk, talk with the locals, and enjoy the scenery.

Quanzhou Tianhou Palace (Tianhou Gong)

Located on Tianhou Road near the south gate of the city, the palace was built in the Southern Song Dynasty in 1196 in honor of a sea goddess who was believed to watch over the sailors at sea and provide them safety. The palace was given the name of "Shunji" by Emperor Ningzong. It means "sailing down the wind." In 1680, Emperor Kangxi of Qing Dynasty designated the goddess, a daughter of the Lin family, as "Tianhou guarding the country and protecting the people." Thus the palace was renamed "Tianhou Palace."

Qingyuan Mountain Scenic Area

Covering an area of 24 square miles, this scenic area includes Qingyuan Mountain, Lingshan Saint's Tomb, and Nine Sun Mountain (Jiuri Shan). Also called North Mountain, Spring Mountain, and Qiyun Mountain, Qingyuan Mountain is in the southeast of Fujian Province on the north bank of the lower reaches of the Jinjiang River, facing Taiwan. The highest peak in the mountain range is 1,634 feet. The most appealing attractions here are Duanxiang Rock, Amitabha Rock (Mituo Yan), and the stone statue of Lao Zi (the Most Exalted Lord Lao), a Taoist deity. The Amitabha statue in the Mituo Rock, 16 feet tall, is a treasure of stone carving from the Song and Yuan Dynasties.

The statue of the Most Exalted Lord Lao (Lao Zi) on Qingyuan Mountain (From ImagineChina)

The seated statue of Lao Zi is the largest Taoist stone statue in China.

Maritime Museum

Located at the east of East Lake Park in Quanzhou, the Maritime Museum is the only museum dedicated to the history of Chinese sea transportation. The museum was renovated in 1991 and covers an area of more than 323,000 square feet.

The museum has three theme halls, the most appealing of which is the Quanzhou Bay Exhibition Hall of Ancient Ships. It is well worth more time to have a closer look at these ships.

Thatched Hut (Cao'an) Manichean Historic Site

Located at the foot of Huabiao Mountain in Sunei Village on the Jinjiang River, 8 miles from the south gate of Quanzhou, the Thatched Hut is the only intact Manichean historical site in China. The most precious treasure here is a sitting statue of the Buddha of Litht embossed in a round Buddhist niche in the main hall. The face, body, and hands of the statue are skillfully designed to take advantage of various natural hues of the rocks. It is the only stone "Buddha of Light" statue in the world.

Chongwu Ancient City of Ming Dynasty

Chongwu Peninsula played an important role in the history of coastal defense in ancient China. Located on the Chongwu Peninsula in Hui'an County, Chongwu Ancient City of the Ming Dynasty is the most well-preserved granite coastal stone city in China.

The wall of Chongwu Ancient City is 8,061 feet long, and the foundation of the city is a bit more than 16 feet high. (From Colphoto)

A nice view of the mountain and river at the Wuyi Mountain Scenic Area (From CFP)

Nanping Region

Best Time to Travel

Nanping does not have extremely cold winters or hot summers, which makes it an ideal place to visit any time of the year.

Wuyi Mountain Scenic Area

Located in south Wuyishan on the border of the three provinces of Fujian, Zhejiang, and Jiangxi, the Wuyi Mountain Scenic Area is known as one of the top scenic wonders in southeast China. Mount Huanggang, outside of Wuyishan City, has the highest peak (7,080 feet) of Wuyi Mountain, which includes 36 peaks, 99 rocks, 72 caves, and 108 scenic spots. Wuyi Mountain is famous for its historical and cultural landmarks, which feature the Wuyi Palace, Ziyang School, a boat-coffin burial site, and inscriptions on the cliffs.

Longyan Region

Best Time to Travel

Longyan has a warm and humid climate, with warm winters and cool summers. Any season of the year is a good time to visit.

Longkong Cave (Longkong Dong)

Longkong Cave, located in the village of Longkang of Yanshi in the Xinluo District of Longyan, is 30 miles from the downtown area. Featuring a karst landform, Longkong Cave was formed during the Paleozoic Era about 300 million years ago. After three major crustal movements of the ocean floor, the cave gradually evolved into the current form and is listed as the one of the most enormous caves in China. There are 8 halls and 16 subcaves in the cave and the passage inside is more than 6,500 feet long.

During the annual Lantern Festival, the villagers of Longyan hold a ceremony called "walking with ancient things" (Zou Gushi).

Guanzhi Mountain

Also known as Dongtian Rock and Pengfeng Mountain, Guanzhi Mountain is located in the east of Liancheng County. The entire area comprises numerous stones and woods, wandering paths and streams, and a tranquil atmosphere with beautiful natural scenery. In the middle of the mountain is Banyun Pavilion, which was inscribed with the two Chinese characters "Guan Zhi" (name of a kind of cap worn by ancient Chinese judges).

The attractions of the Guanzhi Mountain Scenic Area include hills, streams, grottos, springs, temples, and parks. (From CFP)

Quanzhou chest tapping dance (From CFP)

Fujian Style

Quanzhou Chest Tapping Dance

During the Lantern Festival, the Quanzhou people stroll on the street where the festival procession is held and participate in the chest tapping dance. It is said that both the chest tapping dance and the lion dance were originally from the central part of China. These forms of entertainment were brought to Fujian from Guangzhou by Henan in the Tang Dynasty, who led the army that invaded Fujian. As the most important dance of the Lantern Festival in Quanzhou, the chest tapping dance is performed by a dozen young men. Nowadays the chest tapping dance can only be found in Quanzhou. Therefore, it's considered a typical example of Quanzhou's culture.

Gaojia Opera

As the local opera of southern Fujian, Gaojia opera came into being in the middle of the Qing Dynasty. It's said that at first the opera's plots used to be concerned with stories of Song Jiang, a peasant rebel leader of the Song Dynasty. That's why it's also called "Song Jiang Drama." The shows of Gaojia opera have multiple origins, most of which are puppet opera, Liyuan opera, or Peking opera. Famous shows include *Promoted Three Times* and *Mandarin Duck Fan*. Gaojia opera mainly uses southern music for its scores, but it also incorporates some folk tunes. A lot of acrobatic fighting and clown techniques are also involved.

Hui'an Woman

The most striking aspect of Quanzhou is the Hui'an women's fancy dress. Well-known for their simplicity, kindness, and hard-working spirit, Hui'an women play an important role in both agricultural labor and housekeeping. Their dress is very unique and colorful. The clothes are tight in the sleeves and the chest, barely long enough to cover the navel. Their head decoration is mainly a scarf and

She ethnic group youth in a singing contest. (From CFP)

a bamboo hat. Except for eyes, nose, and mouth, their faces are totally covered by their scarves.

She Ethnic Group

The majority of the She ethnic group live in Fujian and Zhejiang, and Fujian is the province most densely populated by the She. Ninety-nine percent of them speak a language similar to the Hakka dialect but Chinese is generally used too. The She refer to themselves as "shanha" (San-Hak), in which *ha* means "guest." So *Shanha* means "guests residing in the mountain." Since the founding of the People's Republic of China, they have been called "She." As to their origin, there have been different opinions. Generally speaking, the She started to live in the mountainous areas bordering Fujian, Guangzhou, and Jiangsu provinces as early as the seventh century. They didn't start to migrate to the central and northern parts of Fujiang until the Song Dynasty. During the Ming and Qing Dynasties, they started to move to eastern Fujian and southern Zhejiang in large numbers. The She are mainly engaged in agricultural production and are quite experienced in growing rice and tea. She women are good at embroidery and weaving. Mountain folk songs epitomize She culture. The dragon head carved on the She's ancestor cane is their totem symbol.

Gaojia opera draws materials from life. The posture of the performers is refined and graceful while the acting is humorous, witty, and lively. (From CFP)

Henan

Geography at a Glance

Henan Province is located in east-central China in the middle-to-lower reaches of the Yellow River, neighboring Hebei, Shanxi, Shaanxi, Hubei, Anhui, and Shandong provinces. It covers an area of more than 62,000 square miles and has a population of 92,560,000 (2000 census). As most of the province lies to the south of the Yellow River, it was given the name Henan (South River). Geographically, the province is higher in the west than in the east, with plains and mountainous areas. Henan has many rivers that flow into the Yellow, Huaihe, Weihe, and Hanshui rivers.

Henan is located in the northern subtropical and temperate zone with a mild climate, ample sunshine, and plenty of rainfall. It has an average temperature range of 55–60°F with hot, rainy summers; dry, inclement winters; warm autumns; and windy springs.

(From ImagingChina)

Featured Cuisine

Zhengzhou stewed noodles, Luoyang swallow dish, water banquet of Luoyang, Kaifeng steamed stuffed bun, Kaifeng spring chicken in salt, fried dumplings, mashed sweet potatoes, braised fish, fried chicken at Yanqing Taoist temple, three "non-stick" sweets in Anyang (made of egg, lard, and flour), roast chicken, Anyang three roasts, deep-fried eight-spice dumplings, cake with egg, Luoyang noodles.

Folk art of cloth tiger (From Colphoto)

Featured Commodities

Luoyang

Tricolor Tang pottery, Dukang wine, bronze wares, palace lanterns.

Kaifeng

Bianjing embroidery, Bianjing silk, Zhuxian New Year prints, watermelon, Chinese gooseberry, pickled carrots, mashed sweet potatoes, Kaifeng painting and calligraphy.

Nanyang

Jade carvings, pyrograph, Chinese health wine.

Xinyang

Maojian tea.

Transportation Tips

By Bus

The highway network of Henan extends in all directions, joining all the other provinces and cities nationwide, as well as towns and rural areas within the province. There are 11 national highways and 94 provincial highways, among which National Highways 105, 106, and 107 run from Beijing to Guangzhou, Shenzhen, and Zhuhai, with Zhengzhou the transitional point. Zhengzhou and Xinyang are also transitions of the Lianhuo Speedway (Lianyungang—Huo'erguosi) and the National Highway 312 (Shanghai—Yining). County and rural highways constitute a network with Zhengzhou, Kaifeng, Luoyang, Nanyang, Xinxiang, Shangqiu, Pingdingshan, and Zhoukou as the centers. The Kailuozheng Highway is already completed, and the Jingguang Speedway has been partly opened to traffic.

Notes 

❶ Luoyang is noted for all kinds of delicious food. The cuisine here is characterized by a strong local flavor and low prices.

❷ The dishes are served in large portions, so be careful not to order too many dishes before you see the size of the plates.

❸ Scallions and ginger are staple seasonings in the dishes.

❹ Tourists must not miss the Museum of East Zhou (770–221 BCE) Royal Horses and Chariot Pits, located next to the East Zhou Royal Palace, in the center of Luoyang.

By Train

The two main railways of China meet in Zhengzhou, the provincial capital of the central province of Henan. Major lines include the Jingguang, Longhai, Jingjiu, Jiaoliu, Xinjiao, and Xinhe. With the largest number of railways among the provinces, Henan has become one of the largest transportation hubs in China.

By Plane

Three civil airports have been constructed in Henan Province: Zhengzhou, Luoyang, and Nanyang. Thirty-two national airlines as well as some international tourist charter flights have been put into use, leading to the 56 major cities in the mainland and to Hong Kong and Macau. Up to 560 flights are available each week.

Fuyi Quadripod, a Yin artifact (From Colphoto)

POPULAR FESTIVALS

The Qinglong Festival

On February 2 of the Chinese lunar calendar, women in Henan rural areas do not use the scissors or do any needlework. The usual activity on that day is picking potherbs in the field, making dumplings and pancakes, stir-frying soybeans, frying preserved meat, and making steamed buns with dates.

Peony Flower Festival

Held in Luoyang April 15–25, the activities include peony shows, competitions, lantern shows, painting and calligraphy exhibitions, photography, seminars, and an investment and trade symposium.

The International Yellow River Tourism Festival

It is held in Sanmenxia April 20–22. Tourists can take a sightseeing tour in the Yellow River Scenic Area, and experience the folk customs of the Central Plain.

The Ancient Song Capital Culture Festival

Held in Kaifeng, an ancient capital, April 22–26, the main activities are sightseeing in places of interest in Kaifeng, sampling the royal feast, viewing the court dances and musical performances, and a cock-fighting contest.

The Draught Animal Festival

Held on 15th day of the seventh lunar month, it is also called the Ghost Festival among the local people. In the rural households on the Central Plain, various activities celebrate the heritage and utilization of farm animals.

The Zhengzhou International Shaolin Wushu Festival

It is held in Zhengzhou September 10–15 every two years. There are different kinds of martial arts performances and contests, as well as exchanges among wushu fans all over the world.

The Anyang Yinshang Culture Festival

Held in Anyang September 16–25, the main activities are professional entertainment, sightseeing in the historical spots in Anyang, and an excellent local products fair, all highlighting the Yinshang culture.

Recommended Routes

Classic Routes

Twelve-day tour of the travels of Confucius

Day 1 Arrival in at Zhengzhou. Lodging: Zhengzhou Hotel.

Day 2 Old City of State Zheng and State Han→Xuansheng Platform→Home village of Xuanyuan. Lodging: Zhengzhou Hotel.

Day 3 Kongkui→Zilu Tomb→Weihui, staying overnight on the Limousine bus.

Day 4 Bigan Temple→Site of Striking Inverted Bell→Weihui→Hundred Spring→Confucian Temple. Lodging: Weihui Hotel.

Day 5 Confucian cliff→Platform of Drying Book in the Sun→Wenya Platform→Sandalwood Pit→Confucius native place→Temple of Confucius returning to his native place. Lodging: Shangqiu Hotel.

Day 6 Xuange Platform→Old City of State Chen→Shangcai. Lodging: tour bus.

Day 7 Site of Making Inquiries→Old City of State Cai→Temple of Confucius returning to his native place. Lodging: Shangcai.

Day 8 Confucian copper statue→Site of Making Inquiries→Xinyang. Lodging: tour bus.

Day 9 Zigong Temple→Academy of Classical Learning→Fuhan. Lodging: Xinyang Hotel.

Day 10 Changju→Jieni Tomb→Platform of Drying Book in the Sun→Sacred Well→Village of Making Inquiries. Lodging: Pingdingshan.

Day 11 Wangcheng Park→Lord Zhou's Temple. Lodging: Youyi Hotel.

Day 12 End of tour.

Ten-day tour of cultural artifacts

Day 1 Arrival in Zhengzhou. Lodging: Zhengzhou Hotel.

Day 2 Dahe Village remains→Yellow River scenic spot. Lodging: Zhengzhou Hotel.

Day 3 The Provincial Museum→Shang City remains (taking part in the on-the-spot excavation under the directions of experts). Lodging: Zhengzhou Hotel.

Day 4 Zhengzhou→Kaifeng. Lodging: Dongjing Hotel.

Day 5 Song Dynasty Imperial Street→City Museum. Lodging: Dongjing Hotel.

Day 6 Kaifeng→Luoyang. Lodging: Peony Hotel.

Day 7 Longmen Grottoes→City Museum→Emperor Driving on Six Museum. Lodging: Peony Hotel

Day 8 Luoyang→Anyang. Lodging: Anyang Hotel.

Day 9 Yin Ruins Museum→cultural artifact excavation spot→Sanmanxia (Chariot and Horses Pit). Lodging: Mingzhu Hotel.

Day 10 End of tour.

Traditional Routes

Seven-day tour of Luoyang→Zhengzhou→Kaifeng

Day 1 Arrival in Luoyang.

Day 2 Longmen Grottoes→Guan Lin (Graveyard of General Guan Yu)→Guose Peony Garden.

Day 3 Baimasi (The White Horse Temple)→Yellow River Xiaolangdi Hydro Project→Zhengzhou.

Day 4 Dahe Village remains→Huanghedaguan (the Yellow River Scenery Garden)→Yellow River scenic spot.

Day 5 The Provincial Museum→Shang City remains→Kaifeng.

Day 6 Qingming Riverside Landscape Garden→Longting Park→Baogongci (Memorial Temple of Lord Bao)→Baogongfu (Residence of Lord Bao)→The Iron Pagoda→Xiangguo Temple.

Day 7 End of tour.

Three-day tour of luoyang scenic spots

Day 1 Longmen Grottoes→Guan Lin (graveyard of General Guan Yu)→Guose Peony Garden.

Day 2 Luhun Lake scenic spot of Song County→The Luanchuan Jiguan (cock crown) Cave.

Day 3 Longyuwan National Forest Park. End of tour.

Ten-day tour of Luoyang—Dengfeng—Zhengzhou—Anyang

Day 1 Arrival in Luoyang.

Day 2 Longmen Grottoes→White Horse Temple→Shaolin Temple.

Day 3 Dengfeng →Zhengzhou.

Day 4 Dahe Village remains→Yellow River scenic spot.

Day 5 The Provincial Museum→Shang City remains

Day 6 Zhengzhou→Native place of Xuanyuan (Tangquan Hot Spring).

Day 7 Zhengzhou→Anyang.

Day 8 Yin Ruins Museum→Li City artifacts →Tomb of Yuanshikai.

Day 9 Anyang→Linzhou→Hongqiqu Youth Tunnel.

Day 10 End of tour.

Self-Guided Tours

Tour of Three Kingdoms artifacts

Start from Kaifeng, end in Luoyang via Zhengzhou, Xuchang, Nanyang, and Luoyang. Major scenic spots: Caozhi Tomb, Ancient Battlefield of Hulao Pass, Guandu ancient battlefield, Old City of State Han and State Wei, Platform of Abdication, Yuxiu Platform, Eight-dragon Tomb, Spring and Autumn Pavilion, Baling Bridge, Guandi Tample, Wuolong Mound, Wuhou Temple, Hansang City, Discussion Platform, Bowang Ancient Battlefield, Yiqve Pass at Longmen, Guan Forest.

A tour of inscriptions of Tang poetry and Song Ci

Start from Zhengzhou, end in Sanmenxia via Kaifeng, Dengfeng, and Luoyang. Major scenic spots: Yellow River scenic spot, Yuwangtai, Hanyuan Pillar Forest, Shaolin Temple Pillar Forest, Songyang Academy, Shicong's Contemplation Place, Zhongyue Temple, Qiantangzhizhai (Epitaphs from the Tang dynasty), Shanyuan Pillars, Baiyuan Pillar Forest of Hangu Pass.

Custom of funeral, Henan. (From Jin Yongji)

Addresses and Phone Numbers

Zhengzhou Hotel	8 Xinglong Street, Zhengzhou	0371-66760222
Anyang Hotel	1 Youyi Road, Anyang	0372-5922219
Weihui Hotel	103 Qian Street, Weihui County.	0373-4472338
Xinyang Hotel	373 Shengli Road, Xinyang	0376-6223231
Bianjing Hotel	109 East Street(Dongdajie), Kaifeng	0378-2886699
Peony Hotel	15 West Zhongzhou Road, Luoyang	0379-64680000
Xinyouyi Hotel	6 Xiyuan Road, Jianxi Distrcit, Luoyang	0379-64686666
Dapeng Hotel	Inside the Shanzhou Scenic Spot	0398-2966000

Zhengzhou, Jiaozuo, and Xinxiang Region

Best Time to Travel

Spring and autumn are the best seasons to travel. The overall climate is warm and somewhat humid, but there are four distinct seasons.

Shopping Tips

The largest commodity market in Henan Province, Zhengzhou Commodity Market, is located in the east part of Zhengbian Road, which is the only road entering Zhengzhou.

China's earliest astronomical graph, the earliest weiqi board (a game something like "Go"), and the Simuwu Three-legged Vessel are in the Henan Provincial Museum. (From Colphoto)

Henan Provincial Museum

Henan Provincial Museum lies on the intersection of Jinshui Road and Renmin Road in Zhengzhou. As a modern historical and art museum, it was officially opened on May 1, 1998. More than 130,000 cultural artifacts have been collected in the museum. Among the most famous are prehistoric cultural artifacts, Shang and Zhou bronze wares, pottery and porcelain wares, and jade.

At 10:00 a.m. and 4:00 p.m. every day, there is a free concert with ancient musical instruments, such as chime bells and stone chimes.

The Yellow River Scenic Spot

This spectacular and famous scenic area is situated in the suburb of Zhengzhou,

The Yellow River runs across the Central Plain. (From Quanjing)

Dufu in the Tang dynasty, is located in the village of Nanyaowan, Zhanjie, 6 miles from the eastern part of Gongyi. There used to be a Dufu Memorial Temple, and in 1727 a Dufu's Native Place Pillar was erected in its place.

Inside the exhibition hall there is a rare edition of Dufu's poetry and paintings.

18.6 miles from the city. It is about 3.4 miles long and about 3 miles wide. Its main scenic spots are Wulong Peak, Yueshan Temple, Camel Ridge, and the City of King Han and King Ba, with Wulong Peak at the center. Zijin Pavilion in Yueshan Temple is an ideal place for viewing the sunrise. Between the cliffs on the east side of Yueshan Mountain lies the Yellow River Chain Bridge.

Bus No.16 from the train station goes directly to the Yellow River Scenic Spot.

Shikusi (the Grottoes Temple)

The temple lies at the foot of Dali Mountain in the village of Siwan, Duhe, Gongyi. It was built in the Northern Wei Dynasty and now has a Hall of Sakyamuni, 255 cliff engravings, 7,743 Buddhist statues, and dozens of inscriptions.

Dufu's Native Place

Dufu's Native Place, the birth place of the great poet

Mausoleum of Emperors in Northern Song Dynasty

It is situated between the northern Songshan Mountain and the Luo River, covering an area of about 12 square miles. Seven of the nine emperors of the Northern Song Dynasty are buried there. There are also 91 tombs of the royal family.

On both sides of the path there are magnificent stone engravings arranged in line. (From Quanjing)

There are up to 80 different designs of figures and flowers. Creating these can take more than four years. (From Quanjing)

Kang Baiwan's Mansions

In the village of Kangdian, 2.5 miles northwest of Gonyi, it was built in the late Ming–early Qing Dynasty, 500 years ago. Kang Baiwan's Mansions in Henan, Liu Wencai's Mansions in Sichuan, and Mu Erhei's Mansions in Shandong are called the "Three Mansions of China."

The Kang Memorial Temple is a little more than 800 feet northeast of the mansion, and has nine buildings and an engraved brick memorial archway.

Songshan Mountain Scenic Area

Songshan Mountain, located in Dengfeng, is 46.5 miles from east to west, 6 miles in width, with an altitude of almost 5,000 feet. Shaoshi Mountain and Taishi Mountain make up the whole mountain, with 72 peaks and a combined view that is magnificent.

A fresco of 500 arhats in the Hall of a Thousand Buddhas in Shaolin Temple. (From Quanjing)

Shaolin Temple

Shaolin Temple is located at the foot of Wuru Peak, north of Shaoshi Mountain, 56 miles from Zhengzhou. It was built in 495 in the Northern Wei Dynasty. The temple forest lies at the foot of Shaoshi Mountain, and is a large group of tombs and pagodas.

Zhongyue Temple

Zhongyue Temple is seated at the foot of Huanggai Peak, south of Taishi Mountain, about 2 miles north of Dengfeng. Taishi Memorial Temple was its original name. It was built in the Qin Dynasty and enlarged in later dynasties. The 400 buildings in Zhongyue Temple make it the largest temple complex in the Five Mountains area.

Songyang Academy

Situated in the south of Songshan Mountain, Songyang Academy was one of ancient China's higher educational institutions. It was built in the Northern Wei Dynasty and remained a disseminator of Confucianism in ancient China. Many famous scholars have been invited to give lectures, for

The waterfall of Yuntai Mountain, once the secluded home of seven hermits in the Wei and Jin Dynasties. (From CFP)

example, Sima Guang, Fan Zhongyan, Cheng Yi, and Cheng Hao, and others.

Yuntai Mountain (Yuntaishan) Scenic Area

Yuntai Mountain (Yuntaishan) Scenic Area is in Xiuwu County of Jiaozuo, on the south foot of Taihang Mountain. The mountain got its name because the terrain is steep, and the clouds and mist curl up around it throughout the year. The scenic area covers about 73 square miles, with 36 peaks and more than 20 limestone caves.

Star Observation Platform

Star Observation Platform is in Lord Zhou's Temple of Gaocheng, 8 miles southeast of Dengfeng. It was built from 1264 to 1294 in the Yuan Dynasty. The first emperor of Yuan ordered a calendar reform and appointed Guo Shoujing to undertake the job. Guo established the Star Observation Platform, the oldest in China and famous worldwide.

Star Observation Platform comprises the observation tower, the stone tablet, and the surface trough. It is made of stone and brick, with a square surface with a large base and a small top. There is now a China Star Observation Platform Museum, with the observation platform as its center. (From Colphoto)

Jiaying Taoist Temple

Jiaying Taoist Temple is the only one in China that records the history of regulating the Yellow River. It is one of the best preserved large-scale architectural complexes from the Qing Dynasty. Located in the village of Yangzhuang, 8 miles southeast of Wuzhi County, Jiaozuo, it was built in 1723 during the reign of Emperor Yongzheng as a memorial to the outstanding officials who built embankments on the river bank and offered sacrifices to river gods.

Bigan Temple

Bigan Temple is 4.5 miles northwest of Weihui in Xinxiang, covering an area of about 473,369 square feet. The general layout is an oblong, with the tomb more than 65 feet high. It was built in the Zhou Dynasty more than 3,000 years ago. In the Northern Wei and Ming Dynasties, it was repaired and enlarged. Over 100 magnificent stone pillars tower aloft in the temple.

About 64 stone engravings from the Song to the Qing Dynasties are preserved in Bigan Temple. Among them are "Grieving for Bigan," "A Memorial for Bigan" by Emperor Xuandi of the State Chen in Five Dynasties, "To Bigan the Prime Minister" by Emperor Taizong in the Tang Dynasty, and a pillar with the funeral oration and engravings of Emperor Qianlong. (From Colphoto)

East Yue Temple

The East Yue Temple is in the central part of Pingyuan Road of Weihui, Xinxiang. It was built in the year 935 in Five Dynasties and reconstructed in later dynasties. The Great Hall, the Worshipping Hall, and the gallery remain. Inside the temple are stone inscriptions of past dynasties, which are important materials for studying history and calligraphy.

Kaifeng Region

Best Time to Travel

The ample sunshine in Kaifeng makes September and October the best months for admiring the beauty of chrysanthemums, which grow everywhere.

Shopping Tips

Situated in the center of Kaifeng, Madao Street (Madaojie) is the busiest part of the commercial area. The stores there mainly sell general merchandise, silk, textile, clocks and watches, medicine, hardware, fruits, local products, and clothes.

The South and North Bookstore Street in the center city of Kaifeng is a busy commercial section as well. There are many bookstores and stationery stores along the both sides of the street.

The Iron Pagoda

The Iron Pagoda lies in the Iron Pagoda Park in the northeast part of Kaifeng. Originally it was a wooden pagoda named Fusheng Pagoda, built in 982, but it burned down in 1043. In 1049, it was reconstructed and named Kaibaosi Pagoda for the brown glazed tiles inlaid around the pagoda, making it look like iron from a distance. As one of the oldest glazed pagodas in China, the Iron Pagoda enjoys the reputation of "China's first pagoda." Despite floods, earthquakes, and wars over

The Kaifeng Iron Pagoda is 180 feet tall, 13 stories, and is octagonal in shape. (From CFP)

the past 1,000 years, the pagoda is still standing erect.

> The stairway to the top of the pagoda is quite narrow and low; tall visitors might have to bend over to climb.

Xiangguo Temple

In the west part of Ziyou Road in Kaifeng, this temple was originally the mansion of Xin Ling, a feudal prince of Wei in the Warring States period. It was built in the year 555 of the Northern Qi Dynasty but was destroyed in wars over the centuries. In 711 it was reconstructed, and the following year it was given the name "Great Xiangguo Temple" by Emperor Ruizong in the Tang Dynasty. In the late Ming Dynasty it was again ruined in the great Yellow River flood, and rebuilt in 1766 in the Qing Dynasty. Today's Xiangguo Temple retains the earlier construction style of the Ming and Qing Dynasties.

Statue of Avalokitesvara with Thousand Hands and Eyes (From CFP)

The inscription on the wooden board of the "Guchuitai" of King Yu's Terrace was left in the Qing Dynasty. Inside the hall, there is the stone inscription of the Yuwangtai poem by Kang Youwei. (From Colphoto)

Dragon Pavilion

It is located in Dragon Pavilion Park, northwest of Kaifeng, next to the Song Imperial Street in the north, covering an area of around 207 acres. It was originally a part of the palace of the Jin Dynasty, which was later damaged by flood. In 1692, the Wanshou (Longevity) Pavilion was built to house the memorial tablets of the emperors and was called "the Dragon Pavilion." The present Dragon Pavilion was the audience hall of the Wanshou palace.

> On the west bank of Longting (Dragon Pavilion) Lake in the park is the Chinese Hanyuan Pillar Forest, known as China's first and biggest pillar forest. Comprised of over 3,700 inscribed pillars, the pillar forest is well worth a visit.

King Yu's Terrace (Yuwang Tai)

Located in the southeast of Kaifeng, King Yu's Terrace was built in honor of the legendary King Yu in the Xia Dynasty, who devoted all his life to taming the floods of the Yellow River. In 1523, the emperor of the Ming Dynasty built King Yu's Temple, the former name of King Yu's Terrace. Erected high on the peak, the terrace is surrounded by King's

Library, Temple of Three Saints, King Yu's temple, and the Water Virtue.

As the major horticultural area for the Kaifeng chrysanthemum, there is no better place to view the flower in all its glory.

Po Pagoda

As the most remotest above-ground construction in Kaifeng, Po Pagoda is located on the west of King Yu's Terrace Park. When originally built in 974 (Song Dynasty), it had nine stories. In the Yuan Dynasty, the top six floors of the pagoda were destroyed by lightning. In the Ming Dynasty, the ruined six floors were rebuilt into six smaller pagodas, which were preserved. Inside the pagoda there are 178 well-preserved engraved stone tablets, which are highly important to the study of Buddhism.

The name of the pagoda "Po" comes from the surname of the local residents.

Yanqing Taoist Temple

Yanqing Taoist Temple, formerly known as Chongyang Taoist Temple, is in the southwest of Kaifeng. Built to commemorate Wang Chongyang, the founder of the Quanzhen sect of Taoism, this temple was destroyed in the Jin Dynasty but rebuilt in the Yuan Dynasty. With its magnificent halls and temples, it was given the name of "Longevity Palace" by a Yuan emperor. In the Ming Dynasty, it was renamed Yanqing Taoist Temple.

Shan Shaan Gan Guild Hall

Shan Shaan Gan Guild Hall is a rare treasure-house of ancient Chinese architecture, displaying some of the highest achievements in engraving and painting. Located on Xufu Street of Kaifeng, the hall was founded by Shanxi, Shaanxi, and Gansu merchants living in Kaifeng at that time. Inside the hall there are a great number of brick, stone, and wood engravings, embodying vividly many Buddhist stories.

Lord Bao's Ancestral Temple

Lord Bao's Ancestral Temple, on the west bank of Lord Bao's Lake, covers an area of 3,861 square miles. As a series of typical Song temple complexes, this temple consists of an entrance gate, a second gate, a screen wall facing the gate of a house, east and west exhibition halls, a pavilion housing a tablet, a main exhibition hall, a second exhibition hall, a winding corridor,and a hundred-dragon stone carving pavilion. The bronze statue in the main hall, which is 10 feet tall and weighs 2.5 tons, is the most conspicuous.

The exhibition halls at the east and west sides of the temple display Lord Bao's legends and anecdotes.

Lord Bao, named Bao Zheng, was a famous official in the Northern Song Dynasty, known for his incorruptibility and integrity. (From Colphoto)

In the park, all the staff are dressed in Song Dynasty costumes. As this is a "living history" theme park, tourists can also dress up and shop with Song currency. (From CFP)

Historical Theme Park of Song Dynasty

This lovely park lies in the northwest of Kaifeng. Based on the famous painting *Up the River on Qingming Festival* by Zhangzeduan in the Qing Dynasty, the park reproduces vividly the life and scenery in the Song Dynasty. The main buildings in the park include city gate, bridge, streets, shops, rivers, wharfs, and boats.

There are often performances in the park. For example, a file of "Song soldiers" can be seen riding through the streets on horses.

Luoyang, Pingdingshan, Jiyuan Region

Best Time to Travel

Autumn is the best season. If you want to see the famous peonies, April is the best choice.

Shopping Tips

Luoyang Department Store is located in the center of the city. With a business area up to 236,806 square feet, it is the largest shopping mall in Luoyang.

Museum Featuring the Emperor's Chariot Drawn by Six Horses

Located at the East Zhou Royal Plaza, in the center of Luoyang, the main part of the museum is a chariot pit of the Eastern Zhou Dynasty, and a supplementary part exhibits the general history of that era, the latest archaeological discoveries, and theme exhibits of artifacts from the Eastern

Zhou Dynasty. The museum covers an area of over 18,300 square feet. The magnificent chariots form two lines, with one drawn by six horses, documented by ancient writings.

White Horse Temple

The White Horse Temple lies 7 miles east of Luoyang, with a history of more than 1,900 years. Built in 68 CE, it was the first temple built since the introduction of Buddhism into China. The White Horse Temple now covers an area of 32 acres, with a huge bell in the Great Buddha Hall. The White Horse Temple Bell Park in Luoyang is named after it.

> On December 31, *Masi Zhongsheng* (tolling the bell in the White Horse Temple) is held here. The bell is struck to pray for happiness as well as safety and luck for the next year. Tourists are also allowed to strike the bell at other times.

Luoyang Ancient Tomb Museum

Luoyang Ancient Tomb Museum is in the northern suburb of Luoyang, with an area 2,934 square miles, including the aboveground and underground parts. There are 23 restored typical ancient tombs, ranging from the West Han to the Northern Song Dynasties.

The gate of the Luoyang Ancient Tomb Museum is designed as two ancient watch towers. (From CFP)

Guanlin

Guanlin, also known as the Graveyard of General Guan Yu, is in Guanlin Town, southern suburb of Luoyang. Originally built in the Ming Dynasty and rebuilt several times in later dynasties, this site covers an area of over 23,166 square miles, with more than 800 pine trees, 150 rooms and halls, 4 stone archways, 110 stone lions, and 70 stone engravings.

Longmen Grottoes

Longmen Grottoes are located 7 miles south of Luoyang. Originally built in the Northern Wei Dynasty and rebuilt in the Eastern Wei, Western Wei, Northern Qi, Sui, Tang, and Northern Song Dynasties, these grottoes have a history of over 1,500 years. It is about a half-mile from south to north, with 2,345 grottoes, 2,800 engraved inscriptions,

The Longmen Grottoes, the Dunhuang Mogao Grottoes, and the Datong Yungang Grottoes are known as the three foremost treasures among China's grottoes. (From Quanjing)

The ceremony worshipping Heaven initiated by the ancient Chinese Emperor Huangdi. (From CFP)

more than 40 pagodas, and over 100,000 statues. In 2000 it was listed by UNESCO as a World Heritage Site.

Take Bus 81, 53, or 60 to the grottoes.

Wangwu Mountain

Wangwu Mountain lies 28 miles northwest of Jiyuan, adjoining Taihang Mountain and the Yellow River. It is a famous Taoist pilgrimage site as well as one of the nine famous mountains in China. This is where the well-known Chinese fable "Old fools moving away the mountain" is set.

Take a bus from Luoyang to Jiyuan, then change to an express bus to the scenic spot.

Anyang Region

Best Time to Travel

Anyang has a very hot summer. Autumn and spring are its optimal tourist months.

Yin Ruins

The Yin Ruins are located in the village of Xiaotun, northwest of Anyang. With a history of more than 33,000 years, these are the ruins of the late Shang Dynasty's slave society. It is famous for the oracle bone inscriptions and for the bronze wares unearthed in great quantity, documented since the Han and Tang Dynasties. The oracle bones were discovered at Xiaotun in 1899 (Qing Dynasty), confirming the Yin Ruins documented in the ancient records. The Simuwu Quadripod, an ancient ritual vessel, was unearthed here.

In 1987 the Yin Ruins Garden was established on the ruins of the Yin palace. It displays not only the layout and construction of the Yin palace but also the features of its formal gardens. This tourist resort integrates archaeology, gardening, ancient structures, and tourism.

Yin Ruins Garden (From CFP)

Wenfeng Pagoda

Situated at the site of Tianning Temple, at the northwest corner of the old city of Anyang, Wenfeng Pagoda was built between 601 and 604 of the Sui Dynasty (581–618), with the original name of Tianning Temple Pagoda. The 127-foot-tall, octagonal five-floor pagoda is seated on a round lotus base, with the stupa-style top larger than the base, like an umbrella, rare among Chinese ancient pagodas.

On the semicircular front of the arch gate of the Xiuding Temple Pagoda are engraved Buddha niches as well as Tang and Song inscriptions. (From Colphoto)

Xiuding Temple Pagoda

Xiuding Temple Pagoda, also known as Tang Pagoda, is on Qingliang Mountain, 22 miles northwest of Anyang. Built in the Northern Wei Dynasty, the pagoda has three courtyards, all facing south. The main halls include the Hall of Lokspala, the Great Buddha Hall, the Second Buddha Hall, and the Iron Tile Hall. The pagoda itself, a pavilion-shaped brick structure, lies between the Great Buddha Hall and the Iron Tile Hall. Built in the Tang Dynasty, the orange-colored pagoda is also called the Red Pagoda.

Red Flag Canal

The Red Flag Canal lies at the foot of Taihang Mountain, west of Linzhou. The construction of the canal was begun in February 1960 and completed in July 1969. Built on the cliffs of Taihang Mountain, the 4,921-foot-long canal is known as a "man-made heavenly river" and symbolized the spirit of that era. Today's Red Flag Canal is a tourist destination with three parts–Watershed Cave, Youth Cave, and Luosi Pool.

To come here, tourists can get off the train at Anyang of Henan and take a bus to Linzhou, which is more than 30 miles away, about a one-hour ride. It is about 25 miles from Linzhou to the Youth Cave of the Red Flag Canal.

Jiuli

As the birthplace of *The Book of Changes* (*I Ching*), Jiuli lies 2.5 miles north of Tangyin County, at the vast conjunction of the Jiu and Tang Rivers. Here, Emperor Zhou of the Yin Dynasty imprisoned Emperor Wen of the Zhou Dynasty.

The Red Flag Canal passes through the mountains. (From Colphoto)

Nanyang Region

Holding a feather fan and wearing a silk hat, sitting still and musing, the colorful clay figure of Zhuge Liang in the Dabai Hall of the Wuhouci Temple fully demonstrates the elegance of this great strategist. (From Colphoto)

Wuhouci Temple

Located on Wolong Mound, west suburb of Nanyang, the temple was the farmstead of Zhuge Liang, a famous politician and strategist in the Three Kingdoms Period. It was built in Wei and Jin Dynasties and rebuilt in later dynasties. The present Wuhouci Temple (now the the Nanyang Museum) retains the construction style of late Ming and Early Qing Dynasties. Among the 300 existent epigraphs, the seal character, the regular script, and cursive handwriting are well preserved.

In the Nanyang Museum by the Wuhouci Temple there are cultural artifacts of the Han Dynasty, which reflect the history of Nanyang in the period.

Nanyang Han Painting Museum

Nanyang Han Painting Museum lies on the west of the Chezhannan Road, opposite Wuhou Ci. It was built in 1935 and rebuilt in 1959 and 1988. Covering an area of 14 acres, the present museum is the earliest and largest museum specializing in the collection, exhibition, and study of paintings and stone engravings of the Han Dynasty. There are more than 2,000 paintings in the museum, with the best of them exhibited in the 64,583-square-foot exhibition hall in the main building.

Zhang Heng's Tomb

Zhang Heng's Tomb lies in Shiqiao, 15.5 miles north of Wancheng District, Nanyang. The tomb is 2 feet high, with a perimeter of 259 feet. Around the tomb there are brick-paved paths and

Zhang Heng's Tomb in Nanyang. (From Colphoto)

The stone carvings of the Han Dynasty in Nanyang are cut in relief with a wide range of subjects—dances, juggling, historical anecdotes, astronomy, and fairy tales. (From Colphoto)

walls, and in front there are three pillars that tell of the virtues and academic achievements of Zhang Heng as well as the discovery of the tomb.

Medical Sage's Temple

Situated on the bank of the Wenliang River in the eastern suburb of Nanyang, the Medical Sage's Temple holds the tomb of Zhang Zhongjing (150–219), an outstanding herbal doctor in the Eastern Han Dynasty. In the western corridor of the temple, there are 117 stone engraved paintings of famous doctors since Fuxi, the first legendary doctor in Chinese history.

Neixiang County's Yamen

Located on the East Street of Neixiang County, Neixiang County's Yamen was once a local government office in feudal China. It was built in 1034 of the Yuan Dynasty and destroyed and rebuilt in the Ming and Qing Dynasties. As one of the best preserved yamen structures, Neixiang County's Yamen generally maintains the construction style of the Ming and Qing Dynasties. It faces the south and has 117 rooms.

Shan Shaan Guild Hall

Shan Shaan Guild Hall lies at the center of Sheqi, 45 km east of Nanyang, also known as "Shan Shaan Temple" and "General Guan's Temple." It was built in 1782 of the Qing Dynasty and funded by the Shanxi and Shaanxi merchants living in Sheqi. It covers an area of 42,640 square feet, facing the south, with a magnificent view. The Shan Shaan Guild Hall is a wooden construction of the Qing Dynasty, with three parts, each of which is symmetrical.

The Bat Cave

The Bat Cave lies in Baihewan, 75 miles west of Nanyang. The cave is about 2 miles long, with five halls big enough to hold 1,000 people. It has more than 50 scenic spots, including the White Bat Hall and the Bat Palace. More than 100,000 bats of 7 different breeds live in the cave. They fly out for food at night and fly back at dawn.

The back gate of the guild hall has a single-eaved, gable-and-hip roof, and three gate arches. The decorations with totem figures and the gate sides are exquisitely executed. (From CFP)

Door God of woodcut painting, Zhuxian. (From CFP)

Henan Style

Pan Drum of Kaifeng

The Pan Drum of Kaifeng can be traced back to the period of Five Dynasties. It was said that when Zhao Kuangyin, the founder of the Northern Song Dynasty, ascended the throne, the pan drums were beaten to celebrate the emperor's great victory. The drums were praised as "Yellow River royal drums." The Pan Drum of Kaifeng is the largest and heaviest of the drums that are carried on the human body. When it is beaten, it sounds like thunder and billows with an awesome momentum. The Pan Drum of Kaifeng is one of the "Five Drums of China." The others are the awe-inspiring Gong and Drum of Shanxi, the Ansai Waist Drum of Shaanxi, the Lanzhou Taiping Drum of Gansu, and the Feng Yang Drum of Anhui.

Henan Opera

Henan Opera was once called "Henan Bangzi" and "Henan Gaodiao." In earlier times, the actors sang in their normal voice and raised the tune to falsetto when starting and ending. As a result, Henan Opera was called "Henan Chorus." Because the stage was usually built near the hill when performing in the western region of Henan, it was also called "roar near the hill." Henan Opera is one of the major local operas of Henan Province and is popular in some areas of Shaanxi,

The costumes of Henan Opera are now almost the same as those of Beijing Opera due to the influence of the latter. (From ImagingChina)

Gansu, Shanxi, Hebei, Shandong, Jiangsu, Anhui, and Hubei.

Henan Opera is unique in its colorful music, smooth melody, and strong rhythm. The presentation as a whole is tender and smooth while the military segment of acrobatic play is full of enthusiasm. The structure of its arias is variable and its libretto is easy to understand. Henan Opera can be categorized into four types: Lento, Liushui Ban, Er-ba Ban, and Flying Ban. The accompanying instruments are different for the tender story and the lively military part. Those used for the former are Er Xian, Shan Xian, and Yue Qin (which are called "three string players"). Later the Er Xian was replaced by Banhu. The instruments for the military piece include Bangu, Tanggu, Daluo, Xiaoluo (also called Tangluo or Shouluo), Bangzi, and Shouban.

Woodcut Painting of Zhuxian

The town of Zhuxian in Kaifeng of Henan Province was one of the four most famous towns in the Song Dynasty. The other three are Hankou of Hubei, Foshan of Guangdong, and Jingde of Jiangxi. Zhuxian is famous for its woodcut *Nianhua* (New Year paintings). The paintings printed with woodblocks take on the characteristics of rough lines, exaggerated images, and bright and flamboyant color. With their contents mostly originating from the historical operas, historical novels, fairy tales, and folk legends, the woodcut paintings express unique rural flavor and style. The woodcut paintings have great artistic value.

Pan Drum of Kaifeng (From CFP)

Hubei

Geography at a Glance

Hubei, or "Er" for short, is situated in the central part of China. It adjoins Henan on the north, Anhui on the east, Jiangxi on the southeast, Hunan on the south, Chongqing Municipality on the west, and Shaanxi on the northwest. Located north of Dongting Lake (Dongting Hu), it is called Hubei (Chinese for "north of the lake"). Covering an area of 71,776 square miles, the province has a population of 60,270,000 (2000 census). Wuhan is its capital city.

Hubei is located in the transitional region from the second, to the third terrace in the terrain of China; thus, it has a variety of landforms such as mountains, hills, hillocks, and plains. It is surrounded by Wuling, Wushan, Daba, Wudang, Tongbai, Dabie, and Mufu mountains on the west, north, and east. Hills and hillocks spread out in front of these mountains. Lying in the central and southern part is the Jianghan Plain, which extends to Hunan Province to link with the Dongting Lake Plain. The terrain of Hubei is configured like an open basin with three rising sides, a plain central part opening wide to the south, and a breach in the northern part. It is known as the "province of 1,000 lakes" for its crowded river networks, watercourses, and lakes.

Hubei has mainly a northern subtropical monsoon climate, which characterizes the transition from the subtropical zone to the warm-temperature zone. It enjoys abundant

(From Quanjing)

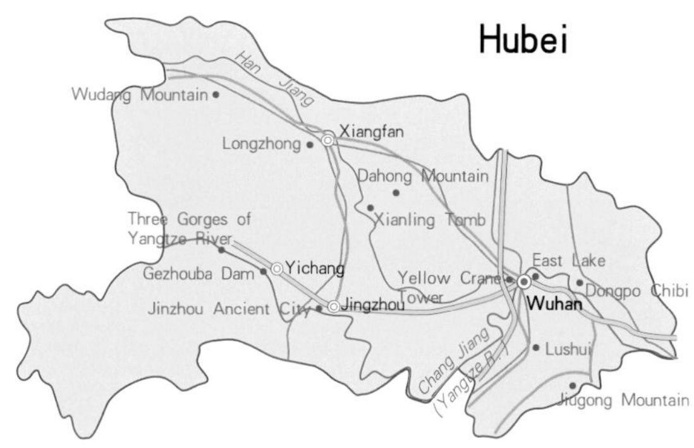

Boat trackers tracking along the Shennong River, Hubei (From CFP)

sunlight, ample heat, a long frost-free period, plentiful precipitation, and a combination of water and heat, favorable for agriculture. Hubei has an annual rainfall of 31.5 to 63 inches, which decreases from the southeast to the northwest.

Golden snub-nosed monkeys in Shennongjia (From CFP)

Featured Cuisine

Wuchang Fish, Laotong bean curd crust, Xiaotaoyuan soup, Sha Lake salted eggs, Jingzhou eight treasures rice pudding, stir-fried smoked pork with Hongshan caitai, fried pheasant in soy sauce, peach blossoms with mashed chicken, three steamed dishes of Mianyang, long-life soup, king-size steamed soup buns with crab roe stuffing, Mianyang steamed meat.

Featured Commodities

Herbal Medicines

Many Chinese herbs and spices are used for herbal remedies; be sure to ask your tour guide for translations.

Special Local Products

Osmanthus (royal palm) flavored candy, sesame candy, Huangshixiang cakes, Gexian rice, Shihua yeast wine, Huanghelou wine, garden rice wine, Bailiubian wine, Hong Lake lotus root, Zhongxiang rice tea, Zhongxiang coiling-dragon tea, Zhongxiang tea, Dengcun tea, Shanling wild arrowroot, Jingshengqiao rice, Xiaogan sesame candy, mushrooms, Wuchang fish, Xianning osmanthus.

Notes 

❶There are round-trip limousine buses between Wuhan and Beijing on festivals and holidays; buses take longer than trains to reach the area.

❷People in Wuhan tend to speak very quickly; therefore, they may not be understood by strangers.

Local Handicrafts

Horse-mouth china, Hubei turquoise carvings, Hong Lake feather fans, enamel bell chimes.

Transportation Tips

By Bus

Hubei has a well-developed transportation system of 9 national highways, 2 national trunk highways, and about 91 provincial highways. Hubei has become a key transportation hub for the national highways. The Shanghai-Chengdu and Yinchuan-Fuzhou expressways are the main routes of the Western Development Program. This highway network connects provinces, cities, counties, towns, main ports, and railway hubs with Wuhan and the central cities of each region.

By Train

Wuhan and Xiangfan, where Beijing-Guangzhou, Jiaozuo-Liuzhou, Beijing-Kowloon, and Wuhan-Chongqing lines intersect, are the most important hubs in Hubei. The intensive railway network reaches all the important cities of China.

By Plane

Hubei, as the transportation hub of central China, has a highly developed air industry. There are five civil airports in Hubei: Tianhe, Sanxia, Shashi, Enshi, and Xiangfan (one civil and military airport); 72 international, domestic, and district airlines fly into these airports, and 57 cities in China can be reached directly now. Wuhan Tianhe International is the most modern and largest airport in central China.

By Water

The Yangtze River and the Han River traverse the whole territory of Hubei, which makes them the two main water transport courses in the province. There are many important ports such as Wuhan, Huangshi, Shashi, Yichang, Xiangfan, and Laohekou, with Wuhan as one of the largest inland ports in the middle and lower reaches of the Yangtze River.

POPULAR FESTIVALS

Buffalo Festival

This is held every year on April 8 of the lunar calendar in the Tujia Ethnic district in western Hubei. Traditional music and sacred dances are performed during the festival.

God of Silkworms Festival

A district festival held in silkworm-breeding areas. The time varies according to the location. It is held every year on the first day of summer in northeastern Hubei. This festival is called the Birthday of Canhua in Jiangsu and Zhejiang.

International Dragon Boat Festival

Held in Zigui every year on May 5 of the lunar calendar. There are dragon boat competitions, Zongzi throwing, and local feasts.

Three Gorges Arts Festival

Held every singular year in Yichang between September and October. Activities such as bell-chime performances and colored pottery exhibitions are held during the festival.

Recommended Routes

Classical Routes

Three-day tour of New Three Gorges—Shennong River—Shennongjia

Day 1 Arrival in Hanyang. Lodging: Suqing Holiday Hotel.

Day 2 Hanyang→Yichang→Xiling Gorge→Three Gorges Dam. Lodging: On the boat.

Day 3 Shennong River→Longchang Gorge→Parrot Gorge→Xuangguan Gorge→Wu Gorge→Qutang Gorge→White Emperor City→Xiangxikou. Lodging: On the boat.

Day 4 Shennongjia Natural Reserve→Tianshengqiao Ecological Tourism Zone→Gold Monkey Mountain Virgin Forest→Alpine Meadow→Shennong Peak→Hanyang. Lodging: On the boat.

Day 5 End of tour.

Four-day ecological tour of Shennongjia

Day 1 Arrival in Yichang. Lodging: Yichang International Hotel.

Day 2 Yichang→Muyu Town of Shennongjia→Tianshengqiao Ecological Tourism Zone→Shennongtan Scenery Park. Lodging: Caiyuan Hotel.

Day 3 Muyu→Yantian Scenery Park→Swallow's Cave→Rainbow Ferry→Savage Cave→Cow's Nose Cavern→Shennong Peak Nature Reserve→Savage Park→Gold Monkey Mountain Virgin Forest→Fengjingya→Watching Tower→Banbiyan. Lodging: Caiyuan Hotel.

Day 4 End of tour.

Four-day tour of Enshi's Tujia and Miao ethnics

Day 1 Wuhan→Enshi. Lodging: Qingshui Hotel.

Day 2 Enshi Qipiao Port→Chuangtan of Qing River→Enshi. Lodging: Qingshui Hotel.

Day 3 Enshi→Suobuya Stone Forest→Dragon's Scale Palace. Lodging: Qingshui Hotel.

Day 4 End of tour.

Traditional Routes

Three-day tour of Three Gorges

Day 1 Yichang→Three Gorges Dam.

Day 2 Three Gorges Dam→Fengjie→White Emperor City→Qutang Gorge→Wushan Mountain→Little Three Gorges (Longmen Gorge, Bawu Gorge, Dicui Gorge).

Day 3 Three Gorges→Yichang. End of tour.

Four-day tour of Yichang

Day 1 Arrival inYichang.

Day 2 The Three Visitor's Cave→Zigui.

Day 3 Site of Changbanpo→Dangyang Bridge→Guangyu's Tomb and Temple→Mai Cheng.

Day 4 End of tour.

Six-day tour of Jing Men

Day 1 Arrival in Jing Men.

Day 2 Holyland Mountain→Zhang River Scenery Park.

Day 3 Xian Tomb of the Ming Dynasty→Yuan Palace→Dakou National Forest Park

Day 4 Guanyin Island→Lijia Zhou→Letian Chu→Frog Stone→Five Peaks Village→Huangji Island.

Day 5 Nine-Dragon Vale→Laojun Platform→Golden Peak→Immortal Cave.

Day 6 End of tour.

Four-day tour of Wudang Mountain

Day 1 Arrival at Wudang Mountain.

Day 2 Wudang Mountain→Golden Peak →Taihe Palace→Zhuanyun Hall→Lisidao →Grounding-Needle Well→Yuxu Palace→ Yuexuan Gate.

Day 3 Nanyan Palace→Longtouxiang→ Making-up Platform→Ancient Plant Path of Feisheng Cliff.

Day 4 End of tour.

Enshi's Tujia youngsters in a singing contest. (From CFP)

Self-Guided Tours

Tour in Wuhan City

Known as the "hub of nine provinces" from ancient times, Wuhan has many historical and scenic sites. Main scenic sites: Second Bridge of the Yangtze River in Wuhan, East Lake, Mountain-Climbing Ropeway, Ever-Spring Tao Temple, Yellow Crane Tower, Ancient Lute Platform, Guiyuan Buddhist Temple, Qingchuan Pavilion, Tortoise Mountain Three Kingdoms Park.

Adventurous tour of Shennongjia

Start from Wuhan at Shennongjia Natural Reserve via cities including Yichang and Zigui. Main scenic sites: Yellow Crane Tower, Ancient Lute Platform, Little Three Gorges, White Emperor City, Gezhouba Dam, Birthplace of Wang Zhaojun, Qu Yuan Temple, Shennongjia Nature Reserve.

Addresses and Phone Numbers

Eastern Hotel	Hankou Railway Station Square	027-85888668
Tian'an Holiday Hotel	868 Liberation Road, Hankou	027-85867888
Qingchuan Holiday Hotel	88 Xima Street, Hanyang	027-84716688
Asian Hotel	616 Liberation Road, Hankou	027-83807777
Lakeside Garden Hotel	115 Geyu Road, Wuchang	027-87782888
Yichang International Hotel	121 Riverside Road, Yichang	0717-6222888
Gezhouba Dam Hotel	3 Yiling Road, Yichang	0717-8866666
Qingjiang Hotel	264 East Wind Road, Enshi	0718-8222281
Enshi Asian Hotel	122 1 Alley, Wuyang Road, Enshi	0718-8279888
Wudang Hotel	33 Ever-happy Road, Wudangshan Mountain, Shiyan	0719-5665548

Wuhan Region

Best Time to Travel

Summer is not the best season for visiting Wuhan because of the hot and humid weather. Spring and autumn are the best times to visit Wuhan.

Shopping Tips

Wuhan Square Shopping Center, a luxurious mall for shopping, entertainment, restaurants, businesses, and recreation, is the largest single shopping center in southern and central China.

New People's Paradise, on Zhongshan Street, is a place crowded with young people. With unlimited entertainment, food, clothes, photography, cosmetics, and fashion elements, it has become the most popular place in Wuhan.

The rebuilt Yellow Crane Tower is made of reinforced concrete, but the surface has been painted in trompe l'oeil, making it appear to be wood-brick. (From CFP)

Yellow Crane Tower

Situated at the top of Snake Hill, Yellow Crane Tower is one of the most beautiful sights in this area The tower was built in 222 in the Wu Kingdom. In 1884 it was destroyed by fire. The new tower, with five stories and 161 feet tall, was rebuilt in 1985.

Take Bus 1, 4, 10, 401, or 413 to Yellow Crane Tower. If taking other buses, you can get off at Yuemachang and walk to the destination.

Hubei Museum

Located at 88 Eastern Lake Road, Wuchang District, Wuhan, this museum was established in 1953. With a floor area of about 97,000 square feet, it contains 200,000 artifacts and materials of various kinds. There are four major exhibits: relics from the Tomb of the Marquis of Zeng, ancient musical artifacts from Hubei, handicrafts of the Imperial Palace of Qing, and the One Hundred Years of Hubei.

The museum is not far from East Lake Scenic Park, so both places can easily be visited.

The site of the Wuchang military government is in Yuemachang. A copper statue of Sun Yat-sen stands before the gate. (From ImagineChina)

Site of Wuchang Military Government

Located north of the former Wuchang Yuemachang and called "the red mansion," this site was originally the Parliament Tower of Hubei, built in 1909 by the Qing government.

East Lake Scenic Area

East Lake Scenic Area, in the eastern suburbs of Wuchang District, Wuhan, covers an area of 34 square miles, with a water-surface area of 13 square miles. The largest scenic spot in Wuhan, East Lake Scenic Area is known as the "99 bends [in the shape of its bank]," with picturesque scenery, clear water, and blue mountains.

Guiyuan Temple

Guiyuan Temple, at 20 Cuiwei Street, Hanyang, Wuhan, was built in 1658 (Qing Dynasty), and is regarded as the first temple of Hubei. It is also one of the four famous Buddhist temples of Hubei. There are 500 clay arhats in the temple.

The shaded dike winding across the surface of East Lake looks like a jade belt floating on the water. (From CFP)

Inside the Arhat Hall of Guiyuan Temple, there are also statues of Sakyamuni and other Buddhist gods. (From Colphoto)

Inside the Hanyan Workers' Cultural Palace, west of Turtle Mountain (Guishan) and alongside Moon Lake (Yuehu), stands the famous Guqintai construction complex, which creates a broad and deep artistic view by ingeniously "borrowing" the landscape of Turtle Mountain and Moon Lake, a skill frequently employed in the designs of the Chinese.

Tongl Mountain Ancient Mining Ruins

Tonglü Mountain Ancient Mining Ruins, a bit less than 2 miles west of Daye County, Hubei, are some of the largest ancient mining ruins unearthed in China so far, covering an area of 31,000 square miles.

Wuzu Temple

Wuzu Temple, also known as Dongshan Temple or Shuangfeng Temple, lies on Shuangfeng Mountain, 7 miles from Huangmei County. It was founded by and named after Hongren, the Fifth Originator of Zen, and was rebuilt in the Qing Dynasty, after being destroyed in wars. Situated halfway up the mountain, the pavilions, galleries, and halls inside the temple are all connected by paths.

Sizu Temple

Sizu Temple lies on West Hill (also known as Po'Er Mountain), 9 miles northwest of Huangmei County. It was one of the largest Buddhist temples in China, with the greatest number of monks and worshippers, and held the highest reputation. It was also the first temple where the monks lived in groups, learned the sutra, and worked on adjacent farms. Built in 624 (Tang Dynasty), the temple was named after Daoxin, the Fourth Originator of Zen, who once lectured there. Acording to legend, the three pine trees at the temple were planted by Daoxin himself.

The ancient street of Yanglou-dong near the Martial Chibi is reminiscent of the Chu region. (From CFP)

Chibi War Relics

The site of the Chibi war relics lies on the southern banks of the Yangtze River, 22 miles northwest of the city of Chibi, opposite Wulin. It is a famous ancient war site, where the army of Liu Bei, joining the army of Sunquan, defeated Cao Cao in the Eastern Han Dynasty.

The Dongpo Chibi in Huanggang is known as the "Wen (intellectual) Chibi"; the Three Kingdoms Chibi in Chibi City is known as the "Wu (martial) Chibi."

Jiugong Mountain

Jiugong Mountain, the middle section of the Mufu Mountain Range, lies in Tongshan County, Xianning. Laoyajian, the main peak of the mountain, is 5,435 feet above sea level. The scenery is extraordinarily beautiful, with green springs, cool summers, autumns full of colored maples, and snowy winters. Yunzhong Lake, 4,035 feet above sea level, is a spectacularly beautiful mountain lake.

Lushui Lake Scenic Area

Situated east of Chibi, Lushui Lake Scenic Area covers 22 square miles, with more than 400 islands scattered in the clear water of the lake. The lake is known as "the Pearl of Chu" for its quiet mountains, green forests, clear water, and serenely beautiful islands.

Zeng Marquis Yi's Tomb

Situated at Leigudun, Suizhou, Hubei Province, this tomb is the grave of Yi, King of the State of Zeng in the early Warring Period in China. Zeng Marquis Yi was buried in 433 BCE or later. When the tomb was unearthed, nearly 15,000 cultural artifacts were found, including bronzeware, musical instruments, gold ware, jade ware, horse-carriage accessories, painted bambooware, and bamboo slips. The largest and best-preserved artifact is a set of 65 bronze chimes weighing 2.5 tons. Although buried underground for about 2,400 years, the chimes still make beautiful music.

Most of the cultural artifacts unearthed from Zeng Marquis Yi's tomb are in the Hubei Museum.

Dahong Mountain Scenic Area

Dahong Mountain Scenic Area lies in the mountainous region of northern Hubei, 40 miles from Suizhou. The mountain stretches in a long line, peak after peak. The summit of Dahong Mountain is 5,367 feet above sea level. Within the scenic area there is a virgin forest, with verdant ancient trees and rare flowers. White Dragon Pool, 2,789 feet above sea level, is known as the "Heavenly Pool in Middle Er."

Zeng Marquis Yi's bronze chimes in the Hubei Museum (From Colphoto)

Xiangfan Region

Best Time to Travel

Spring and autumn are the optimal months to travel throughout Xiangfan.

The Xiangyang ancient city at sunset (From Colphoto)

Xiangyang Ancient City

On the southern bank of the Han River, this ancient city was built in the Han Dynasty and rebuilt in the Qing and Ming dynasties. The square-shaped city wall, with a perimeter of about 4.5 miles, was once surrounded by a moat. The moat has often been referred to as the first moat in China.

At the northwest corner of Xiangyang ancient city is Furen City.

Duke Mi's Temple

Duke Mi's Temple, formerly known as the Mi Family Temple, is located at Guizi Gate Tower in ancient Xiangfan, facing the Small Northern Gate of Xiangyang across the Han River. It was built in the Yuan Dynasty and totally rebuilt in the Qing Dynasty. Constructed to commemorate Mi Fu, an outstanding calligrapher and painter in the Song Dynasty, there are over 100 stone inscriptions by famous ancient calligraphers such as Mi Fu, Su Shi, Huang Tingjian, and Cai Xiang, as well as over 30 pieces of calligraphy by contemporary calligraphers.

Guangde Temple

Guangde Temple lies 6 miles west of Xiangfan, Hubei Province. Its original name was Yunling Temple. Built in the Tang Dynasty, it was famous for its size and the Duobao Buddhist Pagoda, built in the Ming Dynasty. The four halls—Buddha Hall, Avalokitesvara Hall, Big Four's Temple, and Main Hall—are all single-eaved, rebuilt in the Qing Dynasty. The 56-foot-high Duobao Pagoda is made of bricks and stones resembling wood; there are five small pagodas on the top of the main pagoda, making it unique.

Shiyan Region

Best Time to Travel

Shiyan has a particularly vertical climate, with the temperature dropping with the altitude. Spring and autumn are the optimal months to visit Shiyan.

Wudang Mountain

Wudang Mountain, the famous Taoist Mountain with its ancient name of Taihe Mountain, lies in Shiyan, Hubei Province. It joins together Qinling Mountain and Bashan Mountain. During the Tang Dynasty, Five Dragons Taoist Temple was built on the mountain.

> Be sure to take shelter if caught in a storm on the mountain. Lightning strikes and avalanches are common.

View of the Wudang Mountain (From ImagineChina)

Cargo ships waiting to pass in the navigation lock of the Gezhou Dam (From ImagineChina)

Yichang Region

Best Time to Travel

Yichang has an agreeable climate: warm in winter, and pleasant in spring, summer, and autumn.

Tanzi Mountain Scenic Area

Tanzi Mountain Scenic Area, affiliated with the Three Gorges Project of the Yangtze River, lies on Zhongbao Island in Sandou Ping, Yichang, Hubei Province. It is well known for its unusual mountains, clear water, and the unique stones and mountains along both banks of the Yangtze River. It is the embodiment of thousands of years of human history and culture.

Gezhou Dam

Gezhou Dam, at the exit from the Three Gorges of the Yangtze River, Yichang, is 8,402 feet long, 176.5 feet high, with a capacity of more than 8,644.8 billion British gallons (or, 10,382 billion American gallons), ranking it among the largest hydroelectric stations in the world.

Take Bus or Minibus 3 or 9 to Gezhou Dam and get off at the navigation lock.

Jade Spring Mountain

Jade Spring Mountain, in the Jing Mountain Range, lies 9 miles southwest of Dangyang. The spring is known for its clear, sweet water; a stone lion's head over the spring forces the water to flow out through the lion's mouth. Temples, green forests, clear streams, and long mountainous vistas make this a wondrous place to visit.

Three Visitors' Cave

Three Visitors' Cave lies in the middle of the cliff, near the northern peak of Xiling Mountain. It is strategically situated and difficult to reach; it is just 6 miles east of Yichang. Many cultural artifacts are found on the mountain, and those from the Three Kingdoms Period are the most renowned.

Shennongjia

Shennongjia, a wild and remote virgin forest, covers the slopes of the Daba Mountain Range, with an average altitude of 3,281 feet above sea level. It is the only complete subtropical ecosystem at the middle latitude as well as a prominent ecotourism site. Big Shennongjia is 10,000 feet above sea level and is known throughout the country as "the roof of central China." Many myths revolve around the sightings of a primitive ape-like creature, the Chinese equivalent of Bigfoot, and there is a small museum dedicated to evidence of this creature. The scenery is perhaps the most beautiful in the world, with thousands of acres of misty mountains and lush forests.

Shenglong Creek is a great place for river rafting, extending for about 12 miles through the forest. Visitors can see remarkable views such as the ancient plank roads, cliff coffins, limestone caves, and, perhaps, glimpses of leopards, bears, wild boar, and best of all, the endangered Golden snub-nosed monkeys. There are also scattered villages of the ethnic Tu people.

The statues of Bai Juyi, Bai Xingjian, and Yuanzhen in the back room of the Three Visitors' Cave (From ImagineChina)

Qu Yuan's Birthplace

In Zigui County, on the northern bank of the Yangtze River and outside the eastern gate of the county is Lepingli, the birthplace of Qu Yuan. The temple was built in the Tang Dynasty and was moved and rebuilt in 1978 during the construction of Gezhou Dam.

A boat ride from Yichang takes about 3 hours to get to this site.

On the gate there are majestic towers, from which the caves for hiding soldiers can be seen. The picture is the East gate of Jingzhou ancient city. (From CFP)

Jingzhou and Jingmen Region

Best Time to Travel

Spring and autumn are the optimal months for visiting this area.

Longevity Pagoda

Longevity Pagoda is situated on the Bodhisattva Rock (the first rock projecting out of the surface of the Yellow River) at the Jing River Dam. It was built in the Ming Dynasty and took four years to complete. Longevity Pagoda is 134 feet high and built with bricks in an imitation-wood style. The Vajracchedika sutra engraved on the top of the pagoda ranks among the rare cultural artifacts in China.

Bodhisattva Rock at Jing River Dam (From CFP)

Baling Mountain Ancient Tomb Group

This ancient tomb group lies in Baling Mountain National Forest Park, about 7.5 miles northwest of Jiangling County. Situated among the three ancient cities—Jingzhou, Jinan, and Wancheng—it is a concentrated area of the tombs of emperors and marquises. There is Gou Jian's famous sword and an exquisite color-painted wood screen.

Jingzhou Ancient City

Situated in Jiangling County, Jingzhou ancient city, with a history of more than 2,000 years, is among China's best-preserved ancient cities.

Wenfeng Pagoda

Wenfeng Pagoda its on Dragon Mountain, Zhongxiang city. It was built in the Tang Dynasty, with three bronze Chinese characters spelling *Yuan* (meaning "to pass an exam") at the bottom of the pagoda, meaning that examinees can pass the three exams at three different levels. The top of the pagoda looks like an iron brush pen writing toward Heaven.

Ming Xian Tomb

Ming Xian Tomb, on Songlin Mountain, 4.5 miles north of Zhongxiang, was the multiburial tomb of Zhu Yuanyou and Madam Jiang, father and mother of Emperor Jiajing of the Ming Dynasty. As the largest single imperial tomb in China, it is the only imperial tomb from the Ming Dynasty in the six provinces of southcentral China.

Enshi Region

Best Time to Travel

Enshi has a very temperate climate but abounds in fog and rain. Anytime during the year is a good time to visit, except in the summer rainy season.

Qing River Drift

The Qing River begins in western Hubei Province, runs through Enshi, Changyang, and Badong, and empties into the Yangtze River at Zhicheng. The river is 263 miles long and as beautiful as a landscape picture. The river segment for rafting is about 24 miles long, with a drop of 6 to 13 feet. Rafting and drifting are extraordinarily exciting and not dangerous. Along the river there are tall cliffs, waterfalls, clear springs, and green trees. Tourists can not only appreciate the beautiful primitive scenery but also

According to historical records, the exquisite Xian Tomb is nearly perfect. (From ImagineChina)

have a view of the hanging coffins and the cliff planks of the Tu ethnic people.

> Tourists on rafts may not carry any valuables except waterproof cameras.

Lianzhu Pagoda

Lianzhu Pagoda lies at the top of Five Peaks Mountain, east of Enshi on the middle reaches of the Qing River. It was built in 1831 in the Qing Dynasty (1616–1911) and completed in one year. The seven-story pagoda is 138 feet tall. The octagonal base was made from several huge stones. There is a stone giant on each end, whose various poses render the pagoda as stable as Mount Tai itself.

In front of Lianzhu Pagoda there are stone gates and walls. (From CFP)

Tenglong Cave

Tenglong Cave is situated in the near suburb of Lichuan, on the upper reaches of the Qing River. It is a cave group with a dry cave and a wet cave at an altitude of 3,576 feet above sea level. The dry cave is the largest cave in Asia; the stalactites in the wet cave are exquisite and various.

Big Well Ancient Construction Group

The Big Well Ancient Construction Group in Well Village, in the town of Baiyang, Lichuan, Hubei Province, was built in the late Ming Dynasty and Early Qing Dynasty. The complex features both Western style and the Tu ethnic architectural style.

Yumu Stockaded Village

Yumu Stockaded Village is located in Moudao, 37 miles from western Lichuan via National Highway 381 (Lichuan to Wanzhou). The village has ancient tomb groups, pillar forests, cliff planks, an impressive village gate, and other interesting sights. It may indeed be the center of the Tu ethnic culture.

Dragon boat race in wuhan. (From CFP)

Hubei Style

Dragon Boat Festival

Tradition had it that Qu Yuan died on the 5th day of the fifth month according to the Chinese calendar and the Dragon Boat Festival has been celebrated for thousands of years on that day to commemorate him. In Qu's hometown and many southern regions, people eat zong zi (pyramid-shaped dumpling made of glutinous rice wrapped in bamboo or reed leaves) at Dragon Boat Festival. Originally, civilians living adjacent to the Mi Low River dropped zong zi into the river to feed fish in order that the fish would not eat Qu's corpse; Later on, the tradition was spread throughout the country and even to Korea, Japan, and Southeast Asian countries. The festival is best known for its dragon boat races. It was said that people raced their boats to search for Qu Yuan. Nowadays, all tourists can take part in this athletic cultural activity. Dressed in dragon boat clothes, the guests board the boat accompanied by a boatman and travel in the river. It is a particularly magnificent sight. The champion receives a precious souvenir.

During the festival, song and dance performances are held, mainly focused on Qu Yuan culture and reflecting the local situation and customs of the Three Gorges region. Many programs, such as Evoking the Spirit of Qu Yuan and Zhaojun Going West, display great artistic charm, strong local flavor, simple folk customs, and profound cultural depths, from which tourists can enjoy the unique charm of Ba Chu culture.

Zong zi (From ImagineChina)

Hunan

Geography at a Glance

Hunan Province is located to the south of the middle reaches of the Changjiang River. The word *hunan* means "south of the lake," for it is also situated to the south of Dongting Lake. Another name of the province is Xiang, because the biggest river running through the province is called the Xiang River. To the north of Hunan is Hubei Province on the other side of the Changjiang River; to the south are Guangdong and Guangxi provinces; to the east is Jiangxi Province; to the west are Chongqing and Guizhou provinces. Hunan enjoys a strategic geographical position between the southern coastal economic zone and the Changjiang River economic zone. It has an area of 81,000 square miles and a population of 64,400,000 (2000 census). The east, south, and west of Hunan are surrounded by mountains of different altitudes (1,600 to 4,900 feet), while the northern part of it is the Dongting Plain. It can be very rainy in Hunan, and the summer temperature varies greatly from that of the winter.

Featured Cuisine

Hot and spicy fish heads, smoke-dried chicken and fish, Dong'an vinegar chicken, pepper and bacon, Yueyang fish feast, "purple meat" of the Dong ethnic group, fried sticky rice paste of the Tujia ethnic group, mustard-sliced meat, steamed fish on lotus leaf, spicy chicken.

Notes

❶ There are many different plants in Zhangjiajie National Park, some of which are poisonous. Do not touch any plant that you are unfamiliar with. We recommend that you also bring along insect repellent.

❷ Watch out for snakes when you walk in the forests.

Featured Commodities

Special Local Products

Peppers, Xianghuang chickens, Huaihua sugar candies, rice noodles, ramie, Xiang Tea, Junshan Silver Needle Tea, Changsha jasmine tea, dried bamboo shoots, dried bean curd, fermented bean curd.

Local Handicrafts

Xiang embroidery, Liling porcelainware, fine straw mats, Longshan brocade, flower skirts of the Yao ethnic group, Liuyang cloth, Shaoyang bamboo carvings, Yiyang bamboo mats, Liuyang chrysanthemum stone carvings, Changsha black crystal carvings, Changsha Gushan inkstones.

(From Jin Yongji)

Transportation Tips

By Bus

There are nine national highways running through Hunan and a road network connecting all the cities and towns in the province. You can get to almost every tourist city and scenic spot by bus.

By Train

There are five national trunk lines running through Hunan, making travel convenient from almost every tourist city and scenic spot.

By Plane

There are three major airports in Hunan-Changsha Yellow Flower Airport, Zhangjiajie airport, and the Changde airport.

By Water

You can reach many large or middle-sized cities in the province by water, including Changsha, Hengyang, Zhuzhou, Xiangtan, Shaoyang, Huaihua, Changde, and Yueyang.

Recommended Routes

Featured Routes

Three-day tour of Heng Mountain

Day 1 Arrival in Changsha. Lodging: Huatian Grand Hotel.

Day 2 Changsha→Heng Mountain→Sutra Temple→Virgin Forests→Fangguang Temple.

Day 3 Fuyan Temple→Guangji Temple→Changsha.

Five-day tour of Zhangjiajie–Son of Heaven Mountain–Maoyan River

Day 1 Arrive at Zhangjiajie.

Day 2 Zhangjiajie→Baofeng Lake.

Day 3 Son of Heaven Mountain→Western Sea→Heaven Platform→Fairy with Flowers→Mount of King's Pen→General Helong's Park→Crouched Dragon Mountain→Ten-Mile Gallery.

Day 4 Valley of Four Rivers→Zhangjiajie National Park→Jinbian River→Yellow Stone Village.

Day 5 Hundred-Mile Gallery→Maoyan River Rafting.

Traditional Routes

Six-day tour of Zhangjiajie–Shaoshan–Changsha

Day 1 Arrival in Zhangjiajie.

Day 2 Zhangjiajie→Baofeng Lake.

Day 3 Son of Heaven Mountain→Western Sea→Heaven Platform→Fairy with Flowers→Mount of King's Pen→General Helong's Park→Crouched Dragon Mountain→Ten-Mile Gallery.

Day 4 Valley of Four Rivers→Zhangjiajie

POPULAR FESTIVALS

Tujia New Year's Eve

The major festival of the Tujia ethnic group, held on New Year's Eve in Zhangjiajie, Yongshun, and Longshan. There are traditional Tujia folk dances and singing contests.

Sheba Festival

The major festival of the Miao ethnic group, held on April 8 of the lunar calendar in Jishou, Phoenix Village, and other locations. This is a time to worship ancestors, play traditional games, and enjoy feasting.

Dragon Boat Festival

Held every year on June 10 to 14 on the South Lake of Yueyang. Teams from different provinces of China take part in the competition.

Firecracker Festival

There is no fixed date for this major festival of the Dong ethnic group. Be sure to check your travel guide.

Addresses and Phone Numbers

Zhongyin Hotel	1 West Zhanqian Road, Yueyang	0730-8270666
Huatian Hotel	300 East Jiefang Road, Changsha	0731-4442888
Xiangquan Hotel	168 North Shaoshan Road, Changsha	0731-4439999
Tongcheng International Hotel	159 North Shaoshan Road, Changsha	0731-4168888
Jiacheng Hotel	215 West Laodong Road, Changsha	0731-5118888
Shennong Hotel	269 Middle Furong Road, Changsha	0731-5218888
Jinyuan Hotel	279 Middle Furong Road, Changsha	0731-5558888
Fu Lihua Hotel	88 Bayi Road, Changsha	0731-2298888
Yinyuan Hotel	189 North Zhurong Road, Nanyue District, Hengyang	0734-5662271
Chenzhou International Hotel	17 West People's Road, Chenzhou	0735-2320232
Zhangjiajie International Hotel	42 Sanjiaoping, Yongding District, Zhangjiajie	0744-8222888
Baofeng Lake Hotel	Baofeng Lake, Wulingyuan, Zhangjiajie	0744-5619999

National Park→Jinbian River→Yellow Stone Village→Changsha.

Day 5 Changsha→Shaoshan→Former Residence of Chairman Mao→Dripping Cave→Bronze Statue Square.

Day 6 Shaoshan→Changsha→Ma Wangdui Tomb→Yuelu College→Orange Sand Bar.

Six-day tour of Changsha–Shaoshan–Heng Mountain–Yueyang

Day 1 Arrive at Changsha.

Day 2 Ma Wangdui Tombs→Yuelu Mountain→Yuelu College→Orange Sand Bar.

Day 3 Changsha→Hua Minglou Village (former residence of Liu Shaoqi) → Shaoshan→Heng Mountain.

Day 4 Half-Moutain Pavilion→South Heaven Gate→Zhurong Mount→Yueyang.

Day 5 Yueyang Pavilion→Dongting Lake →Jun Mountain.

Day 6 End of tour.

Four-day tour of Changsha–Shaoshan

Day 1 Arrive at Changsha.

Day 2 Ma Wangdui Tomb→Yuelu College →Evening Pavilion→Orange Sand Bar.

Day 3 Changsha→Shaoshan→Hua Minglou Village.

Day 4 End of tour.

Self-Guided Tours

Tour of the ancient town of Phoenix

Southern Great Wall, Former residence of Shen Congwen, Suspended Bamboo Houses (Diaojiaolou).

Tour on Heng Mountain

Heng Mountain is famous for its beautiful landscapes. There are many temples on the mountain to visit.

Western Xiang tour

Changsha–Zhangjiajie–Mengdong River Rafting–Folk Customs Park–Ancient town of Phoenix–Southern Great Wall–Ancient town of Huangsi Bridge.

Changsha, Xiangtan, and Hengyang Region

Best Time to Travel

Spring, autumn, and winter are all good times for visiting Changsha. Summers are extremely hot and uncomfortable.

Shopping Street

South Huangxing Walking Street in Changsha is a new pedestrian area with many brand-name shops, restaurants, and recreational places.

Yuelu Mountain

Yuelu Mountain is on the western side in the Xiang River, Changsha. Besides the splendid natural scenery, there are also many places of learning, such as Yuelu College, Yuelu Temple, the Evening Pavilion, and others.

Shaoshan

Shaoshan is a beautiful town surrounded by green mountains. It is well known in the world as the hometown of Mao Zedong.

Mao's Ancestral Temple in Shaoshan was originally built in 1741 when Emperor Qianlong reigned. It was restored just before the one-hundredth anniversary of Mao Zedong's birth and has been open to the public since 1993. (From CFP)

The Evening Pavilion on Yuelu Mountain is named for the famous poem by Du Mu, a Tang Dynasty poet, who wrote: "Stopping my cart, I get off to enjoy the beautiful evening. The maple leaves are even redder than the flowers in Feburary." (From CFP)

From Changsha you can take train 5365 or 5366 to Shaoshan. It takes about three hours.

Former Residence of Mao Zedong

Located in Shaoshan, the former residence of Mao Zedong is just an ordinary farmhouse. The interior of it replicates the original dwelling as closely as possible.

To visit Changsha No. 1 Normal School, where the young Mao Zedong studied, take Bus 1 and get off at Dachun Bridge. You can walk from the school to the Xiang River, and then get to the Orange Sand Bar by boat.

Hunan Museum

This museum in Changsha has a total of 110,000 exhibits. There are also highly regarded exhibits of 3,000 extremely precious cultural artifacts, including bronzeware from the Shang Dynasty, and articles excavated from the Ma Wangdui Tombs.

Former Residence of Liu Shaoqi

This residence is located in Hua Minglou Village, Ningxiang County, 31 miles from Changsha. Liu Shaoqi, the second president of the People's Republic of China, was born here on November 24, 1898. There is a statue and a memorial museum dedicated to Liu Shaoqi near the residence.

> The former residence of Liu Shaoqi is not far from the Orange Sand Bar, so you can visit both on the same day.

Heng Mountain Scenery Park

Heng Mountain is also called South Mountain, one of the Five Mountains of China. It is famous for its splendid natural landscape and Buddhist and Taoist temples. It is said that the mountain has 72 peaks, among which the most well-known are Zhurong Peak, Heaven Column (Tianzhu) Peak, Lotus (Furong) Peak, Zigai Peak, and Shibing Peak. It has long been an attraction for great men of letters, who left their poems there.

> Wild Goose Peak is the best known of the 72 peaks. It is said that when wild geese coming from the north arrive here, they feel the spring and fly no more.

Yueyang Region

Best Time to Travel

From May to September are the best months to visit. Dongting Lake is at its best at this time. The coldest month is January; the hottest is July.

Yueyang Mansion

Yueyang Mansion sits beside Dongting Lake. In ancient times, Yueyang Mansion was regarded as the most magnificent tower in the world and Dongting Lake as the most beautiful lake in the world. Its reputation is due largely to the famous essay "The Yueyang Mansion," by Fan Zhongyan (989–1052), a distinguished man of letters living during the Northern Song Dynasty.

The main tower of Yueyang Mansion has three floors, and the weight of the entire building is supported by four wooden pillars. (From Quanjing)

The picturesque scene at Dongting Lake. Here you may see birds, dark green mountains, and the red sunset, which dyes the sky and the lake an orange color. (From CFP)

Dongting Lake

Dongting Lake is one of the five largest lakes in China and consists of East Dongting, South Dongting, West Dongting, and Datong Lake. It is a natural reservoir for the Yangtse River and features the beautiful scenery of lakes and mountains. Its appearance changes with the seasons, and it takes on a different look at different times of the day.

Jun Mountain in the Dongting Lake area features Liuyi Well, the Tomb of Two Concubines, and speckled bamboo.

Zhangjiajie Region

Best Time to Travel

The best months for visiting Zhangjiajie are April and October, when the landscape is at its most beautiful.

Wuling Yuan Scenery Park

Situated in the Wuling Mountain Range in northwestern Hunan, the park consists of Zhangjiajie, Son of Heaven Mountain, Suoxi Valley, and Yangjiejie, each with unique and natural scenery. The park covers an area of 193 square miles.

It is not a good idea to climb the mountains on rainy days; the trails are slippery, and fog often screens the views.

Suoxi Valley

Situated northwest of the town of Cili, this spectacular valley is also called "the Hundred Zhang Valley" (Bai Zhang Xia), and it is about 18 miles long. Yellow Dragon Cave in the valley is one of the ten largest caves in China.

Scenery in Wuling Yuan (From CFP)

Some 1,200 miles from Son of Heaven Mountain, there is a rural area at an altitude of 3,281 feet above sea level. (From ImagineChina)

Western Xiang Region

Best Time to Travel

All four seasons are suitable for traveling in western Xiang.

Dehang Scenery Park

This scenic spot is a village inhabited by the Miao ethnic group. Start from the town of Ai Zhai and wind your way up along the brook. You will see water carts, small boats, and the suspended bamboo houses that are typical of the Miao ethnic group.

Dehang has many traditional festivals, among which the Miao New Year is the most ceremonious.

Son of Heaven Mountain

Situated in the hinterland of Wuling Yuan, this mountain is the highest spot in the area. Standing on Son of Heaven Peak or Seven Star Mount, you get a panoramic view of the mountain.

Maoyan River

Maoyan River is about 30 miles long. There are cliffs on both sides of this river and many riptides, waterfalls, and ancient trees.

Gate of Heaven Mountain

This mountain has a huge cave through which one can walk from north to south, just like passing through a gate.

Nine-Sky Cave

This cave has nine skylights, 40 smaller caves, and three underground rivers. The view is magnificent.

Ancient Si Town (Lao Si Cheng)

Located 9 miles east of Yongshun County, this town is the capital of the Tu Si Dynasty, which lasted 800 years. There are hundreds of places of interest in the town and it is known as the "museum of the Tujia nationality in the open air."

Lion dance in Dehang (From Colphoto)

The picturesque view of the Phoenix ancient city (From Quanjing)

Mengdong River Scenery Park

Located in Yongshun County, this park is a newly developed tourist attraction. There are high cliffs, torrents and waterfalls, caves, and rare plants. You can also witness and learn about the local folk customs.

The Mengdong River raft trip takes about five hours.

The exciting Mengdong River trip (From CFP)

The Ancient City in Phoenix

About 33 miles south of Jishou, this ancient town still retains the architectural style of the Ming and Qing dynasties. The town is characterized by primitive simplicity and elegance.

Huaihua Region

Lotus Mansion (Fu Rong Lou)

Lotus Mansion is in the town of Qiancheng, Hongjiang, and is a fascinating and famous traditional mansion. It was built in honor of Wang Changling, a distinguished poet of the Tang Dynasty.

Taro Village

Inhabited by the Dong ethnic group, this village was built during the Hongwu Years (1368–1398) of the Ming Dynasty. Although it has been restored several times, it still retains its original flavor.

Huilong Bridge (Huilong Qiao)

Originally built in the Qing Dynasty, this bridge was destroyed twice by flood. Today's bridge, about 200 feet long, was rebuilt in 1931.

Matian Drum Tower

As a symbol of the Dong ethnic group, this tower has a history of more than 300 years. It is 51 feet tall, with 9 floors. On the four eaves of the roof, there are sculptures of kylin, phoenix, peacock, lion, and deer, regarded as propitious animals. The roof beam of the tower is also painted.

Ancient trading town in Hongjiang, Huaihua (From CFP)

Miao women in traditional costume, Phoenix City in Hunan. (From ImagineChina)

Hunan Style

Spicy Girls

Hunan people are famous for enjoying spicy food. Anyone who does not eat spicy food is not considered a native of Hunan. As validated by modern science, chili peppers have some efficacy in improving the looks. So it is no wonder there are so many beauties in Hunan, called "Spicy girls." Spicy girls are not only fearless in eating chili peppers, but also "spicy" by nature. They have an enchanting manner like other southern girls, and making an even bigger impression, they are extremely brisk and straightforward. Contact with them is like eating a chili pepper because you feel warm and bright from the bottom of your heart although your face is streaming with sweat.

Hunan Embroidery

Hunan embroidery (Xiang embroidery), one of the four famous embroideries of China, is notable for its time-honored history, excellent craftsmanship, and unique style. In its long development, Hunan embroidery skillfully integrated different artistic forms from traditional Chinese paintings, embroidery, poetry, handwriting, and inscriptions, and formed its own unique style. More than 70 stitches and threads of more than 100 colors are used in this embroidery. It is characterized by precise composition, vivid images, brilliant colors, a strong sense of reality, and the combination of appearance with spirit.

Hunan embroidery can be bought in many places in Hunan. Jinhuali Embroidery Shop in the city of Changsha is a good choice. With a history of more than 100 years, the shop is located in Huangxing Road. You can get valuable works of art as well as materials for daily use in this shop.

Address: No. 30 Middle Huangxing Road, Changsha.

Hunan Cuisine

Hunan cuisine has enjoyed a long history. More than 2,000 years ago, Hunan cuisine

(From Colphoto)

was famous for its preserved ham. The local flavor of Hunan cuisine is marked by its spicy dishes, and smoked and preserved food are its main feature. Hunan cuisine is characterized by its hot and sour flavors. The cooking methods include stewing, steaming, frying, and sautéing. It consists of regional cuisines from the Xiangjiang River Valley, the Dongting Lake region, and the western mountainous area. Hunan cuisine is typically represented by cuisine from the Xiangjiang River Valley, which in turn is mainly represented by Changsha cuisine, which is aromatic, delicious, sour, spicy, and delicate in flavor and employs a variety of cooking methods. The cuisine from the Dongting Lake region is known for seafood, livestock, and fowl. The dishes are particular about their greasy, salty, spicy, aromatic, and soft flavors. The cuisine from the western Hunan area uses charcoal as fuel. It is characterized by the very strong rural flavors of the mountainous area as well as delicacies from the mountains, preserved meat and salted meat. The most famous dishes in Hunan cuisine are sautéed Dong'an chicken, steamed varieties of preserved food, sautéed chicken with hot spicy sauce, braised shark's fin, Jishou sour pork, braised dog meat, sautéed preserved duck fillet, and stewed lotus seeds with mushrooms and crystal sugar.

Steamed Varieties of Preserved Food

Preserved food is popular in the western Hunan area, and it employs a storage method

(From ImagineChina)

that the local inhabitants worked out in order to preserve fresh chicken, duck, fish, and pork. It includes three procedures: pickling, smoking, and drying. As a famous traditional dish of Hunan cuisine, steamed varieties of preserved food uses preserved chicken, duck, and fish as its ingredients and has a unique flavor. The thick aroma, savory taste, bright color, and luster make it quite delicious.

Stewed Yellow Cartfish

Stewed Yellow Cartfish uses a special fish from the mid-Hunan area and stews it with chili peppers. The dish is oily and spicy. The little fish tastes very delicious and is easy to eat since there is only one bone in its body. It is really a treat to order stewed yellow cartfish and a bottle of beer on a hot summer day. But be careful—it is very spicy!

Sautéed Dong'an Chicken

Sautéed Dong'an Chicken is a famous traditional dish in Hunan cuisine. It can be traced back to the Tang Dynasty when three elderly women ran a small restaurant in Dong'an County in Hunan. The chicken they cooked was so savory that the chief of Dong'an County arrived himself to have a taste and named it "Sautéed Dong'an Chicken." With a history of more than 1,000 years, Sautéed Dong'an Chicken has become one of most famous Hunan dishes. Its bright color, red gravy, savory taste, and strong aroma are an indisputable attraction for tourists.

Customs in Western Hunan

Tulaosi

Tulaosi, called "Tima" in the Tujia language, is an experienced and knowledgeable wizard who helps people to pray for a son, pray for wealth, avert calamities, cure diseases, and pray for rain by means of superstition, mythology, and medicine. The main job of Tulaosi is to offer sacrifices to the Tujia king and ancestors in order to pray for the protection of the gods of the Tujias. Tulaosi possesses great power and is in charge of all the religious activities of the Tujias. He never goes in for farm work. He is ancestral and is respected by all the Tujia people. The Tujias are well known for the sacrificial ritual of the Waving-Hands Dance held annually by Tulaosi, who sings the "Holy Song of Tima." The "Holy Song of Tima" might have originated in the horn of the ancient Tujia tribe, while the Waving-Hands Dance might have originated in the Ba Yu Dance of the ancient Ba people. The "Holy Song of Tima" tells of the origin, reproduction, war, and migration of the Tujias and is considered a living history lesson on the music, literature, language, and customs of the Tujia ethnic group.

Marriage Customs

Most Miao people have freedom about whom they marry. Mass courting occasions often take place during social activities such as going to a fair and meeting girls. Wedding rituals include "crying for marriage," "opening the face"(cutting off the fine hair around the bride's face, meaning she is married), "sitting in a bridal sedan chair" (the bride's elder brother carries her on his back to go out the door), "blocking gifts" (the groom's family sends a team with the bridal sedan chair and a band to fetch the bride on the day before the wedding; the bride's family puts a large table in front of the door. When the team arrives, the bride's party asks for gifts by singing), and "smearing ashes" (after the team has their meal, the bridesmaids smear black ashes on the face of the young man who has come to fetch the bride on behalf of the groom). On the wedding night, the groom is not permitted to stay in the bridal chamber, which is a ritual that allows the bride to meet with her sisters. Crying for marriage means that the bride is reluctant to leave her parents' home. There are many conventional practices for crying for marriage including the mother and daughter crying, the aunt and niece crying, sisters crying, the uncle and niece crying, sisters-in-law crying, and scolding the matchmaker. Crying for marriage lasts for 3 to 5 days, and sometimes even for 10 to 15 days.

Funeral Customs

When somebody passes away, the Miao people express their condolences for three to five days. Lusheng (a reed instrument) is played unceasingly. People hold a memorial ceremony with animal sacrifices, for which cattle is considered the best. The Miao people practice interment with a wooden or stone coffin. Death due to murder, accident, childbirth, or suicide is considered infelicitous, and a funeral is not to be held. The deceased is cremated or buried for a second time and cannot be buried in the communal graveyard.

On the funeral day, many relatives and friends sing mourning songs around the coffin, with one taking the lead and others singing an accompaniment in turn. Some of the words of the songs are fixed, and some extemporized. The words often pay tribute to the morality and personality of the dead. The Tujias refer to a deceased person as "old" or "passed away," and the word "dead" is taboo.

After a person dies, the sons burn paper spirit money while the daughters wash the body and extremities with a white cloth, which is known as "washing five hearts." The deceased is dressed in burial clothes and shoes. His belt is made of cotton yarns that number the same as his age. An oil lamp burns beside his feet, and he holds a peach branch in his left hand and a rice ball in his right hand.

The old man offers sacrifices to the Miaojia king and ancestors to pray for the protection of the gods of the Miaojia. (From Colphoto)

Guangdong

Geography at a Glance

Guangdong, also called "Yue," is located in the southern part of China. To the north lie the Southern Ranges (Nan Ling), Jiangxi Province, and Hunan Province; to the south is the tropical ocean; to the southwest is Hainan Province across the Qiongzhou Straits; to the east is Fujian Province; to the west is the Guangxi Zhuang Autonomous Region. Guangdong covers an area of 64,500 square miles and has a population of 86,420,000 (2000 census).

Guangdong has a semitropical humid monsoon climate—warm and rainy days all year. The average temperature in January is 55°F, and that of July is 82°F. The annual precipitation measures 59 to 78 inches. Guangdong has a long coastline, many hot springs, and complex terrain. For example, Zhaoqing has karst features, and Shantou has sea-eroded features.

Lingnan Gardens in Guangdong has a unique style. The four most famous gardens are the Garden of Morning Sunshine (Qing Hui) in Shunde, the Garden of Yuyin Mountain (Yuyin Shan) in Panyu, the Garden of Loveliness (Ke Yuan) in Dongguan, and the Garden of Liang in Foshan. There are also many historical sites in Guangdong.

Featured Cuisine

Dongguan sausages, crab casserole, pork with salted vegetables (*meicai*), rice rolls, Guangdong bacon, sampan porridge, Guangzhou wonton, roast pork, milk custard, braised snake and chicken, fiery drunken shrimp, sweet-and-sour pork, stir-fried shrimp with fresh milk, ginger milk, salted dried cabbage.

(From Quanjing)

Guangdong

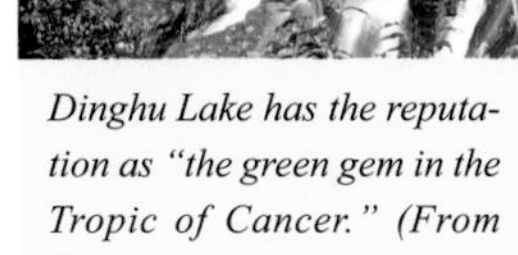

Dinghu Lake has the reputation as "the green gem in the Tropic of Cancer." (From CFP)

Miao girls dressed up in silver ornaments, in Guangdong (From ImagineChina)

Featured Commodities

Chinaware

Guangzhou gold-inlay porcelain, Dapu Gaopi porcelain.

Everyday Commodities

Jiangyang knives, Guangdong rosewood furniture, Gaoyao straw mats, Xinhui straw mats.

Local Handicrafts

Dongguan straw mats, Jieyang bamboo mats, Yue embroidery, Chaoshan embroidery, Gaozhou horn sculpture, Chaoshan wood sculpture, Shawan brick sculpture, Jiangyang lacquerware.

Transportation Tips

By Bus

There are many highways in Guangdong; 12 national highways interconnect in the province.

By Train

There are many trunk railroads running through Guangdong. The Guangzhou main station is the southern end of the Beijing-Guangzhou Line, which is the heart of China's north-south corridor. Shenzhen Station, Guangzhou Eastern Station, and Dongguan Eastern Station are the southern ends of the Beijing-Kowloon Line.

By Plane

There are a number of passenger airports in Guangzhou, Shenzhen, Shantou, Zhuhai, Zhanjiang, Foshan, Huizhou,

Notes 

All tourists need border permits fo travel to Zhuhai or Shenzhen. When you travel in the cities, bus travel is your best bet, as it is convenient and fast. Choose licensed hotels for the sake of safety.

and Meizhou, and 16 international airlines with flights from Guangzhou to Los Angeles, Amsterdam, Sydney, Melbourne, and many cities in Southeast Asia.

By Ship

Zhujiang (Pearl River), the second largest navigable river in China next to the Yangtze River, is in Guangdong Province. Shipping lines link Hong Kong, Macao, Shenzhen, and Zhuhai directly with Guangzhou, Zhaoqing, Wuzhou, and other cities. Shantou is an important port between Hong Kong and Taiwan.

Recommended Routes

Featured Routes

Three-day tour of Meizhou

Day 1 Arrival in Meizhou. Lodging: Kedu Grand Hotel.

Lingguang Shi→Former residence of Marshal Ye Jianying→Memorial Hall of Ye Jianying→Wild Geese-Flying-South Scenery Park. Lodging: Kedu Grand Hotel.

Day 2 Mundane World Cottage (Renjing Lu, former residence of Huang Zunxian)→Thousand Buddha Tower→Hakka Round-Dragon House (Weilong Wu)→Sightseeing and shopping. Lodging: Kedu Grand Hotel.

Scenery in Zhaoqing in Guangdong. (From CFP)

Day 3 End of tour.

Six-day tour of famous cities in Guangdong

Day 1 Arrival in Guangzhou. Lodging: Grand China Hotel.

Day 2 Memorial Hall of Sun Zhongshan →Yuexiu Park→Five Goats Sculpture→East Mountain Square→Pearl River→

POPULAR FESTIVALS

Qingming (Pure Brightness) Festival

On April 5, people offer sacrifices to their ancestors at home first, then go to the tombs of those who have died. In the old days, people would put a willow wicker in front of their ancestors' tablets four or five days before the festival.

Lychee Festival

Held in Shenzhen from June 28 to July 8.

Chinese Valentine's Day (Qi Xi)

Held on the 7th day of the seventh lunar month. It is the most important festival for single women in Guangzhou.

Double Ninth Festival (Chongyang Festival)

Held on the 9th day of the ninth lunar month. It is said that your bad luck will change into good if you climb to high places. It is the custom of the Guangzhou people to climb local hills and fly paper cranes hoping for good luck.

Xinghai Odeum→Guangdong Art Museum. Lodging: Grand China Hotel.

Day 3 Guangzhou-Zhuhai Lodging: Gulf Hotel.

Day 4 Sun Wen Park→Macao Tour→Meixi Memorial Archway→Jiuzhou Mansion→Lovers' Road→Runfeng Pearl Market. Lodging: Gulf Hotel.

Day 5 Shatoujiao Town→Sino-British Street→Minsk Aircraft→Statue of Deng Xiaoping in Lotus Mountain Park→Guangzhou. Lodging: Grand China Hotel.

Day 6 End of tour.

Five-day tour of historic sites in Guangzhou

Day 1 Arrival in Guangzhou. Lodging: Grand China Hotel.

Day 2 Orchid Garden→South Yue King's Tomb→Yuexiu Park→Guarding the Border Mansion (Zhenhai Lou)→Three Element Temple (Sanyuan Gong)→Memorial Hall of Sun Zhongshan. Lodging: Grand China Hotel.

Day 3 Chen's Ancestral Temple→Guangxiao Temple→Liurong Temple→Huaisheng Temple→Five God Temple. Lodging: Grand China Hotel.

Day 4 The Site of Guangzhou Soviet Government→Wanmu School (Caotang)→Guangdong Museum→Cemeteries of Martyrs→Tomb of 72 Martyrs. Lodging: Grand China Hotel.

Day 5 Danshuikeng Scenery Park→South Sea God Temple→Huangpu Military School. End of tour.

Traditional Routes

Four-day tour of Guangdong Province

Day 1 Arrival in Guangzhou.

Day 2 Lovers' Road→Jiuzhou Mansion→Macao Tour→Shijingshan Park.

Day 3 Tiger's Gate Bridge→Crystal World→Lotus Mountain Park→The World Park→East Gate Evening Market.

Day 4 Sino-British Street→Minsk Aircraft→Guangzhou. End of tour.

Four-day tour of Guangdong Province

Day 1 Arrival in Guangzhou.

Day 2 Guangzhou→Shantou→Nan'ao Island.

Day 3 Qing'ao Bay→Treasure Island→Former residence of Chen Cihuang→Kaiyuan Temple→Taifo Palace→Xiangzi Bridge→Fengxi Chinaware.

Day 4 Kongfu Tea Café→Sea Corridor→Shantou University→Guangzhou. End of tour.

Self-Guided Tours

Shenzhen-Yangshuo

When you arrive at Yangshuo, you can walk from Yangdi Dock in Lijiang to Xingping. Along the way, there are many beautiful scenes: Wave Stone Forest, Nine-Horse Stone Wall, Eight Gods Crossing the Sea, the Goddess Peak, and others. Next day visit the famous Ten-li Gallery and head toward Moon Mountain. You will pass through Butterfly Spring, Dragon River, and Big Rong Tree. When you return to Guilin, make sure not to miss Elephant Nose Mountain (Xiangbi Shan) and the Reed Flute Cave (Ludi Yan).

Guangzhou-Daxu Mountain Waterfalls Scenery Park

Major sights in this scenery park are Natural Oxygen Bar, White Crane Rock Falls, Wild Banana Forest Falls, Tortoise Pool Falls, Gem Falls, and Hidden Gold Cave Falls.

Guangzhou, Dongguan, Jiangmen, Zhaoqing, Foshan Region

Best Time to Travel

October, November, and December are the optimal months to visit.

Shopping Tips

Shangxiajiu Street is located in the western part of Liwan District, Guangzhou. This is an old business street in Guangzhou.

Beijing Road pedestrian street is located at the center of Guangzhou and is also the commercial center of Guangzhou.

Memorial Hall of Sun Yat-sen is one of the most representative buildings in Guangzhou. It is also where big events or performances take place. (From CFP)

Yuexiu Park

Located at the crossing of Liberation Road (Jiefang Lu) and Middle Round-the-City Road (Huanshi Zhonglu), this is the largest park in Guangzhou. The elegant scenery is represented by Yuexiu Mountain and the many historic sites such as

Addresses and Phone Numbers

Grand China Hotel	22 Liuhua Road, Guangzhou	020-86666888
Summer Palace Hotel	Summer Palace Villa, Tongtai Road, Guangzhou	020-83918698
Guangzhou Garden Hotel	368 East Round-the-City Road, Guangzhou	020-83338989
Kedu Hotel	West Lidu Road, Meizhou	0753-2190288
Dihao Hotel	188 East Jinsha Road, Shantou	0754-8199888
Sunshine Hotel	1 Honored Guest's Road Shenzhen	0755-82233888
Shangri-la Hotel	1002 Jianshe Road, Shenzhen (east of the train station)	0755-82330888
Yindu Hotel	1150 East Yuehai Road, Gongbei District, Zhuhai	0756-8883388
Gulf Hotel	245 Shuiwan Road, Gongbei District, Zhuhai	0756-8877998
Huangchao Hotel	95 Duanzhou Road, Zhaoqing	0758-2238238
Yincheng Hotel	48 Guantai Road, Nancheng District,Dongguan	0769-22818888
Haiyue Garden Hotel	East Houjie Road, Houjie District, Dongguan	0769-85885888
Jiahua Hotel	No. 1, Jiabei Avenue	0769-85928888

Guarding the Border Mansion, Ming Dynasty City Wall, Yuexiu Mansion, and Five Goats Sculpture.

> The park contains Yuexiu Mountain Stadium, which can hold 30,000 people, and the Yuexiu Natatorium, where international swimming and water sports take place.

Shamian

Located on the north side of Pearl River White Goose Pool, in the Liwan District, Guangzhou, Shamian is an elliptical island, on which there are more than 150 structures in European style.

> Nighttime in Shamian is very beautiful and romantic. The bars and cafés are filled with people.

Grand World Scenic Park

Located in Guangzhou, this park has lifelike replicas of the world's most famous buildings, statues, landscapes, and gardens. Tourists can travel all around the world and never leave China.

Cemetery of the 72 Revolutionary Martyrs

Located on East Martyr's Road, Dongshan District, Guangzhou, on Yellow Flower Hill (Huanghua Gang) at the southern foot of White Cloud Mountain (Baiyun Shan), this cemetery is the resting place of 72 revolutionary martyrs who gave their lives in the Guangzhou Uprising on April 27, 1911.

Memorial Hall of Sun Zhongshan

Located at the southern foot of Yuexiu Mountain, Guangzhou, this hall was once the office of Sun Yat-sen. It is an immense, octagonal, palace-like building. The Guangzhou Horticultural Expo is held in Yuexiu Park.

> Take Bus 2, 6, 24, 27, 41, 193, or 217.

Chen Ancestral Temple

Also called Chen's College, this temple was originally built between 1890 and 1894 during the Qing Dynasty (1616–1911). The large mansion is composed of 19 rooms and is elaborately decorated.

White Cloud Mountain (Baiyun Shan)

Situated in the northern part of Guangzhou, 10.5 miles from the city center, White Cloud Mountain is part of the Jiulian Mountains. Clouds hang over it in autumn, thus its name. The highest peak of the mountain is Moxing Ling with an altitude of 1,253 feet above sea level, the highest point in Guangzhou.

The luxurious Chen Ancestral Temple. (From CFP)

The recently restored figures of Sakyamuni and Shanxian Buddha in Guangxiao Temple. (From ImagineChina)

Guangxiao Temple

Located between North Haizhu Road and Jinghui Road in Guangzhou, this temple, built 1,500 years ago, occupies an important place among the many Buddhist temples in southern China. Many Buddhist monks come from all parts of the world to study and preach here.

Liurong Temple

Located in the center of Guangzhou, this Buddhist temple was built around 537. There are three large statues of Buddha in it.

Huangpu Military School

Located on the Changzhou Island of Huangpu, about 12 miles from southeastern Guangzhou, the school was founded in 1924 by Sun Yat-sen to train and educate army officers.

Conghua Hot Spring

Located in the hot spring town of Conghua, 46.5 miles northeast of Guangzhou, this is a well-known resort. There are 12 separate springs with an average water temperature between 97 and 160°F.

Garden of Loveliness (Ke Yuan)

Located in Wancheng town in Dongguan, this exquisite garden complex was built during the Qing Dynasty (1851–74). It is one of the four most beautiful gardens in Guangdong. There are many buildings, pavilions, ponds, and bridges in the garden, most of which are named by the character *Ke* (meaning "lovely").

Fortress of Tiger Gate

Located on both sides of the Tiger Gate Waterway, Dongguan, at the mouth of the Pearl River, the fortress was built in the Ming Dynasty (1368–1644). It is also the site where the Opium Wars took place.

> There is a well-known street in the fishing village of Xinwan in Tiger Gate that sells fresh seafood.

The Garden of Loveliness displays natural scenery in limited space. (From ImagineChina)

The blockhouses in Kaiping (From ImagineChina)

Swimming Tortoise Village

Located in White Sand (Baisha) Precinct, the layout of the buildings in the village resembles a swimming tortoise.

Kaiping Blockhouses

These local buildings, specific to Kaiping, are used for both dwelling and defense. Once there were more than 3,000 buildings; now there are about 1,800.

> The Kaiping people live a rustic life. Many of them cannot speak Mandarin (Putonghua) but rely on their native dialect.

Li Garden (Li Yuan)

Located in Genghua village in Kaiping, this private garden was built in 1926 by the American Chinese Xie Liwei. It has the characteristics of a traditional Chinese garden, Western architecture, and southern river villages, forming a unique style of its own.

The Deity's Temple (Zu Miao)

Located on Zumiao Road in Foshan, this is the temple of the Taoist Xuantian god.

Star Lake (Xing Lake)

Located in the northern suburbs of Zhaoqing, the lake area is divided into five smaller lakes: East, Blue Lotus, Seven-Star, Wavy Sea, and Red Lotus. In the Seven-Star Lake area, there are seven cliffs with a layout like the Big Dipper, so they are called "the Seven-Star Rock."

Dinghu Lake

This beautiful lake is in the northeastern suburbs of Zhaoqing. It has been a holy site in Buddhism since the Tang Dynasty.

Xiqiao Mountain Scenery Park

Located near Guanshanyu in Nanhai, this park has 72 mountains, 36 caves, 28 waterfalls, and 207 springs. White Cloud Cave is the most spectacular sight in the park.

Shenzhen and Zhuhai Region

Best Time to Travel

Summer lasts as long as six months in Shenzhen, and cold weather is rarely seen. You can visit Shenzhen at any time of the year and enjoy comfortable, pleasant weather.

Sino-British Street

Located in Shatoujiao, Shenzhen, this street is 1,640 feet long and 6.5 feet wide. There is a boundary stone in the middle of the street, dividing Shatoujiao into two parts. The east part belonged to China, while the west part belonged to Britain (Hong Kong). The street is now a corridor connecting Hong Kong with the inner land.

The boundary stone in Shatoujiao, which has witnessed much history. (From Colphoto)

Chinese Folk Customs Theme Park

Located in Shenzhen and next to the Splendid China Theme Park, this is the first large-scale theme park in China, focusing on folk arts, ethnic customs, and traditional houses of all the ethnic groups.

Jiuzhou City

Located between the Shijingshan Tourist Center and the Zhuhai Hotel in Zhuhai, Jiuzhou City is a shopping park integrating shopping with tourism. It covers an area of nearly 215,000 square feet and features a combination of classical appearance and modern interior design.

This impressive building is now the Municipal Museum of Zhuhai. (From Quanjing)

Shenzhen Wild Animal Park

Located beside Xili Lake to the east of the town of Xili in Shenzhen, this park is a purpose-built semitropical area with an ecological garden environment system, the first of its kind in China. Here you can not only see wild animals but also tropical and semitropical trees and plants.

Window of the World

Located in the Overseas Chinese Town of Shenzhen, and covering an area of more than 114 acres, Shenzhen's Window of the World features the world wonders, historical interest sites, scenic spots, natural landscapes, folk dwellings and customs, and world-renowned sculptures and drawings. Even folklore and theatrical performances are available here. The park is composed of 118 magnificent attractions on different scales from 1:1 to 1:100, which, based on geographical position and category of scenes, is

The glass pyramid standing on the square of the Window of the World. (From CFP)

divided into nine scenic areas: the World Square, Area of Asia, Area of Oceanic, Area of Europe, Area of Africa, Area of America, Recreational Center of Modern Science & Technology, Sculpture Park, and International Street. Every evening there are exotic shows and parades performed by artists from home and abroad. This is very much like an Epcot Center in China.

Shaoguan Region

Nanhua Temple

Located at Caoxi, 15 miles from Shaoguan, this is a famous Buddhist temple originally built in 504, known as the "ancestral court" (Zuting) where Buddha Lord VI Huineng preached on Zen in southern China. The three Buddha figures in the temple are 26 feet tall, and the Kwan-yin figure is 13 feet tall.

Take the bus from the Shaoguan train station.

Kowloon Eighteen-Shoal River

Also named Hanlong, this river section is about 37 miles long, starting from Pingshi in Dayao Mountain, ending at Wujiang River in Lechang. On a river raft journey, there are 18 shoals, including Qierou, Sanceng, Heshang, Dayuan, Longtou, and Zhantan.

The raft trip takes about 3 hours.

Danxia Mountain (Danxia Shan)

About 30 miles northeast of Shaoguan, this is one of the four most famous mountains of Guangdong. The mountain rocks are as red and bright as the sunglow, which makes for an enchanting scene. Formed of the red sandy rock, the Danxia Mountain area is characterized by steep red

Red Clouds Mountain is also called "the Red Stone Park of China." (From ImagineChina)

cliffs with precipitous peaks and flat valleys. Since 1988, Danxia Mountain has been designated as a National Scenic Spot, a National Natural Protection Zone for Geology and Geomorphology in China, a Grade AAAA National Tourist Spot, and a National Geological Park of China.

The plank road along Yangyuan Cloud Cliff is very narrow and steep. It is thrilling but somewhat dangerous to climb it.

Bibei Yao Village

This village is located on Dayao Mountain 33.5 miles to the northeast of Ruyuan Yao Autonomous County. Tourists can enjoy the beautiful landscape and learn the old and traditional customs of the local Yao people.

Gold Cock Mountain

Located in Pingshi of Lechang, a city on the border of Hunan and Guangdong, this is a magnificent and strategically located mountain. An old saying goes, "If one man guards the pass, ten thousand cannot get through."

Meizhou Region

Best Time to Travel

Meizhou has a subtropical monsoon climate with plenty of sunshine and sufficient rainfall, making all four seasons suitable for tourism.

Thousand-Buddha Tower (Qianfo Ta)

Located in the suburbs of Meizhou and surrounded by mountains, the octagonal tower was originally built in 965 and rebuilt in 1991. It is 118 feet tall and has nine stories.

The rebuilt Thousand-Buddha Tower comprises many towers, one on top of another. (From Colphoto)

Mundane World Cottage (Renjing Lu)

Located on East Mountain in the Meijiang District, Meizhou, the cottage is named for a poem by Tao Yuanming, a distinguished poet from the East Jin Dynasty. Built in 1884, it is the former residence of Huang Zunxian, the patriotic Chinese poet and politician.

Lingguang Temple (Lingguang Shi)

Located in Yinna Mountain, 28 miles from Meizhou, this temple was built in 861 in memory of a respected monk of the Tang Dynasty. Originally called Shengshou Temple, the present name has been used since 1385, in the Ming Dynasty.

Former Residence of Ye Jianying

Located in the village of Huxing 20.5 miles from Meizhou, this is a typical Hakka cottage made of clay and lime with 15 rooms, preserved in memory of Ye Jianying, one of the ten founding marshals of the People's Republic of China.

Chaozhou Region

Best Time to Travel

It is humid and warm all through the year, making all four seasons suitable for tourism.

Han Yu's Temple

Located on Penholder Mountain on the eastern bank of the Han River, this is the oldest and best preserved temple built in memory of Han Yu, the great poet who lived in the Tang Dynasty. The temple is home to 40 well-preserved ancient inscribed pillars and many plaques written by prominent modern personages.

Phoenix Tower

Located on a sandbank in the Han River, this Song Dynasty tower was built with bricks and stones. The octagonal tower is 153.5 feet high, with seven stories. Tourists can climb to its top for a bird's-eye view of the scenery below.

Mansion of Emperor's Great-Grandson-in-Law Xu

Located in Dongfucheng, Grape Lane, Zhongshan Road, the mansion was built in 1064 and was home to Xu Jue, born of a distinguished family in Chaozhou and great-grandson-in-law of Emperor Taizong of the North Song Dynasty. The mansion has a simple and unsophisticated style, and is one of the well-preserved Song buildings in Chaozhou.

The gate of the mansion of the emperor's great-grandson-in-law. (From Colphoto)

Kaiyuan Temple

Located at the midpoint of Kaiyuan Road, this Buddhist temple was built in 738 (Tang Dynasty). The temple is one of the outstanding examples of Chinese architecture and art. The two pagodas that stand opposite each other in front of the main hall in the temple, Purple Cloud Hall, are octagonal five-tier stone buildings with exquisite carvings. Two images of Buddha are carved on each of the eight sides. Forty ancient Buddhist tales are inscribed on the walls of one pagoda. Here are preserved various cultural artifacts: the Song Dynasty Bronze Bell, the Yuan Dynasty Incense Burner, the Ming Dynasty Thousand-Buddha Pagoda decorated with gold paintings and wood carvings, the Qing Dynasty Dazang Buddhist Scripture granted by Emperor Yongzheng, and other amazing sights.

> The Guangji Gate Tower, generally known as East Gate Tower (Dongmenglou), is located at the East Gate of Chaozhou city to the west of the Xiangzi Bridge. As the piers of the Guangji Bridge were built in succession over a span of more than 300 years, they have different styles and sizes.

Typical Cantonese dish (From CFP)

Guangdong Style

Yue Opera

Yue Opera is a kind of opera that uses Guangzhou dialect. It came into being at the end of the Ming Dynasty and the beginning of the Qing Dynasty. Later, after repeated practice, Yue Opera gradually used "clapper spring" as its basic singing tune while assimilating the folk music and melodies of Guangdong. It developed further and became an important opera at today's scale. Nowadays, it is popular not only in Guangdong Province, but also in the coastal regions of mainland China and overseas. The traditional Yue opera performances of early times included *A Precious Jade Cup Named Scoop of Snow* and *Huanghua Hill*. Later, there were shows like *Daiyu Buries Fallen Flowers*. Contemporary shows of considerable influence include *Lotus Lantern*.

Cantonese Cuisine

Cantonese cuisine is one of the eight major cuisines in China. It includes Guangdong cuisine, Chaozhou cuisine, Dongjiang (Hak-Ka) cuisine, and Hainan cuisine. Cantonese cuisine uses a wide variety of ingredients including some that are complex and highly valued. The Cantonese are innovative with

A Yue Opera performer and an instructor demonstrate how to apply performance makeup. (From CFP)

Yue Opera (From Colphoto)

their dishes, and imitate and draw upon the strong points of other cuisines, including Beijing cuisine, Sichuan cuisine, Jiangsu cuisine, Shandong cuisine, Zhejiang cuisine, and western cuisine. People of other provinces joke about Cantonese cuisine: anything that flies (except planes), crawls (except trains), or swims (except submarines) might be listed on a Cantonese menu.

Tea-Picking Opera

Tea-picking opera, also referred to as "tea song" and "tea-picking song" is a kind of Chinese folk dance, popular in China's southern tea-growing regions, such as Guangdong, Guangxi, Jiangxi, Fujian, Zhejiang, Jiangsu, Anhui, Hunan, Hubei, Yunnan, and Guizhou provinces populated by the Han ethnic group. A tea-picking opera performance usually involves a pair consisting of a man and a woman or a group consisting of one man and two women. Later, it developed into a group dance performed by several or even a dozen people. The movements in tea-picking opera mimic those of picking tea leaves and, later, those of life activities such as combing hair and applying makeup; or they depict the romantic sentiments of a young man and woman in love.

Humor dance—Aizibu, in tea-picking opera (From Colphoto)

Guangxi Zhuang Autonomous Region

Geography at a Glance

Guangxi Zhuang Autonomous Region, "Gui" for short, was founded on March 15, 1958. It is located in the southwest of China's coastal area. To the east is Guangdong Province; to the north are Hunan and Guizhou provinces; to the west is Yunnan Province; to the south is Beibu Bay; to the southwest is Vietnam. It covers an area of about 88,800 square miles and has a population of 44,890,000 (2000 census), one-third of whom are of the Zhuang ethnicity. It is the most convenient passage to the ocean in southwest China.

Guangxi has more mountainous regions than plains, with 76 percent of it covered by mountains and highlands. Most of its rivers are tributaries of the Pearl River. Guangxi is endowed with plenty of ocean resources because it borders Beibu Bay. In most areas, the average temperature in winter is above 50°F. The annual precipitation range is 47–71 inches.

Featured Cuisine

Rice-wrapped coconut dumplings, Guilin nun noodles, crispy-skinned pork, braised mutton with southern bean curd, Wuzhou paper-wrapped fried chicken, Lipu taro braised meat, steamed Li River fish, Yangshuo river snails, stir-fried beef with bamboo shoots, steamed bean curd balls, Nandan sweet glutinous rice cakes, pingle lily pow-

der, stewed water chestnuts and Xianggu mushrooms, Nanning rice noodles, roasted pork.

Featured Commodities

Special Local Products

Oysters, green crabs, prawns, seahorses, pearls, sea cucumbers, abalones, sleeve-fish, cuttlefish, Lipu taro, Dongyuan wine, Guilin wine, lemongrass.

Local Handicrafts

Cattle-horn carving, shellwork, weaving, batik.

Fruits and Delicacies

Juicy peaches, grapes, bananas, pineapples, longan, lichee, mongo, sugarcane, sweet dates, snow-pear.

Transportation Tips

By Bus

There are eight national highways and many expressways in Guangxi. The hubs of the road network are Nanning, Liuzhou, Qinzhou, Yulin, Wuzhou, and Lipu.

By Train

The Xiang-Gui line is the major railroad in Guangxi. The eastern end is connected to the Beijing-Guangzhou Railroad. Other important lines are the Nanning-Kunming, the Nanning-Fangchenggang, and the Qinzhou-Beihai. Liuzhou is also an important city for rail transportation.

By Air

There are five airports in Guangxi, located in Guilin, Nanning, Beihai, Liuzhou, and Wuzhou, with Guilin International

The Yao ethnic group constitutes 60 percent of the population in Guangxi Province. (From Colphoto)

Notes 

❶ Be sure to take rain gear with you when you travel to Guangxi.

❷ The best opportunity to enjoy the mountains and waters of Guilin is the rainy season, when the area is shrouded in mist and fog. After visiting the Li River, don't miss the Huaping Nature Reserve in Longteng.

(From Jin Yongji)

Airport being the largest. There are over 80 airlines and regular flights from Guilin to Hong Kong, Macao, and Japan.

By Ship

There are river transport lines such as Wuzhou-Zhaoqing-Guangzhou-Hong Kong, and ocean lines such as Beihai-Haikou.

Recommended Routes

Featured Routes

Six-day tour of Baise

Day 1 Arrival in Baise. Lodging: Ruifeng Grand Hotel.

Day 2 Chengbi Lake→Shuiyuan Cave→Sister Luo Cave→Nine Dragon Columns Lodging: Local residence in Leye.

Day 3 Leye→Moli Village→Buliu River→Leye Main scenes are Thousand-Year Tree, Celestial Bridge (Xianren Qiao). Lodging: Local residence in Leye.

Day 4 Leye→Heaven Delve Groups→Baise→Steaming Cave→Heaven Delve Lookouts→Underground Forests. Lodging: Ruifeng Grand Hotel.

Day 5 Baise→Jingxi→Tongling Grand Canyon. Lodging: Ruifeng Grand Hotel.

Day 6 Detian Falls (world's second-largest border-crossing falls)→Green Island

POPULAR FESTIVALS

Chili Festival

On the eve of the lunar new year, the Zhuang people celebrate their hot and spicy dishes with feasts, singing, lion dances, dragon lantern dances, and general hilarity.

Tuwang Festival

Two or three days before the Grain Rain (around April 19, 20, 21), the Dong people hold singing games, arm wrestling, and other traditional activities. Young men and women sing in antiphonal style to express love.

Firecracker Festival

Held on the 3rd day of the third lunar month. The main event on this day is scrambling for firecrackers, which is like a football game in Western countries.

Singing Festival

Held in spring and autumn by the Zhuang people. The spring festival starts on the 3rd day of the third lunar month, and the autumn one is around Mid-Autumn Day (August 15 of the traditional Chinese lunar calendar, which occurs with the first full moon within half a month around the autumn equinox). The festival is held in memory of Sister Liu, who overcame many difficulties and adversaries by singing witty folk songs.

Tiaogong Festival

Held on the 3rd day of the fourth lunar month and lasts for three days. The Yi people dance, sing, visit friends, and worship ancestors.

Fenlong Festival

Also called Wuyuemiao (or "Worship in May"), it is a festival of the Maonan people held on the last Chen day after the summer solstice. The first two nights of the festival are for worshipping in the temple and the last day for sacrificing a bull.

Addresses and Phone Numbers

Grand International Hotel Nanning	88 East Minzu Road, Nanning	0771-2111888
Ming Yuan Hotel	38 Xinmin Road, Nanning	0771-2118988
Yong Jiang Hotel	1 Linjiang Road, Nanning	0771-2180888
Tao Yuan Hotel	74 Taoyuan Road, Nanning	0771-2096868
Nanning Hotel	38 Minsheng Road, Nanning	0771-2103888
Zhong Jiao Hotel	1 North Jiefang Road, Liuzhou	0772-2832888
Di Yuan Hotel	186-1 Linjiang Road, Guilin	0773-5688888
Jun Hao Hotel	28 Guanlian Road, Yangshuo, Guilin	0773-6910088
Guilin Hotel	14 South Ronghu Road, Guilin	0773-2823950
Fubo Shan Hotel	27 Binjiang Road, Guilin	0773-2569898
Yu Lin Hotel	133 Park Road, Yulin	0775-2830168
Rui Feng Hotel	5 Chengbei Road, Baise	0776-2881688
Jiatianxia International Hotel Beihai	8 West Beihai Road	0779-3065666

Clouds→Spring Return Border River→No. 53 Sino-Vietnam Boundary Stone→Shatun Falls→Black Water River. End of tour.

Traditional Routes

Five-day tour of Guilin

Day 1 Arrival in Guilin→Seven-Star Park.

Day 2 Guilin→Yangshuo.

Day 3 Multicolor Mountain→Fubo Mountain→Elephant Nose Mountain→Seven Stars Rock Group.

Day 4 Reed Flute Cave.

Day 5 End of tour.

Five-day tour of Nanning

Day 1 Arrival in Nanning.

Day 2 South Lake→Ethnic Cultural Relics Park→Guangxi Museum→Herb Garden.

Day 3 Yiyan Mountain→Mingxiu Garden→Lingshui Lake.

Day 4 Qingxiu Mountain→Bailong Park.

Day 5 End of tour.

Three-day tour of Beihai

Day 1 Beibuwan (Beibu Bay) Square→Beach Park→Silver Beach (Yin Tan).

Day 2 Weizhou Island.

Day 3 Hepu Star Island→Forest on the Sea.

Six-day tour of northern Guilin

Day 1 Arrival in Guilin.

Day 2 Guilin→Longsheng.

Day 3 Longsheng→Sanjiang.

Day 4 Sanjiang→Rongshui→Longsheng.

Day 5 Longsheng→Ziyuan.

Day 6 End of tour.

Self-Guided Tours

Weekend on the border roads

Start from Nanning, via Ningming, Pingxiang, Longzhou, Detian, end at Jingxi. Major sites are Ningming Huashan Cliff Painting, Friendship Pass (Youyi Guan), Puzhai Border Trade Center, site of the French Consulate, Xiaoliancheng Emplacement, Mingshi River, Detian Falls, Tongling Grand Canyon.

Western Gui and Western Xiang

Start from Liuzhou, via Sanjiang, Tongdao, Jingzhou, Huitong, Hongjiang, Zhongfang, Huaihua, Phoenix town, Jishou, Yongshun, Zhangjiajie, end at Changsha. Major sites are Chengyangqiao Dong Ethnic Village, ancient town of Phoenix, former residence of Shen Congwen, Tuo River, Southern Great Wall, ancient town of Yellow Ribbon Bridge (Huangsi Qiao), Furong town, Mengdong River, Suoxi Valley, Ten-li Gallery, Tianzi Mountain, Henglong Park.

Nanning Region

Best Time to Travel

In Nanning, the temperature varies between 53 and 82°F, neither too cold nor too hot. Any month is suitable for travel in Nanning.

Shopping Tips

Xiguan Road has the busiest evening market in Nanning. It opens at 6 p.m. and sells various goods such as clothes, jewelry and accessories, and toys.

Xingning Street is an ideal place for buying gold ornaments. The ornaments sold in these shops are of good quality, varied design, and reasonable price.

Chaoyang Road is the center for shopping in Nanning. There are many shops and shopping malls here, in addition to stores such as Wal-Mart.

There are many brand-name shops on Qixing Road.

Huashan Scenic Park (From CFP)

Ningming Huashan Cliff Paintings

Located on Zuojiang Cliffs, 15.5 miles from Ningming County, these paintings date back to the Warring States period and took shape in the East Han Dynasty, about 2,000 years ago. They are the works of the ancient Luoyue people living in the area and the like is rarely seen elsewhere in the world.

Tourists can get to Huashan by boat from Nanning, which takes 2 hours.

Guangxi Herb Garden

Located in the eastern suburbs about 5 miles from the center of Nanning, this herbal paradise supplies herbs and spices to China and Southeast Asia.

Qingxiu Mountain Scenic Area

Located southeast of Nanning, Mount Qingxiu is renowned for its beauty and the clear waters that run through it. It comprises 18 peaks including Qingshan Peak and Phoenix Peak. It covers a total area of 1.6 square miles, including a water area of 158,000 square feet and a greenbelt area of some 269,000 square feet. The undulating chains of mountains, verdant trees, liquid springs, and historic sites make Qingxiu a good place to enjoy tranquil beauty and charm. Because of the many lakes and the emerald green trees on the mountains, Qingxiu is the primary source of fresh air for the downtown Nanning area. Accordingly, it is referred to as "the lungs" of Nanning.

Detain Falls

Located on the border between China and Vietnam, these are the largest cross-national falls in Asia and the second-largest in the world. The headwater of the falls is the Guichun River in Guangxi, which flows into Vietnam and back into Guangxi. The falls are 131 feet high and 328 feet wide, forming a spectacular view.

> Detian Falls are about 124 miles from Nanning. There are tour buses from Nanning to Detian Falls every day, and the best time to see the falls is in June.

Headquarters of the Red Army

Baise and Chongzuo are home to two old headquarters of the Red Army. The first one is the Yuedong Guild Hall in Baise, which is the site of the headquarters of the Seventh Corps of the Red Army and also the memorial hall for the Baise Uprising. The other is the Qingfeng Tower in Chongzuo, a well-preserved two-story brick-and-wooden construction, the site of the headquarters of the Eighth Corps of the Red Army.

Yiling Rock Cave

Located in Yiling Village, Wuming County, 11 miles from Nanning, this is a limestone cave and has been called an "underground palace." Amid the multicolored, lighted

The spectacular Detian Falls amid the beautiful scenery. (From ImagineChina)

stalactic formations, tourists may feel as if they are in a fairy tale. The average temperature is 64°F, so, it is wise to take along a light sweater to wear even during the warm seasons. According to geologists, the cave formed about one million years ago and it contains various forms of stalactite, stalagmite, and stone pillars.

Memorial Tomb of Liu Zongyuan. (From CFP)

Liuzhou Region

Best Time to Travel

All four seasons are suitable for traveling in Liuzhou.

Memorial Tomb of Liu Zongyuan

Located in Liu Zongyuan Park in Liuzhou, the tomb contains the personal effects of Liu Zongyuan, a distinguished man of letters who lived during the Tang Dynasty. The tomb was built in the Song Dynasty and restored in the Qing Dynasty.

Fish Mountain (Yu Feng Shan)

Located in Liuzhou, this is believed to be the place where Sister Liu (Liu San Jie) lived and became immortal. In popular legend, Sister Liu was a Zhuang ethnicity girl who could sing extremely well and was called "the goddess of songs."

Duleyan Scenic Area

Located in the southern suburbs of Liuzhou, this scenic area features beautiful mountains, waterfalls, strange caves, and rocks. There are 46 caves and more than 10 viewing pavilions.

Government Office of the Zhuang Leader Mo (Mo Tusi' Yamen)

Located on the north side of Cuiping Mountain in Laibin, this was the headquarters of the local government of the Zhuang ethnicity, appointed by the emperor of the Qing Dynasty. The leader went by the surname of Mo. It is the largest and best preserved building of its kind in China and is called "the Imperial Palace of the Zhuang People."

Chengyang Yongji Bridge

Also called Chengyang Wind and Rain Bridge (Fengyu Qiao), it is located in Chengyang village, Dong Nationality Autonomous Region, Sanjiang. There is a picturesque veranda bridge that shelters people from wind and rain.

> From Yongji Bridge, you can take a side trip to explore Pingpu, a rustic Dong ethnic village. The drum tower not far from Chengyang is also worth a visit.

Chengyang Yongji Bridge is very intricately structured. (From CFP)

Ma Pang Drum Tower

Located in Mapang Village, Dong Nationality Autonomous Region, Sanjiang, this tower is the most representative of its kind in Guangxi. In the shape of a pagoda, the tower is 65 feet high. Besides the four main posts, which symbolize safety and fortune, it has 24 other posts. The pedestals of those posts are made from fine bluestone and are carved with various patterns.

Guilin and Hezhou Region

Best Time to Travel

Guilin is free from hot summers and cold winters. Flowers bloom throughout the year, making all four seasons suitable for tourism.

Multicolor Mountain (Die Cai Shan)

Originally called Gui Shan, the mountain is situated beside the Li River and stretches across the city. Composed of Bright Moon (Ming Yue) Peak, Crane (Xian He) Peak, Si Wang Peak, and Yu Yue Peak, the mountain abounds in beautiful views.

Du Xiu Mountain

Located at the center of Guilin, this is only one of the mountains in Guilin. It is 709 feet high and boasts splendid views such as Snow Cave and Moon Pool.

Fubo Mountain

Located by the Li River, this mountain was named for Fu Bo, a general in the Han Dynasty. On the west side of the mountain, there are stone steps leading to the top. On the east side is Listening-to-Waves Pavilion (Ting Tao Ge) and Pearl Cave (Zhu Dong), with many stone inscriptions and Buddha figures in it.

By the river there is a stone column hanging down like a funnel, which is about 18 inches high, with its lower tip a few inches from the ground. It is said that General Fubo of the Han Dynasty used to test his sword here; thus the stone column is called "Sword Testing Stone."

Du Xiu Mountain rises steeply from ground like a huge column supporting the sky. (From CFP)

Reed Flute Cave (Ludi Yan)

Located on the south side of Guang Ming Mountain, this cave is about 700,000 years old, formed as the result of constant water erosion. Reed Flute Cave is the largest and perhaps the most spectacular of the limestone caves in Guilin. Hidden halfway up a mountain, it got its name from the reed that grows near the entrance, which makes excellent flutes. The cave is known as a "palace of natural art." Along its zigzag path are the unusual stalactites and stalagmites that, with colored lighting, look like coral, agate, amber, or jade—a wonderland of formations resembling or-

The magnificent scenery inside Reed Flute Cave. (From CFP)

chards, gardens, or whatever else you care to imagine.

Take Bus 3, Express Bus 4A, or the free Bus 58.

Rich Fish Rock

Situated in Dongli village, San-he Xiang, Li-pu County, this rock takes its name from the underground river in the rock cave, which teems with oil-rich fish. The total length is less than 3 miles. In the cave are many large and small chambers; the biggest covers 269,000 square feet and contains many beautiful scenes. One of them contains a stalagmite 32 feet tall but only 5.5 inches in diameter.

Ancient Town of Huang-Yao

The ancient town of Huang-Yao is in the northeast of Zhao Ping County, about 43 miles from the county seat. The town is only about a quarter of a square mile in area. There are small roads made of green stones, well-kept houses, and temples in the Ming and Qing style.

The ancient town of Huang-Yao is a harmonious, serene place with many beautiful vistas. The photo shows a horizontal inscribed board donated by Emperor GuangXu of the Qing Dynasty. (From ImagineChina)

Huang-Yao County was founded in the Kaibao age of the Song Dynasty. During the Wanli era (1572–1620) of the Ming Dynasty it developed quickly, and during the Qing Dynasty it reached its peak of splendor. Because the majority of the residents' family names are Huang and Yao, the town was called Huang-Yao. At present, there are still eight complete gravel roads, with a total length of 6 miles. The width of the roads ranges from 6 to 16 feet. There are more than 300 ancient buildings of the Ming and Qing dynasties in the town and dozens of kiosks, temples, and bridges. There are about 100 horizontal boards, the most famous of which is the Xingning temple board. This ancient town is an exhibit of the cultural history of East Gui Province.

At the foot of Elephant Nose mountain, the clear blue water runs through Water Moon cave. The water mirrors the cave, and people can see the image of two caves linked together. (From Jin Yongji)

Elephant Nose Mountain

Elephant Nose Mountain is also called Elephant Mountain. Situated where the Peach Blossom River meets the Li River, it is one of the most famous mountains in Guilin, resembling an elephant standing at the river, taking up water with its nose. On the mountain is Elephant Eye Rock, which tourists can walk through. Other scenes on the mountain include Water Moon Cave, Puxian Tower, Cloud Peak Temple, and the exhibition hall of the Taiping Rebellion site inside the temple.

Seven Star Park

Seven Star Park is situated at the foot of Seven Star Mountain in Guilin city. The Small East River runs through it. The positions of the seven peaks of Seven Star Mountain are like the seven stars in the Big Dipper, hence it is called Seven Star Park. The park has the typical features of karst topography. The mountain is green, the water is clean, the cave is extraordinary, and the rocks are beautiful. As far back as the Sui and Tang dynasties, about 1,000 years ago, Seven Star Park was a famous place.

Tumuli of the King of Jingjiang

The grave mounds of the King of Jingjiang are at the foot of Duxiu Peak in the eastern suburbs of Guilin. The king was Zhu Shouqian, the grandson of Emperor Zhu Yuanzhang's elder brother and this is the cemetery of Zhu and his decendents. The tumuli were built in 1372. The perimeter of the area is about 62 miles and contains more than 300 tombs of kings, princesses, generals, and relatives.

Guilin's Lijiang River

The Lijiang River lies in the northeast of the Guangxi Zhuang Autonomous Region. Also called Li Water, it has the typical features of

Fishing boats on the Lijiang River. (From Jin Yongji)

lmestone peaks. The river, famous for its green mountains, beautiful waters, and wonderful caves, belongs to the Zhujiang water system. Its headstream is on Cat Mountain in Xingan County, north of Guilin. Flowing 215.5 miles through Guilin, Yangshuo, Pingle, and Wuzhou, it finally converges with the West River. The nicest part of the Lijiang River is from Guilin to Yangshuo, about 52 miles in all.

North Sea, Yulin, and Guigang Region

Best Time to Travel

Known as the Hawaii of the East, the North Sea is a good place to visit in any season.

YingLuo Mangrove Protected Area

Situated on the west side of Yingluo Harbor, in Shankou, Hepu County, the mangrove reserve is also called "the forest under the sea." Its total coastline is 31 miles long and provides habitat for many animals, such as the endangered sea cow, and birds. After the tide recedes, people can boat in the mangrove forest on the sea.

Silver Beach

About 6 miles northeast of North Sea City, there is an excellent beach. The sand is fine and smooth, and the color is like silver. About 15 miles long, with no reefs, the beach is an integral part of the Guilin landscape. Silver Beach includes three small sections (Silver Beach Park, Beach Park, Hengli Watersports Holiday Center), villas, and hotels.

A ticket for Silver Beach is food for three days.

North Sea's World Under the Sea

North Sea's World Under the Sea is located in the North Sea Beach Park. It is the biggest undersea

North Sea Silver Beach is an ideal swimming and sunning place, and a wonderful spot for a summer vacation. (From ImagineChina)

Beautiful coral fish in the Undersea World. (From Colphoto)

tourist spot in southwestern China. There are five large water scenic spots. The North Sea aquarium covers about 13,520 square feet and is divided into seven rooms. There are more than 2,800 fish and other sea creatures on display. The aquarium features a large, clear plastic tube through which visitors can walk and watch the fish swim all around it.

Big Vine Gorge

Big Vine Gorge is on the Qian River, in Guiping. About 27 miles long, it is a magnificent gorge, one of the largest in Guangxi. There are cliffs on both sides; a huge vine stretches across the river, which the local residents use as a bridge.

Zhenwu Pavilion on the Jinglue Stand

Zhenwu Pavilion on the Jinglue Stand is in People's Park, east of the Rong County seat. Built as a Taoist temple, it is a three-story structure, made of about 3,000 different wooden parts. Eight pillars support the whole building, but the most amazing part are the four pillars on the second floor that actually support the weight of the building without touching the floor. Having undergone many storms and earthquakes, the pavilion is still intact.

Site of the Jin Tian Village Uprising

This site is about 17 miles north of Guiping city. In and around the village, there are ruins from the Taiping Rebellion, such as the ancient fortress, Rhinoceros Pond, the parade grounds, and Three Circles Temple. The temple has been converted into a museum exhibiting historical literature and artifacts from the Jintian Uprising during the Taiping Rebellion.

Zhenwu Pavilion is the earliest structure of the four famous buildings in China south of the Changjiang River. (From CFP)

A Zhuang native from Jingxi is making "Xiuqiu." (From Imagine-China)

Guangxi Style

Guilin Rice Noodles

Guilin is famous not only for its superior natural scenery, but also for its rice noodles. Guilin residents eat rice noodles the way northern people eat wheat flour meal. They have rice noodles on a daily basis and are only concerned about the taste, ignoring the size and accouterments of the restaurant in which they are eating. Walking along the streets in Guilin, you can see fashionably dressed ladies and handsome gentlemen, who can't wait to be seated, standing there and enjoying steaming bowls of rice noodles. They are so serious about this dish that they are quite unaware of the image they present. Guilin rice noodles are renowned for their unique flavor. The noodles are round, smooth, and pliant. The broth is fresh and tasty. The meat and vegetables are crisp and delicious. Great importance is attached to the making of broth. It is said to be made of pork, pig bone, cassia bark, aging fermented soy sauce, dried tangerine peel, licorice, cumin, aniseed, and mangosteen fruit stewed together. Of course, different food stalls distinguish themselves by their different flavors. Guilin rice noodles are tasty but not expensive. They are so easy and quick to serve that even the American fast-food giant McDonald's relinquishes the market in Guilin.

Yao Ethnic Group

As a typical mountain ethnic group in China's south, the Yao people constitute over 60 percent of the population in Guangxi Province, where there are several branches, including the Pan Yao, Bunu Yao, Jinxiu Yao, Baiku Yao, and Hong Yao. Their language belongs to the Yao branch of the

Guilin rice noodles (From Colphoto)

(From ImagineChina)

Miao and Yao language group in the Sino-Tibetan dialect family. Some other Yao people speak Mandarin, Zhuang, Miao, or Tong dialects. The economy of the Yao is mainly of a self-sufficient kind with a heavy reliance on nature. Besides farming as their main occupation, most of them are also engaged in forestry. Their staple foods include rice, corn, and sweet potatoes. Drinking and smoking are common. Yao women are quite skilled in dye weaving and embroidery.

As a branch of the Yao ethnic group, the Hongyao live mainly in Heping village, Longsheng County, Guangxi Province. Since ancient times, they have had a habit of growing long hair. In the Huangluo Yao village located at the foot of Longji Hill in Guilin, there are over 60 households and a population of 300, among whom there are more than 60 women with hair longer than 55 inches. So this village is called "Number One Long-Hair Village in the World."

Zhuang Ethnic Group

The Zhuang ethnic group has the largest population among all Chinese ethnicities. There are over 14 million Zhuang people in Guangxi Province. As an important branch of the ancient Baiyue tribe in the Lingnan region, the Zhuang boast a splendid history and a colorful culture and are considered a people rich in sparkling wisdom. The area inhabited by the Zhuang is renowned for its bronze drums and cliff drawings (which date back to the Qin and Han dynasties) as well as Zhuang-style brocade (which dates back to the Tang and Song dynasties).

Visitors will be overwhelmed by the Zhuang people's hospitality if they visit a Zhuang household in a village because they will be treated like guests by the whole village. Guests are presented with cups of drinks by crossing their arms through those of the hosts, a ritual which makes for an impressive reception. Zhuang people show great respect to their elders and their religious beliefs are of a primitive origin. Important festivals include the Spring Festival, the Zhongyuan Ghost Festival on the 15th of seventh lunar month, the 3rd of third lunar month festival, the Pure Brightness Grave Visit Festival, and the Mid-Autumn Festival on the 15th of eighth lunar month. Rice and corn are their staple foods, and rice wine is the major drink for holiday consumption as well as for entertaining guests. The wedding ceremony of the Zhuang is of unique interest, and the best places to experience their marriage customs are Longsheng and Longji. After hundreds of years of development, the local folk song fair, Geyu, has become very popular. Most such fairs are now held in the river valleys of the Hongshui, Zuojiang, and Youjiang rivers. According to a survey, in Guangxi Province there are over 600 locations holding folk song fairs which vary in size. However, the one held on the 3rd day of the third lunar month is the most impressive.

Geyu Festival of Folk Song

On the 3rd day of the third lunar month, the folk song fair, Geyu, is observed by the Zhuang people. *Geyu,* which means "mart on a slope of river bank" or "double dragon cave" in the Zhuang language, refers to singing in the field or outside a rock cave. There are two kinds of Geyu: one held in the daytime and another at night. The daytime Geyu is held in the fields and is mainly concerned with match-making by means of singing songs; the nighttime Geyu is held in the village and its themes are production, the seasons, antiphonal work, and history. On the day of Geyu, the older married people bring five-color rice and colorful eggs prepared in advance, while the young people dress themselves in their best. The girls go to the fair with a ball made of strips of silk. The statue of Sister Liu is carried around the fairgrounds once before the singing begins. The girls take part in the singing contest while appraising the male contestants' moral fiber and talent. A girl throws the silk ball to the young man she chooses, and if the young man thinks likewise, he will tie a gift to the silk ball before he throws it back. At some fairs, there is a competition on a stage, which is usually set under a large tree at the foot of a hill. The singers perform one by one on the stage, old and young alike. They sing about their new life and sweet romance.

Firecracker Festival

At this traditional folk festival of the Dong ethnic group, firecrackers are lit. The first firecracker signifies the booming population; the second signifies economic prosperity; the third signifies a bumper harvest. An iron ring, the symbol of happiness, is tied to every firecracker with red and green strings. The iron ring is launched into the sky by the force of the gunpowder. When it falls back to earth, people vie with each other to grab it—called "seizing the firecracker." It's said that whoever gets the firecracker will have a growing family and economic prosperity as well as happiness and health. At the end of the event, young men and women gather together to sing Dong opera, perform color tunes, play Lusheng, a reed-pipe wind instrument, and dance. When dusk comes, campfires are lit and people either sing Dong opera or engage in a freestyle singing contest. The festive scene is full of joy and laughter.

The Dong ethnic group's Caitang dance (From CFP)

Hainan

Geography at a Glance

Hainan, or "Qiong" for short, is in the southernmost part of China. To its north, is the Qiongzhou strait dividing it from Guangdong Province. Hainan is more than 13,000 square miles in area, including the Xisha Isles, Nansha Isles, Zhongsha Isles, and its marine belt. The population is 7.86 million (2000 census).

The center of Hainan is mountainous. The highest mountains are Wuzhi and Yingwu; below are hills, plateaus, and plains. The Songtao and Nandu rivers originate in the central mountains.

Hannan has a tropical monsoon climate: hot throughout the year, with a great deal of rain, distinct dry and wet seasons, frequent tropical storms, and typhoons.

Featured Cuisine

Baoluo rice noodles, Dongshan pancakes, coconut rice, Tangshi clay pot, Xinglong lemon duck, Shishan goat hot pot, Li's sour pickles, Miao's colored rice, Lingao suckling pig, Shishan Yong goat, nutritional soup made of turtle and snake, tender chicken braised with coconut, Pengkou barley, sliced Wenchang chicken, Hele crab in Qiong sauce, Hainan turnip cake, Hainan coconut bread, Wenchang rice cake, coconut-flavored grain sorghum cake.

Featured Commodities

Special Local Products

Xinglong coffee, coconut candies, Dunchang crystal products, bamboo carvings, Shuiman tea, partridge tea, areca tea, Wenchang chick-

(From ImagineChina)

Beach scene at Tianyahaijiao in Sanya City, Hainan. (From CFP)

en, Jiaji ducks, Dongshan goats, Hele crab, coconut chicken, bamboo-tube rice, Xianglan tea, Basha green tea, Kuding tea, deer and turtle wine, Poma wine, areca wine, coral.

Local Handicrafts

Carvings, coral bonsai, wood carvings, wood pictures, vine products, root carvings, textiles of the Li ethnic group.

Transportation Tips

By Bus

There is a well-developed road network comprising highways, expressways, and local roads. National highways 223, 224, and 225 are the main roads in Hainan. The east and west island belt highways are the best routes to the counties and cities of Hainan.

By Train

Yuehai Railway goes from Zhanjiang in the north, through Leizhou Penisula, converging with the West circle railway of Hainan, and terminating at Sanya.

By Plane

Hainan now has two international airports, Haikou's Meilan and Sanya's Phoenix. There are 363 national airlines and 21 international airlines serving Hainan.

By Water

Hainan has two major passenger transportation docks, Haikou Harbor and New Haikou Harbor. Using the national lanes,

Notes 

❶ Tourists can arrange their visit with a travel agency, which can also book rooms, thus avoiding translation problems.

❷ Remember to bring swimsuits and suntan oil.

❸ In cities like Haikou and Sanya, minibuses will take you to scenic areas. You can also rent a motorized three-wheeler, which is locally called a "three legged cat."

POPULAR FESTIVALS

Hainan International Coco Festival

Held on March 3 of the Chinese calendar. There are lantern exhibitions and international dragon boat races in Haikou, Wenchang, Tongshi, and Sanya.

Winter Jasmine Flower Market

In Haikou, there are flower exhibitions.

Flowers Changing Festival

Held on January 15 of the Chinese calendar, in Haikou. People exchange flowers and create wondrous displays.

Li Minority Festival

Held on March 3 of the Chinese calendar in Qiongzhong, Dongfang, Changjiang, and Baisha counties. There are bamboo dances and campfire parties.

Autumn Festival

In Miao villages, there are Moon Dances, feasts, and general festivities.

Zhanzhou Mid-Autumn Singing Festival

Held on Mid-Autumn Day, the folk song festival in Zhanzhou has singing contests, traditional antiphonal folk singing, dancing, and feasting.

people can get to the middle and lower reaches of the Changjiang River and the harbors on the coastline. Via the international lanes, you can get to Russia, Japan, Korea, Africa, and European countries.

Recommended Routes

Featured Routes

Three-day tour in the Wuzhi Mountain Gorge

Day 1 Haikou→Diaoluo Mountain National Forest Park→Qixan Mountain Range Scenic Area. Lodging: Qixian Scenic Area.

Day 2 Wuzhi Mountain National Forest Park →River rafting in the Wuzhi Gorge. Lodging: Wuzhi Mountain Hotel.

Day 3 End of tour.

Five-day tour from Haikou to Vietnam

Day 1 Haikou Xiuying Harbor→Vietnam Xialong Bay. Lodging: Vietnam.

Day 2 Xialong Bay→Guilin on the sea→ Xialong Bay→Haiphong→Fulin Temple→ National Entertainment City of Haiphong-Tushan. Lodging: Haiphong.

Day 3 Haiphong→Hanoi→Bating Square →Chairman's mansion→Huzhiming's former residence→Long-legged houses→One Pillar Temple→Military museum→Ancient streets of Hanoi→Huanjian lake. Lodging: Hanoi.

Day 4 Hanoi→Xialong Bay→Haikou. Lodging: Passenger ship.

Day 5 Xiuying harbor of Haikou. End of tour.

Traditional Routes

Five-day tour in Hainan

Day 1 Arrival in Haikou.

Day 2 Haikou→Boao→Yudai Beach Scenic Area→Dongshan Mountain→

Xinglong→Tropical arboretum→Traditional village of Southeast Asia.

Day 3 Xinglong→Lingshui County→Monkey Island in South Bay→Glancing-Back-Deer Park→Culture Square of the Big East Sea.

Day 4 Tianyahaijiao→Crystal processing factory→Nanshan Culture Park→Tea-making ceremony→Pearl Exhibition Hall→Yalong Bay.

Day 5 End of tour.

Five-day driving tour

Day 1 Haikou→Qionghai→Wanning→Wuzhizhou Island.

Day 2 Wuzhizhou Island→Yalong Bay→Sanya.

Day 3 Sanya→Nanshan Cultural Park→Tianyahaijiao.

Day 4 Sanya→Wuzhishan Mountain→Zhanzhou.

Day 5 Lanze town→Haikou.

Self-Guided Tour

Seashore tour

Start from Haikou to Sanya, passing Qiongshan, Wenchang, Qionghai, Wanning, and Lingshui. The main attractions on the line include Sugongci Temple, Hairui's Tomb, Qiongtai Academy of Classical Learning, redwoods, coconut forest in the Eastern Suburb, Song's ancestral residence, Wanquan River, Nanwan Monkey Island, Coconut Island, Yanlong Bay, Glancing-Back-Deer Mountaintop Park, Tianyahaijiao, Haishan.

Tour of the customs of the Li and Miao ethnic groups

Start from Tongshi to Tunchang, passing Baoting Li and Miao Autonomous County and Middle Guangxi. The main attractions on the line include Hainan Ethnic Museum, Chinese Ethnic Cultural Village, Wuzhi Mountain, Qixianling Hot Spring Resort, Nanguo areca villa, Baihua Ridge, Limu Mountain Forest Park, Yingge Ridge Resort, Maple Deer Range.

Addresses and Phone Numbers

Haikou Hotel	4 Haifu Street, Haikou	0898-65350266
Baohua Seascape Hotel	69 Binhai Street, Haikou	0898-68536699
International Holiday Village	In national forest protected area of Shuiman Township	0898-86550001
Xinglong Pearl Hotspring Hotel	Xinglong Pearl Street, Wanning	0898-62555999
Sanya Hawaii Hotel	Haihua Road on Yuya Street, Sanya	0898-88227688
Golden Palm Hotel	National scenic area of Yalong Bay, Sanya	0898-88569988
Yantai International Hotel	18 Haidianwu East Road, Haikou	0898-66250888
Central Asia Hotel	1 Hedong Road, Sanya City	0898-88246888
Sanhaitian Hotel	88 Haiyun Road, Sanya City Dadonghai	0898-88211466

Haikou and North Qiong Region

Best Time to Travel

The best time to tour in Haikou is from November to April; May to October is the rainy season, and June to September is the typhoon season.

Shopping Tips

Haixiu East Road passes through the center of Haikou. The main business roads such as Datong, Park, and Boai all converge there. There are at least 250 business enterprises and stores on this road.

Souvenir shoppers can visit the East Gate Market on Boai Road. Here you can buy Hainan specialties, such as sea products, special local products, deer products, and palm blankets.

Mangrove is a unique and ecologically important tree on tropical beaches. (From Colphoto)

Qiongtai College is the only college founded officially in Hainan during the Qing Dynasty.(From Colphoto)

Hairui's Cemetery

Situated in the village of Binya, Xiuying District, in Haikou. Built in 1589, this is the cemetery of Hairui, an official in the Ming Dynasty. On the front gate are four Chinese characters *Yue Dong Zheng Qi,* which means "a decent man in east Guangdong." The tomb consists of a stone table, a stone platform, five-bar railings, and a round tomb made of granite with a hexagonal base. In front of the base, there is a monument stating Hairui's name and official position.

 Take Bus 2 and 16.

Qiongtai College

Qiongtai College, on Wenzhuang Road, Fucheng, in Qiongshan, was established

The drum tower is near the college, on the rampart on South Wenzhuang Road.

in 1705. Built in memory of Qiuqun, a scholar of Wuying Palace during the Ming Dynasty and one of the most famous writers of Hainan.

Saddle Mountain Volcano

Situated in the town of Shishan, the mountain looks like a saddle. It is the highest place in north Hainan and may be the most intact extinct volcano in the world. It is believed that the Saddle Mountain volcano dates from 27,000 to 1 million years ago. There are about 30 lofty hills around Saddle Mountain, which were also once active volcanoes.

Guilin Ocean Scenic Area

Located in the coastal area northeast of Qiongshan, this place once belonged to the Guilindu of outer Yifeng in the Ming and Qing dynasties. There are over 360 miles of open water, known as the Guilin Ocean. With pure seawater, and no sharks or reefs, this is also a good spot to swim and enjoy water sports. The 15,780-foot beach is bow shaped; the rocks near the beach serve as seawalls. The sand there is as white as silver, fine and smooth.

There were once 72 villages at the site of the shallow sea to the northeast of Guilin Ocean. In 1605 an earthquake destroyed the area, but the ruins of many of the houses can be seen under the water.

Dongzhai Alley Mangrove Reserve

Dongzhai Alley Mangrove is located in Dongzhai Alley, northeast of Qiongshan. Almost 31 miles long and 15.5 square miles in total area, this is the first mangrove protection area in China. There are 41 species of mangrove growing in the reserve. The convoluted roots of the mangrove protect shorelines from erosion and storm surges, and they also provide an ideal habitat for many varieties of fish and other marine animals.

Speedboats are available in the area. Don't miss a chance to rent a boat and visit the beautiful Wild Pineapple Island.

Mangrove forests in Hainan. (From ImagineChina)

Sanya Region

Best Time to Travel

Winter is the optimal season to visit Sanya.

Shopping Tips

The Tianyahaijiao village in Sanya is a good place to buy souvenirs from Hainan.

Glancing-Back-Deer Peninsula

The peninsula is situated in Sanya Bay about 3 miles south of the city of Sanya. It is shaped like a deer standing on the shore and glancing backward, thus its name. The highest spot here is 935 feet above sea level. The park itself is beautiful and quiet, with a small observatory, the white Listening to the Tide Kiosk, and other unique and serene areas.

There is a huge Glancing-Back-Deer statue in the park. (From CFP)

Between Glancing-Back-Deer Peninsula and Elm Wood Bay, there is the crescent-shaped Dadonghai Bay, well known for its stunning vistas.

Tianyahaijiao (World's End)

Tianyahaijiao, situated at the foot of Horse Mountain, is 16 miles west of Sanya. Its name translates as "the end of the sky and the corner of the sea," and was the farthest place ancient Chinese were able to travel by land. Once it was almost impossible to find another person on the beach, but now there are hundreds of tourists, arriving in tour buses and by elephant. Still, it is a beautiful place to stroll on the beach and watch the seabirds.

Yalong Bay

Yalong Bay is 15.1 miles southeast of Sanya. The climate there is mild, with cool summers and warm winters. There is a vacation resort with exclusive lodgings, restaurants, and many recreational activities.

West Sand Isles

West Sand Archipelago is one of the four major archipelagos in the South China Sea. It is made up of the Yongle Isles and the Xuande Isles. Pure and beautiful, the coral isles cover an ocean area of about 19,3051 square miles. In ancient times, West Sand Archipelago was called "thousand li long sand." Few people visit these far-flung islets, so the water and beaches are extremely clean.

View of West Sand Archipelago (From CFP)

The city of Boao is the site of the Boao Asia Forum, an outgrowth of China's open-door policy. (From Colphoto)

Hainan Eastline Region

Wenchang Confucius Temple

Wenchang Confucius Temple, located at 77 Wendong Road, Wenchang, was originally built in the Qingli era (1041–1048) of the North Song Dynasty. The temple was destroyed but rebuilt in 1375 and moved to its present location. The temple complex is one of the best preserved in Hainan.

Boao Tour Area

The Boao Tour Area is situated in Boao Harbor, at the mouth of the Wanquan River. It is about 12 miles from the town of Jiaji. Boao Harbor is formed by the Wanquan, Longgun, and Jiuqu rivers. The harbor is vastly beautiful and important to the Hainan economy.

> The provincial train and the minibus will take you to this destination. Near the tour area is the Wanquan River and the statue of the Red Detachment of Women in the Red Army. The ballet *The Red Detachment of Women,* written in 1964 and famously performed for then-president Richard Nixon in 1972, tells the story of a peasant girl who rose to prominence in the Communist Party. The music, by Du Mingxian, is based on Hainan folk songs and has been adapted for use in Beijing opera and films.

Wanquan River

Wanquan River is known as the "Chinese Amazon River." The third-largest river in Hainan, its source is on Wuzhi Mountain, and it flows generally northeast for 105 miles, then turns southward, meandering through banana and coconut plantations to the South China Sea.

Dongshan Mountain

Dongshan Mountain is almost 2 miles east of Wancheng, in Wanning. There are three mountain peaks, all of which have pavilions for enjoying the spectacular scenery. The mountain has several well-known Buddhist temples, the most famous being Chaoyin and Pure-Land temples.

Coco Woods of the East Suburb

Coco Woods is situated on the seashore of the East Suburb, in Wenchang. There are a great number of different varieties of coconut

In the East Suburb Coco Woods, the plentiful coconut trees wave in the sea breezes. (From Imagine-China)

trees, and altogether about 500,000 coconut trees of varied sizes, heights, and shapes, forming a natural and beautiful scene.

Here you can sample rare seafood and taste fresh coconut milk. You can also watch harvesters climb the coconut trees.

Xinglong Hot Springs

The Xinglong Hot Springs are found on the Xinglong Oversea Chinese Farm, where there are not only beautiful views but also more than a dozen springs. The high mineral content of the water is said to be beneficial, and bathing in the 140°F water may ease the aches and pains of arthritis. There is a complete and modern spa on the grounds.

Dazhou Island

Dazhou Island in the vast South China Sea, southeast of Wanning, comprises two islands and three peaks, the highest of which is 948 feet above sea level. The largest of the islands in Hainan's coastal area, it is also the only habitat of canaries in China.

South Bay Monkey Island

South Bay Monkey Island is situated 3 miles south of the Lingshui county seat. It is the only macaque protection area on an island. Large, craggy rocks of various shapes dot the island, and 29 groups of macaques make the rock crevices their home. The total number of macaques here is more than 1,800.

South Bay Monkey Island is an ideal habitat for macaques. (From ImagineChina)

The Midwest Line of Hainan Region

Hainan Ethnic Museum

Hainan Ethnic Museum is on Yaxu Mountain to the north of Wuzhi Mountain City. It is a comprehensive museum that collects and exhibits cultural artifacts of the Li, Miao, and Hui peoples, Hainan's history, and the traditional cultures of all the ethnic groups of Hainan.

Fanmao Village in Li Stockaded Village

About one mile north of Wuzhi, this ancient and traditional village of the Li ethnic group still holds to the old ways. Surrounding the village are green mountains and farmland. The thatched roofs of the Li houses are boat-shaped and have been made this way from time immemorial. Weaving and needlework, singing, and dancing are the hallmarks of the Li people's lifestyle. Always be very aware of taboos and customs of ethnic groups, and pay close attention to your tour guide in such matters.

Taiping Mountain Waterfall

Taiping Mountain Waterfall, about 4 miles north of Wuzhi Mountain City, is on the slope of Taiping Mountain. The altitude of the mountain is 2,625 feet above sea level. The waterfall hangs between two enormous rocks, falling 328 feet to a beautiful pool at the base. In rainy seasons, the waterfall is tremendously loud and very impressive.

Wuzhi Mountain

Wuzhi Mountain is located in central Hainan. Because the peaks look like a hand with outstretched fingers, it is also called Five-Finger Mountain. The first peak of Wuzhi Mountain is 4,265 feet high, but the second is the highest, at more than 6,000 feet. The third peak was once the highest peak, but it has been damaged by lightning strikes and earthquakes.

Jianfeng Mountain National Forest Park

Located in Yuedong County, Hainan Province, this small preserve was first recognized in 1976. About 6 square miles in area, it is the first national tropical rain forest park with first-growth trees, primitive ferns, and other prehistoric flora.

Not far from Jianfeng Mountain is the Yingge Sea salt field, the largest in Hainan and important to its economy. Maogong Mountain resembles the profile of Chairman Mao.

The traditional boat-shaped roof thatching of the Li. The roof and the walls join together. (From Colphoto)

Local handwork (From ImagineChina)

Hainan Style

Li and Miao Villages

The Li people were the first to immigrate to Hainan Island, and therefore can be considered the true natives here. Today they have the largest population among all the ethnic groups on the island. The Miao people have the second-largest population after the Li. Folklore customs of Li and Miao villages are the most interesting and distinctive part of Hainan local culture.

Li Ethnic Group

The Li people are the real natives on Hainan Island. As a branch of the ancient Baiyue groups, they crossed the ocean and landed on the island about 4,000 years ago, becoming the first inhabitants here. According to historical records, they were first given the name "Li" at the end of the Tang Dynasty. Like other minority groups, Lis have preserved their own native language, primitive way of life, and unique customs. As a result of ethnic intermingling, the Li people have drawn greatly on the Han cultures and customs, and only those living in the autonomous counties of the mountainous areas in the middle part of Hainan Island are still practicing and continuing the Lis' traditional lifestyle. However, deep in everyone's heart, the Li still represent Hainan's local customs and cultures.

Ship-Shaped Houses

The legend goes that the ancestors of the Li people arrived on the island after a long journey across the sea, only to find that it was a desert island. Finding no shelters, they turned their wooden ships over to make houses. Later, they built their real houses in the shape of a ship.

Water-Splashing Festival

The custom of water splashing is popular with both Li and Miao people. Water play activities, such as sprinkling water on each other, water fighting, and playing ducks and drakes, have been practiced for generations after generations. The water splashed out by people is believed to have the power to bring others happiness and blessings. The government of the Li and Miao Autonomous Prefecture of Baoting in Hainan made the decision that as of 2002, the water-splashing festival would be held every year on July 7 of Chinese calendar.

Bamboo Pole Dance

The bamboo pole dance is a kind of traditional dance of the Li people. When performing it, the dancers first place two bamboo poles parallel to each other on the ground as the "cushion" poles. Across these two poles, several thinner bamboo poles are placed horizontally. Players are divided into two groups to hold the thinner bamboo poles on either side, each person grasping two thin bamboo poles in both their hands. With the accompaniment of music, those holding them open and close the poles rhythmically as they slide them on the "cushions." The dancers jump and hop between the bamboo poles, making various movements.

Miao Ethnic Group

The Miao ethnic population living in Hainan amounts to about 70,000. According to historical records, some of the Miao people on Hainan Island came from Guangxi Province during the Ming Dynasty as a result of conscription, and some came from the central plains areas during the Ming Dynasty and the Qing Dynasty to avoid the wars and chaos there. Most of them now inhabit a compact community in the mountainous areas on southern Hainan Island, and some are scattered around the Han and Li habitats.

Coco Carvings

Coco carvings are handicrafts made by carving on coconut shells. These works are novel and varied in shape, and they look primitive and elegant, having a particular style and employing the strong colors of Hainan. Coco carving in Hainan has enjoyed a long history. It can be traced back to as early as the Tang Dynasty, when some people started

Li ethnic dance to celebrate their traditional festival in Hainan (From ImagineChina)

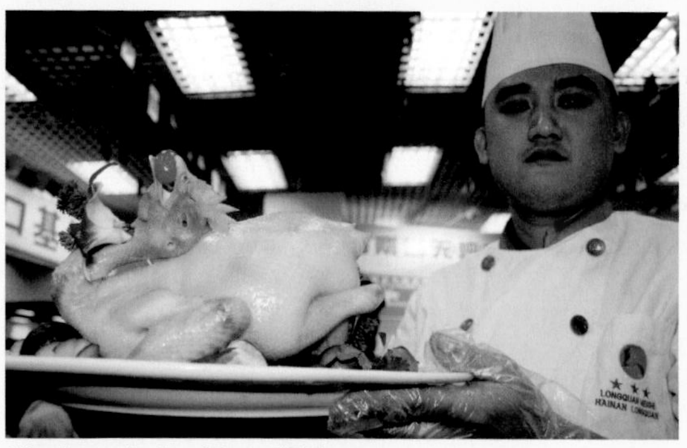

Wenchang chicken (From CFP)

to make wine cups with coconut shells. Lu Guimeng, a poet in the later Tang Dynasty, once wrote the line: "Filling the coco cup with wine to get rid of poisonous fog." In both the Ming Dynasty and the Qing Dynasty, coco carvings served as tributary products to Beijing. There are hundreds of colors and varieties of these coco carvings. Especially popular are the coco sister and the coco monkey, which are made from original coco and are vivid and lifelike, full of natural and simple beauty. In recent years, coco carving paintings have appeared in the market. Their primitive and simple style, ingenious design, and interesting patterns add up to a new look for the traditional coco carvings.

Four Famous Dishes of Hainan

Wenchang Chicken

Wenchang Chicken tops the list of the four most famous dishes of Hainan. It is made from a carefully selected home-fed chicken. It is so named because it was first produced in the city of Wenchang in Hainan Province. The dish is crisp, tender, and fragrant when skillfully cooked; its delicate taste and pleasant texture are best preserved when the chicken is gently boiled and eaten with no other ingredients but soy sauce. In Hainan, the dish is usually served with rice cooked in chickenfat and chicken broth, which is commonly called "chicken rice." When Hainan people refer to "eating chicken rice," they actually mean eating such rice in combination with the tender, boiled chicken. In Hainan, Wenchang Chicken is very popular not only at banquets but also at luncheons and in daily family meals, and it also enjoys great popularity in Hong Kong and Southeast Asia.

Jiaji Duck

Jiaji Duck is one of the most renowned traditional dishes in Hainan. Also called "Fan Duck," Jiaji Duck was first introduced by Hainanese living abroad. Originally, the ducks were fed in the town of Jiaji, in Qionghai, thus acquiring the name "Jiaji Duck." The dish features thin skin, crisp bones, and plump and tender meat. There is a layer of fat between the skin and the meat, which never tastes oily, but is especially delicious. Jiaji Duck can be cooked in a variety of ways, but to best retain its original flavor and traditional reputation you should gently boil the duck and serve it with just soy sauce.

Hele Crab

Hele Crab, another of the four most famous dishes in Hainan, is produced in the town of Hele in Wanning County, Hainan Province. Hele Crab is famous for its hard shell, fatty meat, and rich cream. You can cook it by steaming, boiling, stir-frying, or roasting, but steaming the crab is probably the best method, as it gives the dish its full flavor and retains the shape of the crab. Serve the crab with ginger and vinegar to fully enjoy the unique flavor of this dish with its delicious and tender meat and its golden juices as bright as the yolk of a salted duck egg. This dish is abundantly nutritious as well. According to theories of traditional Chinese medicine, its medical benefits include nourishing the bone marrow, improving the liver and the yin, supplementing the gastric juices, strengthening the muscles and tendons, invigorating blood circulation, and soothing ulcers.

Dongshan Goat

Dongshan Goat is the fourth of the four famous dishes in Hainan. It features jet-black skin, succulent meat, and thick broth. It tastes fresh, and not at all redolent of goat. It is said that it is delicious because the goats eat the rare plants and special products from Dongshan Mountain such as partridge tea. There are various cooking methods for Dongshan Goat. Whether it is braised or cooked with consommé or with coconut milk, the dish is tasty; each method has its special features, but all make for a rare delicacy.

A Li village (From CFP)

These four famous dishes are available in all big restaurants in Hainan. Of course, they are also very expensive, so it's advisable to ask about the price before having a try.

Hainan Beverages

Li's Sweet Distillers' Grain

This beverage is made by fermenting a special local product of the Li called Shanlan glutinous rice. The people put the rice into a bamboo basket and the fermentation process is started with a special kind of herb that grows on Li Mountain. The basket is then covered with fresh, clean banana leaves. After several days of fermentation, the ingredients are transferred to a sealed jar. After half a month more, the sweet distillers' grain is available. This beverage is highly nutritious, and it tastes even more delicious when boiled with eggs.

Deer and Turtle Wine

Deer and Turtle Wine is a kind of tonic wine with low alcoholic content whose ingredients include deer and turtle, two special animals in Hainan, as well as diverse Chinese herbs. The recipe for this kind of wine originated with some very famous herbalist practitioners in Hainan. The wine, with a glowing red color and mellow taste, has won many prizes both at home and abroad. It has become a popular drink with both the Hainan natives and a large number of tourists because of its excellent quality and reasonable price.

Coffee Wine

Coffee wine is a kind coffee-colored light wine made from the high-quality coffee produced in Hainan. It combines the scents of both wine and coffee, and thus has a very special flavor.

Wanhua Tea

Wanhua tea always reminds people of the hospitable Miao people and their custom of serving it to guests. Wanhua tea has a light and refreshing scent. Just have a drink of it, and the pervasive fragrance lingers. Wanhua tea looks bright and translucent, and is a special beverage, which is why the Miaos serve it to their guests.

A special method is used to make this tea: First chop ripe Chinese watermelon and grapefruit peel into different shapes and pieces the size of a finger; then carve the slices into various images of, for example, fish, birds, beasts, flowers, and grass. These images are considered symbols of good luck and blessing, and thus this tea makes a fine offering for guests.

Green Tea and Black Tea

Traditionally, the local green tea and black tea are exported from Hainan to other countries in large quantities. The black tea in particular, with its pure and mellow fragrance, is greatly favored by foreign consumers, especially Europeans. The black tea of Wuzhi Mountain is ranked as top grade by experts and has been sold in over 40 different countries and regions. The green tea of Baisha County is also very popular.

Shuiman Tea

Shuiman tea refers to the wild tea from Wuzhi Mountain. It grows in the mountains and thus has absorbed the essence of its natural surroundings. It tastes mellow and sweet and is also used medicinally to protect against colds, stop diarrhea, strengthen the stomach, and refresh the mind. At present, Wuzhi Mountain wild tea is widely planted and its production has been increased greatly. In the Wuzhi Mountain area, there are still some mysterious and beautiful legends about Shuiman tea.

Zhegu Tea

Zhegu tea, which grows mainly on Dongshan Mountain in Wanning, is made of the leaves of wild tea trees and has a wonderful flavor and aroma. The tea tastes refreshing and sweet, with a light medicinal fragrance. In addition, this magical tea is also effective in lowering blood pressure, reducing weight, strengthening the spleen, and protecting the stomach. As a result, many ancient scholars thought highly of this tea and called it a kind of felicitous herb. It is said that the reason Dongshan goat tastes fresh and has no gamey smell is that the goats eat fresh Zhegu tea leaves on Dongshan Mountain.

Hainan Snacks

Hainan Vermicelli

This is the most distinctive snack in Hainan; it has been passed down throughout history and now is very popular in towns and cities in the north of Hainan Island. Because it represents good luck and long life, it has become a requisite selection for all kinds of festivals and other happy occasions. There are two kinds of Hainan vermicelli; one is thick, and the other is thin. Cooking the thick vermicelli is relatively simpler, for you need very few added ingredients to make the thick vermicelli broth. However, cooking the thin vermicelli is somewhat more complicated. The vermicelli is mixed with a variety of additional ingredients and sauces, thus making a kind of "pickled" vermicelli. Hainan vermicelli usually refers to this kind of "pickled" dish. The right way to eat Hainan vermicelli is to put some plain vermicelli in a bowl or on a plate, add the extra ingredients and sauces to it, mix them and then enjoy this delicious snack. If you are fond of spicy food, you can add some chili paste to it to enhance the flavor. When you are nearly finished with the vermicelli, you can add some hot sea mussel broth to the bowl. This makes a different kind of delicacy that leaves you with a lingering aftertaste.

Baoluo Rice Noodles

Baoluo rice noodles, a popular local snack in Hainan, are made of rice noodles combined with broth and various additional ingredients. It acquired its name because the Baoluo rice noodles made in Wenchang County in the town of Baoluo are the best known. The dish is also called "thick vermicelli broth" in the northern areas of Hainan because the rice noodles used are thicker than those used for Hainan vermicelli. The noodles are white, soft, and slippery; the broth is hot and delicious, and the side ingredients are savory and chewy. This delicious snack with a slight sour-peppery flavor stimulates your appetite, and you'll never get enough of it.

Hainan Lijia Rice in a Bamboo Tube

This is a traditional delicacy of the Li ethnic group in Hainan. Some rice and a measured amount of sauces are put into tube-shaped containers made of fresh bamboo, and then they are baked. The Li people usually bake this dish on charcoal in the mountainous fields or at home. Today, this technique has been improved upon by experienced cooks and the dish has become quite popular. The presentation itself is appealing: The bamboo is a beautiful green color; the rice looks saucy yellow, gives off a pleasant aroma, and tastes delicious. A good beverage with which to accompany this dish is the Shanlan wine of the Li people.

Glutinous Rice Cakes with Coconut

This is a very common snack in Hainan. First, use glutinous rice flour to make a sort of shell. Stuff the shell with a filling made of fresh coconut, sesame seeds, crushed peanuts, and white sugar. Then wrap it with pineapple leaves and form it into a round cake about 2 inches in length. Steam it and eat it while it's still hot for a very distinctive and enjoyable flavor experience.

Lingao Roast Suckling Pig

Lingao pig is a very special kind of pig, with its small size, thin skin and lean meat. The cooked piglet glistens and tastes delicious, with crispy skin and tasty meat. This snack, a major export of Hainan, is in great demand in Hong Kong and Macao and has enjoyed a long-standing reputation.

Lijia rice in a bamboo tube (From Colphoto)

Hong Kong Special Administrative Region

Geography at a Glance

Hong Kong Special Administrative Region is also called Xiangjiang, or Xianghai. It is east of the mouth of the Zhujiang River and consists of Hong Kong Island, Kowloon Peninsula, New Territories, Lantau Island, and all the surrounding water area. Its land area holds a population of 6.78 million (2000 census), among whom 95 percent are Chinese. Hong Kong is at the southeast end of the Euro-Asia mainland. It is one of the main trading, transportation, and financial centers of the Asia-Pacific region. After the Opium War in 1842, it was taken over by the English government. On July 1, 1997, the Chinese government resumed the dominion of Hong Kong and set up the Hong Kong Special Administrative Region there.

Hong Kong faces the South China Sea. There are more than 200 islands off the coast. Hong Kong Island is the economic and cultural center of Hong Kong proper. The average temperature of Hong Kong is 78°F. Spring is warm and foggy, summer is hot and rainy, autumn is pleasant, and winter is dry and cold. The precipitation between May and September is about 80 percent of the entire annual amount.

Featured Cuisine

Boiled pork slices, pork slices fried with pickled mustard, field mouse braised with black beans, rice rolls with dried onion, braised sea cucumber, boiled shrimp, fried sugar shrimp, shrimp rolls with fresh meat and lettuce, spicy salt shrimp, sauced jelly-

(From ImagineChina)

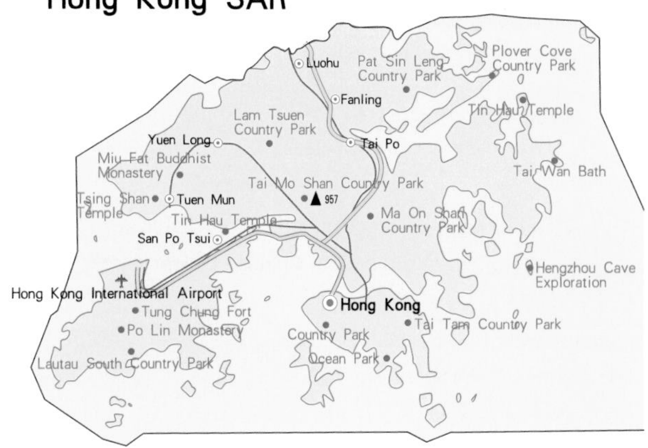

The Hong Kong skyline from Victoria Peak (From ImagineChina)

fish, hot sauced river clams, Yuanyang crisp dishes, braised fish heads, Hong Kong tea meal, Hong Kong rice cakes.

Featured Commodities

Hong Kong has always been a shopper's mecca; its goods and services are world class, and you can find just about anything you want. Shopping malls, department stores, clothing stores, and upscale shops can all be found in Hong Kong.

Transportation Tips

By Bus

Hong Kong's highways and expressways are extremely crowded, and the inner-city streets and suburban roads can be a driver's nightmare. Bus, minibus, or taxi is the best way to get around.

By Train

Railroads play an important role in the economy of Hong Kong and in people's daily life. The mainland's rail network is now linked with Hong Kong: the Jingjiu line from Peking to Kowloon, the Guangjiu line from Guangzhou to Kowloon, and the Hugang line from Shanghai to Kowloon.

By Air

Hong Kong is home to one of the top ten major airports in the world, and is a first-class international airport in southeast Asia. There are nearly 40 airlines in Hong Kong providing flights to every country in Europe, the North America, South Africa, the Middle East, Australia, and all countries of Southeast Asia.

Notes 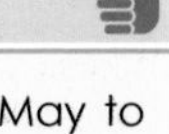

❶ The end of May to the middle of September is the typhoon season. Tourists should be aware of the different levels of typhoon severity and take proper precautions.

❷ Light sweaters, raincoats and hats, and cotton clothing are suitable for most seasons in this semitropical climate.

❸ In Hong Kong, all citizens and tourists must carry an ID card or passport at all times.

POPULAR FESTIVALS

Hong Kong International Film Festival

Held from March to April. New films, documentaries, fabulous parties, and, of course, movie star sightings.

Hong Kong Food Festival

Held from March to April. Chinese specialties, local and ethnic foods, food exhibitions, contests, and hundreds of opportunities to see and taste the best of Chinese delicacies.

The Birthday of the Queen of Heaven

Held on March 23 of the Chinese calendar. In Yuanlang and other places, there are boat-decorating contests, floats, parades, and lion dancing performances.

Hong Kong Arts Festival

Held in October. Drama, music, dancing, art lectures, and other activities.

By Water

There are express ferries between Hong Kong and Macau.

Recommended Routes

Featured Routes

Four-day tour in Hong Kong

Day 1 Ocean Park→Repulse Bay→Times Square→Jambo Sogo→Taiping Hill Top→Lan Kwai Fong.

Day 2 Haver Market→Golden Fish Street→Birds Garden→Wong Tai Sin Temple→Space Museum→Hong Kong Science Museum→Harbor City→Park Lane Shopper's Boulevard→Temple Street Night Market.

Day 3 Sam Tung Uk Museum→Tsing Ma Bridge→Po Lin Monastery →Maritime Square→Ladies Market.

Day 4 End of tour.

One-day tour in Hong Kong

Wong Tai Sin Temple→Chi Lin Nunnery→Shatin Che Kung Temple→Lam Tsuen Tree of Wishes in Tai Po→Yuen Long Folau Hill →Tsing Ma Bridge.

One-day self-guided cultural tour in Hong Kong

Central Ferry Piers 7 and 8→Lantau Island→Po Lin Monastery→Mui Wo Pier→Cheung Chau→Lamma Island→Yang Shue Wan →Golden Bauhinia Square→Hong Kong Convention and Exhibition Center→Repulse Bay→Jinzhizun Jewelry Processing Factory →Clock Exhibition Center→Taiping Hill.

Masses of tourists on the busy Tongluo Bay in Hong Kong (From CFP)

Hong Kong Island Tourist Area

Best Time to Travel

Hong Kong's climate is semitropical, so expect hot, humid weather throughout most of the year. October and September are the optimal months to visit Hong Kong.

The Hong Kong Protocol House (From CFP)

Shopping Tips

In Wangjiao there is a special outdoor market called Women's Street. On both sides of the street, there are more than 200 stands and small fashionable dress shops, hat shops, jewelry shops, and shoe stores.

Beverley Commercial Center is situated in Tsia Sha Tsai; upscale clothing and jewelry are the high-ticket items.

Causeway Bay is the beachhead of Hong Kong's fashion district. Most of the shops and businesses here are open about 12 hours each day.

Addresses and Phone Numbers

Kowloon Xilaideng Hotel	20 Midun Street, Jianshazui, Kowloon	00852-23691111
Kowloon Shangri-la Hotel	64 Dongyao Subway, Jianshazui, Kowloon	00852-27212111
Peninsular Hotel	Salisbury Road, Jianshazui, Kowloon	00852-29202888
Golden Shore Hotel	1 Qingshan Street, Qingshan Bay, New Territories	00852-24528888
Shijihaijing Hotel	508 Hong Kong Circuit Street	00852-29741234
Wanhao Hotel	88 Jinzhong Street, Taigu Square, Hong Kong	00852-28108366
Century Hong Kong Hotel	238 Xiefei Street Wanzai, Hong Kong	00852-25988888
Culture East Hotel	5 Gannuo Street Central, Central Circuit	00852-25220111
Boning Hotel	310 Gaoshida Street, Tongluo Bay, Hong Kong	00852-22938888
Kowloon Rihang Hotel	72 Dongyao Subway, Jianshazui, Kowloon	00852-27391111

The Yajiao area of Ocean Park is the entertainment center, with roller coasters, ferris wheels, games, thrill rides, and food. (From Quanjing)

Hong Kong Government House

Known as the Hong Kong Protocol House, it is situated on Banshan Mountain on the Central Circuit. Built in 1855, it is a white European-style building that shows the English traditional architectural influence. After the return of Hong Kong in July 1997, it was renamed the Protocol House. Now, it is the place where Hong Kong diplomats and VIPs meet foreign guests.

Ocean Park

Ocean Park is situated on Shan Shui Kok Peninsula between Wan Chai and Repulse Bay. Covering about 170 miles, it is one of the largest amusement and theme parks in the world. It is divided into Wong Chuk Hang Park and Nan Wang Shan Park, each section with its special theme (panda pavilion, thrill rides, food courts, international plaza, and the like), and the two parks are linked by cable car. Some people think this is better than Epcot.

Taiping Hill

Taiping Hill, 1,112 feet above sea level, is situated in the western part of Hong Kong Island. Since Hong Kong was founded, Taiping Hill has been seen as its symbol. At night, standing on Taiping Hill, you can see the sparkling panorama of Hong Kong and Kowloon.

> Take the cable car to the top of the mountain. It takes eight minutes for the 900-foot trip. The cable cars run every ten minutes or so from 7 a.m. to midnight.

Mo luo Street

The antiques center of Hong Kong is on Moluo Street. Several other streets in this area (West Queen's Street, Helihuo Street, Ladder Street, and Yuegu Street) constitute the antiques distribution district. The well-known Moluo Street Antique Market is there.

> On Moluo Street, there are not only real goods but counterfeits. Be aware of what you buy, and ask your travel guide for help in translating information.

Kowloon and New Territories Region

Shatian Racecourse (From CFP)

Best Time to Travel

Hong Kong's climate is semitropical, so expect hot, humid weather throughout most of the year. October and September are the optimal months to visit Hong Kong.

Huang's Temple

Huang's Taoist Temple is in Qiangse Park in the Zhuyuan district, Kowloon. The temple was originally built in Huangsha, Guangzhou, and moved to Hong Kong in 1921. It was built in the memory of the Taoist god Huang. In 1915, Liangrean and his followers came to Hong Kong as missionaries in Wanzai.

Placed strategically among the skyscrapers, Huang's Temple draws many pilgrims. (From CFP)

This temple serves as a learning and worship center for Taoists.

Shatian Racecourse

Shatian Racecourse, managed by the exclusive Hong Kong Jockey Club, is situated on the reclaimed land on the north bank of City Gate River. Covering about 247 acres, the track and nearby Penfold Park have state-of-the-art racing equipment and facilities. This is a good place to spend a summer afternoon.

Hong Kong International Airport at night (From Quanjing)

Space Hall

Space Hall is located in Jianshazui, Kowloon. Opened to the public in 1980, this air-and-space museum is spectacular. It has a celestial phenomena hall, a general exhibition hall, and a sun science hall. The museum is comparable to the Air and Space Museum in Washington, D.C.

> If you arrive in Hong Kong by air, take the express bus from the airport to the Central Circuit. There are only two stops, Qingyi and Kowloon. The bus runs every ten minutes from 6:00 a.m. to 1:00 p.m.

Tin Tan Buddha Figure

The Tin Tan Buddha Figure is located on Dayu Island to the western part of Hong Kong on the 1,581-foot Muk Yue Peak. The Buddha Figure depicts the sitting figure of Shakyamuni, the lotus flower seat, and the base. Because the base of the Buddha Figure is modeled after the Circular Mound Altar in Beijing Tiantan (Temple of Heaven), this statue is locally known as the Hong Kong Tin Tan Buddha.

The Buddha Figure is 76 feet tall. (From Quanjing)

Hong Kong Disneyland

Hong Kong Disneyland opened on September 12,

2005. At 311 acres, it not the largest Disneyland, but it certainly is impressive. Three official languages are spoken at this fifth iteration of Disneyland: English, Mandarin, and Cantonese. Here tourists can visit American Town Street, Fantasy World, Exploration World, and Future World, in addition to special dance and parade performances, thrill rides, and fireworks.

Monday to Friday: HK$295 for each adult, HK$210 for each child (3–11 years old). Saturday, Sunday, and special holidays: HK$350 for each adult, HK$250 for each child; senior citizens enjoy a preferential price Monday to Friday of HK$170, and Saturday, Sunday, and special days of HK$200. Children under 3 years old get free admission.

Bird's-eye view of Space Hall (From Colphoto)

Entrance to Hong Kong Disneyland (From ImagineChina)

Macau Special Administrative Region

Geography at a Glance

Macau Special Administrative Region, also called Haojing, Xiangshanao, or Haojiang in ancient times, is composed of the Macau Peninsula, Taipa Island, and Coloane Island and is situated to the south of Canton Province, on the west bank of the Pearl River. To the north is Gongbei, Zhuhai; the South China Sea is to its south; to the west is Wanzai of Zhuhai; Hong Kong is to the east. The Macau Special Administrative Region is 99 square miles in area and has a population of 440,000 (2000 census). Most of Macau is plateau and hills, and a few plains. Coloane Island is itself a granite mountain with the highest elevation in the entire region. The main peak is Tashitang Peak at 571 feet high, which is also the highest peak in Macau.

Macau is in the subtropical monsoon area, giving it a warm and humid climate. The humidity is generally 73 to 90 percent, and the average temperature is 68°F. The annual precipitation runs about 80 inches. From the end of May to mid-September, Macau is subject to tropical storms and typhoons.

Macau was invaded and occupied by Portuguese colonists in 1553. On December 20th, 1999, the Chinese government resumed the sovereignty of Macau and set up the Macau Special Administrative Region.

(From Quanjing)

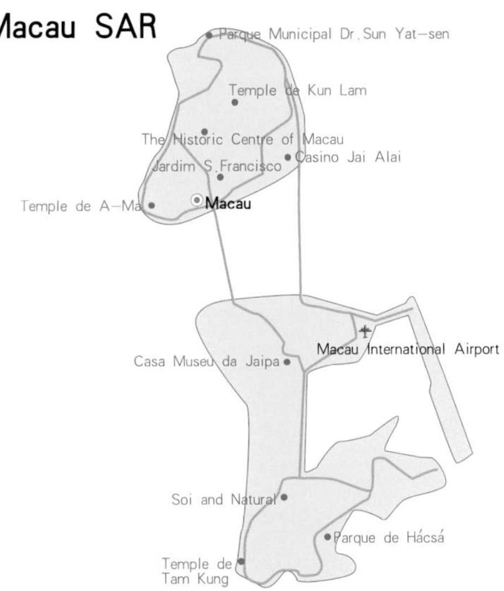

As one of the three biggest casino centers in the world, Macao is reputed to be the "oriental Monte Carlo." Local tourism actually developed from its world-renowned gaming and entertainment industries, which have become Macao's pillar industries. Macao residents refer to casinos as "entertainment places," and they usually located in hotels, as affiliates. (From ImagineChina)

Featured Cuisine

In addition to Chinese specialties and local items, there are a lot of delicious Portuguese foods available in Macau.

Feature Commodities

Macau is shopping panadise for tourists. Antiques, jewelry, crafts, and herbal medicines are are widely available. Jewelry is the most sought-after commodity here.

Transportation Tips

By Bus

Buses and taxis are the only means of public transportation on Macau. Macau–Taipa Bridge, Friendship Bridge, and Cotai Road are the main highways. There are no trolleys or trains on the island.

By Air

Macau International is the second international airport built on reclaimed land in the New Area. At present, the airport has 29 airlines with scheduled flights to Beijing, Shanghai, Nanjing, Fuzhou, Xiamen, Haikou, Wuhan, Chongqing, Xi'an, Zhengzhou, Ningbo, and Sanya. There are daily flights between Xiamen, Fuzhou, and Macau in adddition to flights between Taipei, Gaoxiong of Taiwan Province, and Macau. Asia Pacific Airlines provides convenient helicopter flights between Hong Kong and Macau.

Notes 

❶Remember to always carry an ID card, passport, and visas with you, as it can be an enormous amount of trouble if you are caught without them.

❷Special travel guildes can arrange for ID cards and visas, lodging, and transportation.

POPULAR FESTIVALS

Mazu's Birthday

Held during the Spring Festival on March 23 of the Chinese calendar in Mazu Temple. Feasts, sacrifices, family gatherings, and rituals take place.

Macau Lantern Festival

Held March 15 of the Chinese calendar. Lantern displays, special foods, parades, and performances of various kinds take place.

Macao Arts Festival

Sponsored by the Cultural Agency, this festival runs March 6–28 and includes music, dance, arts performances, and film exhibitions from many countries.

Dragon and Lion Dancing Festival

Held on April 8 in Yuxing, Macau. The main activities are dragon and lion dancing, feasting, and parades.

Dragon Boat Festival

Held in June, highly decorated dragon boats from many areas compete and parade.

Yulan Festival

Yulan Festival is also called the Ghost Festival. Held on August 29 or July 14 of the Chinese calendar. Macau is one of the few areas where this custom is still prevalent. Many households place rice and meat in front of their doors for their ancestors' spirits.

By Water

As a harbor city, water transport is very important for Macau. The passenger transportation by sea between Hong Kong and Macau is very busy. There are about 200 boats between the two cities daily.

Recommended Routes

Featured Routes

Five-day tour in Macau and Hong Kong

Day 1 Arrive in Macau. Lodging: Pujing Hotel.

Day 2 Macau–Taipa Bridge→Ruins of St. Paul Church→Symbol of Returning (Lotus Base)→Pujing Gambling House. Lodging: Pujing Hotel.

Day 3 Reach Hong Kong. Lodging: Kowloon Hotel.

Day 4 Lotus Base→Taiping Mountain →Huang's Temple→Jewelry processing factory→Duty-free shop→Hong Kong Ocean Park→Qianshui Bay. Lodging: Kowloon Hotel.

Day 5 End of tour.

One-day tour of Macau

Macau Peninsula Line in the morning: Guanzha→Guanyin Hall→Puji Zen Court →Ruins of St. Paul Church→Macau Museum→Memorial of Sun Yat-sen→ Dongwangyang Fort and Lighthouse→ Lulianruo Park→Barra Temple→Maritime Museum→Xiwangyang Church→City Hall→Conference Hall→Rose Hall.

Leave via the Island Line in the afternoon: Zai Village→Horse race→Guanyin Rock→Cotai Dockyard→Luhuan City→ Shengfangjige Church→Tangong Shop→ Zhuwan Beach→Heisha Village and Beach.

Macau Region

As a traditional event in Macao, drunken dragon dance is held at the Bathing Buddha Festival, 8th day of the fourth lunar month. Made of and weighing about 10 kilograms, the dragon comprises two sections: the head and the tail. The performers, who must drink some liquor before the dance, are seen to be half intoxicated and half sober, fighting a dragon vigorously and making it plunge, leap, and swerve about as though it is flying in midair. (From CFP)

Best Time to Travel

October to December are the optimal months to visit Macau. From May to September it is very hot, with daily rainstorms and the occasional typhoon, but this is the best time for swimming and surfing.

Shopping Tips

Central Mall is located on Yin Prince Street. Here you can shop for world-famous name brands.

Gaoshide Street is near Erlonghou Park at the foot of Songshan. Street vendors and small shops sell all kinds of inexpensive goods.

St.Paul's Outdoor Market is near Ruins of St.Paul Church . You can find all kinds of pottery, small statues and figurines, souvenirs, and antiques.

Kanggong Temple Outdoor Market, near the Kanggong Temple, is the center of the secondhand goods market.

Addresses and Phone Numbers

Pujing Hotel	Pujing Road	00853-28883888
East Hotel	Floor 3, 11 Fulong New Road	00853-28572710
Lijingwan Hotel	2 Dangzaishibotai General Street	00853-28831234
New Century Hotel	889 Dangzai Xurishengyangong Street in Dazai	00853-28831111
San Diego Hotel	Macau Republic Street	00853-28378111
Fuhao Hotel	70-106 Dr. Luoliji Street	00853-28782288
Beijing Macau Hotel	199 Beijing Street in Xinkouan	00853-28781233
Haojing Hotel	Gaokening Gentleman Street	00853-28339955
Weisiting Holiday Hotel	1918 Heisha Street, in Luhuan	00853-28871111
President Hotel	355 Friendship Street	00853-28553888

Ruins of St. Paul Church

Ruins of St. Paul Church are situated on the Small Hill near Daba Street. Built in 1637, it is now one of the symbols of Macau. The ruins were a part of St. Paul Church, which was the largest Roman Catholic church in Macau. In 1835 it was destroyed by fire, leaving just the front part, now the Memorial Arch.

Monte Fort

Monte Fort is also called St. Paul Monte Fortess, Central Monte Fortress, or Great Samba Monte Fortress. Situated at the top of Shi Mountain in the center of Macau, it is the biggest and oldest military emplacement in Macau.

At the Macau Observatory in the center of Big Emplacement Castle, tourists can see the military charts and equipment. At the northeast end of the castle are stone carvings from ancient Macau.

Barra Temple

Barra Temple is also called Mazu Pavilion or the Queen of Heaven Temple. Located in the southeastern part of the Macau Peninsula, this lovely historic temple is about 500 years old.

St. Paul Church's Memorial Arch has extremely beautiful paintings, statues, and sculptures. (From Quanjing)

At the emplacement, there are about a dozen huge cannons like the one in the photo. (From CFP)

Maritime Affairs Museum

The Maritime Affairs Museum at Mazu Temple Front Street No.1, very near the beach, resembles a ship. It was built in 1987 to exhibit the history of maritime affairs of China, Macau, and Portugal. The museum is said to be situated at the place where the Portuguese first landed on Macau. The Maritime Affairs Museum is open from 10:00 a.m. to 6:00 p.m. and is closed on Monday and Tuesday.

Lu Garden

Located at the intersection of Raleigh Old Road and Holland Garden Road, the Lu Garden is the only Suzhou-style garden in Hong Kong

Barra Temple is composed of four major buildings: the main palace, the stone palace, Hongren Palace, and Guanyin Pavilion. (From Quanjing)

and Macau. Here, the pavilions, towers, pools, rock formations, small bridges, waterfalls, and winding corridors present an intoxicating view, much like the beautiful scenery south of the Yangtze River.

Puji Temple

Puji Temple, also called Guanyin Hall, is located on the Feifujiang Road in Macau. Built in the Tianqi years (1621–1627) of the Ming Dynasty, the temple is one of the three Buddhist temples in Macau. There are three Buddha statues in Daxiong Hall, and several other figures strategically placed throughout the temple complex. There is also a statue of Marco Polo in one of the courtyards.

Casino Lisboa

Casino Lisboa is inside the Lisboa Hotel. It is the biggest gambling house in Macau. The casino is open 24/7 and tourists and locals alike spend their leisure time trying to win at cards and slots.

> Banks and hotels in Macau all provide money exchange and withdrawal services. Macau International Airport and Pujing Hotel also provide these services around the clock.

Taipa Island

Taipa Island is situated about 1.5 miles southeast of Macau Peninsula. To its west is the Small Hengqin Island. The Taipa Island is shaped like a whale, with an area of about 1.58 square miles and a population of 7,000. An ancient village known for its fireworks, it developed into a small but lively town. Hyatt Regency Hotel, New Century Hotel, and Macau University are the highlights of the island.

Macau–Taipa Bridge

Macau–Taipa Bridge is the first sea bridge between Macau Peninsula and Taipa Island. It was designed by the Portugese bridge designer Gado. It was opened on October 5, 1974. The bridge, 6,857 feet long and 30 feet wide, is supported by six piers.

Casino Lisboa is a column-shaped building. The crown-shaped marquee made of neon lights is a symbol of Macau's gambling economy. (From Quanjing)

Taiwan

Geography at a Glance

Taiwan, or "Tai," is situated on the southeast China Sea. To its east is the Pacific Ocean. To its west is Fujian Province on the other side of the strait. Taiwan, with its 88 islands including Taiwan Island, Penghu Isles, Fishing Island, Chiwei Island, Lan Island, and Burning Island, has a total area of 13,900 square miles. Taiwan is the largest island in China and is an inseparable part of the country. The Northern Tropic zone goes across Taiwan, giving it a tropical and semitropical climate. It is like summer all year, with quite a bit of wind and rain. Except for the west side of the island, which is a plain, the rest of Taiwan is mountainous. Taidong Mountain, Central Mountain, Yushan Mountain, Snow Mountain, and Ali Mountain are the major mountains on the island. Yushan, the peak of the Yushan Mountain, is called Taiwan's roof, at nearly 13,000 feet above sea level.

Chiang Kai-shek, also known as Jiang Jieshi, served as leader of the Kuomintang after the death of its founder, Dr. Sun Yat-sen, in 1925. After the Communists gained control of the Chinese mainland in 1949, Chiang retreated to Taiwan, where he established a government in exile.

Featured Cuisine

Xiaobei fermented tofu, *dingbiancuo,* Duxiayue noodles, flavored glutinous rice dumplings stuffed with meat, wontons in thin broth, *guancaiban,* Heiqiao sausage, *laotianlu,* Shenkeng Miaokou tofu, Zhanghua meatballs, Danshui Age (fried tofu with stuffing), Beidou meatballs, Danshui fishballs, Yanlin meat rice.

(From Quanjing)

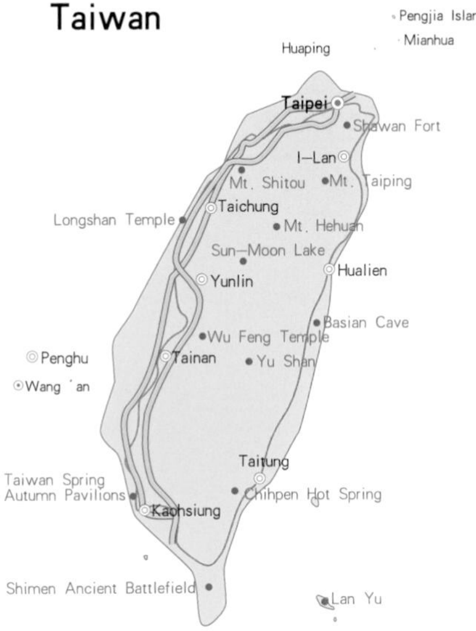

Tourists admire the sunrise over Alishan Mountain, in central Taiwan's Nantou County, 250 kilometers (155 miles) south of Taipei. The Alishan area exerts a special fascination for mainland Chinese, who see it as a rustic escape from the cares and travails of everyday life. (From Quanjing)

Shopping Tips

Gangshan's three treasures are soy sauce, honey, and mutton dishes.

Penghu's four treasures are Huangwen stone, coral, sea trees, and Maogong stone.

Other special products include Yingge pottery, Hualian jade, Peitou art pottery, Xinzhu Christmas lamps, Green Island shell pictures, Taipei Shilin knives, Tainan Guan Temple vine products, Dajia straw weavings, many different varieties of tea, Hualian stone carvings, and Meinung paper umbrellas.

Transportation Tips

By Bus

Road transportation is extensive and convenient. Highways, expressways, island circuit roads, and small lanes create a network of ways to get around on the island.

By Train

Rail transportation in Taiwan Province is well developed and convenient. A circular railway network has been formed around the whole island, from Western Longitudinal Main Line, to Pingdong Branch Line, Huadong Railway, Beihui Railway, Yilan Branch Line, and then back to the Western Longitudinal Main Line. As the main artery of the Taiwan rail-

Notes 

❶ Most businesses and government offices are open from 9:00 a.m. to 6:00 p.m. Banks are open from 9:00 a.m. to 3:00 p.m. and are closed every other Saturday.

❷ The Island Circuit Railroad, roads, and passenger buses are very convenient for tourists. Public transportation is inexpensive and a good way to see all the sights of Taiwan.

ways, the Western Longitudinal Mainline has been electrified. As the main line in the east, the Yilan line links transportation between the east and the west of Taiwan Province.

By Air

There are 16 airports in Taiwan; among them, Taoyuan, Gaoxiong, and Hualian are the largest and best equipped. Taoyuan and Gaoxiong are international airports. Taiwan has 93 airlines to Japan, North America, the Philippines, Singapore, Thailand, Indonesia, and Hong Kong.

By Water

Sea transport is the lifeline of Taiwan's economy. The main ports are the international ports of Jilong, Giaoxiong, and Hualian.

Water lanterns are released on a river flowing through Taipei on August 26, as people mark the annual ghost festival, which begins on the 1st day of the seventh lunar month. People present food to honor the spirits of the underworld on August 27, or the 15th day of the lunar month. (From ImagineChina)

Recommended Routes

Featured Routes

Five-day tour to Taiwan places of interest

Day 1 Arrive in Taipei. Lodging: Guobin Hotel.

Day 2 Zhongzheng Memorial Hall→Ximenting→Longshan Temple→Night Market in Huaxi Street. Lodging: Guobin Hotel.

Day 3 Imperial Palace Museum→Wild Willow, Strange Stone Park→Yangming Mountain→Shilin Night Market. Lodging: Guobin Hotel.

POPULAR FESTIVALS

Dajia Matsu International Tour Festival

From February to April, held in Dajia, in Taizhong County. It features studies of traditional crafts and ethnic culture, performances of ethnic singing and dancing, and cultural artifacts of Dajia Matsu.

Shimen International Kite Festival

Held in September in Xinzhu, Taiwan. There are hundreds of kite-flying contests, and many kinds of music, drama, and artistic performances.

Chiayi International Wind Music Festival

Held in Jiayi at the end of the year, it features indoor and outdoor music performances, a marathon of wind music, street performers, an exhibition of wind music instruments and music books, contests, competition, and feasting.

Gaoxiong Container Festival

Held in Gaoxiong from December to January, it includes activities such as a container arts fair, a container café, and a contest of cake-shaped containers.

Addresses and Phone Numbers

Guobin Hotel	63 North Zhongshan Road,Taipei	00886-2-25511111
Far Eastern Plaza Hotel	201 South Dunhua Road, Taipei	00886-2-23788888
Jindian Hotel	1049 Jianxing Road, Taizhong	00886-4-23288000
Changrong Guiguan Hotel	6 Taizhonggang Road, Taizhong	00886-4-23139988
Tainan Hotel	1 Chenggong Road, Tainan	00886-6-2289101
Huawang Hotel	42 Wufufour Road, Gaoxiong	00886-7-5518211
Hanlai Hotel	266 Chenggongyi Road, Gaoxiong	00886-7-2161766

Day 4 Taipei→Sun and Moon Pond→Wenwu Temple, Dehua Society, Xuanzhuang Temple, Cien Tower, Xuanguang Temple. Lodging: Huawang Hotel.

Day 5 Sun and Moon Pond→Gaoxiong→Liuhe Night Market. End of tour.

Traditional Routes

Seven-day tour around Taiwan

Day 1 Yangming Mountain National Park →Imperial Palace Museum→Zhongshan Memorial Hall→Jinghua.

Day 2 Sun and Moon Pond→Round the Lake Tour→Yunguang Temple, Cien Tower →Wenwu Temple→Taizhong.

Day 3 Jiuzu cultural village→Shuili→Alishan→Sisters Pond→Ciyun Temple.

Day 4 Sunrise on Zhu Mountain→Tainan →Chiqian Tower→Anping ancient castle →Foguang Temple in Gaoxiong→Gaoxiong Harbor→Xizi Bay Tour Section→Liuhe Night Market.

Day 5 Gending National Park→Hejianbi Beach Park→Maobitou reefs tourist area →Zhiben→Hot springs.

Day 6 Zhiben→Huadong Beach (Small Wild Willow, Flowing on Water, Sanxiantai, Baxian Cave)→Hualian.

Day 7 Hualian→Tailuge National Park→Beiben Road→Jilong Harbor. End of tour.

Three-day tour to the best tourist areas in Taiwan

Day 1 Zhongzheng Memorial Hall→Ximenting→Longshan Temple→Huaxi Street Night Market

Day 2 Imperial Palace Museum→Zhonglie Temple→Yangming Mountain→Shilin Night Market.

Day 3 Taipei→Jilong→Wild Willow Strange Stone Park→Bitoujiao Park→Jilong Night Market. End of tour.

This is a three-generation tree which seemed to be dead and was revived twice, on Alishan Mountain. (From CFP)

Taipei Region

Best Time to Travel

Taipei's climate is semitropical. All months are good for travel here except July, August, and September.

Shopping Street

Taipei Xinwang is the largest pottery factory along the Old Street. Here you can watch pottery being made, take a class in pottery making, and buy as much as you can carry with you.

Taipei Taixiang Shop was established in 1938. Having an excellent reputation for buying, drying, and selling tea, this shop is a must-see. You can purchase many different kinds of tea and tea sets here.

Taipei Mainland Bookstore was built in 1938. It is one of the two main bookstores selling Japanese academic books on agriculture, engineering, and science.

Taipei National Palace Museum

Taipei Imperial Palace Museum is in Out Double Creek, Shilin. Modeled on the Imperial Palace Museum in Beijing, it was formerly called Zhongshan Museum. The collections are mainly from the Imperial Palace Museum in Beijing, the Imperial Palace Museum in Shenyang, and Chengde Summer Villa. There are about 60,000 cultural artifacts on display.

Take Bus 213, 255, or 304, and get off at the Imperial Palace Museum.

Zhinan Palace

Zhinan Palace is situated on Monkey Mountain in the Muzha district, the southeastern suburb of Taipei. It was built in 1881 and has been renovated many times since. It was built mainly in memory of Lüdongbin. The

The Taipei Imperial Palace Museum is elegant and offers many ethnic exhibits and artifacts. (From Quanjing)

temple is well known and revered as a holy site of Taoism. In accord with Lüdongbin's tenet, "the three churches are the same in nature," the temple honors Taoism as its center, along with Confucianism and Buddhism.

Longshan Temple

Longshan Temple, located near Wanhua Night Market in Taipei, was built in 1738 and is the oldest temple in Taipei. It was constructed in the shape of the Chinese character *Hui* (meaning "return") and consists of the front palace, rear palace, left and right halls, and central hall. The temple is open only for important ceremonies.

Palaces of the Taipei Confucius Temple. (From Quanjing)

Taipei Confucius Temple

Situated in Dalongdong, this is a traditional Confucian temple, and it resembles the Confucius Temple in Quanzhou. Built in 1879, it was demolished after the Japanese invasion. In 1925, it was moved to the present site. Dacheng Palace is the main palace of the temple complex and is an impressive and magnificent example of traditional Chinese architecture.

On Wild Willow Beach, there are many odd-shaped rocks. (From Quanjing)

Beitou Hot Springs

Located in the northern suburb of Taipei, these hot springs originate in north Taiwan near Longfeng Valley under Xingyi Road. The temperature of the water is a steady 185°F and is suitable only for bathing and other spa activities. Because of the sulfur content in the water, it cannot be drunk. Legend says that this water can cure arthritis, muscle aches, and dermatitis.

Yangming Mountain

Yangming Mountain, 1,453 feet high, is also called Straw Mountain and is located 10 miles north of Taipei. In Yangming Mountain Park, there are the volcano lake, gushing springs, sulfur springs, and other unique features, which make this a major tourist destination.

Wild Willow Natural Beach Park

Wild Willow Natural Beach Park is in the Wild Willow Village, in Wanli township, Taipei County. The beach is actually a narrow, long cape stretching out to the sea. It is 5,577 feet long and 656 feet wide. The beach itself was created by thousands of years of wave action and water erosion on sandstone.

Site of Hongmao City

Hongmao city is on Zhongzheng Road in Danshui, Taipei County. The city was built buy the Spanish, after they invaded Taiwan, and named Sengruogu city. The castle was built in traditional Spanish style with a square and a round top. The former English Consulate within the city was built in 1891. All of the building materials were shipped here from the mainland.

Shimen Reservoir

Shimen Reservoir, in the southeastern part of Taoyuan County, is part of the Dahanxi River system. Here, the water formed a broad, deep pond between two mountains, Shimen Mountain and Xizhou Mountain. These act like an immense stone gate, thus the reservoir was called Shimen (Stone Gate). The top of the dam also serves as the center for the Reservoir tourist area. From here you can see all the beautiful sights around the Dahanxi River and the Taoyuan plateaus.

The main dam of Shimen Reservoir is impressive. At 436 feet tall, it is the largest earth-and-stone dam in Taiwan. (From ImagineChina)

Peace Island

Peace Island, originally called She-liau Island, is 2.5 miles from Keelung city center. It spreads over 163 acres of natural rockface coast. Due to its unique natural features, the area is now designated as a national park. There are three main unique features: rock terrain formed by ages of ocean current erosion, fossils, and a 66-foot-deep cave, which is said to have been the last retreat of the Dutch during the war led by Taiwan's Koxinga.

Taoyuan Mini

Lying on the boundary between Longtan, Taoyuan County, and Guanxi, Hsinchu County, this 74-acre mini is the largest mini in the world. It is a comprehensive recreation center well known for its collection of different kinds of mini structures. It appeals to all kinds of people, including children and the elderly.

Taichung Region

Best Time to Travel

Descending in altitude from north to south and facing the sea in the west, this area is blessed with a mild climate which is favorable for tourism all year round.

Sun Moon Lake

This renowned resort is located at the center of Suishih Village, in the town of Yizhir (Fish Pond), in Nantou County. Surrounded by mountains, this natural lake spreads over an area of 45 square miles at an altitude of 2,454 feet. Kuanhua Island on the lake marks the boundary. From the south the island looks like a half moon, whereas from the north it

The scenery at Sun Moon Lake varies with time and season. (From Quanjing)

resembles the corona of the sun. Thus, it is called Sun Moon Lake. The scenic beauty here is breathtaking and truly magnificent.

➡ Direct buses to the lake are available from Chiayi. The journey takes about one hour.

Taroko National Park

Taroko, which means "beautiful" in the aboriginal Atayal language, is one of the most beautiful national parks in Taiwan. Established in 1986, this park in Hualien County is well known for its narrow road with unique scenic spots. Surrounded by mountain peaks and deep valleys, this park is the best place to view such amazing sights. It also features diverse species of animals, plants, birds, and butterflies. Half of the mammal species that are found in Taiwan are present here, and the vegetation in the park includes broad-leaved forests and mixed broad-leaved and coniferous forests. In addition, 90 percent of the resident species of birds in Taiwan and over half the butterfly species can be found in the park.

➡ It would be more convenient to self-drive or hire taxis to visit the Taroko Gorge in the park, since few buses are available.

Hsitou Forest Recreation Area

Located in the foothills of Phoenix (Fenghuang) Mountain in Luku Village, Nantou County, the Hsitou Forest Recreation Area is one of the seven Alpine Botanical Centers in Taiwan. It covers an area of some 6,170 acres and is surrounded by mountains on three sides, while the north is fringed by valley. Rain levels are high, and vegetation is dense. Due to the varying climates and scenery, this area attracts visitors all year round. In addition, there are more than 1,200 species of trees in this area. Some are among the rarest and most precious in the world.

The cliffs along the Taroko Gorge are virtually vertical, with a height of more than 3,280 feet. (From Jin Yongji)

Chiayi Region

Best Time to Travel

The temperate marine climate in Chiayi is favorable for tourism all year round.

Alishan (Mount Ali) Scenic Area

Alishan, the most popular mountain resort in Taiwan, is a branch of the Yushan Mountain

Range, Taiwan's highest mountains. The area is famous for its five picturesque sights: the mountain train, the forest, clouds, sunrise, and sunset. The Three-Generation Tree stands as a symbol for Alishan. It is so named because it has withered and come back to life three times. The alpine railway, built by the Japanese in 1912, at an altitude of 7,185 feet, is one of the three highest mountain railways in the world. Due to the varying altitude, the train passes through tropical, subtropical, and temperate zones within a range of about 45 miles, making for distinct views and experiences. Finally, Chushan is the best place to go for the Alishan sunrise. Visitors can get there by train or walk along the stone steps near the post office for about 2 miles, passing through the forest. The walk takes about 40 minutes.

The Alishan forest train, popular with Chinese tourists, Chugs his way on the mountain slopes. (From CFP)

Beigang Chautyan Temple

Beigang Chautyan Temple is also called Tyanhou Temple and was built in the third year of Kangsyi in the Qing Dynasty, dedicated to Meijou Madzu (also called Queen of Heaven, a goddess worshiped by seamen, fishermen, travelers and merchants). It's the primary temple of the more than 300 Madzu temples in Taiwan. It's ranked as class-2 ancient ruins. Chautyan Temple is magnificent, with its wealth of delicate carved ornaments. From the first to the third lunar calendar month is the time of the commemorating festival, which attracts pilgrims from all over Taiwan. In particular, on the 23rd of the third lunar month, which is Madzu's birthday, the whole street in front of the temple fills with pilgrims and the cacophonous din of gongs, drums, and exploding firecrackers all day long.

Tainan Region

Best Time to Travel

The semitropical climate here, which renders it warm in winter and cool in summer, is favorable for tourism all year round.

Anping Castle

Located between Guosheng Road and Castle (Gubao) Street in Tainan, this the first castle in Taiwan, built in 1624 by the Dutch. Its original name was Relanzhe Castle. At present, most of the structures within the castle are ruins from the period when Taiwan was occupied by the Japanese.

Anping Castle. (From Quanjing)

Kaiyuan Temple

Located in the northeastern part of Tainan, this is one of the oldest Buddhist temples in Taiwan. It houses a 1,760-pound bell, which is the oldest and most precious one in Taiwan. Funds to pay for the bell came from donations collected by the first abbot of the temple.

Zhuxi Temple

Originally called Little Western Paradise Temple (Xiaoxitian Si), it took its present name from the nearby Zhuxi River. The temple lies in the southern district of Tainan. Built in 1684, it is the oldest temple in Taiwan.

Daitianfu Memorial Temple

Located in Beimen, Tainan County, this temple was built in memory of five nobles; thus, it is also called Five Nobles Memorial Temple by the local people. Constructed in 1662, it is the oldest among such temples in Taiwan.

Koxinga Memorial Temple

Located along Kaishan Road in Tainan, the temple was built in honor of Koxinga (1624–1662), who defeated the Dutch and recaptured and developed Taiwan. Since Koxinga was loyal to the Ming Dynasty and against the Qing Dynasty, the temple was later renamed Kaishan Temple to avoid finding fault with the Qing government.

Kaohsiung Region

Best Time to Travel

October and November are the best months to visit this area.

Drumming Mountain (Dagu Shan)

Lying along the western coast of Kaohsiung County, this mountain is 3.4 miles long and 1.5 miles wide, with a highest altitude of 3,730 feet. It is a natural boundary for the city of Kaohsiung as well as a great summer resort for tourism.

Fokuang Shan

Fokuang Shan is a huge Buddhist temple cum monastery built in 1967. It is located west of Kaoping River, northeast of Tasueshien (Big Tree Village) in Kaohsiung County. It is now the center of Buddhism study in Taiwan and Asia. Crowning the entire area is none other than a gigantic

The Dragon and Tiger Towers in the northern suburb of Kaohsiung city. (From Jin Yongji)

120-meter-tall, golden statue of Buddha. It stands proud and smiling, with its right hand extended, left hand held down, and eyes half closed. It is flanked by 480 other, smaller Buddhas, each over 6 feet tall. They glitter in the sunshine, which makes a truly spectacular sight. In the vicinity is another temple called Big Buddha City, where you will find more than a thousand statues of Buddha of various sizes.

Cheng Ching Lake

About 4 miles northeast of Kaohsiung, Cheng Ching Lake is a 222-acre, man-made reservoir surrounded by greenery. Originally called Big Shell Lake or Big Parapet Lake, the reservoir was redesigned in 1954. When it reopened in 1959, it became a popular tourist area and was renamed Cheng Ching Lake, meaning "clear water lake."

> July and August are the best months to appreciate the numerous lotuses in the lake.

Olungpi Lighthouse (From Quanjing)

With more than 1,000 species of tropical plants, Kenting National Park is the number one tropical forest in Taiwan. (From Colphoto)

Kenting National Park

Kenting National Park, established in 1984, is one of the most popular recreation centers in Taiwan. Situated on Hengchun Peninsula, at the southern end of Taiwan, the park faces the Pacific Ocean, Taiwan Strait, and Bashi Channel. The coastal area stretches across 37,507 acres and the total area of the park is 82,175 acres. Kenting National Park features various natural views, such as sand seashores, fringing reef shores, rock seashores, limestone tableland cliffs, isolated mountains, slumping cliffs, river mouths, rivers, and lakes.

Olungpi Lighthouse

Olungpi Lighthouse is situated on Hengchun Peninsula, the southernmost part of Taiwan. Lying on the navigation route between the South Sea and the Pacific Ocean, the lighthouse is not only a landmark of Olungpi, but also a symbol of Taiwan. It is the largest lighthouse in the Far East. Its light, flashing every ten seconds, is strong enough to cover a range of 20 nautical miles, thus winning the reputation at the "Light of East Asia."

Followers dressed in deity costumes dance in front of an inflated Matsu to promote the Dajia Matsu Festival, in Taipei. The festival is on from April 9 to 30 and is expected to attract more than 300,000 people annually. (From ImagineChina)

Taiwan Style

Gaoshan Ethnic Group

The Gaoshan people are the most primitive ethnic group living in Taiwan. They are bold and unconstrained, good at singing and dancing, and one of the branches of descendants from the ancient Yue ethnic group in southern China. The Gaoshan ethnicity includes nine tribal groups—the Taiya, Amei, Paiwan, Saixia, Bunong, Cao, Beinan, Lukai and Yamei—that have slightly different languages and customs. In addition, there is the Pingpu tribe, which has settled on the western plain, after generations of migration, and integrated into modern civilization. Except for the Paiwan tribe, which practices the hereditary nobility system, the tribes have kept some features of clanship, while the Amei tribe maintains the customs and practices of a matrilineal society. The language of the Gaoshan people belongs to the Indonesian language group of the southern island phylum. There are roughly 400,000 people of Gaoshan ethnicity around China; 82 percent live in Taiwan while, the rest are mostly in coastal cities in Fujian.

Drinking Wine from Interlinked Cups

This is a traditional custom among the Gaoshan people. The wine is first poured into interlinked wooden cups; then a person holds each side so that two people drink wine at the same time. The two can be both female or one male and one female.

(From CFP)

Index

C

D

E

H

I

J

K

L

M

N

R

S

U

V

W

X

Y

Xia	1994–1766 BCE
Shang	1766–1027 CBE
Zhou	1122–256 BCE
Qin	221–206 BCE
Early Han	206 BCE–9 CE
Xin	9–24 CE
Later Han	25–220
Three Kingdoms	220–280
Sui	589–618
Tang	618–907
Sung	969–1279
Yuan	1279–1368
Ming	1368–1644
Manchu/Qing	1644–1912

Editor in chief

Chen Xuejian, Lijun

Subeditor

Jin Yongji, Zhou Xinghua

Editor

Xie Aiwei, Wanghua, Zhangna

Designer

Sun Yangyang

Map information sources

Star Map Press

Photo Number

JS(2008)01-020

FIRST EDITION

Designed by Blue Sky Publishing

Library of Congress Cataloging-in-Publication Data is available upon request.

ISBN 978-0-06-1473548

08 09 10 11 10 9 8 7 6 5 4 3 2 1